NATIONAL GEOGRAPHIC

TRAVELER

California

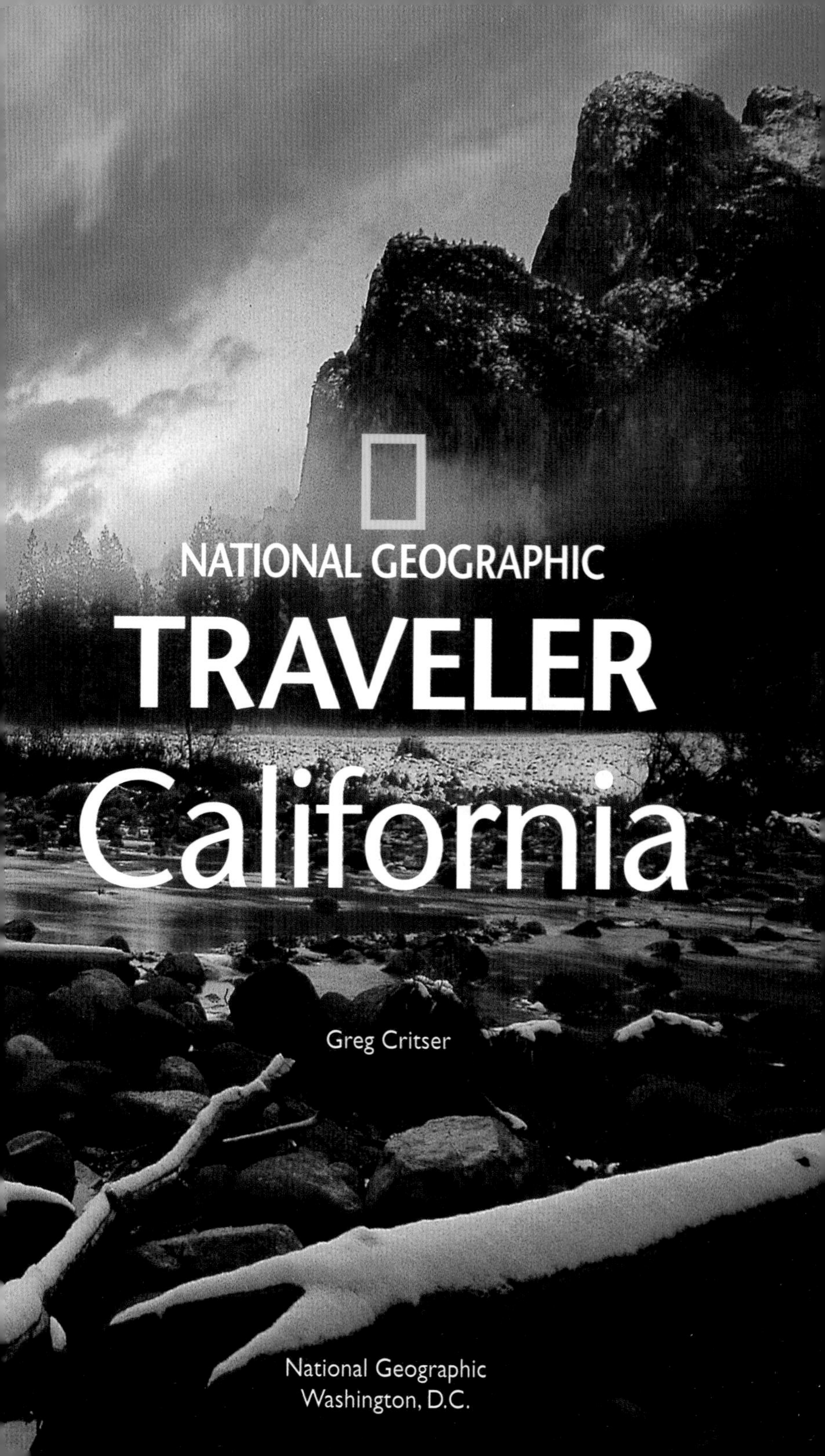

NATIONAL GEOGRAPHIC

TRAVELER

California

Greg Critser

National Geographic
Washington, D.C.

Contents

Page 1: Lone cypress, near Carmel
Pages 2–3: Winter sunrise, Yosemite Valley
Left: San Clemente Beach

How to use this guide

See back flap for keys to text and map symbols

The *National Geographic Traveler* brings you the best of California in text, pictures, and maps. Divided into three main sections, the guide begins with an overview of the state's history and culture. Following are 11 regional chapters with featured sites selected by the author for their particular interest. Each chapter opens with its own contents list.

The regions and sites within the regions are arranged geographically. Some regions are further divided into smaller areas. A map introduces each region, highlighting the featured sites. Walks and drives, plotted on their own maps, suggest routes for discovering an area. Features and sidebars give intriguing detail on history, culture, or contemporary life.

The final section, Travelwise, lists essential information for the traveler—pre-trip planning, special events, getting around, and emergencies—plus a selection of hotels, restaurants, shops, activities, and entertainment.

To the best of our knowledge, all information is accurate as of the press date. However, it's always advisable to call ahead whenever possible.

204

Color coding

Each region is color coded for easy reference. Find the region you want on the map on the front flap, and look for the color flash at the top of the pages of the relevant chapter. Information in **Travelwise** is also color coded to each region.

San Francisco Museum of Modern Art
www.sfmoma.org
151 3rd St.
415/357-4000
Closed Wed.
$$. Free 1st Tues. of month
Bus 5, 9, 12, 14, 15, 30, 38, 45

Visitor information

Practical information for most sites is given in the side column (see key to symbols on back flap). The map reference gives the page number of the map and grid reference. Other details are address, telephone number, days closed, entrance charge in a range from $ (under $4) to $$$$$ (over $25), and nearest public transport. Other sites have information in italics and parentheses in the text.

TRAVELWISE

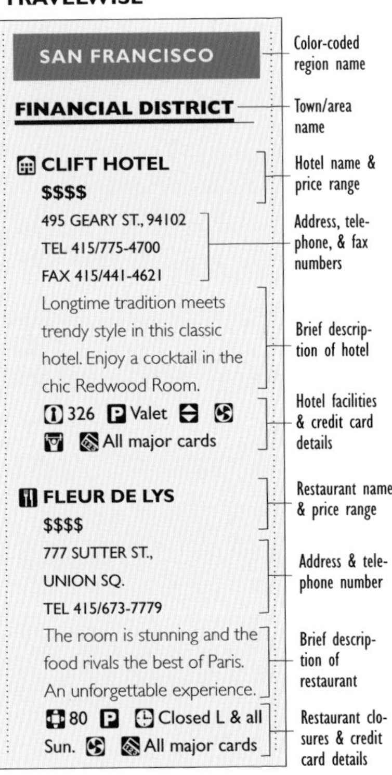

Hotel & restaurant prices

An explanation of the price bands used in entries is given in the Hotels & restaurants section (beginning on p. 346).

REGIONAL MAPS

- A locator map accompanies each regional map and shows the location of that region in the state.
- Adjacent regions are shown, each with a page reference.

WALKING TOURS

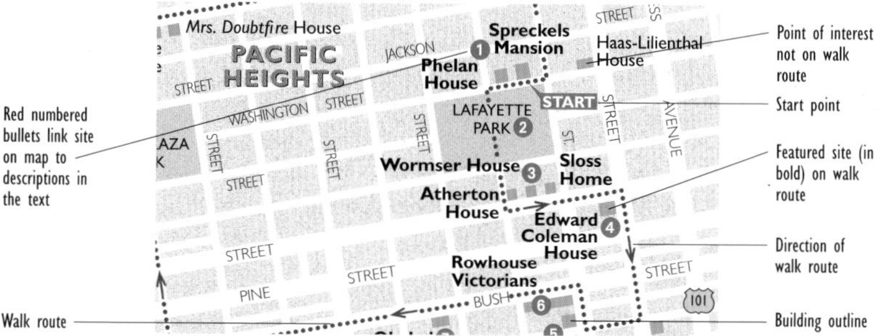

- An information box gives the starting and ending points, time and length of walk, and places not to be missed along the route.
- When two walks are marked on the map, the second route is shown in orange.

DRIVING TOURS

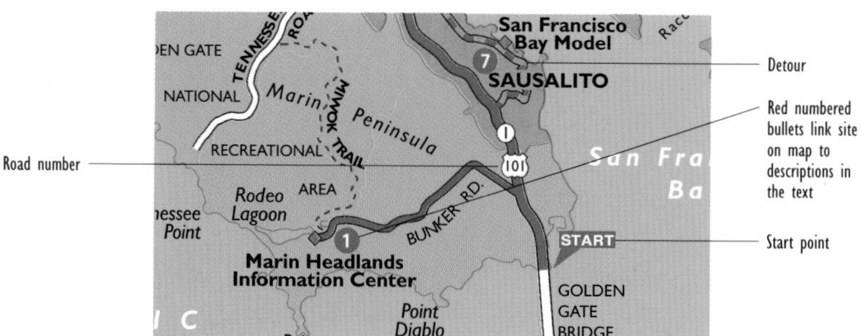

- An information box provides details including starting and finishing points, time and length of drive, places not to be missed along the route, and tips on the terrain.

NATIONAL GEOGRAPHIC

TRAVELER California

About the author

Greg Critser was born in Steubenville, Ohio, and raised in Whittier, California. He received his B.A. in History at Occidental College in Los Angeles, and his M.A. from UCLA. His biographical research about the California author and social activist Carey McWilliams has appeared in the American Historical Association's *Pacific Historical Review* and the *UCLA Historical Journal.* Greg has worked as a senior editor at four magazines: *California Business, California* (formerly *New West), Buzz,* where he edited an award-winning stable of young Los Angeles writers, and *Worth,* where he was responsible for the magazine's first National Magazine Award nomination in public interest journalism. His own work has appeared in *Harper's,* the *Washington Post Magazine,* the *Wall Street Journal,* the *Los Angeles Times,* the *Washington Monthly,* the *New Yorker,* and *Worth.* Greg's acclaimed study of obesity, *Fat Land: How Americans Became the Fattest People in the World,* was published in 2003.

History & culture

Modoc petroglyph, Lava Beds National Monument

California today

CALIFORNIA. ICON OF AMERICAN PROSPERITY AND EVEN THE "AMERICAN Dream." The popular image of the "Golden State" as a place of bikini-clad surfers and glamorous film stars has been nurtured, if not created, by Hollywood. Mother Nature has ably assisted by blessing California with unparalleled beauty. Third largest state (after Alaska and Texas) in the United States, but by far its most populous, California comprises a dizzying potpourri of superlative landscapes. This, and a famously carefree yet polyglot lifestyle, have drawn to its bosom an accentless, outdoorsy, entrepreneurial, experimental, forever upbeat, multi-cultural people inspired by California's open and inviting horizons. It's all part of the enviable California mystique.

Purely from a standpoint of numbers, Californians are remarkable: There are now more than 36 million of them, representing one in every eight U.S. residents. So great is California's allure to migrants that the state's population is expected to top 50 million well before the year 2050.

Ethnically, Californians comprise the nation's most diverse population. While blacks represent less than seven percent of the population—only half that of the U.S. average—and 44 percent are Caucasians of northern European descent, today fully one-third of the state's population identify themselves as Hispanic, a reflection of the state's geographic and historic intimacy with its neighbors to the south. More than one in ten Californians is Asian, ranging from Hmong villagers to Hindu software programmers to Chinese financiers. While fewer than half of Californians were born in the state; fully one quarter were born outside the United States.

The result of this compressed ethnic migration, according to the California novelist and social observer Donald Waldie, is a *mestijaze*, "the promiscuous amalgamation of Hispanic, African, Asian, and Native American peoples." It is little wonder, then, that one California university recently renamed its old 1960s-inspired ethnic studies program as, simply, American studies.

Geographically, Californians are still largely a coastal people—more than one out of four reside in the five major metropolitan areas of Los Angeles, San Diego, San Francisco, San Jose, and Long Beach—all close to the sea. Yet a great many the newer arrivals, together with a large number of second- and third-generation Californians, have been moving eastward to thriving inland suburban and new-town destinations with names like Rancho Bernando and Santa Clarita. Meanwhile, new arrivals from abroad continue to coalesce where their native peers are established, resulting in high concentrations of specific ethnicities: thus, for example, Vietnamese Americans constitute an astounding 31 and 21 percent, respectively, of the populations of Westminster and Garden Grove.

Californians are as diverse in lifestyles as in heritage and skin tones. The rusticity-seeking dwellers of the forested far north have more in common with the cowboys of Idaho than they do with California's urban sophisticates. And few commentators would argue with the observation that San Franciscans differ markedly from Los Angelenos. The state's multi-faceted nature is epitomized by the differences (and rivalries) between the two urban centers. Progressive, heavily gay San Francisco (birthplace of anti-Vietnam War hippiedom) has always been open-minded, even non-conformist, despite being the West Coast's bespoke suited "Wall Street." Sprawling and slightly narcissistic laid-back L.A. is more self-possessed and money-oriented, as befits the world capital of Hollywood fame and glamour.

Money—the pursuit of money!—and boundless optimism wed to an entrepreneurial spirit and individuality drives Californians ever forward. In the past two decades they have reinvented their state's economy—the seventh largest in the world—weaning it from its onetime dependence on defense spending and redirecting it towards high technology

Deep in naturalist John Muir's Range of Light, Yosemite's Vernal Falls glows in its own mist.

and finance. Silicon Valley, centered around San Jose, is the birthplace and epicenter of the computing industry—Apple, Google, Hewlett Packard, and IBM are among the behemoths headquartered here—and the spawning ground of not only the technological future but also of overnight fortunes. Los Angeles' economy and culture remain heavily dependent on the movie industry, and the fascination with youthful looks has spawned its own industry—cosmetic surgery! Meanwhile, California is the world's fifth largest producer of agricultural produce, although agriculture accounts for only two percent of the state's economy. Indeed, the vast San Joaquin/Sacramento Valley—colloquially known as the Central Valley—is the most productive and profitable agricultural center in the world, thanks to incredibly fertile soils and a constant stream of migrant labor (much of it illegal and thereby cheap).

While the very name "California" is synonymous with Hollywood movies and TV sitcoms, the cultural milieu runs broader and deeper than *Mad Max* movies and *The*

From palms to basin to the looming mountain ranges, Los Angeles at sunset remains the nation's most futuristic city—the Oz of America.

Simpsons. Highbrow art looks back with pride to the plein art movement, birthed here, while radiant works by L.A. adoptee, British-born David Hockney, have helped secure California's artistic place in the sun. In music, too, there's something to sing about. Los Angeles and San Francisco are bastions of classical music, as well as the spawning grounds for contemporary sounds, from the Beach Boys and Grateful Dead to rappers and the Red Hot Chile Peppers.

There is, of course, a cost to all of this growth and creativity, and much of it is borne by the environment. While it is true that the major part of the state remains pristine and unimaginably beautiful, it's also true that water quality in many urban areas has worsened. And to improve the air that Californians breathe; even the Central Valley is now mired in smog as foul as anywhere else in the nation. But

Surfers, with their vintage car, at Orange County's Huntington Beach

California, always at the forefront of national trends, is a trend-setter in efforts to legislate on behalf of a cleaner environment—a process accelerated under the tenure of pioneering Governor Arnold Schwarzenegger. The "gubernator" has spent much of his time in recent years responding to natural disasters. Fires, floods, and earthquakes have always been part of the bargain of being Californian, but they seem to grow ever more calamitous each year as the cities grow bigger and more crowded. One senses that the more thoughtful Californian may be just a little bit on edge, wondering what Mother Nature has up her sleeve next.

Yet Californians cannot be bowed down. Like the common concept of California's Mediterranean climate, their vision is always sunny. It is hard not to be so, one assumes, when blessed with such an abundance of sunshine and natural beauty. Southern Californians' boast of being able to ski in the morning and sunbathe the same afternoon is the envy of anyone who doesn't actually live there. And East Coasters shivering through midwinter blizzards shovel snow while the inhabitants of Palm Springs sunnily sip iced martinis

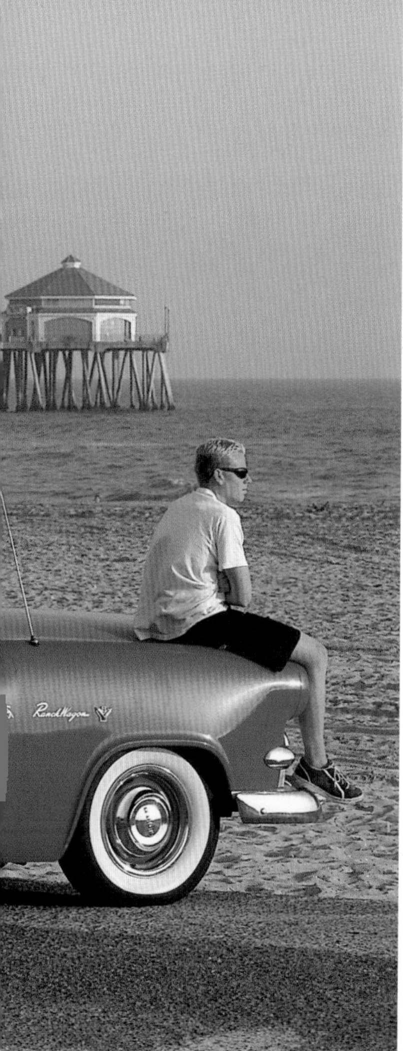

poolside in finger-snapping Sinatra style. True, chilling fogs smother much of the Pacific shoreline: famously, San Francisco's coldest months are actually August and September, much to many ill-equipped tourists' surprise. Anyone believing that even California's winter clime is always sunny should read up on the fate of the Donner party (forced to resort to cannibalism to survive when trapped by snowstorms in 1846 while attempting to cross the Sierra Nevada). And only mad dogs and Englishman venture into Death Valley in the killer heat of mid-summer.

But therein lies a deeper beauty. The physical diversity of both climate and terrain is astounding. North America's iconic low-point, Death Valley (282 ft below sea level), lies within a few hours' drive of the Sierra Nevada, where 15 peaks soar more than 14,000 feet. California's scale is big enough to guarantee amazing variety yet small enough to permit visitors to switch in a single day between mountain, coastline, desert, and forest. No wonder Californians are passionate about outdoor recreation. Mountain biking first evolved some 20 years ago on the steep, winding trails of Mount Tamalpais. Whitewater rafting was birthed on the sparkling rivers that spill from the Sierras like effervescent champagne. And weekends are given to the health-conscious hedonism of sailing, snowboarding, surfing, or sundry other active pursuits.

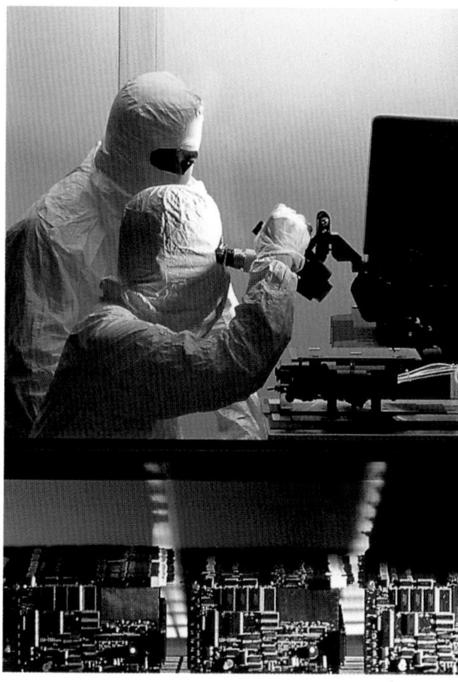

Technicians in a Silicon Valley "clean room" inspect microchips.

All this and more awaits visitors keen to sample the individual elements that combine to define the uniquely Californian quality of life. ■

The land

NOT EVERYONE WHO COMES TO CALIFORNIA REACTS TO ITS SOOTHING AND tranquil climate the way Charles Dudley Warner, a 19th-century traveler, did when he exclaimed "Here is our Mediterranean! Here is our Italy!" *(Our Italy,* 1891). But few who have driven the state's byways and taken in the smells of orange blossom and pines and sage and sea remain impartial to its natural charms. If there ever were an American Mediterranean, California would be it.

The climate, in part, proceeds from the land, and the land—158,000 square miles of it—proceeded from a series of giant tectonic collisions that began some 250 million years ago, when the offshore Farallon plate began to slip underneath the North American continent. In the process it formed a mountain range. Then: more collision, more mountains. And so, very gradually, the basic basin-and-range geography of the state was formed.

About 130 million years ago, these collisions heated up the underlying mantle of the Earth, liquefied it as lava and, eventually, formed the Sierra Nevada. Once the North American plate overtook the Farallon, it bumped (this time laterally) into the Pacific

plate. This formed what is known as a transform fault, the San Andreas, a network of terrestrial stresses and cracks that stretches northwest from the Gulf of California to Point Arena, above San Francisco Bay. The Pacific plate and the North American plate slide past each other along this fault, sometimes imperceptibly, at other times explosively in an earthquake.

The result of this upheaval is a land of extremes. At 14,495 feet, Mount Whitney, in Sequoia National Park, is the highest point in the coterminous United States. Badwater, in Death Valley, at 282 feet below sea level, is the lowest. The consequential extremes in temperature and precipitation are aided and abetted by two major oceanic currents along the state's 1,100-mile coastline. The deep, cool California Current sweeps south bringing frigid Arctic waters and is thus responsible for San Francisco's long, cool summers and legendary fogs. A secondary current, shallower and fragmented, flows along the eastward-veering southern California Bight, thereby accounting for the south of the region's remarkably balmy weather.

At the continent's end, the dramatic Big Sur coast takes a constant battering from the Pacific Ocean.

What fails to thrive here? Not much. Botanists estimate that, because of the abundance of singular habitats, more than one-third of California's 5,000 native flora may be unique to the state. In the foothills you can find the live oak, *Quercus agrifolia*, its tiny, hollylike leaves ingeniously suited to the high temperatures and low humidity of the region. *Sequoia sempervirens*, the coast redwood, thrives in the moist conditions near the coast. *Sequoia gigantea*, the giant sequoia, grows higher up in the Sierra Nevada. The pickleweed, *Salicornia,* has adapted so successfully to the harsh and salty waterline of inland estuaries that, from afar, its clusters appear as swaths of russet-colored snow. And there are the imports—date, orange, and madrone. California has made them all its own.

Weather changes with the land, flora and fauna adapt to weather—and Californians to all three. Witness, if you are lucky enough to travel here at the right time, the quintessential California rite of nature worship: the grunion hunt (see p. 131). A slim fish, 5 or 6 inches long, with an eerily green body and a silvery belly, the grunion spawns in shallow waters upon each high tide during every full or new moon between March and August. The grunion is an unremarkable fish for eating, yet its lunar swan song is irresistible to teenagers everywhere. Thousands throng to their favorite beaches to frolic with it.

No one knows quite why, but the activity is somewhat appropriate: Young people thinking of mating while trying to grab a slithery fish that spawns and swoons where the great Farallon plate smashed against the North American continent, giving rise to the natural wonder that is California. ■

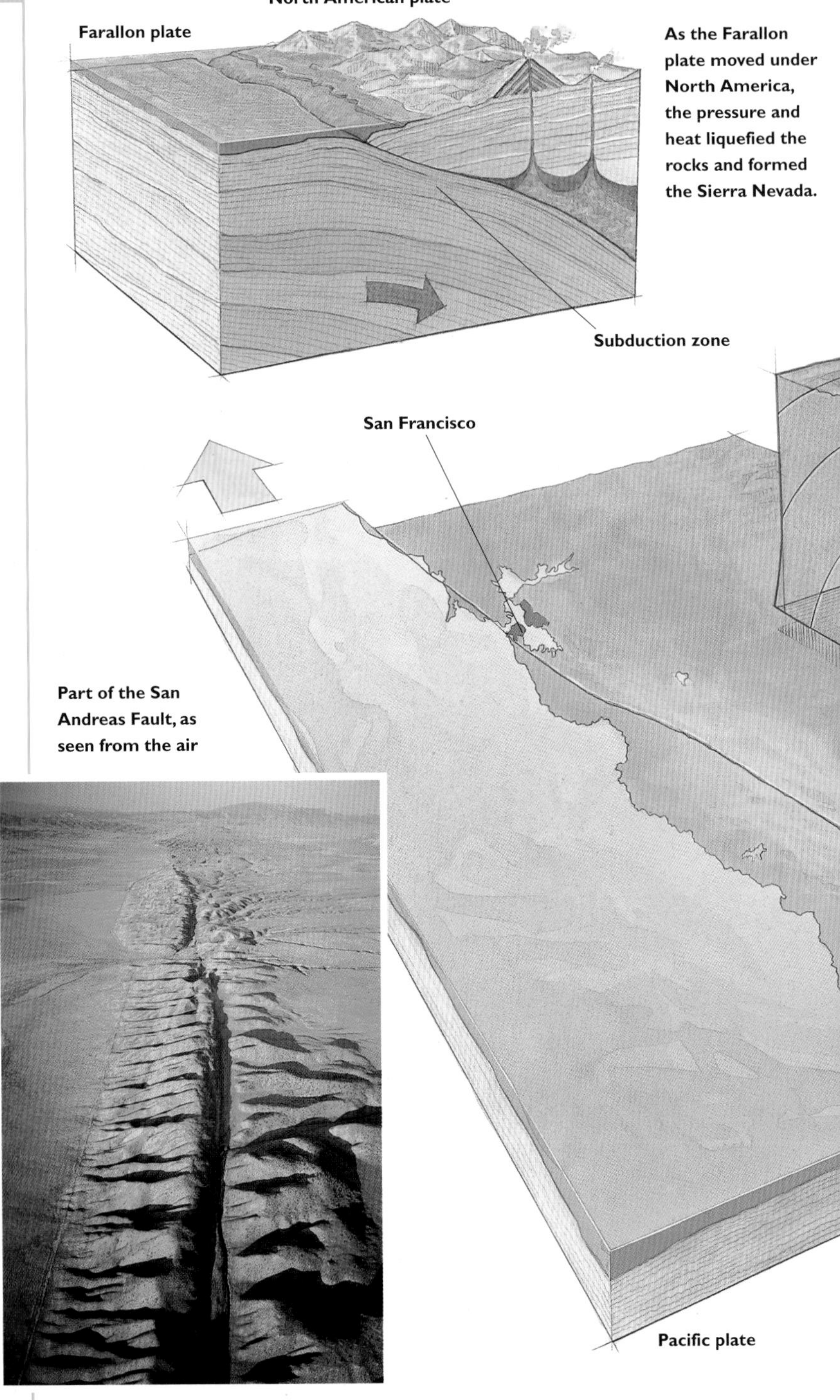

As the Farallon plate moved under North America, the pressure and heat liquefied the rocks and formed the Sierra Nevada.

Part of the San Andreas Fault, as seen from the air

The North American plate and the Pacific plate slide past each other along the San Andreas Fault. Arising deep in the Earth's crust, earthquakes send primary waves (P-waves) pulsing through nearby rock; these set up slower, secondary waves whose shearing action can buckle the surface rocks and open up cracks and fissures along the fault line.

San Francisco residents view the fire that followed the 1906 earthquake; in terms of destructiveness, this is still the granddaddy of them all.

San Andreas Fault

North American plate

Los Angeles

The 1994 earthquake near Northridge paralyzed Los Angeles, pulling freeways apart and demolishing thousands of buildings. Left: the remains of an I-5 exchange near Simi Valley

Food & wine

FOR THE PAST TWO DECADES CALIFORNIA HAS LED THE WAY IN TODAY'S increasingly eclectic culinary world. It is the ultimate foodie mecca, with a host of different cuisines. This diversity makes California cuisine hard to classify, but three historic themes resonate.

The first of these themes is the embracing of various ethnic traditions. The earliest sustained effort to create a California cuisine was made by *Sunset*, the "Magazine for Western Living." The publication was launched in 1898 by the Southern Pacific Railroad, whose aim was to exhort Easterners to "colonize the west and...travel in style to a new life of year-round sunshine and agricultural bounty." Almost immediately *Sunset*'s founders embraced the state's Mexican culinary past, launching an endless campaign to educate Golden Staters on everything from "Try a Mexican Dinner" to "Making Mexico on Your Table." Here was a way for a new Anglo migrant to invent a culinary history, a cuisine partly of memory and partly of psychological need.

Another theme—also one of *Sunset*'s editorial missions—was the merging of nature and home through kitchen and garden, the notion that even middle-class Californians should have their own kitchen garden. This, as the editors liked to put it, was "Sunshine as Power." No issue of the magazine was (or, for that matter, is) complete without an extended monthly garden column and several articles on topics like what to do with all those kiwi fruits or how to grow an Asian spice garden. Eating your own freshly grown food was not only pragmatic and thrifty; it could increase vigor, the key to fully appreciating all that California had to offer.

The third theme could be called the "search for pure flavor," an activity born of the vast agricultural abundance and the belief among California chefs that theirs is a quest for absolute essence—of basil or orange or tomato or plum.

The first great modern synthesizer of these themes was Alice Waters, founder, in 1971, of the Berkeley restaurant Chez Panisse. Having just returned from a trip to France, Waters applied the principles of Provençal cooking to California ingredients. As she later wrote, "My one unbreakable rule has always been to use only the freshest and finest ingredients; [my] quest led to Amador County for suckling pigs and peppery watercress; to Napa for Zinfandel made especially for our restaurant; to Gilroy for garlic; to Sonoma for locally made goat cheeses; to the ocean daily for oysters...."

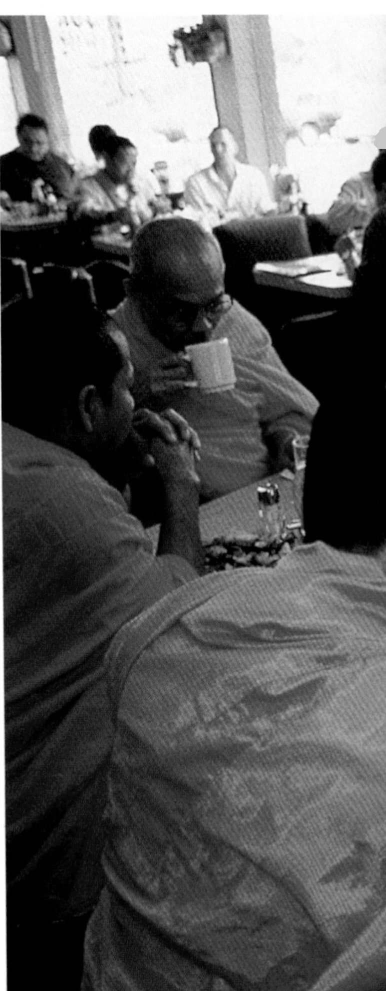

Buddhist monks breakfast in a Denny's restaurant, Los Angeles.

Inspired by Waters's injunction to "eat fresh from the garden," chefs from around the state literally reinvented all the classic cuisines—and a few nonclassic ones as well. In 1979 a young San Francisco Zen Buddhist named Annie Somerville, determined to make vegetarian cooking more, well, vegetarian, opened a new restaurant called, simply, Greens. It was a refreshing contrast to the gloppy mess of overcooked grains and soy cheese that through the years had come to symbolize the genre.

In Los Angeles the innovators looked southward. The young chefs Susan Feniger and Mary Sue Miliken took up the old *Sunset* injunction about the importance of Mexico and started the Border Grill, where intense *poblano* chilies met the mesquite-grilled flavors of modern Santa Fe. In 1984 cooks Viana La Place and Evan Kleiman opened Angeli, an Italian café/pizzeria, which sought to reinvigorate traditionally heavy Italian-American restaurant food by treating the tastes of the southern Italian kitchen "in a light, modern manner." Rather than following the convention of serving foods either hot or chilled, they served theirs at warm-to-room temperature because "we know that the true flavors of food can be best appreciated at these temperatures." And, of course, there was Wolfgang Puck's celebrated Spago restaurant in Los Angeles, where California's entire ethnic archipelago fell onto a delicate pizza pie. No one would ever think of Beijing duck and goat cheese in quite the same way ever again.

If the 1970s and '80s were about freshness and ethnic fusion, the 1990s were about the primacy of flavor, often in more traditional fare. At Napa Valley's French Laundry, considered the "best restaurant in the United States" by the discriminating Ruth Reichl of the *New York Times,* chef Thomas Keller draws from the surrounding countryside—and beyond

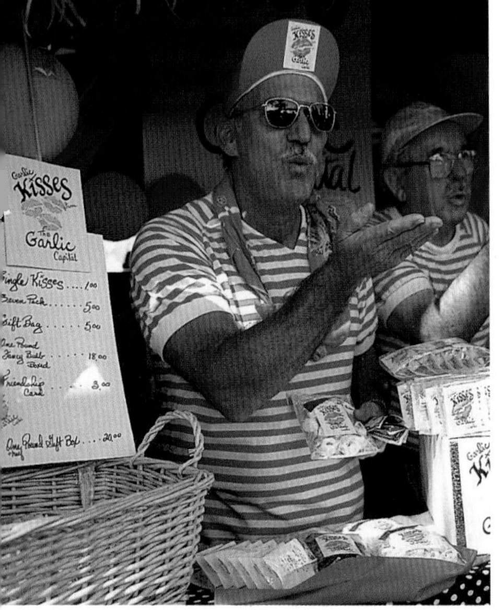

A vendor of "garlic kisses" plies his customers at the annual Garlic Festival in Gilroy, near Santa Cruz.

from France and Italy—to create such startling dishes as white truffle custard, lobster in vanilla-saffron *sabayon* sauce, and pomegranate sorbet with champagne gelée. In San Francisco, Reed Heron's Rose Pistola restaurant in North Beach captures the essence of rustic Genoese cooking in its chickpea-flour breads and whole roast snappers.

In Oakland, there is a thriving farmers' market where Hmong villagers hawk fresh lemongrass and fiery Thai chilis, while African Americans offer big bean pies and homemade barbecue sauce. Nearby, at a little place called Café 817, an Italian man named Sandro Rossi has pared his menu to the purest and freshest of what makes Italy Italy and California California. Over tiny Napa lettuce he drizzles only the freshest of local olive oils; over that, the most intense cured Italian ham the founders of *Sunset* could ever have imagined. A sliver of parmesan. A sprig of lemon basil. It is the cuisine of dreams. *Perfetto!*

WINE

With more than 500 wineries across the state, perhaps the only thing more surprising than the variety of California wines is their overall quality. As John Doerper writes in *Wine Country,* his influential book on the subject, "The quality of the *average* wines produced in Napa and Sonoma is now so high that the gap between them and premium wines has narrowed.... Winemakers now feel they have to widen that gap—to keep distinctive wines truly distinct—by raising the quality of premium wines ever higher." For the aficionado of wines, whether experienced or amateur, the situation spells bonanza. Today more than ever California is a wine-lover's heaven, unparalleled anywhere in the word except for the ancient stands of France and Italy.

The modern history of California winemaking dates from as recently as 1966, when the Robert Mondavi Winery was founded in Oakville, near Napa, by Robert Mondavi and his elder son, Michael. Obsessed with elevating Napa Valley wines to world-class status, the Mondavis began experimenting with one of the mainstays of local viticulture, wines known as California sauternes. Soon they were applying contemporary European techniques learned during fact-finding expeditions across the Atlantic. The most important of their innovations involved sauvignon blanc grapes; like their friends in France, the Mondavis began to leave the skins on the grapes after the crush, then ferment them in a stainless steel tank and transfer them to French oak barrels for aging. The result was one of the state's first blockbuster premiums—a new twist on an old favorite dubbed *fumé blanc* by Mondavi the elder.

What followed was an explosion of vintners adapting similar classic techniques to California grape growing. Within ten years Mondavi's dream came true. At the Paris Wine Tasting of 1976, two California wines edged out French reds and whites. *Sacré bleu!*

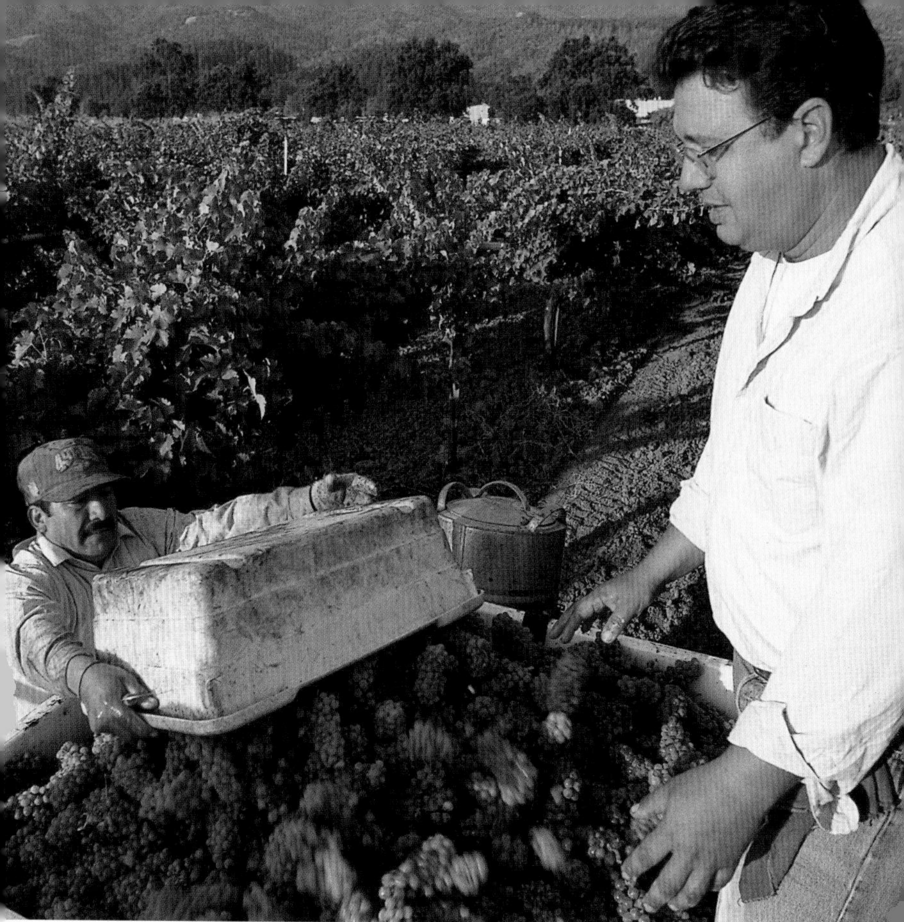

The grape harvest in Napa Valley, where the microclimate and soil conditions are perfect for viticulture. Since the 1960s, California winemaking has become world renowned.

The story since then has at times bordered on the tragicomic: So many nouveau winemakers have set up shop in the Napa and Sonoma Valleys that, during the summer tourist peak, there may be more traffic jams there than in the cities. And there has been, predictably, a small but notable Disney effect, with some large wineries becoming so adept at marketing and branding that one might wonder which comes first, the wine or the label.

Such cynicism evaporates when one returns to first principles—making world-class wines. Perhaps the most important trend in recent years is the increasing value placed on a wine's appellation, the special geographic and climatic area from which it comes. These regions—some vast, some only a few hundred acres—possess microclimates capable of producing wines of extra high quality that have special taste characteristics.

A particularly popular appellation at present is the Carneros region of southern Napa, which runs westward into Sonoma County. Here, the cool breezes and fogs from nearby San Pablo Bay help produce some of the state's most spectacular Pinot noirs, as well as several outstanding chardonnays. Farther north and west, the Benziger family have used the various shade and sun combinations at their Sonoma Mountain vineyard to make a deep cabernet sauvignon. Still farther west, the nearly continuous cool weather of the Anderson Valley not far from Mendocino has helped produce world-class gewürztraminer and Riesling. ■

History of California

"IN CONTRAST TO HISTORY, THE STORY OF MAN IN CALIFORNIA WOULD have different proportions, would take a longer view and recognize the Indians as the largest minority for a generation after 1849, heavily in the majority through the preceding 80 years, and the only residents for centuries and millennia prior to 1769. In other words, from man's first appearance in this area the Indian monopolized the scene for at least 97 percent of the time span."—John W. Caughey, *California*

EARLY CALIFORNIANS

If California's eccentric geography wrought an equally unique botany, its impact on human settlement was even stronger. Consider the archaeological record. Mainstream scholarship has long held that the first Californians probably arrived around 6,000 to 7,000 years ago (a small but important group places the date as far back as 10,000 years). By the time Europeans arrived in the 16th century, however, Native Americans numbering about 300,000 had fragmented into some 105 linguistic groups dispersed widely throughout the state.

These groups fell loosely into one of three linguistic families. The Penutian resided largely in the north and included the Miwok and the

Wintun, who may have been among those greeting the Spaniards in the late 18th century. Among the Hokan, occupying the central coast, were the Chumash, perhaps the most technically sophisticated of the southern tribes. The Uto-Aztecan in the south were distant descendants of Mexico's Aztecs and the American Comanche; their numbers included the so-called Gabrieleños, one of the first fully Christianized, or missionized, Indians.

Details of daily life in pre-Columbian California remain scarce, but relatively new data suggest some compelling conjectures. Radiocarbon dating of inscribed animal bones found in the La Brea Tar Pits in Los Angeles, for example, indicates that the carvings were done on "green," or fresh, bones of now extinct animals, suggesting that early L.A. man led a life intricately tied to packs of wildly aggressive wolflike creatures. Reconstruction of the only complete human remains on the same site—those of a young woman—indicate that violence was not uncommon: Her skull had been bashed in with a blunt object. Close examination of the boats used by the Santa Barbara Chumash indicate that the tar pits were part of an important trade route. Modern-day Wilshire Boulevard in Los Angeles lies directly over the path they took to gather tar to waterproof their crafts.

Still, the original Californians lagged significantly behind the Aztecs, their brethren to the south, in several key areas. They had no organized system of agriculture, kept no domesticated animals (except for dogs), and were neither builders of roads nor creators of metallurgy. Their priesthood was relatively informal. Not surprisingly, these traits led the first European colonists to brand California's natives as rustics—"diggers" who lacked the self-sufficient backbone that Europeans considered a hallmark of civilization.

Yet there was little evidence that hunger was a problem for these people—at least until the Europeans came. This has led modern scholars to reconsider what, exactly, constitutes a "civilized" material culture. One item under their microscope is deer hunting as practiced by the Rumsen people of southern Monterey Bay. Far from being a simple, unplanned activity, Rumsen deer hunting involved not only high levels of skill, training, and knowledge, but also demanded such religious and social preparations as praying, sexual abstinence, dietary restrictions, and even various mind-sharpening techniques. As the scholar Malcolm Margolin points out, the hunter would usually give away part or all of his catch to elders and neighbors so that "hunting, in short, did not render a man 'self-sufficient,' but like other aspects of Indian life served to bind the hunter closer to others in a strand of reciprocity."

A fair question, then: Why did the Native Americans gravitate toward the mission system so easily and so freely (as was usually

Paintings by ancestors of the Modocs, at Fern Cave in Lava Beds National Monument, near Tulelake

the case, despite assumptions to the contrary)? The answer must be found in what the Spaniards—with their legions of armored soldiers, exotic foods, elegant white horses, and sonorous-voiced padres—brought to the meeting when the two groups first encountered each other on a lonely beach in San Diego in 1769.

Padre Junípero Serra, the 18th-century Father of California, founder of a chain of 21 missions for the Spanish crown

SPANIARDS & MEXICANS

With few exceptions (among them the discovery of Point Reyes in 1579 by the English freebooter Sir Francis Drake), the pioneering of California was largely a Spanish undertaking. As such, its context was both medieval and colonial: medieval because it immediately followed the Spanish Inquisition and the expulsion of the Moors; colonial because it grew directly out of Cortés's 1521 conquest of the Aztecs in Mexico.

The new Pacific outpost derived its name from a 16th-century popular fantasy of chivalry, *The Exploits of Esplandian* (1510), by Garci Rodríguez de Montalvo. In it, the Christians of Constantinople must confront a great unknown: a force of Amazons led by a certain Queen Califia from the island of California, where everything was made of gold. Frustrated in his search for the fabled Seven Cities of Gold, the Spanish explorer Francisco de Bolonas first applied the name to Baja in 1541—an allusion to a paradise, yet unfound.

Bolonas was followed in 1542 by the more well-known Juan Rodriguez Cabrillo, who discovered San Diego Bay in 1542. Then came 125 years of benign neglect as Spain concentrated its resources on the silver and gold strikes in Mexico and the development of the Manila-Mexico spice trade. Only when incursions of British and Russian explorers threatened Spanish hegemony did Charles III of Spain finally make California a priority again: In 1768 he dispatched Gaspar de Portolá to secure the coast for Spain.

To do so, Portolá implemented the three most powerful elements of Spanish colonialism: the pueblo, the presidio, and the mission. The pueblo represented civil authority and was based on the medieval notion of a secure clustering of towns. The presidio, a fort, represented the military elite. The mission was the vehicle for the religious authorities charged with converting the Indians to Christianity.

Spain's most influential imperial cleric was the Franciscan Padre Junípero Serra, who founded the first mission, in San Diego, in 1769. A native of Mallorca, Serra entered the priesthood at 16, developed a reputation as an outstanding preacher, and was dispatched to the Americas in 1749. A stubborn, spirited, and often combative man, he was also a classic medievalist, believing, among other things, that pain and discomfort purified the soul. (Once he deliberately exposed himself to a swarm of insects, which caused an infection that left him permanently lame in one leg.) Serra's passion led him and his successors to establish 21 missions in California by 1821.

While few scholars doubt Serra's sincere religious motives, few also doubt that it was the mission system that led to the dramatic decline in the Indian population. This was tragedy laced with irony: The padres believed that they could only protect their neophytes from outsiders and often brutal Spanish soldiers by concentrating their wards together in large numbers. Yet by doing so, the padres also introduced the Indians to new European diseases. By the advent of the gold rush in 1848, Indian numbers had dropped from a pre-Columbian high of 300,000 to fewer than 35,000; and to fewer than 20,000 a decade later.

To this day, the destruction of the Indians in California is regarded as the original sin of the Golden State. Serra was eventually beatified by Pope John Paul II, but only after a 30-year, multimillion-dollar public relations campaign by some of California's richest and most influential Roman Catholics.

After Mexico won independence from Spain in 1821, California drifted under a succession of weak Mexican governors, who increasingly viewed the faraway colony as a drain on internal resources. To reward settlers and placate the ambitious, Mexico began granting large tracts of land to locals, or Californios. The result was the growth of an affluent rancho culture, of grizzly bear hunts and fiestas and rodeos. Eventually, these local land barons—the *gente de razón*—grew hostile to interference from Mexican authorities. In 1836, the Californio Juan Bautista Alvarado led a revolt against Mexican authorities and proclaimed California a free and sovereign state. Mexico soon regained sovereignty, but the stage was now set for independence—and eventual U.S. statehood.

STATEHOOD OF GOLD

By 1846, two more potent elements had entered the amalgam of forces setting California on the path to independence and, eventually, statehood. Both of them resided among the 800 Anglo-Americans then living in the Mexican California.

The first was mountain men, fur trappers and reckless fortune seekers of mixed degrees of gentility, who resented Mexico's control. The second was Yankee settlers and entrepreneurs looking for opportunity. Among them were William B. Ide, who led a party of a hundred over the Sierra to the Sacramento area; James Wilson Marshall, the eventual discoverer of California gold; Sam Brannan, a Mormon pioneer and real estate entrepreneur; and John Sutter, a Swiss American who founded a colony named New Helvetia that later became the state capital. These Americans, of various stripes of religiosity, were united in their plan to remake Mexican Catholic California into a more American Protestant version of paradise—Yankee paradise.

Into this cauldron of ambition and prejudice rode a young Army commander, John C. Frémont, the leader of a secret 1845 government investigation into California's political affairs. President James Polk had provoked the Mexicans on the Texas border and needed to know how the Californios would react to a declaration of war. Under the guise of a scientific expedition (although he could not explain the presence of a howitzer in its midst), Frémont and his small band were staying in the capital, Monterey. José Castro, the *gobernador* in Monterey, grew suspicious and threw out the protesting Frémont, who retreated to Hawk's Peak overlooking the town and hoisted an American flag before going on to Oregon.

John C. Frémont, leader of the 1846 U.S. Army occupation of California, which paved the way to statehood

Frémont's camp soon became a magnet for disaffected mountain men and entrepreneurs, many of whom had heard of the Hawk's Peak incident and feared eviction by Mexico.

On June 14 a band of these men descended on the Sonoma quarters of Mariano Vallejo, the *commandante* of Alta California, to demand his surrender. Vallejo, a longtime supporter of independence, entertained the men generously with *aguardiente;* he had been expecting them. Arriving later to find his comrades drunk, William B. Ide, the leader of the insurgents, negotiated Vallejo's surrender and then raised a quickly improvised flag featuring a grizzly bear and blazoning the words "California Republic."

A few weeks later Frémont rode in and declared the republic a "permanent territorial possession" of the U.S., under military rule. Commander John Sloat sailed into Monterey Bay and, without firing a shot, took formal possession from Castro. A year and a half later, upon victory in Mexico proper, the Treaty of Guadalupe Hidalgo formalized Frémont's coup, and California was part of the U.S.

Before clear heads could begin to reckon how to organize this new U.S. possession, California exploded in gold fever. The discovery by James Wilson Marshall at Sutter Creek on January 24, 1848, represented the ultimate slap in the face to the Old World, which had begun its exploration for the Seven Cities of Gold more than 300 years before. In the first months of excavation at Yuba alone, five California argonauts took out more than $75,000 worth of ore every month. At Placerville, the average daily yield per man often topped five pounds, while a group of seven men from Monterey, using 50 Indian laborers, took out 273 pounds of gold in just seven weeks.

When the world beyond California heard of the strike, the young state's population began to soar. In San Francisco alone, more than 40,000 migrants arrived during the last weeks of 1848. The greatest and most lasting wealth was made by the business people who rose to service this new population—from Levi Strauss, the inventor who (with a partner) patented the process for putting rivets into denim and so created an enduringly popular form of clothing, to hoteliers, bankers, and lawyers. Nonwhites played a substantial role in the gold rush. The number of black miners tripled to 2,000 during the first three years of the strike—literally a golden opportunity for men still not recognized as full U.S. citizens. Many so-called Free Negroes, for example, used their gold to buy freedom for other members of their families. And while racism was rampant throughout Gold Country, it was often tempered by the intimacy of side-by-side labor with whites, something quite new to many Free Negroes. As one free man wrote to his wife from Cosumne Diggins mine, "This is the best place for black folk all over the globe. All a man has to do is work and he will make money."

The gold rush also ushered in official statehood. In 1849, a group of 48 men drew up a draft state constitution; one-quarter of them had come with the gold rush. Perhaps just as important was their youth: Only four of them were over 50, 30 were under 40, and 9 were still in their 20s. The 31st state, admitted in

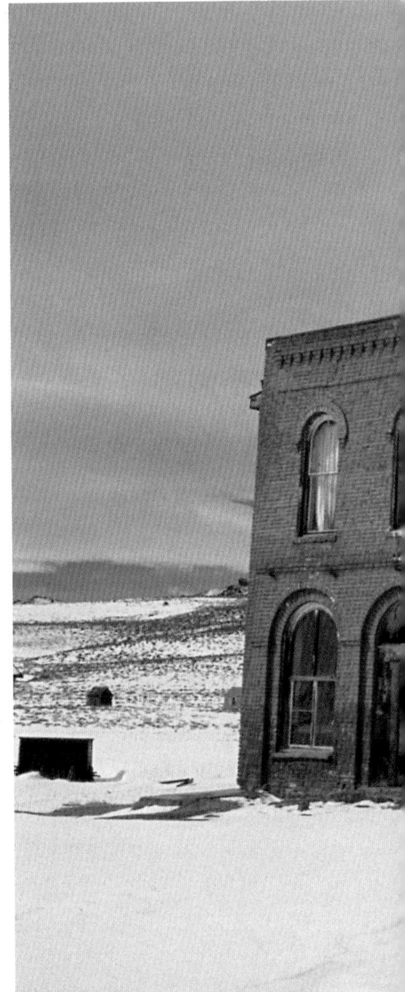

The DeChambre Hotel in the ghost town of Bodie. The gold gone, no one wanted to live here.

1850, would be run by some of the youngest old-timers in the country.

BOOM YEARS

The 70-year period following California's admission into the Union witnessed a series of economic, demographic, and technological booms unparalleled in the nation's history. These booms were to shape the character and the image of the new state, which was perceived as a land of daring individualism and serendipitous success. California was where the young nation was able to act out its most youthful fantasies.

The story of the Central Pacific Railroad and the men who profited so mightily from it is a case in point. The line was originally the passionate vision of Theodore Judah, a young civil engineer who had successfully presided over the construction of the state's earliest line, the Sacramento Valley Railroad. As the gold rush towns rose around him, Judah was the first to connect California's economic dreams with the prevailing East Coast dream of a transcontinental railroad. Judah's idea (eventually fulfilled) was the so-called Dutch Flat route over the Sierra. Rebuffed by San Francisco politicians and private investors alike, he finally called a meeting of investors inside a Sacramento hardware store owned by Mark Hopkins and Collis P. Huntington. With Leland Stanford, a wholesale grocer, and Charles Crocker, a dry goods merchant, these men eventually convinced the increasingly

desperate Judah to sell them one-hundredth of Central Pacific's outstanding stock and make them president, vice president, secretary, and treasurer of the new company. In 1863, as Judah traveled back east through Panama to stake his claim to the California leg of the transcontinental, he contracted yellow fever and died. Control passed to the men who would later be known as the Big Four.

Between 1880 and the onset of World War I, the number of miles of railroad in California increased from 2,195 to more than 8,000, creating new markets and fueling new industries.The boom in California agriculture—until then a small, regional affair—was led by the wheat growers, who planted such vast acreages that reapers would often have to camp at the end of a field, having completed but one pass during the day. Newly accessible markets led to all kinds of innovation. By the end of the 1880s, orange growers had figured out how to cool a railroad car sufficiently well

to ship their goods to the East Coast; by 1892 they had succeeded in shipping their fruit to England.

The constant influx of immigrants from the rest of the U.S. and abroad also brought new ways of doing things. Where old-timers near Sacramento saw swampland, for example, the Japanese pioneer George Shima saw a veritable Eden for growing the potatoes he so loved in his homeland. Such was the road to success for the "Potato King." The expatriate

"The Road to California," an 1871 lithograph of the Central Pacific's line into the Sierra Nevada, along the Truckee River

Hungarian Count Agoston Haraszthy became the "father of California wine" when in 1857, reveling in the pleasant climate and rich soils of Sonoma Valley, he created the state's first winery, spurring on the labors of Charles Krug, Jacob Schram, and Paul Masson, who would make California wines world famous.

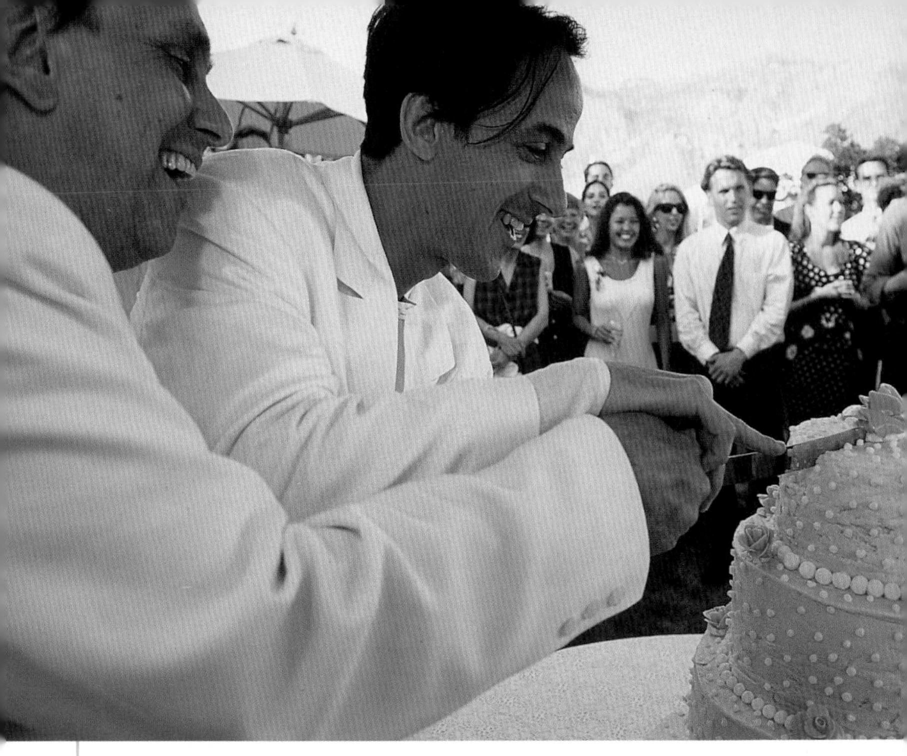

In San Francisco, gay weddings are now common—and very communal—events that boast many of the traditional features.

Luther Burbank set up his horticultural laboratory in Santa Rosa, devoted to grafting and seed selection. The aggressive lending and collateral strategies of the Italian-American banker A.P. Giannini made his Bank of America the financial undergirding for generations of the state's farmers.

All these new ways of doing things seemed to congeal in the explosive growth of the early 20th century's ultimate boomtown: Los Angeles. The semidesert city used the latest engineering techniques to secure water from a faraway place called the Owens Valley (which was left an environmental wreck). Advertising and the new motion picture industry lured new residents to newly irrigated suburbs.

But how long would it look like that? Such growth might nurture the collective and the private pocket, but its price was the scarring of the landscape by mining and dumping and construction, the damming of great rivers, and the felling of great forests. A partial antidote was found in the activities of the Sierra Club and its rugged-mystic founder John Muir.

Muir, a Scot by birth, came to California in 1868. As a boy he had gone blind and, having regained his sight, had vowed to dedicate his life to the witnessing of nature. For decades he trekked the Yosemite Valley and other natural wonders, writing about them for various national newspapers and magazines. In 1892 he helped found the Sierra Club, was made its first president, and promptly went to war with the government over a plan to permit mining, lumbering, and grazing near Yosemite. Muir convinced the state to deed Yosemite to the federal government for use as a national park. It remains an international symbol of a paradise rescued.

POSTWAR SUBURBAN PARADISE

One would hardly have expected the good life to grow out of California's experiences in the Great Depression and World War II, yet that is precisely what happened. The Depression proved to Americans that California's much celebrated economic resilience was no fiction. The million new migrants who came here during the 1930s experienced it for themselves. And what the Depression served to bolster, the war years cast in figurative and literal steel. Fueled by War Department contracts, California's total annual income almost tripled during the war. The Cold War kept the defense economy buoyant in the 1950s, and by 1960 California had a population of 15.8 million.

This growth and affluence, in proximity to the style-creating movie industry, helped give birth to the nation's first lifestyle culture. Here one could break with the past and, through personal consumer choices, become the person one wanted to be. A hypothetical composite of "California man" in 1960 might have read something like this: He works as a machinist or junior engineer at Douglas Aircraft, producing equipment for the U.S. Air Force or TWA. He holds a mortgage on a modern tract house in Lakewood, an "instant community" built from blueprint to landscape in two years. On weekends, dressed in a Hawaiian shirt and "zories," he attends a pool party in Palos Verdes—his idea of being hip. There, over barbecued steak and taco salad, he discusses contemporary politics—not conventional party politics, but specific ballot issues: a new tax to build the state university system into a world-class institution or a measure to control handguns.

In the late 1960s and all through the 1970s, personal lifestyle culture broke new frontiers. California universities pioneered ethnic studies centers—one way for their students to regain the sense of personal history lost in the original race to become American. On the same campuses the farmworker-rights leader Cesar Chavez found some of his most dedicated organizers—youth who truly believed in the justice of *la causa,* but who could also use the involvement to rethink traditional laissez-faire notions about economics and poverty. San Francisco became the world's first gay metropolis, with gay power parades and the country's first openly gay political figure, Supervisor Harvey Milk.

The conventional middle class also asserted the primacy of individual rights, first with the passage of Proposition 13, which severely limited the growth of property taxes, then in their overwhelming support of antitax political conservatives, from President Ronald Reagan to Gov. George Deukmejian. Bold new ventures by and for the spiritually aware ranged from open-air churches (one formed by the Rev. Robert Schuller later became the Crystal Cathedral) in drive-in theaters to Zen Buddhist centers. Outdoor enthusiasts demanded and got several new state and national parks.

Yet the most important contribution of the 1970s and '80s lay not in social or political developments, but in business. Heavy investment in education, combined with the stop-go nature of post-Vietnam defense spending, created a growing class of techno-whiz kids, concentrated around San Jose and the rest of the Bay Area. They included Steve Wozniac and Steven Jobs, who founded Apple Computer; William Millard, an IBM dropout who started ComputerLand, the world's first computer retail chain; and Andrew Grove, a Hungarian immigrant who helped build Intel into the world's largest maker of microchips. Presiding over them all as father figure and mentor was David Packard, the founder of Hewlett-Packard.

To the south, the boom in L.A. and San Diego was due not so much to a substantial technological base but to an unstructured, fluid business establishment. With traditional banking concentrated in San Francisco, L.A. attracted the financial experimenter. Michael Milken, the brilliant (if felonious) inventor of the junk bond, underwrote hundreds of successful but undercapitalized firms that later created thousands of new jobs.

By the late 1980s, however, several new challenges confronted Californians. Although the state had already begun to wean itself from defense contracts, it was unprepared for the enormous cuts that followed the end of the Cold War. Nor was it primed for the social costs of unchecked immigration, regardless of the net gain these new Latin and Asian immigrants brought to the economic table. The population was still increasing, and constrained state spending (largely the legacy of the antitaxers) exacerbated old inequities by beggaring poor school districts, libraries, and social welfare programs.

When the biggest race riot in the nation's history broke out in L.A. in April 1992, many Americans felt that Californians were finally

getting their comeuppance. Referring to the faltering Golden State, the social critic Michael Kinsley summed up the prevailing sentiment. "Ha-ha!" he wrote in his nationally syndicated newspaper column. "Ha ha ha ha ha!"

PERMANENT FRONTIER

From 1989 through the first half of the 1990s, its economy adrift, California suffered a series of punishing environmental and social disasters. In 1989 the Bay Area was struck by the most severe earthquake since 1906. A section of the Bay Bridge fell, and the Cypress Freeway collapsed, sandwiching traffic, while the Marina District crumbled, then burned. In October 1991 a wildfire hit the Oakland hills, destroying 3,000 homes.

Things were no better in Los Angeles. The 1992 riot was the worst race riot in U.S. history, erupting after an all-white jury acquitted four police officers accused of brutally beating Rodney King, an African American. The beating, captured on videotape and broadcast to a world audience, assumed epic proportions. When the acquittal was announced, the racially mixed south-central part of the city erupted in four days of lootings, burnings and shootings, leaving 58 dead and nearly 2,000 wounded. There followed four days of looting, burnings, and shootings, leaving 58 dead and nearly 2,000 wounded. The National Guard was brought in to restore order. In 1991 a series of wildfires paralyzed the region from Malibu to Laguna. In January 1994, the city was hit by a 6.7 earthquake originating in the San Fernando Valley. Some sections of freeway collapsed; neighborhoods of older tract housing crumbled. More National Guard

Nearly given up for dead after the 2001 Internet bubble burst, Silicon Valley is now enjoying renewed life.

troops and billions in federal aid were required. Measures taken to deal with race issues included changes in the police services and plans to build better schools in the inner city.

In fact, by 1995 new migrants were again arriving in droves. The most important reason was the state's economy, which was beginning to sing again. Dwindling trade barriers and a soaring global economy had created huge new markets for Californian products: wine, rice, computer chips, electronic games. Another critical component was Hollywood. While the 1930s and '40s are traditionally thought of as the film industry's Golden Age, the 1990s became its Platinum Age. Pushed by worldwide demand for "entertainment product" and the flourishing of cable and pay-per-view TV, new jobs created in the entertainment industry had, by 1997, replaced nearly all the jobs lost in the defense cutbacks.

California—and specifically San Francisco—was the hub of the Internet boom of the late 1990s, when the Bay Area grew giddy on the most spectacular growth since the 1849 Gold Rush. The California Dream took on new meaning as tech-savvy youngsters became millionaires at the blink of an eye. The multiplying economy fostered a massive new wave of migration from out of state, adding fuel to a concomitant real estate boom. Californians had good reason to celebrate the new millennium. By 2002, however, they were suffering an almighty headache following the collapse of the Internet and stock-market bubbles. Employee stock-option fortunes evaporated overnight, along with jobs. With housing prices continuing to skyrocket, California witnessed a net exodus as residents headed out for greener pastures. In 2003, those that remained ousted the incumbent governor and voted in Arnold Schwarzenegger on a "no new taxes" promise to resolve the state's overwhelming budget problems.

Schwarzenegger has proved a popular governor, not least for his environmentally friendly agenda and his hands-on management of several natural disasters—devastating fires mostly—that have struck California in recent years. He was reelected to a full four-year term in November 2006. In 2007, the housing and mortgage crisis impacted southern California severely, with home prices in many cities crashing by 20 percent. Meanwhile, the state has continued to see a huge influx of predominantly Hispanic migrants, while many high-tech jobs have been "outsourced" to Asia.

Demographically, the 1990s continued trends evident since the 1970s, with Latinos increasingly dominating the traditional core cities and a multiethnic middle class moving to the older suburbs. Newer so-called ex-urbs, still farther from the core, continue to attract the upper middle class. One new phenomenon is the popularity of "urban core boutique cities"—places like downtown San Francisco, which increasingly relies on San Jose for its main economic sustenance while marketing itself as the fashionable place to live. ■

The arts

IN THE MID-1880s, ARTIST JOHN GUTZEN BORGHUM WAS ASKED WHY SO many of his fellow painters were drawn to California. Borghum was nonplussed. It was, he said, because "such pure and living color is found in but few parts of the world, and such variety of strange and 'paintable' matter does not exist elsewhere." Today, California's vibrant art scene continues to draw sustenance from the state's diverse landscape.

PAINTING

That nature, with either a capital or a small letter *n,* should preoccupy every generation of California artists is hardly surprising. The state covers more than 158,000 square miles, much of it undisturbed to this day by the hand of humankind. Yet scale and remoteness alone do not quite explain the appeal. California as a phenomenon does. The state appeared at a critical period of time for the United States, a time when conventional frontiers were perceived as settled and when new lands were deemed necessary for the reinvigoration of the Democratic Experiment. It was the impact of Americans on the land, and vice versa, that bolstered the self-confidence of the young nation. There was a name for it: Manifest Destiny.

The first art to trickle out of the gold rush consisted largely of genre paintings of everyday life, a preoccupation among American artists all over the country. Yet these early works veered from the period's aesthetic norms by consistently portraying everyday scenes from heroic daily life. "Miners in the Sierras," the 1851 work by Charles Nahl and Frederick Wenderoth, shows four miners shoveling dirt into a sluice box. The work is hard, the earth yielding only to mighty swings of the pickax. But the real point of the painting is what lies ahead of the miners—an enormous rocky valley, unsettled but for one ramshackle cabin in the distance. Only a hero could work on, undaunted.

As the first impressions of California circulated—some of them accurate, many surely "stretchers," as Mark Twain would have it—more and more artists packed their bags and palette boards and set out for the West, where they would render the state's abundant natural wonders. Although many of these first landscape painters were amateurs, not a few were professionals skilled in techniques of detail and illumination. Albert Bierstadt (1830–1902), a New Englander famed for his 1868 painting of Yosemite Valley, was overwhelmed by his subject. "We are now here in the Garden of Eden," he wrote to one friend, "the most beautiful place I was ever in."

A sense of the mystic infuses his paintings. Trees seem ready to burst with colorful saps; the folds of great mountain faces appear still pliable, the Creator not yet finished with them. The High Sierra, explains the scholar Illene Susan Fort in the book *Paintings of California*, "epitomized the idea of divine immanence that had become central to the American concept of nature."

Younger artists soon transformed the genre. Impressionism's preoccupation with light combined with a growing sense of regional uniqueness. The underrated William Keith (1839–1911), for example, began his career using Bierstadtian detail in his 1869 "San Anselmo Valley Near San Rafael"; by 1880 his style had mutated into a more van Gogh-like evocation of the "Sand Dunes and Fog, San Francisco." In the former, giant eucalyptuses loom over plucky explorers. In the latter, the solitude of nature triumphs, the competing ecologies of sea grass, shrubs, and ocean quietly resolved. Urban versions of this trend were rendered by William Hahn (1829–1887), in "Market Scene, Sansome Street, San Francisco" and by Theodore Wores (1859–1939), in "New Year's Day in San Francisco Chinatown."

These two impulses—localism and impressionism—made up a variety of movements spanning the period from the late 1890s through the late 1930s. The first recognizable group, the tonalists, focused on the Monterey Peninsula. Inspired by George Inness's "California" (1894), these artists looked to

New Englander Albert Bierstadt's "Half Dome, Yosemite" evoked what he called "the most beautiful place I was ever in."

Postwar British artist David Hockney (above, "Le Plongeur," 1971) was so taken with the "private moments" of California life that he moved to Los Angeles permanently.

somehow evoke the essence of a scene via the use of tone, or, as Fort writes, "a narrow range of muted colors that emphasized spareness of land, solitary nature...."

Yet localism did not imply timidity; Inness's gold-toned scene of a small rural settlement dominated by two gnarled trees is, after all, titled simply "California," as if it were somehow the final word on the subject. A similar sense of authority resounds in "The Summer" (1932), by Gottardo Piazzoni, who once answered the question "What is your religion?" with the reply "I think it is California." By 1933, the San Francisco painter Arthur F. Mathews had pushed the tonalist form to a point of precision. His "Monterey Cypress #3" has the authority of a five-color woodblock print—brown, gray, green, blue, and an unforgettable butter gold.

The well-documented works of the Bay Area's Society of Six show just how profoundly European trends came to inspire big-city California painters. The Society's "simple" use of brilliant hues and glowing palettes conspired to one end: to evoke the modern experience of nature. Yet, even in the works of one artist, the tactics of the typical Society of Six painter could be remarkably diverse. Was Selden Connor Gile (1877–1947), in his "Boat and Yellow Hills," a Postimpressionist? Or was he, as is suggested in his almost hallucinatory "The Soil" (1927), a modernist? How about a tonalist-modernist? The exercise in labeling may be silly, but it is irresistible, given the grandness of the work.

If the "modern experience of nature" was what enthralled the Society of Six, it was nature's pure "sensation" that preoccupied the southern California plein air scene. Painters such as Joseph Kleitsch and William Wendt seemed to proceed from a simple premise: that the invariably perfect weather of southern California made for a perfectly invisible backdrop, allowing the subject of any painting there to vibrate with feeling. There is a wistful surrender to the everyday in Kleitsch's "Old Laguna" (1924), a surrender we would not trade for the world. In Wendt's "Where Nature's God Hath Wrought" (1925), a "typical" southern California hillock embodies the unknowable, the jagged geometry of purple rock rising forcefully from rolling green sage knolls. God's fist, raised in silent remembrance.

The onset of the Great Depression shook this Homeric idyll to its roots. The social and economic tumult of the nation was being played out on California's landscape, particularly upon its farms and orchards. Even before Steinbeck's groundbreaking *Grapes of Wrath* appeared in 1939, however, modern social realism flowed. Frances Brooks's "The Picnic" (circa 1930–40) depicted the simple joys of the toiling class dancing in the evening shade after a long day in the fields. Painter Maynard Dixon's "Oakie Camp" and "No Place To Go" (both 1934) bear the indelible influence of his photojournalist wife, Dorothea Lange, known for her haunting photographs of the Depression dispossessed.

Watercolorist Millard Sheets (1907–1989) did some of his most memorable work in collaboration with Lange and fellow photographer Horace Bristol. Sheets's spare but charmingly forlorn "Miggs (Migrants), 1938" was used, in tandem with Lange and Bristol's works, by *Fortune* magazine to illustrate two 1939 articles on the plight of migrant field-workers.

As in the rest of the country, the postwar period witnessed the rise of several modernist genres, from abstract expressionism to conceptual art. The content has been increasingly figurative, from the smudged impressionism of Elmer Bishoff (1916–1991) and Richard Diebenkorn (1922–1993). Landscape—the public landscape—subsided.

Yet landscape—the private, personal landscape—remains at the core of the works of David Hockney (1937–), the preeminent figure of postwar Californian art. Using a self-described "playful" style of bold color and strong line, Hockney has consistently portrayed his, and by extension everyone's, private California. Intimate California. These are places that could only "feel" private in a state blessed with so much space and wealth: swimming pools ("A Bigger Splash," 1967), backyards ("A Lawn Being Sprinkled," 1967), even roads through deserts ("Pear Blossom Highway," 1986), and roads to Hollywood Studios ("Mulholland Drive," 1980).

This last reveals how an artist's personal growth is tied to the region itself. As Hockney tells it in his 1996 autobiography *That's the Way I See It*, "I'd moved to Los Angeles and was working on a painting of the view outside my studio on Santa Monica Boulevard. And it wasn't working. It was still stuffy, still asphyxiated by that sense of supposedly 'real' perspective. I gave up. I moved up to the Hollywood Hills and I began painting the drive down to the studio. The moment I moved up here into the hills, wiggly lines began appearing in my paintings. The only wiggly lines I'd had on my paintings before were those that were on water. I was painting [Mulholland] from memory—the memory of the drive down—[and it] was beginning to work. You see, it was all about movement and shifting views—although at the time I didn't yet fully understand the implications of such a moving focus."

LITERATURE

About 20 minutes north of Angels Camp in Gold Country, in a quiet stretch of live oak and chaparral, sits a forlorn wooden shack. Here, in 1865, the young Mark Twain (1835–1910) wrote his most famous short story, "The Celebrated Jumping Frog of Calaveras County." The story concerns Jim Smiley, a betting man who is "always ready and laying for a chance," particularly when it comes to animal races. One day Smiley decides to catch a frog and train it to jump for competition. After three months of dedicated training, the frog, Dan'l, becomes Smiley's prize, "whomping" all comers.

One day a stranger in camp, hearing Smiley bragging about his frog, says: "Well, I'm only a stranger here, and I ain't got no frog; but if I had a frog, I'd bet you." No problem, says Smiley, spying an easy mark. He hands Dan'l to the stranger and asks him to hold him while he fetches another frog. Smiley returns, and the race begins. "The new frog hopped off lively, but Dan'l give a heave, and hysted up his shoulders—so—like a Frenchman, but it warn't no use—he couldn't budge: he was planted solid as a church." Smiley pays the man the $40, then discovers the trouble. The "stranger" had filled Dan'l with shotgun pellets.

Scottish poet Robert Louis Stevenson wrote of Napa Valley as "a pleasant music for the mind."

In fewer than three pages, Twain had sketched the elements of what would fascinate him and so many others writing about the Western experience: Here was a place where men made themselves up as they went; freed from the conventions of the East, they could reinvent themselves—and their language—as conditions changed. Environment trumped heredity. Indeed, environment made the man: Bret Harte (1836–1902), one of Twain's contemporaries, would even speak of a place called Roaring Camp, where "the strongest man had but three fingers on his right hand; the best shot had but one eye."

To Harte and Twain, these were minor men—characters—yet somehow universal men as well, creating new lives and new rules in a land they perceived as a blank slate. What could be more American? No wonder the author-raconteur Ambrose Bierce (1842–1914) is best known not for his poignantly beautiful short stories ("An Occurrence at Owl Creek Bridge") but for his bitter truths about life in San Francisco. As in: "A morning newspaper says three unclaimed gold watches are in the hands of the police, and that it is not definitely known who stole them. It is definitely known who *will* steal them."

If the first literary explorers of California were wits who discovered what California was doing to the forty-niners, the next generation rendered precise regional portraits of the new state, seeking the truth in life's detail.

One of these, the Scottish author Robert Louis Stevenson (1850–1894), arrived in Napa for a nine-week honeymoon during the summer of 1880. Having been ill, he was quickly revived by the mild weather of the countryside and soon took to long walks and carriage rides, meeting a host of idiosyncratic fellows who were, by turns, making wine, playing at silver mining, squatting for land, and, like Stevenson, recovering from various ailments. Stevenson had discovered a land of tonics. Standing in Jacob Schram's vineyard one day, he looked over the valley and mused, "In this wild spot, I did not feel the sacredness of ancient cultivation. It was still raw, it was no Marathon, and no Johannesburg; yet the stirring sunlight, and the growing vines, and the vats and bottles in the cavern, made a pleasant music for the mind."

Another self-described literary explorer, Helen Hunt Jackson (1830–1885), was also at work during this period. A writer, traveler, and activist for the much-abused California mission Indians, Jackson published her most influential work, the romantic novel *Ramona*, in 1883. By setting her story of a doomed love affair between a Señorita Ramona and a mission Indian, Alessandro, against the deplorable conditions of the tribes, Jackson hoped to draw attention to the plight of the American Indian.

Instead, *Ramona* was extolled as a glowing evocation of the region's Spanish Catholic past, glorifying the treatment of the Indians under the Spanish and Mexican dons and padres and laying almost all of the blame for Indian woes upon the later Anglo immigrants. To this day, the popularity of the book, along with the pageants, tour guides, and plays that it inspired, account for much of southern California's sweet-and-sour sense of itself—sweet for what once was (but really wasn't), sour for what is (but which may be better, if uglier).

By 1900, the adventure writer Jack London (1876–1916), a former sailor, tramp, and gold miner, had settled down to write in the San Francisco Bay Area. The hard-drinking London cut a wide swath. A self-educated socialist, he ran for mayor of Oakland and lost. He co-authored a book on sexual politics, then one about the underclass of London. Orating frequently on such subjects, he soon became America's best known socialist. Yet it was on the Oakland waterfront that London seemed most at home. His short stories had a diverse cast of local characters: Mexican boxers, Portuguese wharf rats, Irish thieves, Chinese shrimp-catchers. Here were oyster-bed thieves with names like Porpoise, Centipede, and Barchi, who said things like "You better slide outa this here or we'll fill you so full of holes you wouldn't float in molasses." So strong was London's writing—and so ambitious—that many critics believed he would become the West's first truly big author, a California Zola. By the eve of World War I, he had crafted some of the most compelling and memorable stories of his day. But a California Zola he was not to be. In 1916, Jack London died of alcoholism. He was 40 years old.

Writers of the next generation tended—not always successfully—to seek a national stage for their California experience. Poet Robinson Jeffers (1887–1962) evoked such strong admiration for his passionate, violent etchings of mankind's follies that his self-built Tor House, in Carmel, became a place of pilgrimage for writers and critics from around the world. Short story writer and playwright William Saroyan (1908–1981), an Armenian American from farm country in Fresno, won similar fame for *The Human Comedy* and *My Name is Aram.* The characters in the works of Italian-American John Fante, writing in L.A., were luminous enough to garner the praise of even H.L. Mencken.

Yet in John Steinbeck (1902–1968) there would be a California Zola, or at least a California Faulkner. A native of the little farm town of Salinas, Steinbeck wrote about the ways of the "small man, the small woman"—ordinary people trying to make their way in an American Eden where all was not well. Some of his subjects were cannery workers *(Cannery Row),* others tramps *(Of Mice and Men),* and still others the wandering *paisanos* who harvested the state's agricultural bounty *(Tortilla Flat).* Their world was that of the Great Depression. Steinbeck was clearly taken with their plight, making it the basis, even in his most overwrought scenes, of something that was irreducibly brilliant, unforgettable.

Jack London conjured a raw and rough world of fishermen, wharf rats, and thieves—*Homo californius.*

If Steinbeck was California's Faulkner, then Dashiell Hammett and Raymond Chandler would be its double-headed Balzac, peopling its landscape with cynical detectives, long-legged dames, and corrupt cops. Hammett's alter ego, Sam Spade, was the more hard-boiled of the two, although Humphrey Bogart's portrayal of him in *The Maltese Falcon* would forever leave Americans with the notion that he was somehow a good fellow beneath it all; apparently Hollywood did not believe the public could handle such amorality. The character of Philip Marlowe

in Chandler's *The Big Sleep*, however, *was* supposed to be a decent fellow, which of course the studios gladly accentuated. Yet the point of both characters is similar: What other reaction could an individual have to California? As the critic Edmund Wilson later noted, bleak hard minimalism was the only logical reaction to a place where the only constant thing in life was the flat endless line in the sunset called the Pacific Ocean.

Much of California's postwar literature continued in this vein, often embracing the decadent, as with Charles Bukowski's Meat School of inebriate poetry. From the 1970s (although arguably traceable as far back as Christopher Isherwood's *A Single Man*, about gay life, in 1963), new and more optimistic themes began to reassert themselves, principally through ethnic writers. Authors such as Amy Tan, for example, began exploring their interior immigrant worlds, fusing Old Country inheritances with New World domestic drama.

But it is through nonfiction that the newest minorities have made their most noticeable mark. Mexican American Richard Rodriguez, often seen with Jim Lehrer on public TV's *NewsHour*, specializes in the post-postmodern paradox: How does California transform the Old World, and how does the Old World change California and, in turn, the whole nation?

"How shall I present the argument between comedy and tragedy, this tension that described my life?" Rodriguez asks in one memorable essay, "Days of Obligation." "Shall I start with the boy's chapter, then move toward more 'mature' tragic conclusions? No, I will present this life in reverse. After all, the journey my parents took from Mexico to America was a journey from an ancient culture to a youthful one—backward in time. In their path I similarly move, if only to honor their passage to California, and because I believe the best resolution to the debate between comedy and tragedy is irresolution, since both sides can claim wisdom."

Richard Meier's design for the Getty Center in Los Angeles may be the ultimate regional coda to postmodernism.

STYLE & DESIGN

While California's literary impact on the world has been relatively minor, its influence in the world of style and design has been sizable. One reason is one of today's principal makers of "culture"—Hollywood, which is in the business of digesting large amounts of information about audiences and then feeding it back to them in just recognizable forms. This is why one might hear one of today's smart college kids describe a postmodern building in downtown Los Angeles or San Francisco as having "a *Blade Runner* look."

But California's impact on the look of our world does not begin and end with cinema. Henry and Charles Greene, architects of the late 19th-century Arts and Crafts movement, are a case in point. The movement, which called for a return to simplicity and honesty in the arts, already had American proponents (such as the prairie school of architecture under Frank Lloyd Wright). However, it fell to the Greene brothers to find a distinctively Californian version of the style, more suited than the prairie style to the arid desert environs of much of the state. Working in Pasadena from the early 1890s through 1915, the Greenes created a series of homes they dubbed "Ultimate Bungalows." The Gamble House (see pp. 110-11), designed for one of the country's biggest industrialists, may be the best of these efforts. Hallmarks of the style include Japanese-influenced overhanging eaves, the mission-influenced use of tile and stone, and a penchant for simple, handmade natural wooden furniture. The style was so resonant (and so widely imitated) that, to this day, the words "Arts and Crafts" and "Greene and Greene" are often used interchangeably. The style is resurgent, reflected in Disney's Grand Californian Hotel, advertised as being in the "Greene and Greene craftsman style," as are hundreds of new tract homes now being built around the state.

In the U.S., architecture has often carried the extra burden of providing its own historical context; if a place has no past, the architect must evoke one, the better to advertise a client's latest real estate enterprise. In California, this need for a past was exacerbated by the state's late entry into the Union and by its geographic remoteness. Thus the architect

Bernard Maybeck (1862–1957) imposed an imperial beaux arts style on his design for the 1915 Panama-Pacific Exposition, the better to signal to the world the grand ambitions of post-1906 earthquake San Francisco. Architect Bertram Grosvenor Goodhue (1869–1924) improvised a Spanish colonial revival style, replete with churriguresque ornamentation and tile domes, for San Diego's 1915 California Pacific Exposition. More recently, architect John Jerde has raised the profile of the genre, using larger-than-life signs and icons to create such faux landmarks as San Diego's Horton Plaza and the Universal Citywalk in Los Angeles.

Nevertheless, it may well have been the state's paucity of visual history that allowed the internationalist Richard Neutra to create some of the world's best examples of modern architecture, particularly in the realm of private houses. An immigrant from Austria, Neutra had been trained in the modernist school of Bauhaus architecture, which advocated pragmatism, spare clean lines, and functionality. His 1933 V.D.L. House (see p. 106), in the Silverlake district of Los Angeles, represents the epitome of the style. A boxy, angular shape, the house is perhaps most distinctive for its use of large windows to blur the division between the inside and the outside. Copied by generations of major and minor architects, it is the DNA for much of what passes for contemporary architecture in the United States today.

California, by virtue of history and climate, permitted the ultimate experiments in the functional. Where else, after all, could one dress in what came to be called "leisure wear" but in a place where, seemingly, everyone was a newcomer and where every day was as sunny as the one before? In the postwar period, the state produced such fashion and design innovators as Cole of California, known for loose-fitting yet elegant beachwear, which was often worn far from the shore. The popularity of the

The set for the 1941 film *Sergeant York*, starring Gary Cooper, included this camera platform for director Howard Hawks.

singing group the Beach Boys, and the growth of surfing, helped launch such firms as Ocean Pacific, which now sells surfwear and Hawaiian shirts from Topeka to Tokyo.

The focus on comfort and "the essentials" was also a driving force behind the Venice Beach-based designers Charles and Ray Eames, who in the 1950s produced the stripped-down "Potato Chip Chair," still much in evidence in offices around the world. And the need for easy mobility to cover routinely long distances in California soon elevated the automobile to icon status. No wonder that Detroit's most far-reaching innovations come from students at the Art Center College of Design in Pasadena.

Three recent buildings point to California's role in determining the look of tomorrow. With its defiantly bold lines and chock-a-block appearance, Frank Gehry's Aerospace Building for the California Museum of Science shows how functionality and the need for historic reference can be married without the misleading romanticism of earlier practitioners. Conversely, Richard Meier's Getty Center in Los Angeles, with its endless (and blinding) travertine plazas, may establish a new (and possibly troubling) coda for postmodernism.

And what of the Spanish architect Raphael Moneo's Cathedral of Our Lady of the Angels, in Los Angeles? It may well represent what, at least for California, is the ultimate aesthetic achievement: a monument that is more Mexico City than Spanish, and more Golden State than United States.

CINEMA

Although Hollywood, and by extension California, has long been synonymous with the film industry, conventional wisdom now holds that physical location plays only a secondary role in determining what regions will profit most mightily from this economic powerhouse. Citing the rise of computer animation, special effects technology, and sound stages in places as far flung as Austin, Texas, and Raleigh, North Carolina, some pundits have even proclaimed that the old Hollywood—the place where dreams are made—has ceased to exist. Yet time and time again, after flights of fancy to other ports, the film industry has reinvested in California, betting its existence on the combination of talent, technique, and location that the state possesses in such abundance.

Although the first full-length film made in L.A. was produced in 1907, it was not until 1910 that one filmmaker would fully exploit southern California's climatic, geographic, and historic attributes. That man was David Wark Griffith (1880–1948). A Kentucky-born actor who desperately wanted to be a playwright, the tall and lanky Griffith had by 1910 become a dominant director of one-reelers in the budding New York film industry. Taking his acting troupe west on seasonal filming forays, Griffith found that he could save money and time by using the region's abundance of sunlight. In the first four months of 1910, Griffith produced 21 films with southern California locations as background. Location

soon began to dictate content, as the historic missions prompted Griffith to make a version of Helen Hunt Jackson's *Ramona,* among other California-themed films.

In the process of manipulating all that sunlight to dramatic effect, Griffith discovered film's fundamental storytelling techniques: the angle shot, the flashback, and the close-up. All of these he used to stunning effect in his 1915 *The Clansman* (later retitled *Birth of a Nation*), a racist saga of Civil War reconstruction that President Woodrow Wilson called "history written with lightning." The film was so popular that it established Hollywood as the center of moviedom, and by the late 1920s Hollywood accounted for approximately 90 percent of all films made worldwide.

Certainly no one needed to convince Louis B. Mayer that there was money to be made in Tinseltown. A Russian-born Jew, a junk dealer turned Boston theater owner, by the time Mayer moved to L.A. in 1918 he had already

profited handsomely from movies. Among other wise moves, he had bought regional rights to such films as *Birth of a Nation.* California, where everything was new and fluid, imposed none of the social constraints that Jews met in the East; more than money drew Mayer and a generation of Jewish emigré moguls to the West Coast. There, Mayer and his rivals Jack, Harry, Albert, and Sam Warner produced films that were more American than America. Optimistic and

One of the fountains at Universal Studios theme park in the San Fernando Valley

solidly midwestern, the Andy Hardy series, for example, starred Mickey Rooney as a rosy-cheeked teenager who loved sports, his wise "pop," and his nurturing "ma." At a time when the U.S. faced one of its greatest crises—its entry into World War II—Andy was unwavering in his belief that American values would always win out.

Mayer was also the creator of the studio system of film production, signing up young talent for years at a time and then driving them to make dozens of films, a kind of plantation system with champagne and silk scarves. His paternalism, combined with his studio's ownership of theaters, gave him formidable power over an actor's life. The writer Bill Wilder recalls an afternoon spent writing a script at MGM in the early 1940s and seeing Mayer deal with the troublesome Mickey Rooney. "We looked out the window because there was screaming going on, and Louis B. Mayer held Mickey Rooney by the lapel. He says, 'You're Andy Hardy! You're the United States. You're the Stars and Stripes. Behave yourself! You're a symbol!' "

Although elements of this restrictive studio system remained in place until the early 1960s, its decline began as early as 1939, when the Department of Justice began investigating fair trade violations involving studio control of theaters. By the late 1950s, the moguls had been forced to divest themselves of most holdings, stripping them of a lucrative source of capital with which to support their burgeoning stables of winsome stars, cranky directors, and megalomaniac producers. The story of Hollywood since has largely been the story of brilliant individuals—from Robert Towne *(Chinatown)* to Francis Ford Coppola *(The Godfather)*—trying, and usually failing, to refashion certain elements of the old system.

Of all these attempts, DreamWorks, the latest and most ambitious, may well be the one to succeed. At the core of DreamWorks, the first new studio in 50 years, are three men: mogul David Geffen, former Disney mastermind Jeffrey Katzenberg, and producer-director Steven Spielberg. The latter is the linchpin. An accomplished TV producer by his early twenties, Spielberg is the most commercially successful director in film history. Technology, in the form of special effects, has played a large role in making his work shimmer, as in *Jaws, E.T., Indiana Jones, Jurassic Park,* and *Shrek.*

Spielberg has an extraordinary ability to cut through cultural clutter and zero in on tales with mythic resonance: *E.T.* as a coming-of-age in America story; *Jaws* as a modern Moby Dick, replete with Ahab-like shark hunter and an ending (costar Richard Dreyfuss paddling away on a piece of flotsam) evocative of Melville's hero clutching his dead friend's coffin.

Like Mayer, Spielberg and his partners also cultivate the special "people skills" (described by historian Garry Wills as "omnidirectional fawning") needed to secure the best stars, directors, and technicians. This is particularly apparent in the early success and quality of the trio's releases, including the *Shrek* films. However, Spielberg's approach to managing talent is very different from Mayer's. According to the *Wall Street Journal,* he ends every business call with the three words every player in Tinseltown can't get enough of: "I love you."

THEATER

The theater is one of the few enterprises in California to suffer from the presence of the film industry. The reasons are obvious, given some people's preference for wealth and fame. World-class playwrights such as Bertolt Brecht may sometimes take up residence but seldom stay under the palms for long enough to create the consistent audience demand required to sustain a distinct stage community.

Over the past few years, however, progress has been made. The director-provocateur Luis Valdez has pushed his Teatro Campesino to acclaimed performances of his Latino-themed plays, and San Diego's Old Globe Theater has won an international following for its presentations of modern and classical works. The brassy San Francisco Mime Troupe has refined the art of socially relevant drama. Another product of the California theater scene is Anna Deavere Smith, a part-time Stanford professor whose one-woman shows about such incendiary events as the Crown Heights and L.A. Riots have won her critical acclaim and a coveted "genius" grant from the prestigious MacArthur Foundation. A recent project, *House Arrest,* is a play about sex, scandal, and the American Presidency through the ages.

Under the director Gordon Davidson, L.A.'s Mark Taper Forum has launched several Tony Award-winning plays. In 1993 the Forum took a gamble by throwing its weight behind the gay-themed *Angels in America* by Tony Kushner. The result was acclaim and the biggest compliment a California director can receive: a subsequent run on Broadway. ■

No one calls it the Big Orange—but that's about the only thing folks don't call the nation's second biggest city, a sprawl of urban villages filled with art museums, beaches, and a food and music scene that garners vast acclaim.

Los Angeles

Stardom in pink

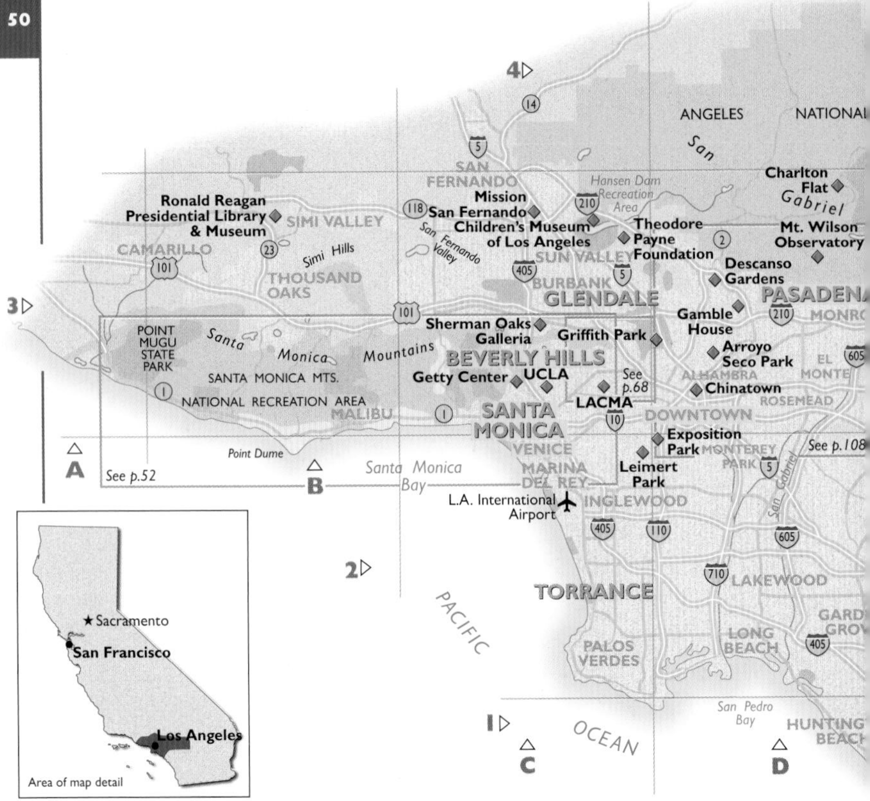

Los Angeles

IT IS, FIRST AND FOREMOST, A FLATLAND—A GREAT DESERT PLAIN. BUT IT IS a desert plain like no other. Irrigated with imported water, surrounded by glistening beaches and verdant foothills, and peopled by nine million dreamers from the ends of the Earth, greater Los Angeles, North America's second largest metropolitan region, may well hold more surprises and delights than any other single destination in the world.

Certainly its short but action-packed history suggests so. Founded in 1781 by a group of Spaniards, Indians, and mestizos, the city was originally claimed for the King of Spain as El Pueblo de la Nuestra Señora la Reina de Los Angeles—the City of Our Lady Queen of Angels. It quickly changed hands to Mexico in 1822, then, reluctantly, to the United States in 1846. (The U.S. troops were initially so unpopular here that local *mujeres*—women—sent one stiff-necked U.S. Army lieutenant packing, along with a poignant sign of their regard: ripe peaches wrapped in cactus needles.)

After a brief period of lawlessness, the region underwent a still continuing pattern of real estate boom and real estate bust. L.A.'s resultant sprawl (now of 80 contiguous towns) would thus reflect the values of the city's predominantly midwestern founders, men and women who sought to re-create the village society they had left behind in places like Iowa or Indiana rather than become part of some looming cosmopolitan cluster.

Today these urban villages persist as identifiable, if constantly changing, regional cultures. The onetime beach resort town of Santa Monica is now a sophisticated, affluent city of

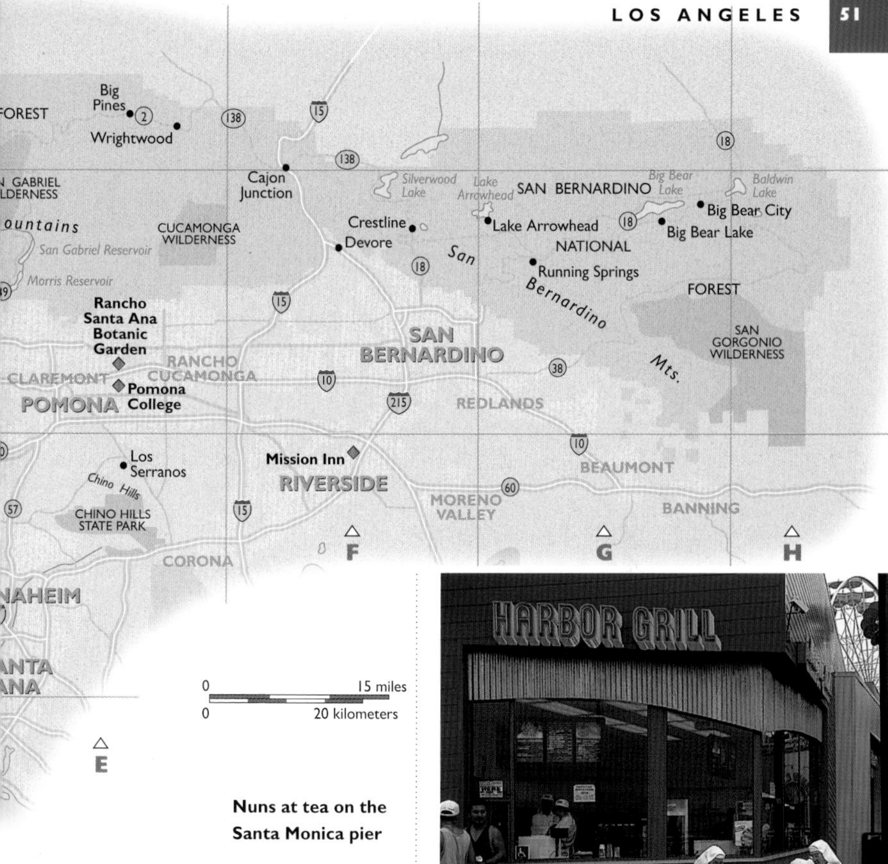

Nuns at tea on the Santa Monica pier

achievers with one of the nation's most inclusive city governments, strong environmental laws, and a culture zone stretching from its historic pier to adjacent places like the Getty Center, which one critic has called the Athens of the West.

The Beverly Hills area offers world-class shopping (on Rodeo Drive), art (at the Los Angeles County Museum of Art), and people-watching (at the bustling original Farmers' Market). And, of course, Hollywood itself.

The late 19th-century "millionaires' retreat" of Pasadena, now a diverse community of Anglos, Asians, and Latinos, similarly thrives with art (the Huntington Library), food (nearby Monterey Park, the first suburban Chinatown), and architecture (as the capital of craftsman home building).

The traveler who settles into any one of these areas, all within 30 minutes' drive of each other, will be richly rewarded. ■

How to see L.A.

Spread out over more than 4,000 square miles, greater Los Angeles is best anticipated as a small European country and best seen using one or more staging areas as your base. This guide presents four of them: "From the beach" (see pp. 52–67), "From Beverly Hills" (see pp. 68–87), "From downtown" (see pp. 88–107), and "From the foothills" (see pp. 108–126). Besides their proximity to key sites, these areas were selected for their access to high-quality hotels, restaurants, streetlife, and nightlife. ■

From the beach

With more than 72 miles of coastline and 30 miles of sparkling beaches, Los Angeles is a sun lover's dream. There is so much beach, in fact, that almost every special-interest group can be amply accommodated. Continentals flock to Santa Monica for the upscale shopping, the food, and the fellow travelers. Die-hard water sports fans go north to surf at Malibu or to windsurf at Will Rogers. Dog lovers can take their pooches to Leo Carrillo still farther north. Young lovers seek out the quiet of Marina del Rey to the south, while bohemians, oddballs, artists, and anyone in need of a laugh and a decent hot dog in-line skate over to Venice.

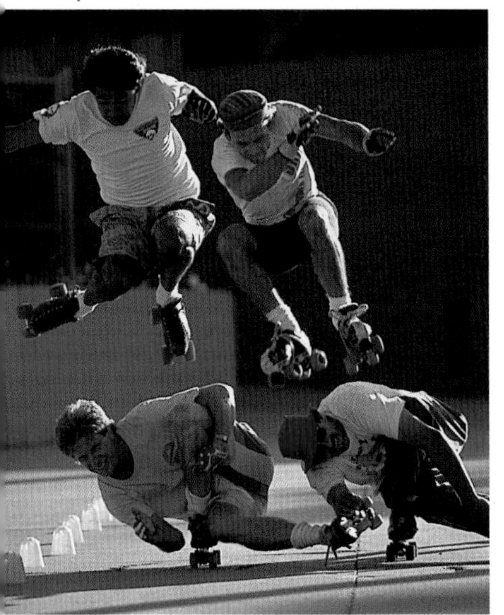

Just inland, pursuits turn to culture. The Getty Center has everything from van Gogh to Rembrandt in painting and outstanding decorative arts, as well as one of the most controversial public gardens in the country. UCLA, one of the state's most striking campuses, has more gardens (one of sculpture, one Japanese-style), as well as a stupendous museum devoted to cultural history. ■

The palm tree

Decades of "creative landscaping" have resulted in L.A.'s towering palm trees. Many strains came from Chile and the Canary Islands; only the fan palm *(Washingtonia filifera)* is native to the Southwest. At more than 50 feet, with fronds up to 5 feet long, this transplant from the Southwest desert serves as unofficial icon to the region. ■

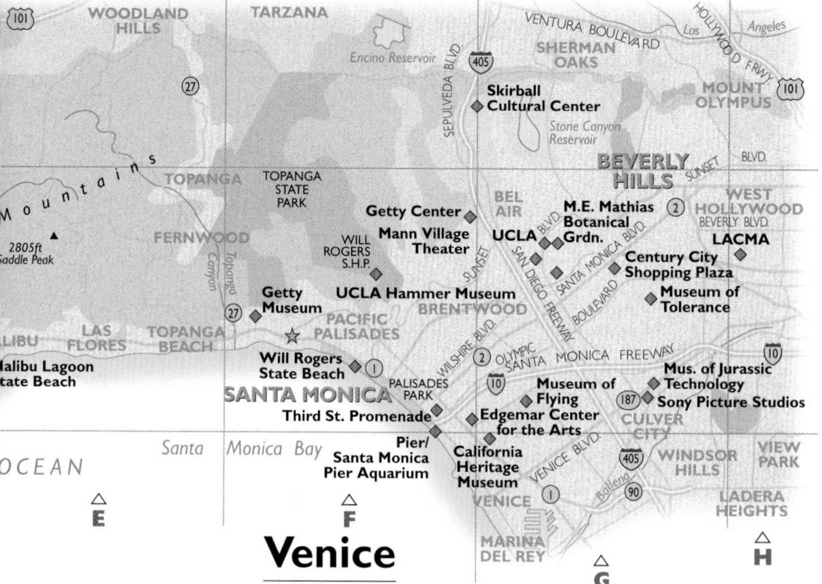

Venice

FOUNDED IN 1904 AS "THE VENICE OF AMERICA" BY enlightened tobacco tycoon Abbot Kinney, this part-bohemian, part-affluent jumble of wooden beach cottages, neo-Renaissance architecture, and idyllic canals is part of Marina del Rey.

Venice harks back to L.A.'s original golden era, when beachgoers rode the Red Car line to Kinney's version of St. Mark's before jumping into a (now razed) saltwater plunge. "Old" Venice architecture can still be seen at **Windward Circle,** and enough remains to make the 3-mile **boardwalk** one of the most frequented destinations for locals and tourists alike. At the southern end, near Venice Boulevard, strollers will see the caged-in outdoor gym known worldwide as **Venice Weight Pen.** Muscle-bound exhibitionists, street artists, palm readers, musicians, religious preachers, and bikini-clad roller-skaters add to the modern day circus that defines Venice Beach. It was here that Arnold Schwarzenegger and a legion of Mr. Americas learned to pump iron.

The area around the last of the Venice canals *(near Dell Ave.)* has become a placid, picturesque home to many of L.A.'s cultural elite, including Matt Groening, creator of *The Simpsons*. At the northern end stands the 30-foot-tall public art piece **"Ballerina Clown"** by Jonathan Borofsky *(corner of Main St. & Rose Ave.)*. Keep with the spirit of Venice by driving east to the **Museum of Jurassic Technology,** where the curator has assembled an eclectic collection of strange phenomena (such as the deprong mori, or "piercing devil" bat) and weird human accomplishments (micro-sculptures of Snow White and the Seven Dwarfs built inside the eye of a needle). The museum's avant-garde program of evening speakers is one of L.A.'s best kept secrets. A tour of **Sony Picture Studios** leads you through sets where *Spiderman* swung from buildings and agents from *Men in Black* battled aliens. You can even sit in on a filming of *Jeopardy!* and *Wheel of Fortune*. ■

Venice/Marina del Rey

Map: 53 G1

Visitor information

www.visitthemarina.com

Address: 4701 Admiralty Way, Marina del Rey

Phone: 310/305-9545

Museum of Jurassic Technology

www.mjt.org

Address: 9341 Venice Blvd.

Phone: 310/836-6131

Hours: Closed a.m. & Mon.–Wed.

Price: Donation

Sony Pictures Studio

www.sonypicturesstudios.com

Address: 10202 W. Washington Blvd.

Phone: 310/244-8687; 310/520-8687

Hours: Tours Mon.–Fri.

Price: $$$$$

Opposite: Roller skaters show off their agility and skills at Venice Beach.

Santa Monica's Third Street is the place to dine and shop.

Santa Monica

SANTA MONICA IS NO LONGER THE SLEEPY BEACHSIDE town so aptly evoked as "Bay City" by the detective novelist Raymond Chandler. With a population of more than 88,000 and some of the best eating and shopping in L.A., Santa Monica now sports a much more European ambience—the Nice of California. The various musicians who perform at the four-times weekly farmer's markets are an indication of another facet of Santa Monica: its prime position on the world music scene.

Santa Monica
53 F2
Visitor information
www.santamonica.com
1920 Main Street, Suite B
310/393-7593; 800/544-5319

Camera Obscura
1450 Ocean Ave.

Fortunately for the seeker of old Santa Monica, there are still all the eternal beachside delights: salty air, tawny beaches, and magical sunsets. Perhaps the best place to take in the city's character is **Palisades Park** *(Ocean Ave.)*. Deeded to the city in 1875 by John Percival (J. P.) Jones, a city founder, this 26-acre strip of green lawn and Washington palm trees sits above Santa Monica Bay. The views sometimes include a glimpse of Catalina Island, some 22 miles away. A morning walk could include several notable stops: The 110-year-old **Camera Obscura** projects images through its rooftop lenses and prisms—a reminder of what passed for wonder before the age of Disney; the statue of **St. Monica** *(Ocean Ave. & Wilshire Blvd.)* by Eugene H. Monrahan is remarkable for its streamlined modern lines, as is the old **Shangri-La Hotel** just across the street.

While the historic **Santa Monica Pier** now houses the reasonably priced Pacific Park amusement park, many come just to see the 1909 **Looff Hippodrome** and its refurbished carousel of hand-carved ponies built by the Philadelphia Toboggan Company, where Paul Newman's character worked in *The Sting*. On the south side of the pier is the original **Muscle Beach,** where the muscle-bound show off to the public. Underneath the pier is the **Santa Monica Pier Aquarium,** where three aquariums educate the public on marine science. Just north of the pier, at 415 Pacific Coast Highway, is the **Marion Davies Guest House,** built for the star in 1929 by noted architect Julia Morgan.

On Main Street, the **California Heritage Museum** is well worth a visit. Housed in the 1894 former home of city founder J.P. Jones, the museum offers a number of exhibits in displays that change regularly. Some of its past shows have featured the work of 1920s California tableware makers, the origins of the Hawaiian shirt, and artifacts of early surfing culture. The architecturally inclined should take in the **Edgemar Center for the Arts,** originally designed as the Santa Monica Museum of Modern Art by Frank Gehry, whose work has included the American Center in Paris and the Guggenheim Museum in Bilbao, Spain. Architectural pilgrims can also see (from the outside only) Frank Gehry's home at 1002 22nd Street.

Although currently closed, the **Museum of Flying** is scheduled to relocate to a new site on the north side of the Santa Monica airport in 2008. The airport is on the old site of the Douglas Aircraft Company which, for more than 60 years, dominated the construction of both commercial and military aircraft. The new museum will feature functioning World War II planes along with dozens of more recent aircraft.

Shopping and people-watching at **Third Street Promenade** *(between Broadway & Wilshire Blvd.)* can be a full-time pursuit. The best time to hit the Promenade is on Wednesday, when the famous **Santa Monica Farmers' Market** convenes at Third Street and Arizona Avenue. This is a "foodie" magnet, and a keen eye might spot celebrities and famous chefs scouting out the best organic mushrooms and brussels sprouts. ■

Santa Monica Pier Aquarium
www.healthebay.org/smpa
✉ Santa Monica Pier
☎ 310/393-6149
🕒 Closed Mon & a.m.
$ $, children free

California Heritage Museum
www.californiaheritagemuseum.org
✉ 2612 Main St.
☎ 310/392-8537
🕒 Closed Mon.–Tues.
$ $

Edgemar Center for the Arts
www.edgemar.com
✉ 2437 Main St.
☎ 310/399-3666

Museum of Flying
www.museumofflying.com
✉ Santa Monica Airport
☎ See website for opening details

Green Los Angeles

More than 25 years of environmental activism has resulted in cleaner beaches, better water, and new state parks dedicated to preserving the ecologies of western Los Angeles County.

The most scenic of these parks is **Malibu Creek State Park** *(1925 Las Virgenes Rd., Calabasas, tel 818/880-0367)*, with reaches of rolling grasslands, sharp gorges, creeks, and towering old trees. You can take a guided horseback ride *(tel 310/457-3730)* through this backcountry.

At the end of its namesake sits **Malibu Lagoon State Beach** *(tel 818/880-0350)*, 35 acres of wetlands where bird-watchers can see egrets, herons, brown pelicans, and the endangered tidewater goby. Farther north is the largest of the parks, the 15,000-acre **Point Mugu State Park** *(tel 818/880-0350)*, where sage and native grassland meet rocky coastline. Closer to L.A. is **Topanga State Park,** *(tel 310/455-2465)* an 11,000-acre park with 36 miles of trails through wildflower pastures and past creeks. ■

Drive: Along Sunset Boulevard

Intrepid travelers can test out their L.A. driving legs by taking a spin up legenda Sunset Boulevard, a scenic, winding road memorably featured in one of moviedom's mc stupidly terrifying chase scenes (*Against All Odds,* 1984). The sane motorist, ho ever, begins the jaunt with a late morning brunch at Gladstone's 4 Fish *(17300 W. Paci Coast Hwy., Pacific Palisades, tel 310/454-3474, www.gladstones.com),* where the French to and orange mimosas (only one, please) get you into the proper self-indulgent mood.

Meditating at the Self-Realization Fellowship Lake Shrine in the unlikely setting of Sunset Boulevard

Heading east on Sunset, the first stop is the **Self-Realization Fellowship Lake Shrine ①** *(17190 Sunset Blvd., tel 310/454-4114, closed Sun. a.m. & Mon.).* Founded in 1950 by the Paramahansa Yogananda who preached that "there must be world brotherhood if we are to be able to practice the true art of living," the shrine underscores the highly ecumenical nature of Hinduism in L.A. With its gardens of miniature roses and hydrangeas the size of basketballs, the shrine is a perfect place for an after-lunch nap. The gift store sells Indian curios, incense, and self-improvement literature, such as the highly unjolly *Overcoming Character Liabilities.*

Still on Sunset, a left turn at Bienveneda Avenue will take you to the **Topanga Trailhead ②,** the start of hikes into the mesquite-and-sage landscape of the Santa Monica Mountains. A nearby sign points to the easily negotiated **Phil Leacock Memorial Trail,** from which the view takes in Pacific Palisades as well as the ocean.

Continue up Sunset and past the famous **Gelson's Market ③** *(Sunset Blvd. & Via de la Paz),* where you can stock up on picnic items. Beyond it, look out for the turnoff for **Will Rogers State Historic Park ④** *(14253 Sunset Blvd., tel 310/454-8212).* The beloved humorist deeded his estate to California, which has maintained his home and polo field; a free audio tour of Rogers's living room and living quarters, with its charming cowboys-and-Indians decor, is a must. A hike up **Inspiration Trail** as the wispy late afternoon fog rolls into the park will put a flush of sun and wind on your face.

On Sunset again, you pass infamous **Rockingham Avenue ⑤** (where noted non-killer O. J. Simpson's house has been razed) and stop for an espresso at Brentwood

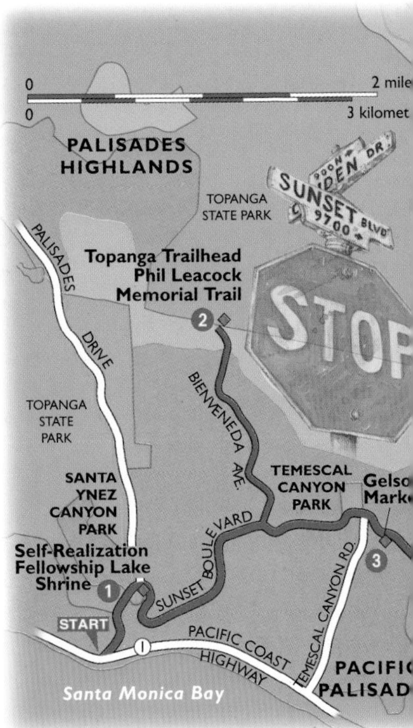

Village *(Barrington Ave.)* before passing the I-405, the San Diego Freeway, and coming to **Bel Air Estates 6,** home of the rich and famous. Either of two ornate "gates" on the north side of Sunset admit the curious to a maze of small streets lined with some of L.A.'s priciest (if sometimes aesthetically troubling) estates. Note that the "star maps" hawked here are likely to be worthless. Content yourself with occasionally exclaiming "That's gotta be Greta Garbo's house!" or "Isn't that where Don Johnson and Melanie Griffith got married?"

You can either end the drive here or continue to **UCLA** (see pp. 64–66) or to **Beverly Hills** (see pp. 68–87). Alternatively, turn right on Beverly Drive to Little Santa Monica Boulevard and the **Century City Shopping Plaza** *(10250 Santa Monica Blvd.)*. ■

- Also see area map p. 53
- ➤ Gladstone's 4 Fish
- 12 miles
- 2 hours
- ➤ Bel Air Estates

NOT TO BE MISSED

- Self-Realization Fellowship Lake Shrine
- Will Rogers State Historic Park
- Bel Air Estates

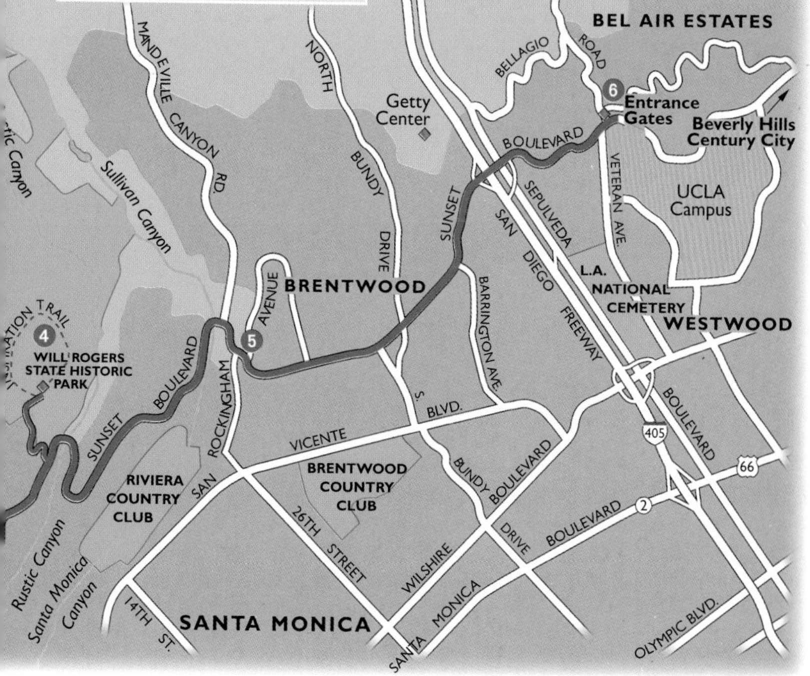

Glowing neon advertising dazzles the early evening drivers in a typical view along Sunset Boulevard.

BEL AIR ESTATES
BELLAGIO ROAD
6 Entrance Gates
Beverly Hills Century City
Getty Center
MANDEVILLE CANYON RD.
NORTH BUNDY DRIVE
SUNSET BOULEVARD
SEPULVEDA
SAN DIEGO FREEWAY
VETERAN AVE.
UCLA Campus
L.A. NATIONAL CEMETERY
WESTWOOD
BRENTWOOD
AVENUE
BARRINGTON AVE.
Sullivan Canyon
Rustic Canyon
Santa Monica Canyon
4 WILL ROGERS STATE HISTORIC PARK
5
ROCKINGHAM
SAN VICENTE BLVD.
RIVIERA COUNTRY CLUB
BRENTWOOD COUNTRY CLUB
S. BUNDY DRIVE
26TH STREET
WILSHIRE BOULEVARD
405
66
2
SANTA MONICA BOULEVARD
OLYMPIC BLVD.
14TH ST.
SANTA MONICA

J. Paul Getty

Getty Center

PERCHED ON ITS 110-ACRE CAMPUS HIGH ABOVE THE drone of I-405, the Getty Center, completed in 1997, inspires conflicting emotions in Angelenos. The dazzling complex of specially cut Italian travertine and very American aluminum bespeaks all the ambitions of the great art institution that it is—a source of pride for many Angelenos. Yet the modernist campus also seems to be at once removed, reinforcing the old notion that in L.A. art has no organic connection with the community.

Getty Center
www.getty.edu
53 F2
1200 Getty Center Dr., Getty Center exit from San Diego Freeway (I-405)
310/440-7300; 310/440-7305 for hearing impaired
Closed Mon. Open Fri. & Sat. until 9 p.m.
Free; parking fee (parking based on availability)

Yet since its opening, the Getty's actions have belied such concerns, and, through an outreach program, the center connects to the cultural life of the entire city. Key features of this process are the ongoing programs with local schools (guided and self-guided tours are offered, but must be reserved in advance) and educational programs covering photography, sculpture, and painting.

THE BUILDING

The first home of oil billionaire J. Paul Getty's growing collection of antiquities and decorative arts was the recently-restored Romanesque **Getty Villa** *(17985 Pacific Coast Hwy.),* based on the Villa dei Papyri at Pompeii, that Getty built in 1953 above Topanga Beach. His superb collection of Greek and Roman antiquities—more than 50,000 pieces in all—are arranged thematically. Today the villa also serves as an educational research center into the study of ancient art and cultures. An eccentric with a reputation for being a skinflint (he once installed a payphone for guests in his English mansion), Getty surprised critics by leaving a 700-million-dollar trust. Astute financial management has increased it to a whopping four billion dollars, enabling its trustees to commit one billion dollars to the building of the new museum.

Their choice of architect was Pritzker Prize–winner Richard Meier, known for his design of the High Museum in Atlanta. The key design issue was how to make a modernist structure that inspired a classical sense of permanence. Meier's answer was to use travertine, a form of limestone quarried in Bagni di Tivoli, Italy. The result is a hulking complex of shifting hues of white, ranging from a retina-scarring *blanc majeur* in the morning to a pleasant, late-afternoon-in-Rome gold by dusk.

An electric tram shuttles visitors from the front entrance and parking to the museum **Arrival Plaza,** dominated by Martin Puryear's 45-foot sculpture, "That Profile." An orientation film is shown.

THE ART

The Getty's five main buildings are arranged with an eye to flexibility and chronology. All of them are connected, by either hallway or overpass, on both floors; at ground level visitors can easily pass from 16th- to 18th-century works, then back to 17th-century, and so on. All of the upper floors are bathed in sunlight. Mobile audio guides are programmed to respond to inquiries about individual paintings.

Paintings in the **North Pavilion,** which highlights art before 1600, include the evocative "Mythological Scene," painted circa 1524 by the Italian Dosso Dossi (room N205). The work not only perfectly illustrates the Venetian

The gleaming Getty complex stands on a hill above Los Angeles.

penchant for dreamscape and allegory, but also gives the museum the opportunity to fulfill its aim of educating the public about the history of paintings. Fra Bartolommeo's "The Holy Family" is a good example of the luminous quality of this early 16th-century Italian's work. A 1330 panel by Bernardo Daddi depicting the Virgin, St. Paul, and St. Thomas Aquinas has been particularly well preserved. According to author Letitia Burns O'Conner, "the conservator who examined it prior to its purchase in 1993 declared he had never seen a *trecento* picture so well preserved, its glazes still intact to modulate the bright colors of the drapery, its punched gold background glowing softly."

In 2003, the Getty acquired Titian's "Portrait of Alfonso d'Avalos, Marchese del Vasto," painted in 1533. Considered the Getty's most important portrait, this masterpiece—of an illustrious noble shown in his suit of armor—by the leading exponent of Venetian Renaissance painting, is considered to have set the standard for court portraiture and the subsequent evolution of Western art.

The **East Pavilion,** continuing the chronological sequence, covers art from the period between 1600 and 1800. While the emphasis here is largely on Dutch and Flemish works, two small 17th-century paintings, Italian and French respectively, show the collection's range: Domenichino's "The Way To Calvary" is done on copper; Valentin de Boulogne's "Christ and the Adultress," (both in room E201) is noted in a museum caption by the neoconceptualist L.A. artist John Baldessari as "a kind of film noir."

What follows is a blur of giants including Rubens ("The Entombment," "The Murder of St. Francis," both in room E202) and Rembrandt ("The Abduction of Europa" in room E205). A memorable piece by a lesser known 17th-century Dutch artist is Hendrick Terbrugghen's "Bacchante with Ape" (room E204). Downstairs, the rotating collection of drawings in Gallery 103 is worth searching out for its spotlighted new acquisitions.

The **South Pavilion** expands the scope of the previous galleries by introducing decorative arts between 1600 and 1800, the core of J. Paul

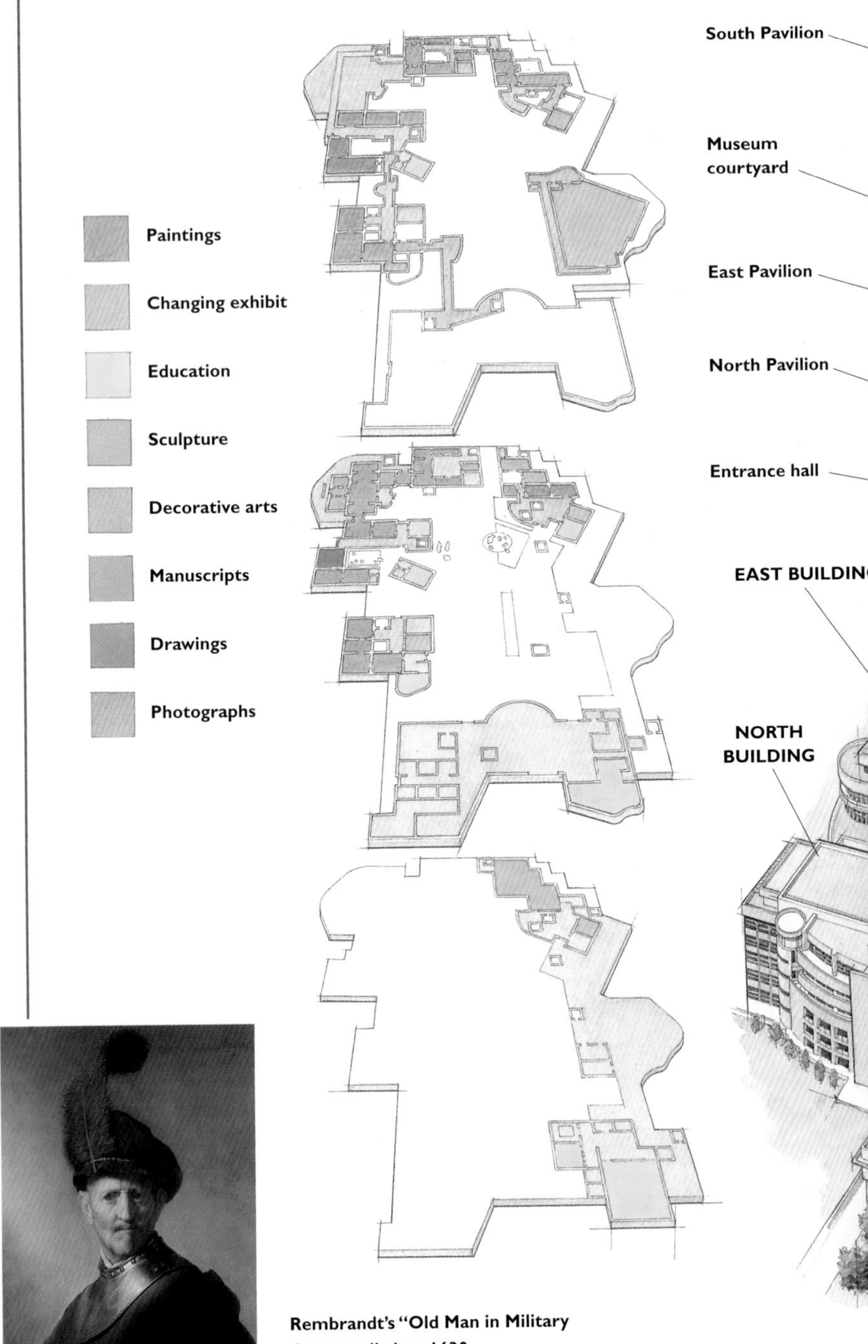

Rembrandt's "Old Man in Military Costume," circa 1630

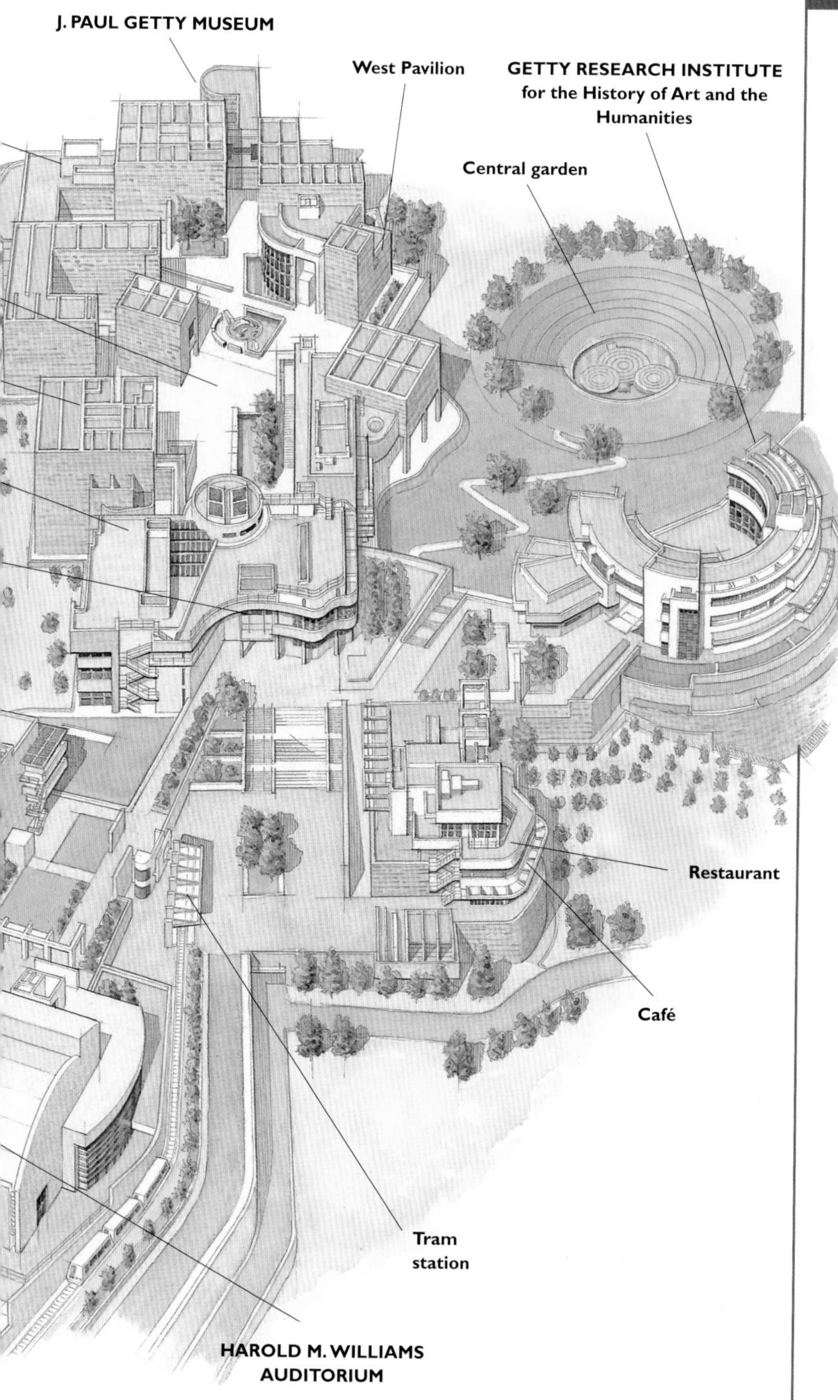
J. PAUL GETTY MUSEUM
West Pavilion
GETTY RESEARCH INSTITUTE for the History of Art and the Humanities
Central garden
Restaurant
Café
Tram station
HAROLD M. WILLIAMS AUDITORIUM

FILM SHOWS

Regular film shows given in the auditorium include: "Art Works: Behind the Scenes at the Getty" (30 mins.) and "Concert of Wills: Making the Getty Center" (90 mins.). ■

Getty's personal collection. To do it justice, the museum brought in New York designer Thierry Despont to craft several period rooms, constituting a "museum within a museum." The effect is priceless, though some find it overwhelming. Despont's pale blue French-paneled room is a perfect medium for the ornate chairs, clocks, and furnishings. The enormous "Cabinet on Stand" (1675–1680) by André-Charles Boulle, in room S103, shows a craftsmanship unmatched by his contemporaries.

Some visitors may prefer, with some justification, to make a separate trip to the Getty Center to see "Art after 1800," the exhibition in the **West Pavilion.** However, to do this would be to miss the effect of the dramatic build-up that the other pavilions provide. While many have cynically criticized this collection as "Europe's Greatest Hits," it is hard to underplay the delight provoked by the works of Monet, Renoir, Cézanne, Manet, and van Gogh that are hung here. "Irises" by van Gogh remains the biggest attraction. See it first thing in the morning before the crowds arrive. Lesser known paintings worth seeing here include the Belgian painter James Ensor's huge 1888 work "Christ's Entry Into Brussels, 1889" (room W204).

Juxtapositions of "smaller" works—a specialty of the Getty—make this gallery sing. Put Cézanne's "The Eternal Feminin" next to his "Still Life with Apples,"

Vincent van Gogh's "Irises," in the West Pavilion

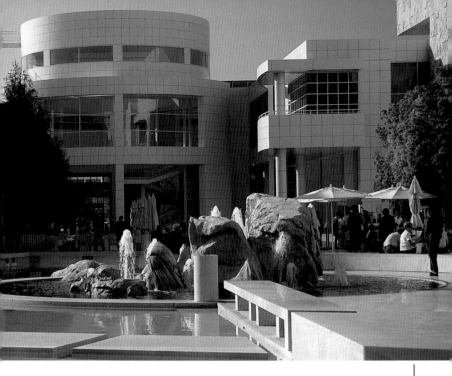

and see if you ever think of fruit in the same way again.

The brilliantly arranged photo gallery on the first floor makes a fitting coda.

Lastly, no visit to the Getty Center would be complete without exploring the **Exhibitions Gallery,** although its most famous and controversial piece, the Getty Kouros is no longer there. It was one of several antiquities returned to Greece and Italy after they were proved to have been stolen or excavated illegally. In 2007, the Fran and Ray Stark Sculpture Garden opened beside the tram station to display the bulk of 28 contemporary outdoor sculptures that Hollywood producer Ray Stark and his wife donated to the museum.

In addition, the Getty offers an eclectic range of events, from artist-at-work demonstrations and poetry readings to an annual Renaissance Family Festival, plus free "Friday Nights at the Getty" concerts featuring Afro-Latino, Cajun, folk, and blues music.

THE CENTRAL GARDEN

While there are many places at the Getty to pause and ponder or relax, nothing conjures the sense of discovery quite like the 134,000-square-foot Central Garden. Created by the artist Robert Irwin, the garden is an example of what he calls "site-generated art." Irwin's notion is that a person's intimate experience of nature can be heightened by accentuating the configuration of foliage, sunlight, and shade.

The focal point of the garden is a maze of floating azaleas, surrounded by a terraced round ravine marked by geometrically arranged cactuses. Irwin interrupts the sense of botanical order with a series of "specialty gardens"—a meadow, a stream garden, terraces of hydrangeas and nasturtiums and irises. Just how well the scheme furthers the museum's aesthetic ideals is up to the individual stroller, but a better place to rest and soak up the sun is nowhere in sight. ■

Pools and fountains cool the museum courtyard.

The statue base is designed to stabilize it in an earthquake.

One of several noted sculptures on the campus

UCLA

FOUNDED IN 1919 AS PART OF THE UNIVERSITY OF California, the University of California at Los Angeles long languished in the shadow of its older sister, UC Berkeley. Eventually, following a period of explosive growth, the 400-acre campus began establishing a profile of its own (the turning point of which is said to have been former Chancellor Franklin Murphy's command to answer the administration phones by saying "UCLA!" rather than "University of California"). Today UCLA ranks among the top ten research universities in the U.S., producing several recent Nobel Prize winners, and is fondly known as the "University of Caucasians, Latinos, and Asians," because of the diversity of its 35,000 undergraduates. South of Bel Air and north of Westwood Village, UCLA is at the heart of L.A.

UCLA
www.ucla.edu
53 G2
Visitor information
405 Hilgard Ave.
310/825-4321

THE CAMPUS

Sitting on a low hilltop and overlooking surrounding valleys and mountain ranges, UCLA's **Central Quad** of four Romanesque-Renaissance-style buildings was built in 1929. Lush grounds and swaying old eucalyptus trees make it a perfect place for weekend strolls. The **Powell Library** *(Quad, southwest corner)* is an architectural gem. Named for the California bibliophile and longtime UCLA librarian Lawrence Clark Powell, the building has been restored to its 1929 grandeur. Soothing mission-tile staircases lead to a reading room crowned by an ornate ceiling. The temporary structure used to house books during the remodeling, nicknamed "Towell," has won several architectural citations for its innovative use of materials.

Also recently restored is **Royce Hall** *(Quad, northwest corner),* another jewel. Named for the California philosopher Josiah Royce, the Italianate auditorium is said to have been modeled on the Church of St. Ambrose in Milan.

THE MUSEUMS

UCLA's main museum, the **UCLA Hammer Museum,** was founded by the late oil magnate Armand Hammer to house his then thin collection of old masters and Impressionist paintings. Since then, the Institution has matured. Among the works in the collection are "Summertime" by artist Mary Cassatt (1844–1926), whose work was exhibited with that of the Impressionists in Paris in the 1880s. Other highlights include Rembrandt's "Portrait of a Man of the Raman Family" (1634) and Renoir's childlike "Grape Pickers at Lunch."

Writings on the Wall displays essays written by prominent people in the arts about their favorite paintings from the Hammer Collection.

Three other collections warrant attention. One is the largest U.S. collection of satirical drawings and watercolors by 19th-century French caricaturist Honoré Daumier. The other star, now also at the Hammer, is the **UCLA Grunwald Center for the Graphic Arts** *(tel 310/443-7078),* which features a wide range of paper works from Dürer and Cruikshank to Picasso and Matisse. Because the Hammer is fond of traveling exhibitions—sometimes at the expense of its permanent collection—it is best to call before visiting for current information. The Hammer's new initiative to amass a collection of contemporary works created since the 1960s focuses on drawing and photographs, with an emphasis on pieces since the Millennium.

The museum's **Billy Wilder Theater,** opened in December 2006, hosts provocative public programs and provides a cinematheque for the UCLA Film & Television Archive's vast documentary and movie collection.

The **Fowler Museum of Cultural History** is a recent addition to the L.A. museum scene, but it has been making waves nonetheless. With its focus on non-European art and its emphasis on anthropology, the Fowler has staged acclaimed shows on subjects ranging from voodoo to the little-known Mochas people of pre-Columbian Peru.

THE GARDENS

The university has three outstanding gardens, all open to the public. The **Mildred E. Mathias Botanic Garden** is a perfect place to read, write, or just sit and contemplate nature's wonder. The habitat diversity covers the spectrum from bamboo groves to streambeds and tropicals—some 4,000 plant species in all. The **Franklin D. Murphy Sculpture Garden,** behind the University

The Romanesque-Renaissance Royce Hall

UCLA Hammer Museum
www.hammer.ucla.edu
✉ 10899 Wilshire Blvd., Westwood Village
☎ 310/443-7000
🕒 Closed Mon. Open Thurs. until 9 p.m.
$ $$

Fowler Museum of Cultural History
www.fowler.ucla.edu
✉ Fowler Hall
☎ 310/825-4361
🕒 Closed a.m. & Mon.–Tues. Open Thurs. until 8 p.m.

Mildred E. Mathias Botanic Garden
✉ Hilgard & Le Conte Aves.

UCLA Hannah Carter Japanese Garden
www.japanesegarden.ucla.edu
✉ 10619 Bellagio Rd.
☎ 310/794-0320
🕒 Closed Sat.–Mon. & Thurs.

UCLA Live
www.uclalive.org
☎ 310/825-2101 (tickets)

Geffen Playhouse at UCLA
www.geffenplayhouse.com
✉ 10886 Le Conte Ave.
☎ 310/208-5454

Museum of Tolerance
www.museumoftolerance.com
✉ 9786 W. Pico Blvd.
☎ 310/553-8403
🕒 Closed Sat. & public and Jewish holidays
$ $$$

Research Library, is a testimony to the former chancellor's breadth of interests. The 5-acre sculpture garden is the largest on the West Coast. Some 70 pieces of sculpture stand in the shade of the jacaranda trees. Among the artists are Auguste Rodin, Isamu Noguchi, Joan Miró, Alexander Calder, and Henry Moore. The **UCLA Hannah Carter Japanese Garden,** located in Stone Canyon, just north of the main campus, completes the botanical experience. In addition to a noted collection of Japanese red maple, pine trees, and a koi pond, there are a traditional bathhouse, a five-tiered pagoda, and a moon-viewing deck. A Hawaiian garden is behind the teahouse, replete with orchids and flowering vines.

PERFORMING ARTS

UCLA Live is one of the city's premier cultural institutions, presenting world-class, cutting-edge works at the vanguard of dance, music, spoken word, and experimental theater. Inaugurated in 2001 with pop music icon Elvis Costello, this year-round program spans the globe with its wildly eclectic offerings intended to nurture the development of experimental endeavors. UCLA Live's programs are hosted at venues around UCLA's campus and beyond, including the Freud Playhouse, with its large proscenium stage, and the restored Royce Hall, known for its state-of-the-art acoustics.

An infusion of funds from the mogul-philanthropist David Geffen and topflight Hollywood talent has propelled the **Geffen Playhouse,** in beautiful Westwood Village, into the top ranks of L.A. theater venues.

AROUND UCLA

Westwood Village, just south of the main campus, serves as the proverbial (but pricey) "college town." Breakfast at Stan's Corner Donut Shop *(10948 Weyburn Ave., tel 310/208-8660)* is de rigueur, if only to experience the chocolate chip–peanut butter crullers. Bel Air Camera *(10925 Kinross Ave., tel 310/208-5150)* is in a building that looks like a camera (stock up here on photographic supplies).

The restaurant scene around UCLA is constantly churning; one constant, on Westwood Boulevard just south of Wilshire Boulevard, is La Bruschetta *(1621 Westwood Blvd., tel 310/477-1052),* which serves up consistently good pasta dishes. Farther down Westwood is Junior's *(2379 Westwood Blvd., tel 310/475-5771),* the "Cadillac of Delis." Almost any of the Iranian restaurants on the east side of the street (known as Little Persia) serve up a decent lamb or chicken dish. To the west on Pico Boulevard is the Zen Bakery *(10988 Pico Blvd., tel 310/475-6727);* the breads and muffins are outstanding. On Pico and Westwood looms the neon-and-concrete Westside Pavilion Mall *(10800 W. Pico Blvd.),* where west L.A.'s deeper pockets find just the right casual wear. Nearby, the Spanish Mission-style **Mann Village Theater** *(961 Broxton Ave., tel 310/248-6266)* is a principal venue for Hollywood's biggest movie premieres.

Driving east for ten minutes on Olympic Boulevard will take you to the **Museum of Tolerance,** a "teaching museum" dedicated to educating the public about racism and ethnic genocide. The focus is the Nazi Holocaust. The 90-minute guided tour of its interactive displays is unforgettable—and emotionally devastating. A recent addition, "Finding Our Families, Finding Ourselves," showcases the diversity and achievements of noted Americans. The museum's Tolerance Center, which includes a film on genocide in Rwanda and Bosnia plus interactive exhibits that teach a message of personal responsibility, closed in 2007 for renovation. ■

Skirball Cultural Center

THIS YOUNG INSTITUTION, SET ON A HILLTOP JUST north of the Getty Center, represents one of the single best developments to come out of the growing trend toward boutique museums. This is because the Skirball has refined its mission—"to present Jewish culture and experience as part of the living fabric of American life as a whole"—and then, as it were, gone for the gold, presenting only the best and most comprehensive shows on the subject. There is a depth and singularity of experience here, matched by few such museums in the country. As its president, Dr. Uri Herscher, says, "The center's programs show that we Jews take seriously the inheritance of the past, but that doesn't mean we remain in the past."

At the core of the 125,000-square-foot center, designed by Moshe Safdie, is the exhibition entitled "Visions and Values: Jewish Life from Antiquity to America." Divided into 12 galleries, this rich display of artifacts, art, photos, texts, and objects from daily life takes visitors from the destruction of the Second Temple in A.D. 70 to modern-day America. Some are monumental: the Hirsch Hannuchah Lamp, from the early 20th century, shows the robust nature of that era's German Jews. Another reference to pre-Holocaust German Jewry is the reproduction of the (later destroyed) New Synagogue of Berlin. Yet often it is the small, odd fragment that is most illuminating: a hand-painted handkerchief from China with the large letters *Ort,* meaning place in German; the "Portrait of Mrs. Sarah Lyons" from Great Britain; Alexander Tyshler's 1917 poster photo, "Anti-Semitism is Counter-Revolutionary!" and an "Ertrog Container" for citron used in the Sukkot (harvest) ceremony.

The center has a program of arts and cultural events, including plays, music (including blues legend John Hammond), and readings. ■

Skirball Cultural Center

www.skirball.org

- Map: 53 G3
- Address: 2701 N. Sepulveda Blvd.
- Phone: 310/440-4500
- Hours: Closed Mon. & a.m. Tue.–Fri.
- Price: $$

Exhibit on Jewish life in America

From Beverly Hills

The great urbanist Reyner Banham once referred to L.A.'s flat basin topography as "the plains of id." Here, life was so calm that anyone who lived in it for long would soon confront—or embrace—all their long-banished desires. Note Banham's use of the plural, "plains." For if there is a "plain of id" in downtown (of midwestern and Latino aspiration) and another at the beach (of body-beautiful aspiration), certainly there is a distinct one operating in and around the greater Beverly Hills area. This is the plain of money, both refined and crude—of money made and money spent.

It has always been that way in Beverly Hills. Founded in 1906 by real estate developer Burton Green, the city grew slowly until the 1920s. In 1920 movie star Douglas Fairbanks purchased a prominent hilltop in the area for $35,000. There he built the legendary Pickfair mansion for "America's sweetheart," actress Mary Pickford. Pickfair attracted all who aspired to be a Fairbanks or a Pickford, and the real estate market boomed.

Be warned: You will probably spend more on accommodations, food, and shopping in Beverly Hills than in other parts of the city. But this is a perfect place from which to explore several adjacent areas. Just south, the Wilshire Corridor leads eastward to the Los Angeles County Museum of Art, perhaps the West Coast's best single art destination. Along the northern boundary of Beverly Hills runs Sunset Boulevard, which also leads eastward, first to West Hollywood, a strip of famous restaurants and gay life, then on to old Hollywood, where so much of the money to sustain Beverly Hills was made in the first place. From there the old Hollywood Freeway (US 101) leads over to the San Fernando Valley, land of the quintessential shopping mall, offering yet more opportunities to part with your money. ■

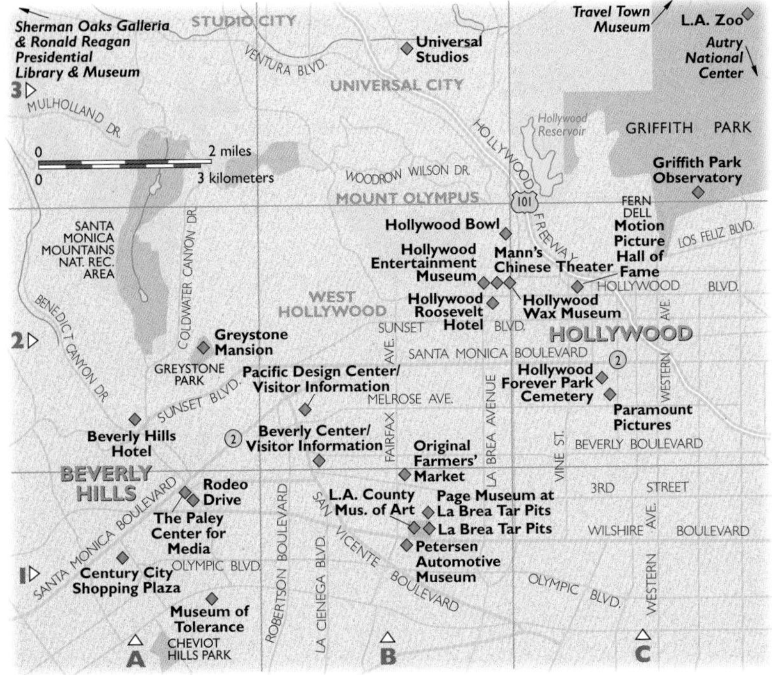

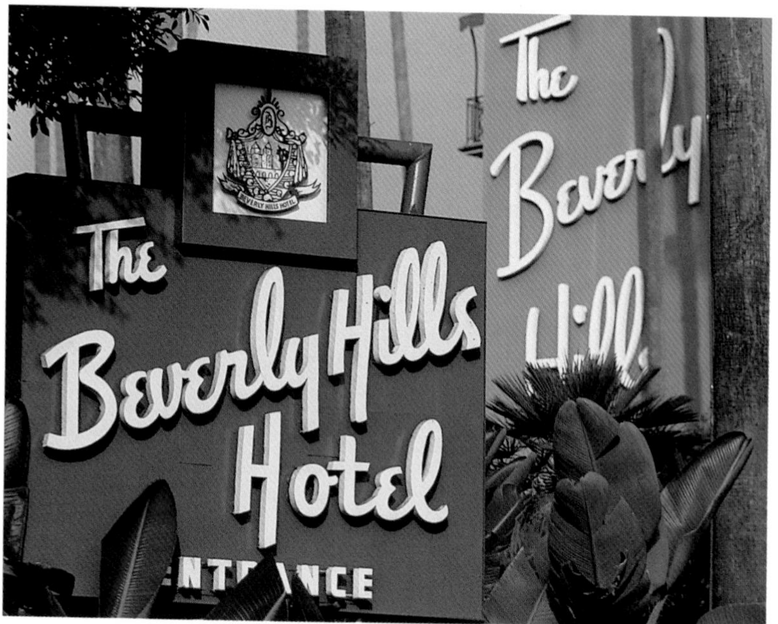

Still stylish Beverly Hills Hotel

Beverly Hills Hotel

THERE WAS A TIME WHEN MANY BELIEVED THAT THE OLD Pink Palace—the Beverly Hills Hotel—had permanently lost its glow, its lovely yet outdated accommodations overshadowed by the gleaming new Peninsula Hotel down the way. No more. Ever since its purchase by the Sultan of Brunei in 1989, the hotel has mounted a strong comeback, investing heavily in a complete makeover. The result is a glamorous retreat that evokes the best of Hollywood's Golden Age while providing all the modern conveniences.

It is not often that a hotel, even a luxury hotel, counts as a "destination." But to see *Homo hollywoodis* in action, there is no better place than under the old pepper tree in the legendary Polo Lounge. Make a reservation for 1:30 p.m. Order the tortilla soup, then the fresh crab plate. Sit back and watch the scene. Later, wander down to the Fountain Café, where you will often see younger stars preening, eating fatty no-no's, or irritably dealing with their equally irritated agents. Next, stroll the grounds and take in the architecture. If the mission-style exterior looks familiar, it may be because it was designed in 1912 by Elmer Grey, who with his partner Myron Hunt also did the Huntington Library. Paul Revere Williams was the architect for the newer Crescent Wing, built in 1949.

As the afternoon wears on and the heat rises, the hotel pool will look appealing. At the poolside, fresh sorbet is served at 4 p.m. After that, jump in. After all, Katharine Hepburn did once—and she had all her clothes on. At night, celebs cluster at Bar Nineteen 12, the hotel's hip new bar. ■

Beverly Hills
[map] 68 A1
Visitor information
www.beverlyhills.org
[mail] 239 South Beverly Dr.
[phone] 800/345-2210

Beverly Hills Hotel
www.beverlyhillshotel.com
[mail] Beverly Hills Hotel, 9641 Sunset Blvd.
[phone] 310/276-2251

JCB
JCB
JCB

Rodeo Drive

THE THREE BLOCKS OF RODEO DRIVE NORTH OF WILSHIRE Boulevard rank among the most famous (and most expensive) shopping districts in the world, comparable with the Champs-Élysées in Paris, or Florence's Ponte Vecchio. The one big difference is style; along Europe's great boulevards one would never think of wearing a sweatshirt and jeans to go shopping for a $1,000 silk blouse. In Beverly Hills, a man in a tracksuit may well drop $15,000 in one afternoon, shopping at, say, Bijans's For Men. This does not mean you should not dress well to shop here—but if you choose to go casual, whip up a good dose of attitude to go with it.

Begin at Saks Fifth Avenue (just southwest of Rodeo), one of four large department stores on Wilshire. With its valet parking and attentive staff, Saks may well be the least snooty of the bunch.

Walking north on Rodeo, the first area to your right is known as **2 Rodeo**, a retail "alley" created in 1990 to house new outlets for Tiffany's and Ferre, along with several tasteful shops specializing in home decor. This was the first new street to be carved out of the city since it became independent from L.A. in 1914. Two Rodeo Drive was started in the 1980s by real estate developer Douglas Stitzel who spared no expense with the imported Italian cobblestones. Several economic downturns later shoppers still visit the Van Cleef & Arpels, Christian Dior, Lalique, or Versace boutiques.

People-watching reaches its peak at the coffee bar in nearby Giorgio. North of that are Hermès, where scarves have become an art form, and Gucci, the Italian purveyor of handbags and accessories. The **Rodeo Collection,** just to the north, features five stories of cafés and stores, including such classy menswear outlets as Stefano Ricci. Guess USA? tops the stroll northward. Witness the plump trying to get into tight jeans here and find out just what that question mark means. Watch for Anderton Court, on the east just north of Dayton. It was designed by Frank Lloyd Wright in 1952. You can take a narrated trolley tour of Beverly Hills architecture by meeting the bus at Rodeo Drive and Dayton Way *(Sat. plus Tues.–Sun. in holiday seasons, hourly 11 a.m.–4 p.m., tel 310/285-2442, $$).*

Once relieved of your excess cash, it might be relaxing to drive over to the **Greystone Park & Mansion.** The 46,000-square-foot English Gothic Revival mansion was built in 1928 by oil baron Edward Doheny and then vacated after his son was found dead there in an apparent love suicide. Today a registered historic landmark it is owned by the city of Beverly Hills, and the public enjoys its 18 acres of terraced gardens for picnics. Classical concerts are hosted each Sunday afternoon, January to May.

The **Paley Center for Media** is a delightful diversion for anyone interested in television and radio. Visitors can view news, entertainment, and sports footage preserved in the collection of 140,000 television and radio programs. Check out the old *Steve Allen Show* for an example of early daytime-audience participation. ■

Rodeo Drive
Map 68 A1

Rodeo Collection
www.rodeocollection.net
Address: 405 N. Rodeo Dr.
Hours: Closed Mon.–Tues.

Greystone Park & Mansion
www.beverlyhills.org
Address: 905 Loma Vista Dr.
Tel: 310/550-4654

Paley Center for Media
www.mtr.org
Address: 465 N. Beverly Dr.
Tel: 310/786-1000
Hours: Closed Mon.–Tues.
Admission: Donation

Opposite: Christmas on Rodeo

The main entrance to the museum

Los Angeles County Museum of Art

"OH! I JUST CAN'T BELIEVE IT. THERE IS SO MUCH GREAT art at that place, I mean great, that sometimes it's overwhelming for the rest of us. You're so lucky to be from a city with that much great art." This telling recommendation comes not from LACMA's public relations crew, but from a public relations person at one of San Francisco's leading art institutions. Anyone familiar with the intense rivalry between the two cities knows that such remarks are rare.

Los Angeles County Museum of Art
www.lacma.org
68 B1
5905 Wilshire Blvd.
323/857-6000
Closed Wed.
$$. Free 2nd Tues. of every month

But rare is perhaps the best word to describe LACMA. In the three decades of its existence, the museum has gathered together the greatest collection of art in the western United States, 150,000 works, most of it of singular taste and quality. One reason for this is curatorial continuity. The American, Modern, and Southeast Asian collections were each largely built under the regime of one passionate curator, Pratapaditya Pal; this makes for a cohesiveness rare in most large mainstream museums.

Initiated in 2004, a new master plan for the LACMA campus has entrusted world-renowned architect Renzo Piano to redesign the museum and transform it both in and out to create more dynamic, light-filled spaces while allowing visitors to navigate easily through galleries featuring work from ancient times to the present. New galleries, public spaces, gardens, and a new building devoted to exhibiting a collection of recently purchased contemporary works will be woven together along a central concourse. The first of the three phases is scheduled for completion in early 2008, when the encyclopedic permanent collections will be rearranged and reinstalled.

The best time to visit LACMA is on a Friday evening, when the museum is open late and a free jazz concert thrums. The museums also hosts Latin Sounds on Saturday evenings, and a classical concert series on Sunday evenings. During blockbuster exhibitions, the museum can become quite congested; if you want to see one of these shows be sure to make reservations.

Visitors now enter the boldly re-imagined campus through the **BP Grand Entrance,** an open-air pavilion featuring landscaped piazzas, with the new **Broad Contemporary Art Museum** to the west. The latter's 60,000-square-feet of exhibition space includes "Band," one of two monumental Richard Serra sculptures of contoured weathered steel. Beyond, **LACMA West,** in a 1938 art deco building that once housed the May Company department store, today houses special exhibitions plus the **Boone Children's Gallery,** an interactive gallery for children and families.

The bulk of the collection is housed in four main buildings, with a fifth, the **Bing Center,** providing an auditorium with an ambitious calendar. Its weekend film series *(tel 323/857-6010)* is the place for film buffs—a legacy of the English author Christopher Isherwood's regular attendance in his later years. There is also a cafeteria, research center, and library *(by appointment only).*

Gateway to LACMA East is the historic **Ahmanson Building,** now transformed into a soaring space connected to the plaza concourse by a Spanish-style staircase. Its three levels exhibit an extraordinary wealth of Far Eastern, South and Southeast Asian, European, African, and American art, but it is Pal's collection of South and Southeast Asian art (on the third level) that is the most delightful and sensual example of LACMA's curatorial brilliance. Countries represented include Cambodia, Indonesia, and Nepal, but it is Indian art that is most exuberantly celebrated. In particular, don't miss the 12th-century Tamilnadu copper statue "Yasoda and Krishna," one of only two or three known representations of the baby Hindu deity and his foster mother done in metal. Compare this with the depiction of the dancing boy Krishna in the 15th-century copper "Destruction of Kaliya" a few galleries away.

The world-renowned Madina Collection of Islamic Art spanning works from the 7th through 19th

Detail from Maruyama Okyo's painted screen, "Puppies among Bamboo in the Snow" (1784), on display at the Los Angeles County Museum of Art

centuries is one of the world's preeminent Islamic holdings. The collection, also on the third level, focuses on decorative arts and calligraphy, and includes a number of rare masterpieces. The ancient world is also well-represented, including an outstanding pre-Columbian collection boasting a rich cross-section of objects from the major civilizations of ancient Mexico.

A full range of American art comes together on the plaza level. Arranged chronologically, this collection highlights the great themes of American art. Key works include Winslow Homer's "The Cotton Pickers," painted in 1876, just before the artist retired to New England. Homer's experience as a correspondent-illustrator during the Civil War for *Harper's Weekly* magazine propelled his rendering of rural America beyond the romantic pictures so preponderant at the time.

A joyful American send-up of Michelangelo and Rubens is all over Paul Cadmus's "Coney Island" (1934). The work succeeds because it is fleshy, resolutely hoi polloi, and yet humane about it all. Also displayed on the plaza are arts and crafts furniture, and examples of work by Tiffany and others in the American decorative arts sections.

To appreciate just how far American artists journeyed from their aesthetic forebears, take a good long look at the second level's majestic collection of European painting and sculpture. Stop at Rosso Fiorentino's "Allegory of Salvation" (1521). Rosso's portrayal of the young St. John, who has fallen faint at his mother's side after learning of her terrible prophecy of what will befall the Christ Child, is a clear comment on Michelangelo's "Pietà."

An ever still spot in these galleries is in front of Rembrandt's stunning "Raising of Lazarus" (1630). So much is captured in the moment the picture portrays, and the artist has rendered it so skillfully, that gazing in silence seems the only appropriate reaction to such mastery. The main spot of light falls on the women at the graveside expressing their unfolding awe. Yet perhaps more arresting is the way the light falls on Christ. Even the Savior of All Mankind looks somewhat surprised at what he has done.

The Ahmanson links east to the **Hammer Building** and to the collection of 19th-century European art, featuring Rodin and Degas, Gauguin and Pissarro. In one hall are three remarkable Cézannes, hung in a group. This floor of the Hammer is also home to a series of temporary and special exhibitions, often drawn from the museum's own collection of prints, drawings, and photographs.

In the prints and drawings collection, one can closely see the bravado strokes of Castiglione's "St. Mark" (1655–1660), in which the emotionalism of the counter-Reformation reaches a crescendo. Typical of LACMA's collection of German expressionism is the 1910 "Standing Child" by Erich Heckel, a pillar of the movement known as Die Brücke, which advocated art as a regenerator of man's natural spirit. The photography collection includes several works by Weston, Steiglitz, Frank, and Siskind.

Leaving the Hammer, walk eastward to reach the **Pavilion for Japanese Art,** an eccentric but perfect building for, among other things, the Shinenkan Collection of Edo period screen art. Donated by the philanthropists Joe and Etsuko Price, these scenes of nature—cranes flying, tigers prowling, roosters and hens foraging—have such a strong emotional impact that one leading Japanese art scholar confessed to having wept when he first saw them. That LACMA and the Prices agreed to build a pavilion with only natural

Winslow Homer's "The Cotton Pickers" (1876) is one of the featured works of American art at LACMA.

lighting is a testimony to their good taste and sense of adventure. Particularly worth seeking out is Suzuki Kiitsu's "Seashells and Plums," painted, like almost all Edo art, without any preliminary sketching. As Price once explained, "He simply had to have the whole painting in his head before he executed one stroke."

To the south of the Hammer Building is the **Anderson Building**, which exhibits art since 1900. Although the building received unfavorable reviews, its layout permits natural light to reach every gallery, an accomplishment that not only complements the art but makes for a pleasant atmosphere, an important attribute given the rather discomfiting nature of most modern art. The quality and importance of some of the work here is open to question: Exhibits range from Alison Saar's indulgent "Sledge-hammer Mamma" to moments of brilliance, such as Ed Keinholz's "Back Seat Dodge" (deemed lurid in the 1960s, when museum trustees voted to ban it, today it seems, well, *quaintly* lurid). The pantheon of contemporary notables represented includes Picasso and David Hockney, whose seven exhibited works here include "Mulholland Drive." LACMA's ongoing effort to collect and display the Mexican modernists is also proving fruitful, with fine examples of the works of Rivera, Orozco, and Siquieros. Look for Rufino Tamayo's "America" (1955) or Rivera's "Women Washing" (1925).

After the Anderson, go left, down the steps to the **Cantor Sculpture Plaza & Garden,** where the late Bernard Cantor's collection of Rodins cavort silently in the grass. A number of large-scale contemporary works were recently added, including Christopher Burden's "Urban Light," incorporating more than two hundred antique cast-iron lamposts.

LACMA's photography department puts on exhibitions drawn from its permanent collection of approximately 6,000 works, from the medium's invention in 1839 to the present, with works from the greats—Henri Cartier-Bresson, Walker Evans, Ansel Adams—to emerging artists. It also administers the Ralph M. Parsons Lectures on Photography series. ■

Mastodon model in La Brea Tar Pits

Around Museum Row

MID-WILSHIRE HAS A NUMBER OF OTHER PLACES TO VISIT around the LACMA. Among these attractions are La Brea Tar Pits. Visitors can stroll the park grounds and watch excavations in process at a number of pits. Don't miss the eerily bubbling tar lake in front of the museum.

Page Museum at La Brea Tar Pits
www.tarpits.org
68 B1
5801 Wilshire Blvd.
323/934-7243
$$ (free 1st Tues. of month)

Petersen Automotive Museum
www.petersen.org
68 B1
6060 Wilshire Blvd.
323/930-2277
Closed Mon.
$$

The **Page Museum at La Brea Tar Pits** displays some of the million fossils recovered from the adjoining **La Brea Tar Pits.** These Pleistocene remains are between 10,000 and 40,000 years old. The displays chronicle the animal life of L.A. in the Ice Age. There are skeletons of the saber-toothed tiger, an imperial mammoth with 12-foot tusks, and a Harlan's giant ground sloth, which once stood over 6 feet tall and weighed about 3,500 pounds. Don't miss La Brea Woman, dated to be more than 9,000 years old. The Paleontology Lab is a must for parents who help on their children's science projects.

Your ticket to the Page Museum is also valid for the **Petersen Automotive Museum**—200 cars from the collection of founder Robert Petersen, the auto magazine tycoon. Covering four floors, the museum traces the entire history of the automobile. For car buffs this is a must, but even car cynics have come away extolling these wonders. Among them are James Dean's 1950 Mercury, the 1948 Tucker, Mel Torme's 1937 Jaguar, and a 1981 DeLorean. A recent exhibition celebrating the 50th anniversary of rock 'n' roll featured 75 classic and custom guitars of the stars, along with Eric Clapton's 1940 Ford Coupe and Janis Joplin's 1965 Porsche. Other special exhibitions have ranged from "Speed: The World's Fastest Cars" to "Hollywood Star Cars" and "Alternative Power: Lessons from the Past, Inspiration for the Future." ■

Original Farmers' Market

ABOUT 15 BLOCKS AWAY FROM MUSEUM ROW (A PLEASANT walk when the weather is cool) is a place just brimming with the simple pleasures of life. Here, at the junction of Third Street and Fairfax Avenue, is a celebration of the pure sensual enjoyment of eating old-fashioned meals in a festive environment. The original Farmers' Market is a complex of more than a hundred shops catering to your every gustatory whim. A kind of 1930s counterpart to downtown's Olvera Street, it is themed, but in a charming, pre-Disney way.

Originated by the oil tycoon E.B. Gilmore in the 1930s, the market serves as a kind of village green in L.A. The phrase "meet me at Third and Fairfax" is still synonymous with meals of ham and eggs, gumbo, fried chicken, fresh fish and oysters, Belgian waffles, gallons of "Joe," tacos and beans, giant peanut butter cookies, submarine sandwiches, Armenian grilled meats, pots of pasta in red sauce—you get the picture. "The Farmers' Market is what they call a 'great good place,'" remarks the longtime L.A. chronicler Catherine Seipp. "It's that increasingly rare but vital locale where you can go to be alone with other people." Some of those others may well be from the film industry. Director Tim Burton *(Beetlejuice, Batman)* is sometimes seen near the waffle bar, Denzel Washington at Kokomo's Café, and a group of regulars led by the director Paul Mazursky near Bob's Coffee and Donuts, near the east end. Stop by and give them a copy of your script. Bob's, by the way, makes about a thousand donuts a day. ■

Farmers' Market
www.farmersmarketla.com
✉ 6333 W. 3rd St.
☎ 323/933-9211

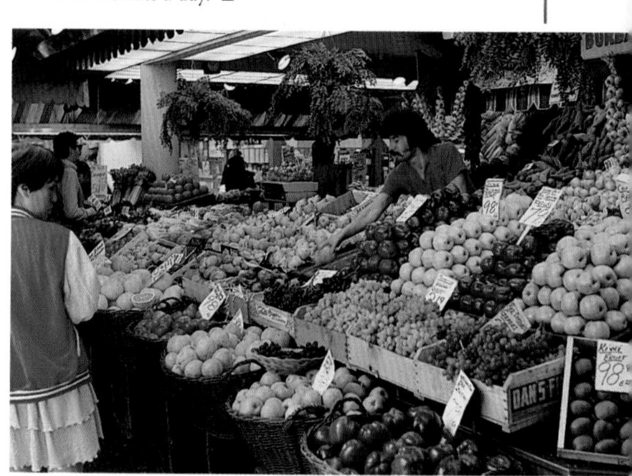

Shopping at the original Farmers' Market

The ultimate schmooze

If you are still hungry after the Farmers' Market (or if it's two o'clock in the morning), a similar scene is reprised, round the clock, just across the street at Canter's Deli *(419 N. Fairfax Ave., tel 323/651-2030)*. Located in the middle of L.A.'s thriving Fairfax District, a hub of the Jewish community, Canter's serves up quintessential deli fare: bagels loaded with red onion, smoked salmon, and cream cheese; potato latkes (pancakes); cheese blintzes; calf brains and eggs; *matzo brei* (a matzo-meal and egg pancake); brisket of beef; corned beef on rye; giant sour pickles; cream soda; and vat upon vat of matzo-ball soup. The bakery counter sells outstanding fresh breads and pastries, but most clients prefer to dine in and be entertained by the waitresses' banter—a long-standing Canter's tradition. ■

Melrose Avenue

On Melrose, neon rules.

NORTH OF THE FAIRFAX DISTRICT, RUNNING EAST–WEST between La Brea Avenue and Robertson Boulevard, is a strip of ultimate urban grooviness. Melrose Avenue is responsible, among other things, for the resuscitation of Heather Lockyear's career (via the hit TV show *Melrose Place*), for the popularity of Harley Davidson motorcycles among film stars (via its Johnny Rocket's Burger hangout), and for the $500 ripped T-shirt (via Comme des Garçons, a Japanese clothier with a penchant for bald-headed models who swear). It's just so swell—where should one start?

Near the district's eastern end at La Brea, have lunch at Angeli Caffe *(7274 Melrose Ave., tel 323/936-9086),* where founders Viana La Place and Evan Kleiman launched a wave of southern Italian trattorias more than 15 years ago—a trend that continues unabated across the U.S. Order the *arancini* appetizers and pizza margherita, or the *insalata forte* of shaved parmesan and fennel.

Farther west are clothing boutiques, specialty stores, and folk art shops that sell affordable and interesting Mexican Day of the Dead works and painted tin *retabla* art. A good place to relax is the well-known Bodhi Tree Bookstore *(8585 Melrose Ave., tel 310/659-1733),* which features an extensive collection of New Age literature and books about world religions and spirituality. You can have a nice cup of tea, enjoy the incense, and find out everything you ever wanted to know about the Rosicrucians.

Nearby is the **Pacific Design Center** *(8687 Melrose Ave., tel 310/657-0800, www.pacificdesigncenter.com),* a collection of 200 showrooms offering furnishings by some of the best-known designers in the world. The behemoth also houses a branch of the Museum of Contemporary Art (see p. 97). Back on Melrose, walk along toward Robertson Boulevard for some outstanding tile, lighting, and furniture outlets.

From here, choose where to go next: north to West Hollywood, deemed the "Castro District of L.A." south to the **Beverly Center** *(3rd St. & La Cienega Blvd., www.beverlycenter.com)*, the sine qua non of all galleria shopping experience; or east Hollywood (see pp. 79–82). ■

West Hollywood Visitor information
www.visitwesthollywood.com
✉ 8687 Melrose Ave., Suite M-38
☎ 310/289-2525

Johnny Rocket's '50s diner

Hollywood

Hand- and footprints at Graman's (now Mann's) Chinese Theater

FOR A CITY THAT IS RIGHTLY CONSIDERED THE VERITABLE engine of the world entertainment industry, Los Angeles is something of a letdown in this regard for most tourists. The reason is that the studios are no longer geographically concentrated in old Hollywood, but spread about—some in the Valley, some in Burbank, others in Culver City and other unsexy destinations. Hollywood itself, that stretch of boulevard so often photographed, has for years looked quite down at heel, the remnants of its glamour dulled by the reality of a gritty street culture. Although there have been, and continue to be, several worthwhile redevelopment projects designed to "bring Hollywood back to Hollywood," the results are often disappointing, thinly veiled attempts to unload second-class tourist souvenirs.

So, these pages offer a selective iconic tour of Hollywood, covering few of the oft-cited theme museums and restaurants but, instead, a few choice destinations, real places that function now as they did in the old days. Those seeking the quintessential "studio tour" with plenty of fanfare and special effects will be more than satisfied by a day at Universal Studios (see p. 87).

To get a good sense of "working on the lot," as studio life is called, the best place to begin is **Paramount Studios** (see p. 80). The longest continuously running film studio in old Hollywood still holds some of the old magic, and two-hour guided tours grant an exciting behind-the-scenes look at operations of a movie facility. Visitors can also make reservations to watch a sitcom taping but, alas, the studio grounds—where moments and monuments from movie-history are laid on thick and fast—are now off-limits. From Melrose, you can pause for a photo-op of the famous Bronson Gates entrance, with its palm trees nodding in the wind and

Hollywood
www.hollywoodchamber.net
Map 68 C2

Visitor information
✉ 6541 Hollywood Blvd.
☎ 323/468-1376

Mann's Chinese Theater
www.mannstheaters.com
6925 Hollywood Blvd.
323/464-8111

Hollywood Entertainment Museum
www.hollywoodmuseum.com
7021 Hollywood Blvd.
323/465-7900
$$

Motion Picture Hall of Fame
www.filmfame.com
1608 North Vine St.
323/465-2300

Hollywood Wax Museum
www.hollywoodwax.com.
6767 Hollywood Blvd.
323/462-8860

Opposite: The palms and traffic of Santa Monica Boulevard

fountains gurgling in the background; these are the portals through which the limousine drove in *Sunset Boulevard* (1950). These are also the grounds where Fred Astaire and Ginger Rogers danced and where Lucille Ball and Desi Arnaz literally invented the modern television production company.

For a relaxing, elegant lunch, drive north on Vine Street to the **Musso & Frank Grill** *(6667 Hollywood Blvd., tel 323/467-7788, closed Sun–Mon)*, a Hollywood landmark where hip Angelenos take their out-of-town relatives who want to eat "flannel cakes" à la Philip Marlow detective movies.

Sated, make a beeline for a true monument, **Mann's Chinese Theater.** Built in 1927 by Sid Grauman, this may well be the most famous movie theater in the world. While many of the old landmarks are gone, the theater's extensive patio will certainly take you back a few years, containing as it does the hand- and footprints of many legendary movie stars. Even Roy Rogers's horse, Trigger, is honored here.

More commercial, or themed, enterprises abound in this area. Tacky or tantalizing, there is no denying the appeal of **Frederick's of Hollywood** *(6608 Hollywood Blvd., tel 323/957-5953, www.fredericks.com)*, the legendary lingerie shop and museum that sells all manner of saucy ladies undergarments and, inevitably, boasts the Frederick's Celebrity Lingerie Hall of Fame. Nearby, the **Hollywood Entertainment Museum** offers famous props and other exhibits about filmdom and its major players; "trekkies" might get a thrill from the original sets from "Star Trek: The Next Generation." The **Motion Picture Hall of Fame** honors film legends—great accomplishments, movies, and actors—spanning a century of moviemaking. The recently expanded **Hollywood Wax Museum** lets you feel part of a red carpet event with its exhibits of movie stars like Halle Berry and Angelina Jolie shown arriving for the Academy Awards. It also has a horror exhibit, plus recreations of scenes from such movies as *Men in Black*, *The Matrix*, and *Star Wars*.

No visit to Hollywood is complete without stepping the sidewalk of stars known as the **Hollywood Walk of Fame.** A series of orange signs mark the route, which forms a loop and features almost 2,000 bronze stars. The Hollywood Visitor information center provides a map.

The Hollywood Walk of Fame

How to see a star

"Alright, all that culture is just fine. Now, how do I see Tom Cruise or Pamela Anderson Lee?"

For the more ambitious celebrity seeker, the Entertainment Industry Development Corporation produces, free of charge, a daily location shooting agenda for all projects being filmed in L.A. This list is available at 1201 W. 5th Street, Suite T-800 *(tel 323/957-1000, www.eidc.com)*. Audiences Unlimited *(tel 818/753-3470, www.tvtickets.com)* can arrange free admission to more than 40 live shows, sitcoms, and one-time-only entertainment events.

CBS Television City *(7800 Beverly Blvd., Los Angeles, CA, 90036, tel 323/575-2345)* offers free tickets for a number of sitcoms, game shows, and talk shows.

Paramount Pictures *(5555 Melrose Ave., tel 323/956-1777, www.paramount.com)* supplies tickets at its visitor center up to five days in advance of tapings. ■

July 4th at the Hollywood Bowl

Hollywood History Museum
www.thehollywoodmuseum.com
✉ 1660 N. Highland Ave.
☎ 323/464-7776
🕒 Closed Mon.–Wed.

Hollywood Forever Park Cemetery
www.hollywoodforever.com
✉ 6000 Santa Monica Blvd.
☎ 323/469-1181
Map available at office

Hollywood Bowl
www.hollywoodbowl.com
✉ 2301 N. Highland Ave.
☎ 323/850-2000 or 323/480-3232 (Ticketmaster)

Hollywood Bowl Museum
✉ Hollywood Bowl, 2301 N. Highland Ave.
☎ 323/850-2058

More fulfilling is the recently opened **Hollywood History Museum,** in the Max Factor Building, now restored to original 1935 splendor and chock-full of mementos regaling fascinating lore of the Hollywood region and movie industry. The world-famous **Mel's Drive-In** *(tel 323/465-2111, www.melsdrive-in.com)* all-American diner is next door.

Late afternoon might suggest a few quintessentially Hollywood outings. One is a visit to **Hollywood Forever Park Cemetery,** where many big names from movie history, from Rudolph Valentino to Cecil B. De Mille, are buried.

When evening approaches, head to the **Hollywood Roosevelt Hotel** *(7000 Hollywood Blvd., tel 323/466-7000, www.hollywoodroosevelt.com),* where the first Academy Awards were held, a location chosen perhaps because its investors were Charlie Chaplin, Mary Pickford, and Douglas Fairbanks. The Roosevelt has been revived in recent years, and its Cinegrill is a nice place for a martini and live music. One thing not to miss is the swimming pool, which David Hockney painted in the mid-1980s.

The perfect end to a summer day in Hollywood would be a concert at the **Hollywood Bowl.** Founded in 1922, the Bowl is the summer home of the L.A. Philharmonic, which offers an affordable evening concert series ranging from the classics to show tunes to unlikely star vocalist combinations. The season is also peppered with several world-class special events, such as the International Mariachi Competition and the Playboy Jazz Festival.

Just as important—some would say more so—is the scene at the Bowl. On July 4, for example, longtime box seat holders turn out for the "1812 Overture" and a fireworks display. Among them will be dozens of movie and TV stars and, often, the very cream of old L.A. society, men in white pants and bow ties, ladies in pastel linens and cashmere wraps, for the cool night air.

Bring a picnic dinner, or you will end up quite ravenous. Arrive at least an hour early to see the **Hollywood Bowl Museum,** where you can watch famous Bowl performances on film, from the Beatles to Judy Garland. ■

Griffith Park

THE BEST KEPT SECRET IN LOS ANGELES, FAR FROM BEING small or tucked away, is right under everyone's nose. Griffith Park, whose more than 4,000 acres make it the largest urban park in the United States, is five times the size of New York's Central Park. That the park remains undiscovered by many would hardly surprise its founder, Col. Griffith J. Griffith. For years, he attempted to persuade the city fathers to turn his 1896 bequest of land, once part of Rancho los Feliz, into the hub of a city-wide park system. (Of course, Griffith's circumstances at the time may not have helped his cause: The hard-drinking Welshman had just returned from a two-year term in San Quentin prison for trying to kill his wife.)

While earlier generations of Angelenos periodically embraced the park, only recently has it become a preferred spot for weekend outings. In fact, the park is now a preferred spot for an estimated 10 million visitors each year. There are children's museums, a zoo, a museum for adults, an old-fashioned merry-go-round, and, perhaps best of all, a place from which to gaze at the stars above and the city below.

That place, the renowned **Griffith Park Observatory,** is located at the top of Observatory Road. As recounted by local historian Letitia Burns O'Conner, the colonel had been so stunned by his experience of looking through the Mount Wilson telescope that he proclaimed, "If all men could look through that telescope, it would revolutionize the world!" Griffith was long gone before his dream finally came true here, in 1935. Since then, the observatory and its grounds have attained iconic status. Its exterior and the bronze statues of Galileo and company formed the backdrop to the famous switch-blade fight in the James Dean movie *Rebel Without a Cause* (1955).

The classic 1935 building re-opened in 2007 after a five-year restoration and now boasts 60 exhibits plus a state-of-the-art theater and a Wolfgang Puck café. The museum on two levels is chock-full of sensational exhibits on astronomic sciences, and includes an enormous rotating globe in the main rotunda. The east dome holds the **Hall of**

Griffith Park
68 C3
Visitor information
www.lacity.org/lacity30.htm
4730 Crystal Springs Dr.
323/913-4688

Griffith Park Observatory
www.griffithobservatory.org
2800 E. Observatory Rd.
213/473-0800
Closed Mon. & a.m. Tues.–Fri.
Laserium shows: call for times
$$ for Laserium

The great outdoors

Griffith Park's 50 miles of trails make it a haven for hikers of all abilities. The **Sierra Club** *(tel 323/387-4287, www.sierraclub.org)* has maps and details of events. For horseback riders there are more than 40 miles of bridle paths through some of the loveliest canyons. The **Los Angeles Equestrian Center** *(480 Riverside Dr., tel 818/840-9063, www.la-equestriancenter.com)* rents horses and has maps of the park's main paths. Several local stables offer a Friday sunset ride. Other leisure activities in Griffith Park include golf on a choice of four courses, two 18-hole and two 9-hole. For golf, you must first buy a parks card from the L.A. City Recreation Department *(tel 888/527-2757, www.laparks.org),* then make reservations a week before you wish to play. ■

Autry National Center
www.autrynationalcenter.org
✉ 4700 Western Heritage Way
☎ 323/667-2000
$ $$

the Eye Exhibits, displaying a camera oscura; the **Hall of the Sky Exhibits,** in the west dome, focuses on the sun and moon and holds solar telescopes. The central dome forms the **Samuel Oschin Planetarium,** known for outstanding laser-light and music shows, as well as more standard planetary projections. The lower levels feature exhibits relating to deep space, and the new **Leonard Nimoy Event Horizon** theater, with hourly shows.

Later, as the sun dips into the Pacific, the denizens of the City of Angels stroll onto the observatory's terrace to watch the horizon boil with pinks and reds and purples before it finally falls dark, winking with a million lights below and billions above.

Those who visit the observatory earlier in the day might instead turn left on Los Feliz to Western, where a right turn will take you to shady, brook-riven part of the park where more than 140 types of ferns make for a cool (and botanically fascinating) afternoon stroll.

The great surprise of the Griffith Park's more recent additions is the **Autry National Center,** formed in 2003 by the merger of the Southwest Museum, the Women of the West Museum, and the Museum of the American West. The center today comprises a first-class educational institution plus two outstanding museums featuring permanent collections and special exhibitions dedicated to exploring the life and times of American cowboys and Native American Indians. Don't miss it.

The **Southwest Museum of the American Indian,** with 250,000 pieces, is closed to the public while a new state-of-the-art facility is under construction. The sibling **Museum of the American West,** founded in 1989 with a 54-million-dollar gift from late cowboy film star Gene Autry, is arranged thematically. Starting on the ground floor, the **Romance Gallery** relies on the special quality of its objects rather than gallery themes. Paintings include John Gast's 1872 work "American Progress," Charles Deas's 1847 "Indian Warrior," Albert Bierstadt's "Sunset Over the Plains," as well as several Frederic Remington oils, and statues and animal figures by Charles Russell. In the same section you will also find Buffalo Bill's own saddle, later used in Robert Altman's film *Buffalo Bill* (1876). Hollywood informs the **Imagination Gallery.** There are breakaway chairs, ricochet guns, bottles that shatter but don't cut, even Tom Mix's personal pistol. A collection of Western movie posters begins with *Cimarron* and ends with *Thelma and Louise.* It is a testament to Gene Autry's restraint that the display of his own film legacy is both strong in quality and modest in size.

The top floor is arranged thematically, beginning with the **Opportunity Gallery,** which strikes a particularly brave note in its presentation on pre-cowboy-era Native Americans. "With little thought for native peoples," one display states, "they [Anglo migrants] aggressively began to populate and exploit the West." The impeccable collections of Native American weaponry make for imaginative conjecture about the practice of battlefield medicine at the time. The **Conquest Gallery** shows meticulously preserved Gatling guns juxtaposed with displays on Plains bison culture. Also on view is Bierstadt's memorable "Herd of Buffalo and Indian" (1859). The **Community Gallery** looks at how emerging Anglo immigrant culture shaped already-existing Indian and Mexican culture. There is an original of the Cherokee Nation Constitution (in Cherokee) and a series of early photographs, while the **Colt Firearms**

Opposite: The view of downtown Los Angeles from the balcony at the Griffith Park Observatory

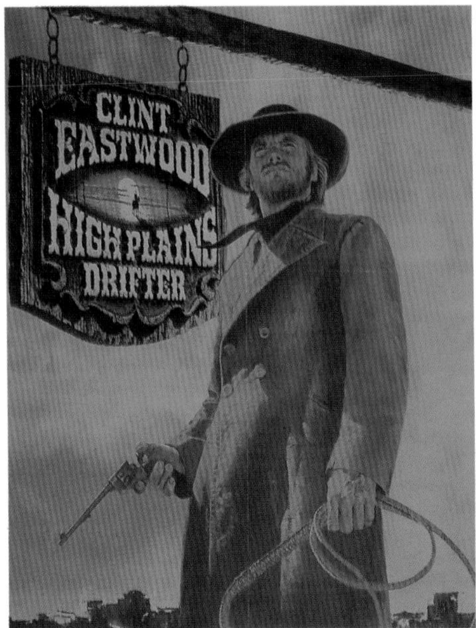

A classic movie poster at the Museum of the American West

Los Angeles Zoo
www.LAZOO.org
5333 Zoo Dr.
323/644-4200
$$

Travel Town Museum
5200 Zoo Dr.
323/662-5874

Live Steamers Railroad Museum
www.lals.org
5202 Zoo Dr.
323/661-8958
Open Sun.

Symphony in the Glen
www.symphonyintheglen.org
213/955-6976

Collection spans firearms from tiny Derringer's and early Smith and Wessons to Winchester rifles. The **Cowboy Gallery** thoroughly examines the relationship between horse and rider. There is a large exhibit of historical saddles, from the *vaquero*-style ones used by Mexican cowboys to today's highly technical saddles. Art in this gallery includes N.C. Wyeth's 1903 *Saturday Evening Post* cover "Bucking Bronco"; the masterful but largely underappreciated 1945 watercolor "California Vaquero," by former Hollywood stuntman Joe DeYong; and work by the well-known Maynard Dixon. The **Family Discovery Gallery** honors the contribution of the Chinese and includes hands-on exhibits for children. The museum offers several special tours, and there is a restaurant-café.

The **Los Angeles Zoo** has been busily bringing its facilities up to international par in recent years, with major new climate-controlled environments for its animals. L.A.'s collection of more than 1,200 mammals, birds, amphibians, and reptiles is beginning to attract increasing flocks of *Homo sapiens*. One reason is the zoo's ongoing experiments with novel habitats. One of them, called "Chimpanzees of Mahale Mountains," presents several dozen chimpanzees frolicking on an acre of grass and streams. Sea Lion Cliffs—a salt-water habitat with underwater viewing—and the Pachyderm Forest for the zoo's elephants, hippos, black rhinos, and other large game, are popular attractions. The most recent attraction is Campo Gorilla Reserve, bringing gorillas back to the zoo for the first time in four years, although the zoo's hottest stars are three Sumatran tiger cubs born here in October 2007. The zoo also features a botanical garden.

For railroad buffs both small and large, the park's **Travel Town Museum** is a must-see. Travel Town is home to 14 steam locomotives, a number of specialty cars (as in the Union Pacific's luxurious "Little Nugget"), and two operating diesel locomotives. A free miniature train takes visitors around the grounds, and in addition to the museum's own historical exhibits and fire engines there is an enormous N-gauge model train track maintained by a local group of rail enthusiasts. It is up and running on weekends.

A different free train ride can be had by going to the nearby **Live Steamers Railroad Museum,** whose enthusiasts operate an elevated 2-mile line on which 7-inch-gauge model trains run on Sundays.

Another free event in the park is the Symphony in the Glen, a program of concerts that aims to provide people from all walks of life with the opportunity to enjoy classical music. ■

San Fernando Valley

EARTHQUAKES SUCH AS THE 1994 ONE CENTERED IN Northridge have brought a certain notoriety to the San Fernando Valley, between Hollywood and San Fernando. This, the essential valley, is home to almost one-third of L.A.'s population, and to one of its most popular attractions, Universal Studios.

The huge success of the themed **Universal Citywalk** has been something of a shock to L.A.'s self-proclaimed arbiters of cool. After all, the two-block-long congeries of neon and pop architecture is the kind of urban confection that most deep thinkers love to hate. Citywalk has become one of the leading destinations in the area precisely because it entertains people so well. The entertainment lies in three activities: eating, shopping, and people-watching. There are also street performers, including fire-jugglers, musicians, puppet masters, and all manner of eccentrics. Citywalk is eclectically hip enough to hold the attention of child, parent, and the most jaded of eyeball-rolling teens.

Next door, Hollywood meets Disneyland at **Universal Studios,** where backlot tours are a must do. Its movie-themed rides, "The E.T. Adventure," "Jaws," "Jurassic Park—The Ride," and the multi-sensory "Shrek 4-D" are visitor favorites. The high-tech "Revenge of the Mummy" promises scary thrills. The Backlot Tram Tour is the way to see the huge studio site and its dozens of movie and TV locations, including "Crossing Jordan" and the top-rated "CSI: Crime Scene Investigation" both new in 2007, and a ride based on the blockbuster hit, *The Simpsons*, opened in spring 2008, with Bart and family sharing the ride. A visit to Universal is an all-day affair, and you can stay on in the Valley into the evening, perhaps to take in a concert at the **Universal Amphitheater** *(tel 818/622-4440).*

Iconic signage at Universal Citywalk

Another recommended activity is a spin along **Mulholland Drive,** accessible from several of the north–south thoroughfares including the I-405 and Sepulveda Boulevard. A winding, scenic drive that cuts between the Valley and L.A. proper, Mulholland gives breathtaking views of celebrity mansions, mountains, and the ocean. Back down on Ventura Boulevard, a 2-mile strip of stores and restaurants culminates in Jerry's Famous Deli *(12655 Ventura Blvd., tel 818/766-8311, www.jerrysfamousdeli.com)*, frequented by celebrities.

Farther west, in the Simi Valley you might visit the **Ronald Reagan Presidential Library & Museum.** Displays show every era of the late president's life, as well as a Gallery of Presidents honoring the Presidency spanning two centuries. The museum also hosts rotating exhibitions. Visitors can also tour Air Force One, the Boeing 707 that served seven presidents. ■

San Fernando Valley
Map 50 C3

Universal Studios Hollywood
www.universalstudioshollywood.com
Map 68 B3
Universal City Dr. (off US 101)
Tel 800/864-8377
$ $$$$$

Ronald Reagan Presidential Library & Museum
www.reaganfoundation.org
Map 50 B3
40 Presidential Dr., Simi Valley
Tel 8805/577-4000 or 800/410-8354
$ $

From downtown

Almost every pundit worth his or her salt has cadged a cheap laugh over downtown L.A. "An enormous village" is how author Louis Adamic saw it in the 1920s. A "harlot city" said author Carey McWilliams, viewing its "mob mad" yokelry intoxicated on cheap religion and bad movies. "It is as if one tilted the nation on its side and let all the loose nuts roll down into one corner," proclaimed Frank Lloyd Wright.

Much of this hostility derives from the fact that Los Angeles has little of a traditional downtown social scene. Yet even early on, L.A. did have an identifiable core, still present today, bounded by the Old Pueblo district to the north, the Santa Monica Freeway to the south, Central Avenue to the east, and the Pasadena Freeway to the west. So why all the jokes?

One answer may be that downtown L.A., either then or now, cannot be considered an American city at all, but rather a city of the desert. Moreover, this desert city was, and is, a Latin-American phenomenon. None has caught its essence as well as that of Mexican Nobel Laureate Octavio Paz. "When I first arrived in the United States I lived for a while in Los Angeles, a city inhabited by over one million persons of Mexican origin," Paz wrote in his 1961 masterpiece, *The Labyrinth of Solitude*. "At first sight, the visitor is surprised not only by the purity of the sky and the ugliness of the dispersed and ostentatious buildings, but also by the city's vaguely Mexican atmosphere, which cannot be captured in words or concepts. This Mexicanism—delight in decorations, carelessness and pomp, negligence, passion and reserve—floats in the air. I say 'floats' because it never mixes or unites with the other world, the North American world based on precision and efficiency. It floats, without offering any opposition; it hovers, blown here and there by the wind...." ■

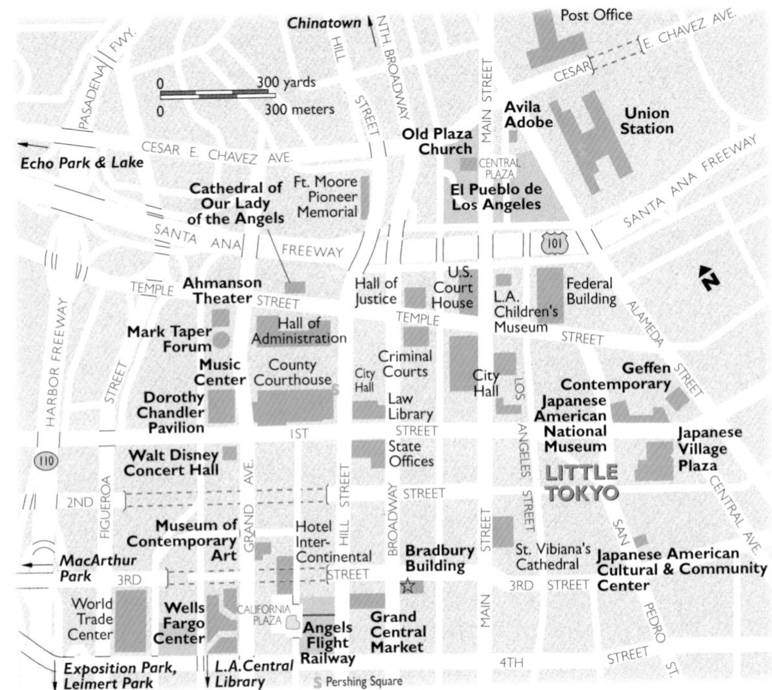

Union Station

Stylish Union Station

ONE MIGHT START A TOUR OF PAZ'S FLOATING WORLD IN the north by parking in the blacktop lot surrounding Union Station *(Alameda St. at Cesar Chavez Ave.).* Erected in 1939 (by some accounts on the site of an ancient Indian village), this was the last great train station to be built in the United States. A walk about its interior reveals many elements unchanged since then, from the massive wooden waiting benches to the muted earth tones of the designs modeled on Native American patterns.

Visitors might recognize the glistening travertine and marble interior from scenes in such movies as *Pearl Harbor, Star Trek: First Contact,* and *Blade Runner.* From the station's rear, equally spiffy and super-efficient subway cars offer an air-cooled ride to Long Beach or MacArthur Park. Intended to revolutionize travel in the city, the new Metrorail system is estimated to have cost L.A. taxpayers a billion dollars a mile. Make use of it!

Outside the station, take a moment to look at the cityscape, the palms waving in the breeze, the old pueblo church beckoning, the cars zooming by on Alameda. This was the scene that millions of new Angelenos laid eyes on when they first arrived. To get a better idea of what they saw, take a historical tour offered by the L.A. City Historical Society *(tel 213/891-4600 for reservations, www.lacityhistory.org).* ■

El Pueblo de Los Angeles

THIS 44-ACRE HISTORIC MONUMENT CONTAINS WHAT might best be thought of as the sociological DNA of Los Angeles. In it are not only the remains of the historic pueblo, but also several sites documenting the early presence of Italians, Chinese, Spaniards, and, of course, Native Americans. Though, for these reasons, it hangs heavy with symbolism for so many in L.A., El Pueblo is nevertheless a place increasingly concerned with the present and the future. Its historic Roman Catholic church welcomes a new generation of Angelenos, learning the language and ways of a strange but promising land. Pretty high school girls practice folk dances on the Plaza Pavilion, calling home to *mama* on their cell phones. Toddlers squeal with delight under the blooming jacarandas, tearing apart giant pink clouds of cotton candy proffered by street vendors.

El Pueblo de Los Angeles
See map p. 88

El Pueblo Visitor information
622 N. Main St.
213/628-1274
Closed Sun.

Chinese American Museum
www.camla.org
425 North Los Angeles St.
213/485-8567
Closed Mon.

After crossing Alameda Street from Union Station you reach Placita Dolores, site of many festivals and celebrations, then go past the Indian Garden before arriving at the Central Plaza, built in 1825–1830. The statue in front of you is of Felipe de Neve, the stoic *gobernador* who led the original settlers to the site in 1781; the one behind you is of his employer, King Juan Carlos III of Spain. To the east is the Biscailuz Building, which now houses a Spanish language library and bookstore. Follow the sign to the **Mexican Cultural Institute,** which often stages exhibitions by contemporary Mexican artists *(125 Paseo de la Paz #500, tel 213/624-3660).*

Don't miss the outdoor shops along **Olvera Street,** named for Augustin Olvera, who fought against Frémont during the war of American conquest. Closed to through traffic since 1930, Olvera Street today is a kind of pre-Disney ethnic theme park, complete with roving mariachis and guys who sell shaved-ice confections from rickety carts. What makes it so jolly today is its lack of slickness; it is a genuine anachronism. The food at the

Siqueiros mural

Between Olvera Street's Hammel Building and the Italian Hall is a remarkable piece of mural painting by the Mexican artist David Alfaro Siqueiros (1896–1974). Entitled "American Tropical," the work was almost immediately covered up after Siqueiros, an ardent trade unionist and onetime revolutionary (he fought to overthrow Porfirio Días in 1910–11), was expelled from the U.S. in 1932. He went on to found the Center for Realist Art in Mexico City, eventually becoming one of the leading artists of 20th-century Mexico. "American Tropical" has in recent years been uncovered and "stabilized" by the progressive Getty Conservation Institute.

A guide to both old and new public art around downtown can be found by searching the Public Art in Los Angeles website, www.publicartinla.com. ■

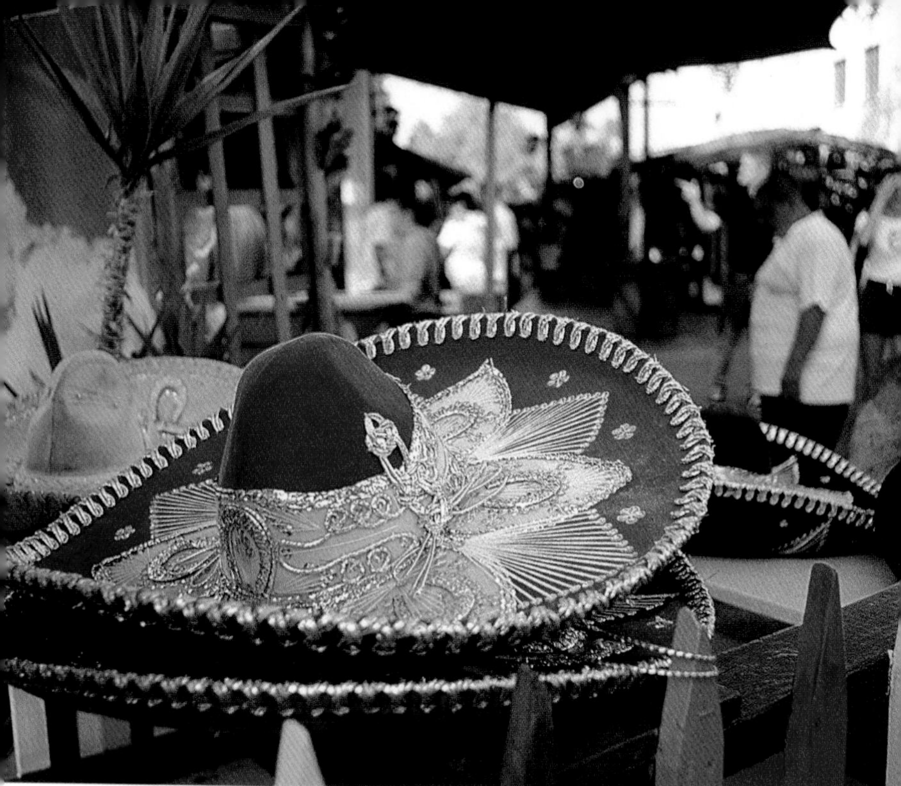

Stall selling Mexican hats

restaurants tends to be pretty average, but the range of Mexican folk art and leather *huarache* sandals on sale here are hard to beat. Buy some before visiting the **Avila Adobe** *(10 E. Olvera St.)*, built in 1818 by one of the first ruling families of Los Angeles, the Avilas. (Francesco Avila was an early Mexican *alcalde*, or mayor.) Many of its beams are said to have been made from cottonwood trees that once grew along the Los Angeles River.

Across from the adobe is **Sepulveda House,** where the visitor center on the first floor shows a free, short film on early L.A. history. The house, built by Señora Eloisa Martinez de Sepulveda in 1887, is in the Eastlake Victorian style—an early sign of the region's troubling aesthetic malleability. The center offers free tours, Tues.–Sat. mornings.

Leaving the house on Main Street and walking westward, one can visit the **Old Plaza Church** (taking care to respect worship hours). Built in 1818 and restored and rebuilt several times since, it is worth walking through, simply to witness how the church continues to be the principal portal into the existing society for new Americans.

On the south side of the park, the restored 19th-century Garnier Building (said to be the last surviving structure from the city's original Chinatown) today houses the **Chinese American Museum,** which opened in late 2003 and is dedicated to fostering an understanding of Chinese American heritage. The twin-level museum displays artifacts, photographs, period clothing, jewelry boxes, decorations, musical instruments, and ornamentation from years past to the present day. ■

Top: Chinatown restaurants
Below: Boy marching in Chinese New Year parade in Chinatown

Chinatown

BECAUSE THE EPICENTER OF ASIAN CUISINE IN L.A. HAS shifted farther east, to the San Gabriel Valley, many have taken to asking why they should even bother with the "old" Chinatown, sandwiched between Hill and Broadway just south of Chavez Ravine. The answer is simple: If you haven't eaten dim sum at the Empress Pavilion, you haven't eaten it at all.

Located on the second floor of Bamboo Plaza, the **Empress Pavilion** *(988 N. Hill St., tel 213/617-9898, www.empresspavilion.com)* is the epitome of a classic Hong Kong restaurant, cavernous, air-conditioned almost to the point of hypothermia, and filled with little rolling steam carts stuffed with delectables ranging from *shui mai* (shrimp dumpling) to pork *bao,* a baseball-size bun filled with sweet pork and golden nuts. In between, watch the guy outside spin little sugar candies out of thin air.

Just down Hill Street is **Chinatown Central Plaza,** marked by the wildly gay **Gate of Filial Piety.** Both were built in the late 1930s. Inside is a statue, erected in 1966, of Sun Yat-Sen, the father of independent China, whose daughters were later on to invest heavily in California banking and real estate.

On the Broadway side of the plaza is the **Phoenix Bakery** *(969 Broadway),* packed at night with families from all over town buying almond cookies, gooey Rice Krispy bars and, of course, fortune cookies. A mark of L.A.'s diversity is a store with a 6-foot plaster rooster on top, on the east side of Broadway, called Live Poultry, with signs also in Spanish (¡Pollo Vivo!) and Chinese.

If the north end of Chinatown still evokes the era of Suzy Wong and *Flower Drum Song,* the south end feels more like something out of a John Woo film, with plenty of up-to-the-minute multistory mini shopping malls and ginseng parlors on every corner. ■

Chinatown
Visitor information
www.chinatownla.com
727 N. Broadway, Suite 208
213/680-0243

Chinatown
See map p. 88

Little Tokyo reverts to traditional dress in the annual Nisei Week festival, held around July/August.

Little Tokyo

IF L.A.'S CHINATOWN FEELS A BIT LIKE AN EMPTY STAGE, Little Tokyo, the heart of the nation's largest Japanese American community, feels like the third act in a Busby Berkeley musical. Once threatened by the tragic aftereffects of World War II internment of Japanese Americans, it now hums with a revived community spirit, not to mention millions in Japanese and local real estate investments.

The eastern anchors of Little Tokyo area consist of two thriving arts complexes, the **Geffen Contemporary** (see pp. 97–99) and the **Japanese American National Museum.** This thoughtfully curated institution occupies two spaces, one inside a 1920s Buddhist temple, the other in a modern center on the corner of First Street and Central Avenue. Particularly moving is the permanent exhibition of old home movies on the ground floor of the old church. Two blocks south and one block west, the **Japanese American Cultural & Community Center** has exhibits on aspects of Japanese culture such as bonsai and ikebana and is considered one of the best such centers in the United States. A must, if time permits, is one of the performances sponsored by the center, which often include world-class acts such as the Grand Kabuki of Japan.

Return to First Street to find **Fugetsu-do** *(315 E. 1st St., tel 213/625-8595),* a traditional Japanese candy store that still uses antique wooden forms to press sweets into delicate patterns. In Weller Court, a small plaza midway between San Pedro Street and Los Angeles Street, you can experience two culinary pleasures. One is the sweet bean-filled pancakes known as *imagawayaki,* cooked up on a century-old griddle in the window of Migawa's. Next, try the Flying Fish Restaurant, just across the way, which serves sushi via a conveyor belt. ■

Little Tokyo
See map p. 88

Japanese American National Museum
www.janm.org
369 E. 1st St.
213/625-0414
Closed Mon.
$$

Japanese American Cultural & Community Center
www.jaccc.org
244 S. San Pedro St.
213/628-2725 or 323/680-3700 (performances)

Buy fresh food or visit one of the many eateries at bustling Grand Central Market.

Broadway walk

Nowhere is the floating world of Octavio Paz's Los Angeles better illustrated than in the greater Broadway area. You can best appreciate this part of Los Angeles by taking a walk through its heart. In the 1930s this was the closest thing the city had to a "traditional" American city center, complete with stock market, big law firms, expensive restaurants, and opulent movie theaters. Today, Broadway is the undisputed capital of Latin L.A., an exuberant Les Halles in the making. There are Bible-thumpers on every corner, and thrumming, bopping music emanates from a dozen discount audio stores where you can buy classic rumba and mambo at one-third of the usual prices.

Having parked at Third Street and Broadway, start at the **Bradbury Building** ❶ *(304 S. Broadway)*, the extraordinary 1893 structure now best known for its appearance in the movie *Blade Runner*. With its five stories of glorious glazed brick, ornamental iron, and filigreed windows, the Bradbury's design was inspired by its architect's eerie session with a Ouija board ("Take the Bradbury!" it allegedly commanded), and by the 1887 science fiction novel *Looking Backward*, by Edward Bellamy. The book posited the typical commercial building as a "vast hall full of light, received not alone from the windows on all sides, but from the dome, the point of which was a hundred feet above." After walking about the lobby, jog across the street and visit the **Botica/Farmacia.** Here you will find one of

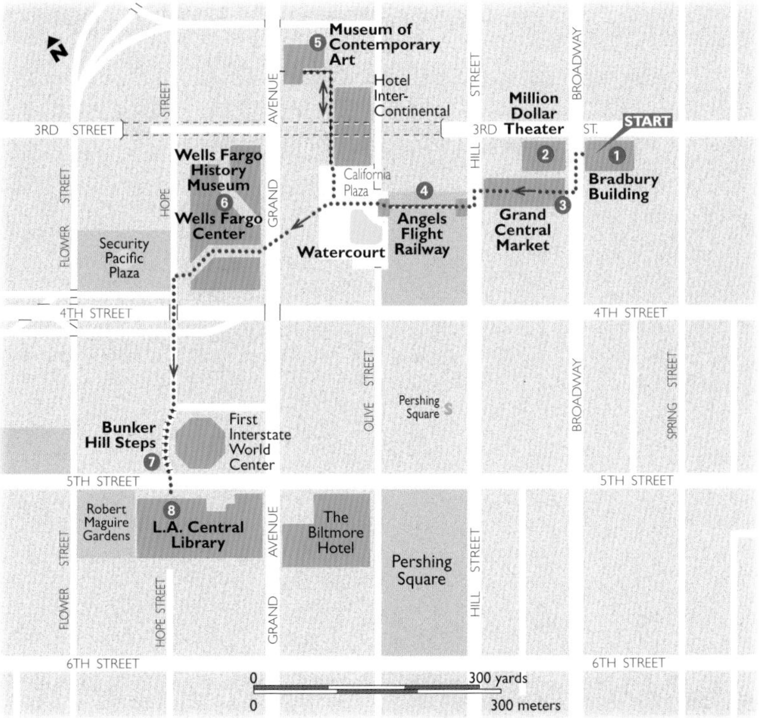

N
Museum of Contemporary Art
5
Hotel Inter-Continental
Million Dollar Theater
START
3RD STREET
STREET
AVENUE
STREET
BROADWAY
3RD
ST.
Wells Fargo History Museum
6
Wells Fargo Center
California Plaza
4
Angels Flight Railway
2
1
Bradbury Building
3
Grand Central Market
HILL
HOPE
GRAND
FLOWER STREET
Security Pacific Plaza
Watercourt
4TH STREET
4TH STREET
OLIVE STREET
Pershing Square
BROADWAY
SPRING STREET
Bunker Hill Steps
7
First Interstate World Center
5TH STREET
5TH STREET
Robert Maguire Gardens
8
L.A. Central Library
The Biltmore Hotel
Pershing Square
FLOWER STREET
HOPE STREET
GRAND AVENUE
HILL STREET
6TH STREET
6TH STREET
0
300 yards
0
300 meters

Also see area map p. 88
- Bradbury Building
- 1 mile
- 1 hour
- L.A. Central Library

NOT TO BE MISSED

- Bradbury Building
- Grand Central Market
- Angels Flight Railway
- Museum of Contemporary Art

the biggest and most colorful collections of traditional Santeria folk medicines in the country, with more than 60 different types of "spiritual baths" alone. If not too busy, the presiding pharmacist will gladly explain items and their uses.

Go past the **Million Dollar Theater 2**, built by Sid Grauman in 1918 with a Hollywood baroque fantasy terra-cotta facade. It is now a mission hall.

ANGELS FLIGHT

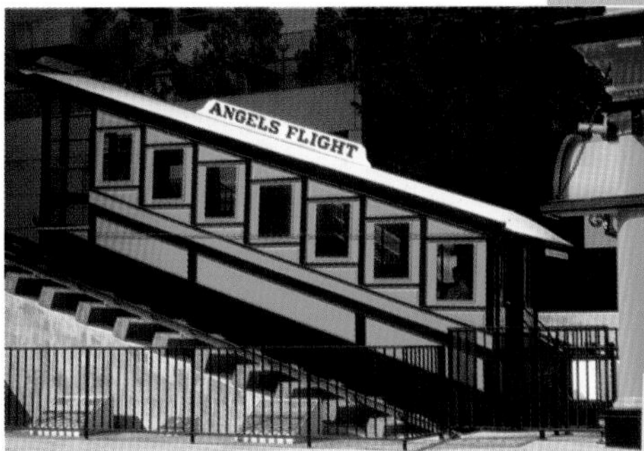

The restored Angels Flight Railway

Walk south on Broadway to reach the back entrance to **Grand Central Market 3**, where all manner of foodstuffs, both raw and cooked, are for sale. Try the tasty El Salvadoran *pupusas* (stuffed tortillas) at Sarita's Pupuseria, or stand in line at the old-fashioned China Café, where you can get a plate of traditional fried rice. On the second floor, past the bargain

One of the 19th-century stagecoaches preserved in the Wells Fargo History Museum

spices at Del Rey Productos Latinos, is the Tropical Zone, where you can buy any of a hundred different combinations of fresh juices. Sitting in Grand Central Market watching everybody eat reaffirms the writer Carey McWilliams's 1932 observation that Los Angeles "is a nation of munchers. In L.A., no one misses a meal."

Cross Hill Street from the market to the **Angels Flight Railway 4,** a beautifully restored 1901 funicular, which will whisk you up historic **Bunker Hill** to the **California Plaza** on Grand Avenue. To the north, next to the Hotel Inter-Continental, is the **Museum of Contemporary Art 5** (see pp. 97–99), and in the distance the Music Center (see p. 100), home to the renowned L.A. Philharmonic and the L.A. Opera.

Circular steps lead to the sun-filled **Watercourt at California Plaza,** a lunch spot with entertainment provided by syncopated water spouts and fountains. Across Grand is the **Wells Fargo Center 6,** where several large pieces of public art include works by Louise Nevelson, Robert Graham, and Jean Dubuffet. The **Wells Fargo History Museum** *(333 S. Grand Ave., tel 213/253-7166, closed Sat.–Sun.)* houses a perfectly preserved 19th-century stagecoach.

Go down the escalator to Hope Street, past the Calder sculpture, and on to the Hope Street overpass to the **Bunker Hill Steps 7,** L.A.'s version of the Spanish Steps in Rome. At the top is the highly symbolic sculpture by Robert Graham entitled "Source Figure" (1992). Down the steps and through the lush landscaping is the pride of modern downtowners, the newly restored **L.A. Central Library 8** *(630 W. 5th St., tel 213/228-7000, www.lapl.org)*. Designed by Bertram Goodhue, who also worked on Caltech and Balboa Park, the building displays many elements that might be called neo-Byzantine, neo-Spanish, or neo-Egyptian. Inside the second-floor rotunda is a chandelier representing the solar system, and a 1933 mural by Dean Cornwell depicting the romance of L.A.'s past.

Outside, the art deco sculptures of Homer, St. John, Shakespeare, and others are by Lee Lawrie, best known for his sculpted main entrance to the RCA building in New York's Rockefeller Center. The **Robert Maguire Gardens** to the west has been restored to Goodhue's basic design, embellished by modern elements, including the Grotto Fountain.

The L.A. Conservancy *(523 W. 6th St., tel 213/623-CITY, www.laconservancy.org)* offers many great and reasonably priced tours. ■

Museum of Contemporary Art (MOCA)

Entrance to the Museum of Contemporary Art

IT HAS OFTEN BEEN OBSERVED THAT WHEN YOUNG artists want to make a name for themselves, they go to Manhattan. When they want to make art, however, they go to L.A., where the lack of a clear arts hierarchy and a less corporate culture has always made dreaming a respected art form in itself. But it was not until 1984, when MOCA opened, that L.A. had the clout, the will, and the money from younger patrons that is necessary to make a modern art museum anything more than a dream. Fueled by generous contributions from Hollywood's younger moguls, MOCA has quickly established itself as an institution with which to be reckoned, amassing in just a few years the most prestigious collection of postwar art in the western United States.

The works are displayed in the **MOCA Gallery at the Pacific Design Center** (see p. 78), the **Geffen Contemporary** (see p. 99), and the main **MOCA campus** itself, which hunkers down in two red sandstone pavilions on Grand Avenue, north of California Plaza. While it pays to phone for an exhibition schedule, the cavernous Geffen ensures that some of the museum's permanent collection remains on display for at least part of the year.

The best strategy for seeing the two main facilities (one ticket admits you to both) is to start in Little Tokyo at the Geffen, where you can buy your ticket and enjoy the capacious, light-filled building before eating lunch at one of the affordable restaurants on First Avenue. Then walk or drive over to MOCA *(parking available in the garage under California Plaza).* If you are more interested in the MOCA building, designed by the Japanese architect Arata Isozaki, reverse the order. But you may then regret that you spent too much time in MOCA's ill-lit exhibition space when you could have lingered at the Geffen.

The core collection was procured by the museum trustees in

Museum of Contemporary Art (MOCA)

www.moca.org

- See map p. 88
- 250 S. Grand Ave.
- 213/626-6222
- Closed Tues. & Wed.
- $$ (ticket valid for all venues)

Styled chairs by Isozaki

1984 from Giuseppe and Giovanna Panza; by most critical measures, the acquisition is considered a coup. Among the 80 pieces in the Panza collection are works by Robert Rauschenberg, Mark Rothko, Roy Lichtenstein, and Claes Oldenberg. The latter's installation piece, "The Store" (1961–62), grounds the collection in the 1960s, in this case underscoring the era's emergent genres of pop art and "happening" art. Roy Lichtenstein's "Man With Folded Arms" (1962) shows the fullness of the Panzas' taste, opting for a subdued, almost woodblock-print illustration rather than one of the artist's more over-the-top, comic-book style works.

The museum has aggressively entered the fray over photographic art, scooping up 2,000 prints in 1995 alone. This makes for one of its best standing displays—the works of Larry Clark, known most recently for his disturbing film *Kids*. In a series of 50 black-and-white photos taken in 1980, Clark, in pieces such as "Tulsa," documented the world of young white Texas outcasts: among them drug addicts, boozers, and gun freaks. The pictures are spooky, not just for their content but also for the way they seem to prefigure the age of video.

In 1989, MOCA received perhaps its single most discerning collection, 18 works of sculpture, painting, and drawing from Rita and Taft Schreiber. Two bronze figures by Alberto Giacometti, "Tall Figure II" and "Tall Figure III" (1960), are at its heart; redolent of the Etruscan-era *Uomo sull'Ambras* found in Italy's oldest towns, the delicate forms cast one of mankind's oldest fears—that of evaporating in sunlight—and render it permanent. Some of the other pieces from the Schreibers are by Alexander Calder, Arshile Gorky, Joan Miró, Piet Mondrian, and Jackson Pollock.

The **Scott D. F. Spiegel Collection** is more problematic, perhaps reflecting the fact that some members of this group of "emerging artists" are still alive. The works by Jean-Michel Basquiat, with their icons of urban tribalism, are still vexing: Were they the work of a genius whose life was cut tragically short, or was it simply Basquiat's mentor Andy Warhol's longest-running joke? Robert Longo's series of falling men surely provokes ("It makes me want to choke him," was one recent comment), as does Susan Rothenberg's "The Hulk."

To its credit, MOCA has made a strong commitment to site-specific artworks, something requiring an enormous effort in audience education. This has created a platform for the works of Robert Irwin. Irwin is principally concerned with the manipulation of light and space, as his seminal garden at the Getty illustrates (see p. 63). MOCA's openness to experiment with new forms has led to other nontraditional shows. Unlike its brother on the

This Claes Oldenburg exhibition typifies the many special shows held by MOCA.

hill, the **Geffen Contemporary** is free from the obligations of being an institutional showplace. Named for mogul-contributor David Geffen, this is a more flexible venue, its size and light allowing a number of configurations to accommodate large-scale works. Initially dubbed the "Temporary Contemporary," the giant old warehouse, just up the street from the Japanese American National Museum, has taken on a life of its own in recent years, often outperforming MOCA itself.

One major exhibition featured the large-scale works of the sculptor Richard Serra. A Californian who worked in Paris and Florence before settling in New York, Serra's principal medium is sheet steel. This the artist uses to produce highly minimalist works of huge dimensions—giant cubes of steel plates leaning against each other, and acres of sheet metal winding around city blocks. Usually encountered outdoors as public art, Serra's works take on a strangely fragile quality when shown in the Geffen. Similarly, L.A. performance artist Chris Burden, known for shooting himself and hammering nails through his hands—and videoing the whole affair—has a rare permanent exhibit here, a whimsical site piece entitled "Exposing the Foundations of the Museum," which he did with pick and shovel.

The Geffen has also expanded MOCA's ability to present architectural subjects, as in its successful "Blueprints for Modern Living: The History and Legacy of the Case Study Houses," which highlighted an important theoretical architectural movement with L.A. roots.

In 2001, MOCA opened the **MOCA Gallery at the Pacific Design Center,** with an emphasis on contemporary architecture and design. Housed in the "Blue Whale" building, designed by Cesar Pelli, its inaugural exhibition surveyed a tendency in Japanese art, animation, fashion, and graphic design toward two-dimensionality. The museum has staged a number of large-scale exhibits documenting some of the century's most visionary architects, from Isozaki himself and Geffen designer Frank Gehry to Louis Kahn. ■

Geffen Contemporary

See map p. 88

152 N. Central Ave., Little Tokyo

213/626-6222

MOCA Gallery at the Pacific Design Center

8687 Melrose Ave., West Hollywood

310/289-5223

The new Walt Disney Concert Hall at the Music Center of Los Angeles County

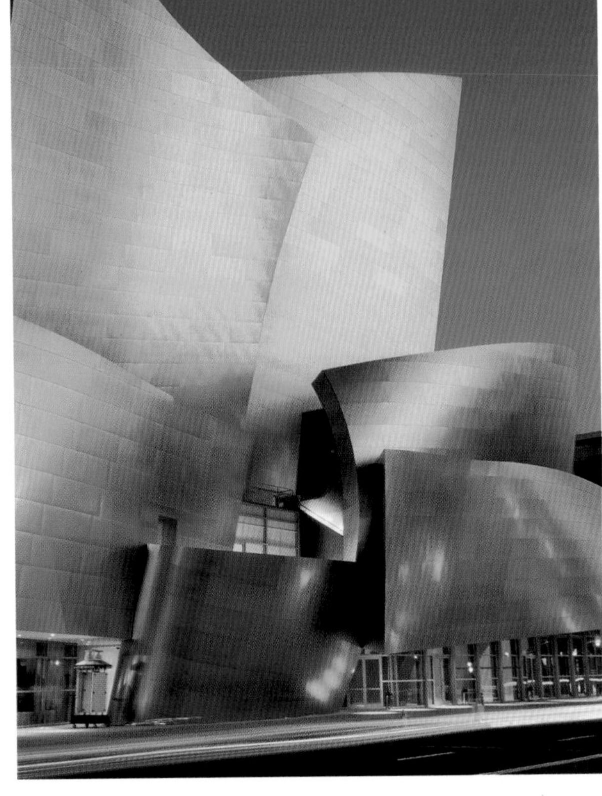

Music Center of Los Angeles County
www.musiccenter.org
See map p. 88
135 N. Grand Ave.
213/972-7211; 213/972-4399 (tours); 213/972-7211 (tickets for Dorothy Chandler Pavilion, Ahmanson Theatre, & Mark Taper Forum)

Walt Disney Concert Hall
111 S. Grand Ave.
323/850-2000; 213/972-4399 (tours)

Cathedral of Our Lady of the Angels
www.olacathedral.org
555 W. Temple St.
213/680-5200

Around downtown

THE MUSIC CENTER OF LOS ANGELES COUNTY IS THE West's preeminent performing arts venue, offering a critically acclaimed, year-round program of music and theater. The center itself is worth visiting during a trip downtown; its public art includes sculptures by Robert Graham and Jacques Lipchitz, the latter perched inside an inviting water sculpture.

The 7-acre complex of the **Music Center of Los Angeles County** comprises four separate forums. The **Dorothy Chandler Pavilion** is home to the L.A. Opera, and the L.A. Master Choral. The **Ahmanson Theater** presents large-scale theatrical blockbusters, and the **Mark Taper Forum** is a more intimate house for innovative drama. The jewel in the crown is the **Walt Disney Concert Hall,** designed by Frank Gehry and opened in 2003 as the new home of the L.A. Philharmonic. Recalling the Guggenheim in Bilbao, this bold statement in stainless steel is one of the most acoustically sophisticated concert halls in the world. Completing the complex is the new, cubist-inspired **Cathedral of Our Lady of the Angels,** by architect

Opposite: One of several fountains in and around MOCA

Echo Park & Lake
www.historicechopark.org
☎ 323/860-8874
$ Donation for walking tours

José Rafael Moneo. Replacing the old cathedral, damaged beyond repair by the earthquake of 1994, it has an adjoining plaza and gardens with a **Native American Memorial.**

A drive west along Sunset to Echo Park Avenue will take the adventurous to a delightful, if often overlooked, section of old Los Angeles, **Echo Park & Lake.** Here it is possible to get an idea of what early Angeleno civic planners hoped would be the heart of the city, a kind of West Coast Central Park under the palms. Today the park is a center of the thriving Central American community. Strollers can buy colorful shaved ices, roasted corn, and mango sticks sprinkled with chili powder and lime juice. Pedal boats can be rented for an invigorating turn about the lake. The 21-acre park hosts two yearly events, the Cubafest L.A. music fair in May *(Dept. of Cultural Affairs, tel 213/202-5500, www.culturela.org)* and the Lotus Blossom Festival in July. Just to the park's east is **Carrol Avenue,** one of the city's earliest Victorian neighborhoods; tours can be arranged through the L.A. Conservancy *(523 W. 6th St., tel 213/623-CITY, www.laconservancy.org)*. A bit farther to the west, down Sunset Boulevard, are numerous *panaderias*, Latino bakeries. ■

The first electronic evangelist

Sitting in the northwest corner of Echo Park, just beyond the quacking ducks, is the historic **Angelus Temple** *(1100 Glendale Blvd., www.angelustemple.org)* founded in 1923 by the Foursquare Gospel preacher Aimee Semple McPherson. One part actress, one part evangelist, and one part entrepreneur, "Sister Aimee" attracted thousands to her church by using highly theatrical techniques to engage their imaginations.

The Works Progress Administration guide to California gives this description of the temple in its heyday: "The ceiling of the huge unsupported dome is sky-blue behind fleecy clouds, and light enters through tall stained glass windows. The temple has four robed choirs, several orchestras, bands, and smaller musical organizations, an expensive costume wardrobe, a vast amount of stage scenery, and a 5,300-glass communion set. Also in the structure are the technical room and studio of Radio Station KFSG—the 'Glory Station of the Pacific Coast'—the Choir Studio and the Prayer Tower, where alternating shifts of men and women have prayed in continuous session night and day since the Temple opened in 1923. A display of X-ray photographs and discarded crutches is offered as testimony to the 'healing power of prayer.'"

Today the church has a television show, featured on the Trinity Broadcasting Network, that airs the theatrical ministry. ■

Exposition Park

The California Science Center in Exposition Park

JUST WEST OF I-110, THE HARBOR FREEWAY, AND SOUTH OF the University of Southern California stands a cluster of buildings and greens known as Exposition Park. Originally designated in 1872 as a place to hold agricultural fairs, it became a public park at the turn of the 20th century.

On the northern edge of the park are its two main attractions: the **Natural History Museum of L.A. County** and the **California Science Center** encompassing almost 500,000 square feet.

With more than 35 million specimens, the natural history museum is the second largest natural history and cultural museum in the United States, outranked only by the Smithsonian. Faced with the prospect of seeing such a huge collection, you would be well advised to do some advance planning. The museum's website is extremely useful, outlining upcoming exhibitions and talks and detailing much of the permanent collection. The museum has a wealth of child-centered exhibits, as well as reading areas.

Of all the museum's permanent exhibits, none brings visitors back as often as its hallmark "Dueling Dinosaurs," the complete, full-scale skeletons of a *Tyrannosaurus rex* and a *Triceratops* posed in deadly battle. This memorable exhibit had its roots in a decision by museum trustees more than 30 years ago to fund a series of expeditions to Hell Creek in Montana. By 1969 the venture had reaped a treasure trove of dinosaur remains, including an enormous *Tyrannosaurus* skull that, after five years of reassembly, proved to be the largest ever found (a distinction only recently conceded to a new find in South Dakota's Black Hills). In 2003, another whole T. Rex skeleton arrived from Montana to become the best preserved, most complete specimen currently in any collection on the West Coast.

Exposition Park
50 C2

Natural History Museum of L.A. County
www.nhm.org
900 Exposition Blvd.
213/763-3466
$$

California Science Center
www.casciencectr.org
✉ 700 State Dr.
☎ 323/724-3623
323/744-7400 for IMAX
$ $$$ for IMAX

The museum has several adjacent dinosaur halls dedicated to other rare finds: a duckbill *Edmontosaurus*, which coexisted in the Late Cretaceous period with *Tyrannosaurus*; a *Stegosaurus tenops*, a Jurassic period herbivore; another fighting scene, this one between the vicious *Allosaurus* and *Camptosaurus*; and a cast of the longest necked dinosaur yet discovered, *Memenchisaurus hochuanensis*, another Cretaceous period plant eater.

For the less "dinocentric," there is the **Gem and Mineral Hall,** displaying more than 2,000 gem and mineral exhibits, including one of the largest gold exhibits in the world; and the **Times Mirror Hall of Native American Cultures.** About 800 pieces from the museum's permanent collection are always on display here. Exhibited is the William Randolph Hearst Collection of Navajo textiles, Southwest pottery, Great Basin basketry, Plains beadwork, and a reproduction of a pueblo cliff dwelling.

Those with an interest in ornithology will enjoy the **Schreiber Hall of Birds.** This collection includes more than 500 birds and 27 separate learning stations. Similarly, the **Marine Hall** caters to the Cousteau in us all, with dioramas of sea life in California waters, plus one of only 17 rare megamouth sharks found since the first one was discovered in 1976.

Finally, the **Ralph M. Parsons Discovery Center** takes the current fad for interactive museum displays to a wonderful and unusual extreme. The 6,000-square-foot pavilion not only lets visitors touch dinosaur bones, mammal furs, and fish scales, but it also has a live insect zoo stocked with tarantulas, scorpions, Madagascan hissing cockroaches, and dung beetles.

Fresh from a recent remake, the museum now features the **Ancient Latin America Hall,** with spectacular exhibits of ancient South American and Meso-American cultures, while the **Lando Hall of California History** traces events and culture since the 1500s.

In the northeast section of Exposition Park is the **California Science Center (CSC)**, which teaches scientific and technological literacy in interactive ways.

The many marvelous exhibits include the **Air and Space Gallery,** dedicated to explaining the principles of air, space, and flight and how humans design aircraft and spacecraft. Housed in a 1984 Frank Gehry structure with an F-104 Starfighter bolted to its facade, the gallery displays stunning exhibits, including a full-scale model of the 1894 Lilienthal glider that inspired the Wright brothers' flight, the Bell X-1 (the world's first supersonic aircraft), a Gemini capsule, and a full-scale model of Sputnik. Visitors can examine spacesuits, peer through telescopes, and marvel at a vast assortment of exhibits that details the ways in which humans explore outer space. In an **Air and Space Discovery Room,** kids can learn about the moon, explore the planets, and pretend to be pilots on an airplane or space shuttle. The **Science Court** features hands-on demonstrations ranging from molecular science and energy to an exciting high-wire bicycle.

One central exhibit, **"World of Life"** (in Edgerton Court), draws rave reviews. Divided into several mini-pavilions, this is a high-touch, high-tech exploration of how living things function and survive. The emphasis is on the human cell, highlighted in a huge multimedia Cell Lab and Cell Theater, where audiences are surrounded by enormous projections of cell functions.

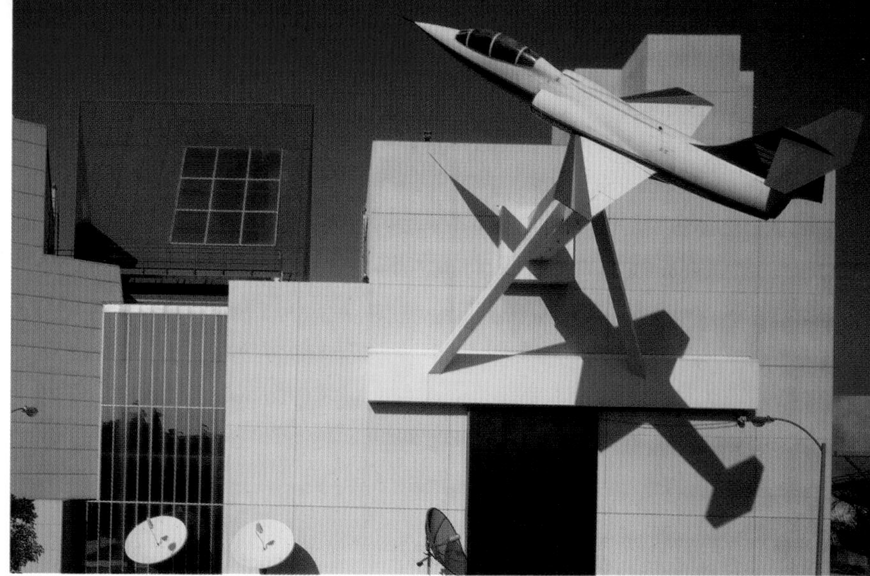

Five life process galleries dramatize how organisms defend themselves, reproduce, make energy, and control interaction with their environments. In the gallery showing how organisms are supplied with food, visitors can compare the effort needed to transport blood from the heart to the brain of a boy with that needed to do the same for a giraffe.

Another state-of-the-art exhibit, **"Creative World,"** looks at the ways in which human endeavor has shaped—and will shape—the world around us. In its three galleries, visitors can help to build structures which then undergo various environmental tests to see how they might fare in natural disasters. There are interactive displays about "smart highways," robotics, comp-uter technology (through a "virtual volleyball" exhibit) and long-distance communications, and even a child-size TV studio.

In the **IMAX Theater,** a variety of science films are projected both three-dimensionally and at several times their normal size.

At the center of the park is the 15-acre sunken **Rose Garden,** planted in 1913 as part of the City Beautiful movement.

Just to the north of Exposition Park is the campus of the **University of Southern California,** where the architecturally inclined can enjoy a free one-hour walking tour *(tel 213/740-6605, www.usc.edu)* past several graceful Gothic- and Renaissance-style buildings.

Set at the eastern edge of Culver City, where much of Los Angeles's African-American community lives, Exposition Park is also home to the **California African-American Museum,** with changing exhibitions honoring the contribution of blacks to American settlement and culture.

From Exposition Park it is but a short drive to **Leimert Park** *(1 block E of Crenshaw Ave. at 43rd Pl.),* a residential community originally laid out in the 1930s by architects Olmsted and Olmsted. This neighborhood has become the centerpiece of the black community's cultural renaissance, with festivals, world-class jazz *(World Stage, tel 323/293-2451),* Museum in Black *(4331 Degnan Blvd., tel 323/292-9528),* and the Dance Collective *(4327 Degnan Blvd., tel 323/291-1538).* ■

An F-104 on the front of the California Science Center's Aerospace Hall lets you know at once what is here.

California African-American Museum
www.caam.ca.gov
600 State Dr.
213/744-7432
Closed Mon.

Architecture drive

Between 1920 and 1950, perhaps no single region in the United States produced as much first-rate modern architecture as did L.A.'s Los Feliz-Silver Lake area. Why this is so is still the subject of debate. There was, of course, the sheer critical mass of Richard Neutra and R.M. Schindler, who took up residence there early in the 1920s. There was the great cerebral ferment inspired by the migration of European intellectuals in the 1930s. Lastly there was the sun, which heightened the angularity of modern architecture, just as the lushness of Southern California's year-round garden afforded a vast, green, leafy backdrop by way of contrast for these boxy, functional houses of steel, glass, asphalt, and concrete. Whatever the reason, few areas of the world seemed to grasp with such intensity the words of the leading Bauhaus architect Walter Gropius, who in 1926 declaimed: "Modern man, who no longer dresses in historical garments but wears modern clothes, also needs a modern home."

This drive takes in a selection of these buildings—still architecturally stunning, though it is perhaps harder now to grasp just how innovative they were when first built. (Remember that they are private residences, so look at them from your car or from the sidewalk.)

Travel north from downtown on I-110 to the Los Feliz Boulevard exit, then head west to Commonwealth Avenue. Turn right to find 2648 N. Commonwealth, Raphael Soriano's **Schrage House** ❶, built in 1951. Soriano was a Neutra-mentored modernist known for his experimentation with steel and aluminum framing.

Return to eastbound Los Feliz. Make a quick right on Rowena Avenue and a quick left on Lowry Road to see two houses by Frank Lloyd Wright, Jr., Frank Lloyd Wright's son: the **Carr House** ❷ at Lowry and Rowena, and the **Farrell House** ❸ at 3209 Lowry. While Wright's son was building these fine small private houses in 1925–26, his father had just finished four of his enormously weighty "cast-block" houses.

Continue south on Rowena, past Hyperion Avenue, to Glendale Boulevard and turn left, then right on Waverly to Nos. 2717–2721. Here, R.M. Schindler's **McAlmon House** ❹ of 1935 reflects the architect's search for a style that could be judged "not by the eyes, but by living." Return to Glendale and proceed south to Silver Lake Boulevard. Here, turn right, follow the boulevard to the left to a cluster of houses by Richard Neutra, who began developing the area into a modernist housing colony in the late 1940s (Nos. 2250, 2242, 2238, and 2232 East Silver Lake Boulevard are just four of the houses he built between 1948 and 1961). The architect's own home, the **V.D.L. House** at 2300 Silver Lake ❺, was originally built in 1933 with funds from a client named Van der Leeuw. Tours can be arranged by appointment (*tel 323/953-0224, www.neutra.org/tours.html*). The house has an interesting history; it was completely rebuilt after a fire by Neutra's son, Dion, who added some questionable elements such as the reflecting pools while trying to outdo papa.

The easiest route (albeit longer) to the next stop is simply to proceed south on East Silver Lake to Sunset Boulevard, turning right to Micheltorena Street, where you will see two outstanding examples of houses designed in 1939 by Gregory Ain, the **Daniels House** ❻ at 1856, and the **Tierman House** at 2323. Ain used space, particularly small spaces, in a particularly masterful way, "framing" a home's volume to accentuate capacities, both functional and emotional.

Also on Micheltorena are two houses by John Launer, a Frank Lloyd Wright apprentice who attempted to create highly individualized modern houses. He often integrated water features and the garden into the plan, as with the **Lautner House** ❼ (1939) at 2007 Micheltorena, and the **Silvertop House** (1957) at 2138. At 2265 Micheltorena is the **Alexander House** (1940) by Harwell Harris. It reflects Harris's unique blending of craftsman concern for natural materials with the modular configurations of Neutra, who was his mentor in the early 1930s.

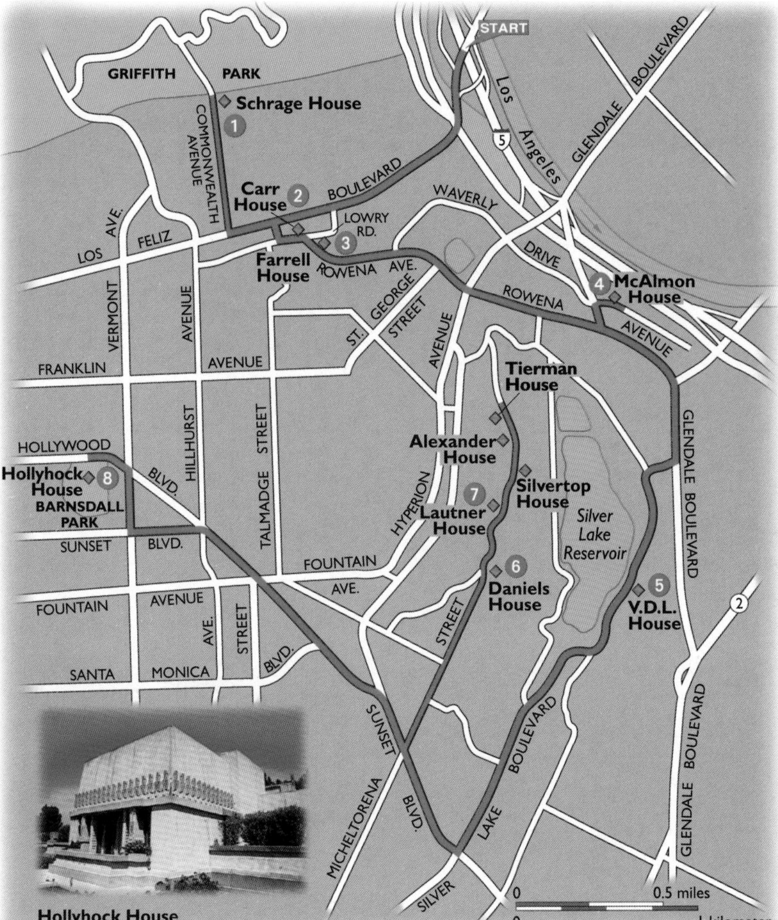

Hollyhock House

Return to Sunset and follow it westward past Santa Monica Boulevard and Hillhurst where it becomes Hollywood Boulevard. Go past Vermont Avenue and on the left you will see the sign for Barnsdall Park. Here is the last and most famous stop, Frank Lloyd Wright's **Hollyhock House** 8, a spectacular concrete block residence built for an oil heiress in 1917–20. The wonderfully light and airy interior is still complete with its original Wright furniture *(tel 323-644-6269, www.hollyhockhouse.net; tours daily, $$)*.

For more information about these and other L.A. architects, try the website at www.greatbuildings.com. ■

Also see area map p. 50 C3
- Los Feliz Blvd.
- 6 miles
- 1 hour
- Barnsdall Park, Hollywood Blvd., & Vermont Ave.

NOT TO BE MISSED

- Schrage House
- V.D.L. House
- Daniels House
- Alexander House
- Hollyhock House

From the foothills

Along the foothills of the San Gabriel Mountains lies a swath of forests, unique architecture, and a lively cultural life. No wonder that famous people from all walks of life—from Albert Einstein to Jon Bon Jovi—have chosen to call it home.

Dotted with sage and live oak, the foothills of the San Gabriel Mountains form one of the primordial historic landscapes of California, redolent of old Spanish dons on horseback, padres nodding in siesta after Mass, señoritas with the local Matalija poppy behind one ear. With that as a backdrop, today's foothill culture, located mostly on the borders of the Angeles National Forest, can be thought of as a hybrid: part Midwestern migrant, part Latin, and part Asian. Where else could one find a stucco office building with a sign on it saying "Chinese Rotary Club of San Gabriel"? ■

Rose Parade float

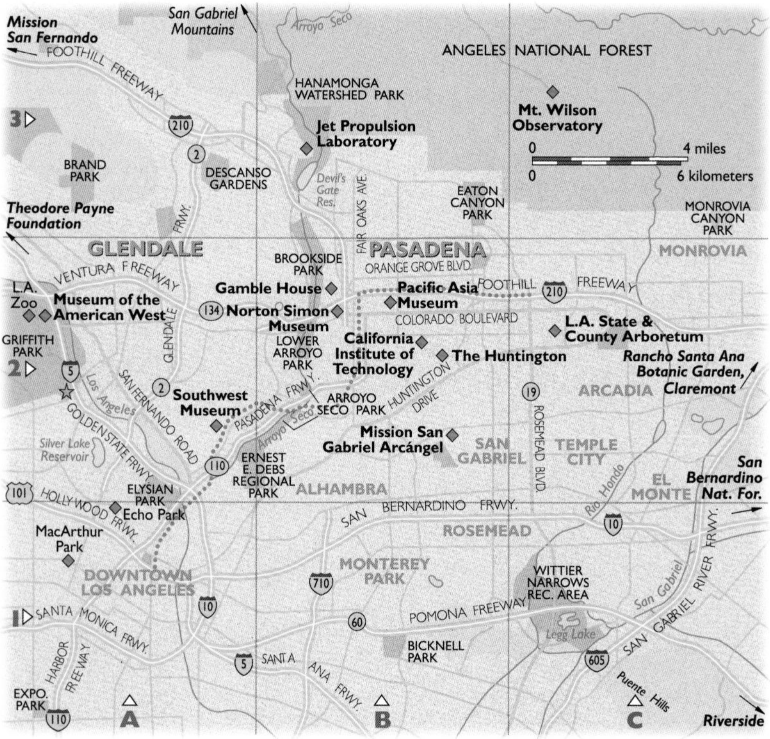

Mission San Fernando
San Gabriel Mountains
Arroyo Seco
ANGELES NATIONAL FOREST
FOOTHILL FREEWAY
HANAMONGA WATERSHED PARK
Mt. Wilson Observatory
Jet Propulsion Laboratory
0 4 miles
0 6 kilometers
BRAND PARK
DESCANSO GARDENS
Devil's Gate Res.
FAIR OAKS AVE.
EATON CANYON PARK
MONROVIA CANYON PARK
Theodore Payne Foundation
GLENDALE
BROOKSIDE PARK
PASADENA
ORANGE GROVE BLVD.
MONROVIA
VENTURA FREEWAY
L.A. Zoo
Museum of the American West
Gamble House
Pacific Asia Museum
FOOTHILL FREEWAY
Norton Simon Museum
COLORADO BOULEVARD
L.A. State & County Arboretum
GRIFFITH PARK
LOWER ARROYO PARK
California Institute of Technology
The Huntington
Rancho Santa Ana Botanic Garden, Claremont
GLENDALE
SAN FERNANDO ROAD
Los Angeles
Southwest Museum
PASADENA FRWY.
ARROYO SECO PARK
HUNTINGTON DRIVE
ARCADIA
GOLDEN STATE FRWY.
Silver Lake Reservoir
Arroyo Seco
Mission San Gabriel Arcángel
SAN GABRIEL
ROSEMEAD BLVD.
TEMPLE CITY
ERNEST E. DEBS REGIONAL PARK
Rio Hondo
EL MONTE
San Bernardino Nat. For.
HOLLYWOOD FRWY.
ELYSIAN PARK
Echo Park
ALHAMBRA
SAN BERNARDINO FRWY.
ROSEMEAD
MacArthur Park
SAN GABRIEL RIVER FRWY.
DOWNTOWN LOS ANGELES
MONTEREY PARK
WITTIER NARROWS REC. AREA
San Gabriel
SANTA MONICA FRWY.
POMONA FREEWAY
Legg Lake
HARBOR FREEWAY
BICKNELL PARK
SAN GABRIEL
SANTA ANA FRWY.
Puente Hills
EXPO. PARK
Riverside
A B C
1 2 3

Pasadena

Pasadena City Hall

AT THE CENTER OF THE REGION IS PASADENA, "CROWN OF the Valley." Founded in the late 19th century by high-minded folk from Indiana who wanted "to get where life is easier," Pasadena evolved as one of southern California's wealthiest communities, complete with a Millionaires' Row (south on Orange Grove from Colorado), a Valley Hunt Club (still private), and more debutantes than there are flowers on a Rose Parade float.

Although conservative, Pasadena could be politically tolerant, putting up with radicals such as writer Upton Sinclair in the 1930s. World War II made Pasadena a more representative town, open to light industry and affordable housing.

The city has experienced a renaissance in recent years as a hub of commerce, education, and the arts. Much of the impetus has come from neighborhood groups and architectural preservationists known as "bungalow huggers" for their defense of the small craftsman houses that, at one time, were only considered fit for the bulldozer. As a result, the city's **Old Town** *(Fair Oaks Ave. & Colorado Blvd.)* is one of the best examples of downtown renewal in the state.

To the east, the new **Plaza Las Fuentes** *(N. Los Robles Ave. & N. Euclid St.)*, consisting of a hotel and restaurants, successfully merges with the historic revivalist architecture of **City Hall** *(100 N. Garfield Ave.)* by Bakewell and Brown, and the **Pasadena Library** *(285 E. Walnut Ave.)* by architect Myron Hunt. The ornate tile and plaster **Pasadena Playhouse** *(38 S. El Molino Ave., tel 626/356-7529, www.pasadenaplayhouse.org)* is one of the top stages in the area. ■

Pasadena Visitor information

www.pasadenacal.com

Map 108 B2

171 S. Los Robles Ave.

626/795-9311

The Gold Line

800-266-6883

A light rail system, inaugurated in 2003, now links Old Pasadena with downtown Los Angeles' Union Station.

Patio and koi pond behind the Gamble House

Gamble House

BUILT IN 1908 BY THE ARCHITECT BROTHERS CHARLES Sumner Greene and Henry Mather Greene for wealthy industrialist David Gamble, the Gamble House represents the epitome of the American Arts and Crafts movement. One can imagine the satisfaction the Greenes might now experience were they to rematerialize some sunny weekend afternoon and surreptitiously take one of the meticulous and informative afternoon guided tours of their "Ultimate Bungalow."

Gamble House
www.gamblehouse.org
108 B2
4 Westmoreland Pl. (off Orange Grove Blvd.), Pasadena
626/793-3334
Closed a.m. & Mon.–Wed. Soft-soled shoes recommended (coverings provided otherwise)
$$

With all the hype surrounding the craftsman aesthetic (fueled in no small part by the actress Barbra Streisand's $250,000 purchase of a Stickley side cabinet), it is easy to forget that the original impulse of the bungalow movement was rather mundane. It was, above all, an attempt to create an affordable, regionally appropriate architecture. In southern California, this means three things: a patio, a covered porch, and large rooms with no dark hallways. It is a form that peppers the landscape here in countless stucco houses around Pasadena.

In the Gamble House, however, the architects were given the resources to explore the outer limits of naturalism, emphasizing simplicity of construction, honesty of materials, and a deference to the designs of Mother Nature. "In a sense," California historian Kevin Starr has eloquently written, "the craftsman bungalows were themselves planted on the landscape as arboreal forms."

With its Japanese-inspired overhanging eaves and wooden shingles, the exterior of the Gamble House certainly suggests a radical departure from the fussy Victorianism that prevailed in late 19th-century Pasadena home building. Gone are the tiny, lace-puddled windows, the faux English gardens, the gingerbread crenellations above lintel and column. In their place are wide windows, spare lighting fixtures, and Japanese koi ponds amid river stones and creeping mint. One can almost hear John Ruskin and William Morris cheering in the background.

The Gamble's **interior,** however, may be the greater masterpiece. One highlight is the Tiffany doorway and entry room. The rear of the hall is the best place from which to admire the cumulative effects of sunlight beamed through stained glass onto an endless variety of wood and glass surfaces. The interlocking wood casements and panels become structure and decoration, harmonizing organically with the light fixtures that were inspired by Japanese lanterns.

The spare **master bedroom** on the second floor carries the Japanese nature theme forward. Finished in rare Port Orford cedar, the room gets indirect lighting via wooden light fixtures dangling on leather straps and embedded with abalone shells. The fireplace is done in an earthy brown—a stone cedar, in effect. The furniture is linked together by a repeating oval shape inspired by the handguard on a Japanese sword known as a *tsuba*. A door leads to three open-air sleeping porches. The butler's pantry and its tile wall and wooden cabinets represent the pinnacle of careful hand craftsmanship, everything fitting as if it had grown together.

No tour of the Gamble is complete without a brief tour of its **grounds.** The old garage now serves as a gift store, well stocked with books on California home building and reproduction Arts and Crafts tiles, lamps, clocks, and bric-a-brac. You can also buy a map of the surrounding neighborhood which shows the location of dozens of Greene brothers houses within walking distance of the Gamble, and identifies several Ultimate Bungalows in other parts of Pasadena—well worth the drive. Please remember that they are private houses, to be viewed only from the sidewalk.

Kitchen, Gamble House

One nearby house, behind a shrub-lined fence at 645 Prospect Crescent, is **La Miniatura,** Frank Lloyd Wright's first adobe-block house. The architect once described it as a "genuine expression of California in terms of modern industry and American life." Unfortunately it is now a genuine expression of dilapidation.

Also in the area, on Grand Avenue, is the restored **Arroyo Hotel** *(129 S. Grand Ave.),* in its heyday a gathering place for wintering millionaires. Converted, it now hosts the U.S. Ninth Circuit Court of Appeals. Nearby is the **Colorado Street Bridge,** which sweeps over the Arroyo Seco riverbed and park. Once known as "suicide bridge" for the convenient height it afforded despairing financiers of the 1930s, the bridge is a focal point for preservationists. ■

Arroyo culture

Stand in the middle of the sweeping Arroyo Seco Bridge and, instead of looking toward the mountains, look southward. There flows the old *arroyo*, down a cement flood-control culvert and on into the ocean some 20 miles away. It was this landscape, wilder than it is now and certainly without the cement, that inspired L.A.'s unique turn-of-the-century culture, the arroyo movement.

Like their upscale brethren up on Millionaires' Row, the rustic bohemians who lived along the arroyo were transplants from the east, men and women who had come here, first tentatively, then with enthusiasm, only to discover that good air and omnipresent oranges do not make a culture. But if the Valley Hunt Club types on Orange Grove sought to replicate eastern institutions, the rustics of the arroyo sought roots in the region's real and mythic past, with its innocent natives and Spanish dons, its life lived close to the wild. The millionaires—even the Arts and Crafts types—had lawns and fountains. The Arroyoans had…river boulders and elderberry.

The acme of the "Arroyo type" was Charles Fletcher Lummis, an itinerant newsman who, in 1885, walked to L.A. from Ohio, sending missives along the way to the *L.A. Times*, where he was later to become city editor. Lummis used boulders taken from the arroyo to build his home, El Alisal *(200 East Ave., tel 323/222-0546, www.socalhistory.org, closed a.m. & Mon.–Thurs.)*, now home of the Historical Society of Southern California. The floor plan was one of rustic simplicity, with a patio to conjure a kind of *terra española* and every manner of native basket and blanket he could lay his hands on. By 1907 his efforts to save Indian folk art had become so extensive that he founded the Southwest Museum for its preservation and study *(234 Museum Dr., Avenue 43 exit, off I-110, tel 323/221-2164, www.museumsofthearroyo.com, closed Mon.)*. Lummis's deep feeling for the region permeated his own writings. Speaking of the "old days," he once wrote: "There was no paying of $5 to be seen chattering in satin while some Diva sang her highest. There was no Grand Opera—and no fool songs. There were Songs of the Soil, and songs of poets and troubadours in this far, lone, beautiful happy land; and songs that came over from mother Spain and up from Stepmother Mexico. Everybody sang…they felt music, and arrived at it."

His friends were of like romantic mind. The bookseller John Vroman, whose store *(695 E. Colorado Blvd., tel 626/449-5320)* is still central to Pasadena literary life, took to photographing the Southwest Indians, confecting close-ups of Hopi mothers as Madonnas-in-buckskin. The period's leading plein air painters took up residence just upriver from Lummis, rendering the canyon rock and sumac in faded yellow and pale sage. Painter Maynard Dixon designed "Don" Lummis's enormous hand-carved doors. His friend, the university dean William Lees Judson, whose stained-glass studios became a center of the local Arts and Crafts movement, even emulated Lummis's home-building techniques.

By the 1920s, however, Lummis's star had fallen. Los Angeles had entered the 20th century with a great surge of urbanity; the simple precepts of Arroyo culture could certainly no longer contain it. Increasingly ill—first losing his eyesight, then contracting brain cancer—Lummis lived out his final years at El Alisal, dying in 1928.

Yet everywhere in southern California one finds remnants of the rustic bohemianism Lummis preached. It is found in the ubiquitous patio outside even the tiniest apartment or condominium; in the inexpensive Tijuana serape hanging on a restaurant wall; in the "mission" roof tiles atop the cheesiest strip mall in the San Fernando Valley or Chinatown.

Most recently it is found in the Arroyo Seco Park itself, where, through the efforts of city government and business, the old riverside habitats are being revived. Parts of the concrete arroyo have been redirected to natural streams and ponds; exotic plants have been weeded out and replaced with native coffeeberry, elderberry, and willows. Horses from a local stable clip-clop along the trails. There are hawks, killdeers, and mallards. Hikers, dog-walkers, and bird-watchers have appeared.

For more information, contact the Arroyo Seco Foundation *(tel 626/584-9902, www.arroyoseco.org)*. ■

Norton Simon Museum

Sculpture by Rodin grace the entrance to the Norton Simon Museum.

THOUGH PASADENA HAD LONG NURTURED ITS OWN ART museum, it was not until 1974, when the brilliant industrialist Norton Simon entered the picture, that the city's museum scene finally came to the fore. It was Simon who agreed to acquire the foundering Pasadena Art Museum and infuse it with talent, funds, and, most importantly, his own collection. Called "picture for picture, the greatest painting collection in town—indeed the Western United States" by the discerning *L.A. Times* critic Christopher Knight, the selections also demonstrate Simon's affinity for what might be called the primary example. That aesthetic informs the entire museum, from its stunning choice of old masters to the bronze gods and goddesses in the South Asian section. Simon's dedication has been carried forward by his widow, actress Jennifer Jones, who presided over the museum's recent three-million-dollar redesign.

The fine art collection commences with works from the 14th century. The choice of "Saints Benedict and Apollonia," by Filippino Lippi (1483), is indicative of Simon's eye for color, texture, hue, and tone. Robes enfold all but the essentials—only the strong hands and purposeful gaze of the saints are revealed. The Simon likes to mix media, standing four gold panels by Giovanni di Paolo and Pietro Lorenzetti near the oil paintings of Raphael, Bassano, Cranach, and Memling. The depth and breadth of the collection is greatest in the baroque period, with works from Spain, Italy, France, Holland, and Belgium. Francisco de Zurbarán's "Still Life with Lemons, Oranges

Norton Simon Museum

www.nortonsimon.org

108 B2

411 W. Colorado Blvd., Pasadena

626/449-6840

Closed a.m. & Tues.

$$

and a Rose" (1633) is an outstanding example of the period, its sensuous rendering of oversize fruits approaching realism. The rococo is represented by 18th-century French and Venetian works by Fragonard, Chardin, and Canaletto. One can nearly smell the baby powder in Giovanni Battista Tiepolo's glorious "Triumph of Virtue and Nobility over Ignorance" (1740–1750).

The museum's holdings from the modern period remain the envy of the American curatorial world. Paul Cézanne's "Tulips in a Vase" (circa 1890–92) is a wistful, light-filled evocation of a humble glazed vase and imperfect flowers, the biomorphic agitation of the leaves a reminder of the obviously hasty arrangement of the flowers, the *ma'mselle* perhaps rushing off to scold an errant child. Monet, Renoir, and van Gogh follow. The 20th-century exhibit also holds all the touchstones—Picasso, Klee, Braque, Kandinsky. The bohemian woman in Matisse's "Odalisque with Tambourine (Harmony in Blue)" (1926) is at once bawdy and delicate. Picasso's "Woman with Hairnet" documents the artist's fascination with the female form.

Below: Sculptures include this one by Henry Moore.

Later in his life, Simon took an interest in Southeast and South Asian art. Fortunately, he was living in L.A. where the great curator Pratapaditya Pal (see p. 72) was monomaniacally amassing the L.A. County Museum of Art's collection from that part of the world. In an age when so many Asian antiquities were flooding into American institutions, Pal was brave enough to play the role of dour editor, throwing out showier, second-rate items and investing heavily in high-quality essentials. That attitude simply reinforced Simon's own picky tendencies. The result is a splendid group of sculptures, primarily from Nepal, Thailand, Cambodia, and India. The 14th-century Nepalese bronze gilt "Tara" is a favorite.

The Garden Café in the sculpture garden (closed during rains), part of a 79,000-square-foot garden planted in 1870, is a delightful place of repose. The museum also offers a film series and lectures (tel 626/844-6980). ■

Galleries at the Norton Simon Museum

Pacific Asia Museum

Housed in a 1924 building in Chinese imperial style, the Pacific Asia Museum *(46 N. Los Robles Ave., Pasadena, tel 626/449-2742, www.pacificasiamuseum.org, closed Mon.–Tues., $$)*, a long-standing Pasadena institution, takes a rare pan-Asian approach to exhibitions. Its displays have included Burmese, Nepalese, Chinese, Thai, and Japanese art complemented by nontraditional showings of art from New Guinea and "Oriental" woodblock prints by western artists such as Paul Jacoulet and Lillian Miller. Visit the serene Chinese garden in the inner courtyard and the bookstore, and take a look at the small permanent collection, all well worth the time. Walk up the street to Plaza Los Flores for lunch or a drink afterward. ■

Opposite: Sculptures include this one by Henry Moore, entitled "Family Group #1" (1948–1949), a bronze work that is part of an edition of four.

Descanso Gardens

FOUNDED IN 1939 BY LOS ANGELES PUBLISHER MANCHESTER Boddy, the 160-acre Descanso Gardens sit in a natural bowl at the foot of the San Rafael Hills, once prime food-gathering territory for the Gabrieleño Indians, who used the nut of the live oak as a dietary staple. The unique location—a cool spot in the middle of hot foothills—has afforded Descanso a remarkable range of plantings, from its internationally recognized camellia garden to its native plant garden. This results in a succession of year-round colors.

Descanso Gardens
www.descansogardens.org
108 A3
1418 Descanso Dr., La Cañada-Flintridge
818/949-4200
$$

Note: Regular plant sales, flower shows, and lectures: check for dates.

Begin your tour in the **Camellia Forest,** the pride of Descanso. Situated under the canopy of a 25-acre live oak forest (some of the trees are more than 300 years old), the camellia collection is the largest in North America, with more than 700 varieties. Filtered light and fertile soil collaborate to produce some truly remarkable specimens. Several varieties of the red Chinese camellia are the result of founder Boddy's tenacious negotiations with the Chinese for propagation rights.

The **Japanese Garden,** next, contains authentic Japanese structures and its own Japanese teahouse, garden bridge, and ponds—the perfect place for a rest and a cool drink. Not far away is the **Lilac Garden,** featuring some 350 of the fragrant shrubs, among them Sierra Blue and Mountain Haze, developed especially for the mild southern California climate. From the Lilac Garden, walk to the 5-acre **International Rosarium,** where much of the work of the famous hybridizer Walter E. Lammert remains in such classic cultivars as Sunny June, Bewitched, High Noon, and Chrysler Imperial. The **Iris Garden** is a seasonal delight, as is the **Spring Promenade,** with acres of tulips and other spring bulb plantings.

The 9 acres of **California Native Plants,** developed with naturalist Theodore Payne, are well worth the walk. In the **Lake and Bird Sanctuary** grebes and mallards are commonly spotted from a bird observation station.

The gardens provide a number of guided tours, both on foot and by tram. A delightful children's railroad takes families to the home of founder Boddy, now a display area for the work of local artists. ■

Other botanical wonders

The **Los Angeles County Arboretum & Botanical Garden** *(301 N. Baldwin Rd., Arcadia, tel 626/821-3222, www.arboretum.org)* has stretches of Australian and African plants, tropical greenhouses, and herb gardens.

Farther out of the city, off I-210, there's a sizable display of desert flowers at **Rancho Santa Ana Botanic Garden** *(1500 N. College Ave., Claremont, tel 909/625-8767, www.rsabg.org)*, with 86 acres dedicated solely to California native plants. Closer to Pasadena are the Huntington Botanical Gardens (see pp. 118–19) and **Burkard's Nursery** *(690 N. Orange Grove Blvd. & Lincoln Ave., Pasadena, tel 626/796-4355, www.burkardnurseries.com)*. ■

Spring in Descanso Gardens

The Huntington

The Huntington
www.huntington.org
108 B2
1151 Oxford Rd., San Marino
626/405-2100
Closed Tues. (call for hours)
$$$

LIKE ITS MODERN EQUIVALENT THE GETTY CENTER, THE Huntington represents nothing if not huge ambitions. And, like the Getty, these ambitions—research library, art collection, and garden—are realized with elegance, taste, and, for the most part, depth. What makes the Huntington something the Getty should strive for can be described in only one word: consistency. For more than 80 years, this brainchild of Henry E. Huntington, nephew of railroad baron Collis P. Huntington, has single-mindedly pursued excellence of the caliber found only in some of Europe's best-edited collections (the Musée d'Orsay in Paris comes to mind as one).

Huntington was a great booster of early 20th-century L.A.; his mark, in fact, is everywhere discernible in the routes of the modern freeway system, which still often follow the tracks of his Red Car line, a once popular trolley car system. (Urban legend—revived in the movie *Who Framed Roger Rabbit?*—has long blamed its demise on an evil oil company–car company lobby, but scrutiny reveals that, ultimately, Angelenos simply preferred cars to rail trams.) The Huntington was one of Henry's later passions, coming after his divorce from his first wife and his marriage to Annabelle Huntington, his aunt, in 1914.

Thomas Gainsborough's portrait of Jonathan Buttall, known as the "Blue Boy" (1770)

The Huntington complex is set on 207 acres of breathtaking gardens. Its three art galleries and library preserve and show such masterpieces as a Gutenberg Bible, Rogier van der Weyden's "Madonna and Child," Gainsborough's "Blue Boy," Mary Cassatt's "Breakfast in Bed," and Edward Hopper's "The Long Leg," among many other treasures.

The botanical gardens range from an extensive collection of old roses to tropical plants and desert landscapes (look for the creeping devil cacti in the Baja California desert bed). Each individual attraction is covered by an outstanding free brochure. Smart travelers will allocate an entire leisurely day to take in all the Huntington's sights, lunching at the restaurant near the Shakespeare Garden and having late afternoon tea as a relaxing finale. Bring a hat or umbrella in the summer—even with all that greenery the Huntington can be hot, hot, hot.

Passing through the **Entrance Pavilion** on Allen Avenue, bear right past the Palm Garden and into the **Library Exhibition Hall.** The high ceilings and large galleries in this building are a perfect place to cool off while taking in the remarkable Ellesmere manuscript, from 1410, of the *Canterbury Tales*. These pages, with their colorful border ornaments and renderings of the Wife of Bath, remind how far away is the world that first moved Geoffrey Chaucer to pen the great mythical yarns. Their foreignness is a reminder that the stories may well have origins not in Western civilization at all, but in the great Hindu tales of the *Pancatantra*, written in about A.D. 200. Rarely does mere type prove so moving.

After looking at the Gutenberg Bible and admiring Audubon's exquisite illustrations in *Birds of America*, move on to the beaux arts **Huntington Gallery,** the onetime residence designed, with

nods to the Mediterranean, by Elmer Grey and Myron Hunt. By 2006, the mansion, completed in 1911, had deteriorated markedly. Hence, the Huntington Gallery closed in 2006 to reopened in May 2008 after extensive restoration. This huge gallery contains the country's largest collections of British and French painting from the 18th and 19th centuries. But don't spend too long in front of Gainsborough's "Blue Boy" or Lawrence's "Pinkie." The gallery has so many treasures, and with a few inquiries to the hovering guards, you might see some of William Blake's watercolors, which the museum owns in quantity.

A walk through the **Shakespeare Garden** will take you to the **Scott Gallery,** which traces the history of American art over three centuries. Here you may recognize Gilbert Stuart's "George Washington"(1797), the stern visage forever emblazoned on the memory of American schoolchildren everywhere. Adjoining the Scott Gallery, the **Erburu Gallery** opened in 2005 as a showcase for the institution's growing collection of American art, while nearby, Henry Huntington's garage has been transformed into the **Boone Gallery,** a world-class art venue for changing exhibitions.

On the way out, pass through the rose and herb gardens and linger for a while in the **Japanese Garden.** It has four main features: a formal garden, a Zen rock garden, a 19th-century Japanese teahouse, and an ikebana pavilion. Don't miss the view from the Zen garden to the house, where the zigzag bridge affords a rare Western insight into the spare, asymmetrical aesthetic of Japan.

Another must, particularly in spring when it is in flower, is the peach tree and stone pagoda in the canyon of the Japanese Garden proper. Intrepid strollers will also delight in the Australian and Desert Gardens, and the new **Chinese Garden,** opened in February 2008 with 12 acres—the largest such garden outside of China—complete with lake. ■

The Japanese Garden

Caltech

California Institute of Technology
www.caltech.edu
108 B2
1200 E. California Blvd., Pasadena
626/395-6811

Caltech Science Museum
626/395-6520
Open by appointment only

LONG SYNONYMOUS WITH TECHNOLOGICAL PROWESS, THE California Institute of Technology produced some of the 20th century's biggest scientific breakthroughs. This was where, in the 1930s (while a fuzzy-haired fellow named Einstein rode around the campus on an old bicycle), Theodore Von Karmen pioneered the mathematical principles of aeronautics and where the Richter system for measuring earthquakes was developed. More recently, the subatomic particle dubbed the quark was discovered here. That the grounds should be such a marvelous repository of architectural finds makes them all the more worth a visit, perhaps on a Saturday afternoon between visits to the Gamble House and Pasadena's Old Town (see p. 109).

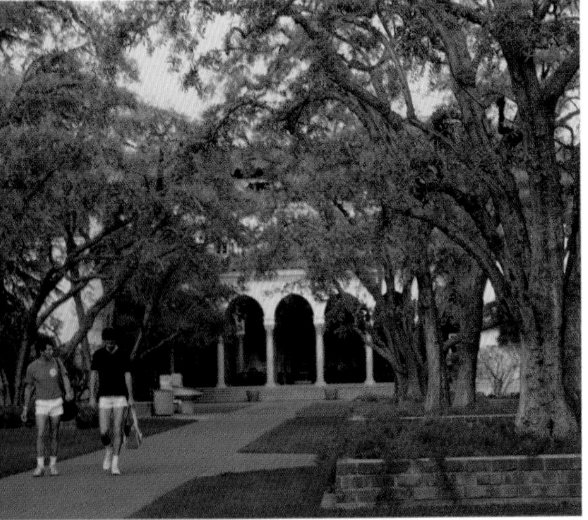

Students on the Caltech campus pass the Spanish Renaissance cloisters.

Caltech originated as a vocational school in the late 19th century. It evolved along a master plan by the great architect Bertram Grosvenor Goodhue, who went on to do such memorable projects as the L.A. Central Library (see p. 96) and San Diego's Balboa Park (see pp. 150–53). Goodhue envisioned a dual-axis campus with portals, cypresses, and a central pool...something of the effect of the one leading to the Taj Mahal in India. Certainly Goodhue was into Spanish Renaissance, as indicated by his floral volutes and sculptured shells around the entry to the **Parsons-Gates Hall of Administration.** Two remaining structures by Goodhue are the **Bridge Laboratory of Physics** and the High Voltage Research Laboratory (now called the **Sloan Laboratory**). Both of these structures have been modified, but close inspection reveals many of the signature Goodhue touches: vaulted ceilings, water fountains, large expanses of plain exterior wall punctuated by regular patterns of windows. In fact, architectural detail plays a huge role in maintaining the campus's muted religious bearing, as in the old Alexander Calder sculptures preserved in the current facade of the **Beckman Laboratory of Chemical Synthesis.**

Campus social life centers on the **Athenaeum,** built in 1930 by British architect Gordon Kaufman. Again, a kind of eclectic Mediterranean style reigns. The **Beckman Institute** maintains the **Caltech Science Museum** devoted to Caltech alumnus Arnold O. Beckman, a pioneer of scientific instrumentation, including a re-creation of the chemistry lab when he was a student. The college offers talks by visiting scholars, plus regular musical and cultural events *(tel 626/395-4652).* ■

Mission San Gabriel Arcángel

FOUNDED BY SPANISH FRANCISCANS IN 1771 AS THE fourth in a chain of 21 California missions, Mission San Gabriel Arcángel has a rich heritage. It was from here that Gobernador Felipe de Neve led a party of soldiers and settlers in 1781 to establish El Pueblo de Nuestra Señora La Reina de Los Angeles. It was from this mission (once dubbed San Gabriel de los Temblores for the area's frequent earthquakes) that the padres ruled over 1.5 million acres of farmland making them a formidable economic power. As for all the missions, secularization in 1833, and Americanization subsequently, led to San Gabriel's decline. For the past century it has been subject to restoration efforts, the latest in 1996.

Mission San Gabriel Arcángel
www.sangabrielmission.org
108 B2
428 S. Mission Dr., San Gabriel
626/457-3048

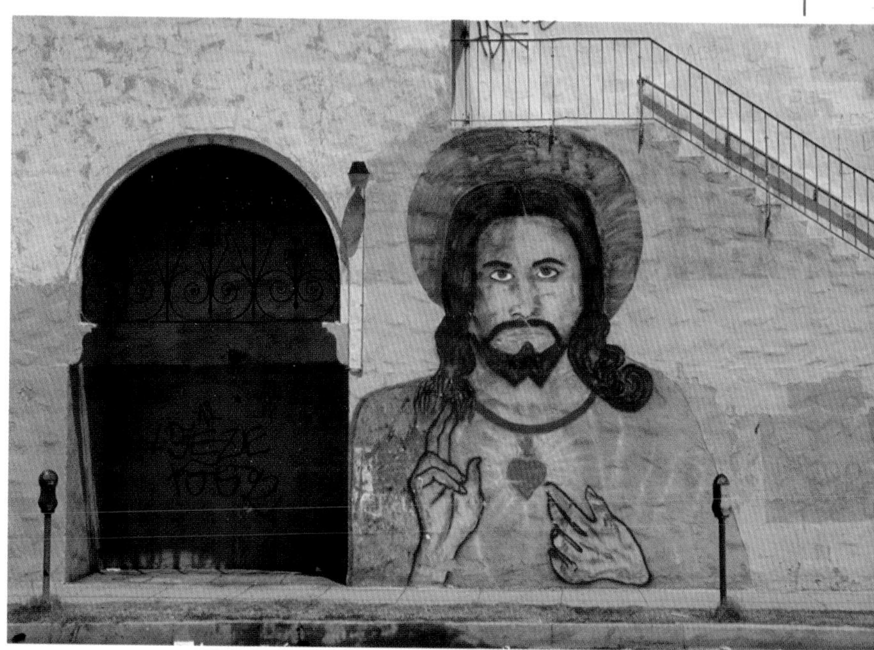

Modern mural on a 19th-century mission wall

What remains of the original church has been carefully restored. The main chamber consists of a simple rectangular vault with an altar of Spanish design. The colorful sculptures of various saints, one donated by Queen Maria in 1773, are in remarkably good condition. The capped buttresses of the belfry underscore a decidedly Moorish subtext to San Gabriel. Scholars have noted its resemblance to the cathedral of Cordoba, birthplace of Padre Antonio Cruzado, who is credited with building the mission. As with many of the missions, the surrounding grounds and cemetery provide ample opportunity to ponder the mixed legacy of Spanish colonization. Underneath are said to be the remains of some 5,000 Gabrieleño Indians. ■

Monterey Park

For travelers who consider food as a destination in itself, the four-city area of Monterey Park, Alhambra, San Gabriel, and Rosemead may well be heaven. This area of the San Gabriel Valley, known as Monterey Park, is home to L.A.'s burgeoning Asian populations, many of whom come from Taiwan, Hong Kong, mainland China, and Vietnam. The result, as the august *Atlantic Monthly* pronounced, is that the "best Chinese food in the world is now being served in Los Angeles's new Sino-suburbs."

It was not always thus. Until the mid-1970s, Monterey Park was just another of southern California's largely Anglo middle-class suburbs, where adventurous eating began and ended at the local taco house. Beginning in the early 1970s, however, a few Chinese immigrants began promoting the area's real estate in overseas Chinese newspapers. Loosened immigration laws made sales easier, and Hong Kong's imminent return to the People's Republic of China increased the heat on the middle-class to move. By the mid-1980s, Monterey Park was 60 percent Asian, a booming Chinese-American suburbia with its own supermarkets, banks, and restaurants.

Travelers take note: This is not the Chinese food of your youth. While elements of the old "sweet-and-sour pork" menu remain, by and large this is the cooking of modern China, highly regional and very fresh. This means you must remain open-minded and willing to ask questions. While their employees may occasionally struggle with the vexing English language, most shops will have someone fluent enough to answer basic questions. But the watchword is *experiment*, rather than ordering as though you were taking a legal deposition. Unless you are into bird's-nest soup and platypus beaks, the food here is inexpensive, so try several different dishes.

Ready? To get the full range of the experience, start at San Gabriel Square, once a drive-in theater and now lined with restaurants and dubbed the Great Mall of China. A good

introduction to Taiwanese cuisine can be found here at Happy Family *(608 N. Atlantic Blvd., tel 626/282-8986)*, where the L.A. food guru Jonathan Gold recommends the pan-fried string beans and the home-style tofu. The less adventurous can try any of the fish and seafood entrées, and the spicy eggplant is memorable.

Farther down Valley Boulevard, directly across from the Turning Point Spaghetti Disco House, is one of many smaller plazas; in it is Mei Long Village *(301 W. Valley Blvd., San Gabriel, tel 626/284-4769)*. Presided over by its businesslike but congenial owner, the restaurant is usually packed with Chinese families and the occasional round-eyed foodie. Order the crab dim sum for starters. Now order another—they're that good. The stir-fried pea greens are a must, as is the pièce de résistance, a huge piece of the most delicious pork, rather uncharmingly named Pork Pump.

Now try something different—perhaps at An Lac Restaurant *(1281 E. Valley Blvd., Alhambra, tel 626/282-8033)*, a Vietnamese café that serves outstanding red rice chicken and two versions of spring rolls—one fried, one not. Eat both.

Walk around the Valley Square place and entertain yourself at the Chinese supermarket, an experience which is like going to Hong Kong without getting all sweaty. Five blocks east, stop in at the Saigon Sandwich & Bakery *(718 E. Valley Blvd., San Gabriel, tel 636/288-6475)*, one of colonial France's few contributions to the culinary world. This is the place to buy perfect, fresh-baked baguettes (crunchy exteriors and cloud-soft innards) and Vietnamese *bahn mi* sandwiches with fresh veggies and jalapeños, and the flan is delicious. Buy three sandwiches and get a free baguette.

The penultimate, and slightly more pricey, seafood meal can be had at Empress Harbor Seafood *(111 N. Atlantic Blvd., tel 626/300-8833)*. Here the food is so fresh that it prompted the following passage from Jonathan Gold: "We had an almost perfect Chinese meal here. First there were giant prawns, fished out of the tank one by one with a net, tossed thrashing into a bucket. Then, a few seconds later, shrimp, steamed, the flesh of the banana-sized creatures sweet and firm. Next, a live lobster, which splashed everyone at the table when it was scooped from the tank." You get the idea. Now get going! ■

Far left: Cooking at Yuet Lee restaurant
Above: In the middle of a New Year's dinner; Below: Dim sum and desserts arranged for a Sunday breakfast

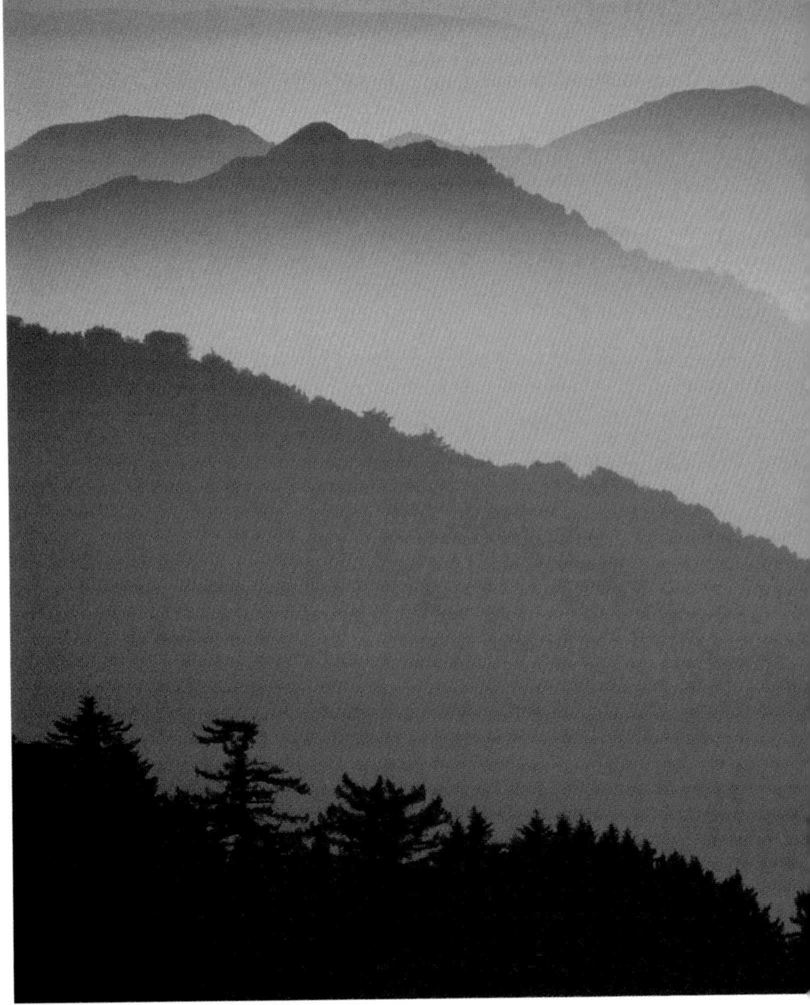

San Gabriel Mountains at dusk

Around the foothills

LOOMING ABOVE THE FOOTHILLS AND STRETCHING FROM the San Fernando Valley east to San Bernardino is **Angeles National Forest.** This 650,000-acre area features hiking trails, picnic sites, and ski areas. Devastating fires often blaze through the forests, as in 2007.

Angeles National Forest
108 B3
Visitor information
www.fs.fed.us/r5/angeles/
626/574-1613

Mission San Fernando
50 C3
15151 San Fernando Mission Blvd., Mission Hills
818/361-0186

At the old **Mount Wilson Observatory** *(tel 310/476-4413, www.mtwilson.edu, open April–Nov.)*, on the Angeles Crest Highway, one can see the telescope used by generations of Caltech scientists to probe the mysteries of space or watch the hang gliders jump off the cliff and sail home to Altadena below. The **Charlton Flat** picnic area, farther up, is a prime spot for bird-watching. Still farther on, at **Jarvi Memorial Outlook,** watch for bighorn sheep.

Back down the mountain, a worthwhile side trip to the west is

to the **Mission San Fernando.** Founded by Padre Fermin Lasuen in 1797, this mission served early L.A. in much the same way as its counterpart in San Gabriel, by providing the new pueblo with food, clothing, and fuel. Lasuen was a masterful inculcator of the faith, and by 1819 San Fernando had a neophyte population of more than a thousand. The fully restored chapel is worth viewing for its use of Indian and Spanish colors and ornamentation. The wide, tiled walkways under the mission loggia are a pleasure to stroll along, particularly on a hot, dry summer day when the stillness all around encourages contemplation.

On the way back from the mission, everyone interested in the flora of the Southwest should visit the **Theodore Payne Foundation,** a shrine to native botany that is a must for those interested in buying and cultivating Californian plants. In the spring, the 23 acres are ablaze with wildflowers. Nearby, the **Children's Museum of Los Angeles** *(tel 818/686-9280, www.childrensmuseumla.org)* opened in 2008 as a highlight of the **Hansen Dam Recreation Area.**

Theodore Payne Foundation
www.theodorepayne.org
- Map: 50 C3
- Address: 10459 Tuxford St., Sun Valley
- Tel: 818/768-1802
- Hours: Closed Mon. mid-Oct.–June & Sun.–Wed. July–mid-Oct.

Hansen Dam Recreation Area
www.laparks.org
- Address: 11770 Foothill Blvd, Lake View Terrace
- Tel: 818/899-3779

Hang gliders at Mount Wilson

Driving eastward back into Pasadena on I-210, you will pass the exit for the **Jet Propulsion Laboratory.** You need to make reservations at least a month in advance in order to visit this wonderland of real space pioneering. It was from here that NASA explored the solar system with missions ranging from the first *Explorer* to the latest *Sojourner.*

Jet Propulsion Laboratory
www.jpl.nasa.gov
108 B3
4800 Oak Grove Dr.
818/354-4321; 818/354-9314 (tours, reservations required)

The road farther eastward (I-210) is dotted with small, down-home towns full of yesteryear charm. A stop in the town of **Monrovia** (Myrtle exit) finds clusters of inexpensive antique stores. The quaint college town of **Claremont,** a 20-minute drive farther east, has a New England feel and several artistic and architectural places of pilgrimage, from Myron Hunt's Bridges Hall of Music at **Pomona College** *(N. College Ave., tel 909/621-8000, www.pomona.edu)* to the first mural painted in the U.S. by José Orozco, at the school's Frary Hall.

Big Bear Lake
50 G3
Visitor information
www.bigbearinfo.com
909/866-6190

San Bernadino National Forest
www.fs.fed.us/r5/san bernardino
909/382-2600

It is an hour-long drive to the city of **Riverside,** where the restored **Mission Inn** *(3649 Mission Inn Ave., tel 909/784-0300, www.missioninn.com)* is a prime example of blended Mexican and Spanish architectural styles, with ornate loggias and fountains.

Farther east again is the **San Bernardino National Forest** *(tel 909/382-2600),* an everlastingly popular vacation destination. In the 1920s, such stars as Charlie Chaplin made **Lake Arrowhead** the resort destination of preference. Now it is home to numerous mountain water-sports outfits in the summer and skiing in the winter.

The particularly scenic **Bluff Meadow,** at the end of **Champion Lodgepole Pine Trail,** can be found south of neighboring **Big Bear Lake,** where you can see bald eagles during the winter months. Good for biking and hiking in summer, Big Bear wears a snowy shawl for much of the winter, drawing skiers and snowboarders to **Big Bear Mountain Resorts** *(tel 909/866-5766, www.bigbearmountainresorts.com),* offering southern California's premier downhill ski runs. ■

Southern California's balmy evening breezes and azure blue skies conjure a Mediterranean feeling. In the south, San Diego's Balboa Park is a major cultural draw; to the north, Santa Barbara beckons with fine architecture and good food.

Southern California

Lighthouse, Santa Barbara

Southern California

DESPITE OCCASIONAL EFFORTS TO REPACKAGE ITS NAME INTO SOMETHING more memorable (or marketable), "Southern California" remains the moniker of choice for the vast region unfolding south from the Tehachapi Mountains to the Mexican border.

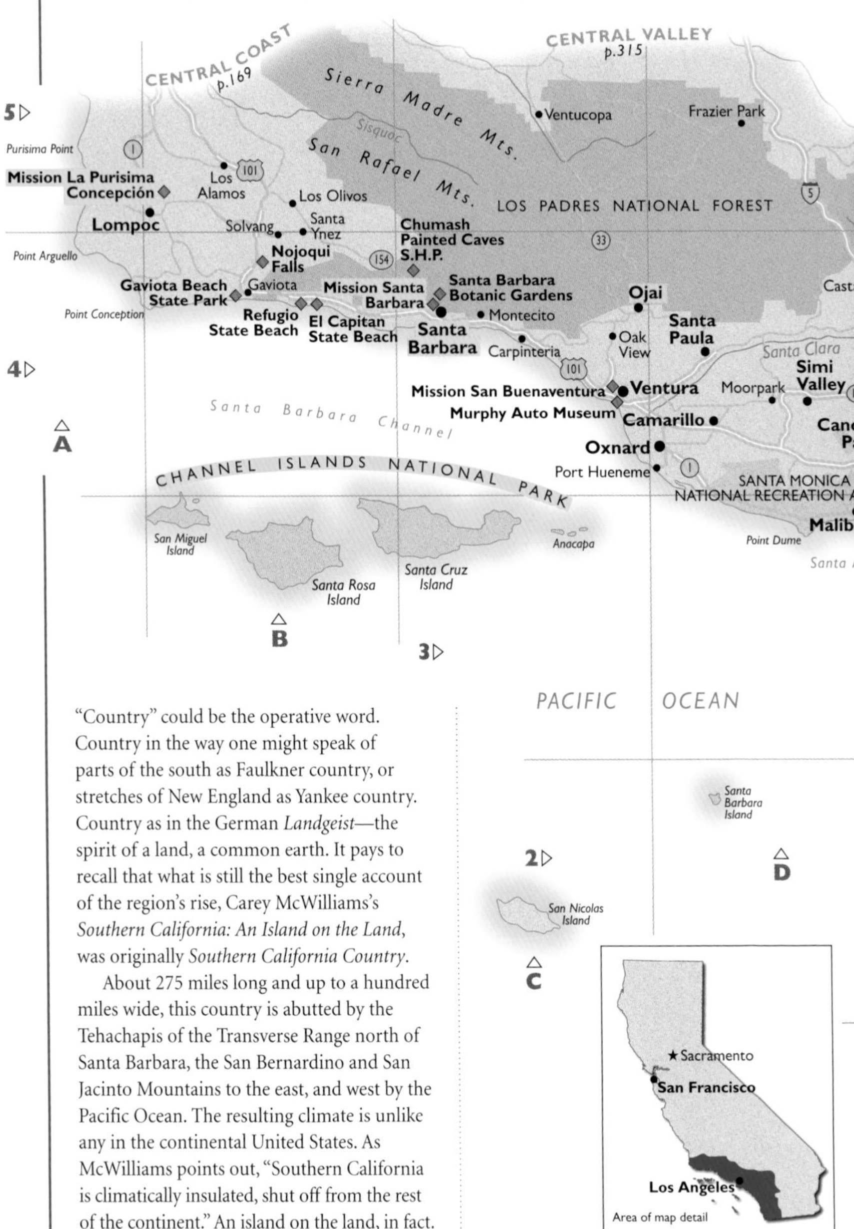

"Country" could be the operative word. Country in the way one might speak of parts of the south as Faulkner country, or stretches of New England as Yankee country. Country as in the German *Landgeist*—the spirit of a land, a common earth. It pays to recall that what is still the best single account of the region's rise, Carey McWilliams's *Southern California: An Island on the Land*, was originally *Southern California Country*.

About 275 miles long and up to a hundred miles wide, this country is abutted by the Tehachapis of the Transverse Range north of Santa Barbara, the San Bernardino and San Jacinto Mountains to the east, and west by the Pacific Ocean. The resulting climate is unlike any in the continental United States. As McWilliams points out, "Southern California is climatically insulated, shut off from the rest of the continent." An island on the land, in fact.

The islanders, as already stated, are increasingly a great and grand mix of tribes from the ends of the Earth. Yet a keen-eyed traveler to Santa Barbara or Laguna or San Diego will note that this is a mixed tribe that has *picked* its ideal climate and settled in here. One result is that most of its memorable cultural places are natural places: tidal pools and hot springs, swimming coves and surfing beaches, botanical gardens and sprawling onetime ranchos. Is beach spelled with a capital "B" anywhere but in southern California?

The beaches to the south, from Long Beach to San Diego, are nirvana to sun worshippers the world around; inland from them are theme parks galore (Disneyland, Knott's), a new wine country (Temecula), several great art and culture palaces, and a number of wonderful fruit orchards for the picking. The beaches to the north, from Santa Barbara on, are cooler, more urbane places to stroll and explore history, then to eat great food. If you can tear yourself away from these beaches, inland you will discover still another new wine country, lots of horses, and a bucolic little gem of a place called Ojai, where the intrepid might find the roots of the region's vaunted new spirituality. ■

Long Beach at night, with the *Queen Mary* outlined in lights

Long Beach

SITUATED ON THE 8-MILE COASTLINE OF SAN PEDRO BAY, Long Beach has always been in the shadow of Los Angeles, its more glamorous sister to the north. Early settlers at Long Beach had giant land grants, but L.A.'s had access to power in Spain, Mexico, and then the United States. By the late 1930s, L.A. was known as the palm and sunshine city of the Pacific; Long Beach, with more than 89 percent native-born Anglos at the time, was known as "Iowa by the Sea." By the late 1970s, it was generally seen as a run-down port, full of colorful if somewhat ripe characters.

Long Beach
129 E3
Visitor information
www.visitlongbeach.com
1 World Trade Center, #300
562/436-3645 or 800/452-7829

Aquarium of the Pacific
www.aquariumofpacific.org
100 Aquarium Way
562/590-3100
$$$

Queen Mary
www.queenmary.com
1126 Queens Hwy.
562/435-3511
$$$

In recent years Long Beach has resuscitated itself. It now claims one of the best ports in the world, a high quality of life, and several worthwhile attractions for visitors. At its hub is the new multibillion-dollar Queensway Bay project, the largest seaside development in California history.

Anchoring Queensway, and worthy of a good morning, is the outstanding **Aquarium of the Pacific.** The aquarium, one of the country's largest, displays 12,500 marine creatures in 19 major habitats. The vast Shark Lagoon is worth the visit alone.

From the aquarium entrance, you can catch the aquabus to Long Beach's other big attraction, the ***Queen Mary.*** This imperious ocean liner, launched in 1936, has undergone notable renovations that have restored it to its art deco glory. Admission includes a shipwalk tour and access to such special exhibits as "Russian Cold War Submarine *Scorpion.*"

For shopping or dining, return downtown to **Pine Avenue,**

Hands on at the Cabrillo Marine Aquarium

where Melrose meets the Pacific. Alternatively, go to the **Long Beach Museum of Art.** This little jewel, located in a historic house overlooking the ocean, presents exquisitely curated shows on Western artists; one exhibition presented the works of Clinton Adams, credited with rescuing the art of lithography post-World War II.

Also in Long Beach is the **Museum of Latin American Art,** which focuses on the art of the area's Latinos. Many of them draw inspiration from David Siquieros, who painted in the Los Angeles area in the 1930s, and Jose Orozco.

For a unique bibliophilic experience, head over to **Acres of Books** *(240 Long Beach Blvd, tel 562/437-6980, www.acresofbooks.com)*. Here you can obtain some of the best bargains on the West Coast, with a huge choice.

Around the bay, the one outstanding destination, often overlooked, is the town of **San Pedro.** This was once the hub of maritime culture in the Los Angeles area, with a colorful cast of Japanese, Slav, and Croatian fishermen. Many remain around the quaint shopping areas and local seafood cafés. Worth a visit is the **Cabrillo Marine Aquarium,** focusing on the local marine life.

Travelers arriving between March and August can enjoy a true southern California treat. During nighttime high tides, the museum provides guided viewings of the grunion runs, when millions of small fish land on local beaches, burrow into the sand to mate, and then retreat to die in local waters.

A popular jaunt is the helicopter or ferry ride to **Catalina Island,** 22 miles offshore. Once favored by famous figures from gum magnate William Wrigley to Zane Grey (his home is now a hotel), this rugged island is surrounded by pristine waters abounding in marine life. Ashore, visitors can explore the 42,000-acre **Catalina Island Conservancy** *(tel 310/510-2595, www.catalinaconservancy.org)*, home to fox, buffalo, and even bald eagles, and setting for the **Wrigley Memorial & Botanical Garden.** The art deco Casino Building houses the **Catalina Island Museum** *(tel 310/510-2414, www.catalina.com/museum.html)*, with an outstanding archaeological collection. ■

Long Beach Museum of Art
www.lbma.org
✉ 2300 E. Ocean Blvd.
☎ 562/439-2119
🕒 Closed Mon.
$ $$

Museum of Latin American Art
www.molaa.com
✉ 628 Alamitos Ave.
☎ 562/437-1689
🕒 Closed Mon.
$ $$

Cabrillo Marine Aquarium
www.cabrilloaq.org
✉ 3720 Stephen White Dr., San Pedro
☎ 310/548-7562
🕒 Closed Mon.
$ $$

Catalina Island Visitor information
www.catalina.com
✉ #1 Green Pier
☎ 310/510-1520

Disneyland Resort

Disneyland Resort
www.disneyland.com
129 F3
1313 Harbor Blvd., Anaheim
714/781-4565 or or 714/781-4400 (tickets only)
$$$$$ (children under 3 free)

FOR MANY TRAVELERS THE PRINCIPAL DESTINATION IN southern California, Disneyland has been the subject of so many interpretive essays in recent years that one might think that the Happiest Place on Earth, founded in 1955, had lost its happy sense of innocence and wonder. The park has been excoriated for operating unsafe rides (the subject of extensive liability litigation), discrimination (leading to a touchy debate over whether gays should be allowed to dance in conservative Walt's family-oriented attraction, answered finally with a "yes"), and cultural imperialism (for a "lack of ethnic diversity" among its cartoon characters). The result? People keep coming in record numbers, spending tons of cash, and feeling happy happy happy!

There are ways to maximize your enjoyment and minimize your discomfort during a visit to this 85-acre park (see box below), comprising **Disneyland Park** and **Disney's California Adventure** park (see p. 136).

Disneyland Park is organized into eight themed "lands." The first is **Main Street, U.S.A.,** organized as a typical American burg of around 1890. Favorite attractions here are the various coin-operated games and the **Great Moments with Mr. Lincoln,** in which an Audio-Animatronics Abe delivers his greatest oratory. The experience proves moving, even to Nintendo-jaded teens. While you are on Main Street, be certain to take in one of the park's many elaborate

The battle plan

Treat a visit to Disneyland as an art aficionado might treat a first-time visit to the Louvre. Get an idea of what your family absolutely must see in the park the night before you go. The company's website is quite helpful, with maps, hotel and food information, and a list of rides scheduled to "go dark" for repair and cleaning. Now think about what you want to eat—you can't bring it in with you, so consider a hearty breakfast at one of Anaheim's 450 local eateries before entering the park, preferably as early as possible. Once you have entered, you are in Disney-foodland, not bad but not great either. You may want to make sure you will have a decent dinner by employing one park fanatic's plan: "Whenever we go we make an immediate beeline for the Blue Bayou Restaurant in New Orleans Square and make a reservation for later that day," she says. "It is the most comfortable, appetizing, sit-down eating place in the park, and you can't beat it after eight hours on your feet." Another strategy, for the ride-oriented, is to take in the park's live attractions, shopping and dining during the day, saving the more popular—and more crowded—rides for the cooler nights, when they are generally less crowded. Lastly, there are now a number of specialized guidebooks to the park for families with small children. ■

Opposite: Sleeping Beauty Castle in Fantasyland

© Disney/Lucasfilm Ltd.

Indiana Jones Adventure attraction

parades; at night, they end with a memorable fireworks show.

Adventureland was once considered one of the park's quieter sections, dominated by such low-tech attractions as the **Enchanted Tiki Room** and the **Jungle Cruise.** But Adventureland's character was revved up with the addition of the **Indiana Jones Adventure.** This ultrafast, well-reviewed attraction has some of the most consistently long lines in the park. Late evening may be the best time for this popular attraction.

Fantasyland enchants with a Sleeping Beauty castle, **Peter Pan's Flights,** and **Snow White's Scary Adventures,** while **Mr. Toad's Wild Ride** is well attended by teenagers and even young adults. For children, two must-rides are: **It's a Small World,** the theme song of which you *will memorize*, and **Dumbo the Flying Elephant.** More ambitious is the fast and wet **Matterhorn Bobsleds**. A word of warning: Don't ride too soon after eating.

Tomorrowland, Walt's idea of the future, puts the emphasis on action, though there are still some attempts at education. **Innoventions,** for example, has guests board a slowly rotating "loading pod," where they are introduced to the exhibits in five thematic areas: transportation, health and sports, home, work and school, and entertainment. Guests are then free to play with hundreds of hands-on displays of new products and technologies. One typical of Tomorrowland is **Honey, I Shrunk the Audience,** based on the popular series of movies. Situated in a 500-seat theater, the show takes its audience on a three-dimensional misadventure in which special effects are used to make the theater appear to shrink to the size of a shoebox. This attraction may be too scary for some small children. **Autopia**—where a second generation of supercharged cars hits the street—is best seen as a mechanized rendition of Disney cartoon characters. New in 2007, **Finding Nemo Submarine Voyage** is an underwater adventure. Hop aboard the submarine to experience a sub-shaking volcanic eruption and explore coral reefs while Nemo and his fishy friends go along for the ride thanks to a futuristic projection technology.

To get a sense of the "old" park, the **Disneyland Monorail** is a classic choice.

Critter Country is one of the younger sections of Disneyland, and its slower pace and gentler entertainments make it perfect for tots and burned-out parents. The **Many Adventures of Winnie the Pooh** fun ride for honey is one highlight here. Another is the more action-oriented **Splash Mountain,** a highly recommended ride in the form of a superslick log flume. You can get wet on this ride.

Frontierland is one of the more traditional sections of the park, with such rides as a **Mark Twain Riverboat, Raft to Tom**

The Astro Orbitor in Tomorrowland

Sawyer Island, and the **Frontierland Shootin' Exposition** show. **Fantasmic!** is a classic park showcase for special effects as well as new and old Disney characters. Fantasmic! takes the viewer on a trip "through Mickey's imagination" along the many rivers of America. Also popular is **Stars of Toy Story,** where kids can meet face-to-face with Sheriff Woody, Jessie, the Yodeling Cowgirl, and other fave stars from the movie. If you become bored by such fare, wake yourself up with a ride on the **Big Thunder Mountain Railroad.**

Perhaps the most memorable ride in the park is **Pirates of the Caribbean,** found in lively **New Orleans Square.** "Pirate" guests ride on a "floating" boat that, after two hair-raising plunges, lands them in a bawdy, pirate- and damsel-filled land of Audio-Animatronics boozers, wenches, and assorted ne'er-do-wells. The line moves quickly, but waits of an hour are not uncommon. The square is a good place to hop

The Mad Tea Party

aboard one of four steam-powered locomotives that tour the park.

Mickey's Toontown, a three-dimensional cartoon world, benefits from new technologies and a younger, more aesthetically sophisticated group of designers and architects. The **Roger Rabbit's Car Toon Spin** is an old-fashioned pod ride in the tradition of Mr. Toad; guests can spin their vehicles as they career through various cartoon worlds. Other attractions here include **Goofy's Bounce House, Donald Duck's Boat,** the **Jolly Trolley,** the **Chip 'n' Dale Treehouse,** and **Gadget's Go Coaster.**

Visitors to Disneyland can also choose **Disney's California Adventure Park.** According to Barry Braverman, its producer, the idea behind this attraction is to "immerse guests in compelling stories, evocative places, and fantastic adventures that will bring the California dream to life." This it does through a series of elaborately themed California districts—from beach to deserts to mountains—that capture northern, central, and southern California on a mere 55 acres. One ride, Soarin' Over California, allows guests to virtually "soar," using hang gliders, over a re-creation of Yosemite National Park, while another attraction conjures up the "Hollywood of the imagination."

The Twilight Zone Tower of Terror, will make the hair stand up on your head. The setting is the once-glamorous Hollywood Tower Hotel, now vacant and full of "ghastly ghostly guests." Adrenalin junkies experience a fateful night when lightning strikes and you are plunged 13 stories down an abandoned elevator shaft into the "most thrilling recesses of The Twilight Zone."

Also here is **Downtown Disney,** a dining, entertainment, and shopping district placed between the entrances to the two theme parks and including a megaplex theater. And if you need a place to rest your head after all this excitement, consider the Grand Californian, a 751-room deluxe hotel, built in a style reminiscent of the Arts and Crafts movement. ■

Around Orange County

The massive Crystal Cathedral in Garden Grove

IF YOU HAVEN'T RUN OUT OF ENERGY AND MONEY BY THE time you have finished with the Magic Kingdom, you may want to explore some of Orange County's other attractions.

The best single destination is the **Bowers Museum of Cultural Art** in Santa Ana. With a mission to preserve, study, and exhibit the fine arts of the Americas, Africa, and the Pacific Rim, the Bowers turns a fine curatorial eye on everything from late 18th-century Mexican copper brandy stills to the massive, cold-rolled steel sculptures of L.A. artist Betty Gold. In downtown Anaheim, **The Muzeo** *(251 S. Anaheim Blvd., tel 714/956-8936, www.muzeo.org, $$$)* cultural center, art gallery, and museum for world-class traveling exhibitions opened in 2007 with a lavish exposition on Imperial Rome.

If you need some non-Disney inspiration, head to the remarkable **Crystal Cathedral** *(12141 Lewis St., Garden Grove, tel 714/971-4000, closed Sun. except services),* where 10,000 panes of glass were arranged in prism-like architecture for the Rev. Robert Schuller, who started here 30 years ago. If you need a dose of reality, however, the **Richard Nixon Presidential Library & Birthplace** will prove fascinating, with galleries on Nixon's life, World Leaders, the Berlin Wall Freedom Presentation, and Pat Nixon's rose garden with the tiny house where the President was born.

For more entertainment, try **Knott's Berry Farm.** Knott's started in 1934 when Cornelia Knott set up a fried chicken restaurant on her husband's berry farm. Today it is a sprawling park with themed areas (many concerning the Wild West), and high-tech roller-coaster rides (The Boomerang, Montezuma's Revenge). ■

Bowers Museum of Cultural Art
www.bowers.org
✉ 2002 N. Main St., Santa Ana
☎ 714/567-3600
🕒 Closed Mon.
$ $$$

Richard Nixon Presidential Library & Birthplace
www.nixonlibrary.org
✉ 18001 Yorba Linda Blvd., Yorba Linda
☎ 714/993-5075
$ $$

Knott's Berry Farm
www.knotts.com
✉ 8039 Beach Blvd., Buena Park
☎ 714/220-5200
🕒 Call for hours
$ $$$$$

Laguna Beach

HOMESTEADED BY MORMONS IN THE 1870S, DEVELOPED AS an artists' retreat and resort town in the early 1900s, Laguna has long proven irresistible to both visitors and natives seeking respite from inland heat and noise. All crisp sea air and primal canyonland, its geography holds a clue to why.

Laguna Beach
129 F2
Visitor information
www.lagunabeachinfo.org
252 Broadway
949/497-9229

Crystal Cove State Park
www.crystalcovestatepark.com
N of Laguna Beach off Pacific Coast Hwy. (Calif. 1)
949/494-3539 or 949/497-7647 (interpretive walks)
$

The town is fronted by a series of stunning coves with waters sometimes shimmering a light blue and sometimes brooding, nearly purple. Rising from the coves are a series of sculpted cliffs, which give way to a small basin flat enough for what many have called "a permanent village." Looming behind that are the *cañons de los lagunas*, or canyons of the lakes. Water, sand, canyon. Such are the features that attracted California's plein air painters, many of whom set up here in the early 1900s. Although the Hollywood crowd soon followed, Laguna has always retained a strong identification with the arts, as represented by its **Pageant of the Masters** *(tel 949/494-1145 or 800/487-3378, www.foapom.com)*, a live staging of masterpieces from Tiepolo to Toulouse-Lautrec.

The modern visitor might begin an exploration of the coves at any number of beaches. **Main Beach,** situated at the foot of Laguna Canyon Road, is the epicenter of the city's beach culture, with a thriving volleyball and skateboarding scene. Its waters are often calm enough for a pleasant swim. Main Beach is also within walking distance of downtown Laguna, fine for strolling and shopping in the summer months.

A more tranquil beach experience can be had by driving about a mile north of Main Beach to **Crescent Bay.** This aptly named stretch of sand is known for its great body surfing waves and ample sunning areas. The tidal pools to its north are easily explored (take some old tennis shoes), and on a good day visitors may see the rare

red sea anemone, sometimes bigger than a baseball glove. The more aquatically skilled can rent snorkeling or scuba equipment and swim out to **Seal Rock,** a protected sanctuary for the honking, boisterous California sea lion. The beds of giant sea kelp around the rock are particularly mesmerizing when viewed through a diving mask.

The unique ecology of Laguna's cliffs is the focus of the relatively new **Crystal Cove State Park,** to the north off the Pacific Coast Highway. Situated on 3.5 miles of onetime cattle-grazing land, the park has undergone extensive vegetation with native plants. An extended boardwalk takes guests through the park and onto the beach below, and it serves as an educational nature trail. You may spot red-tailed hawks and northern harriers swirling above; below, roadrunners career about. Down on the beach, explore Reef Point for more tide-pooling adventures.

One benefit of a disastrous 1992 fire that ravaged Laguna's canyons was the creation of the 19,000-acre **Laguna Coast Wilderness Park.** Two walks justify taking the trouble to make a reservation. The first is the 3.5-mile **Laurel Canyon Nature Trail** *(closed Mon.–Fri.)*, its air perfumed with wild sage and sycamore, its undulating rockscape as dramatic today as it was in the early 20th century, when such painters as Guy Rose and Norman St. Clair depicted the area in their plein air canvases.

Farther up Laguna Canyon Road, past groves of old eucalyptus trees, is the **James Dilley Greenbelt Preserve** *(closed Mon.–Fri.)*. Visitors follow a trail around a landscape of bulrushes, prickly pear, hemlock, and sycamores. Egrets and ospreys are common in the main lake to the north (known as lake number one).

Just north of the Inn at Laguna Beach (the preferred vacation residence) is **gallery row,** on North Coast Highway. The work of many local painters, some doing a form of neo-plein air painting, is worth a look; prices are reasonable for good living room art. Some of the originals that inspired this work can be seen at the **Laguna Art Museum.** The delight of seeing William Wendt's original of "Spring in the Canyon" is just one thing that makes a visit here worthwhile. ■

Laguna Beach and its shoreline at night

Laguna Coast Wilderness Park
www.ocparks.com/lagunacoast
✉ 18751 Laguna Canyon Rd., near El Toro Rd.
☎ 949/923-2235
$ $

Laguna Art Museum
www.lagunaartmuseum.org
✉ 307 Cliff Dr.
☎ 949/494-8971
$ $$$

Beach life at Newport

Beach cities

NORTH AND SOUTH OF LAGUNA BEACH, A STRING OF beach cities edges the coast. Huntington Beach offers the casual visitor an extreme close-up of the southern California surfing scene. Most of the action in this intense youth culture occurs around the pier. On virtually any morning, the earlier the better, you can watch the practice sessions of some of the world's most skilled wave riders. Later in the day, check out the surfwear shops and health food cafés in the old shopping district behind the pier. There is even a surfing museum for those keen to explore every detail of this activity.

Huntington State Beach
129 E3

International Surfing Museum
www.surfingmuseum.org
411 Olive Ave.
714/960-3483
Closed in winter

Newport Beach
129 F3
Visitor information
www.newportbeach-cvb.com
110 Newport Center Drive, Suite 120
949/719-6100; or 800-94-COAST

Bolsa Chica State Beach & Ecological Preserve
www.bolsachiga.org
3842 Warner Ave.
714/846-1114
Closed Mon.

NORTH OF LAGUNA

To the south of central L.A., the wide, clean stretches of **Huntington State Beach** beckon sunseekers; a bike path extends the entire length of the beach. Those interested in marine and waterfowl life can drive the few miles to **Bolsa Chica State Beach & Ecological Preserve.** Here a 1.5-mile trail leads around a tidal lagoon where stingrays and least terns are among the wildlife to be seen. Overlooks provide vistas of the restored wetlands.

Farther south, in an area once marketed as "The Gold Coast" (an indication of the "Beverly-Hills-by-the-Sea" aspirations of those who live here), is the fast-paced, glamorous, and highly tanned community of **Newport Beach.** The principal social activity here is boating, which takes place in the "largest small craft harbor in the world." Even for those who can't afford the $200 deck shoes (let alone the boat), **Newport Harbor** provides ample sun-filled entertainments, from the historic Balboa Pavilion and old-fashioned Fun Zone (somehow bumper cars at the beach are more fun) to the **Newport Harbor Nautical Museum,** located on the 190-foot paddle wheeler *Pride of Newport.* For shopping, Fashion

Island *(Jamboree Rd., off E. Pacific Coast Hwy.)* offers ultra-exclusive shops that rival those of Rodeo Drive. For deeper thinkers, the permanent collection of postwar California art at the **Orange County Museum of Art** may be worth a trip. If the stock market is booming, this museum is known for doing what it takes to gather some rather remarkable exhibitions.

Farther inland, the ornithologically inclined can revel in the **Upper Newport Bay Ecological Reserve & Regional Park** *(2301 University Dr., tel 949/923-2290, www.ocparks.com)*. The Audubon Society estimates that approximately 70 percent of the remaining population of the light-footed clapper rail make their home in this lush 750-acre salt marsh.

Back south on the Pacific Coast Highway (Calif. 1), you'll find two remarkable beaches. The first, **The Wedge,** is known mainly for its huge, bone-crunching waves; on any day you can witness the spectacle of otherwise sane young people hurling themselves into its churn. The second, **Corona del Mar State Beach,** is the epitome of the southern California bathing beach: swimmable waters, pristine sands, and a backdrop of palms, seagulls, and even the occasional pelican. Perfect for picnics.

SOUTH OF LAGUNA

The picturesque coves and rugged cliffs of Laguna continue southward well beyond the city's limits. There is public access to all of these beaches, and they are well worth the effort to escape the summer crowds. The pier and marina are the main attractions at **Dana Point** *(Pacific Coast Hwy. & Street of the Golden Lantern)*. There are several outstanding seafood restaurants here, and a walk to the lookout point yields memorable views.

Inland, off I-5, is the **Mission San Juan Capistrano**, perhaps the most picture-perfect of all the 21 California missions. Founded by Padre Serra in 1776, its simple adobe church is the only building in the entire chain where it is certain that the great man said Mass. The Moorish-style architecture and the burnished bells and arcades of the building lend a romantic hue to Mission San Juan, while the gardens make a pleasant stroll. Migratory swallows return here every spring and are welcomed with a festival on March 19.

Returning to the Pacific Coast Highway, three contiguous beaches give you a choice for a day of sunning and swimming: **Doheny State Beach, Capistrano Beach,** and **San Clemente Beach.** San Clemente was the California location of the western White House, the building to which President Richard Nixon repaired after his resignation. ■

Newport Harbor Nautical Museum
www.nhnm.org
✉ 151 E. Pacific Coast Hwy. (Calif. 1)
☎ 949/675-8915

Orange County Museum of Art
www.ocma.net
✉ 850 San Clemente Dr.
☎ 949/759-1122
🕒 Closed Mon. & Tues.
$ $$$

Mission San Juan Capistrano
www.missionsjc.com
✉ Ortega Hwy., San Juan Capistrano
☎ 949/234-1300

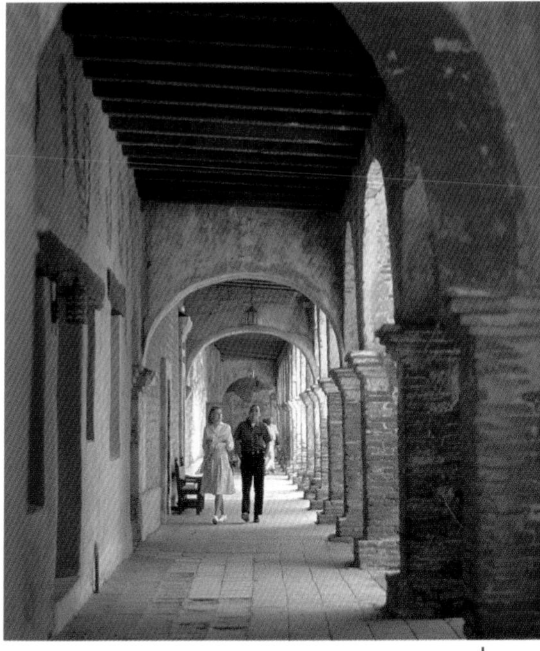

The shady arcade at Mission San Juan Capistrano

Torrey Pines State Reserve

OF ALL SOUTHERN CALIFORNIA'S RESERVES, THIS 1,750-ACRE area of seaside cliffs and lagoons north of La Jolla may well be the most sensuous. The scents of wild fennel, sage, and pine combine with sand, sun, and spray to make a heady mixture. Alas, the pine that gives the reserve its name, *Pinus torreyana*, is the rarest of its genus; only 9,000 of these drought-tolerant trees remain in all America.

Torrey Pines State Reserve
www.torreypine.org
129 G1
Carmel Valley Rd. (exit off I-5)
858/755-2063

Mount Palomar Observatory
www.astro.caltech.edu
129 G2
35899 Canfield, Mount Palomar
760/742-2119 (reservations required for tours)

San Diego Wild Animal Park
www.wildanimalpark.org
129 G2
Calif. 78, Escondido
760/480-0100
$$

Temecula Visitor information
www.temeculawines.org
951/699-6586

Start with a short hike (about two-thirds of a mile) around the **Guy Fleming Trail** *(leaflets from the visitor center)*. Botanizing around the eerily eroded cliffs and twisted pines is a joy, particularly from February through May when the California native flowers blossom in hues of red and orange and purple and green. Omnipresent is the "sticky" monkey flower, its tiny orange trumpets waving in the breeze; here is the yellow mariposa lily, the lemonade berry, and the purple coast cholla.

Near the bottom of the **Broken Hill Trail** is the overlook for Flat Rock, dramatic in its simplicity. From January through March you may spot a California gray whale on its annual migration. Seals, cormorants, and gulls add to the spectacle. Red-throated loons and great blue herons are found year-round.

On the north edge of the park is **Los Penosquitos Marsh,** once a Native American encampment, but now an extensive mudflat whose inhabitants include fiddler crabs and jackknife clams. Access is controlled, but check with the ranger station for tours.

For golfers there is the **Torrey Pines Golf Course** (see p. 386), considered one of the most scenic places in the world to tee off; rates are reasonable.

When you've had your fill of nature and feel in need of some more sophisticated pleasures, the seaside resort of **Del Mar** *(Visitor information, tel 858/755-4844)* lies at the mouth of the Dieguito River north of Torrey Pines. Long famous for its horse-racing track *(tel 858/755-1141)*, balmy summer evenings are pleasant here even when Lady Luck isn't going your way. ■

Away from the coast

The coast may be the great draw, but there are pleasures inland too. **Mount Palomar Observatory** *(Calif. 76 to Cardy Rd., then Cty. Rd. 6)*, where Caltech runs its 200-inch Hale Telescope, lies 6,000 feet up in the Aquanga Mountains.

Or you could visit the wine country of **Temecula** *(I-15 to Rancho California Rd., then E)*. The region's 1,500-foot elevation makes for an interesting Petite Syrah. Try the **Cilurzo Winery** at Rancho California *(41220 Calle Contento, tel 909/676-5250, www.cilurzowine.com)*. Temecula offers plenty of entertainment, including balloon rides with **D&D Ballooning** *(tel 915/303-0448 or 800-510-9000, www.hotairadventures.com)*.

In the **San Diego Wild Animal Park** near Escondido, the Bush Line Monorail travels through the park, allowing you good close-up views of the elephants, lions, and rhinos. ■

Opposite: Wind-carved bluffs and *Pinus torreyana*, the namesake of the Torrey Pines State Reserve

La Jolla

FOUNDED AS ONE OF EARLY 20TH-CENTURY CALIFORNIA'S more exclusive suburbs (think: Bel Air by the sea), La Jolla shimmers with the essence of the Good Life. Its homes, done in a fusion of modernism and recherché mission style by the great architect Clifford May, seem perfectly matched to the always changing ocean sky. Its shopping arcades along sunny Prospect Street are vaguely European, punctuated with steak houses advertising surf 'n' turf and clothiers offering the latest in casual wear (as if there were anything else one *would* wear here). There is the seductive cocktail hour on the Latinate patio at La Valencia *(1132 Prospect St., tel 858/454-0771, www.lavalencia.com)*, overlooking stunning La Jolla Bay, before a play at La Jolla Playhouse.

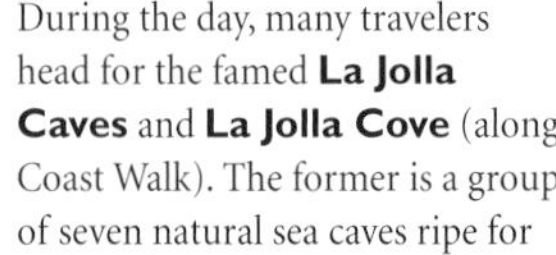

During the day, many travelers head for the famed **La Jolla Caves** and **La Jolla Cove** (along Coast Walk). The former is a group of seven natural sea caves ripe for exploration by the romantic; the latter one is of the most picturesque, albeit tiny, beaches on the coast, its deep blue waters attracting many snorkel divers.

Back up on Prospect, the **Museum of Contemporary Art San Diego at La Jolla** turns a fine curatorial eye upon a constantly changing palette of postwar art and design, from the giant canvases of Leon Golub to the sleek lines of great Italian designers. Many make a visit to this museum just to bear witness to the architecture of Irving Gill, who designed the sleek but site-sensitive building. The collection—full of Ellsworth Kelly, Billy Al Bengston, and Robert Irwin—is extensive enough to evoke such rare praise as that of *L.A. Times* art critic William Wilson, who has called it "an outpost of the New York establishment and a haven for local contemporary art." Its works by Charles Eames, Ludwig Mies van der Rohe, and Marcel Breuer alone warrant a stop.

Those with a certain literary inclination should take time to walk over to **Windansea Beach** *(Neptune Pl. & Bonair St.)*, which was immortalized in journalist Tom Wolfe's essay "The Pump House Gang."

La Jolla
129 G1
Visitor information
www.lajollabythesea.com
7966 Herschel Ave.
619/236-1212

La Jolla Playhouse
www.lajollaplayhouse.org
2910 La Jolla Village Dr.
858/550-1010

Museum of Contemporary Art San Diego at La Jolla
www.mcasd.org
700 Prospect St.
858/454-3541
Closed Wed.
$$$

Spectacular sums up the **Birch Aquarium at Scripps** *(N on Torrey Pines Rd. to Expedition Way)*, the interpretive center for the marine research establishment, the Scripps Institute of Oceanography.

Go first to the **Hall of Fishes,** where state-of-the-art tanks cover the marine life of the Pacific, from the Pacific sardine (the entryway sardine tank is endlessly entertaining) to southern California jellies. Of hypnotic interest here is the giant kelp forest, located inside a sunlit 55,000-gallon tank equipped with a wavemaking machine. The **Art of Deception** gallery displays marine creatures that use camouflage for survival; interactive exhibits help you see what's not so evident at first glance. **The Tropical Seas Gallery** has especially lively exhibits on coral reefs. New in 2007, **Feeling the Heat: The Climate Challenge** addresses issues of global warming.

The extensive **Learning Center** also has all the requisite bells and whistles, with interactive science exhibits, a "submarine dive" video show, and a New Perspectives Gallery for changing exhibitions. Those interested in the truly interactive should take an advance look at the aquarium's activities schedule, which includes such field trips as "Snorkel with the Sharks" (non-man-eating) and "Tidepooling for Tots." A visit to the **Tide Pool Plaza,** with its panoramic view of the La Jolla shoreline, is a stunning coda to the visit, and perfect preparation for any planned tidal pool explorations (see pp. 146–47). ■

Birch Aquarium at Scripps
www.aquarium.ucsd.edu
✉ 2300 Expedition Way
☎ 858/534-FISH
$ $$$

Opposite: Arch-shaded café in La Jolla

Below: Fog blows in over La Jolla's cliffs.

In the tide pools

The typical southern California tide pool consists of five zones, each with its own ecology. The topmost is the spray zone; then come, in descending order, the high, medium, and low intertidal zones, where most of the action is. The last is the subtidal where many of these creatures live when not looking for food in the intertidal.

With its warm waters and accessible cliffside pools, La Jolla provides some excellent opportunities for tide pooling. Linda E. Tway, author of *Tidepools of Southern California*, is a local expert. Her advice is to prepare by checking the local tide tables (in the newspaper daily). Remember that removing any marine life from the pools is against the law.

Although there are several outstanding tide-pooling sites in La Jolla, the location known as Big Rock *(enter from Camino de la Costa between Cortez Place & Via del Norte)* offers the opportunity of seeing some rare and colorful species. Come at low tide—but watch for strong surf surges.

The most continually exposed of the zones, the spray zone, is a treasure trove of thriving marine life. Outstanding examples of creatures that are numerous at Big Rock include the periwinkle, a snail-like mollusk usually about five-eighths of an inch long and spherical in shape, and the striped shore crab, a crustacean normally two inches long with green stripes.

Inhabitants of the high intertidal zone must be able to tolerate a good deal of sun and air; one response is for them to close up or seal themselves with a shell, preventing dehydration. The masters of this, found in abundance at Big Rock, are the California mussel and the leaf barnacle. The mussel grows to six inches in length and is brown to purple-black. It attaches itself to a rock with a single foot. The barnacle, up to five inches long, white and more or less leaf-shaped, clings with grayish brown stalks in large numbers, sometimes one on top of another. Also watch for the giant keyhole limpet, a shell-covered conical oval, gray to brown, clamped to the rock with a single yellow-orange foot.

As exposure to air decreases in the medium intertidal zone, coralline algae transform the gray-green sandstone into a wonderland of pinks and purples. Into this surface burrows the troglodyte chiton, brown and one-and-a-half inches long. These remnants from dinosaur days spend their 20-year lives scraping into the sandstone. The result is the pockmarked surface of Big Rock.

Because the low intertidal zone is mostly submerged, more permanent "homes" are built. One of the most remarkable is that of the sandcastle worm. Two inches long, cream colored with a black tip and lavender tentacles, *Phragmatopoma californica* builds honeycomb-like clusters of delicate sand tubes (watch your step). Another star of this zone is the giant green anemone. A member of the same class of invertebrates as corals, anemones use their tentacles to catch passing prey. The green anemone can grow as large as seven inches wide. Also look for the giant acorn barnacle, which resembles a tiny volcanic crater.

The subtidal zone is where you will see fishes and the larger seaweeds of the area. ■

KEY TO DIAGRAM

1 rough limpet
2 sea lettuce
3 striped shore crab
4 giant owl limpet
5 striped sea slug
6 California mussels
7 pink encrusting coralline algae
8 volcano barnacles
9 velvety red sponge
10 Spanish shawl nudi branch
11 leaf barnacles
12 common surfgrass
13 sandcastle worms
14 rockweed
15 giant green anemone
16 Hopkins' rose
17 California sea hare
18 bat star
19 Panama brittle star
20 ochre star
21 warty sea cucumber
22 sea urchin
23 rock crab
24 spiny lobster
25 black abalone
26 sargasso weed
27 coralline red algae
28 giant keyhole limpet
29 chestnut cowry
30 chitons

Looking across the San Diego marina to downtown

San Diego

IF ITS NEIGHBOR TO THE NORTH, LA JOLLA, REPRESENTS the ultimate California Good Life, then San Diego conjures the ultimate California Outdoor Life. With its huge range of water-sports facilities, its giant municipal culture parks, and the largest zoo in the United States, it is a giant adult playground. The fact that it is surrounded by frontierland—desert to the east, the Mexican border to the south, and the Pacific to the west—only underscores the city's relatively late development. Though it sprawls, it has yet to break out into megasprawl.

San Diego
129 G1
Visitor information
www.sandiego.org
1040 1/3 West Broadway
619/236-1212

From its birth in 1769 as the first Spanish settlement in Alta (Upper) California, San Diego has followed much the same pattern of development as other great Californian cities. The initial spurt of missionizing was so aggressive that, in 1775, the neophytes at Mission San Diego openly revolted and slew Padre Luis Jayme, making him the first martyr of Alta California. A period of Mexican neglect and wildcat Anglo fur trading was followed by a spate of Yankee entrepreneurialism, much of it focused upon the area's climate and natural harbor.

The Yankees stuck. In 1870, Alonzo Horton, considered the founder of modern San Diego, began touting the city as a mecca of tourism and health; eventually he built one of the most celebrated hotels of his time. Nowadays Horton is honored in the popular Horton Plaza outdoor mall.)

By 1915 the city was confident enough to enter the "world exposition" game, hiring the gifted architect Bertram Grosvenor Goodhue (who was responsible for Caltech and L.A.'s Central Library) to design Balboa Park (see pp. 150–53), where the city fathers promoted the 1915 Panama-California International Exposition.

John D. and Adolph B. Spreckels, sons of a sugar magnate, caught the alfresco bug as well, building in 1915 the largest outdoor organ in the world. To this day, on any warm Sunday afternoon, numerous San Diegans and visitors can be found in Balboa Park's open-air Spreckels Organ Pavilion, the music and sun washing over them as they sit like seals on a sandy beach.

During the mid-20th century San Diego boomed. A heavy dose of federal government largesse, largely coming through the burgeoning naval complex, allowed the city to avoid some of the planning mistakes made by its northern neighbors, cities that often sabotaged their own zoning laws in order to attract new corporate residents. In San Diego, debate over growth has traditionally been framed by the phrase "Smokestacks versus Geraniums." Even the conservative former governor of California Pete Wilson, who was the mayor of San Diego in the late 1970s, is remembered as a proponent of restrained growth in the city.

More recently, huge population gains and economic shifts (the naval presence has been replaced in part by high-tech industries) have made planned growth more difficult. San Diego is now the sixth largest city in the United States. Urban sprawl, as in the awful area surrounding Qualcomm Stadium near the old mission, is becoming more common.

Yet any discerning visitor would be hard pressed to come away from San Diego unhappy. The old California Tower in Balboa Park shines in the sun *and* in evening spotlights. Old San Diego is joined with new Tijuana in Mexico via an efficient, low-cost trolley car system and new Bridge of the Americas. There are plays and concerts under the stars every night. Out on Mission Bay, water-skiers skip over lacy wave crests like dolphins leaping. Don't forget the suntan lotion. ■

Girls in Mexican costumes wait to dance at a festival.

Balboa Park
www.balboapark.com
129 G1

San Diego Museum of Art
www.sdmart.org
1450 El Prado
619/232-7931
Closed Mon.
$$$

Balboa Park

OF THE TWO MAJOR "EXPOSITION CITIES" BUILT IN 1915 to commemorate the opening of the Panama Canal—in San Francisco and San Diego—1,100-acre Balboa Park is unquestionably the best preserved and most culturally vibrant. In it are 19 distinct museums and art institutes, three theaters, formal and informal gardens, the nation's largest zoo, and more Spanish colonial architecture than anywhere else in the state. It is, in short, an adult theme park. Think: Walt Disney in 17th-century Spain.

Fountain statue "Azteca Mujer," at Balboa Park

Opposite: Aerospace museum and skyline of San Diego

Arranged in a series of plazas along the main road, El Prado, with the landmark Tower at the east end, the park was designed with two purposes, one pragmatic, one aesthetic. By building a giant Pacific "Dream City," the park's founders hoped to establish San Diego as the preferred port of call for ships arriving through the newly built Panama Canal. By bringing in the architect Bertram Grosvenor Goodhue, known for his flashy Mediterranean style, the city fathers also sought to communicate San Diego's unique vision of itself as a merging of garden and city.

If Balboa Park's official purpose was, as its founders said in one 1930s pamphlet, "to illustrate the progress and possibility of the human race," the unofficial one was not unlike that of today's sophisticated relocation ads used to lure new companies to new cities. This effort was redoubled in 1935, when the city held another world exposition, adding Moorish and Italianate elements to the original Mediterranean aspects. As the state librarian Kevin Starr notes, this was architecture as "romantic text." The text was written by the Chamber of Commerce.

Yet it was the continuing enlistment of the city's mercantile elite that saved Balboa Park and preserved it for what it is today: one of the best kept secrets in American tourism. To take full advantage, set aside at least two days. A Passport to Balboa Park, on sale at any of the park's museums, affords onetime access to each venue and is good for one week. Park near the zoo and walk in, take the tram, or stroll the new landscaped **Park-to-Bay Link** bridge, linking the park to San Diego Bay. Ask your hotel concierge to make reservations for you at one of the three evening theater performances in the park.

MUSEUMS

Although all of them are worth a visit, three Balboa Park museums warrant particular note. The first is the **San Diego Museum of Art.** The largest of the city's museums, it has a significant collection of Renaissance and post-Renaissance works by Spanish artists. The best known work is "Quince, Cabbage, Melon, and Cucumber," painted in 1602 by Juan Sanchez Cotan. One wonders how a man could produce such a realistic depiction of fertility, and the following year, as Cotan did, renounce the world and become a monk. An outstanding work is Bartolomé Murillo's "Mary Magdalene," another display of sensuousness restrained by the artist's preference for flat frontal poses. Although born in Greece, El Greco, who did his best work in Toledo, belongs here among the

Timken Museum of Art–Putnam Collection
www.timkenmuseum.org
1500 El Prado
619/239-5548
Closed Mon. & Sept.

Mingei International Museum
www.mingei.org
1439 El Prado
619/239-0003
Closed Mon.

Museum of Photographic Arts
www.mopa.org
1649 El Prado
619/238-7559

San Diego History Museum
www.sandiegohistory.org
1649 El Prado
619/232-6203
$

Reuben H. Fleet Science Center
www.rhfleet.org
1875 El Prado
619/238-1233
$$

San Diego Air & Space Museum
www.sandiegoairandspace.org
2001 Pan American Plaza
619/234-8291
$

San Diego Automotive Museum
www.sdautomuseum.org
2080 Pan American Plaza
619/231-2886
$$

Spaniards. "The Penitent St. Peter," painted in 1600, startles with its use of dramatic light, reminiscent of Rembrandt's "Raising of Lazarus."

The museum has also put together a notable grouping of American painters, chief among them Thomas Eakins. His "Elizabeth Crowell with a Dog," painted in 1871, will strike a chord with any animal lover.

Just east of the museum of art, the **Timken Museum of Art–Putnam Collection** is housed in the only nonrevivalist building in Balboa Park, a cool modern temple of marble and glass. This somewhat eccentric grouping of European and American masterworks is marked by its even more eccentric juxtaposition with a world-class collection of Russian iconography. From late 16th-century Russia, the wood panel "St. Basil the Great and Scenes from His Life" is full of the quiet power that any good religious icon must possess; it was, after all, conceived as a medium for meditation upon God's kingdom, both here and in heaven. From 1838 comes a painting by Jean Baptiste Camille Corot. Entitled "View of Volterra," the work is a masterful evocation of the long approach from Siena to the old Etruscan town of Volterra, which Corot first sketched during a summer visit to Italy in 1834. The sensuous realism of late 19th-century American painters is found in "The Magnolia Flower," painted in 1888 by Martin Johnson Heade.

Scholars and folk art buffs come from around the world just to see the most dynamic of the park's museums, the **Mingei International Museum,** which is dedicated to world folk art, both contemporary and historical. Titles of past exhibitions hint at the diversity: "American Expressions of Liberty"; "India: Village, Tribal, Ritual Arts"; "Folk Toys of the World"; and "Viva Los Artisanos!" If you are lucky, you may catch one of Niki de Saint Phalle's exhibitions. French-born, New York City raised, now residing part-time in La Jolla, Saint Phalle is known for her colorful and fantastic images, some as big as a small house.

Other museums in the park include the **Museum of Photographic Arts,** which offers an extensive collection of the 20th-century's leading practitioners. The **San Diego History Museum** has a somewhat worn permanent exhibit, but its changing exhibitions display a passionate curatorial bent. The Space Theater at the **Reuben H. Fleet Science Center** contains a planetarium and IMAX theater. The **San Diego Air & Space Museum** has a decent collection of historic aircraft and exhibits on aviation and space exploration. The **San Diego Automotive Museum** has a collection spanning late 19th-century horseless carriages, muscle cars, and cars of the space age. The **San Diego Hall of Champions** *(2131 Pan American Plaza, tel 619/234-2544, www.sdhoc.com)* looks at San Diego's contributions to more than 40 sports. The **Model Railroad Museum** *(Casa de Balboa, tel 619/696-0199, www.sdmrm.com, closed Mon.)* specializes in train scenes of San Diego and southern California. The **Museum of Man** *(1350 El Prado, tel 619/239-2001, www.museumofman.org)* looks at human-kind's evolution from cultural and physical perspectives.

Lastly, the **San Diego Natural History Museum** *(1780 El Prado, tel 619/232-3821, www.sdnhm.org)* specializes in exhibits explaining and illustrating broad habitats and in the geology of gems and minerals.

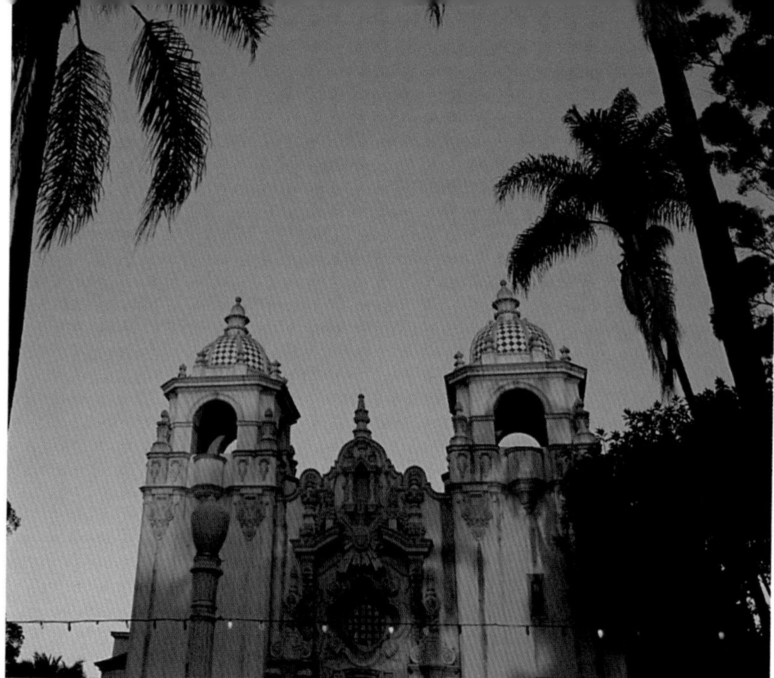

GARDENS & ORGAN PAVILION

The **Spreckels Organ Pavilion** *(just S of the Plaza de Panama on El Prado)* also harks back to a simpler time, when, in 1915, civic leaders John D. and Adolph B. Spreckels spent the then huge sum of $100,000 on building the world's largest outdoor organ. On Sunday afternoons young musicians try out this old classic. Free **Twilight in the Park** concerts are held on mid-week evenings in summer.

East of the organ pavilion, the **Japanese Friendship Garden** is one of the more recent additions to the park. Its 11-acre site features winding pathways, stone lanterns, and raked Zen rock gardens.

The **Botanical Building & Lily Pond** *(between Casa del Prado & museum of art)* is truly something from another era. Built with more than 12 miles of redwood lath, it houses a wide variety of exotic plants. The enormous lily pond has proven highly adaptable over the years. During World War II, when many park buildings were used as troop hospitals, it served as a rehabilitation pool. In the blistering summer of 1945, the pond became a swimming pool for 22,000 local children.

THEATERS

Some of the best theater on the West Coast takes place at Balboa Park's three-venue complex. Built for the 1935 California Pacific International Exposition, the **Old Globe Theatre** was dedicated to abbreviated performances of Shakespeare. After a series offires, the Globe was incorporated into today's triplex to make this San Diego's largest arts institution. The other theaters are the **Cassius Carter Center Stage** and the **Lowell Davies Festival Theater,** each with its unique seating configuration (one in the round, one open-air, respectively). The theaters won a Tony award for excellence in 1984 and have since launched several new works. ■

Balboa Park's Casa del Prado, built for the 1915 Panama-California Exposition, is now home to diverse groups, including a junior theater.

Balboa Park theaters
www.oldglobe.org
✉ El Prado
☎ 619/23-GLOBE

San Diego Zoo

FOUNDED IN 1916 BY THE ENTERPRISING DR. HARRY Wegeforth, the San Diego Zoo has grown far beyond even its founder's grandest dreams. Resting on a hundred acres of northern Balboa Park, this state-of-the-art animal park now displays and cares for 3,900 animals representing more than 800 species. Its botanical credentials (more than 6,500 plant species) startle as well; with only a little imagination one can, within one park, experience jungle, tundra, and rain forest. Many come to San Diego to see this attraction alone. Only excessive marketing detracts from the experience.

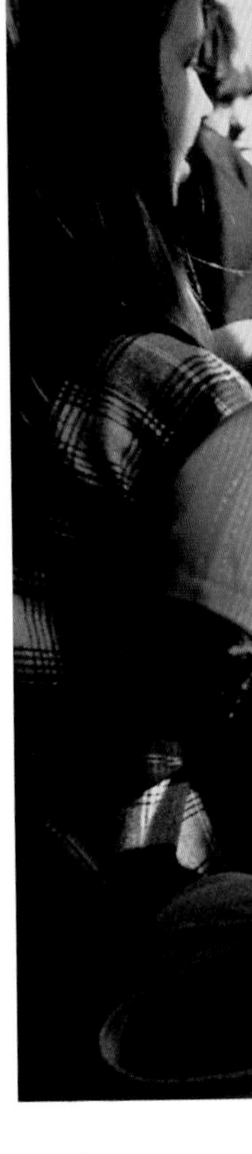

Three different tours (by double-decker bus, aerial tram, or "kangaroo bus") offer visitors different views of the park and its inhabitants. Among the most memorable sites are **Gorilla Tropics,** located just beyond the Bird and Primate Mesa near the park entrance. This is one of the zoo's top attractions—2.5 acres of simulated African rain forest within an 8,000-square-foot enclosure that is home to a troop of western lowland gorillas. Inside the same compound is the **Scripps Aviary,** with more than 200 African birds in free flight—at least until they fly into the netting above.

Just beyond, you'll find the **pygmy chimps** at Bonobo Road. Considered the most intelligent of the primates, these long-legged, slender chimps with odd center-parted hair live in an enclosure of giant rocks and gnarled palms.

Farther to the left, at **Hippo Beach,** visitors can view these remarkable 4,000-pounders both above ground and underwater, through a special two-inch-thick window of laminated glass.

If the weather is hot the **Polar Bear Plunge,** located at the outer boundary of the park, provides a soothing scene. Conjuring two acres of Arctic tundra, complete with Siberian reindeer and arctic foxes, the plunge features a group of playful polar bears busily cavorting in a 130,000-gallon tank. Their underwater antics are visible through a large acrylic window. Many swim right up to the glass, apparently curious about the strange creatures on the other side.

If you backtrack, the **Giant Panda Research Station** is

San Diego Zoo
www.sandiegozoo.com
2920 Zoo Dr., Balboa Park
619/231-1515 (guided tour reservations)
$$$

Studying caterpillars

next. The zoo keeps adding to its population of these endangered creatures: Bai Yun, who arrived from China in 1996, has since given birth to four cubs, most recently in August 2007. A new exhibit area includes an interactive **Giant Panda Discovery Center.**

Nearer the entrance is stunning **Tiger River,** where visitors walk down a misty forest path before coming to ten enclosures housing more than a hundred animals (including Burmese pythons, narrow-snouted crocodiles, and Malaysian tapirs). The tigers prowl about on a grassy hillside, their appearance made all the more dramatic by the rain forest environs.

A new habitat—**Monkey's Trails & Forest Tales**—is home to 30 species of African and Asian mammals, reptiles, birds, etc. and features ground-level and treetop canopy trails. Clouded leopard, pygmy hippos, mandrills, and dwarf crocodiles are among the species to look for. Nearby, orangutans and siamangs cavort in their arboreal habitat, **Absolutely Apes;** visitors can view the apes through a massive glass window.

Between these major stops are dozens of specialized habitats, each designed for the particular needs of its inhabitants. There are the requisite kangaroos and elephants and rhinos and giraffes.

To your left upon entering is an outstanding **children's zoo,** complete with Raintree Grove and a display of the increasingly rare Galápagos tortoises. A **Nighttime Zoo** is open in summer only. ■

A hippo eyes visitors through the window of its pool.

The William Penn Hotel in the Gaslamp Quarter

Historic San Diego

AS THE OLDEST SPANISH SETTLEMENT IN CALIFORNIA, SAN Diego and its environs are full of historic places, some major, some minor. The City of San Diego has made visiting several nearby sites both easy and comfortable. A trolley system offers an outstanding two-hour narrated tour, with the advantage that you can unboard and reboard the trolley all day long.

Junípero Serra Museum
✉ 2727 Presidio Dr.
☎ 619/297-3258

Maritime Museum
www.sdmaritime.org
✉ 1492 North Harbor Dr.
☎ 619/234-9153
$ $$$

Among the attractions are the revived **Gaslamp Quarter** *(Broadway & 4th–6th Aves.)*, where Wyatt Earp ran such a bawdy operation as to cause his more uptight neighbors to move north. Since the 1980s, the quarter has become the place to shop and eat. **Old Town State Park,** protected as the site of the early settlement, also offers the splendid **Junípero Serra Museum,** which holds relics and pieces of art from the original mission.

Nearby you can view the restored **Victoriana of Heritage Park** *(2455 Heritage Park Row)* while kids can romp amid interactive displays at the new **Children's Museum** *(First St. & Front St., tel 619/233-8792, www.sdchildrensmuseum.org)*.

Besides taking you to **Balboa Park** (see pp. 150–53) and the **Coronado Peninsula** (see p. 159), the trolley also travels along San Diego's seafront. There maritime buffs can explore the

Maritime Museum, where the spectacular "San Diego's Navy" exhibit opened in 2007, depicting the history of the U.S. Navy in San Diego; the 1860s *Star of India* is another highlight. Nearby is the **USS *Midway* Aircraft Carrier Museum** *(Navy Pier, www.midway.org),* which berthed here permanently in 2004 after an illustrious 47-year career and today rewards visitors with a virtual reality flight experience, plus military aircraft spanning five decades.

An ongoing redevelopment of downtown San Diego is transforming the long-dormant area into a vibrant neighborhood anchored by the new 46,000-seat **PETCO Park** baseball stadium *(tel 888/697-2373, www.padres.com)* and the award-winning **Horton Plaza Shopping Center,** replicating a European market with more than 140 shops and cafés. Also in the downtown area is the **Museum of Contemporary Art,** a counterpart to the one in La Jolla.

FARTHER AFIELD

From San Diego, take Calif. 209 to Cabrillo Memorial Drive and head to the **Cabrillo National Monument** at the tip of the Point Loma Peninsula. As the name suggests, this is where Juan Rodriguez Cabrillo, the great Portuguese explorer—in service to Spain—became the first European to set foot in California. More appealing than the monument and the **Cabrillo Museum** is the surrounding parkland, 144 acres offering spectacular views of city and bay, as well as extensive hiking trails. You may also visit the lower rooms of the 150-year-old **Old Point Loma Lighthouse,** a short walk from the monument.

Heading out of town eastward on I-8, the scenery brightens as you enter Cleveland National Forest and **Cuyamaca Rancho State Park,** where you can ride horses or bikes, or just walk, on 130 miles of scenic trails. Go north on Calif. 79 to the quaint historical town of **Julian,** where an apple festival attracts visitors in October.

From here go west on Calif. 78, to the old **San Pasqual Battlefield,** just east of the town of Escondido, where U.S. troops defeated rebel Californios in 1846. Turn south, down I-15, to return to San Diego.

Turn north here and follow Hwy. 821 to the quaint seaside village of **Carlsbad,** where **Legoland** *(tel 719/918-5346, www.legoland.com),* a 128-acre theme park, offers innovative rides and models—including replicas of famous cities—made from millions of Lego bricks. Hot new additions include a Jurassic-themed roller-coaster and **Pirate Shores,** with water-based rides. ■

Museum of Contemporary Art
www.mcasd.org
✉ 1001 Kettner Blvd.
☎ 858/454-3541
Closed Wed.
$ $$$

Cabrillo Museum
www.nps.gov/cabr/
✉ 1800 Cabrillo Memorial Dr.
☎ 619/557-5450

Old Point Loma Lighthouse, Cabrillo National Monument

Cuyamaca Rancho State Park
www.parks.ca.gov
✉ 12551 Hwy. 79
☎ 760/765-3020

San Pasqual Battlefield
www.parks.ca.gov
✉ 15808 San Pasqual Valley Rd.
☎ 760/737-2201
Closed Mon.-Fri.

Mission Bay

Mission Bay
129 G1
Visitor information
2688 Mission Bay Dr.
619/276-8200

SeaWorld Adventure Park
www.seaworld.com
500 Sea World Dr.
619/226-2901 or 800/257-4268
$$$$

ALTHOUGH THE SEA PROVIDES THE DOMINANT PHYSICAL atmosphere here, many also detect a decidedly midwestern cast to the outdoor life of jubilant Mission Bay. Jubilant because this 4,600-acre aquatic park, dedicated to just about every water-based activity imaginable, is where San Diegans go to stay healthy and let rip. If you are in relatively good shape and have not tried ocean waterskiing, do not let the opportunity slide by. Several ski shops offer lessons, and you will likely be up and skimming in less than an hour. Numerous rental outlets supply powercraft, sailboats, and every other kind of water sports equipment you are likely to need.

Killer whale show at Sea World

The bay has 17 miles of beaches open to the public; many are home to long-standing beach volleyball rivalries. (Don't be surprised to see a few of your favorite volleyball stars spiking a few for one of the many charity benefits that take place here year-round.) In April of every year, the bay hosts the **San Diego Crew Classic,** a boisterous affair that attracts collegiate teams from around the United States and Canada. In September comes the **World Series of Power Boat Racing.** Even the avid nonboater can enjoy these events, which foster an unbridled festive spirit.

SeaWorld, located on the south side of the bay, remains at the leading edge of themed marine parks and is constantly upgrading its shows and interactive displays in its 150 acres. New in 2006, the **Wild Arctic Interaction** lets you slip into the water to get personal with beluga whales, while **Believe** features high-tech underwater cameras and giant LCD screens as killer whale Shamu and friends perform acrobatics. "Penguin Encounter" and "Shark Encounter" are two long-time favorites. There are also places where one can pet dolphins, pick up a sea star, and even feed a bat ray. Meanwhile, manatees bumble about in a 215,000-gallon freshwater naturalized-environment tank. SeaWorld also has the largest water-fowl collection in the United States.

Two sky rides hoist the visitor high above the surrounding bay, the Coronado Peninsula, and the city; the panoramic views from up here are unforgettable. ■

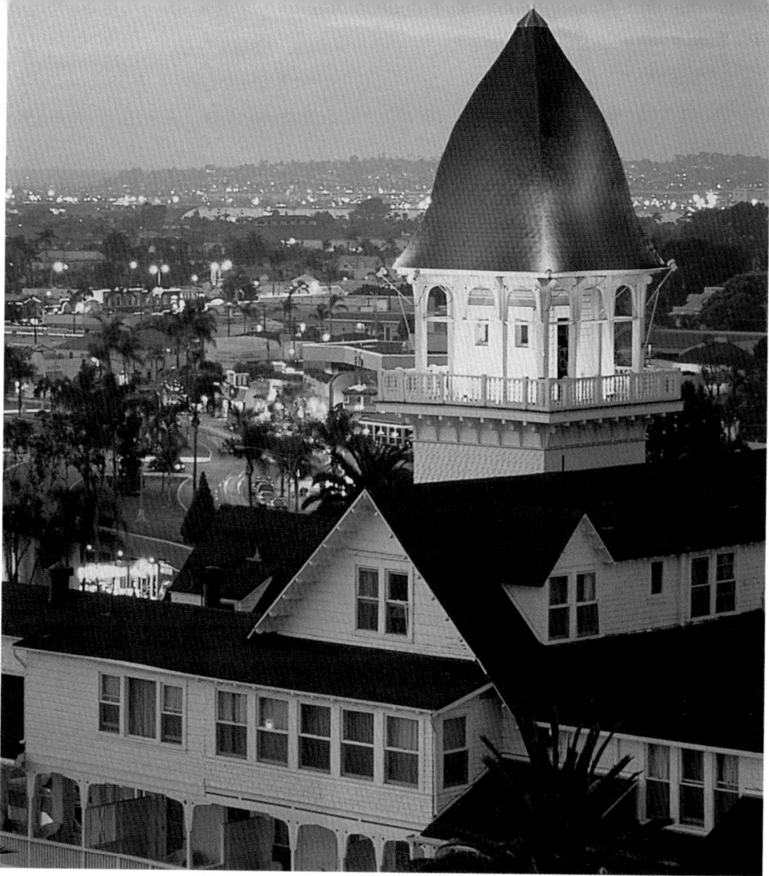

The Victorian Hotel del Coronado still receives guests, though it is now also a tourist attraction.

Hotel del Coronado

The centerpiece of the 4,100-acre Silver Strand Peninsula that separates San Diego's harbor from the Pacific Ocean is the fanciful Victorian Hotel del Coronado *(1500 Orange Ave., tel 619/435-6611 or 800-HOTELDEL, www.hoteldel.com).* Built in 1888 by the enterprising Elisha Babcock, Jr., and H.L. Story, the hotel has been an enduring attraction ever since.

A favorite getaway of blue bloods and Hollywood doyens, the gleaming white structure oozes dated opulence and has hosted the likes of the Duke and Duchess of Windsor, Henry James, and L. Frank Baum, who wrote the *Wizard of Oz* here and supposedly modeled his Emerald City on the view from his room. Most famously, Marilyn Monroe paraded the hallways in *Some Like It Hot.*

While the hotel is still a fanciful place to visit, with historical tours available, the wise traveler will limit outings here to the off-season or mid-week, when the tour buses dwindle in number.

Today's "Hotel Del," often busy and crowded, is a place to see but not one to linger in, even for a meal. Instead, enjoy a drink in the woodsy old lobby bar, then jump back on the San Diego trolley and return across the water to see a play at Balboa Park (see pp. 150–53). ■

Painted papier-mâché on sale in a Mexican market

Mexican folk art

The Mexican city of Tijuana is just a 15-minute trolley car ride south from San Diego's Old Town. These days many come to this once rough border town not for the illicit delights of drink, dames, and gambling—although those still abound—but for Mexican tribal art.

The origins of this industry lie in 18th-century Mexico, when village priests and lay artisans began crafting ornamentation for new churches. These pieces often combine colorful pre-Columbian nature worship and traditional Old World religious iconography. The result is rustic, hallucinatory, festive, and even provocative.

To get there by car, take I-5 or Calif. 805 south past San Ysidro to the International Border Crossing; there you may park, cross the bridge on foot, and pick up a cab on the other side. (Ask the driver how much he charges for the trip downtown.) If you choose to drive your own car, one-day insurance is available at several sites. A better way to see "TJ" is by trolley, available at a number of sites around the city. For the closest, call San Diego Trolley *(tel 619/233-3004)*. The inexpensive journey takes just 45 minutes. U.S. citizens should carry proof of citizenship for reentry.

While folk art of varying quality, new and old, can be found throughout Tijuana's many shopping arcades, one of the better shops is Tolan *(between Calles 7 & 8 on Avenida Revolucion, tel 011 52 66/88-3637)*. It is a good idea to go there first to get an idea of top price and top quality, *then* explore alternatives along the various *calles* to make comparisons. The key is to have fun. Bargain, but don't take it seriously.

Among the most popular items are *retablos*, painted tin-and-wood plaques used as votives in tiny household shrines across Mexico. They often bear the likeness of the Virgin of Guadalupe. Some of the best come from the state of Oaxaca. Look, too, for *ceramicas festas*, brightly colored ceramics used to commemorate the Day of the Dead. These range in size from the tiny clay skulls made in Oaxaca to the fantastic candelabra and Nativity scenes made in Puebla or the wild fusion of biblical and tropical scenes from Jalisco. Renderings of various mythical beasts are usually made in Metepec, outside Mexico City. You will also find *santos* and *bultos* ("saints" and "figures") in tin, clay, wood, and ceramic, and *milagros*, tin representations of parts of the body, often pinned to statues of saints in hope of a healing miracle.

Woven goods, both everyday and precious, include the *sarapes* of northern Mexico, *rebozos*, and *huipils*, tunics made popular by the Mixtec peoples, who dye them with colors from insects and sea snails. The Zapoteca people are known for their copying abilities. Huipils and *quechquemitls*, or capes, made during the 1920s and '30s, often display such European influences as Escher and Miró. ■

Santa Barbara pier at sunset

Santa Barbara

NORTH FROM LOS ANGELES, SANTA BARBARA REMAINS THE favorite weekend getaway spot for Angelenos. Its near-perfect climate of sunny skies, refreshing sea breezes, and temperatures in the 70s persists nearly year-round. Outdoor enthusiasts come here to enjoy some excellent places for horseback riding, surfing, camping, and bicycling. There are botanical gardens to explore, and interesting wine country. Downtown, the street scene thrives with a diverse crowd of students, couples on holiday, and old-timers who stay for the late afternoon breeze. Santa Barbara has a hint of the pleasantly deshabille; more than a hint of Nice, France, in late June.

Santa Barbara is where Angelenos come to get in touch with their Californiano identity. This is not to say that Santa Barbara is 100 percent genuine; the city revels in red-tiled roofs and mission revival architecture. But the atmosphere is not kitsch. It is sincere, pre-TV. Perhaps this is because the city fathers of early 20th-century Santa Barbara, creators of the existing city plan, still had blood ties to the old Hispanic town. The result is a kind of pre-Disney Hispanic dream city.

Santa Barbara has so nurtured its Hispanic roots that you can still easily imagine yourself as a proud don or doña, moving gracefully along its paseo at dusk. The Chumash word *anacapa* (pleasant illusion), now the name of a main street, seems to sum it all up.

MISSION SANTA BARBARA

Not surprisingly, Mission Santa Barbara occupies center stage. Founded in 1786 but not completed until 1820, the Queen of the

Santa Barbara
128 C4
Visitor information
www.santabarbaraca.com
1601 Anacapa St.
805/966-9222

Mission Santa Barbara
www.sbmission.org
2201 Laguna St. (via Alameda Padre Serra)
805/682-4149
$

The classical facade of the mission church

Missions deserves its nickname. Certainly it is one of the most architecturally distinguished, its Ionic columns and Roman facade taking their cues from the drawings of Vetruvius Pollio, dating from 27 B.C. The Roman connection derives from St. Barbara, the mission's namesake, an early Christian martyr said to have been beheaded by her pagan father. The mission also figures in the later fortunes of the city, having educated some of the leading hidalgos and Americanos of the era in its mid-19th-century boys' school. A big attraction is the mission's interior colors, which still glow. Be sure to see the baptismal font. A stroll about the grounds will reveal an extensive Native American aesthetic influence, on the lower

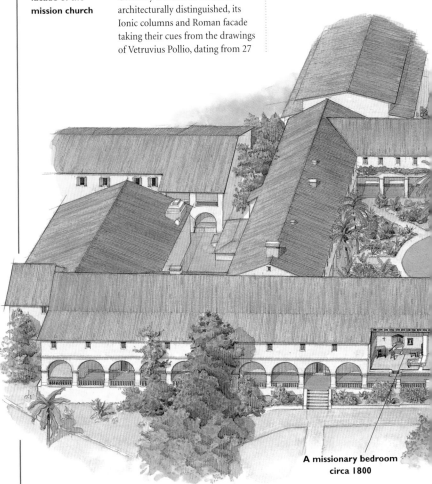

A missionary bedroom circa 1800

walls, in corners, on porticoes, and in murals. The mission fathers still minister to the remaining Chumash in the area, and the commemorative seal to "Juana Maria," a Chumash woman, is the only such plaque dedicated to a Native American in the entire mission system.

THE CITY

The focal point of Santa Barbara's street scene is **El Paseo,** built in the Spanish colonial style in 1922 as part of the city's attempt to convert a rather half-hearted Anglo main street back into a Spanish plaza. The plaza works beautifully as a central gathering place, perhaps because it has at its center the **Casa de la Guerra Historic House Museum** built in 1819 by the Spanish commandante José de la Guerra. It was de la Guerra who, after Mexico won California from Spain, became the small pueblo's commercial leader. He had extensive contacts in the Spanish community through his wife, the daughter of Don Raimundo Carrillo, who was a

Casa de la Guerra Historic House Museum
15 E. De La Guerra St.
805/966-6961
Closed a.m. & Mon.–Wed.
$

The buildings of Mission Santa Barbara

Santa Barbara Museum of Art
www.sbmuseart.org
1130 State St.
805/963-4364
Closed Mon.
$$

Santa Barbara County Courthouse
www.sbcourts.org
1100 Anacapa St.
805/568-2220
Guided tours twice daily

Santa Barbara Botanical Gardens
www.sbbg.org
1212 Mission Canyon
805/682-4726
$$

Santa Barbara Zoological Gardens
www.santabarbarazoo.org
500 Ninos Dr. (off Cabrillo)
805/962-5339
$$

Ty Warner Sea Center
www.sbnature.org/seacenter
211 Stearns Wharf
805/962-2526
$

veteran of the Sacred Expedition of 1869 that had founded the city. The fortune that he accumulated as a result included as much as 200,000 acres of rancho land alone. The adobe is now a museum. A look at the highbrow European furnishings so lovingly acquired by the Carrillo family brings to life the early days of the community here.

The immediate area is filled with other well-preserved remnants of Spanish days, including the **Hill-Carrillo Adobe** (1825–26) at 11–15 E. Carrillo Street, the **Lugo Adobe** (1830) at 114 E. de la Guerra Street, and the **Rochin Adobe** (1856) at 820 Santa Barbara Street. Five blocks east is the **Presidio Chapel** (1788), which contains the original fort's 18th-century decor. It offers a short slide show and a scale model of the Old Presidio.

To the north, the outstanding **Santa Barbara Museum of Art** has important holdings of works by O'Keeffe, Sargent, and Hopper. Two blocks east is the pièce de résistance of Spanish colonial revival, the **Santa Barbara County Courthouse** (1929), considered one of the most beautiful municipal gems in the U.S. Designed by the architect William Moser, the courthouse offers daily guided tours. Don't miss it.

North of the mission district, the **Santa Barbara Botanical Gardens** are the most remarkable of Santa Barbara's many public gardens. Over 5 miles of trails wander through 65 acres of California native plants. Directly east of the mission is 18-acre **Franceschi Park** *(1510 Mission Ridge Rd.)*, named for Emmanuele Franceschi, the "Italian Luther Burbank" who lived in Santa Barbara between 1893 and 1912. The panoramic views and old stone pathways through aloe gardens make this one of the city's more intriguing botanical getaways. Southeast, nearer the beach, are the **Santa Barbara Zoological Gardens,** a small zoo in a large garden in an old oceanfront estate—perfect for a picnic. Farther up Cabrillo is the 32-acre **Andre Clark Bird Refuge** *(Los Patos Way, Cabrillo exit from US 101)*, where you can bicycle through lush gardens squawking with waterbirds.

Many of the most scenic beaches are north of the city, but for plain seaside fun try **Leadbetter Beach** or **West Beach,** adjacent to historic **Stearns Wharf.** The wharf itself is a major attraction, with several good seafood restaurants, a vintner's shop, and a **Ty Warner Sea Center.** You could rent a bicycle and take in the newly completed **Chase Palm Park,** also adjacent to Stearns.

NORTH OF SANTA BARBARA

To get a sense of the grandeur of Santa Barbara's hidalgo days of huge ranchos, drive northwest on US 101, passing three remarkable state beaches along the way: **El Capitan, Refugio,** and **Gaviota.** The rangers can tell you where the old **hot springs** are located just to the north off Vandenburg Road.

From here the old highway veers inland through some of the most beautiful oak and chaparral land in the state. Stop at **Nojoqui Falls** *(off Alisal Rd.)* for a short hike up to the area's only major waterfalls. Continuing north, take Calif. 246 to **Solvang** *(Visitor information, 1511 Mission Dr., tel 800/468-6765, www.solvangusa.com)*, a Danish village that is also home to **Mission Santa Inés,** site of an Indian rebellion.

Drive on, through the **Santa Ynez** wine country (more than 40 wineries off US 101 are open

The Spanish colonial revival courthouse in Santa Barbara

to view) before joining scenic Calif. 154. In the tiny wine burg of **Los Olivos,** you can browse through shops full of antiques and California art. Look for prints by California artist Joe DeYong—a kind of cowboy-meets-Zen landscape and figure painter.

Return to Santa Barbara via Calif. 154, which parallels the old stagecoach route. Turn off onto Painted Cave Road to see the glowing colors of the Native American cave art at the **Chumash Painted Caves State Historical Park.**

SOUTH OF SANTA BARBARA

Go southwest on US 101 to the exclusive enclave of **Montecito** where, by appointment, you can visit **Casa del Herrero,** a private, 11-acre estate known for its outstanding Spanish-Moorish-style garden. Then explore the antique shops in nearby Summerland or Carpinteria. At the end of Calle Ocho Road, Carpinteria is a grand lookout point, said to be where Chumash people caulked their canoes with local beach tar.

Farther south on US 101 is the harbor town of **Ventura,** known for its bargain antiques and for the recently-opened **Murphy Auto Museum,** displaying vintage autos spanning the last 100 years. If you have time, visit the little church of **Mission San Buenaventura,** rebuilt in 1809 after being destroyed by fire. ■

Mission Santa Inés
www.missionsantaines.org
✉ 1760 Mission Dr., Solvang
☎ 805/688-4815

Chumash Painted Caves State Historical Park
www.parks.ca.gov
✉ Painted Cave Rd.
☎ 805/733-3713

Casa del Herrero
www.casadelherrero.com
✉ 1387 E. Valley Rd.
☎ 805/565-5653
🕒 Tours Wed. & Sat. By appointment only. Closed mid-Nov. to mid-Feb.
$ $$$$

Ventura
N 128 A2
Visitor information
www.ventura-usa.com
✉ 89C S. California St.
☎ 800/483-6214

Mission San Buenaventura
www.sanbuenaventuramission.org
✉ Main St. & US 101, Ventura
☎ 805/643-4318

Murphy Auto Museum
www.murphyautomuseum.com
✉ 2340 Palma Dr.
☎ 805/487-4333
$ $$

Mission La Purisima Concepción

THERE MAY BE MORE BEAUTIFUL MISSIONS THAN La Purisima Concepción, a humble grouping of adobe buildings, but no other mission better captures the essence of mission life in the early 19th century. Completely restored by the Civilian Conservation Corps in the 1930s, La Purisima—"the most pure"—is a perfect place to spend a meditative morning away from the crowds, wandering among the old mission buildings and delighting in the outstanding garden of herbs and native plants.

The mission campanile

Mission La Purisima Concepción
www.lapurisimamission.org
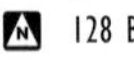
128 B5
2295 Purisima Rd., Lompoc (off Calif. 246, 3 miles NE of central Lompoc)
805/733-3713
$

Completed in 1822 after its original structure was destroyed by the great earthquake of 1812, La Purisima is a repository of colonial history. And while much of its story underscores the tragedy wrought on the Chumash by newcomers to their lands, much also serves to dispel the stereotype of the Indian as a passive rustic.

A **visitor center,** opened in 2007, provides an introductory overview and displays artifacts of the epoch. Beyond, the **cemetery** is the first stop. One-hour guided tours set out from here. Here, one is brought face to face with the blunt fact that more than 500 Chumash died at La Purisima alone, between 1804 and 1807, from exposure to European smallpox and measles. Many of them are buried here.

Next to the cemetery is the long, narrow **church,** which once accommodated up to a thousand for Sunday Mass. Its uneven floors and austere ornamentation reflect the rawness of mission life. Do not miss the "river of life" pattern on the main doors, which suggests that the Chumash were not shy about imbuing the churches they built with their own art.

The nearby **soldiers' quarters, carpenter's shop,** and **weavery** tell of the entrepreneurial nature of the mission system. Each unit was expected to grow and prosper through it own labors. Grain was milled and tallow processed for soap on the back patio. Nearby stands the **dormitory** for unmarried female Indians. The proximity of soldiers' quarters to those of young women is a good indication of what was probably the main social issue in mission life. In 1824 the tension between Indians and soldiers grew so great at La Purisima that neophytes here joined a rebellion that had begun at nearby Santa Inés Mission (see p. 164). Surrounding La Purisima, a group of Chumash seized two cannons, built a wooden wall around the mission, and held their Spanish captives for a month before backup troops arrived to quash the action.

The last major building consists of the **padres' quarters, a convent,** and a small **chapel**. From here Padre Mariano Payeras directed the extraordinary industry of La Purisima, designing his own irrigation system and managing a shop selling candles, wool, and leather goods. The herb and flower garden outside the compound has been completely restored to its original glory. In what might these days be called "Mission Ayurvedic," Chumash and padres created the first bicultural apothecary. ■

Ojai

AMONG THE RITES OF PASSAGE FOR YOUNG ANGELENOS, a trip to Ojai to explore variants of Hinduism and other non-Western religions stands as the only proper antidote to that *other* L.A. rite—the drunken coming-of-age bar crawl in Tijuana.

Ojai positively oozes spirituality. Yet Ojai is far from nineties New Age, as a visit to the venerable **Krotona Institute of Theosophy** will demonstrate. Krotona was founded by American followers of Annie Besant, the 19th-century proponent of Theosophy, a universalistic amalgam of Hindu and Christian thought. The institute was immediately endeared to the independent southern California heart when Besant's protégé, Jeddu Krishnamurti, took the pulpit in 1932 and proclaimed that he was no "great leader" at all but just another fellow trying to figure out life. Every year until his death in 1986, "K," as his students called him, attracted to Ojai seekers bent on hearing him ridicule the charlatans and gurus of popular religion while imparting his own highly rationalistic brand of Hinduism. (Even Nobel Prize-winning scientists from Caltech were known to make the annual pilgrimage to Ojai.) Regardless of one's religious orientation, however, a visit to Krotona will help explain the more complex spiritual landscape behind the region's flighty reputation.

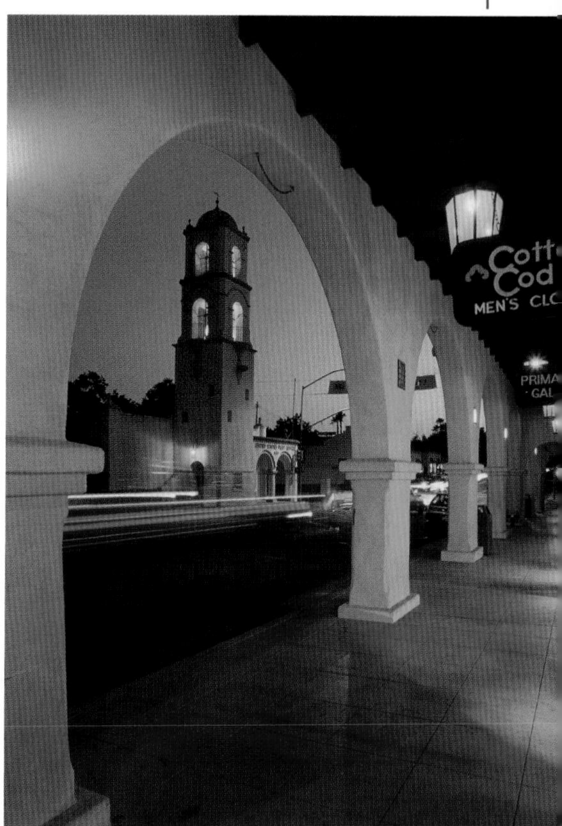

The other culture in Ojai—that of rest and civilized sport—can best be found at the **Ojai Valley Inn & Spa** *(905 Country Club Rd., tel 805/646-1111, www.ojairesort.com).* The renovated hotel, in the mission revival style, sits in spectacular country (cast by Hollywood as Shangri-la in *Lost Horizon*), which you can explore on a rented bicycle. For pure bliss afterward, try a soak at **The Oaks** *(122 E. Ojai Ave., tel 800/753-6257, www.oaksspa.com),* an outstanding full-service spa with decent food.

For real food in classic Ojai fashion, go to **The Ranch House** *(S. Lomita Ave. & Besant Rd., tel 805/646-2360, reservations recommended).* Many food writers credit the Ranch with laying the foundation for modern California cuisine. The roasted pork and the homemade pâté are out of this world. ■

Historic Ojai post office

Ojai
128 C4

Krotona Institute of Theosophy
www.theosophical.org
46 Krotona Hill
805/646-1139
Closed Mon.

Channel Islands National Park

Channel Islands National Park
www.nps.gov/chis
128 B3
Headquarters
1901 Spinnaker Dr., Ventura
805/658-5730

SURROUNDED BY GIANT BEDS OF GLEAMING GREEN KELP, punctuated by deep blue coves and the mysterious remains of ships sunk long ago, the Channel Islands became a national park in 1980. Since then they have become a weekend vacation destination for Angelenos. From January through March, nature adds a further attraction: the gray whale migration. Visitors can spot the 40-foot beasts swimming in schools, often with calves, their spouts shooting high in the air. Bald eagles soar overhead after recently being reintroduced.

To get a closer look, or simply to take in the adventures and scenery offered by these five islands, a little preparation is required. First, make a reservation with the official day boat concessionaire *(Island Packers, tel 805/642-1393, www.islandpackers.com).*

On **Anacapa,** itself composed of three islets, the winter months bring a freshet of new grass. Watch for the whales as well as other migrating species, including the bottlenose dolphin, the California sea lion, and the northern elephant seal. Landing at **Frenchys Cove,** explore the tide pools, then go on to Anacapa, where, just offshore, you can see the remains of the *Winfield Scott*, which sank here in 1853.

The coast of Santa Cruz Island

Santa Cruz Island is the largest in the chain. The Chumash were its principal inhabitants for nearly 6,000 years, fishing and plying the waves in their sophisticated canoes. The island is an ecological miracle, home to 600 plant species, nine of which occur only here.

Santa Rosa Island is home to almost 200 bird species. Keep an eye out for dinosaur fossils; in 1994 explorers discovered the skeleton of a dwarf mammoth.

The giant cross in **San Miguel Island's** Cuyler Bay reminds of the Spanish presence; in 1543 this was a base for Juan Rodriguez Cabrillo, who later died here from an injured leg. A perfect day can be had at San Miguel alone, exploring the beaches with their seals and sea lions and hiking the 3.5 miles to the caliche forest. Here you can see mineral casts of old tree trunks and 10-foot-tall specimens of the yellow flowering plant *Coreopsis*.

Some 50 miles to the southeast, **Santa Barbara Island** got its name from the date that Spanish explorer Sebastian Vizcaino sailed into its waters—December 4, 1602, the Feast of St. Barbara. Because it had no fresh water, Indians did not reside on this island. Attempts aim to restore the island's native flora, once overrun by foreign grasses. ■

From Santa Cruz south to Cambria, the Pacific exerts its hold on the Central Coast. Hearst's fabulous castle, Steinbeck's novels, and Robinson Jeffers's poems reveal its influence as do cozy Carmel, rugged Salinas, and beyond....

Central Coast

Cannery Row mural, Monterey

Central Coast

A SINGLE IMAGE CONVEYS THE ESSENCE OF CALIFORNIA'S CENTRAL COAST. A Monterey cypress, alone, primitive, and defiant, is cast against the bruised blue sky of the Pacific. Fog rolls by in great puffs and swells over Cypress Point in Pebble Beach. First photographed by Carleton Watkins in 1885, the Monterey cypress has become a kind of visual haiku, denoting a primal Eden by the sea. Certainly John Steinbeck, who hailed from here, thought so.

The Big Sur bridge carries Calif. 1 across the Big Sur River.

The drama of the Central Coast grows directly from its geography, particularly its relationship with the sea. Between Santa Cruz and Morro Bay is the nation's largest marine sanctuary. Under the waves, Monterey Canyon (the size of the Grand Canyon) wells with the cold, nutrient-rich waters that start the food chain that reaches up to the sea otter, the elephant seal, and the blue whale. It also has one of the world's largest single kelp beds.

Land and sea together create drama where the Santa Lucia Range tumbles down into the Pacific at Big Sur, or on Point Lobos, where oak-and-cypress-dotted cliffs, their trees cloaked in a pale green moss, finally relent to the turbulence below. Little wonder that photographers Ansel Adams and Edward Weston created some of their most memorable images here (see pp. 176–77).

Travelers in search of drama will be rewarded by many historical sites, most of them well marked and open daily. This area played the central role in 18th- and 19th-century California. Spanish troops and padres settled in 1770, and five years later the king made Monterey the capital of Spanish California. Here, too, the "original sin" of California history was committed. In 1775, Padre Junípero Serra ordered the recapture of a band of Indian converts who had fled his Mission Carmel and returned to the Diablo Mountains to resume their old "pagan" practices. This forced return of indigenous peoples to a European culture that eventually wiped them out has haunted Serra's march toward sainthood ever since. The historical drama concludes in Monterey in 1845–46, when Thomas Larkin, U.S. consul to Mexican California, began a series of intrigues that led to the state becoming a U.S. territory.

The Central Coast offers outdoor delights galore. Golfers can play at outstanding courses such as Pebble Beach. The offshore canyons of Monterey Bay yield spectacular scuba diving, while hikers can spend days exploring the trails of the Santa Lucia Range. Bird-watchers find their mecca a few miles north of Monterey on the Elkhorn Slough National Estuarine Reserve.

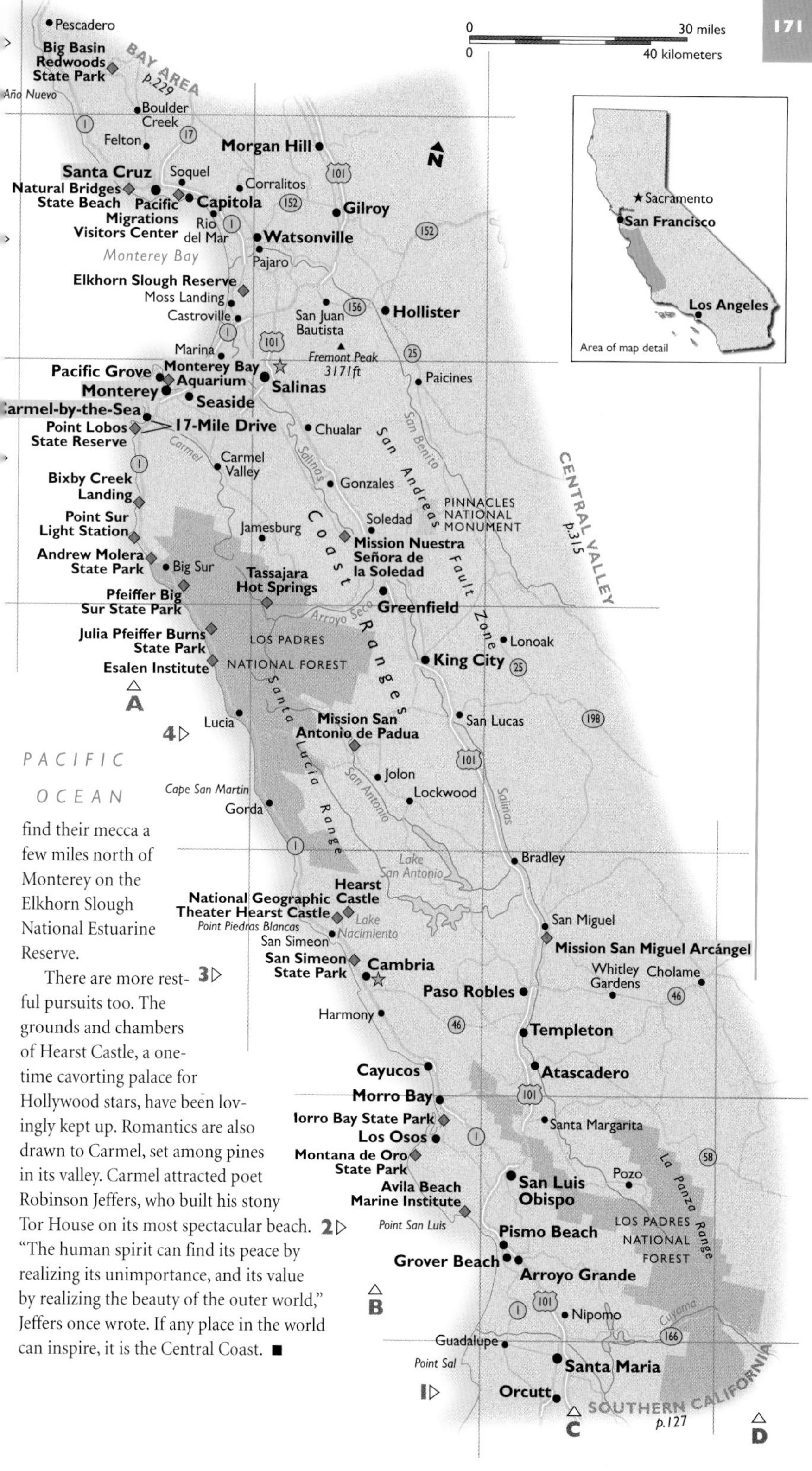

There are more restful pursuits too. The grounds and chambers of Hearst Castle, a one-time cavorting palace for Hollywood stars, have been lovingly kept up. Romantics are also drawn to Carmel, set among pines in its valley. Carmel attracted poet Robinson Jeffers, who built his stony Tor House on its most spectacular beach. "The human spirit can find its peace by realizing its unimportance, and its value by realizing the beauty of the outer world," Jeffers once wrote. If any place in the world can inspire, it is the Central Coast. ■

Hearst Castle

LA CUESTA ENCANTADA—THE ENCHANTED HILL—WAS the name chosen for his 127-acre estate by the publisher-tycoon William Randolph Hearst. Certainly it enchanted him. As a boy traveling in Europe he had told his mother that he would one day occupy Windsor Castle and buy the Louvre. Hearst kept his grand aspirations, and in 1919 commissioned his own *castello grande* to be built 5 miles inland, at 1,600 feet, above the tiny burg of San Simeon. He wanted something reminiscent of his favorite Mediterranean form, the Spanish Renaissance, but also something Californian. "Would it not be better," he wrote to his architect Julia Morgan, "to do something a little different than other people are doing in California as long as we do not do anything incongruous?" The result was an eclectic fusion of Mediterraneanism, tempered by Californian botany and topography.

Hearst Castle
www.hearstcastle.com
171 B3
750 Hearst Castle Rd., San Simeon
805/927-2020 or 800/444-4445 (ticket information; reservations recommended)
$$$$

TOURS

Visitors must take a scheduled tour as road access to the castle is restricted to tour buses. Tour One includes the ground floor of Casa Grande, one of the guesthouses, both pools, and part of the garden. Other tours visit the upper rooms of the main house. The evening tours in spring and fall are guided by docents in period costume. ■

The Hearst-Morgan collaboration (as he saw it) produced **La Casa Grande,** the estate's centerpiece. Choosing acquired elements of European decoration, such as the Spanish and Italian choir stalls used as wainscoting, Morgan fashioned a stunning new aesthetic, "at once suggestive of earlier European creations yet constructed with the most modern techniques," as Hearst curators now describe it.

La Casa Grande was Hearst's salon; here he and Marion Davies entertained stars and celebrities. As one account has it, guests were free to do as they liked as long as they followed four rules: that they congregate nightly in the ornate **Assembly Room** around the 16th-century French fireplace, take dinner in the adjoining **Refectory,** view the evening's motion picture in the theater, and, most important, that they never utter the word "death" in the presence of their host.

A more mono-styled architecture informs the three guest houses, mansions in their own right. These are **Casa del Mar** (often used by the Hearsts during construction of the main house), **Casa del Monte,** and **Casa del Sol.** All are done in Mediterranean style.

Most people's memory of Hearst Castle is the 104-foot-long outdoor **Neptune Pool.** Tiled in deep blue and set in front of a Greco-Roman temple facade, it overlooks one of the estate's most spectacular vistas. Here the Hollywood crowd preferred to cavort. The smaller indoor **Roman Pool** is lined with Venetian and gold-leaf tiles.

Hearst was dedicated to the notion that California's unique climate and topography—vividly recollected from his childhood camping trips—would transform mere Mediterraneanism into something uniquely Californian. The Panama-Pacific International Exposition of 1915 in San Francisco convinced him that this was possible. The exposition's landscape designer John McLaren had transformed a marshy site in the city's Marina District into a Spanish-Italian villa garden—with a good dose of palm trees. Hearst thought he could go one better in his own garden. He dictated that La Cuesta be kept in year-round color. To do so he built five greenhouses and hired a huge gardening staff to raise more than 500,000 annuals for rotational planting. Into these gardens he carefully positioned several gigantic coastal live oaks and California bay trees, and built a one-and-a-quarter-mile pergola—"the longest pergola in captivity," as Morgan called it.

Like many gilded age millionaires, Hearst acquired a collection of European art to decorate his home: antique ceilings, Greek vases, tapestries, and wall panels. Adriaen Ysenbrandt's 16th-century "Madonna and Child" adorns one wall in the main house. In the Gothic Suite sits "La Virgen de la Leche," a tiny statue carved in Spain some 500 years ago. Outside are four colossal stone lion-face goddesses carved in Egypt during the 13th century B.C. Hearst also introduced more recent American art. The renovated **visitor center** features a theater, library, restaurants, and shops, plus space for temporary exhibits. Special evening dinner events include an annual Christmas Holiday Feast. ■

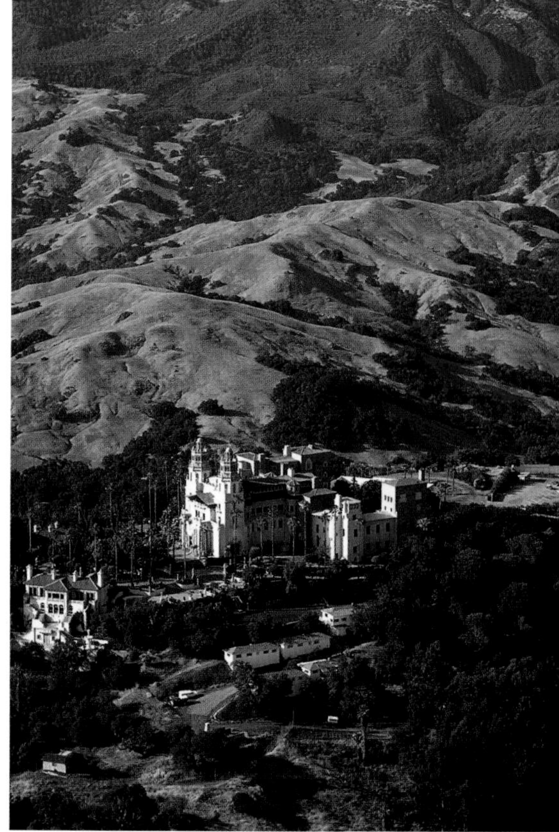

Hearst Castle looks out from its aerie in the Santa Lucia Range.

Around Hearst Castle

An easy side trip from Hearst Castle is to take Calif. 1 south to **San Simeon State Park** *(tel 805/927 2020)*, where some of the most underrated scenery on the West Coast unfolds beneath rocky promontories and jagged cliffs. It incorporates **Pa-Nu Cultural Preserve,** a significant archaeological site dating back almost 6,000 years. The large-format **National Geographic Theater Hearst Castle** *(tel 805/927-6811, www.ngtheater.com)* shows "Hearst Castle: Building the Dream."

Farther south are two more small but spectacular state beaches. One of the ancient volcanic plugs at **Morro Bay** has been dubbed the Gibraltar of the Pacific. Peregrine falcons nest there; elsewhere on the bay is a colony of great blue herons. The mudflats offer fabulous birding.

Near Los Osos, is **Montana de Oro State Park.** Here the Bluff Trail leads to interesting rock formations and tide pools. Inland is the university town of **San Luis Obispo,** a good base for exploring two of California's most exciting new wine regions, **Paso Robles** and **Edna Valley/Arroyo Grande. Pismo Beach,** is a beach community that becomes the clam capital of the West Coast in October. Nearby, the **Avila Beach Marine Institute** *(50 San Juan St., Avila Beach, tel 805/595-7290, www.avilamarineinstitute.com)* educates children in marine sciences with hands-on exhibits. ■

San Luis Obispo Visitor information
www.visitslo.com
✉ 1039 Chorro St.
☎ 805/781-2777

Paso Robles Visitor information
www.pasoroblesschamber.com
✉ 1225 Park St.
☎ 805/238-0506

Pismo Beach Visitor information
www.classiccalifornia.com
✉ 581 Dolliver St.
☎ 805/773 4382

Drive: Cambria to Carmel

With its dramatically twisting roads and stunning scenic promontories, Calif. 1 between Cambria and Carmel is to many Californians a kind of modern pilgrimage, the object of reverence being the Big Sur River (crossed by the awe-inspiring Big Sur Bridge) and its beautiful forested hinterlands.

Begin a trip north on Calif. 1 by first getting gas and a meal in **Cambria** ❶ *(Visitor information, 767 Main St., tel 805/927-3624)*; the distances between the few towns are long, and the road is a workout in itself at times.

Beyond the small town of **Lucia** (the southernmost limit of the redwood tree) lie the three state parks of central Big Sur. First is **Julia Pfeiffer Burns State Park** ❷ *(tel 831/667-2315, www.parks.ca.gov)*. A trail leads to Saddle Rock, location of the only waterfall on the Pacific Coast that falls directly into the ocean. Behind it looms **Anderson Peak,** at 4,099 feet the highest point of the Santa Lucia Range. A few miles farther north is the **Henry Miller Memorial Library** ❸ *(tel 831/667-2574, closed Tues., www.henrymiller.org)*, in the place where the writer spent the postwar years with a coterie of fellow artists.

The star of the Big Sur coast is **Pfeiffer Big Sur State Park** ❹ *(tel 831/667-2315, www.parks.ca.gov)*, the largest of the three state parks, with a substantial stand of redwoods. A good swim in the Big Sur River before making a campsite is an old California tradition.

About 6 miles north again is **Andrew Molera State Park** ❺ *(tel 831/667-2315, www.parks.ca.gov)*, where the scenic Big Sur River ends in a fine habitat for birds and wildlife. Look for mule deer, gray foxes, and raccoons. Much in the way of classic drama surrounds the location of **Point Sur Light station,** built in 1889 after two disastrous shipwrecks *(tel 831/625-4419, www.pointsur.org, walking tours, $$)*. Unfortunately they were not the last. During World War II, the Navy dirigible *Macon* surrendered itself and two crewmen to the legendary Big Sur fog.

The Big Sur area has a series of interesting places to stay or eat. Deetjens Big Sur Inn *(Castro Canyon, tel 831/667-2377, www.deetjens.com)* is a rural sprawl of cabins, each named for various literary figures. It also has a good little Norwegian restaurant. Not far away is the restaurant-bar Nepenthe *(tel 831/667-2345, www.nepenthebigsur.com)*. Designed by a student of Frank Lloyd Wright, it was once bought for Rita Hayworth by Orson Welles. Go for a drink on the deck overlooking the Pacific.

Another enterprise is the Ventana Inn *(tel 831/667-2331, www.ventanainn.com)*, long considered the ultimate in Big Sur lodging. Its spacious, luxury cabins (with kitchens) are built on a sun-flecked hillside. The massages and spa treatments are outstanding, and you can enjoy the Japanese baths, stroll among the trees in Ventana's white bathrobes, and enjoy the peace.

At the Loma Vista Café & Gardens *(tel 831/667-2818)* you can enjoy a cup of coffee and great views of the Santa Lucia Range, and buy exotic and native plants.

Approaching **Carmel** (see pp. 178-79), you reach **Point Lobos State Reserve** ❻ *(tel 831/624-4909, http://pt-lobos.parks.state.ca.us)*, a striking rocky promontory whose coves are home to sea lions, sea otters, and pelicans. Literary experts believe this was the inspiration for Spyglass Hill in *Treasure Island*, which Robert Louis Stevenson wrote after visiting in 1879. Two outstanding walks among several are the **Sea Lion Point Trail,** past stands of wild red buckwheat to a lookout onto Sea Lion Rocks, and the **Cypress Grove Trail,** around a grove of ancient cypress hung with green-blue moss. The environs support delicate coastal orchids, which grow along the branches of fallen trees.

To see something of the hinterland, return from Carmel by taking County Rd. G16 up the Carmel Valley. After 20 miles, Tassajara Road on the right takes you to **Tassajara Zen Mountain Center** ❼**,** with natural hot springs. In summer it is possible to make reservations for an austere but calming overnight stay *(39171 Tassajara Rd., Carmel Valley, tel 831/659-2229, www.sfzc.org/tassajara)*. Return to G16 and continue via Arroyo Seco Rd. to Greenfield. A few miles down US 101,

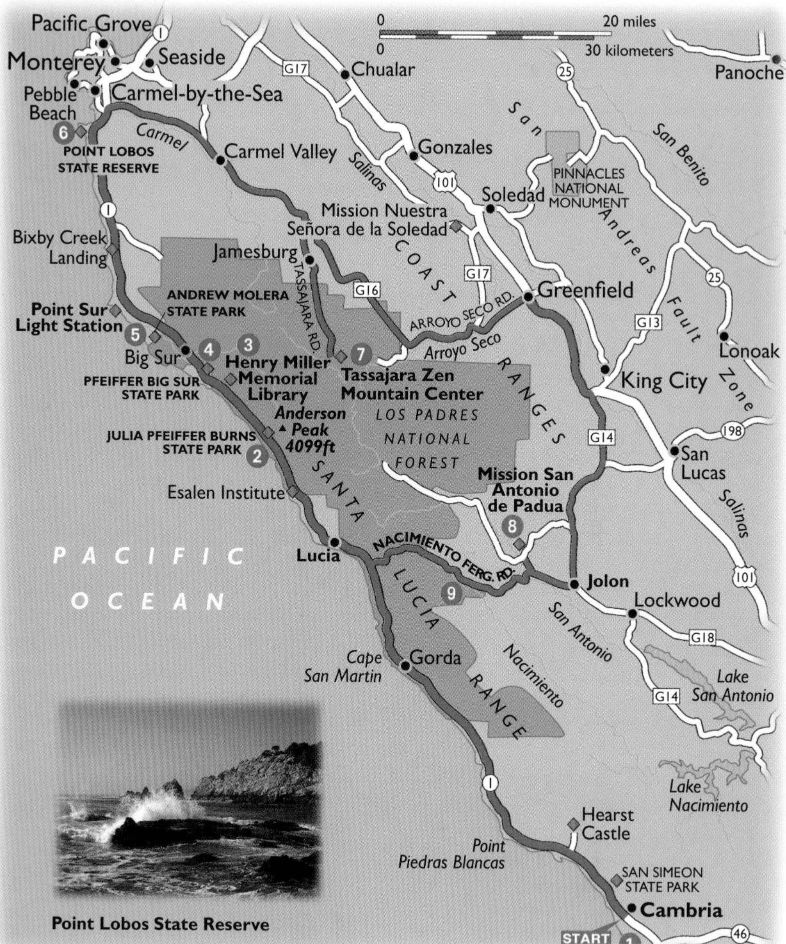

Point Lobos State Reserve

turn off on County Rd. G14 to the small town of **Jolon,** the setting for John Steinbeck's novel *To a God Unknown*, about a pioneering California family. In a quiet valley to the north is the restored **Mission San Antonio de Padua** 8 *(Mission Rd., tel 831/385-4478, www.sanantoniomission.org)*, founded by Padre Serra in 1771.

To see some of the unique botany of the area, return to the coast road down **Nacimiento Fergusson Road** 9**.** In the foothills of the Santa Lucia Range you are surrounded by California wildflowers, particularly in spring. The great variety of plant life here includes wild fennel, a non-native that is slowly dominating the coastal underbrush; white-plumed our lord's candle; bright green-yellow mustard (said to have been sown by the padres); and coastal agave, its tendril-like biomorph twisting and looking like a beached octopus. ■

Also see area map p. 171 B3
➤ Cambria
224 miles
1 day
➤ Carmel

NOT TO BE MISSED
- Julia Pfeiffer Burns State Park
- Point Lobos
- Nacimiento Fergusson Road

Ecology of light, sea, & stone

Ansel Adams, Edward Weston, & Robinson Jeffers

Of the many reasons artists and writers came to the Central Coast, the most important are its physical elements—light, sea, and stone. The evanescence of the first, the promise of the second, the hard reality of the third—these the artists of Big Sur cannot avoid. Their combined hardness, as Ansel Adams once put it, forces the artist to focus on "really seeing."

For photographer Edward Weston, the Central Coast represented both escape and maturation. Born in Illinois in 1886, Weston had by 1917 already established himself as a leading practitioner of his craft, his traditional "soft" style of portraiture gaining him acceptance to the elite London Salon of Photography. Then, in a Gauguin-like moment in 1923, Weston left his wife, took up with an exotic Italian actress, and began a lifelong association with the Mexican art "radicals" David Alfaro Siquieros and Diego Rivera. His style became increasingly direct, documentary, erotic. Portraits of his many lovers, in the nude, were conscientiously unretouched. In the early 1930s he settled in Carmel. With Ansel Adams he founded the much chronicled f/64 Movement, which pronounced that photography should forever be severed from the confining strictures of formalistic art.

Ansel Adams

One particular photo of Weston's captures "his" Central Coast. This is "The Fishing Fleet, Monterey." Any interested traveler can replicate the photograph's perspective by walking about Monterey Marina in the late afternoon. There is a small rock in the foreground, gulls sunning; in the background bob the little work boats, waiting for their masters. The moment evokes not so much Paul Gauguin as Camille Pissarro. This was an exotic, but contained, aesthetic moment.

Weston's young friend Ansel Adams, a hearty man born in 1902 to an affluent San Francisco clan, was less neurotically charged but equally passionate about nature and photography: "I believe in stones and water, air and soil, people and their future, and their fate." This directness with his subjects bursts from all Adams's works, the most well known of which are of Half Dome in Yosemite. Travel down to the shoreline of Point Lobos State Reserve (see p. 174), as Adams did, to see *his* Central Coast. Here shadow and light seem to hold their own vast territories, a block of light here, of darkness there. There is a Zen quality to Adams's Big Sur photographs. They are momentary yet hard—a visual "belief" in stones and water.

It was poet Robinson Jeffers who perhaps best fused Weston's personal coast with Adams's natural coast. Jeffers, born in Pennsylvania in 1887 and raised in southern California, had moved to Carmel in 1914 with his wife, Una. Though he had earned some notice as a young poet in Los Angeles, it was his first work about the Central Coast—the tormented, brutal landscape of his 1925 "Roan

Left: Weston's "Kelp Pattern on Sand" Above: Adams's "Autumn Tree in Cathedral Rocks," one of the many photographs he took in Yosemite

Stallion"—that established his reputation as an authentic modern writer. Jeffers went even further than Adams's and Weston's stripped-down coastal images: *only* nature mattered, mankind being but a passing presence. Only those who understood this had any chance of finding some peace in an increasingly inhumane world.

The Big Sur area's early local population, described by a 1939 guide book as a folk given to "inbreeding, passion, moroseness, and suspicion," filled Jeffers's prose. Bixby Creek Landing, north of Point Sur, was the setting for his "Thurso's Landing," about a woman who takes up with her husband's only friend, a dynamiter for a roadbuilding crew. In one scene the wife, Helen, says to her lover: "Do you ever think about death? I've seen you play with it. Strolling away while the fuse fizzled in the rock." "Hell no," the dynamiter replies, "that was all settled when they made the hills." ■

Carmel-by-the-Sea & around

AN ARTISTS' COLONY DEVELOPED BY TWO NIMBLE REAL estate developers eager to exploit the post-1906 earthquake residential needs of the rich, Carmel has from its very beginnings epitomized what we have come to call the "lifestyle community." Its cachet lies in its "themed exclusivity" as an arts community. Early residents included poet George Sterling and regionalist Mary Austin. In the 1930s the radical Lincoln Steffens and his wife, Ella Winter, took up residence here alongside the increasingly conservative Robinson Jeffers and his Celtically obsessed wife, Una.

Carmel-by-the-Sea
171 A5
Visitor information
www.carmelcalifornia.com
San Carlos, 5th, & 6th Sts.
831/624-2522

Here, too, originated some of the 20th century's earliest "planned growth" communities. In Carmel, business always took a back seat to aesthetics (something even Clint Eastwood had to admit after his mayoral attempt to bring the village into the entrepreneurial age had failed). To this day the recherché tumble of small boutiques on Ocean Street seem to own the franchise on the word "cute." Welcome to the Nantucket of the West.

Not surprisingly, visitors come to Carmel for peace and quiet. That's good, as there is not a lot to do here except admire the scenery and the wildlife, hike, and wander through art galleries. Stock up on outstanding picnic supplies at the Mediterranean Market *(Ocean Ave. & Mission St.)* before heading off to **Carmel City River State Park** *(off Scenic Rd., S of Carmel Beach).* Here, slopes flushed with pine and oak fall to a brilliant white beach, perfect for hiking and bird-watching.

When you tire of the beach, return to town for a browse along **Ocean Street,** where several old shops sell everything from proper nautical wear to handmade cardigans and shawls. For some hearty food in a family-style atmosphere, go to Little Napoli *(Dolores St. near 7th Ave., tel 831/626-6335, www.pepeinternational.com),* where the food is straightforward and

A quiet corner of Carmel

satisfying, the service friendly, and the atmosphere warm and jolly.

As might be expected of a town founded for artists, Carmel offers several outstanding cultural venues. In July and August, the **Carmel Bach Festival** *(tel 831/624-2046, www.bachfestival.com)* takes the spotlight. Concerts and classes on the composer take center stage, and there are several themed events as well.

In October, the **Carmel Performing Arts Festival** offers the works of leading modern playwrights; the well-established **Pacific Repertory Theater** *(tel 831/622-0100, www.pacrep.org)* runs year-round. It is worth checking out the visual works by locals at the **Carmel Art Association** *(Dolores St. between 5th & 6th Aves., tel 831/624-6176, www.carmelart.org)*. The town more than lives up to expectations in this regard, and many visitors end up returning again and again, following and acquiring the works of one artist, year after year.

Since lounging and sitting by cozy fireplaces are two principal Carmel activities, two inns are worth noting (see also pp. 360–61). The first is the Quail Lodge *(8205 Valley Green Dr., tel 831/624-2888, www.quaillodge.com)*, which sits in the Carmel Valley. For a more eco-New Age experience try the Highlands Inn *(Calif. 1, S of Carmel, tel 831/620-1234)*. With their balcony views, in-room hot tubs, spas, personal sound systems, and wood-burning fireplaces, the rooms here make for a memorable experience.

Perhaps the most original feature in all Carmel is **Tor House** and its adjoining Hawk Tower, both built by poet Robinson Jeffers between 1914 and 1930 (with later additions). Jeffers and his wife, Una, were attracted to the site, a *tor* or craggy hill near the outflow of the Carmel River (one of the most dramatic locations on the coast). Constructed of local boulders hauled up from the beach, the structures reflect the idiosyncrasies of the couple. Almost inseparable from the elements to which it is so exposed, the house is an unforgettable California monument to creativity, individualism, and strength.

While here, be sure to visit **Mission Carmel** (see p.181) and take in the stunning **17-Mile Drive** (see p.180). ■

Tor House & Hawk Tower

www.torhouse.org

✉ 26304 Ocean View Ave., Carmel (bet. Stewart Way & Bay View Ave.)

☎ 831/624-1813

🕒 Foundation open Mon.–Thurs. Hourly tours Fri.–Sat. No children under 12. Reservations required.

$ $$

17-Mile Drive

17-Mile Drive
Visitor information
www.pebblebeach.com
☎ 831/373-3304
Motorcycles not allowed.
$ $$

A TOLL-ROAD WORTH EVERY CENT, THE LEGENDARY seventeen-mile, coast-hugging drive along the Carmel peninsula encompasses some of Monterey Bay's most spectacular coastal vistas and natural features. The private roadway snakes through the gated community of Pebble Beach, stippled with luxurious mansions of the rich and famous and a Mecca for golf enthusiasts. Even on foggy days it's hard to get lost thanks to red dotted markings along the route.

The best entrance is the Carmel Gate *(off Calif. 1 at N. San Antonio Rd.)*. Heading north, the road loops uphill to **Huckleberry Hill,** named for its native huckleberry bushes and popular with fruit pickers, smack in the middle of the Del Monte Forest.

The road meets the shore at **Spanish Bay,** where explorer Gaspar de Portola anchored in 1796, believing it to be Monterey Bay. Rising above southern end of the beach, the rocky pinnacles of **Point Joe** lured many a mariner to their fate in the false belief that the point marked the entrance to Monterey. The colliding currents stir up nutrients that feed fishes that in turn bring pelicans, cormorants and other seabirds in vast numbers. **Bird Rock** is a favored roost, and seals and sea lions often haul out to snooze at nearby **Seal Rock** and **Fanshell Beach.**

Nearby, various species of native cypress and pine are a highlight of **Crocker Grove**, a 13-acre nature reserve. At **Cypress Point**, a lone twisted tree sculpted by centuries of merciless wind, must be one of the most photographed and iconic living things in the world.

To end, take time for a drink or meal at **The Lodge at Pebble Beach** *(tel 831/647-7500, www.pebblebeach.com)*, a world-class resort renowned as the setting for **Pebble Beach Golf Links**. Here crooner Bing Crosby launched the Pebble Beach National Pro-Am, which still draws the world's top golfers to play the three-course tournament still known as "The Crosby." And auto aficionados flock in each August for the **Concours d'Elegance** *(tel 831/622-1700, www.pebblebeachconcours.net)*, a spectacular showcase of the world's finest historic cars.

A brochure, available at the start of the drive, spells out all the details. ■

Fanshell Beach from 17-Mile Drive overlook

Three missions

THE SECOND MISSION BUILT IN CALIFORNIA BY THE Mallorcan Padre Junípero Serra, Mission San Carlos Borromeo del Rio Carmelo is historical ground zero for almost all modern discussions of the mission system and its legacy. Built in 1770, this was Serra's place of great toil, the center of his attempt to re-create Spanish civilization in a raw new world. Between 1770 and 1836, he and his successors confirmed more than 4,000 neophytes here.

A vivid literary snapshot of the earliest Mission Carmel survives in the journals of Jean-François de la Perouse, a Frenchman who arrived on a scientific expedition just two years after Serra's death. The huts the mission Indians inhabited, de la Pérouse wrote, "were the most wretched anywhere… eight or ten bundles of straw, ill arranged over stakes, are the only defense against rain or wind." Of the food eaten by both priest and converts, "a kind of soup, made of barley meal," de la Pérouse could only comment that "it would certainly to us be a most insipid mess." And of corporal punishment: "Many sins, which in Europe are left to divine justice, are here punished by irons and the stock." This is how Serra's post-medievalist experiment was perceived by a man of the early Enlightenment.

Today the deep interconnectedness of Serra and California's self-identity can be seen in the statue located in the restored **Old Quadrangle.** Entitled the "Serra Cenotaph," and sculpted in 1924 by local artist Jo Mora, the work portrays a triumphant Serra, a California grizzly bear at his feet.

In the ornate basilica are the graves of the mission's founders, including Serra. (The grave was opened during the 1880s to quell rumors that Serra's body had been stolen; the padre was still there.) **Serra's living quarters,** or cell, has also been restored, albeit with some creative revisionist spin: The leather scourges or whips that used to hang here have been removed, likely out of fear that visitors might "misinterpret" their use. (The padres used them on themselves and, occasionally, on their converts.) On a lighter note, the restored kitchen gives an idea of the simplicity of mission life. The garden possesses a fine collection of native plants and a range of dahlias, some of them as much as eight inches in diameter.

OTHER MISSIONS

Two lesser known missions are within driving distance of Mission Carmel south on US 101. The first is the **Mission Nuestra Señora de la Soledad.** Founded by Padre Lasuen in 1791, Soledad was one of the most remote of the missions. As such, it offered a hiding place to padres and neophytes in 1818, when French pirate Hippolyte de Bouchard was ravaging the other missions. A fine icon is its statue of the Virgin, dressed in the black of a Spanish doña in mourning.

If you are continuing south on US 101, stop at **Mission San Miguel Arcángel.** Founded as an agricultural outpost in 1797, this mission has kept some original interior art. Created by neophytes, it is an original fusion of Old World medievalism and New World fecundity of color. The mission's rafters and corbels were hewn from trees 40 miles away. ■

Mission San Carlos Borromeo del Rio Carmelo
www.carmelmission.org
✉ 3080 Rio Rd., Carmel
☎ 831/624-1271

Mission Nuestra Señora de la Soledad
171 B5
✉ Ft. Romie Rd., off US 101, 3 miles SW of Soledad
☎ 831/678-2586
Closed Tues.

A wall plaque of the Virgin as Queen of Heaven at Mission Carmel

Mission San Miguel Arcángel
www.missionsanmiguel.org
171 C3
✉ 775 Mission St.
☎ 805/467-3256

Two drives in Steinbeck country

It would take too long to list all the many real-life touchstones found in the stories of John Steinbeck. It is enough to say that his writing is inextricably woven into the vast Salinas Valley and points just beyond. These two drives convey much of the atmosphere of Steinbeck country. The Steinbeck Center in Salinas has a brochure with other tours.

DRIVE ONE: SALINAS & THE "LONG VALLEY"

The best place to orient oneself to Steinbeck country is **Salinas** ❶ *(Visitor information, 119 E. Alisal St., tel 831/424-7611).* A good introduction to the drives is the **National Steinbeck Center** *(1 Main St., tel 831/796-3833, www.steinbeck.org),* a modern facility rising out of the author's cherished **Old Town.** The center has an extensive collection of Steinbeck memorabilia (including Rocinante, the pickup truck in *Travels With Charley),* along with several interactive exhibits on his main books and their real-life sources of inspiration. There are also several displays of Hollywood's various renditions of his work, among them *Of Mice and Men* and *The Grapes of Wrath.* A new "Valley of the World" wing celebrates the rich agriculture heritage of the valley.

Just down the street, at 132 Central Road, is the **Steinbeck House,** where the author was born and raised, and where *(with a reservation, tel 831/424-2735, www.steinbeckhouse.com)* one can have lunch. Other attractions here include the **Roosevelt School** *(120 Capitol St.),* the West End School in the epic *East of Eden.* The author attended grades 3–8 here. On Main Street in Old Town are several sites mentioned in the same book, among them the San Francisco Chop House *(No. 116),* Krough's Drug Store building *(No. 156),* and Elk's Building *(No. 247).* The **Garden of Memories Cemetery** *(768 Abbott St.)* is where the author is buried, along with several of the real-life characters in *East of Eden,* including the Hamilton Family, William J. Nesbitt (Sheriff Quinn), and Mary Jane Reynolds (Jenny).

Leave Salinas on US 101 south. The town of **Soledad** ❷ was the setting for *Of Mice and Men;* the general store is still here. Continue on US 101, then turn northeast on County Rd. G13 to **King City** ❸**,** where scenes in *The Red Pony* were set. Return to US 101 and go west to the County Rd. G14 turn off. Take this road to **Jolon** ❹**,** where the action takes place in *To a God Unknown.*

Return to Salinas on US 101, and take Calif. 68 west to pass the scenic **Salinas River basin** ❺**,** where Steinbeck swam and hunted rabbits. Farther along is the mountainscape known as **Corral de Tierra** and Castle Rock. The latter was an inspiration for Steinbeck's *The Acts of King Arthur and his Noble Knights.*

Continue on Calif. 68 and drive into **Monterey** ❻ (see pp. 184–87). Known as Ocean Avenue until 1953, Monterey's **Cannery Row** was the setting for the book of the same name, as well as *Tortilla Flat* and *Sweet Thursday.* The lab of the real-life Ed Ricketts, Steinbeck's raconteur-marine biologist protagonist, is at 800 Cannery Row; Wing Chong's Market (now simply "The Old General Store") is at No. 835. La Ida's Café, from the same novel, is at No. 851 (now called Kaliso's). Over on Alvarado Street you can see the room in which he wrote *The Pearl (399 Alvarado St., 2nd floor).* It was from **Fisherman's Wharf,** on March 11, 1940, that Steinbeck and Ricketts set out for the Gulf of California, the inspiration for *Sea of Cortez.*

DRIVE TWO: THE BADLANDS

This drive takes in fewer novel-specific sites but captures the "Badlands" terrain of so many of Steinbeck's works. Heading north from Salinas on US 101, go east on Calif. 156, and exit at **San Juan Bautista** ❶**.** This small town has Spanish, Mexican, and pioneer California elements. The restored **Mission San Juan Bautista** *(N. side of Plaza, tel 831/623-2127, www.oldmissionsjb.org)* has an altarpiece painted by Thomas Doak, the first American settler in Alta California. Steinbeck was fond of the mission and its stories. Farther east on Calif. 156, exit on San Juan Canyon Road and head to **Fremont Peak** ❷ *(tel 831/623-4255),* the mountain top to which

Also see area map p. 171 B5
Salinas
Drive 1: 152 miles
Drive 2: 95 miles
Drive 1: 5 hours
Drive 2: 3 hours
Drive 1: Monterey
Drive 2: Pinnacles NM

NOT TO BE MISSED

- National Steinbeck Center
- Cannery Row
- Fisherman's Wharf
- Fremont Peak
- Pinnacles National Monument

John C. Frémont retreated (see pp. 27–28). It was on Fremont Peak that Steinbeck, in *Travels with Charley*, chose to go east, never to see his beloved valley again. To the west is the old Steinbeck ranch.

Down from the peak, continue east on Calif. 156, then go south on Calif. 25 for a taste of California Badlands. In the tiny town of **Paicines** ❸ you can still buy a soda at the store where in 1873 the *bandito* Tiburcio Vásquez shot his last victim. **Pinnacles National Monument** ❹ *(tel 831/389-4485, www.nps.gov/pinn)*, a mass of volcanic rock formations with hiking trails, looms to the south. ■

The Monterey waterfront

Historic Monterey

SPOTTED BY JUAN CABRILLO IN 1542, NAMED FOR THE Count of Monte Rey in 1602 by merchant-explorer Sebastián Vizcaíno, and claimed for Spain in 1770 by Portola and Serra, Monterey remained the political, social, and economic core of California until the mid-1850s, when the Americanos decided to locate their new statehouse elsewhere. As an economic force, Monterey kept surging ahead. Its fishing industry was fueled by successive waves of Italian, Portuguese, Chinese, Japanese, and Mexican immigrants.

Monterey
171 A5
Visitor information
www.montereyinfo.org
150 Olivier St.
831/649-1770

Monterey State Historic Park
www.parks.ca.gov
20 Customs House Plaza
831/649-7118

Presidio of Monterey Museum
www.monterey.org/museum
Corporal Ewing Rd., Bldg. 113
831/646-3456
Closed Tues. & Wed.

Today this bayside city teems with new enterprise, museums, art galleries, and an extensive restored historic district. **Fisherman's Wharf** is a favorite place for locals and visitors to grab a bite to eat, shop, and stroll.

Monterey State Historic Park, with headquarters near the Customs House, links more than 30 historical places. Peppered with historical adobes, Monterey-style mansions, and public gardens, its "path of history" is well marked, beginning with the **Customs House,** the oldest government building in California, restored to its 1840s functionality and with a later-added museum. Here, in 1846, Commodore John Drake Sloat proclaimed "henceforth California will be a portion of the United States." (Most of the locals thought him a pompous spy.)

The **Larkin House,** a two-story mud adobe built during the Mexican period, was home to Thomas Oliver Larkin, the first and only U.S. consul to California under Mexican rule. Larkin is credited with much of the local intrigue surrounding Frémont's eventual conquest of California. One of the more remarkable old-time adobes is the **Casa Soberanes Adobe,** also known as the House of the Blue Gate. Built by Rafael Estrada in the 1840s and occupied by the Soberanes from 1860 to 1922, it has been beautifully restored, complete with original furnishings.

The **Pacific House,** a classic Monterey-style building originally used during the 1847 U.S. occupation of California, contains museums on early Monterey and Native American life. Perhaps the best single place to get a sense of early merchant life in Monterey is the **Cooper Molera Adobe,** named for the trader John Rogers Cooper, who married into a prestigious Mexican family. The grounds include barns, farm animals, and vegetable and fruit gardens. **Colton Hall,** where the California constitution was signed, is another outstanding example of Monterey architecture. It now contains a museum about the state's early history.

Originally named the French Hotel, the **Stevenson House** *(530 Houston St.)* is best known for the Scottish writer, Robert Louis Stevenson, who stayed here in the autumn of 1879, recovering from an illness, before marrying and setting off for the Napa Valley.

Away from the historic park, the **Presidio of Monterey** affords access to two important spots: Vizcaíno's 1602 landing site and the location of Padre Junípero Serra's first Mass in 1770. More recent military history is explored at the **Presidio of Monterey Museum,** which houses materials on World War II and one of the fort's colorful inhabitants, Gen. E.O.C. Ord. The **Maritime Museum** contains the Allen Knight collection. Its extensive displays include ships' records, charts, maps, photos, and logs.

Since its early days, Monterey has attracted more than its share of ambitious young artists; the **Monterey Museum of Art** holds an outstanding collection of their work and that of other Californians in its two locations (on Via Mirada and at the Civic Center). Exhibitions have focused on such figures as C.S. Price (1874–1950), a remarkable landscape artist whose life spanned everything from impressionism to incipient abstract expressionism. The museum includes sculptures by Gordon Newhall, Alexander Weygers, and George Rickey. Photographic works by Ansel Adams and Edward Weston are also well represented.

The historic **Edgewater Packing Company** *(640 Wave St.),* on Cannery Row *(see p.182)*, is being converted into an IMAX Theater. Monterey has been the setting for almost 200 movies; a "Monterey Movie Tour" (tel 831/372-6278) visits film locations. ■

The Customs House is California's oldest extant government building.

Maritime Museum
www.montereyhistory.org
550 Calle Principal
831/372-2608
Closed Wed.
$

Monterey Museum of Art
www.montereyart.org
La Mirada location
720 Via Mirada
831/372-3689
Closed Mon.–Tues.
$$
Civic Center location
559 Pacific St.
831/372-5477
Closed Mon.–Tues.
$$

Monterey Bay Aquarium

THIS EXCELLENT AQUARIUM IS CONSIDERED ONE OF THE world's preeminent modern education/research establishments of its kind. It benefits from a consistent unity of purpose: to explore and display the vast realm of Monterey Bay, the nation's largest marine sanctuary, located just outside its door. The result is one of the best single destinations for all ages on the Central Coast. Allow about three hours for your visit. If you intend to see one of the various regular specialty shows such as the feeding of the sea otters, check for scheduled times at the front information desk as you enter. There is a good restaurant (with oyster bar), and also a coffee bar.

Monterey Bay Aquarium
www.montereybayaquarium.org
886 Cannery Row, Monterey
831/648 4800 or 800/756-3737 (advance tickets)
$$$$

The aquarium, recently transformed with dramatic new galleries, provides a tour of the world's oceans and Monterey Bay's four principal habitats. The central attraction of the first section, and gateway to the new **Ocean's Edge** galleries, is the **Kelp Forest.** This huge tank perfectly simulates a kelp environment, complete with surging waters and a variety of ichthyological inhabitants including tightly knit schools of anchovies streaming between the long amber fronds. Try to see the twice-daily feeding show, in which scuba divers descend into the tank to hand feed the creatures. On the second floor, the expanded **Splash Zone,** which uses interactive technology, grants a more detailed look at kelp forest, rocky shore, and coral reef habitats.

The **Deep Reefs** tank reveals the little-known world of oceanic sandy plains, some 100–400 feet deep. These are home to eerie blue sponges, wolf eels, dancing spot prawns, and orange cup corals. The **Sandy Seafloor** exhibit plumbs this seemingly barren world, finding sand dollars and crabs and sea pens and the chameleon-like flatfish. The **Shale Reefs** tank bears several unexpected treasures; the aquarium has used native Monterey Bay rock to reproduce the tunnels inhabited by sea cucumbers, scale-worms, clams, and mussels.

In the **Rocky Shores** tank, visitors can watch the tiny creatures that thrive at the water's edge. Eels slither about between bizarre-looking nudibranches and their whirls of newly hatched eggs. The focal point is a new walk-through acrylic tunnel that let's you experience the power of waves that crash overhead.

The **Tide Pool Life** exhibit uses man-made waves to enliven several tidal habitats, including that of the hermit crab, the sculpin, sea stars, and various forms of anemone. The **Slough** and **Sandy Shore** galleries explore the seven distinct but interrelated habitats of a tidal channel, from mudflats to dune to marsh to beach. These simulate the remarkable marine and ornithological delights of nearby **Elkhorn Slough** (see box p. 187).

Though the aquarium stocks no seals, dolphins, or whales, its outdoor deck provides a perfect spot from which to watch for the various marine mammals that routinely make their way through the bay: harbor seals, harbor porpoises, white-sided dolphins, orca whales, and elephant seals. The 50,000-gallon **Sea Otter** tank gives visitors a close-up look at these playful creatures, which the aquarium obtained as rescued

orphans. And **Wild About Otters,** new in 2007, introduces visitors to non-native species.

Also new is **Mission to the Deep,** combining high-definition video footage with interactive computer animations of underwater robots and other high-tech tools used in underwater research.

Be sure to leave time for the last section, the **Outer Bay,** which contains two of the aquarium's most memorable displays. Focusing on the submerged world beginning 60 miles offshore, the Outer Bay explores a world of light, temperature, and salinity. Perhaps the most spectacular of these seafarers are the drifters, everything from plankton to crab larvae to predatory jellyfish. In dramatically lit tanks, rare jellyfish glow like diamonds against a vast black velvet robe. The purple-striped jelly can reach up to 30 inches in diameter. The one-million-gallon **Swimmers** tank holds giant ocean sunfish, schools of tuna and bonito, and even California barracuda. ■

A diver feeds the fish in the Kelp Forest at Monterey Bay Aquarium.

Elkhorn Slough National Estuarine Research Reserve

Located on a tidal channel teeming with wildlife and fishes, Elkhorn Slough encompasses 1,400 acres of marshland and tidal flats and is home to more than 400 species of invertebrates, 80 species of fish, and 200 species of birds. Leopard sharks and bat rays are often seen cruising these shallow waters. This is one of the last known reaches of the clapper rail. After a morning at Elkhorn, stop at **Moss Landing,** where several stores deal in reasonably priced antique California and Arts and Crafts-era pottery. The cafés offer outstanding oyster dishes. The used bookstore is a dream.

If you are here in early spring, stop at one of the roadside stands and try a fresh artichoke—or have some shipped back home; nearby Castroville is the artichoke capital of the world. ■

Elkhorn Slough National Estuarine Research Reserve
www.elkhornslough.org
1700 Elkhorn Rd., Elkhorn
831/728-2822
Closed Mon.–Tues.
$

Santa Cruz & around

Santa Cruz
171 A6
Visitor information
www.santacruz.org
1211 Ocean St.
831/425-1234 or 800/833-3494

Santa Cruz Surfing Museum
www.santacruzsurfingmuseum.org
In the Mark Abbot Lighthouse, 1305 East Cliff Dr.
831/420-6289
Closed Tues. (closed a.m. & Tues.–Wed. in winter)

FOR THOSE WITH A SLIGHTLY MORE BOHEMIAN APPROACH to travel, the beach town of Santa Cruz is an outstanding destination. The city and its surrounding areas, now fully recovered from the devastating 1989 Loma Prieta earthquake, offer reasonably priced lodging, excellent seafood, and stunning scenery.

In town, the main attraction is the **Santa Cruz Beach Boardwalk** *(400 Beach St., tel 831/423-5590, www.beachboardwalk.com)*, a historic amusement park. Nearby and not to be missed is the **Frans Lanting Gallery** *(207 McPherson St., tel 831/429-1331, www.lanting.com)*, displaying the works of one of the great nature photographers of our time. A favorite activity is to rent a bicycle and ride the bike path on the bluffs above. The exhilarating 5-mile round-trip to the stunning rock formations at **Natural Bridges State Beach** *(2531 W. Cliff Dr., tel 831/423-4609, www.parks.ca.gov)* is unforgettable. On the way back stop by the **Santa Cruz Surfing Museum** for its collection of vintage boards and shark-attack photos.

Sand castle competition, Capitola

Mission Santa Cruz, *(126 High St., tel 831/426-5686)* is but a scaled-down 1931 reproduction of the original. Nearby, at **Roaring Camp Railroads** *(tel 831/335-4484, www.roaringcamp.com)*, steam trains puff to the Bear Mountain summit. The Santa Cruz Mountains are rich in early pioneer history, with sites such as the 1892 **Felton Covered Bridge** *(Calif. 9, 5 miles N of the city)* in the San Lorenzo Valley. Farther north, off Calif. 9 northwest of Boulder Creek, is **Big Basin Redwoods State Park** *(tel 831/338-8860, www.parks.ca.gov)*, where you can rent tent cabins *(tel 800/874-8368)* set beneath towering coast redwood trees. The park has more than 80 miles of trails.

To the east, **Soquel** was the stomping ground of the legendary mail stage driver "Cock-Eyed Charley" Parkhurst, "the toughest looking fellow in the region." He did his part for women's rights, as was discovered at his death when Charley was discovered to have been a "Charlotte." Soquel is now a wine-growing region with more than 70 wineries *(tel 831/685-8463, www.scmwa.com)*; try the **Bargetto Winery** *(3535 N. Main St., tel 831/475-2258, www.bargetto.com)*.

South of Soquel, **Capitola,** once a tuna-fishing village, is now a romantic's redoubt complete with quaint beach cafés and several inns with beautiful views of northern Monterey Bay. The new **Pacific Migrations Visitor Center** *(tel 831/464-5620)* explores the interactions of human and animal migratory patterns in California. ■

Though L.A. may outrank it in size and clout, San Francisco is still the Imperial City of the Pacific Coast, its art museums flush with new acquisitions, its Victorian architecture on bold display, its cuisine supremely gourmet.

San Francisco

The San Francisco–Oakland Bay Bridge and cable car at dusk

San Francisco

AFFLUENT YET BOHEMIAN, COSMOPOLITAN YET PROVINCIAL, GAY YET buttoned-down, old-worldly but youthful—San Francisco has something for every contemporary urban traveler. Part Florence (for its artisanal culture) and part Boston (for its endless ethnic politics), the city is compact, electric, romantic, exotic. To invoke the ancient Costanoan Indians who lived along the bay 500 years ago, it is as if everybody here is "dancing on the brink of the world."

The historic crucible of this unique urban culture was the gold rush. The population of San Francisco rose from a sleepy 500 in 1847 to a raucous 20,000 in 1849. Men (and they *were* almost all men) came here from the ends of the Earth, many of them as honorable as many others were unscrupulous. Following them came the Yankee merchants, intent on making the city, as Richard Henry Dana had observed decades before, "the emporium of a new world." They would succeed beyond their wildest dreams.

Devastation came with the great earthquake and consequent fire of 1906. Not only did the townsfolk—half of them homeless—rally to each other's aid (as they would more than 80 years later during the Loma Prieta earthquake), they also committed themselves

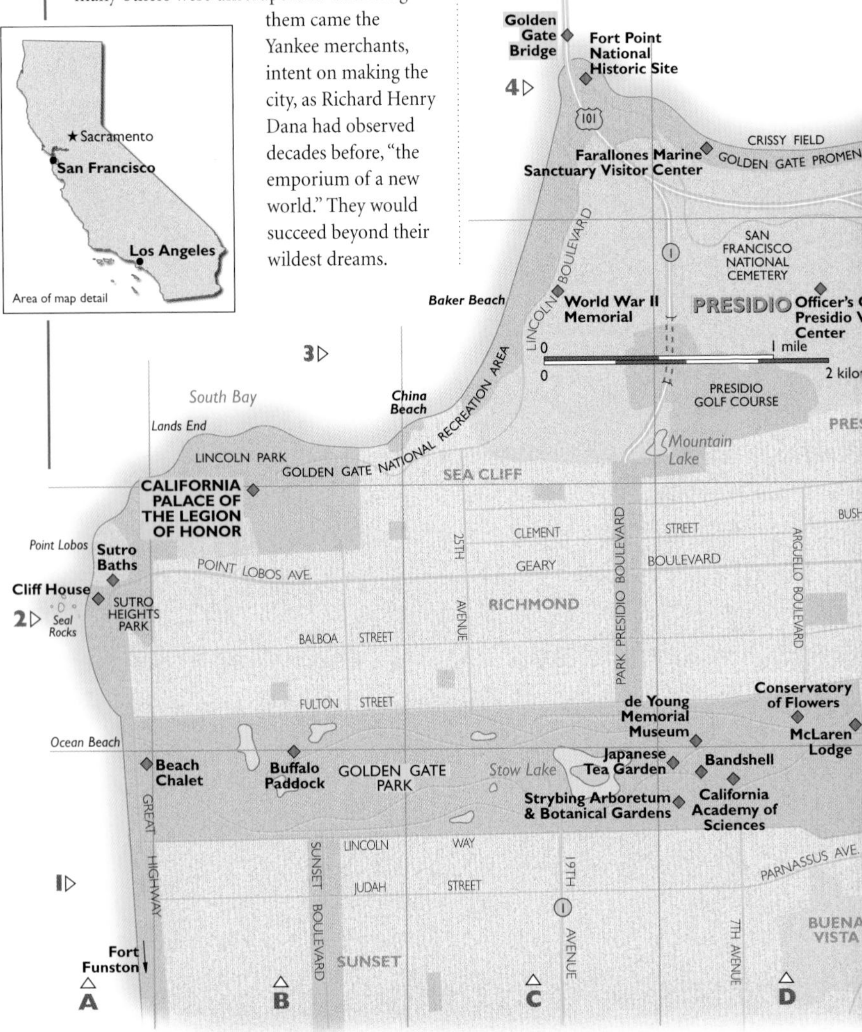

to re-creating San Francisco as the Imperial City of the Pacific. In 1915, the success of the Panama-Pacific Exposition declared that the city was back.

While the Depression certainly burnished the city's Liberal Democratic reputation, it was the AIDS crisis of the 1980s and beyond that again invigorated San Francisco's eclectic character, prompting such traditionally disparate elements as churches, the chamber of commerce, and gay activists to work together.

Travelers in San Francisco today confront a feast of cultural and culinary delights. Fueled in large part by Silicon Valley money, the city has become the site of America's most venturesome high cuisine. Some of the more notable restaurants are the Genoese-inspired Rose Pistola, the California Provençal Jardinière, and Farallon, known for its seafood. Money from "the valley" is also remaking venerable cultural institutions, such as the new Civic Center location of the Asian Art Museum. The fine art museums, showing Californian, modern, Renaissance, and baroque works, have also benefited from public commitment. And the Golden Gate National Recreation Area, a vast expanse of meadows, windswept beaches, gnarled madrone trees, and misty forest trails, beckons.

A final note: San Francisco has a kind of grand boulevardier culture; dressing well here is the norm. ■

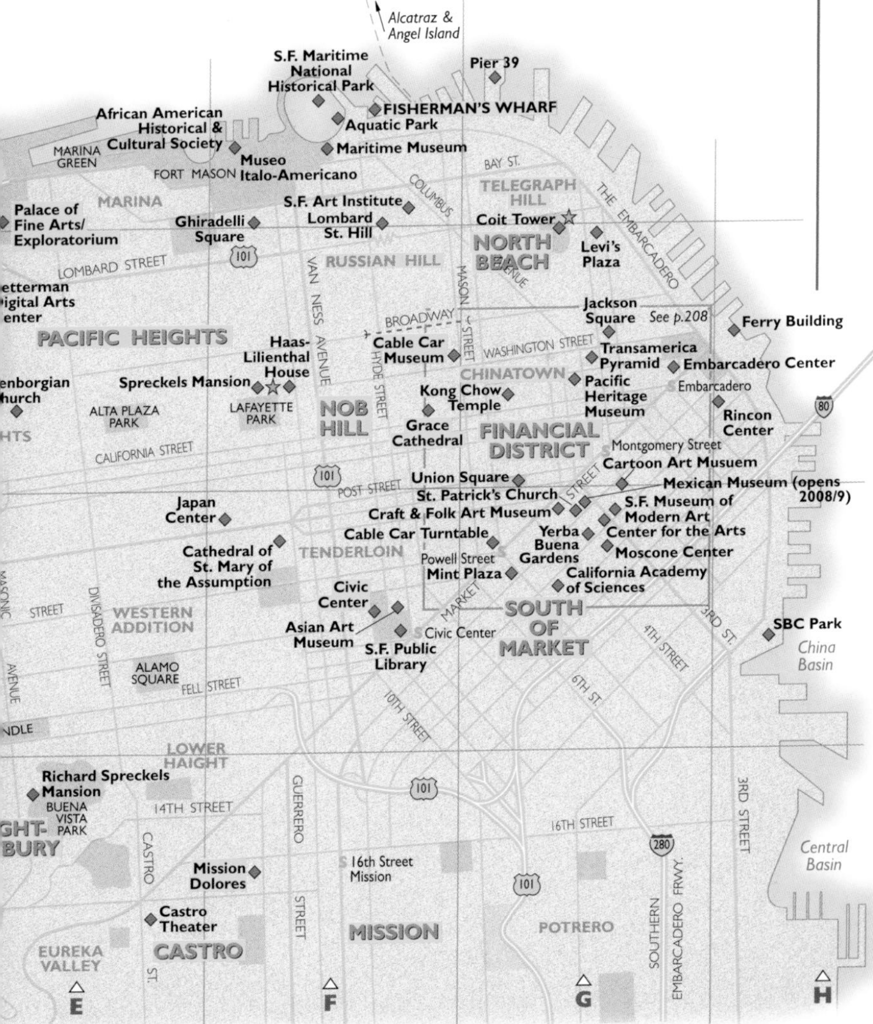

The bridge at dawn, fog rising

Golden Gate Bridge

ALTHOUGH BUILT LONG AFTER THE PARK OF THE SAME name, it is the Golden Gate Bridge that symbolizes San Francisco, both for locals and for people across the world. It is, for one, a remarkable piece of art, an elegant 8,900 feet of concrete and steel supported by just two deftly designed piers. As a feat of engineering, it represents a pure force of wills and is a testimony to the engineering skills of Joseph Strauss, the architectural brilliance of Charles Ellis and Leon Moisseiff, and the financial acumen of A.G. Giannini, whose Bank of America floated the bond issue that paid for it. When the bridge was dedicated in 1937, it was the single largest structure in the world.

Today it would be hard to imagine a better place from which to begin a romantic trip to San Francisco. Mornings, misty and cool, are the perfect time for a bracing walk across the bridge to gain an overview of the city and its setting.

Almost 2 miles long, the bridge is open to walkers (east walkway only) from April through October, and from 6 a.m. to 6 p.m. the rest of the year *(access from Lincoln Blvd.)*. Wear a jacket as winds are often strong. To the northwest, a silvery stream might light up the Marin Headlands, all moody purple and green; behind them stands mysterious Mount Tamalpais (Mount Tam

to the locals). To the northeast are the lonely shapes of Alcatraz and Angel Islands in the bay, their flocks of gulls and pelicans floating on the air as if hanging from invisible rope. Across the bay are Berkeley and Oakland. To the southeast is the skyline of the city itself, perhaps the most memorable in all America. (Certainly Tony Bennett thought so.) Below you, on the south shore, sits **Fort Point National Historic Site.** This red-brick fortress was built during the Civil War to protect San Francisco from confederate attack. Cannon-loading demonstrations are held, and Civil War re-enactments bring the fort to life.

The bridge is a jewel in the crown of the **Golden Gate National Recreation Area.** This stretch of beach, forest, grasslands and promontories runs from **Fort Funston** *(tel 415/239-2366)* in the south, eastward to **Fort Mason** (see p.225) on the inner-city shoreline, and north as far as **Tomales Bay** (see p.245), well beyond San Francisco. The best place to take photographs of the San Francisco skyline is from the aptly named Vista Point, on the Marin side of the bridge. ■

Fort Point National Historic Site
www.nps.gov/fopo
Map 190 C4
Tel 415/556-1693
Closed Mon.–Thurs.

Golden Gate National Recreation Area Visitor Center
www.nps.gov/goga
Fort Mason, Bldg. 201
Tel 415/561-4700

Getting around San Francisco

Though San Francisco is a fine city to visit on foot, there comes a time when you'll want to avoid climbing yet another hill. Luckily, the city is well supplied with user-friendly and affordable public transportation (see inside the back cover).

The Bay Area Rapid Transit *(BART, tel 415/989-2278, www.bart.gov)* is a sleek, well-groomed, 71-mile rail system that links San Francisco and the peninsula with cities in the East Bay (via a 3.8-mile-long transbay tube), making outings to Oakland and Berkeley an easy day trip; a new extension feeds the San Francisco International Airport. The trains run from dawn to midnight. You can purchase multi-excursion passes at any of five BART shops along Market Street—Van Ness, Civic Center, Powell, Montgomery, and Embarcadero.

For information on the Muni bus system and advice on what bus to take, call the Muni information line *(tel 311 within San Francisco or 415/701-2311, or go to www.sfmuni.com).* The historic cable cars (see p. 219), start at Powell and Market and Powell and Van Ness and run from 6:30 a.m. to 1 a.m. daily and go to, or near, many sites. Passes, also accepted on the city's Muni bus system, can be purchased at Muni kiosks. ■

Golden Gate Park

ESTABLISHED IN 1870 ON A THOUSAND ACRES OF SAND AND windswept dunes, Golden Gate Park remains the single best daytime destination in San Francisco. Among its attractions are several world-class art and science museums, gardens representing flora and fauna from near and far, and a wide variety of picnic and hiking areas.

The de Young Memorial Museum puts on special events, like this Tibetan mandala painting exhibition.

de Young Memorial Museum
www.famsf.org/deyoung
- 190 D1
- 50 Hagiwara Tea Garden Dr.
- 415/730-3600
- Closed Mon.
- $$$

The park's varied landscapes—hillocks, glens, lakes, knolls, and meadows—are largely the work of the hard-driving Scotsman, John McLaren, who nurtured it from 1887 to 1943 *(tel 415/750-5442, www.parks.sfgov.org).*

McLaren succeeded William Hammond Hall, the park's first superintendent, after many in the San Francisco establishment ridiculed the notion of creating a park from wasteland. Experimenting with various native grasses and trees, McLaren eventually prevailed over the park's apparently self-destructive tendencies. (As well as its bureaucratic ones: He once faced down his own Public Works board by directing his staff to remove a parking lot and replant it with oaks). So popular was "Uncle John" that an attempt to force him into retirement once resulted in a minor uprising, causing the city fathers to adopt a special exemption for him. He died in 1943, at the age of 96.

A chief concern of more recent times is the lack of parking, so walking (or cycling) is the best way of getting around inside the park. Wear comfortable shoes—the park is three miles long! In mid-2007, the park department began closing many roads within the park on weekends to enhance pedestrian and cyclists safety; trams serve seniors and disabled travelers.

THE MUSEUMS

Often bypassed in the rush to take in the entire park in one day, the museums located here are unmissable, whether it is art that draws you or the excitement of science.

The **de Young Memorial Museum** holds one of the most comprehensive collections of American art on the West Coast. Don't miss it. The de Young is one of those quiet old California institutions that, like an eccentric distant uncle, only slowly yields its treasures—at least at first. Anyone who spends more than an hour here will end up spending a day.

Erected in 1895 in Egyptian

Revival style, the original buildings of this, the oldest public museum in San Francisco, were irreparably damaged by the 1989 earthquake, and the museum is now in a brand-new state-of-the-art structure.

Among the treasures, look for the fine bronze bust of "Mrs. LaChaise" (1912–17). It is by the French-born American sculptor Gaston LaChaise, who worked for Lalique before becoming a U.S. citizen and specializing in the full-bodied *femme américaine*.

Other parts of the collection present a veritable pantheon of 19th- and early 20th-century Americans, including Bill Copley, Paul Revere (silverware), Frederic Remington, Winslow Homer, Grant Wood, John Singer Sargent, and Mary Cassatt. Many expand on Western themes, such as Charles Nahl's troubling 1867 "Sacramento Indian with Dogs," and Thomas Cole's 1847 "Prometheus, Bound," a recent acquisition. Along these lines it is well worth seeking out George Caleb Bingham's "Boatman on the Missouri." William McCloskey's 1890 "Oranges in Tissue Paper" has nothing to do with the West per se, save to make of its main icon a subject fitting for a Jan Brueghel. Do not miss this painting!

Many of these works were given by late 19th-century California's most aggressive capitalists, and were supplemented in 1979 by acquisition of the Rockefeller Collection of American Art.

Recent acquisitions not to be missed include "La Maternité," a Modernist bronze sculpture by Joan Miro; it sits on the lawns in front of the entrance.

Another mission of the de Young is expressed in the Arts of Africa, Oceania, and the Americas collection. Far from the catchall that its title might imply, this collection maintains a fine emphasis on the most primary of pieces, from the Central Asian door rugs in the Wiedersperg Collection to the terra-cotta vessels from 7th-century Teotihuacán in Mexico.

John Singer Sargent's 1884 "A Dinner Table at Night" is part of the de Young's fine collection of American artists.

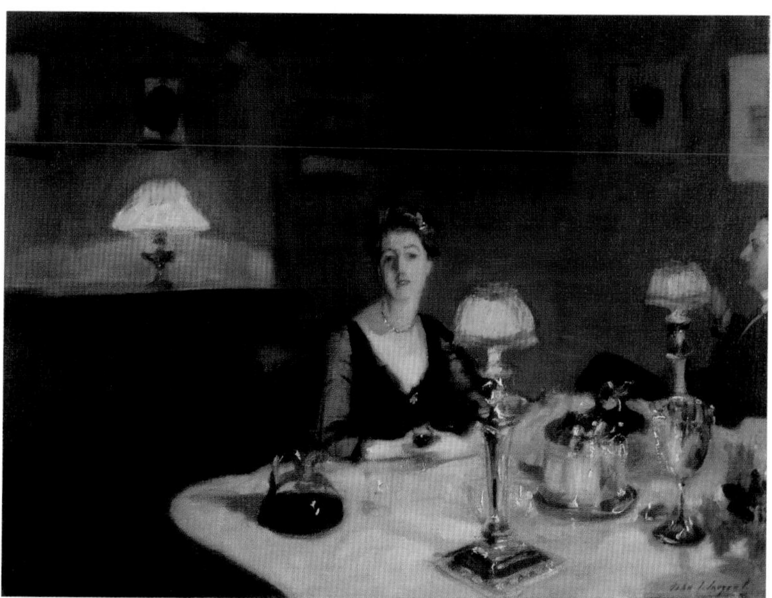

California Academy of Sciences
www.calacademy.org
191 G2
55 Concourse Dr.
415/321-8000
$$

Strybing Arboretum & Botanical Gardens
www.strybing.org
190 D1
9th Ave. & Lincoln Way
415/661-1316
Call for tours
Bus 5, 21 26, 42 47

The textile collection alone includes more than 11,000 items, from European tapestries and oriental silks to fashionable 18th-century dress and fine African costumes. And the encyclopedic Jolika Collection of New Guinea Art, numbering more than 400 extraordinary pieces, many dating back six centuries, is one of the world's great such exhibits.

Across the concourse from the de Young is the **California Academy of Sciences,** established in 1853. After complete rebuilding, the academy has reopened under its new Living Roof with an advanced aquarium, state-of-the-art planetarium, and spectacular natural history museum. Highlights include a rain forest dome where visitors can take a vertical journey; a replication of a U.S. swamp, complete with alligators; and Tusher African Center, with zoological dioramas. The new facility, designed by Pritzker Prize-winning architect Renzo Piano, will have a shape that suggests hills with a roof where native plants thrive.

The lower level of the remodeled facility features exhibits from the academy's former Steinhart Aquarium in a sensational new environment. Visitors can walk through a glass tube inside the Amazon Flooded Forest. Giant octopus, jellyfish, and sharks teems inside the 100,000-gallon California Coast exhibit. A 225,000-gallon coral reef habitat is the world's deepest such interior ecosystem. And the multimedia Water Planet brings to life an array of ocean and freshwater environments. The three-story Planetarium has a real-time NASA data link.

THE GARDENS

One of "Uncle John" McLaren's legacies is the patchwork of special garden-meadows throughout the park. Although not as intensively curated as other attractions, they are pleasant places for picnics and walks. They include the **Redwood Memorial Grove,** the **Heroes Grove,** the **Rose Garden,** and McLaren's own **Rhododendron Dell.** The park service visitor center provides a map of the gardens.

Of the three formal botanical sites, the **Strybing Arboretum & Botanical Gardens** is the most spectacular. The arboretum was founded in 1937 with a gift from Helen Strybing, widow of a wealthy San Francisco merchant. Strybing was particularly interested in indigenous botany and plants with medicinal purposes.

Many of the early collections focused on plants from Mediterranean climates—from coastal California, South Africa, western Australia, the central coast of Chile, and the Mediterranean itself.

One of the most striking of these collections is the **Cape Province Garden,** which displays a number of amazingly well adapted plants from this unique botanical region on the southern tip of Africa. The various heaths (species of the genus *Erica*) can bloom year-round because their small needle-like leaves diffuse heat so well. Another plant family with natural anti-evaporative qualities is the Proteaceae; leaves covered with fine white hairs help the plants retain enough water for their showy blooms. The Cape Province Garden also showcases several varieties of aloe, kniphofia, and ice plant (the last are showier than their freeway-strip cousins might suggest).

One of the more recent additions to the Strybing is the **New World Cloud Forest,** which is a testing ground for some tropical plants, many of which are endangered in their native habitats. The

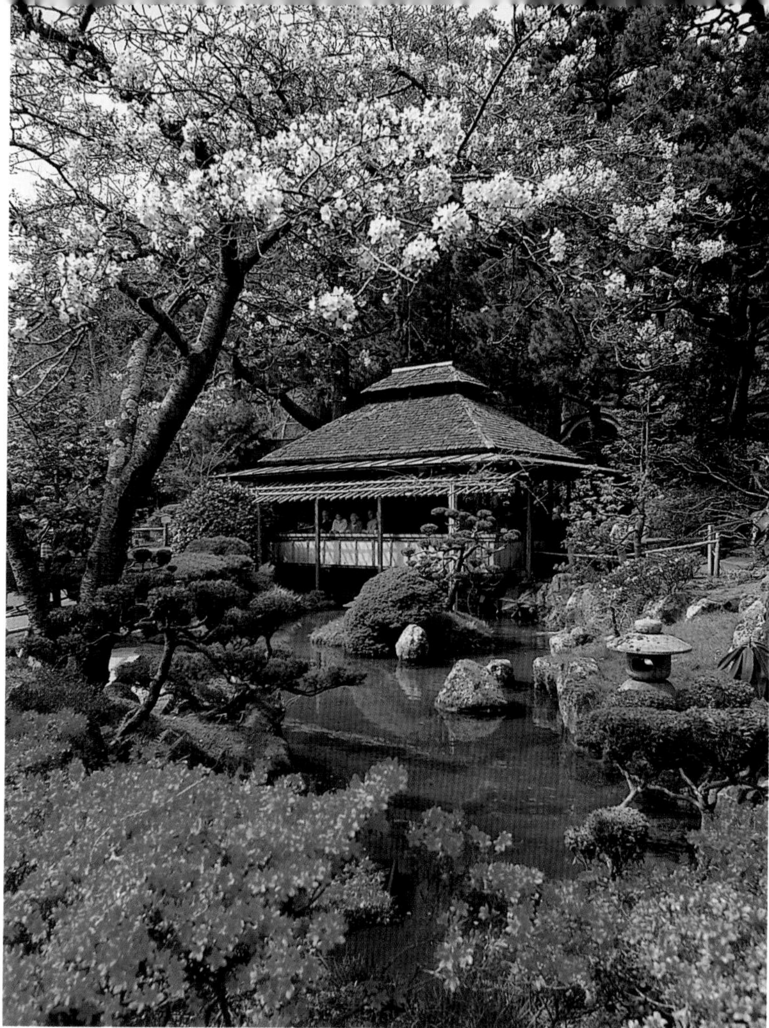

Japanese Tea Garden in bloom

garden is using the Bay Area's natural fogginess to approximate conditions in tropical cloud forests such as those in Chaipas, Mexico. Check out the giant lobelias, salvias, and daisies as large as small trees.

At the north entrance to the Strybing is the **Japanese Tea Garden.** Built for the 1894 Midwinter Exposition, it is the oldest Japanese-style garden in the United States. Today many gather under its old open-air pavilion for tea and cookies after taking in the perfectly manicured grounds. Do not miss Nagao Sakurai's 1953 **Zen Garden,** with its astonishing bonsai cypress. In spring cherry and azalea blossoms explode in a riot of color.

The **Conservatory of Flowers,** which attracts more visitors than any other place in Golden Gate Park, is a huge Victorian greenhouse filled with a riotous profusion of tropical plants from Costa Rican cloud forests, the sweltering Congo, the verdant isles of the Philippines, and many other places. The western hemisphere's oldest existing conservatory, it was erected from a "kit" acquired from the estate of business

Japanese Tea Garden
190 D1
Hagiwara Tea Garden Dr.
415/752-1171 (tour information)

Conservatory of Flowers
www.conservatoryofflowers.org
190 D1
John F. Kennedy Drive
415/666-7001
Closed Mon.
$$
Bus 5, 7, 21, 33, 44, 71; Streetcar N

McLaren Lodge
190 D2
John F. Kennedy Dr. at Stanyan St.
415/831-2700
Closed Sat.–Sun.

magnate James Lick, who had planned to assemble it on his property in the Santa Clara Valley. Erected in Golden Gate Park in 1879, the greenhouse was badly damaged in the 1990s in a 100-mile-per-hour windstorm, closing for eight years and $25 million worth of restoration. It re-opened in 2003. Today, plants from more than four dozen countries—some 1,500 species—are displayed under one vast roof of glass.

There are five galleries. Enter the Lowland Tropics section and you step into a realm of palm canopies and immense leaves (look for the 100-year-old Imperial Philodendron). There are "economic plants"—coffee, chocolate, vanilla—that have had worldwide commercial importance for centuries, as well as cycads, a species that dates back before the age of dinosaurs.

Orchids star in the Highland Tropics gallery, growing among ferns and creepers on gnarled trees. The conservatory boasts the world's best public collection of Dracula orchids. A gallery of Aquatic Plants showcases huge lilies (one variety has leaves that can be six feet in diameter) and flowers that float. Another wing of the conservatory holds potted plants, seasonal flower displays, and special exhibits.

HISTORIC BUILDINGS

Fittingly, the headquarters of Golden Gate Park is in the historic **McLaren Lodge.** "Uncle John" lived in this Moorish-cum-Gothic confection at the eastern end of the park until his death in 1943.

Opposite the Japanese Tea Garden is the ornate Spreckels Temple of Music, now known as the **Bandshell.** Built by the Spreckels family in 1899, it is home to the oldest continuously operating municipal band in the U.S.

Near Stow Lake is the **Pioneer Log Cabin,** a restored 1911 structure made from hand-picked Humboldt redwoods that were floated in a raft down the coast for the Association of Pioneer Women of California. For an example of 1930s Works Progress Administration architecture, see the **Angler's Lodge,** opposite the historic **Buffalo Paddock** with its herd of these shaggy great beasts.

Lastly, if you are heading west, see the **Beach Chalet** *(tel 415/386-8439, www.beachchalet.com),* on Great Highway near the Dutch Windmill. The café, with its Depression-era frescoes, is a great place to eat. ■

Recreation in Golden Gate Park

The park offers all kinds of outdoor pursuits, from soccer to fishing and from jogging to archery. Some roads are closed on weekends for bikers, in-line skaters, and runners. For a comprehensive listing of park facilities, consult the maps available at any major site. Some popular activities are:

Biking: Bikes can be rented in the park, as can in-line skates *(tel 415/668-6699).*

Boating: Pedalboats and rowboats are available for rent on Stow Lake *(tel 415/752-0347).*

Golf: Eccentric nine-hole course *(47th Ave., tel 415/751-8987).*

Tennis: 21 courts *(John F. Kennedy Dr., opposite Conservatory, tel 415/753-7001).*

Lawn Bowling: Easy to learn, free lessons on Wed. *(near Sharon Meadow and the Carousel, tel 415/487-8787).* ■

In a Haight Street shop

Haight-Ashbury

Haight-Ashbury
191 E1

This venerable old neighborhood, named for the two roads that cross at its heart, began life as a Victorian escape from the city center. Growth boomed after the 1906 fire which left the area untouched. In the 1930s it declined, the Victorian houses split into flats. Drawn by low rents, the Beats and blacks arrived in the '50s, followed by the hippies and the flower-power generation. In the '60s, Haight-Ashbury had its 15 minutes of fame. But by the '70s it was a trash-littered ghetto with boarded-up shops.

Remarkably, it made a comeback. Young professionals and gays moved into restored Victorian houses, and interesting shops opened (look for vintage clothes and records). To get the flavor, stroll past the Victorians on Masonic Avenue or by the Queen Anne **Richard Spreckels Mansion** *(737 Buena Vista Ave. W., not open to the public).* Continue up Buena Vista (daytime only) to **Buena Vista Park** and take in the views. South Haight has a fine community of retailers and specialty shops. ■

Castro District

Although well past its prime as "gay capital of the world," the Castro, with its many cafés, clubs, and bars, still offers fast-paced entertainment and busy street life. It was here during the 1970s that gay men first began the often difficult process of leading openly gay lives. Their patron saint was Harvey Milk, a flamboyant and politically astute man who became the city's first openly gay supervisor before being shot, with San Francisco Mayor George Moscone, in November 1978.

Two longtime hangouts are **The Midnight Sun** *(18th St. & Castro)* and **Badlands** *(4121 18th St.).* For film buffs, the ornate **Castro Theater** *(429 Castro St., tel 415/621-6120),* a 1922 film palace, features a Wurlitzer organ that rises from the floor and plays before the featured film. ■

Victorians on the bay

Although many American cities flirted with Victorianism, few reveled in it in quite the same way as 19th-century San Francisco. Victorian architecture was, after all, a perfect synthesis of everything the booming city's new rich craved: status (the style had rich European antecedents); conformity (the Victorian emphasis was on morals, prudence, and the Bible); domesticity (a "lady of the house" dispensed wisdom and discipline); and order (each room had a special purpose, unlike the boardinghouses that were the principal domiciles of the gold rush).

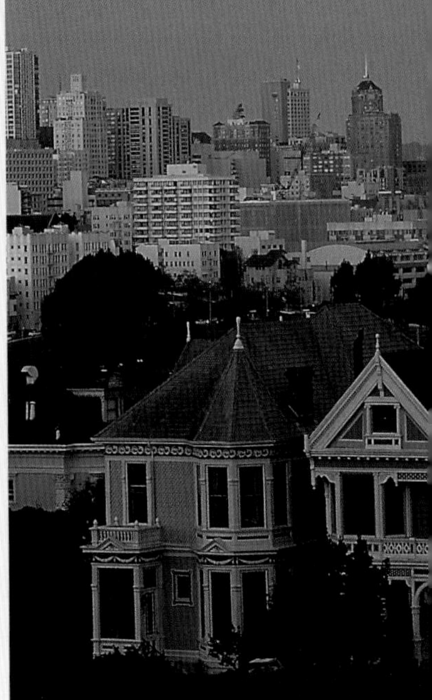

And yet no city confounded, or continues to confound, Victorian stereotypes as much. Consider for example the story of the building now known as the Queen Anne Hotel at 1590 Sutter Street. With its grand domed turret, peaked gables, and gingerbread details, it certainly embodies Victorianism externally. But what happened inside its doors? It was built in 1889 for Senator James G. Fair, one of the Comstock Lode Silver Kings and the force behind the Nob Hill landmark now known as the Fairmont Hotel. At the time the senator had already been sued by his first wife on grounds of "habitual adultery," according to an account by the San Francisco historian Bob Bills.

This was apparently not a happy house. Although the senator kept custody of his two sons, both of them went on to blaze decidedly non-Victorian trails in the annals of family dysfunction. His son James, following a long battle with alcoholism, killed himself in 1892 at the young age of 27. The very next year, the other son, Charles, publicly married one of the era's most prominent prostitutes. In 1890 the building was sold to the Miss Mary Lakes School for Girls, which trained young women in more proper pursuits. It later went through iterations as a men's club and as an Episcopal girls lodge before being boarded up in the late 1950s.

The most pronounced element of the Victorian style was ornamentation—ways to call attention to one's own individual taste while remaining safely inside the framework of Victorian architecture. To do this, the typical San Franciscan could employ several forms of artifice, some interesting, others frilly, and some outlandishly garish. There were the wall textures known as fishscaling and gingerbread, or the window decoration known as puddling, in which one layer of curtain was piled upon another to lend a regal effect. An Italian style could be added to a house by adding a simple eyebrow dormer.

Color, too, functioned as a social barometer. Although the average late 19th-century home might not have been as bright as some of today's candy-colored versions, color was often used to set off various exterior elements.

From the 1930s through the postwar years, as these neighborhoods declined, many of the Victorians became run-down housing stock, rented out on a month-to-month basis and seldom appreciated by their owners. The dominant color was battleship gray. Tour guide Jay Gifford *(tel 415/252-9485, www.victorianwalk.com)* credits the hippie movement with saving the Victorian row houses. "Painting those drab buildings with bright colors saved them because it renewed interest in all those lost and faded details that no one had noticed for so long."

Victoriana, San Francisco style. Top: Victorian row houses on Alamo Square; Left: Roof ornamentation on a Stick-style house; Above: Carved Gothic-style gables on Potrero Hill

But what also transformed "those drab buildings" and made them into what they are today was the combination of two social trends: the remaking of downtown San Francisco as a financial center, and the growing population of gay professionals who worked there and needed housing. Author Richard Rodriguez has noted the irony that "it was thus a coincidence of the market that gay men found themselves living within the architectural metaphor for family."

The late 1990s wrought new changes in San Francisco's Victorian houses. Outrageous colors went out of fashion, but an indicator of the boomtime stockmarket was the use of gold leafing as ornamentation. ■

Mission District

THE MISSION DISTRICT, SITUATED EAST OF THE CASTRO, has made great progress toward revitalization in recent years. The Hispanic murals that have brought life to the streets remain, but new immigrants are the key to the recent change. Their botanicas, flower stands, and produce marts, and the great variety of Salvadoran, Indian, Chinese, and Vietnamese eateries, astound even the locals. The Taqueria Cancun *(2288 Mission St., tel 415/252-9560)* "has the best vegetarian burrito in town—and I'm from the Haight!" one customer reported. Foreign Cinema *(2534 Mission St., 415/648-7600, www.foreigncinema.com)* established an artsy institution by projecting foreign films on an outdoor wall to accompany their popular California/Mediterranean cooking. The neighborhood continues to evolve.

Mission District
191 F1

Mission Dolores
16th St. & Dolores St.
415/621-8203
Muni Light Rail, J car, Van Ness Station

The main attraction of this district is the eponymous **Mission Dolores.** Called by its nickname (a now dried-up creek called Arroyo de Nuestra Señora de los Dolores, *dolores* meaning "sorrow"), its real name is San Francisco de Asìs for its founder's patron saint. Founded five days before the signing of the Declaration of Independence, Mission Dolores is rather plain and spare by the standards of its own era. It is, however, remarkable for its seamless blending of Old World and New World aesthetics, from its colorful roof beams (originally painted by Ohlone Indians) to the statue of the Archangel Michael, dressed as an Indian vanquisher. The reredos, or decorative altar, was made in San Blas, Mexico, in 1796.

The cemetery is also of note. In its center is a statue of Junípero Serra by the California artist Arthur Putnam. The surrounding garden contains many native plants, from huge Mexican sages to Matilija poppies. Here lie the remains of some of early San Francisco's most important personages, among them Don Luis Antonio Arguello, the first governor of Alta California under Mexican rule. ■

The oldest building in San Francisco, the original adobe structure of the Mission Dolores

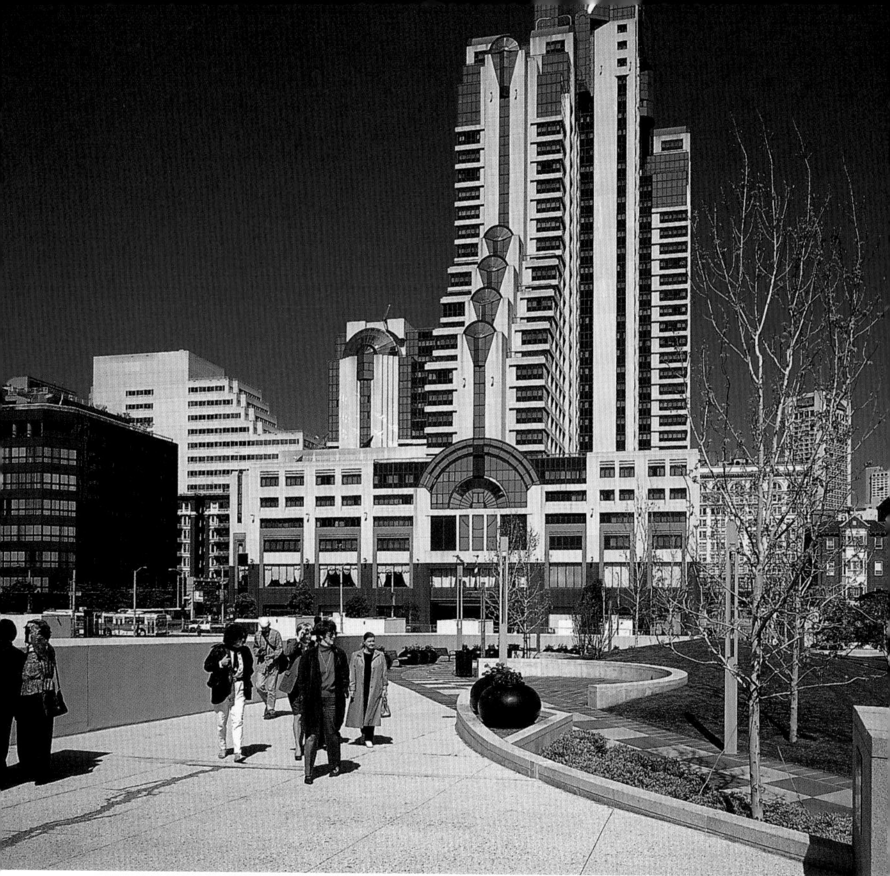

SoMa & Yerba Buena

Yerba Buena Gardens in winter sunshine

SOMA IS THE UNIVERSALLY RECOGNIZED ABBREVIATION for the area of San Francisco that lies *So*uth of *Ma*rket Street. As to Yerba Buena, on the east side of the original 19th-century settlement, now bounded by Market, 2nd, 5th, and Folsom Streets: "They say it means 'good herb,' but if anything good will grow on this soil, I'm mightily mistaken," is how one crew member of the *Brooklyn*, which landed here in 1846, described his bleak surroundings. But what Yerba Buena lacked in agricultural prospects it more than made up for in entrepreneurship. Well into the 20th century the area, named for the landing cove on its seaward side, was the epicenter of San Francisco's business community. In the late 1970s, the city built the Moscone Center here, launching Yerba Buena's present rebirth. As in many post-industrial cities, redundant factories and warehouses have been converted into offices, restaurants, and nightclubs. With museums, playhouses, galleries, a bowling alley, and now the San Francisco Giants' new stadium, SoMa and Yerba Buena easily compete with Golden Gate Park and the waterfront as lively destinations.

SoMa & Yerba Buena
N 191 G2
Visitor information
www.yerbabuena.org

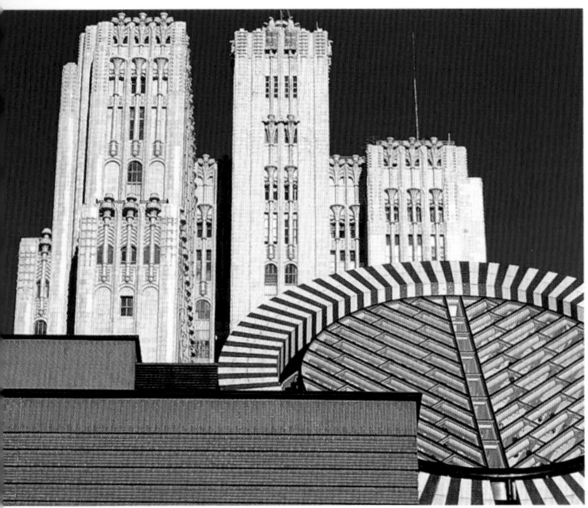

The San Francisco Museum of Modern Art's outstanding contemporary building

San Francisco Museum of Modern Art
www.sfmoma.org
- 151 3rd St.
- 415/357-4000
- Closed Wed.
- $$. Free 1st Tues. of month
- Bus 5, 9, 12, 14, 15, 30, 38, 45

Rooftop at Yerba Buena Gardens
- Between 3rd, 4th, Mission, & Howard Sts.

Yerba Buena Center for the Arts
www.yerbabuenaarts.org
- 701 Mission St.
- 415/978-2787
- Closed Mon.
- $$$ for galleries, free first Tues.
- Bus 9, 12, 14, 15, 30, 45, 76

The main draw in the area is the **San Francisco Museum of Modern Art,** partly housed in a red-orange structure designed by Swiss architect Mario Botta and opened in 1995. With its wide, open galleries and airy interior, it is the perfect place to view this outstanding collection of modern and contemporary art. Its Caffè Museo downstairs is one of the few museum eateries worth its salt and pepper.

Spend the bulk of your time here on the atrium-lit second floor viewing a permanent installation of 250 works dubbed "From Matisse to Diebenkorn," pulled from the museum's 15,000 holdings. A particularly brilliant moment comes early on, with two pieces done in 1916 by Henri Matisse: "Portrait of Sarah Stein" and "Portrait of Michael Stein." The Steins were ardent Bay Area supporters of the artist. It is the only known instance of double portraiture by Matisse, and many scholars believe it to be a high point of his artistic legacy.

Although many modernists created highly idiosyncratic visions using large flat plains and primary colors, none seems so haunting (at least in this collection) as that of Max Beckmann in his 1934 "Landschaft, Cannes." In this simple rendering of palm trees against sea and sky, Beckmann evokes something primordial, even scary. The gray-green palms, so fat and huge as to actually eat up the more diminutive rural features, also seem weirdly frail, as if one good shake of the earth would uproot them instantly.

The museum has a fine representation of Mexican modernists. A triumph is Diego Rivera's 1935 "The Flower Carrier," which fuses the abstract concern for primal shape with the realist's attraction to biomorphism, to how the human body works. Though one can almost count the number of elements in the painting, any geometric staleness is flushed with the blood of Rivera's masterful palette work.

The collection has Hockneys, Lichtensteins, and Diebenkorns, as well as single works by the lesser known. For example, Chinese painter Liu Wei's "Two Drunk Painters" (1990). Another is Robert Colecott work, entitled "Colored TV" (1977). The rendering of a black man watching clearly Anglo-produced TV is, as the curators write, "a brilliant distillation of a moment of cultural tension of American society in the 1970s, as blacks increasingly gained middle class socio-economic status but remained largely excluded from the media."

The newest addition to Yerba Buena's burgeoning culture is across the street at the **Rooftop at Yerba Buena Gardens**. Ten acres of child-size gardens, labyrinths, play spaces, and a glass-enclosed antique carousel are atop the **Moscone Center,** offering some of the liveliest daytime entertainments in town. The latest addition is the **Zeum,** an interactive museum exploring the visual and performing arts, where young people can actually learn to produce their own animated shorts, do 3-D modeling and audio mixing. The Rooftop also runs the **Yerba Buena Ice Skating & Bowling Center.**

Nearby is the **Yerba Buena Center for the Arts,** which features changing exhibitions of local art, and includes the **Center for Arts Theater,** which puts on works reflecting the cultural diversity of San Francisco. Next to it is a great place to relax and picnic, the **Esplanade Gardens.** See the **Martin Luther King Memorial** while you are here. Across the street, historic **St. Patrick's Church** *(756 Mission St., tel 415/777-3211)* presents concerts *($ donation)* on Wednesdays at 12:30 p.m. Behind the church, the **Museum of Craft & Folk Art** *(51 Yerba Buena Ln., www.mocfa.org, closed Mon & holidays, $)* features exhibits from around the world.

The former Jessie Street, adjacent to the historic Old Mint Building, has been redeveloped as pedestrian-only **Mint Plaza** *(www.mintplazasf.org)*, vibrant with cafés and public art. It's a venue for cultural programs, street fairs, a farmer's market, and cinema alfresco.

The **Cartoon Art Museum** is a showcase for selections from its collection of 6,000 pieces of original art—ranging from *Li'l Abner* and *Peanuts* drawings to cels from Walt Disney cartoon features. Highlights: animation drawing from *Gertie the Dinosaur* (1914) by the "father of the animated cartoon," Winsor McCay; underground comix (R. Crumb, *Zippy the Pinhead*); and an early character sheet from Disney's *Snow White* showing some of the seven dwarfs who didn't make it to the film, among them Jumpy and Baldy.

The new **Contemporary Jewish Museum** *(tel 415/344-8800, www.thecjm.org)* occupies the a new building designed by Daniel Libeskind on the site of the former Power Station. The **California Historical Society** puts on some of the best historical shows anywhere. It has 450 oil paintings by such artists as Albert Bierstadt and Thomas Hill, not to mention photos by Carleton Watkins, Eadweard Muybridge, and Arnold Genthe.

The Museum of the African Diaspora looks at the journeys and achievements of Africa-descended people around the world. Permanent exhibitions include the highly moving "Slavery Passages."

While you are in the SoMa area, stroll up Market to the **Rincon Center.** This complex of stores and offices incorporates the 1930s **Rincon Annex Post Office,** done in the art deco moderne style by architect Gilbert Underwood, who also did Yosemite's Ahwahnee Hotel. The draw here is the WPA murals, painted in 1941–48 by Russian artist Anton Refregier. The works were so critical of the San Francisco establishment that the artist had to make 92 changes to placate various interest groups. The murals also withstood a McCarthy-era attempt to destroy them for being "communistic" in tone. ■

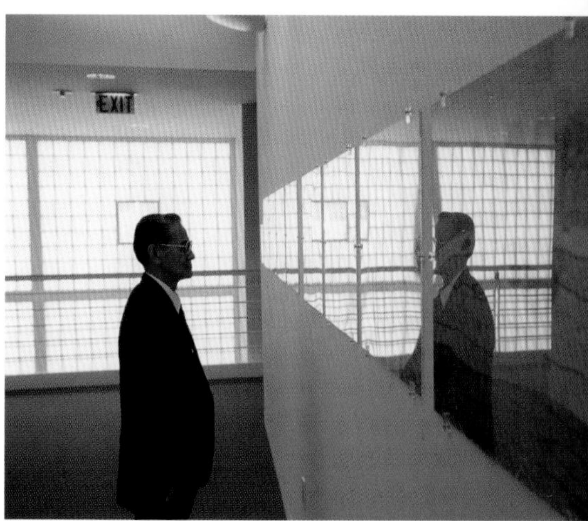

Viewing exhibits at the San Francisco Museum of Modern Art

Cartoon Art Museum
www.cartoonart.org
655 Mission St.
415/227-8666
Closed Mon.
$$

California Historical Society
www.calhist.org
678 Mission St.
415/357-1848
Closed Sun.–Thurs.
$

Museum of the African Diaspora
www.museumoftheafricandiaspora.org
90 New Montgomery St.
415/358-7200
Closed Mon. & Tues.
$$$

Pioneer Monument and City Hall, Civic Center

Civic Center

THE HUB OF SAN FRANCISCO'S GOVERNMENT, THE CIVIC Center is an impressive urban landscape dominated by the classical columns and gleaming dome of the 1915 City Hall. But this is also a neighborhood of serious culture, boasting a symphony hall, the War Memorial Opera House, and most recently the Asian Art Museum, with its treasures of many lands and materials.

Civic Center
191 F2

City Hall
www.sfgov.org/cityhall
Polk St. between Grove St. & McAllister St. For tours go to Van Ness Ave. entrance.
415/554-6023
Tours Mon.-Fri. 10 a.m., 12 & 2 p.m.
Bus 5, 19, 21, 47, 49; BART Civic Center

After the 1906 earthquake and the devastating fire that followed it, San Franciscans vigorously debated how they wanted their rebuilt city to look. Their loftiest hopes for a "City Beautiful," contained in the Burnham Plan, were largely abandoned for more practical ideas, with the lone exception of the splendid Civic Center (between Market, McAllister, and Gough). It is still one of the nation's most complete collections of beaux arts buildings set in a formal plan. Broad red plazas and buildings with gold domes, Doric columns, and masses of California granite, convey the post-earthquake city's regal sense of itself.

After some years of decline, the Civic Center has been revitalized, centering on the **City Hall,** whose recent $300 million refurbishing brought back to life an urban temple of granite, marble, and gilded ironwork.

The 1995 **San Francisco Public Library,** designed by Pei Cobb Freed & Partners, attracts people of all ages who beaver away at their research at computer terminals (the card catalog is online) and in specialized study centers whose scope ranges from Native American and African-American materials to the nation's first library center for gay and lesbian studies.

ASIAN ART MUSEUM

Asian culture and art come to life in a stunning setting: the Italian Renaissance-style old public library designed by Brown and Bakewell and in 2002 given a new interior by contemporary architect Gae Aulenta, known for the Musée d'Orsay in Paris. The museum—the nation's largest devoted entirely to Asian Art, with 15,000 objects—displays works from (in the order they are encountered) India, the Persian world/West Asia, Southeast Asia, the Himalaya/Tibet, China, Korea, and Japan. Exhibits explore three major themes: Buddhism, trade and cultural exchange, and local beliefs.

Among the highlights: Religious statuary illuminates India's diverse religions (Hinduism, Islam, Buddhism, etc.), and an exhibit explains Hindu temples as symbolizing the holy mountains where gods dwell. From Thailand and Southeast Asian islands come ornate daggers (krises), many bejeweled, while Cambodian sculptures show the refined temple decorations created by the Khmer people of the Angkor kingdom. Tibetan arts are represented by monastery scrolls, 15th-century ritual objects of gilded metal, and lacquered wood figures. Works from Nepal include mystical diagrams, or mandalas, that aid meditation.

Chinese exhibits begin with Neolithic oracle bones showing China's first written language. They continue through the first Chinese Buddha (A.D. 338), ceramics, fan paintings, Ming calligraphy, and a large collection of jade objects, ranging from a rare symbolic disk (2,500 B.C.) to openwork carvings and items from the 1930s tourist trade. Also in the collection: textiles, cloisonné, ivory, bamboo, glass.

The finest collection of Korean objects outside their home country includes Bronze Age slate daggers, earthenware vessels, gilded Buddha figures, and paintings on silk. A broad survey of Japanese art takes in painted screens, notably an 18th-century example depicting a scene from the 10th-century poetic narrative *The Tales of Ise*, dry lacquer figures, glazed stoneware and porcelain, bronze ritual bells, carved netsuke, and hanging scrolls. ■

San Francisco Public Library
www.sfpl.lib.ca.us
✉ Civic Center, 100 Larkin St.
☎ 415/557-4400
🕒 Closed Fri. and Sun. a.m. Call for tour hours.
🚌 Bus 5, 19, 21, 26, 47; BART Civic Center

Asian Art Museum
www.asianart.org
✉ 200 Larkin St.
☎ 415/581-3500
🕒 Closed Mon.
$ $$. Free 1st Tues.
🚌 Bus 5, 19, 21, 26, 47; BART Civic Center

The Asian Art Museum's Himalayan Gallery features paintings, bronze sculptures, and rare Tibetan scrolls.

Financial District

THE FINANCIAL DISTRICT (BETWEEN PINE, WASHINGTON, Montgomery, and Drumm Streets) features several interesting buildings. With its foundations in the era of the gold rush, San Francisco's banking industry has long maintained a high profile. Since the late 1960s, its buildings—literally—have too.

The first to scrape the sky (at 52 stories) was the 1969 **Bank of America Building** *(555 California St.)*, soon followed by the distinctive 853-foot **Transamerica Pyramid** of 1972 *(Clay & Montgomery Sts.)*. Older buildings worthy of a second look include the **Pacific Exchange** *(301 Pine St.)*, remodeled in 1930, and the 1903 **Merchant's Exchange** *(465 California St.)*. The 1875 **Palace Hotel** *(2 New Montgomery St., tours tel 415/512-1111, www.sfpalace.com, see p. 265)*, rebuilt in 1909 and now lavishly refurbished, is known as the place where President Warren Harding drew his last breath in 1923. The Garden Court astounds with its

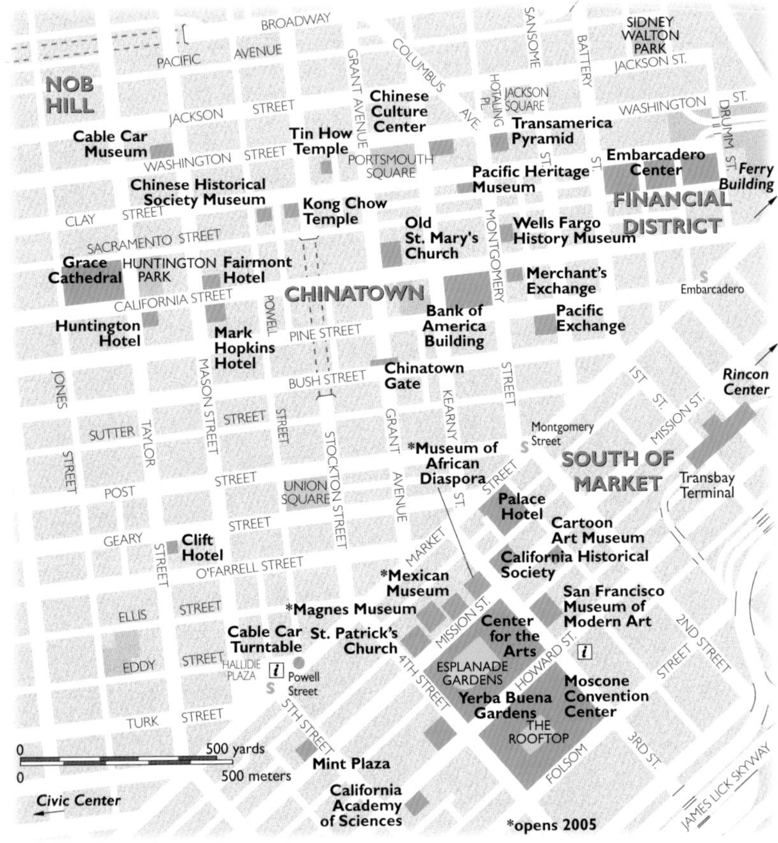

San Francisco's Financial District rises in the heart of the City.

incredible architecture, dome stained-glass ceiling and Austrian crystal chandeliers, and in its early 20th-century heyday was the setting for some of the nation's most prestigious events. Today it's a perfect setting for afternoon tea.

At the modern end of the scale are the headquarters for **Charles Schwab & Co.** *(101 Montgomery St.)*—perhaps, along with Boston's Fidelity Mutual, the most important innovator in modern American finance—and the shopping arcade-cum-plaza known as the **Embarcadero Center,** on Clay between Drumm and Battery.

Access to many Financial District buildings is restricted but looking from the outside is free, as is the lively Montgomery Street scene—watch the brokers either looking depressed or ordering caviar for breakfast. A swell place from which to view it all is the Starbuck's café *(tel 415/788-1363)* at Kearny & Bush. After a double espresso, head up the street to **Jackson Square,** perhaps the best single congregation of buildings from the gold rush era. Take a look at the 1852 **Golden Era Building** *(730–752 Montgomery St.),* then browse among the antiques in the shops in **Hotaling Place.** The shop called W. Graham Arader III *(435 Jackson St.)* has a huge selection of antique prints and rare maps.

Back down Montgomery, stop at the **Wells Fargo History Museum** to see how the West was financed—largely through the efforts of this prestigious bank. The jewels here come in the form of perfectly preserved stagecoaches from the mid-19th century.

The "other" downtown centers in and around **Union Square.** This is the historic center of the downtown retail trade. Exclusive stores, and boutique retailers and tailors, cater to the city's burgeoning financial class.

Nearby, at Powell and Market Streets, is the **Powell Street Cable Car Turntable,** from where you can begin a scenic journey to Nob Hill, Fisherman's Wharf, or Chinatown. ■

Wells Fargo History Museum

www.wellsfargohistory.com

Map p. 208

420 Montgomery St.

415/396-2619

Closed Sat.–Sun.

Cable car California St.; bus 1, 12, 15, 42

Chinatown

Chinatown
Map p. 208
Cable car California St., Powell-Hyde, Powell-Mason; bus 1, 9X, 15, 41, 45, 83

Chinese Culture Center
www.c-c-c.org
Holiday Inn, 750 Kearny St.
415/986-1822
Closed Mon.
Call for tours: hitoric $$$, culinary $$$$

In an herbal pharmacy

Pacific Heritage Museum
www.ibankunited.com/phm
608 Commercial St.
415/399-1124
Closed Mon. & Sun.

Kong Chow Temple
855 Stockton St., 4th floor

FOUNDED NOT LONG AFTER THE FIRST THREE CHINESE immigrants disembarked from the American brig *Eagle* in 1848, San Francisco's Chinatown has long served as a historical touchstone for the city's now highly assimilated but ethnically proud Chinese-American community. It is, to be sure, somewhat faded by age, and many of its older Chinese families have moved to live elsewhere. Yet this noisy quarter *(bounded by Broadway, Powell, Kearny, & Bush Sts.)* remains a vibrant and richly evocative travel destination.

Passing through the ornate, green-tiled **Chinatown Gate** *(Bush & Grant Sts.)* that marks the start of the quarter, those with a bent for shopping can visit the many curio shops along historic **Grant Avenue.** Foodies should take to **Stockton Street,** where produce sellers hawk their wares next to outstanding Chinese herbal medicine stores. Now that such remedies are being recommended on TV by movie stars, a visit to one of the street's many ginseng merchants has become de rigueur. Usually there is a pot of tea made from the herb brewing away, and with patience you can come away with some first-class ginseng.

For some guidance on Chinatown food, it is worth turning to a local expert. An outstanding culinary tour that includes a good dose of local history is conducted by Shirley Fong-Torres *(tel 415/981-8989, www.wokwiz.com).* Ms. Fong-Torres is a knowledgeable host who will make sure you eat only the best dim sum. If you prefer to plan your own food tour, two reliably delicious restaurants are the House of Nanking *(919 Kearny St., tel 415/421-1429)* and Lucky Creation *(854 Washington St., tel 415/989-0818).*

History looms large in Chinatown. To get a sense of its sweep, from gold rush to post-Tiananmen Square, visit the **Pacific Heritage Museum.** The museum is situated inside the 1875 U.S. Subtreasury building, itself built on the site of the original branch of the U.S. Mint. You'll see the literal foundations of the city's financial life downstairs when you look behind glass into the vault. Here are a cart and boxes used in the 1870s to haul bullion, scales for weighing gold dust, and a small collection of beautiful silver coins from the pioneer period. About twice a year a new rotating show exhibits ancient and contemporary works from local and overseas Chinese, illustrating patterns of both artistic continuity and assimilation.

The **Chinese Culture Center** also endeavors, with less success and refinement, to exhibit local art, as well as musical instruments and other cultural items. Its real specialty is its historical walking tours, well worth the cost.

Among the traditional historical stops is **Old St. Mary's Church** *(Grant Ave. & California St.),* one of the few buildings here to survive the earthquake and fire. As the West Coast's first Roman Catholic cathedral, this was a predecessor of the modernistic St. Mary's Cathedral on Gough Street (see p. 215). The park across the street has mah-jongg players and a rendering of Sun Yat-Sen by local artist Benjamin Bufano.

The relatively new (1977) red-brick **Kong Chow Temple** contains one of the oldest Taoist

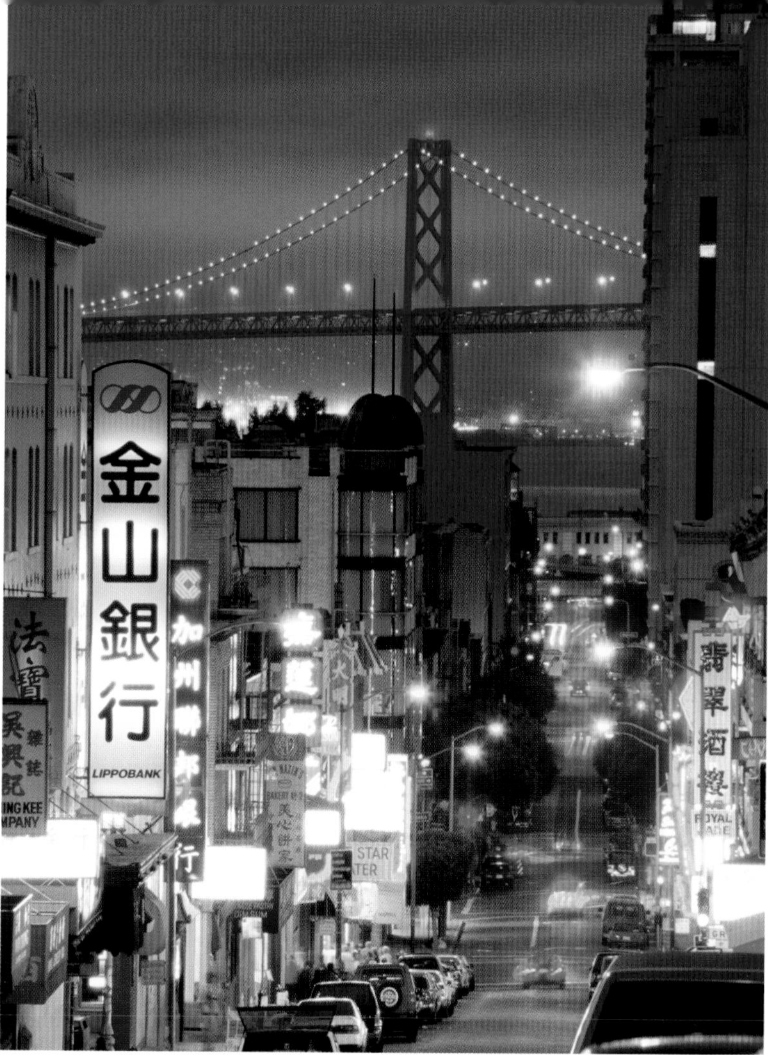

Streets in Chinatown have their own special look.

shrines in America; on its ruby red walls is a 19th-century statue, from Canton, of the patron deity Kuan Ti. The statue was rescued from the ashes of the original temple on Pine Street after the 1906 earthquake and fire. Colorful Waverly Place has restaurants and both churches and temples, including the **Tin How Temple.** Established in 1852 by Day Ju, one of the city's first Chinese immigrants, it is dedicated to the "Queen of the heavens and goddess of the Seven Seas." The remarkable "Life of Confucius" altar has been a spiritual and social core ever since.

The **Chinese Historical Society Museum**—occupying architect Julia Morgan's 1932 Chinatown YWCA, with its towers and painted ceiling panels—focuses on early Chinatown. Other sites offering a sense of the early neighborhood include the **Old Chinese Telephone Exchange** *(743 Washington St.)*, and **Chinese Six Companies** *(843 Stockton St.)*—which once informally "ran" the enclave. ■

Tin How Temple
✉ 125 Waverly Pl.

Chinese Historical Society Museum
www.chsa.org
✉ 965 Clay St.
☎ 415/391-1188
🕒 Closed Sun. & Mon.

Nob Hill

Nob Hill
Map p. 208

AS THE HIGHEST POINT IN THE CITY (338 FEET ABOVE SEA level), it is hardly surprising that Nob Hill has long been San Francisco's most visible indicator of wealth and status. Its name cribbed from the Hindu *nabob*, roughly meaning "big shot," the hill was the residence of choice for such late 19th-century figures as the business and railroad barons Leland Stanford, Charles Crocker, and Mark Hopkins. Men like these led lives of such ostentation as to provoke the Irish labor leader Denis Kearny to lead an angry mob of workers up the hill in protest in 1878. Only the earthquake and fire of 1906 put a (temporary) stop to the bacchanal. The great mansions were replaced—by luxury hotels, city clubs, churches for the wealthy, and parks for the few hoi polloi who made it up the hill for the views.

Doorman at the Mark Hopkins

Today the views are still free and still stunning. Most wealthy residences are now in other parts of the city, but Nob Hill stands as glorious as ever. Its three principal hotels—the **Mark Hopkins** *(1 Nob Hill, tel 415/392-3434),* built in 1926; the **Fairmont** *(950 Mason St., tel 415/772-5000),* saved from the earthquake wreckage by architect Stanford White in 1907; and the **Huntington** *(1075 California St. at Taylor St., tel 415/474-5400)*—all evoke the old era. The Mark and the Huntington warrant consideration by the traveler in search of a memorable San Francisco experience. Given the prices at the deluxe chain hotels, these gracious old piles offer sumptuous spas, unbeatable dining, and often good value.

A good way to take in the main attractions on Nob Hill is to put on some decent clothes and visit the hotel bars, cafés, and restaurants. At the Mark Hopkins, take the elevator up to the art deco-ish **Top of the Mark** *(tel 415/616-6916, www.topofthemark.com),* the hotel's grande dame of a watering spot. It is without peer as a place from which to view the entire cityscape, and has an outstanding wine and mixed drinks list. Sunset is the time to be here.

Across the street at the Fairmont, take in the spacious and ornate lobby, the oldest of the three. The hotel sits on the foundations of the mansion built by "Tessie" Fair Oelrichs in memory of her father, James G. "Bonanza Jim" Fair, an also-ran in the "robber baron" coterie alongside the Big Four: Crocker, Stanford, Hopkins, and Collis P. Huntington. An extensive renovation has restored the Fairmont's lobby, with its Florentine mirrors and gold leaf, as well as the Laurel Court, the Venetian Room, and the façade.

To cap a perfectly opulent day in this perfectly opulent terrain, the restaurant at the Huntington is hard to beat. Named the Big Four in reference to city plutocrats of old, it successfully conjures the best of the old days. Its crab cakes and rack of lamb, not to mention rabbit, quail, and champagne, are exactly what the Big Four would be eating today.

The recently renovated Redwood Room at the **Clift Hotel** *(495 Geary St., tel 415/775-4700, www.clifthotel.com),* boasts the Redwood Room, a moderne-style 1934 cocktail lounge wrought from the wood of a single redwood tree and recently given a overhaul with a mirrored bar, "digital art," and dim lighting—at once romantic and decadent. ■

Opposite: With its swank restaurants and elegant architecture, Nob Hill has been associated with la dolce vita for more than a century.

RAV4
3SRA544

Grace Cathedral

FOR AN UNDERSTANDING OF HOW MODERN SAN Francisco communes with the older, traditional San Francisco, pay a visit to Grace Cathedral, the grand architectural gem of Nob Hill *(California & Taylor Sts.)*. Here, where old-line Episcopalianism meets the globally minded ways of the urban affluent, you will find the focal point of a unique and modern religious culture, one laced with rich tradition, metaphor, and social relevance.

Detail from the "Doors of Paradise" cast, Grace Cathedral

Grace Cathedral
www.gracecathedral.org
Map p. 208
1100 California St. at Taylor St.
415/749-6300
Cable car all lines; bus 1

Officially established in 1853, Grace Cathedral had as its first bishop William Ingraham Kip, a Yale-trained historian. Although orthodox and East Coast urbane, Kip quickly saw a unique opportunity for Episcopalianism in the West. (He was not without a few initial doubts; the bawdy excesses of the gold rush period, he wrote, were "enough to convince one of the doctrine of total depravity.") Kip quickly took to his role as an evangelizing "frontier bishop," delighting in California's Roman Catholic past and Mediterranean climate. By embracing the state's past, aesthetically, oratorically, and socially, Kip believed that Episcopalianism could plant its rich apostolic traditions in an unfolding new world. His would be a Californian Episcopalianism, orthodox but open, its eye on the past yet, as scholar Kevin Starr has noted, "redeemed in futurity...and the aesthetic elaboration of the present." That this doctrine might produce the wide-open, progressive spirit now abundantly in evidence at Grace would likely startle Kip were he alive today. But he would likely come to embrace it. Everywhere here, the modern and the ancient combine in a spirit of mystical openness.

Some highlights of the church bear this out. The classic French Gothic architecture (based on Notre Dame in Paris) is fronted by bronze **entrance doors,** duplicates cast from the originals of Lorenzo Ghiberti's "Doors of Paradise" in the baptistry of the cathedral in Florence. Just inside the doors, to the right, is the **AIDS Interfaith Chapel,** with its altarpiece by the late graphic artist Keith Haring. There is also an AIDS quilt panel, the most universal memorial to victims of the disease.

Inside the cathedral proper, directly behind the **Meditation Labyrinth** (modeled on that of Chartres), is a beautifully wrought statue of St. Francis by the San Francisco artist Benjamin Bufano. An interesting way of linking the 1930s part of the building with the 1960s section can be seen by standing here and looking up and back, toward the entrance. Here you will see the **East Rose Window,** a copy of the "Canticle of the Sun," by Gabriel Loire of Chartres in France. The canticle was inspired by St. Francis's celebratory poem in praise of the Creator and Creation. Looking down at the floor of the nave, you will discover another iteration of that theme, this time on the form of the Chi Rho, a Greek monogram for Christ. Perhaps the ultimate expression of the Grace religious aesthetic, one uniquely Californian and progressive, can be found in the sanctuary. The **altar** is made of granite from the High Sierra and a piece of 2,000-year-old coastal redwood. The altar rail cushions are stitched with wildflowers of various Californian Episcopal dioceses.

Many outstanding original works of Renaissance art in the cathedral include the "Madonna and Child" plaque by Antonio Rossellino, just to the right of the choir stall.

The most memorable and moving works are probably the more recent ones in the **Chapel of Grace Baptistry,** to the left of the choir stall. Two icons done in 1990 by the painter Robert Lenz seem an appropriate coda to the Grace experience. The first, to your left, is of John Donne, the 17th-century mystic poet and preacher, Dean of St. Paul's Cathedral in London. The other is of Mary Magdalene holding in her hand an egg, the instrument by which she is said to have taught the Emperor Tiberius the story of the resurrection. This icon was dedicated in 1990 to Bishop Barbara Harris, the first woman bishop in the Episcopal Church.

A map and walk brochure is on sale in the lobby and gift shop, and afternoon tours are available. ■

The other cathedral

To the south, at Gough Street between Nob Hill and Pacific Heights, is the Cathedral of St. Mary's of the Assumption *(tel 415/567-2020, www.stmarycathedralsf.org).* Designed by MIT architect Pietro Belluschi, the cathedral, completed in 1970, is one of the most dramatic buildings in California. Covering two city blocks, it has a sweeping modern ceiling and outstanding interior sculptures by Mario Rudelli and Enrico Manfridi. The building's remarkable post-modernist shape—a cruciform cone on a square base—evokes the optimistic era of post-Vatican II American Catholicism. ■

Doing tai chi in the park in front of the cathedral

Lombard Street snakes down Russian Hill.

Telegraph & Russian Hills walk

Notable for stunning views of both the bay and the city, Telegraph Hill and Russian Hill hold a number of delights (particularly the singularly crooked **Lombard Street**) within reasonable walking distance.

Chief among the sights on this walk is **Coit Tower** ❶, a 284-foot fluted tower designed by architect Arthur Page Brown (architect of City Hall and the Swedenborgian Church among other buildings) and set at the top of Telegraph Hill. It was built with funds left to the city, after her death in 1929, by the eccentric philanthropist Lillian Coit. The tower is her memorial to the city's firefighters: An obsessive devotion to them was one aspect of Coit's eccentricity. She wore a diamond-studded fireman's badge everywhere she went, even to elegant balls.

Outside of the inevitable elevator ride to the top of the building where the views of the city and the bay are superb, the standouts here

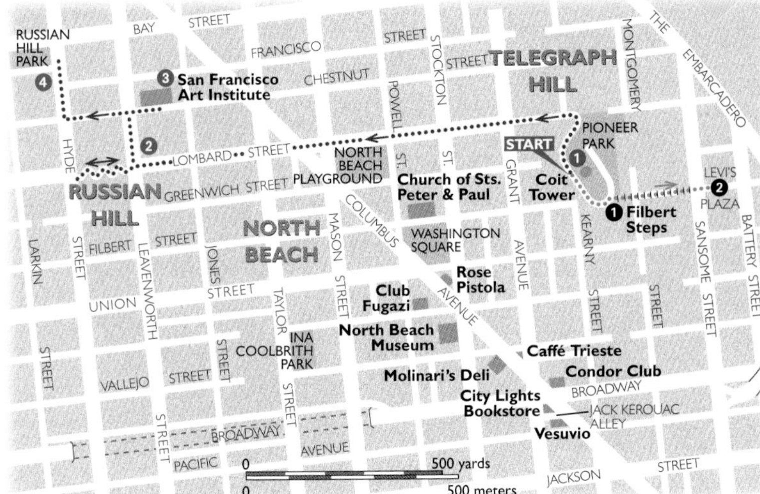

are the **WPA murals,** which line the inside walls. Although controversial in their time, they are nonetheless icons of the city's vaunted tolerance for the politically charged. Particularly arresting is the mural titled **"Banking and Law,"** created in 1933–34 by artist George Harris.

A multimillion-dollar renovation has brought new life to the already splendid Pioneer Park, surrounding the tower, with a series of new terraces and lookout points, making this an even more perfect place for a picnic (buy the makings of it at **Molinari's Deli** down on Columbus Avenue).

From this point, you have two main paths of discovery. The first is the more traditional; strolling down **Lombard Street ②,** across Columbus Avenue and uphill, still on Lombard, to Leavenworth Street. From here, Lombard Street twists and turns up what is called the "world's crookedest street."

A right turn on Leavenworth and again on Chestnut takes you to the **San Francisco Art Institute ③** (see p. 219). The prize here is Diego Rivera's "Making of a Mural" (1931), but the 1926 Spanish Colonial building and all its contents are worth a stop. From here walk along Chestnut to Hyde Street and turn right to **Russian Hill Park ④,** a wonderful place to rest, recoup, and gaze out on the bay.

An alternative walk from Coit Tower, and a splendid end to an afternoon on Telegraph Hill—or perhaps a good prelude to a day on the waterfront—is to go down the **Filbert Steps ❶,** just to the east of the tower. Beginning by a notable art moderne apartment building, the steps descend amid a series of terraced gardens, all of them flush with basketball-size hydrangeas, lush ivies, loquat trees, and magnolias. The steps end at **Levi's Plaza ❷.** Here you will find the headquarters of the legendary jeans manufacturer whose fame stretches from the gold rush to the global era.

"The Irish they live on th' top av it,
And th' Dagoes they live on th' base av it,
And th' goats and th' chicks and th' brickbats
and shticks
Is joombled all over th' face av it."
—Wallace Irwin, from *Telygraft Hill* ■

- Also see area map p. 191 G3
- Coit Tower
- 1.1 miles to Russian Hill Park
- 2 hours
- Russian Hill Park or Levi's Plaza

NOT TO BE MISSED

- Coit Tower
- Lombard Street
- San Francisco Art Institute
- Filbert Steps

Caffè Trieste sells coffee as well as serving it.

North Beach

FROM ITS MID-19TH-CENTURY DAYS AS A POINT OF DISEMbarkation for Italian and French immigrants to its 1950s flourishing as a Beat literary center, North Beach has long been the city's entertaining and unselfconscious theater of street life. With its bounty of hearty food, camp (if now somewhat tacky) sex shows, historic literary cafés, and outstanding boutique shopping, it has travelers returning to it again and again.

North Beach
191 G3

North Beach Museum
1435 Stockton St. in U.S. Bank
415/391-6210
Closed Sat. & Sun.
Bus 15, 30, 39, 45

San Francisco Art Institute
www.sfai.edu
800 Chestnut St.
415/771-7020
Cable car Powell-Hyde, Powell-Mason; bus 30

Bounded by Broadway to the south, Montgomery Street to the east, Lombard Street to the north, and Mason Street to the west, the North Beach quarter was defined by the Genoese Italians who settled here late in the 19th century and claimed it for their own after the 1906 earthquake and fire. Legend holds that when the flames threatened to engulf the district the Italians saved it by breaking open their wine barrels to soak blankets with which to protect their homes. Today the Italian presence is unmistakable in such establisments as **Enrico's** *(504 Broadway)* and **Tosca** *(242 Columbus Ave.)*. Another is **Caffè Trieste** *(601 Vallejo St.)*, where the Giotta Family performs operettas every Saturday.

More recent additions to the Genoese tradition include the number one restaurant draw for locals in the know: the Rose Pistola (see p. 368), which serves such northern delicacies as green Ligurian antipasti, snapper in *aqua pazzo,* and zabaglione cake.

The Italian community's place of worship is the 1922 Romanesque **Church of Saints Peter and Paul** *(666 Filbert St., tel 415/421-0809)*. Here, in 1957, local baseball hero Joe DiMaggio wed Marilyn Monroe. The twin spires of the church overlook **Washington Square,** whose daily parade of Chinese tai chi practitioners and old-style *paisanos* evoke a unique American ambience.

For a bigger draught of the past, visit the **North Beach Museum,** where an extensive photo collection documents the district's history. Recent work by local artists is found at the beautiful Spanish colonial **San Francisco Art Institute** (see p. 217), which also houses the **Diego Rivera Gallery.**

A pilgrimage point for bookish types is the **City Lights Bookstore** *(261 Columbus Ave., tel 415/362 8193)*, just below Broadway. Still owned by the 1950s Beat generation poet Lawrence Ferlinghetti (now somewhat of an "establishment" himself, as the city's former official poet laureate), the store stocks a wide selection of literary fiction and politically charged nonfiction. There is, of course, a deep shelf of Ferlinghetti's fellow poet Allen Ginsberg and the official martyr of the Beat movement, Jack Kerouac, whose *On the Road* fueled the wanderlust of '60s youth. Just across Jack Kerouac Alley is another Beat-era touchstone, **Vesuvio,** still a lively bar.

Clubs and bars line **Broadway;** a walk along the strip is essential, if only to see the **Condor** where, in 1964, when it was the Condor Club, the well-endowed Carol Doda stunned America by dancing topless. In **Club Fugazi** *(678 Green St., tel 415/421-4222, http://beachblanketbabylon.com)* the musical spoof *Beach Blanket Babylon* will tickle you with its outrageous satire and over-the-top hats.

The antique shops of North Beach are worth checking out for their Italo-Americana. Or wander a few blocks up to **Grant Avenue,** where you will discover some highly individualistic shops. Number 1529B was the workshop of Peter Macchiarini, a former WPA artist whose sculptures and jewelry still evoke the best of that period's folk modernism. Across the street, the items at **Aria** range from architectural remnants and figures of saints to antique games. ■

A cable moves under the streets, driven by a central powerhouse. The gripman on the car uses a vise-like mechanism (handle shown blue, above) to grip the cable, which then moves the car. To stop the car, he lets go of the cable grip and puts on the wheel brakes. An additional emergency brake can be used on the rails. ■

Cable Car Museum

The Cable Car Museum *(Mason St. at Washington St., tel 415/474-1887, www.cablecarmuseum.org)* is a small but exquisite collection of cable car artifacts and history. The city's machine-age (but still digital-era functioning) cable cars were originally constructed to solve a transportation problem: how to get people up a hill too steep for horses. San Francisco industrialist Andrew Hallidie came up with the idea of using cable traction to power public transport; the system was inaugurated on August 2, 1873—and hasn't stopped since.

Some of the old cable cars here date from as far back as the 1870s. It is worth going downstairs to see the "brains" of the system. The massive wheels carrying the cable that moves the cars along are beautiful in their early industrial age simplicity.

Present-day cable cars start at Powell and Market, and Powell and Van Ness and run from 6:30 a.m. to 1 a.m. daily *(tel 415/673-6864, www.sfmta.com)*. ■

Pacific Heights walk

During the years following the 1906 earthquake and subsequent fire, the epicenter of wealth and power in San Francisco shifted westward to the hills now known as Pacific Heights. Here, as one WPA writer put it, the rich "could dwell surrounded by gardens overlooking the Golden Gate." In grand style, modern San Franciscans carry on that tradition, everywhere evident during a pleasant morning's walk. Bounded by Union Street's quaint shops on its north side, Divisadero on the west, Geary Street to the south, and Van Ness to the east, Pacific Heights is architecturally eclectic, the result of spasmodic bursts of energy from the city's upper and middle classes.

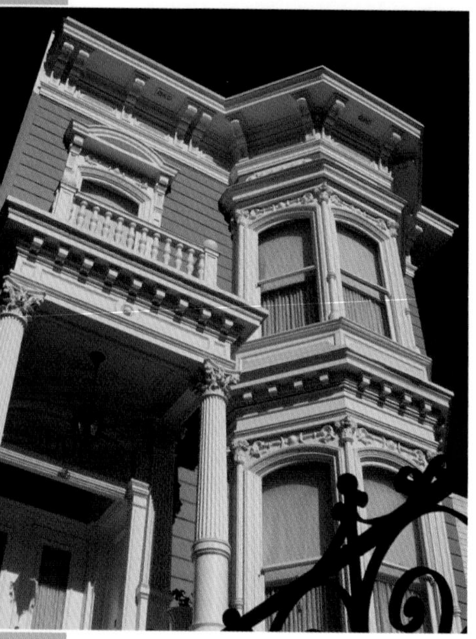

The Italianate facade of one of the handsome row house Victorians on Bush Street

There are some wonderful surprises on this walk and many highlights. (Please remember that nearly all the buildings are privately owned and not open to the public, so view them from the sidewalk.)

The French baroque **Spreckels Mansion 1,** just west of Gough Street at 2080 Washington, is a good starting point. The architect of the Palace of the Legion of Honor, George Applegarth, built the house in 1912 for the sugar magnate Adolph Spreckels. From here Spreckels's wife, Alma, the doyenne of early 20th-century San Francisco, ruled the social scene. Writer Danielle Steel now lives in the "Sugar Castle."

Walk west up Washington, passing the **Phelan House** (four houses up on the right), where Senator James D. Phelan entertained when the city was run by an oligopoly in the late 19th century. Now turn south through **Lafayette Park 2,** from the top of which you will enjoy some of the best views in town. On the southern side, pass the **Atherton House,** at Octavia and California. It is perhaps the most eclectic hodgepodge of Victorian styles anywhere. Proceeding east on California Street past Gough, you will see two outstanding examples of Victoriana. The **Wormser House 3,** at 1834 California Street, was built in 1877 by San Francisco merchant Isaac Wormser. It is interesting for its mix of styles: Queen Anne on the left side and the vertically exaggerated Stick style on the right. At 1818 California sits the **Sloss Home.** Built in 1876 by a fur trade millionaire, it is also in the Stick style, with Italianate lines on the side and cornice.

At 1701 Franklin (and California) is the **Edward Coleman House 4,** built in the Queen Anne style by a Utah mining millionaire in 1895. If you walk south down Franklin you can see the remarkable stained-glass enclosed stairway in the rear. A true historic gem is the former **Century Club,** located at Franklin and Sutter. Its architect was the renowned Julia Morgan, who also designed Hearst Castle and Berkeley's Claremont Hotel. The Spanish consulate now occupies the building.

Go west on Sutter to Gough Street and the **Hotel Majestic 5.** For a while in the 1960s, this 1905 Victorian gem was run as the notorious Brothel, a hotel for gay men. Closed by

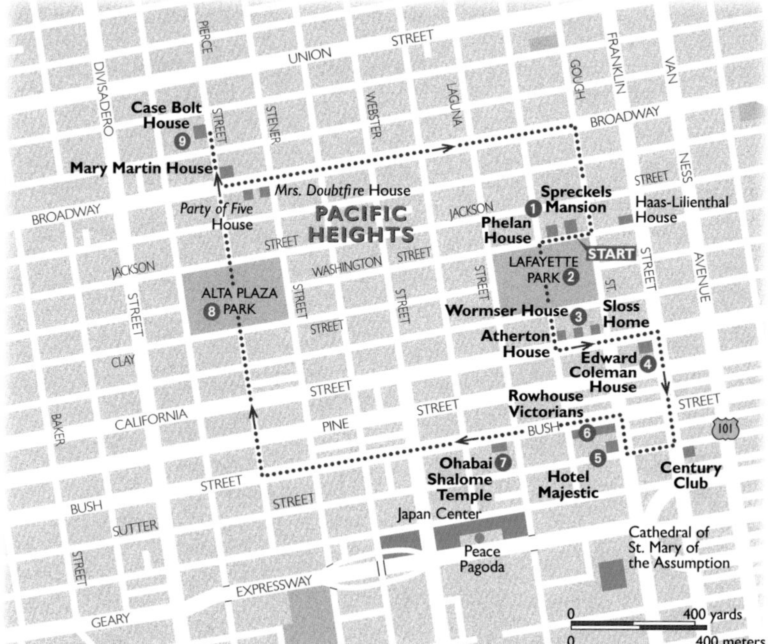

Mayor Dianne Feinstein (along with the bathhouses) during the early AIDS epidemic, it is now an excellent bed-and-breakfast hotel, known for its elegant Butterfly Bar.

Walk north on Gough Street and turn west on **Bush Street** ❻**.** More examples of the area's architectural heritage warrant note on Bush. Houses called **row house Victorians** can be seen here—middle-class houses of mixed styles, ranging (often in one house) from Queen Anne to Stick. The house at 1803 Bush is Italianate; next door is an example of a "smothered" Victorian, a description that refers to mid-20th-century "improving" of 19th-century houses with stucco and brick.

An architectural oddity is the **Ohabai Shalome Temple** ❼ ("Loves of Peace") synagogue near Bush and Laguna. Modeled on the Doge's Palace in Venice, it is redwood right down to its "stone carved" exterior.

Continue west on Bush Street and turn north on Pierce. You can enjoy another aspect of Pacific Heights as you walk northward on Pierce, through **Alta Plaza Park** ❽ with its stunning views, and on north to the junction with Broadway, into the wealthier section of town. Several houses on Broadway have famous associations. At Pierce and Broadway is the house that belonged to actress Mary Martin. The real pièce de résistance of the neighborhood is the **Case Bolt House** ❾ *(2727 Pierce St.)*, built by the hardware magnate in 1915. Appearing to be a kind of inflated Brooklyn brownstone, it is made completely of carved redwood. Its owners came from New York and wanted to feel at home. Return to Broadway. The Victorian at No. 2311 is where the hit TV show *Party of Five* was filmed, while the house at Broadway and Steiner Street was the location of the 1993 movie *Mrs. Doubtfire*. Go east as far as Gough Street and turn south to return to your starting point, the Spreckels Mansion. ■

Also see area map p. 191 G3
➤ Spreckels Mansion
3.2 miles
2 hours
➤ Spreckels Mansion

NOT TO BE MISSED

- Spreckels Mansion
- Century Club
- Row house Victorians

Around Pacific Heights

IF ONE END OF THE SAN FRANCISCO ARCHITECTURAL aesthetic is historicism—the attempt, whether through Victorian homes or a beaux arts civic center, to create a selective European past—the other end is naturalism or Bay Area regionalism.

Swedenborgian Church
www.sfswedenborgian.org
191 E3
Washington & Lyon Sts.
415/346-6466
Bus 3, 12, 22, 24

Haas-Lilienthal House
www.sfheritage.org
191 F3
2007 Franklin St.
415/441-3000
Tours Wed., Sat., Sun.
$$
Bus 1, 12, 19, 27, 47, 49

The prime example of the latter style is the **Swedenborgian Church.** This little structure was built in 1894 for followers of Emmanuel Swedenborg, an 18th-century Swede who preached "reverence for the divine in nature." Although a tiny commission by the day's gilded age standards, the project nonetheless attracted the leading craftsmen of the period. Among them were A.C. Schweinfurth and his boss Arthur Page Brown (who built City Hall), the artists Bruce Porter and William Keith, and the architect Joseph Worcester, who also happened to be pastor of the new church. Another strong influence was Bernard Maybeck, architect of the Palace of Fine Arts.

A stroll through the building and its grounds reveals a central theme: "The interpenetration of the spirit and nature, of the seen and unseen," as the historian Kevin Starr explains. Outside, the garden is planted with olive trees, cedar of Lebanon, elm, pine, plum, and crabapple, "an allegory of the worlds of the Bible, Europe, America, and the Far East." Two circular stained-glass windows by Porter lend a calm glow to the Shaker-simple seating below.

The most vital elements are the madrone tree ceiling supports, which were the young Maybeck's idea. Legend holds that these logs were selected from prime Santa Cruz stock, wrapped in burlap to prevent bruising, and toted by wagon during construction. They heighten the rustic-Zen quality of the church, making a visit here a prized moment for those interested in American architecture.

If you walk north from the Swedenborgian, there's a fine photo opportunity of the bay from the **Lyon Street Steps.** For those interested in Victoriana, it is worth visiting the classic 1866 **Haas-Lilienthal House,** a beautifully restored and furnished Queen Anne structure. Farther to the south, the **Japan Center** *(1730 Geary Blvd.)* is the historic heart of the area's Japanese-American community. This is the place to come for Japanese culture, food, art, and, perhaps most refreshing after a day of walking and shopping, a dunk in the old-style Japanese baths at the **Kabuki Springs & Spa** *(1750 Geary Blvd., tel 415/922-6000, www.kabukisprings.com).* A shiatsu massage and scrub is available by appointment. ■

The rustic entrance to the Swedenborgian Church

Around Fisherman's Wharf

Place of Fine Arts

SECOND ONLY TO CHINATOWN IN POPULARITY WITH tourists, Fisherman's Wharf anchors the waterfront, a triptych extending for five miles from the foot of Market Street westward to Crissy Field and the Golden Gate Bridge. There was a time when the urban shoreline was synonymous with a stroll-and-spend on the highly themed Pier 39. No more. Today, the city's shore can fill an entire day and fit a wide range of interests.

A good starting point for exploring is the historic **Ferry Building** *(Embarcadero at Market St., tel 415/693-0996)*. Opened in 1898 to serve the ferries connecting San Francisco to the East Bay, it entered a long period of desuetude after the opening of the Bay Bridge in 1937. Recently restored, it is now a magnificent marketplace, and the 240-foot-tall clock tower again serves as a welcoming beacon.

Joggers and historic trams run the length of **Embarcadero,** lined with piers used by cruise ships. Further west, **Pier 39** *(Beach St., www.pier39.com)* delights tourists with its shops, restaurants and amusements, including a carousel. Sea lions often laze on the boat docks. At **Aquarium of the Bay** *(tel 415/623-5300, $$$)* a moving

Ripley's Believe It Or Not! Museum
www.ripleysf.com
Jefferson St. 175
415/771-6188
$$

The Cannery
www.delmontesquare.com
2801 Leavenworth St.
415/771-3112

San Francisco Maritime National Historical Park
www.maritime.org
Hyde Street Pier, Hyde St.
415/561-7006
$$ to board historic ships
Cable car Powell-Hyde, Powell-Mason; bus 30, 41, 45; streets: F-line

Fort Mason
www.fortmason.org
Marina Blvd. & Laguna St.
415/441-3400

Mexican Museum
www.mexicanmuseum.org
Bldg. D, Fort Mason, Franklin St.
415/202-9700
Closed Sun.–Tues.
$

Museo Italo-Americano
www.museoitaloamericano.org
Bldg. C, Fort Mason, Franklin St.
415/673-2200
Closed Mon.–Tues.
$

walkway goes through a see-through tunnel while sharks and other sea creatures swim about you. Ferries run from here to Sausalito, Tiburon, Alcatraz and Angel Island (see p.228).

A stone's throw west, **Fisherman's Wharf** is named for the brightly painted fishing fleet that has berthed here since the late 19th century. The area is now mostly a jumble of kitcshy boutiques and tourist traps, but with some splendid restaurants, and the city's famous Dungeness crab is sold at streetside stalls hidden amid sibilant steam. Attractions include **Ripley's Believe It Or Not! Museum,** full of oddities from around the world; and **The Cannery,** a former peach cannery now housing shops, a jazz club, and eateries. All but claustrophobics should be sure to visit the **USS *Pampanito*** *(Pier 45, $$)*, a World War II submarine that can be toured.

The submarine is part of the **San Francisco Maritime National Historical Park.** The mainstay is the **Maritime Museum,** in a streamlined Art Deco building; it exhibits model ships and nautical miscellany that document San Franciso's maritime grandeur. The park's historic vessels include the 1886 *Balclutha* (of Cape Horner style); the 1895 *C.A. Thayer* (a lumber schooner); and the last of the city's paddle-wheeled steam-powered ferryboats, the 1890 *Eureka*. To the south, brick-terraced **Ghiradelli Square** *(www.ghirardellisq.com)*, a 19th-century chocolate factory, today comprises shops and fine restaurants.

The Maritime Museum abuts **Fort Mason** *(www.fortmason.org)*, a former Army barracks, and now a lively cultural center with three outstanding theatrical venues and several small museums. The most engaging are the the **Mexican**

Museum, the **Museo Italo-Americano,** and the **African-American Historical & Cultural Society.**

The **Marina,** with a green next to the seafront, is a fun place to stroll, roller-skate, or fly a kite. The esplanade leads to the **Palace of Fine Arts,** with tan-colored Corinthian columns reflecting in the lake off Lyon Street as a lone but grand reminder of the 1915 Panama-Pacific Exposition. It is well worth a visit, if only to get an idea of how early 20th-century San Franciscans viewed the city's future in the wake of the 1906 earthquake.

The palace's current tenant is the exciting **Exploratorium.** Founded by physicist Frank Oppenheimer in 1969, the Exploratorium utilizes every piece of technological wizardry imaginable to engage young minds in the sciences. Its 800 interactive exhibits, displays, and original artworks include a computer-simulated flight over the city, a distorting room that makes children look bigger than their parents, and even an antigravity mirror. A giant prism teaches the principles of light refraction, while visitors can learn about water dynamics by creating their own vortex in a 7-foot Plexiglas beaker.

The Exploratorium has become something of a media darling in recent years. The science writers at *Newsweek* have declared it an unmitigated smash hit, saying "There are two models for great American amusement centers—Disneyland and the Exploratorium. This place feeds the senses."

Still, it may not be for everybody. Vacationing adults without children should remember something that may not be obvious before entering the museum: This place is *loud.* ■

Fisherman's Wharf and the downtown skyline

African American Historical & Cultural Society

- ✉ Bldg. C, Fort Mason, Franklin St.
- ☎ 415/441-0640
- 🕒 Closed Mon.–Tues.
- $ $

Palace of Fine Arts & Exploratorium

www.exploratorium.edu

- Map 191 E4
- ✉ 3601 Lyon St.
- ☎ 415/561-0360
- 🕒 Closed Mon. except some holidays
- $ $$. Free 1st Wed. of month
- Bus 22, 28, 30, 41, 43, 45

Presidio

Presidio Visitor Center
www.nps.gov/prsf
✉ 50 Moraga Ave.
☎ 415/561-4323

FIRST ESTABLISHED BY THE SPANISH IN 1776, FOR 218 YEARS, the Presidio served as an army post commanding the Golden Gate straits. In 1994, the U.S. Army pulled out and the vast 1,500-acre greenswath was incorporated into the Golden Gate National Recreation Area. Thanks to the restoration of several historic gems and an intelligent conversion of former military installations, the park features well-preserved military installations, a museum, mile upon mile of looping roads, great stands of eucalyptus, plus hiking trails and picnic areas with stupendous views of the Golden Gate Bridge.

The Spanish originally built the Presidio to discourage the Russians; as usual, this was a sad tale for the Ohlone who had lived here for about 5,000 years. In 1822 the site fell under Mexican rule until the U.S. Army took control in 1846. During the next 148 years, the Army transformed the mostly empty windswept dunes and scrub to a verdant jewel-in-the-crown of military posts. The U.S. Army Corps of Engineers planted thousands of cypress and eycalpytuses. The result is a splendid urban forest enclosing sweeping lawns where military history topples over itself.

The logical starting point is the **Presidio Visitor Center,** in the former Officers Club, facing onto the original Spanish parade ground. This Spanish Mission-style building was erected around the original Spanish adobe fort, which can be seen. Nearby, the U.S. Army's oldest general hospital today houses the **Letterman Digital Arts Center** *(closed to the public)*, a division of LucasFilms.

On the bay shorefront, windsurfers launch from beach-lined **Crissy Field** *(Mason St.)*, where tidal marshes have been restored. Here, the **Farallones Marine Sanctuary Visitor Center** *(tel. 415/561-6622, closed Mon. & Tue.)* features hands-on exhibits about local marine life. On the park's south side, the public **Presidio Golf Course** *(300 Finley Rd., tel. 415/561-4653, www.presidiogolf.com)* enfolds **Mountain Lake,** popular with waterfowl and picnickers.

Lincoln Boulevard leads past a series of batteries pointing their cannons toward the Pacific and across the Golden Gate Straits. **Baker Beach** is a popular spot for strolling the sands and offers a stupendous view of the bridge. Before leaving, pay your respects at the **World War II Memorial** *(Lincoln Bvld. & Kobbe Ave)* and at the **San Francisco National Cemetery** *(Lincoln Blvd. & Crissy Field Ave.)*, where more than 15,000 American soldiers killed in battle slumber. ■

The Golden Gate Bridge appears beyond the Coastal Defense Battery.

Denizens of Seal Rock, near the Cliff House

California Palace of the Legion of Honor

THE WESTERNMOST PART OF SAN FRANCISCO, KNOWN AS Lands End, lies within the Golden Gate National Recreation Area. Enshrined in Lincoln Park, this craggy region boasts one of the city's premier art galleries in the neoclassical California Palace of the Legion of Honor—the 1924 gift of San Francisco social doyenne Alma Spreckels.

The stupendous museum, inspired by the Palais de la Légion d'Honneur in Paris, exhibits an extensive collection of old masters, including Rembrandt, Rubens, and Watteau; Impressionist paintings by Monet and Cézanne; works by Picasso and Matisse; and a vast collection of the works by Auguste Rodin, not least an original cast for "The Thinker." One particularly spectacular piece is the "Last Judgement Triptych," from about 1500 by an unknown Triptych master. The palace's exquisite collection of antiquities includes Egyptian, Grecian, and Roman pottery, sculpture, and metalwork. An entire 15th-century Spanish ceiling plus a superb grouping of furniture and decorative items that includes a vast horde of English and French 18th-century porcelain adds up to a collection not to be missed. And the more eclectic offerings include the Reva and David Logan Collection of Illustrated Books. Temporary exhibitions are also hosted, and the museum hosts a Sunday brunch with live music in the Legion Café.

To the southwest, at **Point Lobos,** the newly-renovated **Cliff House,** now a restaurant, overlooks the ocean and you can watch the sea lions and pelicans offshore on **Seal Rock.** Try to visit on Sunday when the restaurant hosts excellent champagne buffets with live harp music. Eastward, the coastal trail takes you to **China Beach,** ideal for picnicking. ■

Cliff House
www.cliffhouse.com
1090 Pt. Lobos Ave.
415/386-3330
Bus 18, 38

California Palace of the Legion of Honor
www.famsf.org/legion
Lincoln Park, near 34th Ave. & Clement St.
415/863-3330
Closed Mon.
$$ (free, 1st Tues. each month)
Bus 1, 18, 38

The islands

A TRIP TO ALCATRAZ HAS BECOME AN ESSENTIAL PART OF any first-time visit to San Francisco. The thrill in walking in the steps of Al Capone and "Machine Gun" Kelly is tempered by the melancholic nature of the world's most famous prison, but visitors agree that it is a uniquely memorable experience. Nearby Angel Island—the "Jewel of the Bay"—provides the freedom that Alcatraz once denied.

Alcatraz Island
www.nps.gov/alcatraz
231 B3
415/561-4900; Ferry bookings 415/981-7625
$$$$

Angel Island
www.parks.ca.gov
231 B4
415/435-1915; Ferry bookings 415/435-2131

Tiburon
231 B4
Visitor information
96B Main St.
415/435-5633

To flesh out a day on the bay, try one of the cruises offered by the **Blue & Gold Fleet** *(tel 415/705-7555, www.blueandgoldfleet.com; reservations recommended).* Boats depart several times a day from Pier 41 on Fisherman's Wharf.

On **Alcatraz** guides tell of escape attempts (all convicts who tried were shot, recaptured, or presumed drowned) and the various criminal personalities. Among these are Robert Stroud, the original "birdman of Alcatraz"; Al Capone, whose five-year stint in isolation left him mentally deranged for life; and the Anglin brothers, who escaped by chipping through the walls of their cells and most likely drowned. In 1887 it held the Indian rebel Kaetena (a friend of Geronimo), who that year had led a mutiny against the government in Arizona. **Alcatraz Cruises** *(tel 415/981-7625, www.alcatrazcruises.com)* offers various themed interpretive tours, including a night trip.

Alcatraz is the background for many a San Francisco sight, here the Hyde Street cable car.

Try to leave time for a walk along the **Agave Trail** through the island's bird sanctuary. Pelicans, for which Alcatraz was named, dominate, but different seasons bring dozens of other species.

Unlike Alcatraz, **Angel Island** remains a relatively untouristy destination. The largest island in the bay, at 1 square mile, it is known for the old **Immigration Station at China Cove,** where hundreds of thousands of Asian and Russian immigrants were "processed" around the turn of the 20th century. During World War II, it was a prisoner of war camp and, later, a missile base. The island also offers miles of outstanding hiking trails and an interesting Civil War camp and fort. A perimeter trail winds about the entire island; a trail near the marina in Ayala Cove takes you to the highest peak, 771 feet, for sweeping views. **The Angel Island Company** *(tel 415/897 0715, www.angelisland.com)* offers tram and Segway tours, plus bike rentals.

The Blue and Gold Fleet also run cruises to **Tiburon** (see p. 242), a quaint, small former railroad town across the bay, good for food and with an excellent bike path. *(Rent a bike when you depart from Pier 41.)* Another option is a cruise along the waterfront, passing such landmarks as the Palace of Fine Arts, Cliff House, and Golden Gate Bridge. ■

The Bay Area offers urbanites Muir Woods in Marin or the coast at Point Reyes. Berkeley, part funk, part professional, has a memorable street scene, Oakland a great museum, and Silicon Valley more than technological wonders.

Bay Area

Seal, Point Reyes

Bay Area

IF THE CHARMS OF SAN FRANCISCO SEEM TO RADIATE OUTWARD, ITS surrounding territories (though substantial in size and at some distance from it) at times seem wholly directed toward the city, as if it were the very reason for their being. That is far from true, but each area's principal attributes do figure heavily in the city's character.

From the east comes much of the region's political, artistic, and literary history. Oakland gave the world Jack London (whose Yukon cabin stands on the bayfront mall) and many of the great plein air painters (whose works hang in the Oakland Museum of California). The much lampooned neighboring city of Berkeley (columnist Herb Caen dubbed it "Berserkeley") still exports the revolutionary impulse, but today it is more likely to be culinary, as at Alice Waters' Chez Panisse restaurant, than political. Still, the university named for the 18th-century Irish philosopher Bishop Berkeley ("Westward lies the course of empire…") remains a great excursion in tolerance, learning, and intellectual inquiry.

From the rugged north—the Muir Redwoods and the Marin Headlands—comes much of the region's avid environmental ethos. There, between the mystical sea fogs and mists, visible from many points in the city, is nature preserved for all…and harvested for all. Travelers here find some of the best produce in the country: the famed oysters of Tomales Bay,

Gray Whale Cove, south of San Francisco, at sunset

found in luxury restaurants around the nation; the cheeses of Point Reyes Station; and the produce of the Marin Farmers' Market. Today's visitors to this whole remarkable area also find an outstanding travel infrastructure, and many small inns and bed-and-breakfasts featuring world-class cuisine, historical ambience, and comforts galore.

And the south? The land south of the city (best seen on the way to the Central Coast, or on a day trip) is still very much the great experiment. San Jose and its environs are the land of technology entrepreneurs, their fortunes, like their mini-mansions, quickly made. Here technology is king. San Jose's most recent sight is the Technology Museum of Innovation, and its most popular tours include that of the giant Intel Corporation, the world leader in semiconductor production.

By contrast, nearby Palo Alto has one of the world's greatest private colleges, Stanford University. Built with a 19th-century railroad fortune, its little university area is a more genteel version of Berkeley. ■

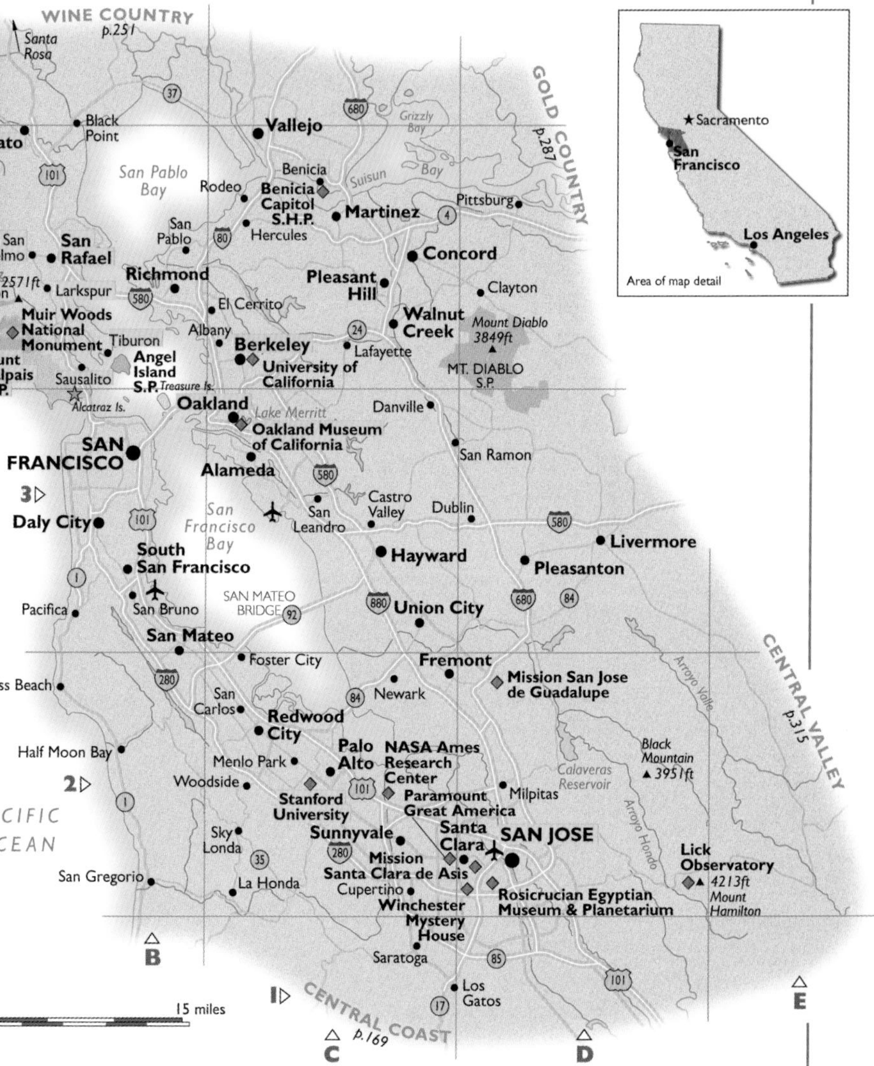

Oakland

OAKLAND HAS LONG LABORED UNDER GERTRUDE STEIN'S memorable, if misquoted, comment—that "there is no *there* there." However, it possesses more than its share of classic American qualities. Oakland's character derives from its history: In 1869 the city fathers accepted an offer from the Central Pacific to become the railroad's western terminus—something its snootier neighbor to the west had fought against with all the money and political might it could muster.

Oakland
231 C3
Visitor information
www.oaklandcvb.com
463 11st St.
510/839-9000

In one sense, Oakland's genius was to turn San Francisco's throwaways into one of the West Coast's most dynamic industrial cities, a distinction it held until well after World War II. If a steel mill, a chemical plant, or a new shipyard was too dirty for the swells across the bay, Oakland would have it. Even today the city's broad harbors and numerous light industrial areas thrum with commerce, though much has been lost to Seattle and Los Angeles in recent years. Under recent mayor, former California Governor Edmund G. "Jerry" Brown, Oakland began to surge forward again. A good notion of the

Heinhold's First and Last Chance Saloon made famous by Jack London

Jack London: Call of the Wild

Not only did Jack London master the adventure novel, his style carried over into other genres. His later reporting of sporting events is also characterized by his trademark inclinations toward the working class, as demonstrated in this excerpt from *The Night Born* (1913):

"To his ears came a great roar, as of the sea, and he saw Danny Ward, leading his retinue of trainers and seconds, coming down the center aisle. Everybody proclaimed him. Everybody was for him. Even Rivera's own seconds warmed to something akin to cheerfulness when Danny ducked jauntily through the ropes and entered the ring. His face continually spread to an unending succession of smiles, and when Danny smiled he smiled in every feature, even to the laughter wrinkles of the corner of the eyes and into the depths of the eyes themselves. Never was there so genial a fighter. His face was a running advertisement of good feeling, of good fellowship. He joked, and laughed, and greeted his friends through the ropes. Those farther away cried 'Oh, you Danny!' It was a joyous ovation of affection that lasted a full five minutes." ■

new Oakland can be found inside the old Oakland, particularly on Friday mornings at the **Oakland Farmers' Market** *(tel 510/745-7100)*. This is an electric scene, vibrant with entrepreneurship of Latinos, Asians, and African Americans. A typical lineup might include an Armenian olive-oil maker from Modesto, a seller of sweet-potato pies and other African-American pastries, a Hmong tribeswoman in bright red selling fresh ginger and lemongrass, and a Vietnamese youngster hawking slippery shrimps and gleaming snapper.

A more historical slice of Oakland can be seen at **Jack London Square** *(tel 510/814-6000, www.jacklondonsquare.com)*, located on the waterfront Embarcadero south of Broadway. Few modern literary figures have been quite so intertwined with a city as was London. Born in 1876 and raised in Oakland, he found fame as a kind of working-class adventure novelist (*The Call of the Wild* and *White Fang*). Jack London's **Yukon Cabin,** from his days in the Klondike gold rush, has been relocated to the square, and you can also visit the oft-mentioned **Heinhold's First and Last Chance Saloon** *(56 Jack London Sq., tel 510/839-6791)*, still a bar. Its floor slants in an unnerving way. The square hosts free concerts, and a weekend farmers' market. Nearby, the **USS *Potomac*** *(tel 510/839-8256)*, Franklin D. Roosevelt's "Floating White House," welcomes visitors at **FDR Pier.**

Lake Merritt, in the city's heart, is a relaxed destination for weekenders. Its pathways frame **Lakeside Park** *(tel 510/238-7275)*, on its north shore, where a wildlife sanctuary draws wild geese and other waterfowl. Here boats can be rented, and Gondola Servicio *(tel 510/663-6603, www.gondolaservizio.com)* will punt you around the lake.

The thickly forested Oakland Hills are studded with giant redwoods, including within the 500-acre **Joaquin Miller Park** *(tel 510/531-9597)*, with hiking trails, equestrian areas, and an amphitheater hosting summertime concerts. ■

Oakland Museum of California

Oakland Museum of California
www.museumca.org
1000 Oak St.
510/238-2200 or 888/625-6873
Closed Mon.–Tues.
$$

IN 1969 THE CITIZENS OF OAKLAND COMBINED THE collections of three older institutions to form the Oakland Museum of California. In so doing, they created one of the finest regional museums in the country. Lodged in a sprawling but spare modern complex, dotted with verdant gardens and placid ponds, the museum brilliantly grounds its patrons in the ecology, history, and art of the state. Its atmosphere is relaxed, and the museum staff is helpful and knowledgeable.

Allocate most of your time to an exploration of the third floor, the **Gallery of California Art.** Although the museum owns more than 80,000 works of this provenance, only about 500 are on display at any time. Divided chronologically and by medium, the gallery lays special emphasis on painting and the decorative arts. The collection hints at the scale and achievement of California's artistic community, who in fewer than 200 years have confronted colonialism, industrialization, the enclosure of the wild, the persistence of Native America, and the emergence of the world's first "permanent" frontier.

Exhibits in the Cowell Hall of California History

Many of these themes are readily identifiable in such spotlighted works as Domenico Tojetti's "Progress of America," an 1875 allegory done in an Italian neoclassic style; Thomas Hill's "El Capitan," an 1866 work with strong leanings toward the impressionist style of later years; the brilliant early tonalism of George Inness's "California, 1894"; the early plein air works of J.H.E. Partington and his 1890 "Lake Temescal." One particularly memorable section is dedicated to the Society of Six, a 1920s group of Oakland-based painters who used a style of bold, simple brush strokes. Aiming to communicate a "joy of vision" via the arrangement of abstract elements, such artists as William H. Clapp (see his "Nepenthe Beach") and Maurice Logan ("Point Richmond") reveled in the primary sky and soil colors of the state. The great Millard Sheets explored the more human dimensions of this aesthetic in paintings such as "Pocket in the Chino Hills" (1931).

One of the great joys of the Oakland is its inclusion of many less celebrated artists from the state's past, many of whom are only now growing in stature and collectability. One of these is Rinaldo Cuneo, whose transfixing "Earth Patterns" (1932) will forever change the way you look at the furrowed landscape of California agriculture. Other delights lie in the

The Cowell Hall of California History

museum's collection of decorative and ceramic arts, a fine example of which is "Teapot" (1941), done by Sargeant Johnson in the famed Magnini Workshop.

Of particular interest to photography enthusiasts is the museum's extensive holding of photos by Dorothea Lange; her 1936 "Migrant Mother"—the closest thing in American art to a Madonna figure—holds a special fascination for those interested in the artistic response to the Great Depression of the 1930s. The gallery is topped off with a significant collection of California moderns, from Richard Diebenkorn and Wayne Theibaud to the lesser known but memorable work of David Park ("Women in a Landscape," 1958) and M. Louise Stanley's "The Functional Family (After Velazquez)," 1993.

Down one level is the **Cowell Hall of California History,** which presents a detailed chronology of the state. To do this, the Cowell employs an abundance of artifacts, including actual covered wagons, gold-mining equipment, and some of the earliest correspondence between pioneers and their "folks back home." Some of the daguerreotypes are particularly entertaining, as in Gabriel Harrison's 1848 "California News," depicting the enthusiastic response of Eastern newspaper readers to the discovery of gold at Sutter's Creek. Early examples of mythmaking also shine, as in the museum's collection of souvenir lettersheets used by illiterate miners to send home "the good news"—even when it was bad.

Down one more level is the **Natural Sciences Gallery,** an extensive (38,000 square feet) display of elemental California, from flora and fauna to lava beds and the Great Basin. The gallery is arranged to simulate a walk across the state's many habitats, with special emphasis on botany and geology and their interplay with water, air, and fire. Try to make time to visit the **Aquatic California Gallery** for an outstanding insight into the state's great variety of marine and freshwater wildlife. ■

Berkeley

ALTHOUGH IT TRACES ITS ROOTS TO THE BREAKUP OF one of California's most powerful 19th-century ranchos, the town of Berkeley did not emerge from the shadow of San Francisco until the early 20th century, when two events helped forge the grand university town that is here today. The first was the 1906 earthquake, which sent many San Francisco folk in search of new homes and lives. These the tiny community across the bay easily provided. The second was the philanthropy of Phoebe Apperson Hearst, mother of William Randolph Hearst. It was Hearst's money that transformed Berkeley, a small college started by Christian clergymen from the East, into one of the nation's preeminent educational institutions.

Berkeley
230 C4
Visitor information
www.berkeleycvb.com
2015 Center St.
510/549-7040

Berkeley Art Museum
www.bampfa.berkeley.edu
2626 Bancroft Way
510/642-0808
Closed Mon.–Tues.
$$

University Botanical Garden
http://botanicalgarden.berkeley.edu
Centennial Dr., off Stadium Rimway
510/643-2755
$

Lawrence Hall of Science
www.lawrencehallofscience.org
Centennial Dr., off Stadium Rimway
510/642-5132
$$$

It was also Hearst money that made the University of California at Berkeley such a fine architectural gem, bringing in such masters as John Galen Howard, Julia Morgan, and Bernard Maybeck to design its key buildings. Of the three it was Howard, with his inclinations toward the Frankish and the monumental, who left the strongest imprint.

A walk through the campus, starting perhaps at the Telegraph Avenue entrance, takes one past **Sproul Hall** and the **Sather Gate,** site of many 1960s free-speech demonstrations. To the north is the principal landmark, Sather Tower, also known as the **Campanile.** Built by Howard in 1914, it is said to have been modeled on the tower of the Piazza San Marco in Venice. Farther north sits the regal **Hearst Mining Building,** built by Howard in 1907. To the east of it is the **Hearst Greek Theater** where, in 1903, Theodore Roosevelt delivered the commencement address. To the west is the **Life Sciences Building,** a massive concrete edifice with lovely external ornamentation in the shape of fishes, reptiles, and mammals. For a relaxing coda, many visitors stroll to the **Faculty Glade,** between Stephen's Union and the **Men's Faculty Club** (itself of Maybeckian inspiration); the glade is flush with oaks and cedars and restful patches of green—just the thing for a picnic and a nap.

Three university museums are also worth seeing. The **Berkeley Art Museum** was established in 1963 by the abstract expressionist painter Hans Hoffman and later housed in this engaging and even playful fan-shaped building. There are the requisite Cézannes and Monets expected of any modern museum, but the Berkeley's unique strength lies in the core collection of Hoffman's own works, 45 of which he donated to the university. See them in Gallery A.

The **University Botanical Garden** showcases another of the university's areas of expertise, with more than 13,000 botanical specimens. The 33-acre site contains a huge variety of exotic species, acquired since the university first began collecting them in 1890. If you plan to visit the Mendocino Coast later, be sure to see the **pygmy forest** to get a scholarly view of the phenomenon so prevalent at Van Damme State Park (see p. 270). For a shot of astronomy, go to the **Lawrence Hall of Science,** where the brains behind some of today's top research put together planetarium shows. The museum and its workshops make science accessible and fun. Its hilltop perch offers spectacular vistas across the Bay as far afield as the Farallon Islands—30 miles out to sea.

The **Hearst Museum of Anthropology** holds the keys to one of the great anthropological puzzles of modern times: How did a lone man named Ishi, the last known representative of the Stone Age Yahi people, come to be discovered in the Central Valley town of Oroville in 1911? A permanent exhibition of his work with UC scholars is on view, along with artifacts from ancient Egypt and Peru. Do not miss this gem.

For those not inclined to meander among the bookstores and cafés of Telegraph Avenue, **Tilden Park** *(N of the university, tel 510/562-7275)* is a tonic. The park's gardens emphasize Californian native plants. Romantics (and their kids) can't get enough of the old carousel and steam trains *(Closed Mon.–Fri. in winter).* ■

Hearst Museum of Anthropology
http://hearstmuseum.berkeley.edu
103 Kroeber Hall, Bancroft Way & College Ave.
510/642-3682
Closed Mon.–Tues.
Bus 7, 40, 51, 52, 64

Students at Sather Gate, UC Berkeley

California cuisine

"All I cared about was a place to sit down with my friends and enjoy good food while discussing the politics of the day. And I believed that in order to experience food as good as I'd had in France, I had to cook it myself." So explains Alice Waters, founder of Berkeley's famed Chez Panisse restaurant, of the inspiration that launched her now famous culinary career.

Anyone who follows food knows that Alice Waters not only far exceeded her own modest goals, some 30 years after the creation of Chez Panisse *(1517 Shattuck Ave.; tel 510/548-5525, restaurant, or -5049, café, www.chezpanisse.com)* she is widely credited for the popularity of California cuisine.

The hallmarks of Waters's cuisine are classic French technique (albeit with a lighter hand with fats) combined with the freshest local, seasonal ingredients obtainable. A sample spring menu might include wild mushrooms on croutons, thin pasta with spring vegetables, charcoal-grilled salmon with grilled red onions, and buckwheat crêpes with tangerines, glacé fruit butter, and eau-de-vie. A summer menu offers yellow squash and blossom soup, grilled whole filet of beef with deep-fried onion rings, and honey ice cream with lavender. Fall offers smoked trout mousse with chervil butter and Champagne sauerkraut. Winter? Try oysters on the half-shell with Champagne sausages and mignonette sauce.

Waters has also deeply influenced the way we think about food, particularly restaurant food. To this day she has kept the European tradition of a single, five-course, prix-fixe menu (a preference shared now by many California chefs, including Thomas Keller at

Alice Waters has always stressed the importance of using fresh ingredients.

Napa's French Laundry). "When people come to the restaurant, I want to insist that they eat in a certain way, try new things, and take time with the food," she writes. "For me food is a totally painless way of awakening people and sharpening their senses. I opened a restaurant so that everybody could come and eat."

You will need to make a reservation if you want to eat at Chez Panisse. Choose between the restaurant itself and the less pricey café upstairs.

Two other brilliant eateries in Berkeley are worth the time and the often inevitable wait. Café Rouge *(1782 4th St., tel 510/525-1440, www.caferouge.net)* offers some of the best bistro meals in the area. Try the steak, the salmon, or even the hamburger. At Bette's Oceanview Diner *(1807 4th St., tel 510/644-3230, closed dinner)*, locals line up for outstanding down-home breakfasts. Afterward, stroll the outstanding Fourth Street Shopping District for some of the city's best gardening, cooking, and design boutiques. ■

Above: Tuna peppersteak with leek coulis at Domaine Chandon restaurant
Below: The kitchen at Chez Panisse

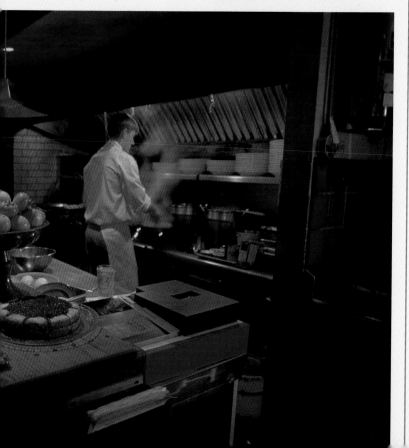

Around Berkeley

NOT SURPRISINGLY, THE HILLS AND GLENS OF BERKELEY hold several one-of-a-kind architectural gems. This is partly due to the free-thinking, creative atmosphere that has long characterized the town's academic community. Another factor is money: This was a wealthy community with the resources to commission some of the top architects of the day. For example, when Phoebe Apperson Hearst underwrote the University of California at Berkeley's early 20th-century expansion, she also made Berkeley into a stage for the era's leading architects. Competition, ego, and inspiration fueled their architectural brilliance.

Julia Morgan's "late medieval" Berkeley City Club

Two examples can be found at the corner of Dwight and Bowditch Ways. If some modern-day architects regard San Francisco's Swedenborgian Church (see p. 222) as the primal altar of the native Arts and Crafts movement, many others revere Berkeley's **First Church of Christ Scientist** *(2619 Dwight Way)*. Built by visionary Bernard Maybeck, who also had a hand in the Swedenborgian, this 1910 structure shows the style in full eclectic, experimental swing. With its great gilded cruciform truss and Romanesque columns of exposed concrete, the church illustrates two of Maybeck's ongoing aesthetic concerns, according to the historian Jefferey W. Limerick: the "love of grandeur, mood and atmosphere" and the "concern for craftsmanship and the rustic."

Opposite is the **Berkeley Baptist Divinity School,** built in 1918–19 by Julia Morgan of Hearst Castle fame. With its slate roof, bay, and turret, the school represents one of the earliest American attempts at an English institutional style (the school's building committee originally requested "not a copy of the Oxford Hall Tower but…that [type of] Tutor Gothic").

Another example of Julia Morgan's work can be found at the **Berkeley City Club** *(2315 Durant Ave.)*, originally the Berkeley Women's City Club. Built in 1929 in what she called the "late medieval style," the club included a 25-by-75-foot pool. As historian Sara Holmes Boutelle writes, "Every aspect of pool life was considered and planned for: changing, swimming, watching, sunning. Morgan's dressing rooms shine in comparison with most of the mildewed dungeons set aside for this purpose."

Hardly of equal caliber, but monumental nonetheless, is the **Claremont Resort Hotel** *(Ashby & Domingo Aves., tel 510/ 843-3000, www.claremontresort.com)*. A giant white castle set against verdant hills, it offers remarkable bay views and boasts a spa and tennis courts. Its fine restaurant, Jordan's, is a worthy dining place, and its Paragon martini bar combines contemporary chic with live jazz. ■

Benicia

Old State Capitol, Benicia

SITUATED NORTHEAST OF SAN FRANCISCO, EAST OF THE entry to the scenic Carquinez Strait, is Benicia—calm, with crisp sea air, a significant history, and abundant small-town delights.

The **Benicia Capitol State Historic Park** *(115 West G St., tel 707/745-3385, www.parks.ca.gov)* is a perfectly preserved piece of California history. Originally built to be City Hall, it housed the state legislature from February 1853 through February 1854, when Sacramento took over. The first Women's Suffrage Act, permitting women to own property under their own names, was passed here. One of the legislators was Mariano Vallejo, who had originally sold the land to the town founders on the condition that it be named for his wife, Francesca; the city fathers later settled on her middle name, Benicia, to avoid conflicts with their growing bay neighbor.

The shops in the **1st Street Antiques District,** stretching from F to C Streets, offer a wide variety of Americana. For military buffs, the **Benicia Historical Museum** displays artifacts from the history of Benicia and the U.S. Army Arsenal. The camels were originally brought to the West to transport troops over desert terrain. ■

Benicia
231 C4
Visitor information
www.beniciachamber.com
601 1st St.
707/745-2120

Benicia Historical Museum
www.beniciahistoricalmuseum.org
2060 Camel Rd.
707/745-5435
Closed a.m. & Mon.–Tues.
$

The lost romance of old California

In Benicia's St. Dominic's Cemetery is a gravestone to Sister Mary Dominica Arguello. This is her story.

Maria Concepcion Arguello, daughter of the military commandante in San Francisco, fell in love with a visiting Russian, Count Nicolai de Rezanov. Her father opposed the union, but Maria won a compromise: If the count went to Rome and received the permission of the Holy Father, then they could wed. The count hurried off, and while crossing Siberia he died of malnutrition and malaria. For ten years Maria pined away, unsure of Rezanov's fate. Finally, in 1816, his death was confirmed. Maria became a nun and died in 1857, "the first native daughter," as her headstone reads, "to receive the Dominican habit in California." ■

Marin Headlands to Mount Tamalpais

Mysterious fogs, lush redwood forests, and dramatic rocky shorelines make the Marin Headlands a popular yet unspoiled destination. That rare combination—the result of a century of environmental activism by Bay Area citizens—yields a seemingly endless parade of spectacular and accessible treats.

Arriving on the Marin Headlands via the Golden Gate Bridge on US 101, go west on Bunker Road to the **Marin Headlands Information Center** ❶ for the **Golden Gate National Recreation Area** *(tel 415/561-4700,* see p.193*)*. Nearby are the starting points for a number of hikes along the **Miwok Trail,** which cut through the landscape of that lost Indian tribe. You can also access some other trails by driving north on US 101 to Tennessee Valley Road. This road will take you to the park's horse stables *(tel 415/383-8048),* a chance to see the area from the perspective of its early European settlers.

Bird-watchers may like to detour via the Redwood Highway south to sleepy **Tiburon** *(Visitor information, 96B Main St., tel 415/435-5633),* an attractive little town noted for the converted houseboats now pulled onto land and used as shops and restaurants. The **Richardson Bay Audubon Center & Sanctuary** *(376 Greenwood Beach Rd., Tiburon, tel 415/388-2524, www.tiburonaudubon.org)* has self-guided nature trails and wetlands full of waterfowl.

Proceeding north again on US 101, take Calif. 1, the dramatic **Shoreline Highway,** west past the famed **Green Gulch Farm Zen Center** *(1601 Shoreline Hwy., tel 415/383-3134, www.sfzc.org/ggf)*. This provides vegetables and inspiration for some of the world's most sophisticated restaurateurs. Courses, Sunday lectures, and retreats are all available. (With advance planning you can arrange overnight stays.)

Farther along Calif. 1, at the **Muir Beach Overlook** ❷ *(tel 415/388-2596),* get your first view of the shore and, in late January to March, possibly of migrating California gray whales. Now drive north to **Stinson Beach** ❸ *(tel 415/868-0942),* popular with surfers and swimmers during the summer months.

Bird-watchers should visit the **Audubon Canyon Ranch** *(tel 415/868-9244),* a breeding site for Great Egrets and Great Blue Herons; and the **Point Reyes Bird Observatory** ❹ *(tel 415/868-0655),* overlooking a restored marshland.

Inland from Stinson Beach stretches **Mount Tamalpais State Park** ❺ *(tel 415/388-2070)*. Mount Tam, as bay folk call it, is a 2,571-foot peak riven by redwood canyons, chaparral-covered ridges, and an abundance of wildlife, from the red-tailed hawk to the black-tailed deer. You can drive to the East Peak of Mount Tam's double peak via the Panoramic Highway, which goes east from Calif. 1 a mile south of Stinson Beach and

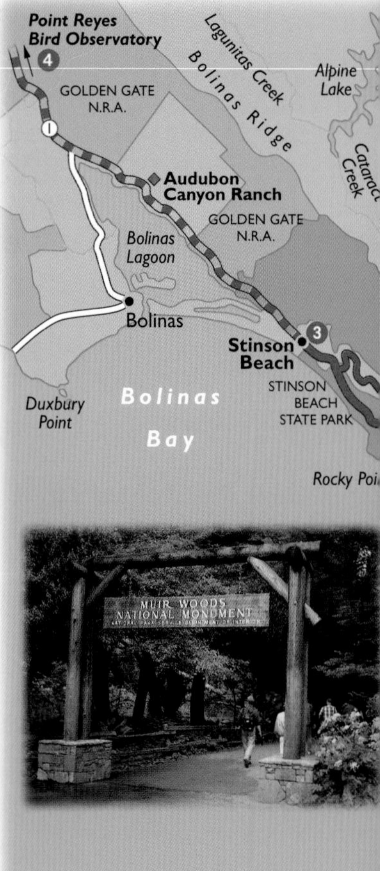

Ridgecrest Boulevard. The **Pantoll Easy Grade Trail,** 2 miles long and aptly named, is perfect for an afternoon hike. Or take to the trails on a mountain bike; locals claim they invented the sport.

Many travelers short of time simply drive past Mount Tam on the Panoramic Highway to the star of the redwoods, the **Muir Woods National Monument** 6 *(tel 415/388-2595, www.nps.gov/muwo)* off the highway on Muir Woods Road. A nature trail takes you through the redwood forest—from the salmon and steelhead trout of the Redwood Creek to the ferns, huckleberries, and violets of the forest floor.

From Muir Woods take the Panoramic Highway to US 101 and back to San Francisco, perhaps making a detour to the quaint waterside town of **Sausalito** 7 *(Visitor information, 780 Bridgeway Ave., tel 415/332-0505, www.sausalito.org).* Don't miss the views across the bay from the steep streets. A unique attraction is the **Bay Model Visitor Center** *(2100 Bridgeway Ave., tel 415/332-3871, www.spn.usace.army.mil/bmvc),* a detailed 1.5-acre hydraulic model of San Francisco Bay complete with tides and currents. ■

Also see area map p. 231 B3
Golden Gate Bridge
42 miles
2 hours
Golden Gate Bridge

NOT TO BE MISSED

- Muir Beach Overlook
- Mount Tamalpais
- Muir Woods NM

Point Reyes

Point Reyes
230 A4
Visitor information
www.nps.gov/pore
Bear Valley Visitor Center, Bear Valley Rd. (off Calif. 1 at Olema)
415/464-5100

Point Reyes Lighthouse
Sir Francis Drake Blvd.
415/669-1534
Closed Tues.–Wed.

AT THE CORE OF THE 75,000-ACRE POINT REYES NATIONAL Seashore is a world-class geological puzzle: How is it that the rocks of this dramatic shore match up with the Tehachapi Mountains, some 300 miles to the south? The answer is that Point Reyes lies on the eastern edge of the Pacific plate, which creeps northwestward past the North American plate at about two inches a year. Multiply that by millions of years and no wonder the Tehachapis were left so far behind. But don't just take the scientists' word for it. At the Bear Valley Visitor Center, visitors to the scenic area can stand on the very spot where, during the 1906 San Francisco earthquake, the peninsula literally leaped 20 feet to the northwest. It is perhaps the most dramatic place in California to view the San Andreas Fault, which has so molded the state's ancient and recent history.

Ruler-straight Tomales Bay runs along the fault line; **Tomales Bay State Park** *(tel 415/669-1140, www.parks.ca.gov)* protects wetlands and surf-free beaches good for picnics. Geology is not the only drawing card here. Full of natural and historic wonders, the point was discovered in 1579 by the English explorer Sir Francis Drake. It was later claimed for the English crown, unbeknown to the Miwok Indians who had helped Drake resupply his ship, the *Golden Hind*.

At the northern end of Point Reyes is the historic **Pierce Point Ranch.** Founded in 1858, it is perhaps the oldest dairy farm in California; the state now manages the original structures and maintains a self-guided trail. Not far away is the **Tule Elk Reserve** where, after a century of near-extinction, this magnificent mammal is staging a comeback. To the south lies **Abbotts Lagoon,** where bird-watchers may paddle canoes to see the annual waterfowl migration. Here the flocks of various rare migratory birds—snowy plover, tricolored blackbirds, and several kinds of raptor—stage a particularly intense display in the fall.

To catch the grand sweep of Drake Bay itself, make the pilgrimage to the **Point Reyes Lighthouse.** The original tower, with a 3-ton lens ground in France, was constructed in 1870 to prevent ships from running aground in the area's notorious fogs. Despite its 24-mile visibility the lighthouse has not prevented several crashes, including at least one involving an airplane. The estuary called **Drakes Estero** *(Pierce Point Rd., canoe rentals tel 415/669-2600 or 415/663-1743),* where the explorer is said to have repaired his ship, is woven with hiking trails; some pass by oyster beds. Bring binoculars in the winter months to scan the horizon for migrating gray whales.

Point Reyes has in recent years become a center of what might be called the "farm-fresh food" movement. In 1994 **Tomales Bay Foods** *(tel 415/663-9335)* started to market locally produced vegetables and cheeses, which can be purchased along with take-away picnic items. A key to its success is access to one of the state's oldest organic dairies, the **Strauss Family Dairy.** Also near Point Reyes, in Point Reyes Station, is **Bovine Bakery** *(tel 415/663-9420),* where you can buy great desserts and breads. Ask local retailers for the best places to buy the noted Hog Island oysters. ■

POINT REYES PICNICS

Michael Bauer, food editor of the *San Francisco Chronicle,* has recommended four picnic spots less than 30 minutes' drive from Point Reyes Station: **Chimney Rock,** on the road to Point Reyes Lighthouse; **Heart's Desire Beach,** located in Tomales Bay State Park; **Drakes Beach,** southwest of Inverness along Sir Francis Drake Boulevard; and **Samuel P. Taylor State Park,** near Olema, with picnic tables under a redwood canopy. ■

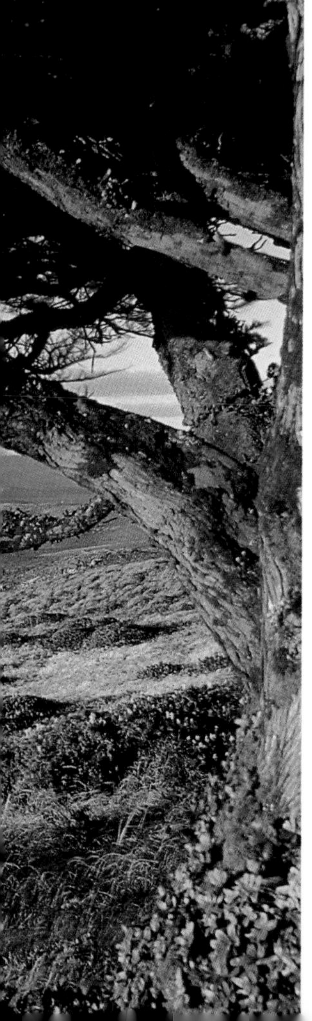

Point Reyes shoreline

Houseboats moored at Sausalito, a popular town in Marin County

Urban Marin County & around

THE HIPPY-TURNED-YUPPY TOWNSFOLK OF MARIN HAVE, over the past few decades, earned for themselves a reputation for being trendy, health-conscious, self-involved, and politically correct. The resulting various farmers' markets, boutiques, New Age galleries, and healing centers all make for pleasant and stimulating outings (whether or not you share the philosophy behind them). Many of the region's towns have outstanding historical and architectural sites too. And Marinites always eat well.

San Rafael
www.sanrafaelchamber.com
231 B4
817 Mission Ave.
415/454-4163

Marin County Visitor information
www.visitmarin.org
Larkspur Landing Circle, Larkspur
415/925-2060

SAN RAFAEL

The site of California's 20th mission, **Mission San Rafael** *(5th & Court Sts., tel 415/454-8141, www.saintraphael.com)* was established in 1817, when the Spanish Lt. Gabriel Moraga convinced the padres at Mission San Francisco to allow their more sickly neophytes to move to San Rafael's warmer and drier climate. The sickly neophytes recuperated, and San Franciscans have ever since sought relief from their winters (and summers) in this gem of a town. Try to visit one of the various weekly **farmers' markets** *(Civic Center, Thurs. & Sun.; 4th St., Thurs. evenings in summer).*

The pristine, small-town atmosphere was not lost on local resident George Lucas, who used it as a backdrop to his classic movie *American Graffiti.* The surrounding geology also fueled one of the last great projects of the architect Frank Lloyd Wright, who called it "one of the most beautiful landscapes I have ever seen." Wright's **Marin County Civic Center** *(3501 Civic Center Dr., tel 415/499-6646),* finished after

his death, was conceived as a "bridge between hills," illustrating the harmony Wright sought to bring between his medium and, as he would have put it, "Nature with a capital *N*."

SAN ANSELMO

Founded in 1875 as the result of a legendary feud between the wives of two railroad men, San Anselmo is now known as the capital of the antiques trade in northern California. Prices are high. The town also has its share of cafés and restaurants, with an especially lively and rather upscale Sunday brunch scene. The New Age has carved out a presence in such stores as Paper Ships Books and Crystals *(630 San Anselmo Ave., tel 415/457-3799, www.paperships.com)*. The Cedarchest Textile Arts for the Home shop *(603 San Anselmo Ave., tel 415/454-5310, www.thecedarsofmarin.org)* sells outstanding handmade works by developmentally disabled people.

LARKSPUR

Brick-lined **Magnolia Avenue,** a colorful shopping district, is listed on the National Register of Historic Places, and the town has a pleasant mix of architecture, ranging from Victorian to log cabin to mission. However, most folk come here for another reason: the **Lark Creek Inn** *(234 Magnolia Ave., tel 415/924-7766, www.larkcreek.com)*, a world-renowned restaurant helmed by chef Bradley Ogden. After one of his brilliant New American meals of, say, pot roast and homemade ravioli, take a stroll to the north end of town to see the remains of the historic **Escalle Winery.** Notice the wildflowers, for which the town is said to have been misnamed (they are actually lupins!).

NOVATO

The north Marin competitor of San Rafael, Novato offers many of the lures of its southern sister, from an **Old Town** district to a summer Tuesday evening **farmers' market.** Above all, it is the town's deep identification with the area's Native American days that distinguishes it for the traveler. An **adobe wall** just outside the Old Town, a former part of the Rancho Burdell, once belonged to the home of Camillo Ynitia, last chief of the Olompali. Ynitia is believed to have been killed by his brother for not sharing the proceeds of the sale of the land to a pioneer family. The **Marin Museum of the American Indian** *(Miwok Park, 2200 Novato Blvd., tel 415/897-4064, www.marinindian.com, closed Mon.)* is a must for anyone interested in the region's pre-European past. ■

Above right: Frank Lloyd Wright's Marin County Civic Center in San Rafael

San Anselmo
Map 231 B4
Visitor information
www.sananselmochamber.org
Tel 415/454-2510

Larkspur
Map 231 B4
Visitor information
1013 Larkspur Landing Circle
Tel 415/499-5000

Novato
Map 231 B4
Visitor information
www.tourism.novato.org
807 DeLong Ave.
Tel 415/897-1164

The turrets and towers of the famous Winchester Mystery House

San Jose

ALTHOUGH ITS HISTORY DATES BACK TO 1777, WHEN THE Spanish attempted to found a mission and agricultural outpost near the Guadelupe River, at the southern end of San Francisco Bay, San Jose clearly takes it cues from a more modern moment. In 1939 two young Stanford graduates, David Packard and William Hewlett, tinkered away in a Palo Alto garage at something called an audio oscillator. Their breakthrough led to the formation of the Hewlett Packard Company, which became the engine fueling the growth of the U.S.'s premier technopolis. Apple, Google, IBM, Intel, Netscape, you name it are all headquartered here, in a one-time piece of farmland now known as Silicon Valley.

San Jose
231 D2
Visitor information
http://sanjose.org
408 Almaden Blvd.
408/295-9600

The Tech Museum of Innovation
www.thetech.org
201 S. Market St.
408/294-8324
$$$

Intel Museum
www.intel.com/museum
2200 Mission College Blvd., Santa Clara
408/765-0503
Closed Sun.

For a long time much of the new wealth tended to travel to San Francisco and other cities. That pattern has changed in recent years with the formation of several new museums and cultural institutions in San Jose. The most glamorous of these is the **The Tech Museum of Innovation,** which offers to feed the "inner techno geek" in all of us, with more than 250 exhibits and interactive displays, an interactive media lab, and an IMAX theater. Four permanent galleries demonstrate every techie aspect of contemporary life—how it works and how it is changing the way society functions. The free **Intel Museum,** located at the Intel world headquarters in Santa Clara, allows visitors to watch chips being made in one of the industry's vaunted "clean rooms," and shows other aspects of the chip process.

While in the Santa Clara area, those committed to seeing all of the California missions can check off another one by visiting the **Mission Santa Clara de Asìs,** on the campus of Santa Clara University *(500 El Camino Real, tel 408/554-40230).* Nothing remains of the 1777 mission, but later buildings can be seen as well as a beautiful facsimile of the original church; many of the old garden's roses—including an 1822 Castilian rose bush—are now classified as antiques by experts. **Mission San Jose de Guadalupe** lies northeast of the city near Fremont. It has an interesting exhibit about the original Ohlone Indians.

In San Jose proper, three museums are worth your time. By far the best is the **San Jose Museum of Art,** located in the old post office building. The museum focuses on works by Bay Area artists since 1980—a much more fruitful endeavor than one might imagine. Particularly engaging are the many artists who attempt to fuse the area's rich agricultural history with its present fixation on technology.

The weird-looking **Rosicrucian Egyptian Museum & Planetarium** was "architecturally inspired by the Temple of Amon in Karnak." The museum houses the largest collection of Egyptian artifacts in the western U.S. It includes a large collection of human and animal mummies, a full-scale reconstruction of an Egyptian noble's tomb, walls of hieroglyphs, and a collection of Coptic textiles. The gardens are extensive, and free hieroglyphic workshops are given on weekends.

About as far from technology and pharaohs as you can get is the **San Jose Museum of Quilts & Textiles** *(520 S. First St., tel 408/971-0323, www.sjquiltmuseum.org, closed Mon.).* The museum prides itself on an international mix, with changing exhibitions and a great gift shop and bookstore.

San Jose is perhaps best known for the **Winchester Mystery House** *(525 S. Winchester Blvd., tel 408/247-2000, www.winchestermysteryhouse.com).* This Victorian mansion is famous for its weirdness: 160 rooms (many too tiny to be useful), and staircases, corridors, and doorways that lead nowhere. The owner, rifle heiress Sarah Winchester, was convinced that she would die if the building was completed...so work continued for nearly 40 years. Look for the huge art glass collection and exquisite period furniture. Special and spooky flashlight tours are given periodically.

Aerospace buffs might like to visit the famed **Lick Observatory,** on 4,200-foot Mount Hamilton, and the **NASA Ames Research Center** *(Moffett Field, tel 650/604-6274, www.arc.nasa.gov).* Here, the NASA Ames Exploration Center lets visitors experience NASA technology and missions first hand and includes an IMAX Theater. Thrill-seekers are drawn to **California's Great America** *(tel 408/988-1776),* a 100-acre theme park. ■

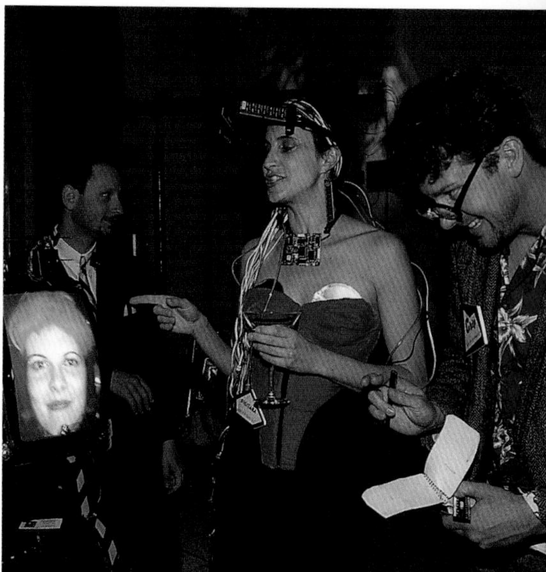

Cyberpartying in San Jose

Mission San Jose de Guadalupe
www.missionsanjose.org
✉ 43300 Mission Blvd., Fremont
☎ 510/657-1797

San Jose Museum of Art
www.sjmusart.org
✉ 110 S. Market St.
☎ 408/271-6840
🕒 Closed Mon.
$ $$

Rosicrucian Egyptian Museum & Planetarium
www.egyptianmuseum.org
✉ Naglee & Park Aves.
☎ 408/947-3636
$ $$

Stanford University

Stanford University
www.stanford.edu
231 C2
Visitor information
Memorial Hall
650/723-2300

Cantor Arts Center
http://museum.stanford.edu
Museum Dr.
650/723-4177
Closed Mon.–Tues.

Hoover Institution on War, Revolution, & Peace
www.hoover.org
Galvez & Serra Sts.
650/723-1754
Closed Sat.–Sun.

STANFORD, ONE OF THE WORLD'S MOST PRESTIGIOUS academic institutions, was founded in 1887 in Palo Alto by the railroad baron Leland Stanford and his wife, Jane, to honor their son Leland Jr., who had died at the age of 16 from typhoid fever. From the beginning it set high-minded goals for itself. According to Kevin Starr's recent history of California, Stanford's early president, David Starr Jordan, "wanted Stanford University to develop into a utopian statement of California possibilities, from which might radiate reforming energy in every direction." With the grand Romanesque architecture, red-tiled roofs, and wide brick plazas, form certainly followed ambition. If you want to visit the campus, the university visitor service offers free one-hour walking tours around it every day from Memorial Hall.

Although there are many interesting historical sites to see, the **Stanford Memorial Church** *(Central Quad)* warrants special note. Completed in 1891, it had to be rebuilt after the 1906 earthquake. The church was the special project of Jane Stanford. She personally commissioned Maurizio Camerino, the great 19th-century Italian mosaicist, to render a reproduction of Cosimo Roselli's fresco of the Last Supper in the Vatican's Sistine Chapel. At the time of its completion in 1903, it was the largest mosaic in the United States. It was entirely rebuilt after it was destroyed in the 1906 earthquake.

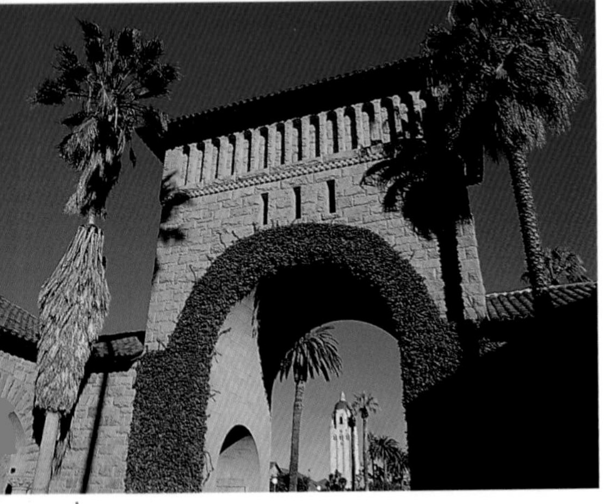

Main entrance to the Romanesque-style Stanford University

A more recent addition (1999) is the beautifully realized **Cantor Arts Center.** The center combines many of the university's older collections—including works by Goya, Piranesi, and Delacroix—with more recent acquisitions. The centerpiece is the Cantor collection of sculptures by Auguste Rodin, the largest in the world. There is also an extensive collection of Asian and American art.

Also at Stanford is the influential **Hoover Institution on War, Revolution, and Peace,** named for its founding president-alumnus. It is a world-renowned archive and library, and one of the first "think tanks." The library holds Herbert Hoover's 150,000-piece collection of manuscripts and documents on international relations. The tower, a 280-foot landmark, was designed by Bakewell and Brown, known for their San Francisco War Memorial Opera House.

A nearby site not to miss is **Filoli** *(86 Canada Rd., Woodside, tel 650/364-8300, www.filoli.org)*, a breathtaking English-style estate with spectacular gardens. ■

Two emerald green valleys, Napa and Sonoma, form the Tuscany of North America, where wine is a way of life and simple outdoor pleasures reign. In the west, the Russian River region conjures quietude, a real tonic for hurried modern life.

Wine Country

Grapes in stained glass, Calistoga

Wine Country

ALTHOUGH IT HAS BEEN THE SUBJECT FOR MANY A FINE SCRIBE, THE grandeur of California's wine country has rarely been captured as well as it was by author Robert Louis Stevenson, who, in the summer of 1880, visited the vineyard of the pioneer winemaker Jacob Schram. "In this wild spot, I did not feel the sacredness of ancient cultivation," Stevenson wrote. "It was still raw; yet the stirring sunlight, and the growing vines, and the vats and the bottles in the cavern, made a pleasant music for the mind. Here...earth's cream was being skimmed and garnered, and customers can taste, such as it is, the tang of the earth in this green valley."

Today, as California wine country increasingly becomes an oenophile theme park, it is easy to forget the primal pleasures of the land itself. True, the crush of summer traffic, the jockeying for dinner reservations, and the collecting of the newest vintages make it exciting. But the joy is in the land—seeing it, smelling it, feeling it connect in your belly with that first drop of a simple Sauternes.

Some planning is worthwhile. First, when to come? California's wine country is best in late fall or early winter, when the crowds thin and the foliage puts on a spectacular show. Second, where to go? Consider staying away from the main action, perhaps in Calistoga, where the food is outstanding and the room rates more reasonable (albeit not cheap). Make reservations if you want to eat at any of the top restaurants. Lastly, bone up on your wine basics. It is hard even for the uninitiated to buy a bad bottle of wine here but a little background knowledge always helps. ■

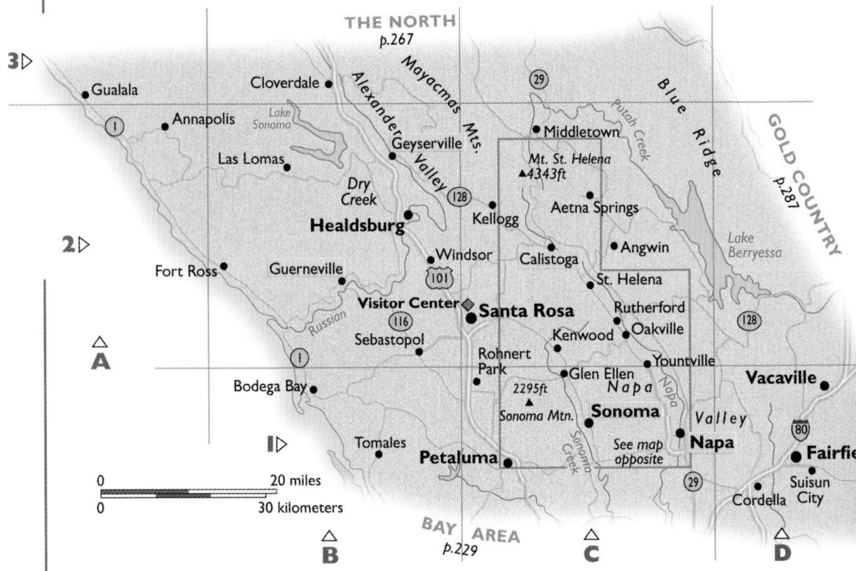

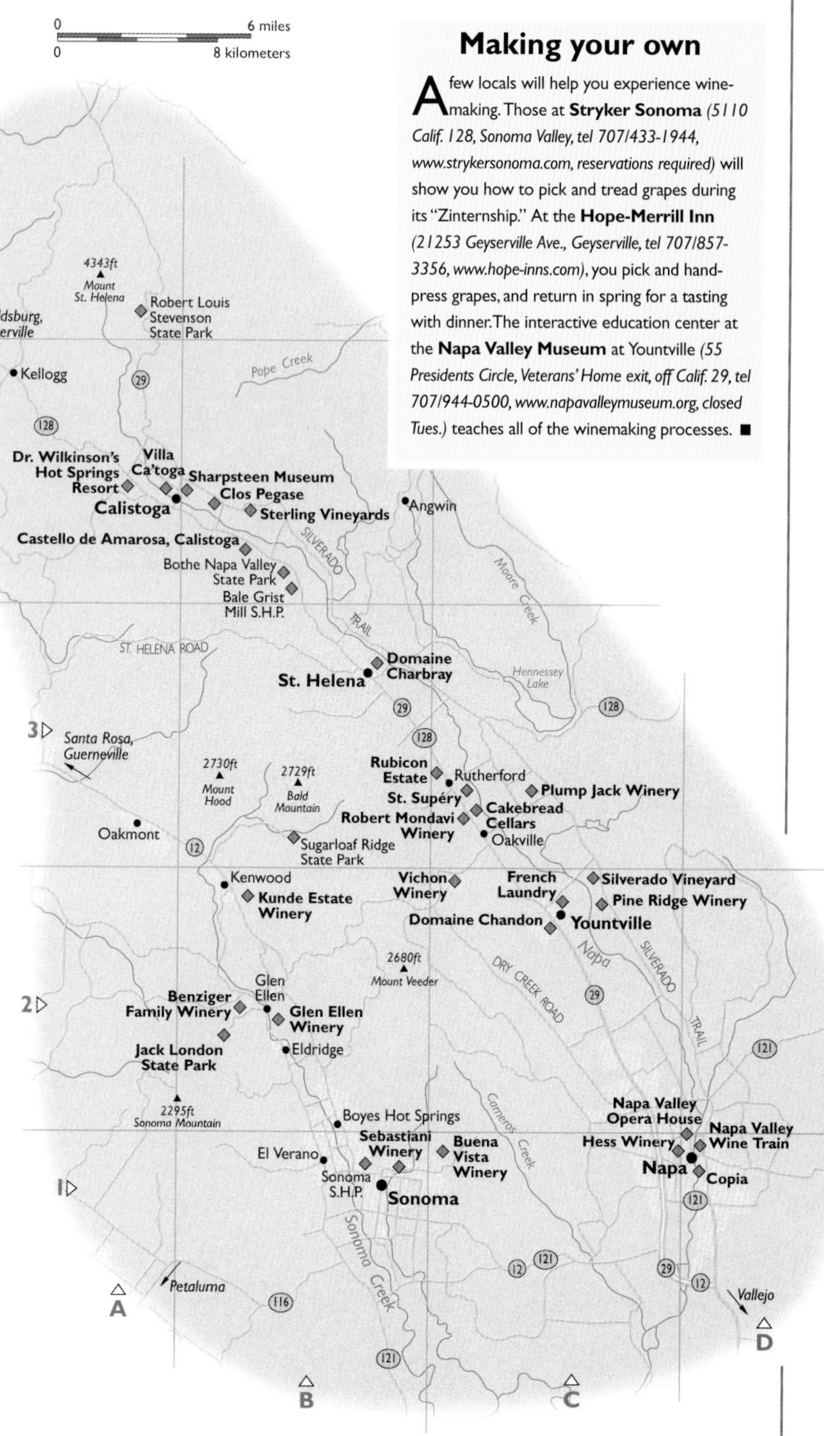

Making your own

A few locals will help you experience winemaking. Those at **Stryker Sonoma** *(5110 Calif. 128, Sonoma Valley, tel 707/433-1944, www.strykersonoma.com, reservations required)* will show you how to pick and tread grapes during its "Zinternship." At the **Hope-Merrill Inn** *(21253 Geyserville Ave., Geyserville, tel 707/857-3356, www.hope-inns.com)*, you pick and hand-press grapes, and return in spring for a tasting with dinner. The interactive education center at the **Napa Valley Museum** at Yountville *(55 Presidents Circle, Veterans' Home exit, off Calif. 29, tel 707/944-0500, www.napavalleymuseum.org, closed Tues.)* teaches all of the winemaking processes. ■

Calistoga's main drag

Napa Valley

THE HEART OF CALIFORNIA'S WINE COUNTRY BEGINS AT Napa, about an hour's drive north of San Francisco. An unremarkable little town now, apart from its courthouse, Napa was a flourishing port until the railways supplanted it. Although it was not officially established until 1848, by the 1860s it had become the epicenter of the region's wineries. Volcanic soils and a favorable climate first attracted vintners to this region in the mid-19th century, but it was well over 100 years before the world began to take California wines seriously. Today, the valley stretching from Napa to the old spa of Calistoga, some 30 miles northwest, has more than 200 wineries, some of them world famous and very much geared to visitors (see pp. 256–59). They need to be. Annually, more than five million people make the pilgrimage up Calif. 29, the backbone of Napa Valley. Inevitably, the restaurant trade has boomed alongside the wineries.

At the heart of the oasis, **St. Helena** is an appropriate home for the **Culinary Institute of America,** located in the historic 1880s Greystone Mansion. With its fragrant herb gardens and food-is-all atmosphere, it would be engaging enough as a travel destination alone. The addition of a restaurant makes it a foodie theme park where you can spend half a day eating, drinking, and relaxing. The seasonal menu is influenced by new Mediterranean cuisine, and the emphasis is on local foods and wines.

The good life continues at the luxury resort of **Meadowood** *(900 Meadowood Ln., St. Helena, tel 800/458-8080, www.meadowood.com)*, where gabled hillside cabins

Napa
www.napavalley.com
253 D2
Visitor information
1310 Napa Town Center
707/226-7459

Culinary Institute of America
www.ciachef.edu
2555 Main St., St. Helena
800/333-9242

Silverado Museum
www.silveradomuseum.org
1490 Library Ln., St. Helena
707/963-3757
Closed Mon.
By donation

are set in a 250-acre valley of oaks, pines, azaleas, and rhododendrons. Many come for the food, the nine-hole golf course, and the outstanding cultural events and outdoor opera in summer.

St. Helena also has associations with Robert Louis Stevenson, who spent his honeymoon near here in 1880. The **Silverado Museum** recalls his stay.

Reposing, in Stevenson's words, "on a mere film above a boiling, subterranean lake," is the spa town of **Calistoga**. Founded by pioneer Sam Brannan as a health resort in 1859, Calistoga offers good bed-and-breakfasts, cafés, boutiques, and restaurants.

For the past 50 years, Calistoga has also provided balm to the weary by means of **Dr. Wilkinson's Hot Springs Resort** *(1507 Lincoln Ave., tel 707/942-4102, www.drwilkinson.com),* which offers reasonably priced spa services: massages, salt glow rubs, and "the mud," a complete immersion in warm volcanic ash and natural hot spring water.

The valley's history is regaled in Calistoga's **Sharpsteen Museum,** displaying eclectic miscellany dating back 200 years. Nearby, Italian-born artist Carlo Marchiori has recreated a feel for ancient Rome at sumptuously decorated **Villa Ca'toga,** a Palladian villa where where Saturday morning tours are offered. At the valley's southern end, the **Napa Valley Opera House** *(tel 707/226-7372)* hosts performances by the American Conservatory Theater. ■

Up to her neck in the soothing mud of Calistoga

Calistoga
253 B4
Visitor information
1458 Lincoln Ave.
707/942-6333

Sharpsteen Museum
www.sharpsteen-museum.org
1311 Washington St., Calistoga
707/942-5911

Villa Ca'toga
253 A4
www.catoga.com
3061 Myrtledale Road, Calistoga
707/942-3900
Closed Nov.-April

French Laundry

A food-lover's dream, Yountville's French Laundry restaurant *(6640 Washington St., tel 707/944-2380, www.frenchlaundry.com)* serves up a menu that many believe is the best in the nation. Some samples from a recent prix-fixe tasting menu: Sabayon of pearl tapioca with poached Malpeque oysters and Osetra caviar; new potatoes and French winter truffles; butter-poached Maine lobster with wilted arrowleaf spinach and saffron-vanilla sauce. These the chef Thomas Keller serves in, as the critic du jour Ruth Reichl put it, "small, intense bites that add up to the valley's most incredible dining experience."

Although the courses are small, there are so many of them that, as one diner remarked, "It was like that movie *Groundhog Day.* Just when we thought we had finished, here came the waiter with another round!"

Reservations can be made between 10 a.m. and 7 p.m., two months to the day before you plan to dine. In other words, make this reservation before you buy your plane ticket. It is worth it. ■

Napa Valley wineries

SITTING IN ONE OF NAPA'S MANY GLAMOROUS BUT RUSTIC tasting rooms or restaurants, it is hard to believe that just a few decades ago the idea that California wineries would ever amount to anything more than a footnote in the annals of wine would have been a joke. But now the footnote is a tome.

To understand the Napa Valley phenomenon takes only one visit to the **Robert Mondavi Winery** in Oakville. Set in a stylish country villa headquarters, the winery was the brainchild of Robert Mondavi, who departed the family's old Charles Krug Winery to experiment with realizing the world-class potential of Napa's rich soils and outstanding climate. So he studied French winemaking techniques with the masters, bringing home new ideas, experimenting, adapting, failing, succeeding. In the 1970s his entries in the Paris Wine Tastings won several important awards, launching Mondavi—and Napa—onto the world stage. Today the Mondavis offer some of the more (deservedly) popular tours in the valley.

If the Mondavis are the quintessential Napa family, born to the land and succored on the grape, the Coppolas seem, at first glance, to be the very antithesis of Napa Valley rusticity. After all, director Francis Ford Coppola only arrived here after the success of two big Hollywood films, *The Conversation* and *The Godfather*. In 1975 he bought part of the Niebaum estate, which had been involved in winemaking since 1872. Three years later he made his first batch of vintage Rubicon.

Now **Rubicon Estate,** formerly Niebaum-Coppola, is known as an outstanding producer of wines, from its trademark Rubicons (labeled by *Wines and Spirits* as "dense, rich, sumptuous—even when young") to its newer Rosso and Bianco line of family-style blends. The winery's Centennial Museum blends artifacts from the early Inglenook winery, which originally stood here, with items from Coppola's films, right down to a real vintage Tucker automobile and Don Corleone's desk.

Another excellent winery tour in the Rutherford area is that of **St. Supéry**. The Pope Valley land that is the winery's core was farmed in the late 19th century. It fell into disuse until 1982, when the French Skalli family purchased 1,500 acres, known as Dollarhide Ranch. For five years the family labored to understand the ranch's unique microclimate, experimenting with various trellising methods and soil management practices. Today its Sauvignon Blanc and Chardonnay are considered outstanding among wines made to be drunk fresh.

The St. Supéry tour includes a visit to the historic Victorian Atkinson House, built in 1881 by the original owners George and Louis Atkinson. Among the other delights here are a display vineyard, and, for the technophile, an exhibit dubbed "SmellaVision," a hands-on display to help one understand the language of aroma, appearance, and taste. A tasting follows, for a moderate fee.

Like Rubicon Estate, **Silverado Vineyard** also has connections with a famous name, for it was founded in the 1970s by the family of Walt Disney. It is situated along the scenic Silverado Trail, a 19th-century Napa Valley mining road that runs along the eastern side of the Napa River, away from the

Robert Mondavi
www.robertmondaviwinery.com
253 C3
7801 St. Helena Hwy. (Calif. 29), Oakville
888/766-6328

Rubicon Estate
www.rubiconestate.com
253 C3
1991 Calif. 29, Rutherford
707/968-1161
$$$$$. Tours by appointment only

St. Supéry
www.stsupery.com
253 C3
8440 Calif. 29, Rutherford
707/963-4507 or 800/942-0809

traffic-ridden Calif. 29 to the west. Grown under the retreating cool air from San Pablo Bay, its merlots and cabernets are especially known for their "rounded" flavors and silky textures. A tour through the winery takes in the dining room, where hang original works by such California painters as Thomas Hill and William Keith. From the back terrace of the house, there is a stunning view of Mount St. Helena, to the northwest, and of the surrounding countryside.

Not far away on the Silverado Trail, the acclaimed daily tours of the **Pine Ridge Winery** concentrate on various aspects of the growing process. A visit to the winery's hillside caves is followed by a tasting of Pine Ridge's fine cabernets, merlots, and chardonnays.

Calistoga (see p. 255) marks the northern end of the Silverado

Ballooning over rows of vines in Napa Valley

Vintners & gardeners

Several Napa Valley wineries take great pride in their gardens. Horticultural buffs should not miss the innovative vegetable gardens at **Cakebread Cellars** *(8300 Calif. 29, Rutherford, tel 707/963-5222, www.cakebread.com)*; the rustic landscaping at **Sterling Vineyards** *(1111 Dunaweal Ln., Calistoga, tel 800/726-6136, www.sterlingvineyards.com)*; and the tomato extravaganza held at the **Robert Mondavi Winery** (see p. 256). **Copia: The American Center for Wine, Food & The Arts** *(500 First St., Napa, tel 707/265-5950, www.copia.org)*, an all-encompassing cultural center dedicated to an integrated celebration of wines, food, and art, features three-and-a-half acres of organic gardens and orchards. ■

Domaine Carneros, a French château in Napa Valley

SilveradoVineyard
www.silveradovineyards.com
6121 Silverado Trail
707/257-1770

Pine Ridge Winery
www.pineridgewinery.com
5901 Silverado Trail
707/253-7500 or 800/486-0503

Clos Pegase
www.clospegase.com
1060 Dunaweal Ln., Calistoga
707/942-4981
Tastings $

Castello di Amoroso
www.castellodiamorosa.com
4045 N St. Helena Hwy., Calistoga
707/942-8200

Trail. A young winery here, **Clos Pegase,** founded by Jan and Mitsuko Shrem in 1987, manages to pull off the proverbial triple treat—art, wine, and architecture—with grace and aplomb. True, the award-winning headquarters, designed by Michael Graves, at first shocked the valley's more traditionally minded vintners. But the Shrems have integrated much tradition into their endeavor as well, the most engaging being their aging caves, 20,000 square feet of venerable wooden barrels buried below a nearby rocky knoll. Throughout the property there is evidence of the couple's other passion: sculptures by Henry Moore, Richard Serra, and Anthony Caro. The winery offers free "Grand Tours" every day, and a presentation by Jan Shrem on the third Saturday of the month except in December and January.

The most sensational newcomer in years is **Castello di Amoroso,** a European-style castle perched on a hill just south of Calistoga. Thirteen years in the making, this 121,000-square-foot inspiration of owner Daryl Sattui features a frescoed great hall, secret passageways, and even a torture chamber. The wines are grown from Italian grapes and sold only on site. Guided tours are offered hourly on weekdays, and every half-hour on weekends, by reservation but drop-ins can enjoy free wine tastings.

The most outstanding art collection belongs to the **Hess Collection Winery,** in the hills west of Napa. Established in 1896 by Swiss entrepreneur Donald Hess on land farmed by the Christian Brothers, the winery occupies a centenarian, three-story stone structure built into the side of Mt. Veeder. The self-guided tour begins in the theater where visitors are introduced to Hess's traditional Burgundian winemaking practice resulting in quality wines of richly satisfying complexity. The second and third floor galleries meld a contemporary redesign into the historic sandstone shell, with 13,000 square feet of art space displaying 115 contemporary pieces, including works by such masters as Francis Bacon and Franz Gertsch.

In recent years many wineries have launched into ancillary endeavors, producing grappa, port, and various trendy spirits. The family-run **Domaine Charbay Winery & Distillery,** a mountaintop aerie outside St. Helena,

leads the spirited pack with such libations as its apple brandy, black walnut liqueur, and award-winning trademark fruit-flavored vodkas. Owner and Master Distiller Miles Karakasevic has parlayed a Yugoslavian family tradition harking back centuries into an enviable success story. Forever concocting, Karakasevic produces the world's only dessert chardonnay, as well as California's first pastis, a California vermouth, and even a sunroot spirit—the first original, purely American spirit—made from sunflower tubers. All are of mind-numbing quality. Centerpiece of the the "Still on the Hill" are two traditional-style copper alambic stills. Family members lead tours for a fee. ■

Viticulture is labor-intensive but uses mechanical methods wherever possible.

Hess Collection Winery
www.hesscollection.com
✉ 4411 Redwood Rd., Napa
☎ 707/255-1144
$ Tastings $$

Domaine Charbay Winery & Distillery
www.charbay.com
✉ Spring Mtn., St. Helena
☎ 800/634-7845
$ $$$$. Visits by appointment only.

Meals on the move

As you might expect, picnics in the Napa Valley are an art form. To get just the right cold chicken, salads, cheeses, and, of course, wine, try the **V. Sattui Winery** *(1111 White Ln., Calif. 29, tel 707/963-7774, www.vsattui.com)*, which offers an extensive deli and a fine picnic area. Among prime picnic spots on the wine circuit for locals in the know are the Vichon Winery in Oakville (which has its own bocce ball court); and the picnic tables at Plump Jack Winery halfway up the Oakville Grade.

As you also might expect, there is no shortage of places to buy picnic supplies. The famed **Oakville Grocery** *(7856 St. Helena Hwy., Oakville, 707/944-8802, www.oakvillegrocery.com)* offers outstanding specialties, from fig-olive tapenade to local fruits and salads. The more commercial (but delightful) **Dean & DeLuca** *(607 St. Helena Hwy., St. Helena, tel 707/967-9980)* has its own charcuterie. In Calistoga try the **Palisades Market** *(1506 Lincoln Ave., tel 707/942-9549)*; in Yountville, **Gordon's** *(6770 Washington St., tel 707/944-8246)* is the place.

If you don't want to picnic, but are tired of the restaurant scene, try a jaunt on the **Napa Valley Wine Train** *(1275 McKinistry St., Napa, tel 707/253-2111, www.winetrain.com)*. A restored 1917 Pullman dining car trundles you through wine country at a leisurely clip as you eat brunch, lunch, or a gourmet dinner. ■

Anatomy of a sparkling wine

Although it is fairly easy to learn about the making of wine in the United States these days, the same cannot be said of champagne or sparkling wine. Its production continues to be a European affair (even to the extent that in recent years there has been bitter controversy over the use of the name "champagne" to refer to wines produced anywhere except in the Champagne region of France). In Napa, however, there is a place where one can get an idea of what goes into a bottle of the drink that, as Woody Allen said, "tingles the tongue as it mangles the brain." That place is Domaine Chandon *(1 Calif. 29, Yountville-Veterans' Home exit, tel 707/944-2280, www.chandon.com)*. Here they still use the ancient and revered *méthode champenoise,* first worked out by a 17th-century monk named Dom Pérignon, to create a sparkling wine.

The first step in the method is the crush or, rather, the press. Sparkling wine requires a lighter hand than still wine in order to

minimize the presence of tannin, a destructive acid that comes from grape skins. The juice then goes into its first fermentation in giant stainless steel tanks. Next comes the blending process, a careful addition and mixing of various grape juices that will produce the desired flavors. To this *cuvée* the winemaker adds a *liqueur de tirage,* a mixture of yeast and sugar that activates another round of fermentation as the liquid is poured into bottles and sealed. This causes the wine to produce more carbon dioxide, infusing itself with champagne's characteristic bubbles. Now the bottles are put in storage for two to five years, depending upon the cuvée.

During this period of autolysis the wine takes on its unique characteristics—its smell, texture, and color. To collect the yeast sediment the bottles are riddled, or turned, several times a day. At Domaine Chandon the process is done by a machine called a *gyropallette,* or by hand. Winemakers have devised an ingenious method to disgorge the sediment by first freezing the neck of the bottle, then unplugging it and letting the built-up carbon dioxide jettison it. The bottle is then corked, wired shut, and labeled. ■

Right: Harvesting the grapes; Bottom right: The first fermentation takes place in steel tanks. Below: Enjoying the result

Sonoma Valley

IF THE NAPA VALLEY IS THE FLORENCE OF AMERICAN viticulture, full of talent, pomp, and wealth, then the Sonoma Valley is its Siena, a place just as deeply committed to the art of wine but with a quieter air about it. In sheer number of wineries, it is outdone by its neighbor; in landscapes and ambition, it is its equal. And as the site of California's most northerly mission and the Bear Flag Revolt, the town of Sonoma has a historical importance that Napa can never match. Six sites at its core comprise Sonoma State Historic Park.

Sonoma Valley
www.sonomavalley.com
252 C1
Visitor information
453 1st St. E.
707/996-1090

Sonoma State Historic Park Visitor information
www.parks.ca.gov
363 3rd St. W., Sonoma

Sonoma Barracks
20 E. Spain St., Sonoma
707/939-9420

Lachryma Montis
Spain & 3rd Sts., Sonoma
707/938-9559

Mission Solano
E. Spain St., Sonoma
707/938-9560

Sonoma Cheese Factory
www.sonomacheesefactory.com
2 W. Spain St., Sonoma
707/996-1931

It is rare to be able to stand in the place where a piece of one country became a piece of another. Such is the case in Sonoma's **Central Plaza,** at the **Bear Flag Monument.** This marks where, on June 14, 1846, a ragtag group of fur trappers and mountain men charged upon the quarters of Mexican commandante Mariano Vallejo, took him into custody and raised a crude flag bearing a star, a grizzly bear, and the words "California Republic." The republicans were independent for less than a month. On July 9, U.S. Captain John C. Frémont declared them part of the territorial United States. The **Sonoma Barracks,** built by Indians for the Mexican army and later occupied by the Americans, is in the plaza, as is **Lachryma Montis,** the Gothic Revival mansion built for Vallejo in 1852. The house was built near a mineral water spring, hence the name, meaning "tears of the mountain."

Just off the plaza is the **Mission Solano,** the last in the chain of missions running up California to be built. Founded in 1819, Mission Solano represented the ambitions of its founder, Padre José Altamira. He hoped to use it to usurp the leadership of Mission Dolores and Mission San Rafael to the south, but his plans were scotched when discovered by his fellows. Altamira nonetheless built a substantial wheat and barley plantation. Unfortunately he so abused his Indian laborers that in 1826 they rebelled and sacked the mission. The chapel on display today was built in 1841.

The simple adobe building of the Mission Solano

Vineyards cover Sonoma Valley.

The gold rush-era **El Dorado Hotel** *(405 1st St. W., tel 707/996-3220, www.hoteleldorado.com)* has been elegantly restored and features a good restaurant, Piatti, offering regional Italian cuisine. For a snack, visit the **Sonoma Cheese Factory,** where you can watch the making of the famed Sonoma Jack through a giant window.

For another welcome side-effect of the ascendancy of California cuisine—the reawakening of the olive oil industry—drive up the valley to **Glen Ellen.** In the center of town is **The Olive Press** *(24724 Arnold Dr., tel 707/939-8900, www.theolivepress.com),* featuring a tasting bar and viewable pressing mill, which can be seen in operation October to early February.

An outstanding place to stay if you are heading in this direction from Sonoma is the **Sonoma Mission Inn** at Boyes Hot Springs (see p. 376), a 19th-century bath-house rejuvenated, tastefully, in grand modern mission style. A good base for Sonoma and Glen Ellen, it is also within reach of **Jack London State Historic Park** *(tel 707/938-5216, www.parks.ca.gov),* just up the road bearing the same name. The author spent his last few years here, building a mansion that burned down before he ever lived in it. Visit the author's grave and a small museum in the house his widow built, displaying memorabilia of the author. His legacy to the Sonoma Valley was a nickname: the title of his book, *Valley of the Moon*, by which the area is still known.

At the northern end of the Sonoma Valley, the historic town of **Santa Rosa** warrants a visit to see the **Charles Shulz Museum,** celebrating the life and art of the eponymous cartoonist; and the **Luther Burbank Home & Gardens,** where for 50 years the famed horticulturist experimented with everything under the California sun. Some of Burbank's great triumphs are on display, including the Burbank Russet potato and the Shasta daisy. ■

Santa Rosa
www.visitsantarosa.com
Map 252 C2
Visitor information
✉ 9 4th St.
☎ 707/577-8674

Charles Shulz Museum
www.charlesmschulzmuseum.org
✉ 2301 Hardies Ln.
☎ 707/579-4452
Closed Tue. Nov-April
$ $$

Luther Burbank Home & Gardens
www.lutherburbank.org
✉ Santa Rosa & Sonoma Aves.
☎ 707/524-5445

Sonoma Valley wineries

Celebration at Viansa Winery

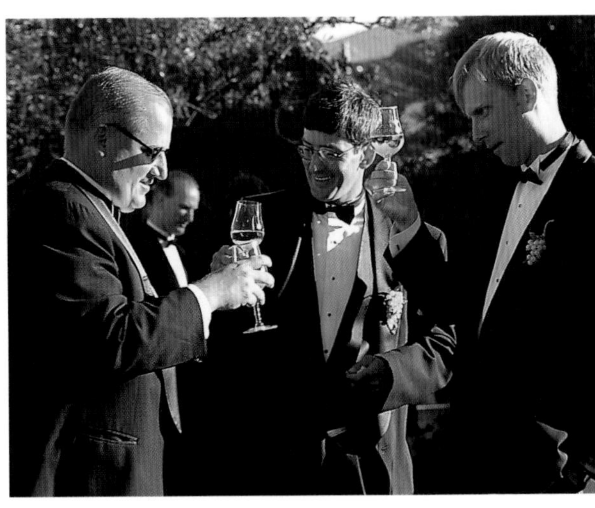

IN RECENT YEARS SONOMA WINERIES HAVE ATTRACTED increasing attention for their diversity of flavor and mood—probably due to the weather, influenced by the Mayacamas Mountains, and to the largely volcanic soils. People come to Sonoma when they just want to embrace Nature and drink a good glass of California vino. Even Robert Mondavi brags about his Sonoma holdings.

Benziger Family Winery
www.benziger.com
Map p. 253
1883 London Ranch Rd., Glen Ellen
707/935-3000 or 888/490-2739

Imagery Estate Winery & Art Gallery
www.imagerywinery.com
14335 Hwy. 12, Glen Ellen
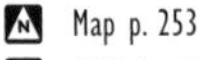
707/935-4515

The best place to start a Sonoma journey is at the **Benziger Family Winery,** near Glen Ellen and Jack London State Park (see p. 263). To quote the prestigious *Wine Spectator* magazine, this is "one of the top ten winery visits in California." The property on Sonoma Mountain was the 1868 homestead of Julius Wegner, carpenter to Gen. Mariano Vallejo. Wegner and his successors engaged in extensive planting, and much of the stunning terracing on the slopes was done by Chinese immigrants in the 1870s.

The present winery was founded in 1980 by Mike Benziger, a native New Yorker who had, in his own words, come west "in pursuit of a dream: to ski and surf on the same day." Later joined by his father and siblings, Benziger has since focused on another dream: building a world-class *terroir,* or soil.

The free tour, winding through unmatched wine country scenery complete with a redwood grove, brilliantly explicates the Benziger mission. Innovative trellising techniques, visible near the Viticulture Discovery Center, allow for maximum regulation of light, which in turn enables the vineyard to produce 25 different wines and 350 different flavors. Inside the rootstock nursery are varieties of rootstock resistant to the phylloxera bug, a bane of grape growers. Visitors also see how vines are grafted, trained, and maintained. There is a fine exhibit on cooperage—the art of barrelmaking—and a working bug farm, where natural methods of

fighting pests are developed. Finally, there is the wine tasting room. The wine seems even better after a few hours spent wandering around in this blissful landscape of flavor.

The Benziger family's **Imagery Estate Winery & Art Gallery** produces rare wines. Its "Artists Collection," numbering almost 200 uncommon varietals, features labels specially commissioned from leading contemporary artists. An on site gallery displays the original art, linked by an interpretation of the winery's Parthenon symbol.

In the Sonoma area, *the* winery to visit is the historic **Buena Vista Winery** in the Carneros Valley east of the town. It certainly lives up to the regal aspirations of its founder, Agostin Haraszthy. This Hungarian noble-turned-émigré farmer came to Sonoma seeking a rustic empire. By 1860, after a tumultuous stint as an official at the U.S. Mint in San Francisco (allegations of light-fingeredness were later dissipated), Haraszthy had amassed some 6,000 acres of pristine valley floor. Not content with the local vines, he returned to Europe in 1861 and sent back more than 200,000 cuttings from 1,400 grape varieties. Among them were some of a pest-resistant strain that would save the nascent industry time and time again in subsequent decades. The result of his labors, much of it in evidence today, has earned him the uncontested title of father of California viticulture.

Buena Vista may be Sonoma's most historic winery, but with 800 acres the largest vineyard owner in the valley is the **Kunde Estate Winery.** The tour here includes a walk through a half mile of hillside caves engineered by Russell Clough, who "dug the tunnel" for San Francisco's BART subway system (see p. 193). Try the family's specialty, Viognier, a white wine from a French grape. If you are lucky they may also have a store of their Zinfandel, made from 114-year-old vines.

To the south in East Sonoma lies the **Sebastiani Winery.** Its tour has been highly praised by the *Wine Spectator* magazine. ■

Buena Vista Winery is the oldest in the Sonoma Valley.

Buena Vista Winery
www.buenavistawinery.com
Map p. 253
18000 Old Winery Rd., Sonoma
707/938-1266 or 800/926-1266

Kunde Estate Winery
www.kunde.com
Map p. 253
9825 Sonoma Hwy.
707/833-5501

Sebastiani Winery
www.sebastiani.com
Map p. 253
389 4th St. East, Sonoma
707/933-3230 or 800/888-5532

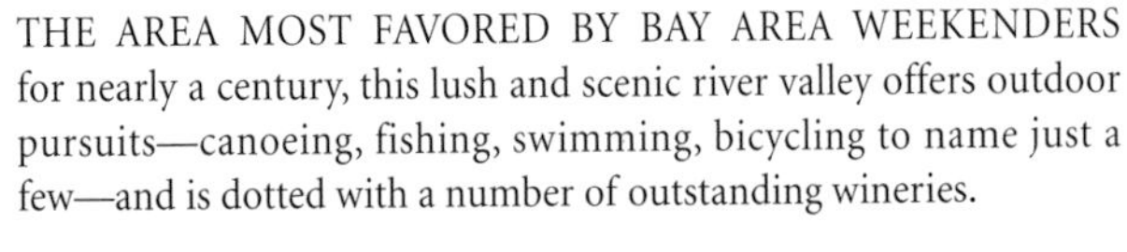

Russian River

THE AREA MOST FAVORED BY BAY AREA WEEKENDERS for nearly a century, this lush and scenic river valley offers outdoor pursuits—canoeing, fishing, swimming, bicycling to name just a few—and is dotted with a number of outstanding wineries.

Guerneville
www.russianriver.com
252 B2
Visitor information
16209 1st St.
707/869-9000

Korbel Champagne Cellars
www.korbel.com
13250 River Rd., Guerneville
707/824-7000

E. & J. Gallo
www.gallosonoma.com
3387 Dry Creek Rd., Healdsburg
707/431-5500

Ferrari-Carano Winery
www.ferrari-carano.com
8761 Dry Creek Rd., Healdsburg
707/433-6700 or 800/831-0381

Stryker Sonoma
www.strykersonoma.com
5110 Calif. 128, Geyserville
707/433-1944

Trentadue Winery
www.trentadue.com
19170 Geyserville Rd., Geyserville
707/433-3104 or 888/332-3032

Russian River offers some splendid kayaking.

Guerneville, the Russian River area's largest town, offers one of the most interesting winery tours: the **Korbel Champagne Cellars.** Founded about 110 years ago by the Bohemian Korbel brothers on the site of their successful lumber mill (which made much of the gingerbread on San Francisco Victorians), the winery is like a tiny piece of company history preserved in amber. An old blacksmith shop and general store remain for viewing. A rose garden, with more than 250 varieties of antique roses, is the subject of a half-hour tour.

Farther north, in the Dry Creek Valley, is the Sonoma operation of the wine giants **E. & J. Gallo.** In the grand tradition of California agriculture (which may horrify some!), the Gallos have literally rearranged the landscape, rebuilt historic bridges, and replanted groves of oaks. The politically correct aspect of their effort is that the farm is entirely organic; it is worth driving by it, even though there are no tours of this clannish family's estate. The Gallo family offers wine-sampling at its new tasting room in charming **Healdsburg** *(320 Center St., tel 707/433-2458).*

For a good sandwich, stop at the Dry Creek General Store on Dry Creek Road just outside of Healdsburg. Then go on to the splendid **Ferrari-Carano Winery.** The wine is outstanding, but so are the 5-acre gardens, with 18,000 tulips in spring.

North again from Santa Rosa is the **Alexander Valley,** a lush region around Geyserville. In summer, **Stryker Sonoma** offers a series of food and wine events; check also for a schedule of evening concerts. The setting alone is worth the drive. **Trentadue Winery,** founded by the Italian-American Leo Trentadue in 1969, is known for its outstanding Sangiovese. ■

Cooler, greener, full of natural wonders, California's north is paradise for outdoors folk. Redwood National Park stars, home to coast redwoods. In Lassen Volcanic National Park fumaroles join postcard-perfect meadows and lakes.

The North

Logging pond in Scotia

The North

IF MUCH OF CALIFORNIA IMAGINES ITSELF AS MEDITERRANEAN IN CAST, ITS northern reaches identify with lands of higher latitudes. This is, after all, a land that Russian settlers tried (and failed) to claim in the early 19th century; it is a coast where Finns and Swedes dominated the fishing and shipping industries. Central to it is a storm system known as the Aleutian Low, which sends icy winds down from the Gulf of Alaska.

This is the California of great natural resources, its rugged terrain sprouting fine woods for the lumber industry, its harbors giving safe haven and bounty to generations of fishermen.

Fortunately for the traveler, much of the remaining bounty has been set aside. In and around Mendocino, great conifers still dominate the coastal rain forests. Farther north, above Eureka, the coast redwoods tower over the junglelike vegetation of Redwood National Park. Here giant ferns and wild orchids create a dream world of filtered sun and foliage. Inland, at Mount Shasta, the manzanitas appear, their red stems hoisting aloft great low clouds of foliage. Then there are the waterfalls. Theodore Roosevelt's favorite was the one called McArthur-Burney.

The north is Lost California. In the Trinity Alps you can drive all day through towering pines blanketed with fresh snowfall. Farther east, in remote Lassen Volcanic National Park, you can explore bubbling volcanic fumaroles,

Old Red Schoolhouse Museum, Orick, Redwood National Park

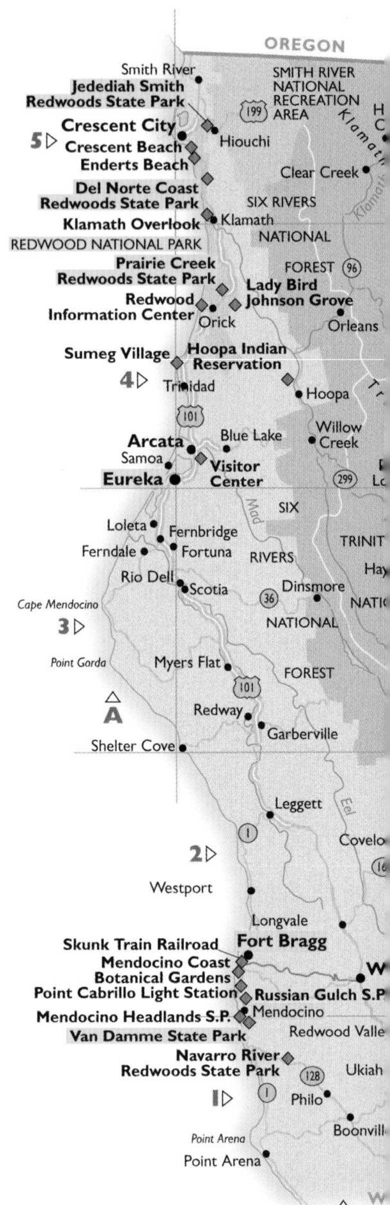

take a horseback ride through wildflower meadows, and stay at an old-fashioned summer lodge where hot springs run through the outdoor swimming pool.

Close to the Oregon border is Lava Beds National Monument, where battles once raged between Native Americans and settlers. Today, amateur cavers can climb through the lava tubes that have been preserved here.

And in the northeastern corner of the state? Alturas, close to several lakes and wetlands, is the capital of California bird-watching. Here you can stay a night, eat at a boisterous Basque restaurant with steaks the size of hubcaps, then wake to the sounds of migrating wildfowl. ■

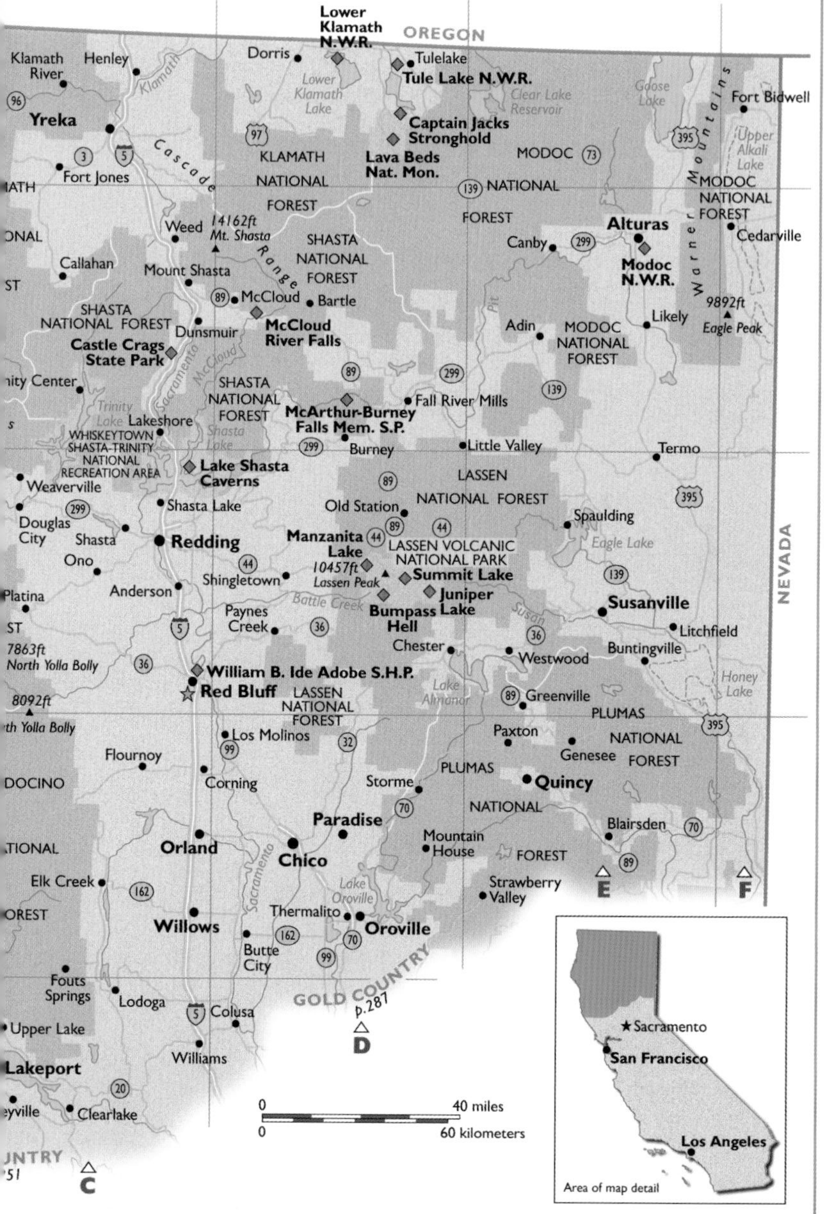

Van Damme State Park

ITS FLOOR CARPETED WITH LUSH FERNS AND REDWOOD sorrel, its paths dotted with little log benches, Van Damme State Park makes for a perfect stopover on the long, windy road between San Francisco and Mendocino. Here, in a small area beside Calif. 1, is a classic northern rain forest with streams containing coho salmon, masses of wild rhododendrons, and one of the world's greatest stands of pygmy pine trees.

For the best views of the park, follow the **Fern Canyon Trail** from the end of the entrance road. Flat and well-marked with a series of numbered salmon sculptures, the trail originated as a logging road in the late 1800s. In 1936 the Civilian Conservation Corps built nine stream crossings and a series of rock embankments along the side of the streams. An idea of the difficulties encountered by the workers comes across in a staff report from the era: "This project is without a doubt the most disagreeable project we are working on… the walls of the canyon are steep and heavily timbered and at this season, the sun seldom reaches that portion of the canyon where the men are working."

An opportunity to view the silvery coho salmon can be had nearby along the **Little River.** They were once so numerous that it was possible to catch them with bare hands, but the coho has in recent years suffered from increasing salinity and dwindling spawning habitats. A few moments spent by the stream will reveal the fish in one of three states. In winter large adult fish begin to spawn, lodging themselves in pebbly basins and laying eggs before drifting down to the sea to die. In spring the eggs hatch, producing dense schools of young. For the rest of the year these young salmon feed, growing to a length of four to six inches. By the next spring they are ready for their journey to the sea; having memorized the scent of their home stream, they develop the silvery color required for survival in salt water. After two years in the ocean, they will return to the Little River to repeat the cycle.

If you visit during May and June, you will witness another remarkable sight: the blooming of the Pacific rhododendron. Long studied for its adaptive abilities, this member of the heath family has leaves that roll under during the summer heat and pink, bell-shaped flowers in six-inch clusters.

The **pygmy forest** is the park's main attraction, reached by the old logging road. A self-guided trail leads through this wonderland of dwarf trees and shrubs; cypresses, Bolander pines, and bishop pines stand only a couple of feet tall, even though they are at least 40 years old. The unique geology, heavy rainfall, and poor soil combine to produce the dwarf effect: Nutrients leached from the topsoil form a hard pan beneath the surface, which the trees' roots cannot penetrate. With reduced nourishment, the trees' growth is stunted.

Various shrubs also grow here, particularly the (edible) huckleberry and the (inedible) manzanita. Be sure to walk the entire circumference for some outstanding photo opportunities. You can rent mountain bikes in Mendocino and ride the trail, but bring a bike rack to avoid having to ride along the perilous Coast Highway. ■

Van Damme State Park
www.parks.ca.gov
268 B1
E side of Calif. 1, 2 miles S of Mendocino
707/937-5804

Pacific rhododendron carpets the ground beneath towering redwoods.

Plant life of the north

Everyone knows about northern California's coast redwoods (see pp. 276–77), but the plant life of the upper reaches of the state offers many other discoveries, too.

Closed-cone pines and cypresses: Four species of pine and ten of cypress dominate this group. All can thrive in infertile soils. Although they grow throughout the state, several species form concentrations in the north, from Van Damme State Park to Humboldt County. The most common are bishop pine, Douglas fir, Mendocino cypress, and Bolander's pine. Their cones open only when exposed to intense sun or fire.

Manzanita *(Arctostaphylos):* A dramatic, low-growing brush with red trunk and lustrous leaves, the manzanita comes in several forms. Inland, at such places as McArthur-Burney Falls, look for the stunning greenleaf manzanita, often growing near magnificent incense cedars. On the coast, look for the low-growing Fort Bragg manzanita or the aptly named hairy manzanita.

Sagebrush *(Artemisia)*: Although widely distributed throughout the state, sagebrush dominates much of the northeastern high desert. The plains are sometimes covered with shrubby sagebrush, while the big sagebrush grows on the eastern edge of the Sierra. Both are highly aromatic, the stuff of Native American and New Age apothecary alike. ■

Mendocino & around

Mendocino & Fort Bragg
268 B1
Visitor information
www.mendocinocoast.com
332 N. Main St., Fort Bragg
707/961-6300

INHABITED BY THE VALLEY-DWELLING POMO TRIBE FROM approximately 9500 B.C., the area was named by 16th-century Spanish settlers for Antonio Mendosa, viceroy of New Spain. At the mouth of the Big River's outflow into the ocean, Mendocino's first Yankee pioneers quickly set up a lumber mill that, by 1853, was producing some 50,000 feet of timber board a day. A town sprang to life, its New England cast and stunning views bringing in not only lumber barons but also a host of tourists and artists, who continue to revel in its many natural delights.

Today, the buffed-up village offers several good bed-and-breakfasts and lovely restaurants located in restored Victorians. Galleries on and around Main Street offer local art, some of it by nationally known landscape painters. Artists here are known for their interesting use of natural materials such as wood and stone.

An excellent way to explore Mendocino's hinterland is by canoe, rentable at the Stanford Inn (see p. 378), itself a grand place to stay. The outrigger-style canoes are fitted with special stabilizing devices, allowing even novices to explore the lush reaches of the **Big River.** Along the way

to the **Mendocino Woodlands,** a wooded upland area, lies a series of breathtaking scenic canyons, salt marshes, and streambeds populated with great blue herons, ospreys and even harbor seals.

There are a number of state parks in the area. If you are here during the winter, go to **Mendocino Headlands State Park** *(off Calif. 1 just S of town)* for gray whale-watching. To the north, **Russian Gulch State Park** *(tel 707/937-5804)* offers 36 miles of coastal trail and the unique Devil's Punch Bowl—a collapsed sea cave through which waves churn with great beauty. Just up the coast, the recently restored **Point Cabrillo Light Station** *(tel 707/937-6122, www.pointcabrillo.org),* dating from 1909, is now open for public tours.

In midsummer do not miss the **Mendocino Music Festival,** *(tel 707/937 2044, www.mendocinomusic.com),* held on the beach!

REDWOOD WINE COUNTRY

Situated southeast of Mendocino along Calif. 128, the wine country of the redwood region is known for its diverse microclimates, producing leading labels of chardonnay, Pinot noir, and sauvignon blanc. Many of the 300 vineyards center on the scenic Navarro River; in recent years the winery that takes its name from it, **Navarro Vineyards** *(5601 Calif. 128, Philo, tel 707/895-3686, www.navarrowine.com)* has received high praise for its Pinot gris and the rarely made (in the U.S.) *verjus,* a tart, green grape juice perfect for the nondrinker and the kitchen, where the French have used it for centuries as a replacement for vinegars and lemon juice.

A nice intermezzo to a day of winery touring would be a picnic at the nearby **Navarro River Redwoods State Park** *(just off Calif. 128 at the posted marker),* an 11-mile-long "redwood tunnel to the sea," as local literature puts it.

FORT BRAGG

The working lumber town of Fort Bragg was founded in 1857 as a military outpost and named for Gen. Braxton Bragg, hero of the Mexican War. On the edge of a redwood forest, it sits between two bodies of running water, the Noyo River to the south and Pudding Creek to the north. A charming way to see much of the hinterland is via the old **Skunk Train Railroad.** Constructed by lumber barons in the 1880s, the 40-mile line takes its passengers through dense stands of redwoods to **Willits,** where the notorious Black Bart robbed 27 coaches between 1875 and 1883, when he was "retired" to San Quentin prison in Marin County.

On the coast to the south are the **Mendocino Coast Botanical Gardens.** Founded in 1961, the gardens specialize in colorful rhododendrons, including hybrids, with collections of heathers, dahlias, camellias, and ivies. There are picnic areas, winding grass paths, and an ocean overlook. ■

Above: Mendocino seen from the sea; Right: A modern-day goat shepherdess

Skunk Train Railroad
www.skunktrain.com
✉ Laurel St., Fort Bragg
☎ 707/964-6371 or 800/866-1690
$ $$$$$

Mendocino Coast Botanical Gardens
www.gardenbythesea.org
✉ 18220 N. Calif. 1, Fort Bragg
☎ 707/964-4352
$ $$$

Eureka & around
268 A4
Visitor information
www.redwoodvisitor.org
1034 2nd St., Eureka
707/443-5097 or 800/346-3482

Humboldt Bay Maritime Museum
www.humboldtbaymaritimemuseum.com
1410 2nd St., Eureka
707/444-9440

Blue Ox Millworks Historic Park
www.blueoxmill.com
1 X St., Eureka
707/444-3437
Closed Sun.
$$

Fort Humboldt Museum & State Historic Park
www.parks.ca.gov
3431 Fort Ave., Eureka
707/445-6567

Fortuna Depot Museum
http://gov.sunnyfortuna.com/museum
3 Park Pl., Fortuna
707/725-7645
Closed Mon.–Wed. in winter

Ferndale
268 A3
Visitor information
707/786-4477

Eureka & around

THE CENTER OF CALIFORNIA'S MASSIVE LUMBER INDUSTRY since the late 1800s, Eureka is like many midsize towns in the state—sprawling, without a core, sometimes pretty and sometimes ugly. Yet Eureka (Greek for "I have found it") holds several delights, both within its city limits and just beyond. Anyone planning to trek through some of the number of memorable national and state parks in this part of northern California will likely end up staying—or at least dining—here.

The **Old Town** area includes three much photographed Victorians, completely restored. The extraordinary **William Carson Mansion** *(143 M St., closed to the public)*, built by a wealthy lumber baron in 1884 and now a private club, is a combination of Queen Anne, Italianate, and Stick-Eastlake styles. Exotic even in its own day, the building was constructed by architects Newsom and Newsom mainly of redwood, using such materials as onyx and white mahogany to accentuate its lines.

Other monuments in Old Town are the **J. Milton Carson House** *(202 M St., closed to the public)*, built by William Carson for his son in 1889, and the **Clarke Historical Museum** *(240 E. St., tel 707/442-1947, www.clarkemuseum.org)*, built in 1888 for the mayor of Eureka, William Clark.

Yurok master woodworker, Eureka

Before looking outside the city limits for travel destinations, try the 75-minute **Humboldt Bay Harbor Cruise** *(tel 707/445-1910; operates summer only; $$$$)* on the old *Madaket*, a 1910 passenger ferry. The **Humboldt Bay Maritime Museum** features a number of exhibits about local shipwrecks. At the **Blue Ox Millworks Historic Park** you can watch craftspeople use vintage machinery to make the gingerbread so evident in regional Victoriana. Finally, look in on the **Fort Humboldt Museum & State Historic Park** and find out about Ulysses S. Grant, stationed in Eureka in 1854.

Several places of interest lie south of Eureka on or around US 101. The first is **Fortuna,** where the **Fortuna Depot Museum** is located inside an 1893 railroad depot. It specializes in antique train, fishing, and logging memorabilia. Off US 101 to the west is the delightful town of **Ferndale,** where one can ride in a horse-drawn carriage through a largely untouched 1890s town. Farther south on US 101, at the riverside town of **Scotia,** visitors can tour the **Pacific Lumber Mill** *(125 Main St., tel 707/764-2222, closed weekends)*, the world's largest working redwood mill, and south again, midway between Eureka and Fort Bragg, lies the little town of **Garberville,** blessed with turn-of-the-century architecture. One not to be missed is the Tudor-style

The hills above Garberville

Benbow Inn (see p. 377), host to the stars in its heyday. Spencer Tracy, Clark Gable, and Joan Fontaine all stayed here. Garberville has a more modern claim to fame: It hosts numerous special events throughout the year.

Across Humboldt Bay from Eureka is the historic **Samoa Cookhouse** *(79 Cookhouse Ln., Samoa, tel 707/442-1659)*, the last logging-camp cookhouse in the western U.S. You can still get a very hearty meal here, and the adjacent museum of logging is intriguing.

On the north side of the bay is the town of **Arcata.** Here the **Arcata Railroad Museum** *(Jacoby's Storehouse, 791 8th St., tel 707/822-4500)* will please railroad buffs with its collection of historic maps and artifacts, and the **Arcata Marsh & Wildlife Sanctuary** is a perfect place for watching northern shorebirds. Just a bit farther north, the beach town of **Trinidad** stands on a dramatic seaside point.

Nearby is **Sumeg Village.** This 1990 re-creation of an ancient village has a working reconstruction of a traditional sweathouse. The Native American tribe based along this part of the coast were the Yurok, while inland were the Hoopa. Today, the large **Hoopa Indian reservation,** about 60 miles inland from Eureka, is home to some 2,000 of the tribe. The **Hoopa Tribal Museum** includes examples of dugout canoes and ceremonial regalia, and offers tours of local villages and ceremonial sites. ■

Local specialties

Regional specialties abound. Visit the **Loleta Cheese Factory** *(252 Loleta Dr., tel 707/733-5470, www.loletacheese.com)*, in nearby Loleta, where you can watch them make their award-winning cheese while trying some free samples. Thin out your blood at Eureka's **Lost Coast Brewery** *(617 4th St., tel 707/445-4480, www.lostcoast.com)*, where they make no fewer than five award-winning brews serving its award-winning Nectar ales and "beer cuisine" in a brew-pub full of football memorabilia. ■

Arcata Marsh & Wildlife Sanctuary
- ✉ 600 S. G St., Arcata
- ☎ 707/826-2359

Sumeg Village
www.parks.ca.gov
- ✉ 4150 Patrick Point Dr., Patrick Point State Park
- ☎ 707/677-3570
- $ $$

Hoopa Tribal Museum
- ✉ Calif. 96, Hoopa Shopping Center
- ☎ 530/625-4110
- 🕒 Closed Sun., plus Sat. in winter

Arcata Visitor information
www.arcatachamber.com
- ✉ 1635 Heindon Rd.
- ☎ 707/822-3619

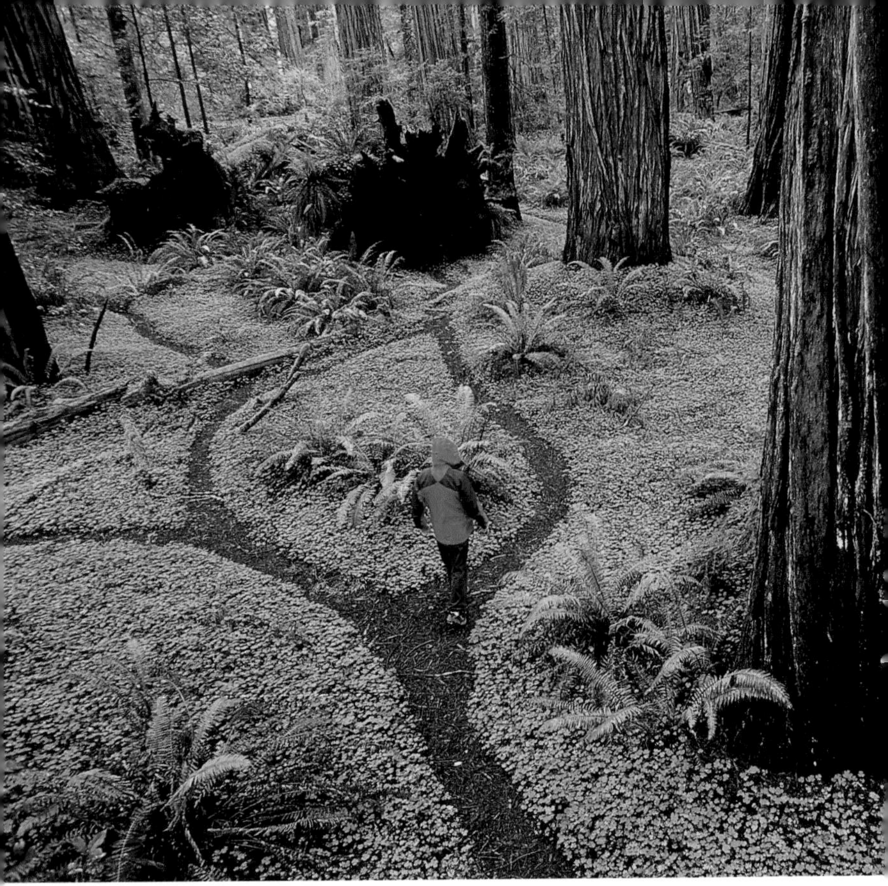

Redwood National Park

A 1968 CARTOON BY THE PULITZER PRIZE-WINNING *L.A. Times* artist Paul Conrad shows a caravan of suitcase-laden cars driving into a tunnel bored through an enormous redwood tree. A sign tacked onto its trunk proclaims: "Redwood National Park." For years, Conrad's vision was not far from the truth. Many travelers rushing along the interstate barely got out of their cars to see the majestic trees; when they did it was merely to snap a photo of the family standing in front of an enormous mass of furrowed bark—the tree, of course, being too big to get into the photo.

Redwood Information Centers

www.nps.gov/redw

✉ 1111 Second St., Crescent City; US 199 at Hiouchi; US 101, S of Orick

☎ 707/464-6101 (information for all redwood parks)

Today, thanks to the renewed interest in the outdoors, California's redwoods are again the subject of human scrutiny. In fact, so many backpackers head into the wilderness that it has become necessary to control their numbers and activities more closely. Yet so far-reaching and awe-inspiring are these parks that, on a hike or even stopping for a picnic, it is still easy to feel you are the only person for miles around.

The four major parks in the northern California area all lie close to the coast north of Orick, on coastal US 101 north of Eureka,

stretching almost as far as the state border with Oregon. **Redwood National Park** (1968) is by far the largest and the youngest. Together with three redwood state parks—**Prairie Creek** (1923) in the south, **Del Norte Coast** (1925) in the middle, and **Jedediah Smith** (1929) at the northern edge—it forms the heart of both a World Heritage site and an International Biosphere Reserve.

The **Redwood Information Center** at Orick should be your first stop. Here you will find maps, books, displays, and helpful park rangers. (Requests for campground reservations should be made several months beforehand, particularly if you are planning a summer visit.)

To see the **Tall Trees Grove,** where the world's second largest tree (368 feet; a 378-feet-tall tree, Hyperion, was discovered in 2007 but is inaccessible by trail), you must first obtain one of a limited number of permits that allow you to drive to the trailhead. To get a permit, arrive at the visitor center early. The round-trip takes about four hours. For those with limited time there are other options, all affording spectacular scenery and rewarding hiking. **Lady Bird Johnson Grove** can be reached by a self-guiding interpretive loop trail, which goes through mature forest and, finally, into the majestic grove dedicated by the former first lady in 1968. A flatter trail to the north, just south of the Prairie Creek park, is **Lost Man Creek.** This fern and moss forest has some outstanding rain forest flora. ■

Above: A hiker in Redwood National Park is like a child among giants. Below: Steller's jay

Redwood flora & fauna

First, a few redwood facts: The coast redwood (*Sequoia sempervirens*) is the world's tallest tree, but not the thickest or the oldest. Those distinctions belong, respectively, to the giant sequoia or Wellingtonia of the Sierra (*Sequoiadendron giganteum*), and the bristlecone pine *(Pinus longaeva),* also an inland species.

Although some specimens have been known to reach more than 2,000 years old, California's coast redwoods average between 500 and 700 years in age. Suffering from no known pestilence or fatal disease, the tree thrives on a vast system of ancillary roots that supports its main taproot. It can reproduce via sprouts as well as seeds, and new stems and roots can shoot from burned or cut-down trunks.

Redwoods are denizens of fog: The mild, moist climate of the dinosaurs was their birthright, a climate somewhat replicated today when warm inland air passes over the coastal lands bordering the Pacific here, which are cooled by the sea current flowing south from the Arctic Ocean.

With a natural rain forest ecosystem feeding it moisture and nutrients, the floor of redwood forests teems with many smaller but equally fascinating and rare plants. Look for deer and sword ferns, redwood sorrel, redwood violet, and western trillium. Chanterelle mushrooms and many other fungi also thrive in this habitat.

Animal life most commonly seen includes Roosevelt elk, chinook salmon, and the huge banana slug, which flourishes in the damp conditions. Among birds to look for in the redwood parks are small seabirds called murrelets, and Steller's jay, a dark blue, noisy woodland bird with a black crest. ■

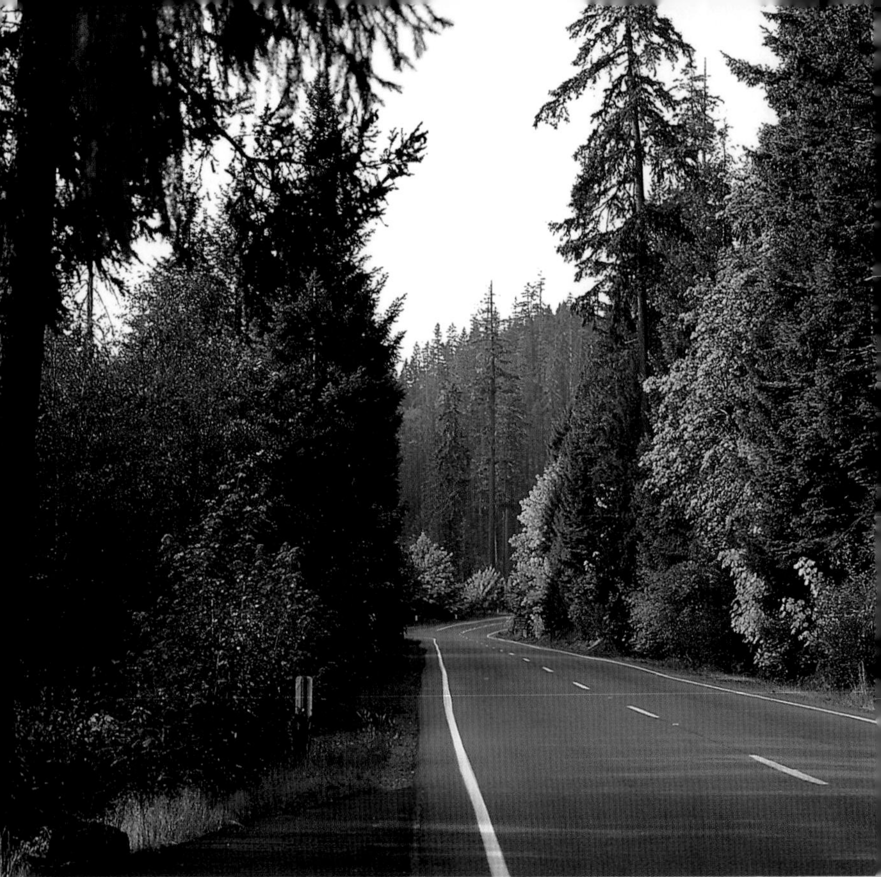

Prairie Creek Redwoods State Park
www.parks.ca.gov
268 B4
Turn off US 101 at Newton B. Drury Scenic Parkway
707/465-7347

Three redwoods state parks

THREE REDWOODS STATE PARKS OF PRAIRIE CREEK—THE farthest south, Del Norte, and Jedediah Smith (in the north), together with Redwood National Park (see pp. 276–77)—spread along the northern coast of California. They offer a diverse range of attractions for forest hikers of all ages and skill levels. Keep in mind that the entire coast redwood area is likely to be damp, misty, and often rainy—these, after all, are the climatic conditions in which the redwoods flourish. But do not let the weather deter you from a thorough exploration of this area. The redwood forests are one of the high points of any tour to the north.

Prairie Creek Redwoods State Park's 70 miles of trails range in difficulty from easy to very strenuous. There is also the scenic, 3-mile drive, **Cal-Barrel Road,** to which any ranger can direct you, as well as the **Revelation Trail,** specially created for blind and partially sighted visitors.

At center stage of the Prairie Creek experience are the Roosevelt elk, which graze placidly on the **Elk Prairie** and on **Gold Bluffs Beach.** A member of the deer

The Indian Jerusalem

North of Prairie Creek, near Klamath at the **Klamath Overlook,** you can visit a place that is the source of an enchanting Native American myth. Walk down the hillside path, past fragrant wild fennel. At the top of an old wooden stairway, as you gaze out onto the mouth of the Klamath River, contemplate the following story.

Once upon a time, according to Klamath oral tradition, the river's outlet was located 6 miles to the north, retained in its path by two sharp parallel bluffs. Then came the Klamath version of Jesus Christ, a man named Po-Lick-O-Quare-Ick. The Wise One, as he was known, had a long and fruitful mission among his people and was greatly loved by them.

When his mission ended, his subjects grieved his departure as he paddled down the river, out to sea. Then, as the Wise One wound his way downriver, he issued a command, obeyed immediately by the twin bluffs, which separated, allowing the river to run a more natural course. Po-Lick-O-Quare-Ick then disappeared into the gold rays of the Pacific sun. Ever since, the Klamath has followed his course, and the Wise One's people have had something by which to remember him. ■

US 199 runs through Jedediah Smith Redwoods State Park.

Camping
Near Elk Prairie. Tel 800/444-7275 for reservations.

Del Norte Coast Redwoods State Park
www.parks.ca.gov
268 B5
US 101, 13 miles N of Klamath
707/465-2146

family, the elk or, as the Shawnee knew them, wapiti, have a tawny brown coat and a thatch of white on their rump. The animal, which is so fat it ought to be called the William Howard Taft elk, is native to the Pacific Northwest, with a population numbering approximately 2,000. Do not approach them. Rather, use the well-marked **Elk Prairie Trail,** a 1.5-mile circuit skirting the eastern edge of the Elk Prairie.

From here begin a number of hiking trails *(maps from the visitor center at entrance to park).* If time is limited try the **Five Minute Trail,** which begins just behind the visitor center. Along this trail are several trees that have been hollowed out by fires; a close look may reveal traces—carved initials, gougings, seat-worn spots—of the families who lived here during the Great Depression.

The **Fern Canyon Loop,** about half a mile in length, takes in a spectacular natural feature where 50-foot canyon walls tower above a mossy floor. Among the many species of fern that grow so luxuriantly in this sheltered, moist spot are the five-fingered, deer, lady, and sword varieties.

A favorite trail is the **South Fork–Rhododendron–Brown Creek Loop,** perhaps the most beautiful of all. A walk of just over 3 miles, it takes in ghostly stands of moss-covered redwoods, ancient tree trunks covered with red, green, orange, and yellow mushrooms, and placid ponds, their surfaces mirrorlike in stillness. For mountain bikers, who are discouraged from most state and national parks, there is a designated 19-mile **Bicycle Trail.** It begins where the Elk Prairie campground road links with the jogging trail.

DEL NORTE COAST REDWOODS STATE PARK & AROUND

This 6,400-acre park stretches along the Pacific shore for some 8 miles south of Crescent City, the most northerly town on the California coast. Del Norte's shoreline is spectacularly wild, and much

Crescent City Visitor information
www.northerncalifornia.net
1001 Front St.
707/464-3174 or 800/343-8300

Jedediah Smith Redwoods State Park
http://redwood.areaparks.com
268 B5
US 199 (off US 101)
707/465-2144
Closed Oct. to mid-May

of it is fairly inaccessible—not to mention foggy. Almost half of Del Norte consists of old-growth trees, from coast redwood to tanoak, madrone, red alder, and bigleaf maple. The dense understory vegetation supports a wide range of wildlife, from bobcat and coyote to bear and deer. Maps and guides for Del Norte, and other parks in the area, are available either from the visitor center in Orick (see p. 276), to the south, or from the main information center for the Redwoods State Parks in Crescent City, to the north.

A tidal wave, triggered by an Alaskan earthquake, swept through much of **Crescent City** in 1964, causing several fatalities and wiping out most traces of the town's history as a focus for the surrounding gold mines.

From Crescent City you can reach the ocean by car, driving south for 2 miles to **Crescent Beach** and **Enderts Beach.** A map of the coastal path known as Damnation Trail is available at the visitor center. During the summer, guided tide-pool walks take place at Enderts Beach, which is known for its teeming marine life.

JEDEDIAH SMITH REDWOODS STATE PARK

Named for the 19th-century pioneer-explorer who opened a trail to Oregon, Jedediah Smith Redwoods (east of Crescent City) is the northernmost of California's redwoods parks. Because of its situation a few miles inland, this park is sometimes sunny when the nearby coast is blanketed in the fog that is such a feature of the Pacific Northwest seaboard. However, the weather is often wet and cold, keeping the **Hiouchi Information Center,** *(tel 707/458-3944, closed mid-Sept. to mid-June),* situated on US 199.

Jedediah Smith, like the other redwoods parks, has established a range of hiking trails. A popular short hike, just half a mile, is the **Simpson-Reed Discovery Trail,** which passes through a remarkable stand of Western hemlock, Douglas fir, and tan oak. Another begins at the trailhead and goes to the 44-acre **Stout Grove,** where some of the coast redwoods are 1,500 to 2,000 years old.

You can also experience the park from the waters of the beautiful **Smith River** on a guided kayak tour. Fishing enthusiasts know the Smith for its runs of chinook and steelhead trout, but it is also popular for swimming and other water-based activities. Rafts, kayaks, and bicycles can be rented in Hiouchi, a little town situated where US 199 crosses the Smith River in the far north of the state. ■

Redwood souvenirs

Chain-saw art—a local specialty with a difference—is wrought almost daily, just outside Orick in Redwood National Park. Screaming eagles made of redwood, little beavers made of oak, and a wide range of bunnies, deer, snakes, and major historical figures are also available at a number of shops in the town. For those who *just have to have* the ultimate souvenir of redwood country—that photo in front of a drive-through redwood tree—you may fulfill this dream at the **Klamath Tour Thru Tree** *(Terwer Valley exit near Klamath)*; the **Shrine Drive-Thru Tree** *(Avenue of Giants exit near Myers Flat)*; or the **Chandelier Tree,** off US 101 in the town of Leggett. ■

Opposite: Driving through the base of Leggett's 2,400-year-old Chandelier Tree

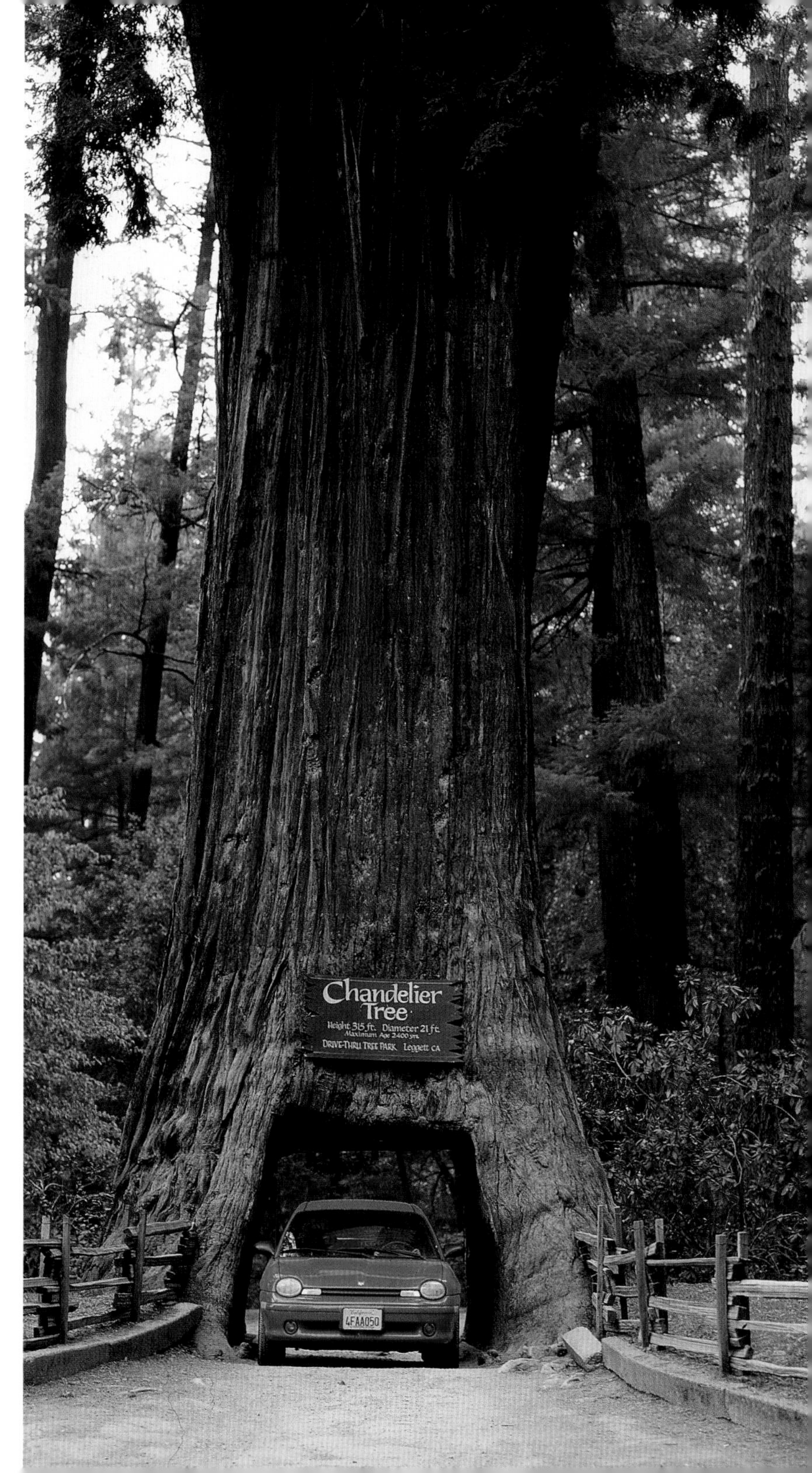
Chandelier
Tree
Height 315 ft. Diameter 21 ft.
Maximum Age 2400 yrs.
DRIVE-THRU TREE PARK Leggett CA
4FAA050

Drive: Mount Shasta

The great northern reaches of California are blessed with some of the state's most stunning scenery and least crowded parks. The north is also cursed with a spare travel infrastructure and, at times, rather daunting drives between attractions. One consequence is that some of the state's most thrilling sites are often overlooked by visitors in a hurry. An advantage of this is that travelers in search of true natural wonders and solitude can have both here, even in summer, when Yosemite and the Napa Valley are packed. This driving tour, lasting up to a leisurely week, will take you to the major attractions of the remote and beautiful north. Depending on your schedule, you can treat it as a series of separate drives, or opt for a shorter circular route by omitting the section north of Mount Shasta. Each major stopping point has accommodations and places to eat.

Start in the small town of **Red Bluff** 1 *(Visitor information, 100 Main St., tel 530/ 527-6220),* reached from the south on I-5, or from the west on Calif. 36, which cuts across the scenic South Fork Trinity River. (If you are coming from the coast, the latter entails a full day's drive. Be sure to check your brakes before departing.) Red Bluff, set on the Sacramento River at the junction of several routes, has a long tradition of hosting travelers. **Turtle Bay Exploration Park** *(840 Auditorium Dr., tel 530/243-8850, www.turtlebay.org, closed Tues.)* is worth a stop. This sprawling campus includes a 200-acre arboretum and garden, plus wildlife exhibits and educational activities tracing the relationship between humans and nature.

Take I-5 north and make a brief stop, about a mile north of Red Bluff, at the **William B. Ide Adobe State Historic Park** *(21659 Adobe Rd., tel 530/529-8599, www.parks.ca .gov).* Ide was an early settler, entrepreneur, and a leader of the 1846 Bear Flag revolt in Sonoma (see p. 262). In early Red Bluff, he literally served as judge, clerk, prosecutor, and defense attorney in trials of horse thieves. After a jury found them guilty, he would invariably sentence them to be hanged. His home has been preserved here, along with some fascinating relics of mid-19th-century ranch culture.

Passing through the towns of Anderson *(Visitor information, 1699 Hwy. 273, 530/365-7500, www.shastacascade.org),* where the U.S. Fish and Wildlife Service runs the **Coleman National Fish Hatchery** *(tel 530/365-8622),* and Redding, I-5 now cuts through increasingly interesting terrain, crossing an arm of the scenic **Shasta Lake** 2**,** California's largest reservoir (29,740 acres). If you have time for a detour, visit **Lake Shasta Caverns** *(tel 530/ 238-2341, www.lakeshastacaverns.com, $$$$, including ferry from Lakeview Marina, E of O'Brien exit off I-5 on Shasta Caverns Rd.),* on the lake's eastern shore. Here, you'll find an illuminated display of stalagmites and stalactites.

Farther north, as you approach Dunsmuir, **Castle Crags State Park** *(tel 530/235-2684)* looms dramatically. Its 6,000-foot spires mark the site of a war, in 1855, between settlers (and their Shasta allies) and the Modoc. The Modoc fled, their numbers greatly reduced.

At 14,162 feet **Mount Shasta** 3 is almost permanently snow covered. A volcanic peak that last erupted more than 200 years ago, it is still considered an active volcano. The mountain left John Muir with a less than pleasant memory—so bad was the frostbite he suffered

Also see area map, p. 269 C3
Red Bluff
431 Miles
3–4 days
Red Bluff

NOT TO BE MISSED

- Shasta Lake
- Mount Shasta area
- Lava Beds National Monument
- Modoc National Wildlife Refuge
- McArthur-Burney Falls Memorial State Park
- Lassen Volcanic National Park

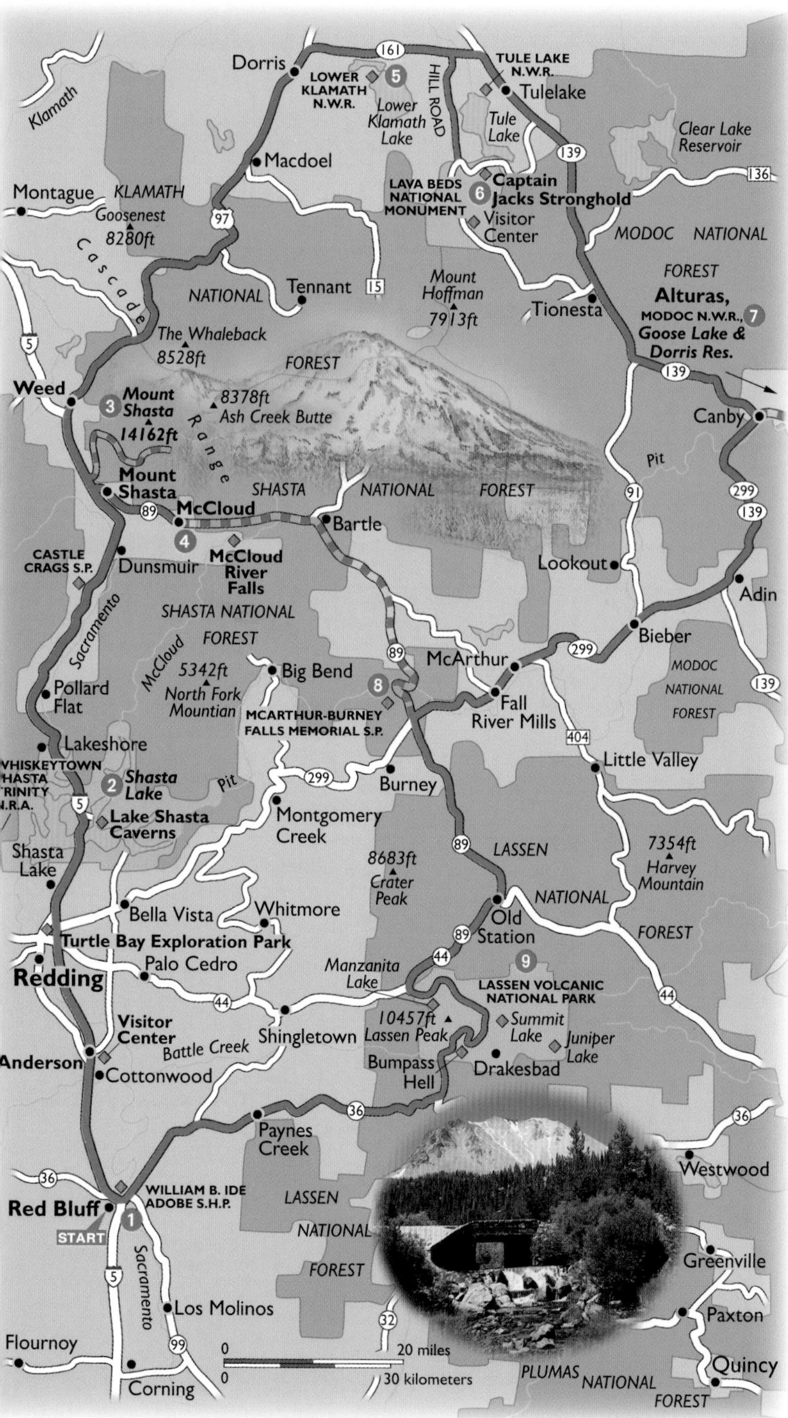
Dorris
LOWER KLAMATH N.W.R.
5
Lower Klamath Lake
HILL ROAD
161
TULE LAKE N.W.R.
Tulelake
Tule Lake
Klamath
Macdoel
Clear Lake Reservoir
139
136
Montague
KLAMATH
Goosenest 8280ft
Cascade
LAVA BEDS NATIONAL MONUMENT
6
Captain Jacks Stronghold
Visitor Center
MODOC NATIONAL FOREST
97
Tennant
15
Mount Hoffman 7913ft
NATIONAL
Tionesta
Alturas, MODOC N.W.R., Goose Lake & Dorris Res.
7
5
The Whaleback 8528ft
FOREST
Weed
3
Mount Shasta 14162ft
8378ft Ash Creek Butte
Range
Canby
Pit
Mount Shasta
SHASTA NATIONAL FOREST
91
299
139
89
McCloud
4
Bartle
CASTLE CRAGS S.P.
Dunsmuir
McCloud River Falls
Lookout
Adin
Sacramento
SHASTA NATIONAL FOREST
McCloud
Bieber
5342ft North Fork Mountain
Big Bend
McArthur
MODOC NATIONAL FOREST
Pollard Flat
8
Fall River Mills
MCARTHUR-BURNEY FALLS MEMORIAL S.P.
404
Lakeshore
Little Valley
WHISKEYTOWN SHASTA TRINITY N.R.A.
2
Shasta Lake
Pit
Burney
Lake Shasta Caverns
Montgomery Creek
Shasta Lake
8683ft Crater Peak
LASSEN
7354ft Harvey Mountain
Bella Vista
Whitmore
Old Station
NATIONAL
FOREST
Turtle Bay Exploration Park
Palo Cedro
Manzanita Lake
44
9
Redding
LASSEN VOLCANIC NATIONAL PARK
Visitor Center
Battle Creek
Shingletown
10457ft Lassen Peak
Summit Lake
Juniper Lake
Anderson
Cottonwood
Bumpass Hell
Drakesbad
36
Paynes Creek
Westwood
WILLIAM B. IDE ADOBE S.H.P.
LASSEN NATIONAL FOREST
Red Bluff
1
START
Greenville
Sacramento
Los Molinos
Paxton
32
99
0 20 miles
0 30 kilometers
Flournoy
Corning
Quincy
PLUMAS NATIONAL FOREST

there one winter that the great man walked with a limp for the rest of his life. Today, with some planning, the area is at least as comfortable—and every bit as scenic—as other ski country. A good place to stay, particularly when you are traveling in the summer, is the old lumber town of **McCloud** 4, a few miles east of I-5 on Calif. 89 *(Visitor information, 205 Quincy St., tel 530/964-3113, www.mccloudchamber.com)*. The restored McCloud Hotel (see p. 378) offers fine bed-and-breakfast with beautiful rooms. During the day, visit one of the three local natural waterfalls in the area where you can swim, picnic, and hike along easy trails *(maps available at the hotel)*. In the evening, enjoy a good meal on the **Shasta Sunset Dinner Train** *(tel 530/964-2142, www.shastasunset.com)* while chugging to the spectacular **MacIntosh Vista.** Mount Shasta may also be of interest for its mystical legends and spiritual vortices.

At this point, you can opt for an abbreviated version of this drive: Rather than heading into the northern section, proceed southeast from McCloud on Calif. 89 and rejoin the drive at McArthur-Burney Falls.

The main drive continues north on I-5 to the old lumber town of **Weed,** of which the tidy town actually has few. Bear northeast here on U.S. 97 to cross the **Cascade Range,** a chain that extends into British Columbia. The Great Basin region is represented here by the **Modoc Plateau—**high, dry, laden with juniper and sage, and flat, flat, flat. The **Klamath Basin National Wildlife Refuges Complex** *(tel 530/667-2231, www.fws.gov/klamathbasinrefuges)*, encompassing six refuges, extends across the Oregon-California border and is home to spectacular bird populations.

Just before the state border, don't miss the turnoff on Calif. 161. Head east, cutting across California's northernmost reaches. A worthwhile first stop is at the **Lower Klamath National Wildlife Refuge** 5 part of a 180,000-acre wetland area under U.S. Fish and Wildlife Service protection. For bird-watchers, this refuge and the nearby **Tule Lake National Wildlife Refuge** are a dream come true. The vast basin of marshes and shallow lakes is a winter haven for bald eagles and for more than a million migrant ducks, geese, and swans. During the breeding season it is common to see herons and egrets, double-crested cormorants and cinnamon teal.

Just to the south of Tule Lake is **Lava Beds National Monument** 6 *(turn off Calif. 161 on Hill Rd. S, tel 530/667-2282, www.nps.gov/labe)*. Be prepared here for extremes: of heat during the day, of cold in the evening. Clustered near the park's visitor center are the famous lava tubes. These 30,000-year-old signs of volcanic activity were formed when the exterior of long lava flows cooled and hardened before their centers. When the flow stopped and the remaining molten lava ran out of the other end, a tube resulted. Many of these tubes contain brightly colored lichens. Some are open for visitors to explore. To do so, you will need warm clothes, hard-soled shoes, a helmet, and a flashlight (the visitor center provides these), and a lot of common sense—for example, do not go alone. Park rangers conduct regular walking tours. They can also direct you to a number of petroglyphs, ancient Native American rock carvings.

Before leaving the park on Calif. 139, take the rare opportunity to visit a battleground most Americans do not even know about—that of the Modoc War. **Captain Jacks Stronghold,** at its center, is named for the ingenious Modoc warrior who in 1872 startled the U.S. Army by beating them in a series of skirmishes over land policy. Two short walking trails take visitors around Captain Jack's fortifications.

A detour for wildlife enthusiasts is to take Calif. 299 east from Canby to the little town of **Alturas** 7 *(Visitor information, 522 S. Main St., tel 530/233-4434, www.cityofalturas.org)*, the focal point of an area that is outstanding for bird- and animal-watching. For a hearty meal while in town, drive over to the Brass Rail (see p. 377), which serves up giant portions of Basque-style cuisine in a family setting.

The big attraction in the Alturas area is the **Modoc National Wildlife Refuge** *(Visitor information, 800 W. 12th St., Alturas, tel 530/233-3572, www.fws.gov/modoc)* a 7,000-acre park dedicated to the management and protection of migratory waterfowl. Don't underestimate its popularity; it may be remote, but professional ornithologists flock here every year. The reason: The refuge is an important resting and feeding area for migratory birds on the Pacific flyway. A total of 246 bird species

Mount Shasta's snow-streaked cone looms over a farm near the town of Weed.

have been spotted on the refuge, including 40 accidentals. In spring and fall, Canada geese and teal, mallard and widgeon are everywhere. In summer come wading birds such as willets and avocets, and several species of gulls and herons. In winter you might spot a bald eagle. On your way, you may see one of the herds of pronghorn that gather on the edge of local wild-rice farms. The best birding is April–May and Sept.–Oct., when the greatest diversity of species is present. **Dorris Reservoir** permits boating and fishing Feb.–Sept.

Anyone interested in pioneer history should make a further side trip north from Alturas on U.S. 395 to **Goose Lake.** Here, close to the point where California, Oregon, and Nevada meet, two important migrant trails converged. One, the **Applegate Trail,** was made in 1846 by a party of 15 men following cartographic information developed by the Hudson's Bay Company's trappers in the 1820s. The second, the **Lassen Trail,** was first trekked in September 1848; after a winter of few supplies and rough weather, the party was rescued, 40 miles north of Sacramento, by Peter Burnett, who later became the first governor of California. Staff of the Modoc National Wildlife Refuge information center will be able to give you detailed information on these trails.

If you do not take the Alturas detour, follow Calif. 299 southwest, then head north on Calif. 89 for the entrance to **McArthur-Burney Falls Memorial State Park** 8 (*tel 530/335-2777, www.parks.ca.gov*). The 129-foot waterfall—Theodore Roosevelt proclaimed it the "eighth wonder of the world"—is easily reached by a well-maintained footpath. Flush with wildlife (the rare black swift nests here) and stands of fantastic incense cedar and ponderosa pine, the park is yet another of this region's under-visited gems. Several campsites are available, as are cabins, and small motels and inns just outside the park offer a restful natural getaway.

On the road once more, drive south on Calif. 89 to reach **Lassen Volcanic National Park** 9**,** which bristles with yet more natural wonders (see p. 286). The spectacular drive across the park on Calif. 89 is closed in winter, and occasionally even in summer in bad weather. Check current conditions with the park.

Continue on Calif. 89 to Calif. 36, and go west to return to Red Bluff. In winter, take Calif. 44 to Redding, then drive down I-5. ■

Lassen Volcanic National Park

ONE OF THE BEST KEPT SECRETS OF THE NORTHWEST IS this 100,000-acre wilderness. Anyone wishing to impress friends with their summer vacation photos and have a great time in truly stunning scenery, away from the crowds of Yosemite, will find this place pure magic.

Lassen Volcanic National Park
269 D3
Visitor information
www.nps.gov/lavo
State Route 36 East, Mineral
530/595-4444
Visitor center closed p.m. & Sat.–Sun.

The park centers on 10,457-foot **Lassen Peak,** a volcano that last erupted as recently as 1915, producing an immense cloud of dust and covering the land around it with deep mud. The effects are still visible more than 85 years later where Calif. 89, or Lassen Park Road, crosses the **Devastated Area** to the north of the peak. The park abounds in extraordinary volcanic landscape features such as hot springs, bubbling mud pots, and gas seeping from holes called fumaroles at **Bumpass Hell** in the southwest. Elsewhere there are blue-green volcanic ponds, crystal-clear lakes, forests, and, in spring, wonderful verdant wildflower meadows. Trails have been laid out by the National Park Service to enable visitors to explore the park's wonders. Keep to them—it goes without saying that hot springs, steam, and unstable ground can be hazardous and that care and common sense are necessary as you follow the trails.

Lassen Peak reflected in the still waters of Lake Helen

Those fond of the outdoor life can choose from six campsites throughout the park. Most of these are located fairly close to dramatic natural features, among them **Manzanita Lake** in the northwest sector, **Juniper Lake** in the east, and **Summit Lake** in the center.

For a more comfortable stay, make reservations at Drakesbad Guest Ranch (see p. 377), a travelers' lodge built by German immigrants in the 1860s to take advantage of the natural hot springs. Later owners built a stone, open-air swimming pool and diverted the water from cold and hot springs to create a plunge pool with a perfect temperature of 95–100°F, ideal for late-night star-gazing. Today Drakesbad offers rustic accommodations in its central lodge (there is only a modest amount of electricity, though the ranch is quite comfortable). As well as outstanding hiking trails there is a horse stable whose hands will escort you through some of the most fantastic scenery in any national park.

The "Lassen Park Guide" includes a list of accommodations. It is available free from the park. ■

The historic—and dramatic—core of California, Gold Country is now mined for (what else?) great wines and stunning scenery. In Grass Valley and Sonora, arts scenes thrive. Mark Twain (his cabin is here) would have approved.

Gold Country

At the end of the rainbow

Gold Country

BASED ON A CHAIN OF PICTURESQUE TOWNS ALONG CALIF. 49, FROM Mariposa to Nevada City, Gold Country is a traveler's delight. Drive through it in a day, or probe, ponder, and explore it for a week. Unlike the far north, Gold Country has a strong tourist infrastructure (perhaps the best visitor centers, prominently posted, of any region), relatively short distances between major points, and (in season) a pleasant, warm climate. No wonder that its beautiful landscapes inspired the plein air painters of the early 20th century.

Panning for gold in Columbia State Historic Park

It is a region of grand, epic history. On January 24, 1848, a New Jersey émigré named James Marshall, working at a wood mill on the American River, spotted a lentil-size speck of yellow ore in the tail race of his operation. He picked it up. Was it pyrite, or gold? He smashed it between stones. It was soft. It was gold. Word spread—to the bay, then back east, then around the world. California was transformed. By 1850 its population had soared from 15,000 to nearly 100,000. As historian J.S. Hallidie wrote, "The world had rushed in."

The refined version of the story adds nuance, tragedy, and color. The gold rush was a triumph for some, but a disaster for the Native Americans routinely stripped of land and made ill with white man's diseases. It was also, in a sense, the end of Latin Catholic California, bringing as it did many Anglo Protestants and Yankee reformers and their very poor food. It was also a multicultural world, where Chinese mixed with Peruvians and blacks and Swedes and mountain men.

Remembering these notions and epic events makes a visit to Gold Country more fulfilling. The towns possess a rich and diverse history that can only be appreciated by walking along their streets. Each town offers mini-excursions and secret histories to visitors.

The Gold Country is a fine lead-in to Yosemite (see pp. 302–306). You could spend

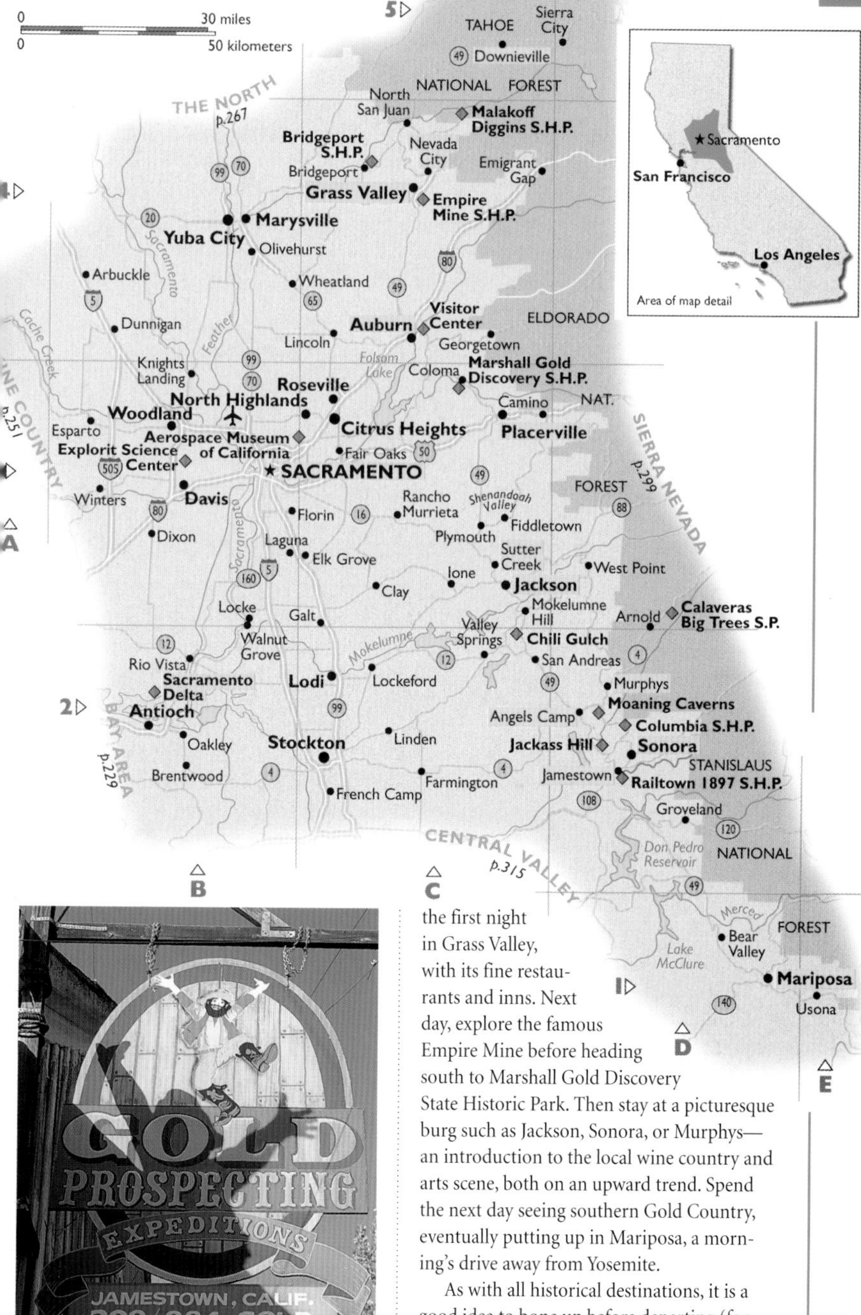

the first night in Grass Valley, with its fine restaurants and inns. Next day, explore the famous Empire Mine before heading south to Marshall Gold Discovery State Historic Park. Then stay at a picturesque burg such as Jackson, Sonora, or Murphys—an introduction to the local wine country and arts scene, both on an upward trend. Spend the next day seeing southern Gold Country, eventually putting up in Mariposa, a morning's drive away from Yosemite.

As with all historical destinations, it is a good idea to bone up before departing (for some suggestions, see p. 345). ■

Old-fashioned advertising in Jamestown

Sacramento

Sacramento
289 B3
Visitor information
www.sacramentocvb.org
1608 I St.
916/808-7777

Sutter's Fort State Historic Park
www.parks.ca.gov
27th & L Sts.
916/445-4422
$

State Capitol
www.assembly.ca.gov/museum
10th St. & Capitol Mall
916/324-0333

Crocker Art Museum
www.crockerartmuseum.org
216 O St.
916/264-5423
Closed Mon.
$$

FOUNDED IN 1839 BY THE SWISS-BORN ENTREPRENEUR Johanne Augustus Sutter, what is now the capital of California began its post-colonial life as one man's attempt to build his own feudal agricultural colony at the confluence of the American and Sacramento Rivers. When the gold rush came the workers on Sutter's estate—a polyglot bunch from the ends of the Earth—abandoned padrone Johanne. The agricultural part fared little better. By the 1850s Sutter was broke.

Much of what remains of **Sutter's Fort,** the center of his New Helvetia colony, can now be viewed on a self-guided audio walking tour of the **Sutter's Fort State Historic Park,** including copper and blacksmith's shops, a bakery, and a prison.

Sacramento's most distinctive building is the elegant 19th-century neoclassic **State Capitol.** Some of its rooms are open to the public, including the one where the state assembly sits. Although Sacramento's social landscape is dominated by politics, the art scene thrives. Do not miss the **Crocker Art Museum.** Located in a 19th-century mansion, the collection grew out of an art-collecting tour of Europe taken by Judge Edwin Crocker and his wife in 1870–72. The collection resulting from their trip was briefly, in the words of art critic William Wilson, "the biggest—if not the most discriminatingly selected—in America." The museum has works by many European painters, from Albrecht Dürer to Hendrick Goltzius, as well as contemporary works by California artists.

Sacramento has revitalized **Old Sacramento,** a 28-acre site on the banks of the Sacramento River, and onetime mercantile epicenter of the gold rush days. Wooden sidewalks in front of historic buildings give a Wild West flavor to the town. The must-see is the **California State Railroad Museum** *(125 I St., tel 916/445 6645 www.california*

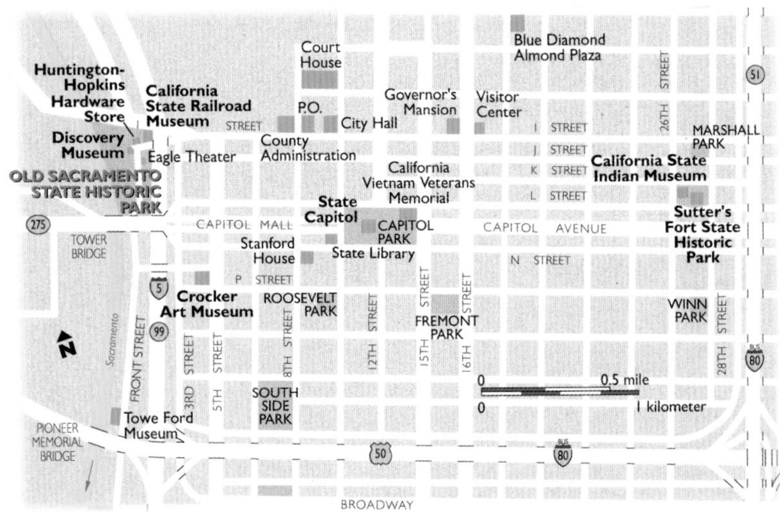

staterailroadmuseum.org) the largest interpretive museum on railroads in North America with 21 locomotives, restored to their 19th-century grandeur. In summer, visitors can take a 6-mile train ride. Adjoining, the **Huntington–Hopkins Hardware Store** *(125 I St., tel 916/323-7234, call ahead)* is the historic spot where the Big Four masterminded the transcontinental railroad.

For a novel and relaxing view of Sacramento, take a ride on the ***Delta King*** stern-wheel riverboat *(tel 916/444-5464, www.deltaking.com).*

The **Discovery Museum** uses interactive computer technology to examine Sacramento's history. The **California State Indian Museum** presents a different perspective on regional history. New in 2007: the **Explorit Science Center** *(2801 Second St., tel 530/756-0191, www.explorit.org),* in the nearby university town of Davis, is a hands-on science museum; and the **Aerospace Museum of California,** on the former McClellan Air Force Base, showcases 30 aircrafts, from early prop planes to supersonic jets. ■

The State Capitol

Discovery Museum
www.thediscovery.org
101 I St.
916/264-7057
$$

California State Indian Museum
www.parks.ca.gov
2818 K St.
916/324-0971
$

Aerospace Museum of California
www.aerospacemuseumofcalifornia.org
3200 Freedom Park Dr., McClellan
916/643-3192

Sacramento Delta

Many of the towns of the Sacramento Delta were founded by Asian immigrants who came here for its agricultural possibilities. The "Potato King" George Shima, a 19th-century Japanese immigrant, created a potato empire on delta soil regarded as wasteland by his Anglo contemporaries.

The tiny town of Locke, out on Calif. 160, was the first community in the U.S. built entirely by Chinese for Chinese. Once a rowdy Wild West town full of booze, prostitutes, and opium, it now stands, picturesque and weathered, as a piece of working history. A museum traces its past. ■

Northern Gold Country

THE TOWNS OF THE NORTHERN GOLD COUNTRY ARE characterized by a cooler climate than those to the south, a strong community spirit, and a local pride in historical continuity, a history that stretches back to the mid-19th century.

Downieville
289 C5

Downieville Museum
330 Main St.
530/289-3423
Closed in winter

Nevada City
289 C4
Visitor information
www.nevadacitychamber.com
132 Main St.
530/265-2692

Malakoff Diggins State Historic Park
289 C4
23579 Bloomfield Rd.
530/265-2740
$

Starting from the north on Calif. 49, interesting places to stop include **Downieville.** Established in 1851 by Maj. William Downie, the place sat on so much gold that, as legend has it, a man boiling a locally caught fish found gold dust at the bottom of the pot. In the town center, on Main Street, is the 1855 **Sierra County Courthouse,** where several men were sentenced to swing from the gallows on Piety Hill, just behind. The **Downieville Museum** displays a wide range of gold-rush artifacts. Amateur gold seekers can buy equipment at Sierra Hardware *(305 Main St., tel 530/289-3582).*

To the southwest on Calif. 49 is **Nevada City,** established in 1849 by miners seeking the rich gravel beds of the Lost Hill section, which yielded eight million dollars in gold dust in two years. The **National Hotel** *(211 Broad St., tel 530/265-4551)* here claims to be the "oldest continuously operating hostelry west of the Rockies." Nevada City is still a welcoming tourist town with comfortable amenities. It is also a base for gold-panning tours at **South Yuba River State Park** *(tel 530/432-2546),* and for visiting **Malakoff Diggins State Historic Park,** to the northeast. The broken landscape there still demonstrates the rapacious nature of the early (and fortunately short-lived) practice of hydraulic gold-mining. For a change of scene, go and admire the beautiful wildflowers along the

Bridgeport Buttermilk Bend Trail off Pleasant Valley Road.

Grass Valley is acknowledged as the richest of California's mining towns, with production of more than 400 million dollars over the course of one century following its founding in 1849. It was the birthplace, in 1855, of Josiah Royce, a Harvard scholar noted for his idealism and emphasis on the importance of the individual. Royce's childhood home, now the site of the city library, is on Mill Street, close to the 1852 home of sultry dance-hall performer Lola Montez, known for her Spider Dance and the fact that she divorced her husband because he killed her pet bear when it attacked him.

The historic **Holbrooke Hotel** *(212 W. Main St., tel 530/273-1353)* was home away from home for Mark Twain, Bret Harte, and several U.S. presidents; the bustling hotel now offers fine cuisine in the restaurant. In fall, rangers from local state parks bring the chef mushrooms and wild lettuce.

Outside the town are **Empire Mine State Historic Park,** the oldest, richest mine in California, and **Bridgeport State Park** *(17660 Pleasant Valley Rd., tel 530/432-2546, $),* which has one of the state's last covered bridges, built to serve the gold mines in 1862.

Going south on Calif. 49, the next place of any size is **Auburn,** at the junction with I-80. The town is surrounded by fruit orchards, which supply its many roadside stands with outstanding local produce in season. Established in 1848 as Wood's Dry Diggins, the town sits on a streamlet named Auburn Ravine, once the site of the richest placer gold mines in the state. The **Placer County Courthouse** *(101 Maple St.),* a handsome 19th-century structure, presides over the Old Town, and its museum *(tel 530/889-6500)* has several interesting historical exhibits.

Coloma, farther south on Calif. 49, was the site of James Marshall's gold discovery. The legendary incident was recorded in one co-worker's diary as follows: "Monday 24th. This

Bourne Cottage, Empire Mine State Historic Park

Grass Valley
289 C4
Visitor information
248 Mill St.
530/273-4667

Empire Mine State Historic Park
Off Calif. 49 E of Grass Valley
530/273-8522
$$

Auburn
289 C4
Visitor information
www.visitplacer.com
13411 Lincoln Way
530/887-2111

The Volunteer Firehouse in historic Auburn

Marshall Gold Discovery State Historic Park
www.parks.ca.gov
Back St., off Calif. 49, Coloma
530/622-3470
$

day some kind of mettle was found in the tail race that looks like gold, first discovered by James Martial, the Boss of the Mill." A fine afternoon can be spent picnicking, hiking, and investigating the historical sites by checking in at the **Marshall Gold Discovery State Historic Park.** The **Monument Trail Hike,** a 1.5-mile loop starting at the Marshall Monument and Gravesite, will take you to the Gold Discovery Site, then along beside the shallow American River to the site of **Sutter's Mill,** and eventually to **Bekeart's Gun Shop,** where you can try your hand at gold panning in a small demonstration tank.

The rolling, oak-dotted hills around the **Shenandoah Valley** are well suited to farms and fruit orchards, which post their wares on roadside signs ("Lambs for Sale," "Heirloom Tomatoes Now!") at the appropriate season. This is also the center of Amador wine country, which lies along Shenandoah and Fiddletown Roads (Fiddletown supposedly got its name from the musical orientation of its Missouri settlers, who were "always fiddlin'"). A beautiful back roads drive can be made northward from Fiddletown (via roads connecting to Shenandoah) to Apple Hill Farms, off US 50 near the little town of Camino. Apple Hill is a collection of farms producing fruits, vegetables, and wines; a more direct route to it runs east from **Placerville** on US 50. Back south, on Shenandoah School Road near the town of Plymouth, the **Amador Flower Farm** *(tel 209/245-6660, www.amadorflowerfarm.com)* specializes in daylilies. Nearby is the tasting room for Deaver Vineyards.

Sutter Creek played a key role in gold-rush history, attracting a number of investors to mine the Widman, Lincoln, and Central Eureka sites. The last, once almost abandoned by Leland Stanford, eventually produced the funds for him to invest in the Central Pacific Railroad. Sutter Creek is now the center of its own thriving mini-wine country, typified by **Sutter Ridge Winery** *(14110 Ridge Rd., tel 209/267-1316, www.sutterridgewine.com)*. The town, formerly a key gold-foundry center, has a fine historic district. Many old mercantile buildings built by Italian immigrants can be toured with the help of a map from the visitor center. The productive **Kennedy Gold Mine** *(tel 209/223-9542, www.kennedygoldmine.com)* can also be explored on summer weekends. ■

The arts in Gold Country

Although there is plenty to do in the area (historical sleuthing, horseback riding, or simply relaxing in the pine- and chaparral-scented air), one other important aspect of life in Gold Country—the arts—should not be overlooked. Events range from wine crushings to music festivals to theatrical and fine arts shows.

Of special note is **Nevada City** which, with its neighbor **Grass Valley**, shares an increasingly well-reviewed arts community. Try the classical "Music in the Mountains" series *(tel 530/265-6124, www.musicinthemountains .org)*, or the Sierra Shakespeare Festival *(tel 888/730-8587, www.foothilltheatre.org)*.

For information on local arts events, a good beginning can be made on www.ncgold.com, but the only way to find out about all the options is to visit each town's visitor center. ■

Southern Gold Country

Main Street, Angels Camp

IT WAS IN SOUTHERN GOLD COUNTRY THAT, WITH THE stakes so palpably high, the gold rush turned violent. Here the "Mexican Robin Hood," Joaquín Murieta, is said to have begun his bloody pillaging. Here the first Chinese Tong wars were fought; here slaves were allegedly sold and race riots fought over mining rights. Today the quiet, picturesque streets of southern Gold Country—from "Moke Hill" (Mokelumne Hill) to Mariposa—betray none of that churning, fugitive, and violent history. Instead there is a placid ambience—that of a wine country in the Sierra.

Once a prominent stopping point on the old Carson Emigrant Trail and now the crossroads of north–south Calif. 49 and east–west Calif. 88, **Jackson** came into its own as a town in 1850. Its early name, Bottileas, was a reference to the many broken whiskey bottles found on its hell-raising streets. The Argonaut Mine, still visible south of Calif. 88, sunk its shafts to an amazing depth of more than one mile below the surface. The town briefly became the seat of Calaveras County after ambitious Jacksonians literally pilfered government archives from nearby Double Springs, only to be out-politicked the next year by neighboring "Moke Hill," which then assumed the title. Today Jackson is a bustling town, full of cafés, Italian restaurants, and bookstores (see p. 298).

Established as a Mexican mining camp in 1849, **Mokelumne Hill,** farther south on Calif. 49, was once one of the most boisterous gold towns, where shootings were a weekly affair. A walking tour map can be obtained from the Hotel Leger *(Calif. 49 & Calif. 26, tel 209/286-1401, www.hotelleger.com)*, but it hardly does justice to the region's eventful

Jackson

289 C3

Visitor information

125 Peek St.

209/223-0350

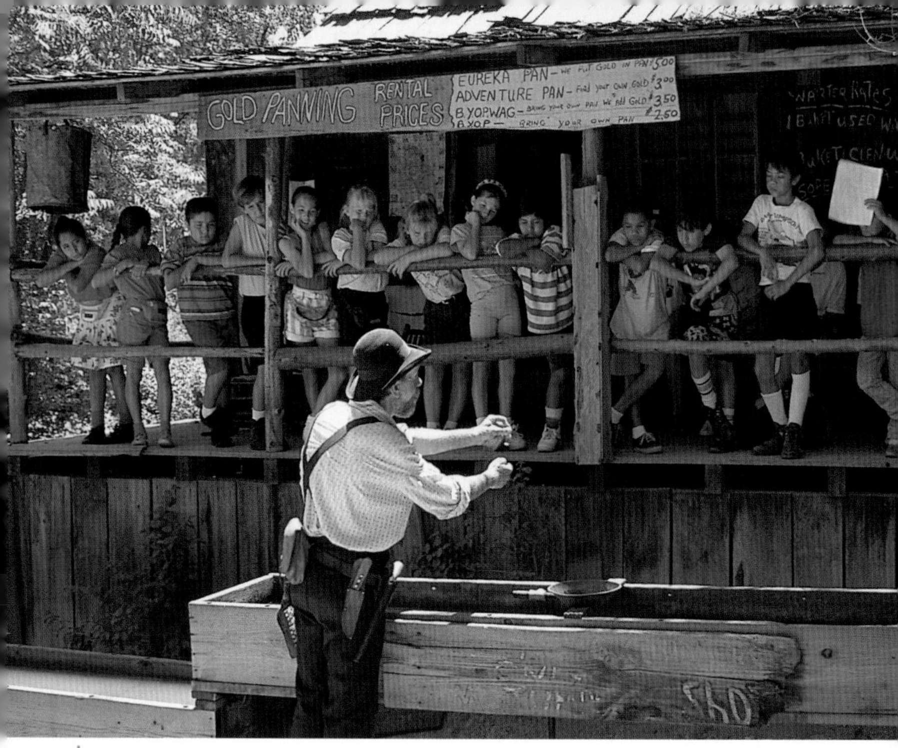

Valuable lessons in gold prospecting at Columbia State Historic Park

past. For example, French Hill, just to the south, is where the so-called French War was fought in 1851 when American miners literally took up their picks to drive off overly aggressive French upstarts. South of there on Calif. 49 is **Chili Gulch,** site of the Chilean War of 1849. This time, the Americans were driven out by Chileans, angered by attempts to expropriate their mining claims.

Another Mexican camp, established in 1848, **San Andreas** may be the site of the tavern portrayed in Mark Twain's story "The Celebrated Jumping Frog of Calaveras County" (see pp. 39–40). Ask at the **Calaveras County Museum & Visitor Center** if you can see the reputedly genuine red sash of the local bandito Joaquín Murieta (see Murphys, below). The museum also has relics of the Miwok, who once dominated the region.

Then again, **Angels Camp,** say locals, is where Twain got the inspiration for the bar scene in "Jumping Frog." ("I found Simon Wheeler dozing comfortably by the barroom stove of the dilapidated tavern in the decayed mining camp of Angel's....") Today this is a rather unremarkable destination, with several boutiques, a few cafés, and a gold rush museum. Fuel up here and drive on to **Murphys,** off Calif. 49 on Calif. 4. Established by brothers John and Daniel Murphy in 1848, Murphys is said to be where Joaquín Murieta got his ire. A three-card monte dealer in 1851, Joaquín had watched as his brother was hanged on a bogus charge of horse thievery. After Joaquín himself was flogged, he embarked on two years of his own brand of bloody thieving, in which, as the Californian author Richard Rodriguez writes in his 1992 book of essays *Days of Obligation,* he "stole horses, beautiful horses. He was like the wind stealing clouds." Murieta was eventually killed near Fresno. So hated was he by the

Calaveras County Visitor information

www.gocalaveras.com

✉ 1192 South Main St., Angels Camp

☎ 209/736-0049 or 800/225-3764

Calaveras County Museum & Visitor Center

✉ 30 N. Main St.

☎ 209/754 4658

Yankees that his captors cut his head off and displayed it in a jar.

Today Murphys is one of the best preserved gold rush towns. **Murphys Historic Hotel** *(457 Main St., tel 209/728-3444, www.murphyshotel.com)* is worth a look—after all, Mark Twain and President Ulysses S. Grant both slept there. The Calaveras Classic Artists performances (tel 209/754-1774, www.calaverasarts.org) feature such well-known musicians as the Stanford String Quartet and harpist Alfredo Rolando Ortiz.

To see giant sequoias close up, travel northeast from Murphys on Calif. 4 to **Calaveras Big Trees State Park** *(tel 209/795-2334)*, near the little town of Arnold.

Murphys is a good place from which to explore Calaveras wine country, particularly the beautiful **Ironstone Vineyards** *(Six Mile Rd., tel 209/728-1251, www.ironstonevineyards.com)*. The winery occupies a stunning building modeled on a 19th-century gold stamp mill. Pick up a picnic lunch in Ironstone's deli and drive south on Parrotts Ferry Road to **Columbia State Historic Park,** a preserved gold rush town with a difference. Here it is not only the buildings that recall the 1850s. A stagecoach, costumed guides, gold panning, live theater, and music in historical saloons all help Columbia to re-create the days when its importance made it a rival of Sacramento in the race to be state capital. On the way you could stop at the **Moaning Caverns,** one of many tourist-oriented natural wonders in this area.

While there may be disputes over aspects of Mark Twain's "Jumping Frog," no one contests its provenance—now a tiny, dilapidated wooden shack perched in a quiet grove of black and live oaks on **Jackass Hill** *(turn left up Jackass Hill Rd. from Calif. 49, S of Carson Hill, N of Turtletown)*. Here Twain, puffing his pipe and worrying over his San Francisco debts, crafted his tale. Anyone with any American literary soul should make this pilgrimage. Few do, making this a lonely and beautiful site.

Established in 1848 by miners from the Mexican state of the same name, **Sonora** teemed with political intrigue during its early years. A riot almost occurred in 1850 when the new U.S. government imposed a $20 tax on foreign-born miners. Eventually the Mexicans fled, but not before a group of Anglo settlers had marched, drum and fife at their front, in a display of bellicosity. Today Sonora is an exciting little town, replete with cafés, restaurants, shops, and cultural events such as the blues festival held here in August *(tel 209/533-3473)*. Visit the **Tuolumne County Museum & History Center** for its gold rush memorabilia.

Angels Camp

289 C2

Visitor information

www.gocalaveras.com

1192 Main St.

209/736-0049

Angels Camp Museum

753 S. Main St., Angels Camp

209/736-2963

Closed Mon.–Fri. (Jan.–Feb.)

Columbia State Historic Park

www.parks.ca.gov

11255 Jackson St.

209/588-9128

Sonora

289 D2

Visitor information

www.thegreatunfenced.com

542 Stockton Rd.

209/533-4420

Tuolumne County Museum & History Center

www.tchistory.org

Bradford Ave., off Washington St., Sonora

209/532-1317

Railtown 1897 State Historic Park
5th Ave., Jamestown
209/984-3953
No trains run in winter

Mariposa
289 D1
Visitor information
www.homeofyosemite.com
Calif. 49 & Calif. 140
209/966-7081

California State Mining & Mineral Museum
www.parks.ca.gov
Off Calif. 49 S of Mariposa
209/742-7625
Closed Tues. in winter

Jamestown, established in 1849 by Col. George James, is now a tiny burg with many cute shops. The main attraction here is the **Railtown 1897 State Historic Park,** an extension of the California State Railroad Museum in Sacramento (see p. 291). A 40-minute, 6-mile ride in an old steam-powered train is a fine way to end a day of exploring, and there is a collection of locomotives, carriages, and railroad mementoes.

Mariposa is best known as one of the gateways to Yosemite; although some 30 miles away, it is the nearest sizable town. But make time for Mariposa itself, which has an interesting old courthouse and jail. Details of its 19th-century days as a mining and railroad center are preserved in two historical collections, at the **Mariposa Museum & History Center** *(511 Jessie St., tel 209/966-2924, www.mariposamuseum.com, $)* and the **California State Mining & Mineral Museum.** Mariposa is where John C. Frémont lived with his literary wife, Jessie, following his defeat for the Presidency in 1858. Their house is on Calif. 140, next to the Odd Fellows Hall. Mrs. Frémont's *Mother Lode Narratives* gives an insight into this remarkable woman's life. ■

Gold Country shopping

Although Gold Country shopping has its requisite share of cute, it also has a great variety of refreshingly down-to-earth establishments.

Antiques: An outstanding antique collective is **Creekside Shops** *(22 Main St., Sutter Creek, tel 209/267-5520),* where you might pick up anything from a McCoy vase to a first edition of an 1896 Bret Harte biography. Two items that are hot among collectors of California memorabilia are turn-of-the-century stereographs and period postcards, many of which bear the scrawl of the era's itinerant sojourners. **Antiques Etcetera** *(S. Washington St., Sonora, tel 209/532-9544)* specializes in early 20th-century dinnerware.

Art: Gold Country is alive with talented artists, many of whom established their reputations in San Francisco before heading upriver. The **Holbrooke Hotel** in Grass Valley has prints by Peggy Swan, a brilliant printmaker. A sampling of the region's talent can be seen at the **Calaveras County Arts Council Gallery** in San Andreas. A coterie of young painters has grown up in and around Sonora. **The Vault** *(42 S. Washington St., Sonora, tel 209/533 1384, www.vaultart.com)* represents many of them. Sonora native Jack Cassinetto's neo-tonalist plein air works echo the early Californian great Gottardo Piazonni.

Books: Several outstanding second-hand book stores include **Hein & Company** *(Main St., Jackson, tel 209/223 9076).* The proprietors have a discerning eye for collectibles; you might snap up a 1930s Maxfield Parrish album or a rare hardcover edition of Gertrude Atherton's *Rezanov.*

Produce: Local produce and many things made out of it are available through the **Apple Hill Growers Association** *(http://applehill.com)* in Camino, east of Placerville. In the fall try **Mill View Ranch** *(Upper Hill Ave., tel 530/644-6885)* for homemade apple pies and jams; the **Marvin Larsen Ranch** *(2721 Mace Rd., tel 530/644-1396)* for cider, pears, and honey; or **Boa Vista Orchards** *(2952 Carson Rd., Placerville, tel 530/622-5522, www.boavista.com)* for fruit, wine, pies, and pastries. ■

Traditional store sign in Columbia

California's Sierra Nevada mountains distill the essence of wildest California, from the wonders of Yosemite, Sequoia, and Kings Canyon National Parks to Lake Tahoe's ski slopes. No one leaves without some sense of nature's might.

Sierra Nevada

Morning mist in Yosemite

Sierra Nevada

THE SIERRA NEVADA MOUNTAIN RANGE RUNS SOUTH OF MOUNT LASSEN to beyond Sequoia National Park. This 400-mile chain is the result of massive volcanic activity some 130 million years ago. Today it is a paradise of deep forests, ice blue lakes, glacier-carved valleys, and snowy mountain peaks.

Travelers interested in the region's flora and fauna (not to mention weather) will need to know the basics of Sierra topography. Ascending the range compares to a trip into Arctic tundra, with every 1,000 feet of elevation equivalent to traveling 300 miles northward.

The Sierra can be broken down into four ecological zones. The mixed conifer zone (3,500–6,000 feet) is a zone of frequent precipitation and dense vegetation. Giant sequoias, Jeffrey pines, and Douglas firs provide cover for deer, bears, and other forest mammals. The lodgepole pine-red fir zone (6,000–8,500 feet) is a region of deeply shaded forests, increasing snowfall, and wet mountain meadow land—perfect for western and lodgepole pine, and Sierra juniper. In the subalpine zone (8,500–10,500 feet), the effects of wind and snow begin to contort the natural landscape; vegetation is low growing, often gnarled and twisted. The alpine zone (from 10,500 feet) marks the timberline; here precipitation falls off dramatically and vegetation grows sparsely. One interesting adaptation by plants is their lack of scent; fragrance uses up scarce water. But the nose's loss is the eye's gain: Many plants compensate by making large flowers to attract pollinators.

The centerpiece of the "Sierra Experience" is Yosemite National Park. But in recent years, the two other national parks—Kings Canyon and Sequoia—have also become first-choice destinations. The great expanse of Lake Tahoe to the north has always been a draw, particularly for those seeking the added distractions across the Nevada border.

One piece of advice: If possible, avoid traveling in summer, when the parks fill up with buses and exhaust fumes. If summer is the only option, consider spending more time in Kings Canyon, which is quite lovely and much less crowded. Another obvious (but often unheeded) piece of Sierra wisdom: Make reservations for a hotel or campsite well ahead. ■

0 30 miles
0 40 kilometers
Loyalton
NORTH TAHOE NATIONAL FOREST
p.267
Soda Springs
Truckee
Donner Memorial S.P.
Granite Chief 9006ft
Tahoe City
Lake Tahoe
Sugar Pine Point State Park
D.L. Bliss S.P.
Emerald Bay S.P.
Desolation Wilderness
South Lake Tahoe
Visitor Center
ELDORADO NATIONAL FOREST
Riverton
Kyburz
Meyers
Woodfords
Kirkwood
Markleeville
Topaz
Walker
Bear Valley
STANISLAUS NATIONAL FOREST
Dardanelle
Sonora Junction
TOIYABE NAT. FOREST
Bridgeport
Strawberry
Pinecrest
NEVADA
SIERRA NEVADA
11755ft Tower Peak
12446ft Excelsior Mountain
Hetch Hetchy Reservoir
YOSEMITE NATIONAL PARK
Tuolumne
Lee Vining
Mono Lake
Mono Lake Tufa State Reserve
Hetch Hetchy Entrance
Tioga Pass Entrance
11123ft Glass Mountain
Benton
Benton Hot Springs
Big Oak Flat Entrance
Yosemite Village
June Lake
Obsidian Dome
INYO NATIONAL FOREST
14246ft White Mountain
Arch Rock Entrance
Devil's Postpile National Monument
Mammoth Lakes
Lake Crowley
Yosemite West
Wawona
Torris Place
Patriarch Grove
Mariposa Grove
South Entrance
Fish Camp
SIERRA NATIONAL FOREST
Ancient Bristlecone Pine Forest
Bishop
Schulman Grove
Oakhurst
Entrance
Aspendell
GOLD COUNTRY p.287
South Fork
Lakeshore
13830ft Mount Darwin
Big Pine
Shaver Lake
Dinkey Creek
10318ft Eagle Peak
THE DESERT p.323
KINGS CANYON NATIONAL PARK
Balch Camp
13125ft Mount Baxter
Pine Flat Reservoir
SEQUOIA NAT. FOREST
Cedar Grove
Grant Grove
Wilsonia
Roaring River Falls
KINGS CANYON NAT. PARK
Big Stump Entrance
Lodgepole
14495ft Mt. Whitney
Crystal Cave
Giant Forest Village
SEQUOIA NATIONAL PARK
Ash Mtn. Entrance
Mineral King
Lookout Point Entrance
CENTRAL VALLEY p.315
11510ft Kern Peak
Camp Nelson
9606ft Blackrock Mountain
SEQUOIA NATIONAL FOREST
Johnsondale
California Hot Springs
Wofford Heights
Lake Isabella
Weldon
Bodfish
Sacramento
San Francisco
Los Angeles
Area of map detail

El Capitan from the Merced River at dawn

Yosemite National Park

FOR MORE THAN 9,000 YEARS, INDIAN COMMUNITIES inhabited the Yosemite Valley. For the last thousand years it was the home of the Miwok, a subgroup of the Ahwahneechee. Ahwahnee means "valley that looks like a gaping mouth," a vivid description of this glacier-carved slash across the Sierra.

Lower Yosemite Falls in full spate in spring

In 1851, the Mariposa Brigade of the U.S. Army was asked by the governor of California to put an end to the conflicts between Indians and miners. Following a group of Indian people into the mountains, the troops came upon this magical valley, the first non-Indians to see it. The great naturalist John Muir (1838–1914) was seduced by Yosemite's spell and spent much of his life defending it. In 1890 the spell conjured a miracle—Congress created Yosemite National Park.

Today, with more than four million visitors each year, Yosemite, a World Heritage site, is one of the world's most famous wilderness areas. The valley at the heart of the park, formed by glaciers and further cut by the Merced River, is surrounded by awesome peaks: the 8,842-foot **Half Dome,** its other half crushed by glaciers; the massive bulk of **El Capitan** (7,569 feet) at the western end of the valley, the world's tallest exposed granite monolith; **Glacier Point,** at the top of a 3,200-foot-high rock wall. These are among the most-photographed natural wonders of Yosemite. Visitors flock to the valley to see them, resulting in traffic jams, pollution, and all the accompanying problems. However, at 7 miles long by 1 mile wide, the valley represents only a tiny fraction of the park's total area of more than 1,000 square miles. In much of the rest of Yosemite, the park's spell is unbroken—especially for those who can leave their cars and walk its trails. **Tioga Pass Road** *(closed spring & winter)* crosses the park from Crane Flat, near the Big Oak Flat entrance. The road climbs to the high country of the Sierra and crosses **Tuolumne Meadows,** dotted with alpine flowers, to Tenaya Lake and on to the 9,945-foot Tioga Pass and the eastern entrance of the park. This is serious hiking country, and the park offers some 800 miles of marked trails, many of which are fine for inexperienced hikers. Discovering Yosemite's colors and smells can be as simple as the stroll to **Mirror Lake** or as taxing as the steep haul up to the top of North America's highest waterfall, the 2,425-foot **Yosemite Falls.** The park is remarkably user-friendly, with major information stations at Yosemite Village, Wawona, and Tuolumne Meadows. The park information service provides excellent trail maps and weather information.

Three outstanding hikes, all requiring moderate effort, are as follows. The **Valley Floor Trek** is a flat, 5-mile loop in the most popular part of the park. Set out early and plan on spending most of a morning. Start by picking up a map at the Valley Visitor Center and take the free bus to the Yosemite Falls stop. After walking the gentle slope up to the foot of the falls, go downhill to **Cooks Meadow,** one of the most lovely in the entire park. From here the entire pantheon of Yosemite icons looms upward like great granite sentries—as well as Half Dome and Glacier Point,

Yosemite National Park
www.nps.gov/yose or www.yosemitepark.com

 301 A4–B5

☎ 209/372-0200 (24-hour updates on weather and trail conditions, plus campground information); 877/444-6777 (campground reservations)

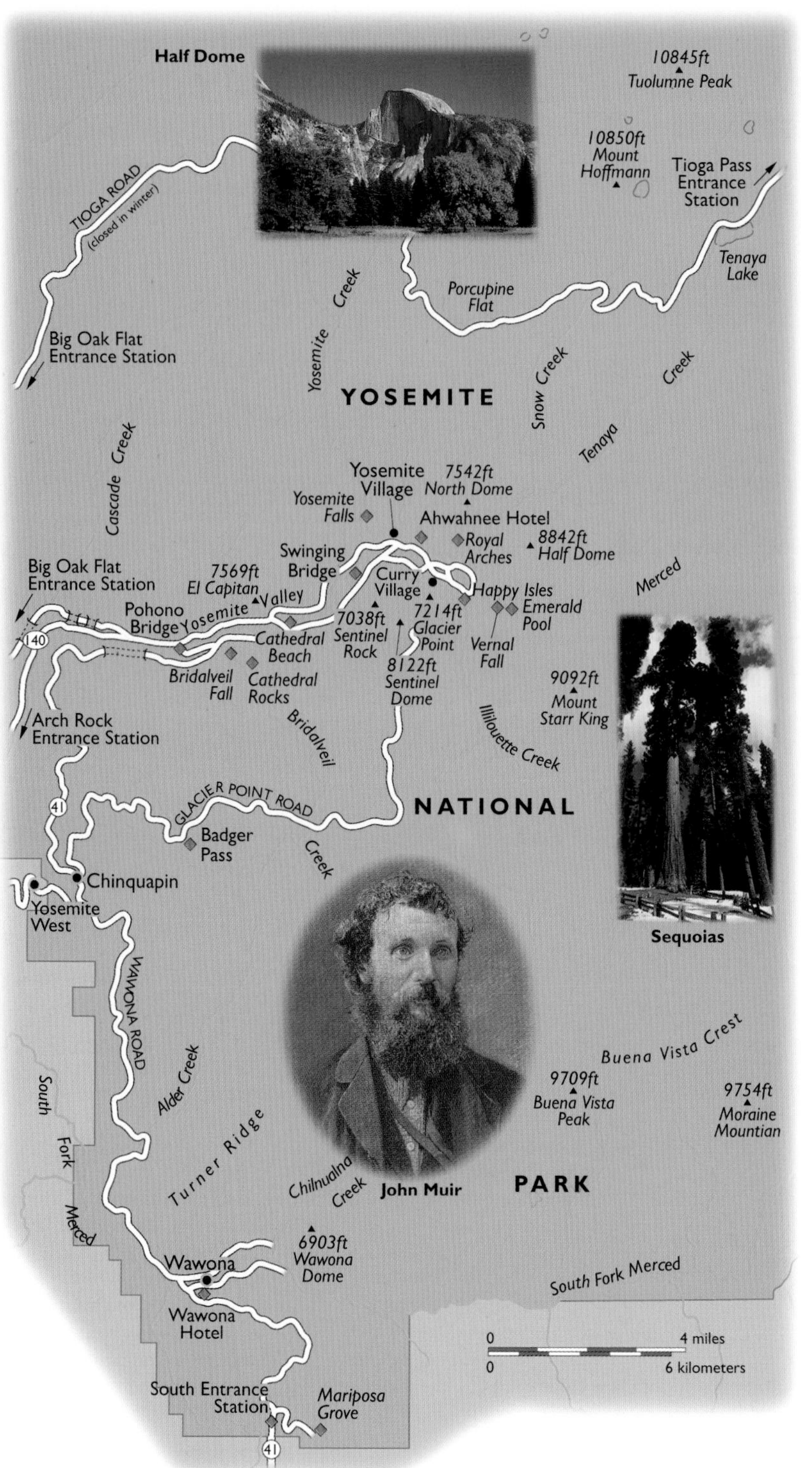

Half Dome
10845ft
Tuolumne Peak
10850ft
Mount
Hoffmann
Tioga Pass
Entrance
Station
TIOGA ROAD
(closed in winter)
Tenaya
Lake
Porcupine
Flat
Yosemite Creek
Big Oak Flat
Entrance Station
YOSEMITE
Snow Creek
Tenaya Creek
Cascade Creek
Yosemite
Village
7542ft
North Dome
Yosemite
Falls
Ahwahnee Hotel
Royal
Arches
8842ft
Half Dome
Swinging
Bridge
Big Oak Flat
Entrance Station
7569ft
El Capitan
Yosemite Valley
Curry
Village
Happy Isles
Merced
Pohono
Bridge
7038ft
Sentinel
Rock
7214ft
Glacier
Point
Emerald
Pool
140
Cathedral
Beach
Vernal
Fall
Bridalveil
Fall
Cathedral
Rocks
8122ft
Sentinel
Dome
9092ft
Mount
Starr King
Arch Rock
Entrance Station
Bridalveil
Illilouette Creek
GLACIER POINT ROAD
NATIONAL
41
Badger
Pass
Creek
Chinquapin
Yosemite
West
Sequoias
WAWONA ROAD
Buena Vista Crest
9709ft
Buena Vista
Peak
9754ft
Moraine
Mountian
Alder Creek
South
Fork
Merced
Turner Ridge
Chilnualna
Creek
John Muir
PARK
6903ft
Wawona
Dome
Wawona
South Fork Merced
Wawona
Hotel
0
4 miles
0
6 kilometers
South Entrance
Station
Mariposa
Grove
41

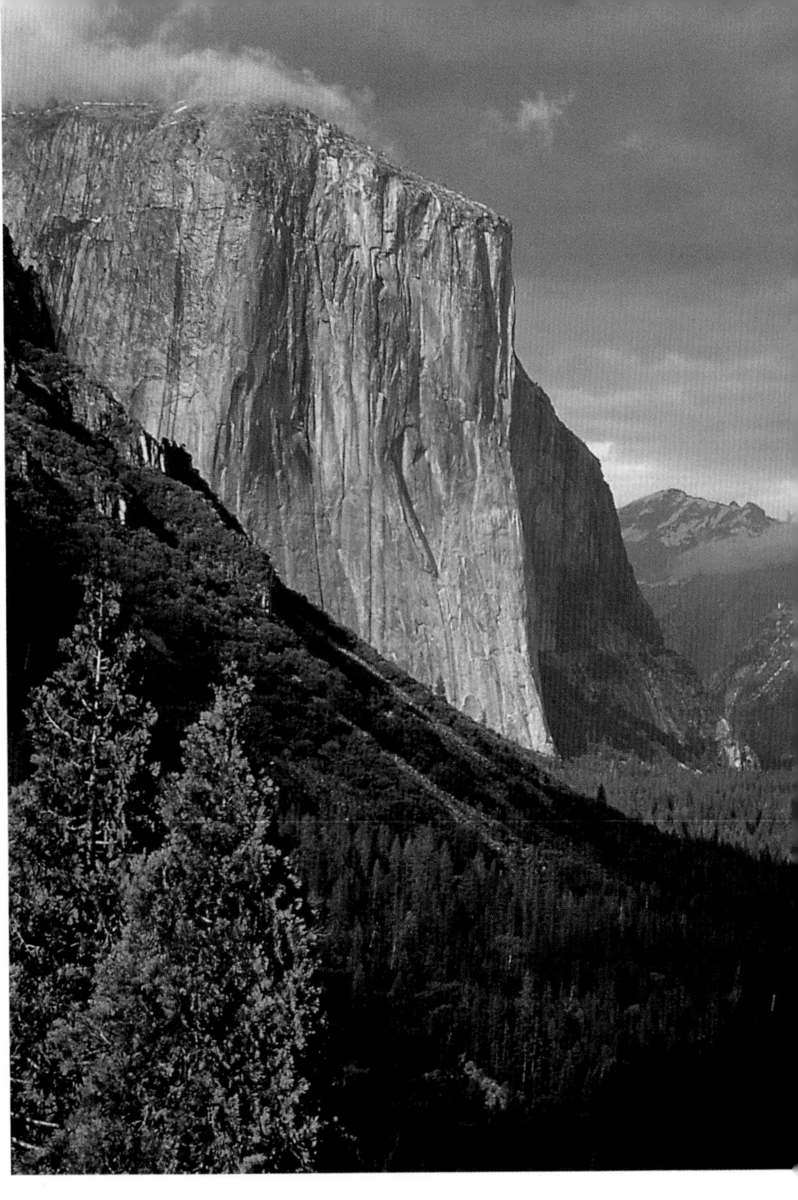

look for **Sentinel Rock** and the **Cathedral Rocks.** Cast your eyes lower and the meadow's flora and fauna come into view. Spring is the best time for the wildflowers here. The meadowlands are often alive with red-wing blackbirds, robins, and Steller's jays; predators such as owls, peregrines and other falcons, and even golden eagles are sometimes spotted hunting over the valley.

Keeping the burbling Merced River to your left, you will come to **Leidig Meadow,** named for Charles Leidig, the first non-Indian male born in Yosemite. This is one of the largest remaining meadows in the valley. Follow the bike path to its edge and to the river, where you may see stunning reflections of **Sentinel Falls.** Follow the trail along the north side of the meadow

to **Rocky Point,** easily recognizable by the rubble at its base, then continue to the river and a large wooded area. Now stick to the trail along the river to an area known as **Indian Swamp.** In spring the meadow here floods, giving amazing reflections of Cathedral Rocks and Spires. The trail then takes you to **El Capitan Meadow,** where you can view the towering sheer slab of granite, the subject of so many Yosemite photos. Across the valley is **Bridalveil Fall,** a spectacular 620-foot vertical torrent in spring. Continue along the riverside to **Gates of the Valley,** one of the best spots from which to view the entire valley.

At **Pohono Bridge,** cross the river to **Fern Spring.** From here you can either follow the trail to the

View up Yosemite Valley: El Capitan on the left, Bridalveil Fall to the right, and Half Dome in the distance

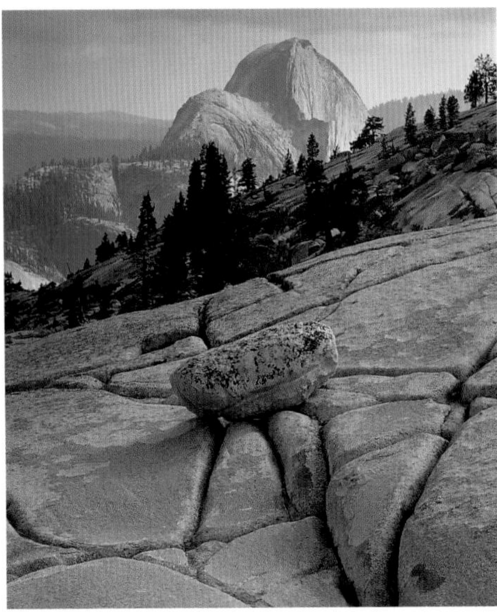

Half Dome, seen from Olmsted Point

base of the fall, or return along the Merced River going through a gate to **Cathedral Beach.** The view of the **Three Brothers** is outstanding. Continue to the **Swinging Bridge.** From here there is a final sweeping view.

The second trek, from **Happy Isles** to **Vernal Falls Footbridge,** is a two-hour, out-and-back trek. Take the bus to Happy Isles, then go along the trail beneath Glacier Point to the **Mist Trail,** one of the most popular in the park. After about 50 minutes of steady climbing, a bridge appears. From here you have your first clear view of 317-foot **Vernal Fall.** You can either return to the Happy Isles bus or go farther up the trail to the brilliant view near **Emerald Pool.** Return on the **John Muir Trail**.

The third trek is the **Mariposa Grove Trail,** a 5-mile hike. If you are on your way south out of Yosemite it is a perfect coda to your trip; no one should leave the park without seeing the giant sequoia. Take the trail just before Calif. 41 leaves Yosemite to the south. Walk through the lower grove until you reach the **Fallen Monarch.** At the 1-mile point you will come upon the **Grizzly Giant,** thought to be more than 2,700 years old. The trail now winds past the aptly named **Faithful Couple** and **Clothespin trees.** A loop at the top passes a log-cabin museum *(open in summer)*, then returns to the trail. ■

Yosemite essentials

There are several entrance stations to the park. The south entry *(Calif. 41)* is the most popular. During peak season you will save time and frustration by using one of the three western gates: Arch Rock *(off Calif. 140)*, Big Oak Flat *(off Calif. 120)*, or Hetch Hetchy *(N of Mather on Hetch Hetchy Rd.)*. To the east is the Tioga Pass entrance *(off Calif. 120 east)*, closed winter through spring. The main sources of information for the park are the entrance stations and the visitor centers. Here one can obtain up-to-date weather and trail condition reports and the "Yosemite Guide."

Camping is allowed only in designated campgrounds. You may need to make a reservation up to three months in advance to be sure of your preferred site at popular times. There are also a number of first-come, first-served sites, for which you register at an entrance.

The three hotels within the park itself (see pp. 380–81) are the Ahwahnee, beyond Yosemite Village, the Wawona which is near the southern entrance, and Yosemite Lodge near Yosemite Falls. All suggest advance booking; for the Ahwahnee make reservations several months in advance. ■

Sequoia & Kings Canyon National Parks

Snow camp on Bullfrog Lake, Kings Canyon National Park

ALL ALONG THE WET, WESTERN SIDE OF THE SIERRA Nevada crest east of Fresno lie two more breathtakingly beautiful national parks, nearly as dramatic as Yosemite to the northwest but not nearly as well known. One reason is elevation. At Sequoia and Kings Canyon, much of the land is perched well above 11,000 feet—about 4,000 feet above the highest road. Fortunately for the non-hiker, several roads wind through the park, with viewing points all along the way. But, as in Yosemite, the best way to see these 862,000 acres is to get out there and sweat a little.

If Sequoia and Kings Canyon were a movie, then the stars would certainly be the giant sequoias. Of the 75 groves of these trees in the world, only eight grow north of the Kings River, and those are scattered over more than 200 miles; the rest are close together in a 60-mile-long area south of the river. The ecology of Sequoia and Kings Canyon—its precipitation, elevation, and soil—is so perfect for these trees that when the giants die, it is not from disease, drought, or pestilence, but from toppling over—they simply get too big!

If you are arriving from the south on Calif. 99, take Calif. 198 northeast to Sequoia or, from Fresno, Calif. 180 east to Kings Canyon. As in almost all national parks, entrance stations provide maps and more detailed trail and climate information.

Sequoia National Park has been organized with a variety of fitness levels in mind. The numerous campgrounds (first come, first

Sequoia & Kings Canyon National Parks

301 C2–C3

Visitor information

www.nps.gov/seki

47050 Generals Hwy., Three Rivers

559/565-3341

served), many of which sit along cool, clear streams, are close to interesting hike destinations, and none are too far from ranger outposts. The popular **Lodgepole Campground** and **Dorst Campground** *(tel 877/444-6777)* require you to book in advance; each offers educational services and rousing fireside entertainment in summer. An attractive new lodging facility, **Wuksachi** *(tel 888/252-5757),* is built of cedar and stone.

Entering Sequoia National Park on Calif. 198 (Generals Highway) from Three Rivers brings you to **Amphitheater Point;** stop for a stunning view of the San Joaquin Valley before driving on to see the astonishing sequoias of the **Giant Forest.** This area is one of the great altars of the American environmental movement. John Muir, who explored and named the Giant Forest, later wrote: "When I entered this sublime wilderness the day was nearly done, the trees' rosy, glowing countenances seemed to be hushed and thoughtful, as if waiting in conscious religious dependence on the sun, and one naturally walked softly and awe-stricken among them." Today the effect is no less striking.

Starting at the **General Sherman Tree,** at 52,500 cubic feet the world's largest living thing (though not the tallest), visitors can take the 2-mile **Congress Trail** past all of the major giant sequoias here, including the **House** and **Senate** groups, as well as the **President** and **McKinley trees.** (The trees were once given the names of heroes of the Paris Commune—the work of a 19th-century utopian society that built a sawmill nearby—but were renamed "when reason prevailed.")

Giant Forest Village is the start of a 3-mile road that will take you, either on foot or by shuttle (in summer), to two outstanding sights. About 2 miles down is the steep, quarter-mile staircase up to **Moro Rock.** From the top of this granite dome is a spectacular view, particularly at sunset. Below stretches the blue-green Kaweah River, while to the west one can see beyond the San Joaquin Valley and over into the Coast Range.

At the road's end is **Crescent Meadow,** perhaps the finest of all mid-altitude meadows. It was here, in 1875, at the lodge of pioneer Hale Tharp, that John Muir spent several nights, later crowning this meadow the "gem of the Sierras." If you get ambitious you can start

The Yokut

Reflect for a moment on the original inhabitants of the Kings Canyon area, the Yokut. Although at first these Native Americans welcomed their mid-19th century pioneer acquaintances, by 1862 the same Anglo newcomers were already forcing the Yokut into the meager back country. Simultaneously the Yokut began to perish from the first infection by the white man's diseases—smallpox, measles, and scarlet fever. A particularly poignant moment came in 1864, when the chief of the remaining Yokut directly asked a leading pioneer, Hale Tharp, to leave. According to the contemporary accounts, when Hale refused, "the chief and his brave sat down and cried."

By the following year all of the Yokut had retreated to the remote back canyons, where they would scratch out only a shell of their former existence. ■

the **High Sierra Trail** here; it finishes at **Mount Whitney,** the highest point in the coterminus United States, 14,495 feet up and 71 miles away.

Four-and-a-half miles north of the Giant Forest is Lodgepole Camp. The **Tokopah Falls Trail** starts here. The walk ascends steadily (but manageably), leading along the magnificent Marble Fork Kaweah River, and on into a series of cliffs and the waterfall of Tokopah Canyon some 2 miles from the start.

A short drive west of Lodgepole is **Crystal Cave,** a series of beautiful underground caverns with outstanding specimens of stalactites, stalagmites, and other geological formations. The 45-minute tour is well worthwhile. In summer, when daytime temperatures can climb to the 90s, the cool interiors of the cave are welcome.

North and west, Generals Highway goes to **Kings Canyon National Park** and reaches the **Grant Grove.** The giant sequoia called the **General Grant Tree** is the world's third largest living tree, at more than 42,000 cubic feet. It is also, in the words of the Park Service, a "designated national shrine" and "the only living memorial to those who gave their lives for freedom."

The 1.5-mile **North Grove Loop** here gives a closer look at the trees. Some relatively easy hikes have their trailheads near here. The **Redwood Canyon Trail,** beginning at Redwood Saddle, is the start of two easy, 6-mile loops through sequoia groves; the **Sugarloaf Trail,** at Sunset Meadow, is a moderate effort for 2 miles along a spectacular glaciated canyon.

North and then east along Calif. 180 (this part is only open in summer) brings travelers into **Sequoia National Forest** and then on to a remote corner of Kings Canyon and **Cedar Grove.** Because of its remoteness, the grove and its surroundings are pleasantly quiet, even during peak season. To get an idea of the glacial history of Kings Canyon, take the **Canyon View** turn a mile past Cedar Grove Village. Another mile east is the entrance to **Roaring River Falls,** where a five-minute walk leads to a waterfall pulsing through a narrow ravine. A farther 1.5 miles east is the scenic **Zumwalt Meadow.** ■

Giant sequoias, Sequoia National Park

Crystal Cave

✉ 12 miles W of Lodgepole Visitor Center

$ $$$ (45-minute tour; tickets at Lodgepole or Foothills Visitor Centers)

Mono Lake & Mammoth Lakes

Mono Lake
301 B5
Visitor information
www.monolake.org
395 & 3rd St., Lee Vining
760/647-6595

Inyo National Forest
Visitor information
www.fs.fed.us/r5/inyo
351 Pacu Ln., Bishop
760/873- 2400

Ancient Bristlecone Pine Forest Visitor Center
White Mountain Rd. off Calif. 168, NE of Big Pine
760/647-6595
Closed winter

ALTHOUGH TECHNICALLY WELL NORTH OF THE OFFICIAL California deserts, Mono Lake bears contemplation as a desertified ecology. Since 1941, water agencies in southern California, thirsty for the liquid gold necessary to grow new suburban communities, have diverted the freshwater streams that used to feed this ancient lake. This has caused the water level to drop by some 45 feet, concentrating already high salt levels. Mono is two-and-one-half times as salty as the ocean. One consequence has been utter havoc for many indigenous birds, fish, and flora.

Another consequence is to the benefit of travelers. As Mono Lake's water level dropped, spectacular geological formations called tufa towers have been exposed. Resembling stalagmites, these towers—formed when freshwater underground springs mix their calcium with the carbonate-rich lake water—conjure the effect of a city skyline against the background of snowy mountain peaks. They are one of the most peculiarly odd and beautiful sights in the state. Some of the best are preserved at **Mono Lake Tufa State Reserve.**

Some species of wader and waterfowl have successfully adapted to the unusual environment here, and it is a popular destination for birdwatchers. Between August and April, the lake is home to one of the largest populations of eared grebes in the Northern Hemisphere; the Audubon Society has estimated their numbers at up to 800,000. Snowy plovers, avocets, and phalaropes also overwinter here, while in spring and summer the lake hosts a large breeding population of California gulls.

ANCIENT BRISTLECONE PINE FOREST

It is something of an effort to visit this remote forest, which lies deep inside the **Inyo National Forest,** south of Mono Lake. But the inconvenience is outweighed by the thrill of seeing the world's oldest living trees. Rival claims are occasionally made, but whatever the current state

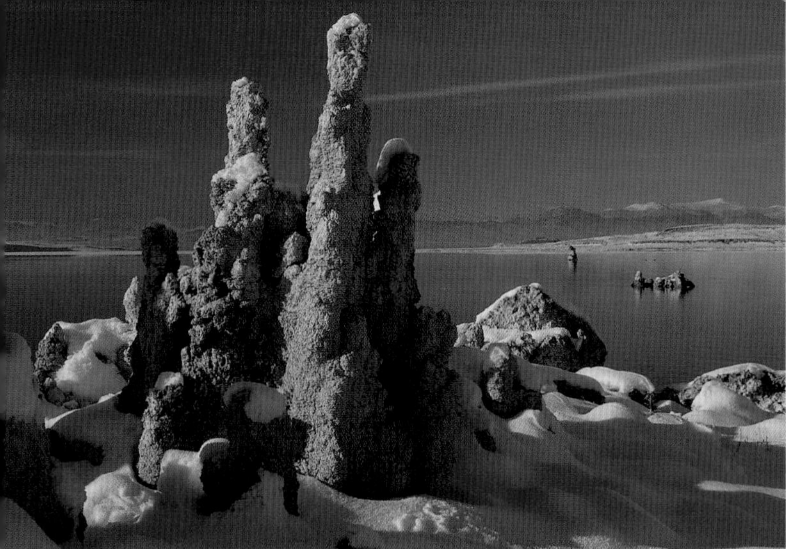

of the scientific debate, these trees are, by any standard, seriously old.

There are two principal groves worth visiting. The first is the 4,000-year-old **Schulman Grove,** named for the naturalist Julius Schulman, who was the first to announce the grove's antiquity in 1958. The Forest Service maintains a **Discovery Trail** off White Mountain Road, which takes you past dozens of the trees. One of the grove's most stunning features is its brilliant palette of primary colors, heightened by the crystal-clear mountain air: cinnamon red trunks against deep blue skies, beige trunks with striking black grain, rich red-orange wood, and purple-black tips to the branches.

The second grove, of even older bristlecones, is the **Patriarch Grove.** It is a few miles farther along White Mountain Road, and several hundred feet higher, just south of the White Mountain Natural Area. In it is the venerable **Methuselah Tree,** whose age is estimated to be over 4,700 years.

The bristlecone pine *(Pinus longaeva)* acquired its twisted, stunted form in response to its extremely cold and windy environment. Trunk bark grows in beleaguered thin strips, forcibly restraining growth and making for the dense cells and abundant resin that are a resilient and necessary life-support system in their inhospitable environment.

MAMMOTH LAKES

One of North America's most volcanically active regions, Mammoth, 20 miles south of Mono Lake, is named for the crystal-clear lakes good for fishing in summer, when wildflowers abound and city-dwellers flock to hike well-maintained trails. In winter, Mammoth is favored for skiing, snowmobiling, and even dog-sled adventures. The **Tamarack Cross-Country Ski Center** *(tel 760/934-2442)* offers 45 miles of trails for Nordic skiers. Aprés ski, head to the new **Mammoth Ski Museum** *(760/934-3781),* regaling the sport's tale in the High Sierra. Hwy. 203 snakes west from Hwy. 395 past **Mammoth Mountain** —California's highest alpine ski area—to **Devil's Postpile National Monument,** a massive column of ancient basalt lava accessible by shuttle bus. North of Mammoth Lakes rises **Obsidian Dome,** a great dome of solid volcanic glass. ■

The calcium carbonate stacks of Mono Lake

Mammoth Lakes Visitor information
www.visitmammoth.com
✉ 2520 Main Street, Mammoth Lakes
☎ 760/934-2712

An ancient bristlecone pine

Lake Tahoe

GERMAN SKIERS HAVE THEIR OWN FOND NAME FOR LAKE Tahoe, *der Blaue*—the blue one. It is often also called one of the most beautiful lakes in the world. Even Mark Twain lost his characteristic bluster when first seeing "the mountains brilliantly photographed upon its surface…surely it must be the fairest picture the whole earth affords."

"Powder hounds" start young.

Lake Tahoe
301 A6
Visitor information
www.bluelaketahoe.com
169 Hwy. 50, Stateline
775/588-5900 or 800/AT-TAHOE

***Tahoe Queen* paddle wheeler**
www.laketahoecruises.com
900 Ski Run Blvd., South Lake Tahoe
775/589-4906 or 800/238-2463
$$$

Heavenly Valley Aerial Tram
Heavenly Ski Resort
775/586-7000

Opposite: *Der Blaue*, so-called for its amazing color

For the record, much of the lake's remarkable color derives from a combination of weather, elevation, and depth. Tahoe is some 1,640 feet deep, making it the tenth deepest inland body of water in the world. Created when the Tahoe Basin sank between parallel faults two million years ago and lava blocked the water's outflow, the lake is now 22 miles long and 12 miles wide. Its environs are an undisputed delight. Golf, fishing, waterskiing, boating, biking, and swimming are among summer activities here; skiing, snowmobile riding, and snowboarding are the area's main winter pastimes. (For skiing information, see Travelwise, p. 387.) The lake's 72-mile shoreline, straddling the California-Nevada border, is home to everything from quiet forest lands on the California side to glamorous gambling venues on the Nevada side. There is something here for everyone.

The traveler looking for peace and quiet will come in spring or fall, never in high summer or winter. The summer peaks with more than 100,000 visitors, so that the lake's shoreline is sometimes completely ringed with car-bound tourists. However, the traveler looking for lots of fun will come in the peak seasons, when there are 36 public beaches to choose from and six golf courses cater to vacationing duffers of all stripes. And there are always the bacchanalian pleasures of the state of Nevada just across the water.

The lakefront on Tahoe's California side includes a number of state parks, historic sites, and ski resorts. **South Lake Tahoe,** the biggest city in the region, is a good place for an overview. Here one can board the authentic *Tahoe Queen* paddle wheeler and sail to Emerald Bay and back, taking in the vast shore and the mountain skyline. Many prefer to spend their first day here doing the **72-Mile Drive,** which will take you around the lake's entire circumference. A fun way to do this is to buy the two-hour audiocassette, "Drive Around Lake Tahoe," available from the South Lake Tahoe Chamber of Commerce *(3066 Lake Tahoe Blvd., tel 530/541-5255, www.tahoeinfo.com)*. The commentary provides a series of colorful facts, tales, and legends about the area as you drive. Another popular way to get oriented is to take the **Heavenly Valley Aerial Tram** at Heavenly Ski Resort, which will whisk you up

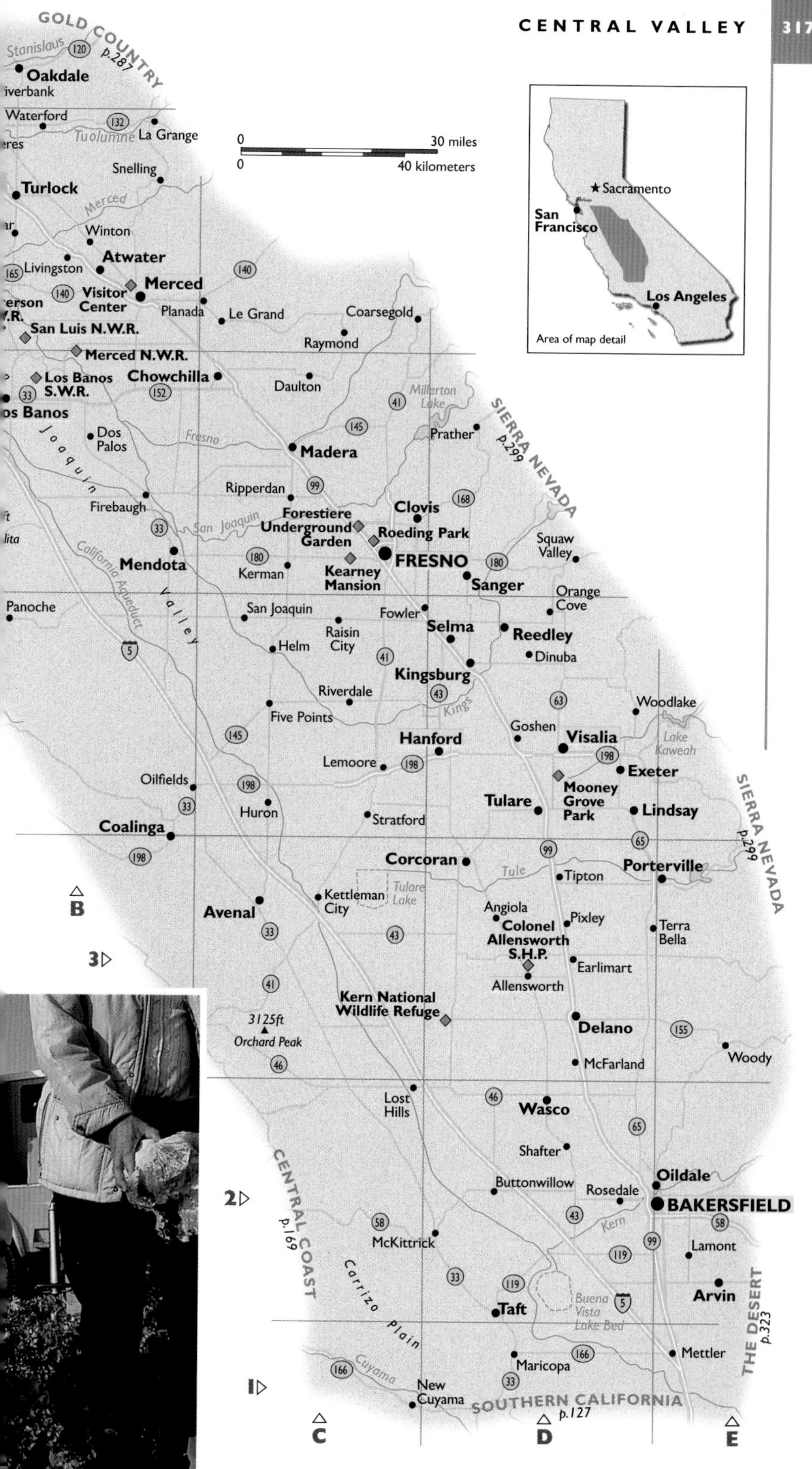
GOLD COUNTRY p.287
Oakdale
Waterford
La Grange
Snelling
Turlock
Winton
Atwater
Livingston
Merced
Visitor Center
Planada
Le Grand
Coarsegold
Raymond
San Luis N.W.R.
Merced N.W.R.
Los Banos S.W.R.
Chowchilla
Daulton
Millerton Lake
Prather
SIERRA NEVADA p.299
Dos Palos
Madera
Ripperdan
Firebaugh
Forestiere Underground Garden
Clovis
Roeding Park
Mendota
Kerman
Kearney Mansion
FRESNO
Sanger
Squaw Valley
Orange Cove
Panoche
San Joaquin
Fowler
Raisin City
Helm
Selma
Reedley
Dinuba
Kingsburg
Riverdale
Five Points
Woodlake
Goshen
Visalia
Lake Kaweah
Hanford
Lemoore
Exeter
Oilfields
Huron
Stratford
Tulare
Mooney Grove Park
Lindsay
Coalinga
Corcoran
Tipton
Porterville
Kettleman City
Tulare Lake
Avenal
Angiola
Pixley
Terra Bella
Colonel Allensworth S.H.P.
Earlimart
Allensworth
Kern National Wildlife Refuge
3125ft Orchard Peak
Delano
Woody
McFarland
Lost Hills
Wasco
Shafter
CENTRAL COAST p.169
Buttonwillow
Rosedale
Oildale
BAKERSFIELD
McKittrick
Lamont
Carrizo Plain
Arvin
Taft
Buena Vista Lake Bed
THE DESERT p.323
Maricopa
Mettler
New Cuyama
SOUTHERN CALIFORNIA p.127
0 30 miles
0 40 kilometers
Sacramento
San Francisco
Los Angeles
Area of map detail

Fresno

THE STORY OF FRESNO, THE RAISIN CAPITAL AND THE central valley's biggest city, goes a long way toward explaining the serendipitous *and* intentional nature of the valley's agricultural success. Founded as a station along the Southern Pacific line in 1872, the town held little allure for its original settlers. They named it Fresno—Spanish for "dry ash." Fruit growing was successful, but the marketing of its biggest cash crop, raisins, was so pitiable that many growers sold them under dubious Spanish labels.

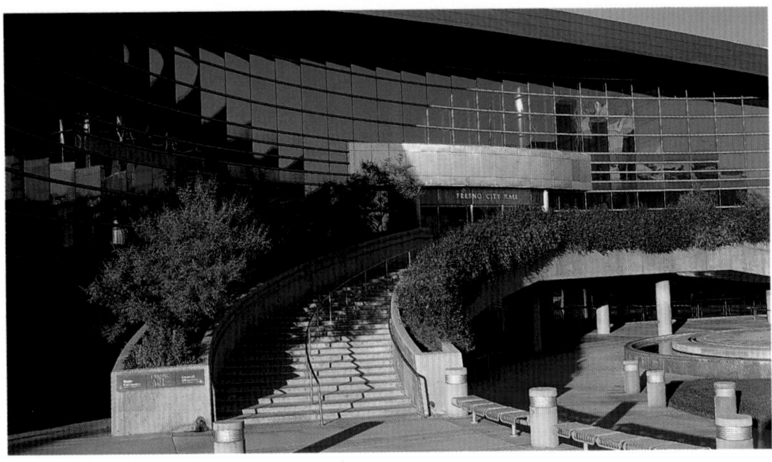

Fresno City Hall

Fresno
317 C5
Visitor information
www.fresnocvb.org
848 M St.
559/445-8300 or 800/788-0836

Mennonite Quilting Center
1012 G St., Reedley
559/638-3560
Closed Sun.

Then, in 1915, a head of the California Raisin Exchange "happened upon a young woman drying her curly jet-black hair under a red bonnet in the front yard of her Fresno home," writes Kevin Starr in *Inventing the Dream* "(The executive) glimpsed what would eventually be one of the most famous trademarks in history…the Sun Maid, a marketing image so successful in its suggestions of health, abundance, and rural charm that in 1920 the Cooperative took Sun Maid as its formal name." The rest, as a glance along the shelf at any grocery store will tell you, is history. Fresno reigns as the nation's most prolific producer of high-value farm products, the Tuscany of the western United States.

As a travel destination, Fresno has improved over the past decade. One attraction is the **Blossom Trail,** a 62-mile self-guided tour *(maps at 2220 Tulare St., www.driveblossomtrail.com)* through orchards, vineyards, and wildflower meadows. March is the best time to view the blossoms. Along the way are growers such as **Simonian Farms** *(S. Clovis St., off Calif. 99, tel 559/237-2294, www.simonianfarms.com),* growing more than a hundred kinds of fruit and vegetables. Also along the drive is the quaint town of **Reedley,** named for the wheat baron Thomas Law Reed, and it's worth a stop at the **Mennonite Quilting Center,** where you can see patient craftsfolk at work on their beautiful—and rare—quilts (buy one, it would make a wonderful family heirloom).

Fresno itself has some (sometimes eccentric) historical sites. The best is the **Forestiere Underground Garden,** part of the underground retreat of Baldasare Forestiere. Between 1906 and 1950, Forestiere sculpted a subterranean home with bedrooms, kitchen, library, and even a walk-under aquarium. More extraordinary still are the huge, productive skylit gardens and orchards from which he not only fed himself but also sold surplus crops. A more conventional shrine is the **Kearney Mansion.** Built by the raisin king Theodore Kearney between 1900 and 1903, the house, in French Renaissance style and furnished in keeping, is on the National Register of Historic Places. It is now a museum of local history.

For a different impression of early Fresno life, see the restored **Meux Home Museum.** Its 19th-century owner T.R. Meux was a Confederate surgeon. Author **William Saroyan** (see box) was born at 3204 E. El Monte Ave. and spent many of his most productive years at 2729 W. Griffith Way. The **Fresno Metropolitan Museum** has a fine collection of Saroyan memorabilia, and the **Fresno Art Museum** is worth a visit for its Mexican and Impressionist works.

The **Chaffee Zoological Gardens,** located in **Roeding Park,** are home to more than 700 birds, mammals, and reptiles. The Tropical Rainforest is outstanding, and the show "Winged Wonders" is a free-flight performance of eagles, hawks, vultures, and parrots. ■

William Saroyan

Saroyan (1908–1981), a Fresno-born Armenian-American author, lived to see many of his plays and novels produced on Broadway *(The Human Comedy)* and rendered in films *(The Time of Your Life)*. But his enduring legacy is his collection of short stories about growing up in rustic Fresno, where immigrant tongues and oddball characters conjured a unique small-town drama, as in this extract from "The Pomegranate Tree":

One night my uncle made a long distance phone call. The produce man, D'Agostino, told my uncle nobody wanted pomegranates.

"How much are you asking per box?" my uncle shouted over the phone.

"One dollar," D'Agostino shouted back.

"That's not enough," my uncle shouted. "I won't take a nickel less than five dollars a box."

"They don't want them for one dollar a box," D'Agostino shouted.

"Why not," my uncle shouted.

"They don't know what they are," D'Agostino shouted.

"What kind of businessman are you, anyway?" my uncle shouted. "They're pomegranates. I want five dollars a box."

"I can't sell them," the produce man shouted. "I ate one myself and I don't see anything so wonderful about them."

"You're crazy," my uncle shouted. "There is no other fruit in the world like the pomegranate."

"What shall I do with them? I can't sell them. I don't want them."

"I see," my uncle whispered. "Ship them back. Ship them back express collect."

The phone call cost my uncle about $17.

So the eleven boxes came back.

My uncle and I ate most of the pomegranates. ■

Forestiere Underground Garden
www.undergroundgardens.com
✉ 5021 W. Shaw Ave., 2 blocks E of Calif. 99
☎ 559/271-0734
⌚ Closed Mon.–Tues. & Nov.–April
$ $$

Kearney Mansion
✉ Kearney Blvd., 7 miles W of downtown
☎ 559/441-0862
⌚ Closed a.m. & Mon.–Thurs.
$ $$

Meux Home Museum
www.meux.mus.ca.us
✉ Tulare & R Sts.
☎ 559/233-8007
⌚ Closed Mon.–Thurs., & Jan.
$ $

Fresno Metropolitan Museum
www.fresnomet.org
✉ 1555 W. Van Ness Ave.
☎ 559/441-1444
⌚ Closed Mon. & Tue.
$ $$

Fresno Art Museum
www.fresnoartmuseum.org
✉ 2233 N. 1st St.
☎ 559/441-4221
⌚ Closed Mon.
$ $

Chaffee Zoological Gardens
www.chaffeezoo.org
✉ 894 W. Belmont Ave.
☎ 559/498-5910
$ $$

North of Fresno

Classic Californian small towns and some excellent wildlife refuges, offering superb opportunities for bird-watchers, characterize the Central Valley country north of Fresno.

Modesto, established in 1870 by the Central Pacific Railroad, was the inspiration for the classic film *American Graffiti*—filmmaker George Lucas, who grew up here, modeled the memorable cruising scenes in his film after Modesto's own teen scene. Another mark of true Californiana is the **Modesto Arch,** one of the few early 20th-century icons of civic pride still extant; its sentiment, "Water, Wealth, Contentment, Health," pretty much sums up the dream of its founders. Lastly, Modesto is yet another foodie paradise—not so much for its restaurants as for its orchards, vineyards, and food producers. An outstanding maker of olive oil is **Nick Sciabica & Sons** *(2150 Yosemite St., tel 800/551-9612)*. The family has been growing olives and pressing fine oil for four generations. Specialties at the **Pure Joy Bakery** *(501 Bangs Ave., Modesto, tel 209/525-3663)* are homemade cider, apple pies, and apple dumplings. Also worth a visit are the **Hilmar Cheese Company** *(9001 N. Lander St., Hilmar, tel 209/667-6076)* and the **Blue Diamond Growers Store** *(4800 Sisk Rd., Modesto, tel 209/545-6229)*, where you can taste locally grown almonds.

South of Modesto is the town of **Merced,** known to most of its visitors as the gateway to Yosemite. There are some excellent wildlife areas just west of the town. Head in the opposite direction from the crowds and visit them—preferably in winter or spring when temperatures are lower. The **San Luis National Wildlife Complex** *(S of Calif. 140 between Merced and Gustine)* consists of three separate refuges, which total some 27,000 acres of grasslands and wetlands around the San Joaquin River. **Merced National Wildlife Refuge** is a haven for flocks of snow geese and sandhill cranes. Similar birdlife, as well as tule elk, flourish farther west at the other two refuges, the **San Luis Reservoir National Wildlife Refuge,** which has a spectacular spring show of wildflowers in the Kesterson Unit; and the **San Joaquin River National Wildlife Refuge.** The latter has a spectacular spring show of wildflowers. For migrating geese and broods of herons, see the **Los Banos State Wildlife Refuge** *(18110 W. Henry Miller Ave., Los Banos, tel 209/826-0463)*. ■

Modesto

316 A6

Visitor information

720 W. 16th St.

209/384-2791

San Luis National Wildlife Complex

www.fws.gov/sanluis

947 W. Pacheco Blvd., Suite C, Los Banos

209/826-3508

Left: Merced County Courthouse

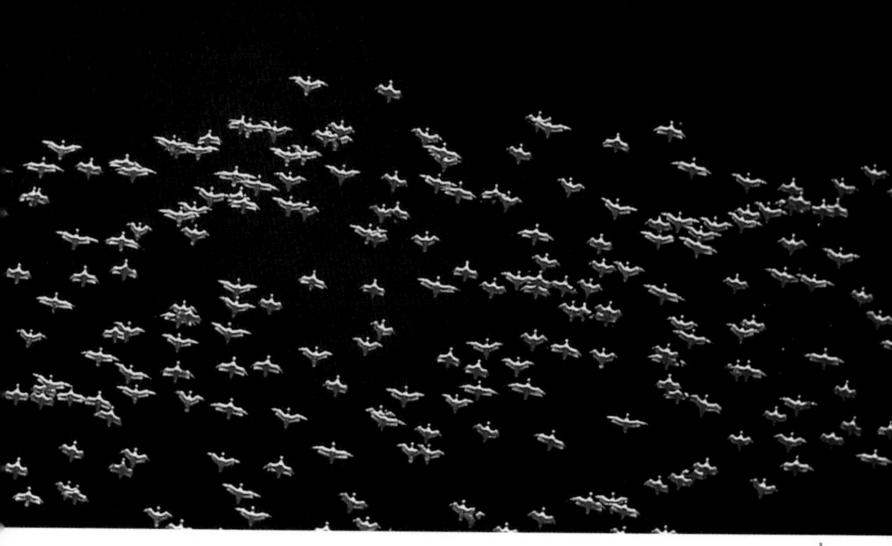

South of Fresno

Ross's geese over fields flooded to re-create their natural habitat

MORE WILDLIFE REFUGES FEATURE SOUTH OF FRESNO, but it is history that draws visitors to this hot, hot area. Agriculture rules and the towns have grown up around packing stations and food-processing companies.

With its pleasant atmosphere, quiet ways, and railroad-era buildings, you would never guess that little **Hanford** *(W from Calif. 99 on Calif. 198)* was the scene of a bloody and historically important feud. In May 1880, a number of settlers in nearby Mussel Slough, understandably believing that the land that they alone had developed belonged to them, were outraged when the Southern Pacific Railroad decided to sell off several parcels from under their feet. When the settlers refused to move out, the railroad arranged for them to be forcibly removed. Guns were drawn on both sides, and seven men died, including two railroad employees. Five surviving settlers were later convicted and sentenced to eight months in the San Jose jail. They emerged as heroes. Later romanticized by Frank Norris in his antibusiness novel *The Octopus*, the Mussel Slough feud marked an important turning point in the campaign to rein in the powerful California railroad barons.

Today Hanford bakes lazily in the California sun. It is best known for the remains of its once thriving Chinatown. You can still tour **China Alley** and the historic 1893 **Taoist Temple** by contacting the Hanford Visitor Agency (*tel 559/582-5024, www.visithanford.com*). Another worthwhile stop is the **Hanford Carnegie Museum,** which focuses on local history and customs.

A few miles to the east of Hanford on Calif. 198 is **Visalia.**

Hanford Carnegie Museum

- 109 E. 8th St., Hanford
- 559/584-1367
- Closed Sun.–Tues.

Tulare County Museum
27000 S. Mooney Blvd., Visalia
559/733-6616

Chinese Cultural Center
500 Akers Rd., Visalia
559/625-4545
Closed Mon.–Tues.

Colonel Allensworth State Historic Park
www.parks.ca.gov
4099 Douglas, off Calif. 43 NW of Delano
661/849-3433

Kern County Museum/Lori Brock Children's Discovery Center
www.kcmuseum.org
3801 Chester St., Bakersfield
661/852-5000

Buck Owens' Crystal Palace
www.buckowens.com
2800 Buck Owens Blvd.
661/328-7560
Small cover charge on weekends

Tehachapi Visitor information
www.tehachapi.com
209 E. Tehachapi Blvd.
661/822-4180

Founded in 1852 by a bear hunter named Nathaniel Vise, this typical midsize agricultural town also played a role in the Mussel Slough incident—it gave the "rebels" sanctuary from the sheriffs and company goons who were hunting them down. Visalia has since grown in classic Central Valley fashion. Packinghouses, food-processing companies, and growers are its dominant economic forces. Two places worth a stop are the **Tulare County Museum,** which has a copy of the famed "End of the Trail Monument" and many artifacts detailing ancient Yokut Indian culture; and the **Chinese Cultural Center.** Distinguished by its two 12-ton marble Tzu-Shih lions, the latter contains several fine holdings of ancient Chinese art and culture.

A popular outing (and a good way to beat the heat) is to head east on Calif. 198 to **Lake Kaweah,** in the foothills west of the Sequoia National Park. Here, during the 1880s, a socialistic experiment called the Kaweah Colony briefly flourished before being stamped out of existence by the state and local opinion.

A utopia of a different kind can be found farther south, west of Calif. 99 near Delano (where Cesar Chavez began the United Farm Workers' most well-known strike). Founded in 1908 by Col. Allen Allensworth, the highest ranking African-American military officer of his day, **Allensworth** was originally envisioned as a "self-governing" town where liberated blacks could live productive, discrimination-free lives. For a short period from 1909 to 1919, Allensworth thrived, attracting many black professionals, from teachers and lawyers to librarians and doctors. Then, in the 1920s, the town's water supplies ran low as large-scale agriculture in surrounding areas drained the water table. A slow exodus to wetter lands commenced and, by the late 1950s, Allensworth was a ghost town. In the 1970s, a group of preservationists began restoring what remained of the town. It is now the **Colonel Allensworth State Historic Park.** Today you can tour the colonel's home, with its original furnishings, before taking a look at the Allensworth schoolhouse and library.

Keen bird-watchers will not want to miss the **Kern National Wildlife Refuge** *(19 miles W of Delano, off Calif. 155, tel 661/725-2767),* to the southwest of Allensworth. This managed wetland in the San Joaquin Valley supports many varieties of shorebirds and, perhaps most notably, a breeding colony of the endangered tricolored blackbird. If it is too hot to hike, there is a 6-mile self-guided driving tour.

The most southerly major town in the valley is **Bakersfield.** Founded in 1862, the city has gone through several economic phases, from agriculture to mining to oil and then back to agriculture. Bakersfield's fine museum complex, the **Kern County Museum/Lori Brock Children's Discovery Center** is a showcase for Native American artifacts and restored and re-created historical Bakersfield buildings. But the real reason to go to Bakersfield is country music. To music buffs, Bakersfield is the Memphis of the West. The star of the scene is the one and only Buck Owens. Listen to live country music and whoop up a storm at his very own place, **Buck Owens' Crystal Palace.** East from Bakersfield, Calif. 58 climbs through the wildly scenic Tehachapi Mountains to Tehachapi, known for its apple orchards and a gateway to Mojave (see p.326). ■

Attracting spiritual and ecological adventurers alike, California's arid lands have become one of the trendiest places to visit. In Joshua Tree the desert blooms; in Palm Springs, it becomes an elegant American Araby.

The Desert

In the Coachella Valley

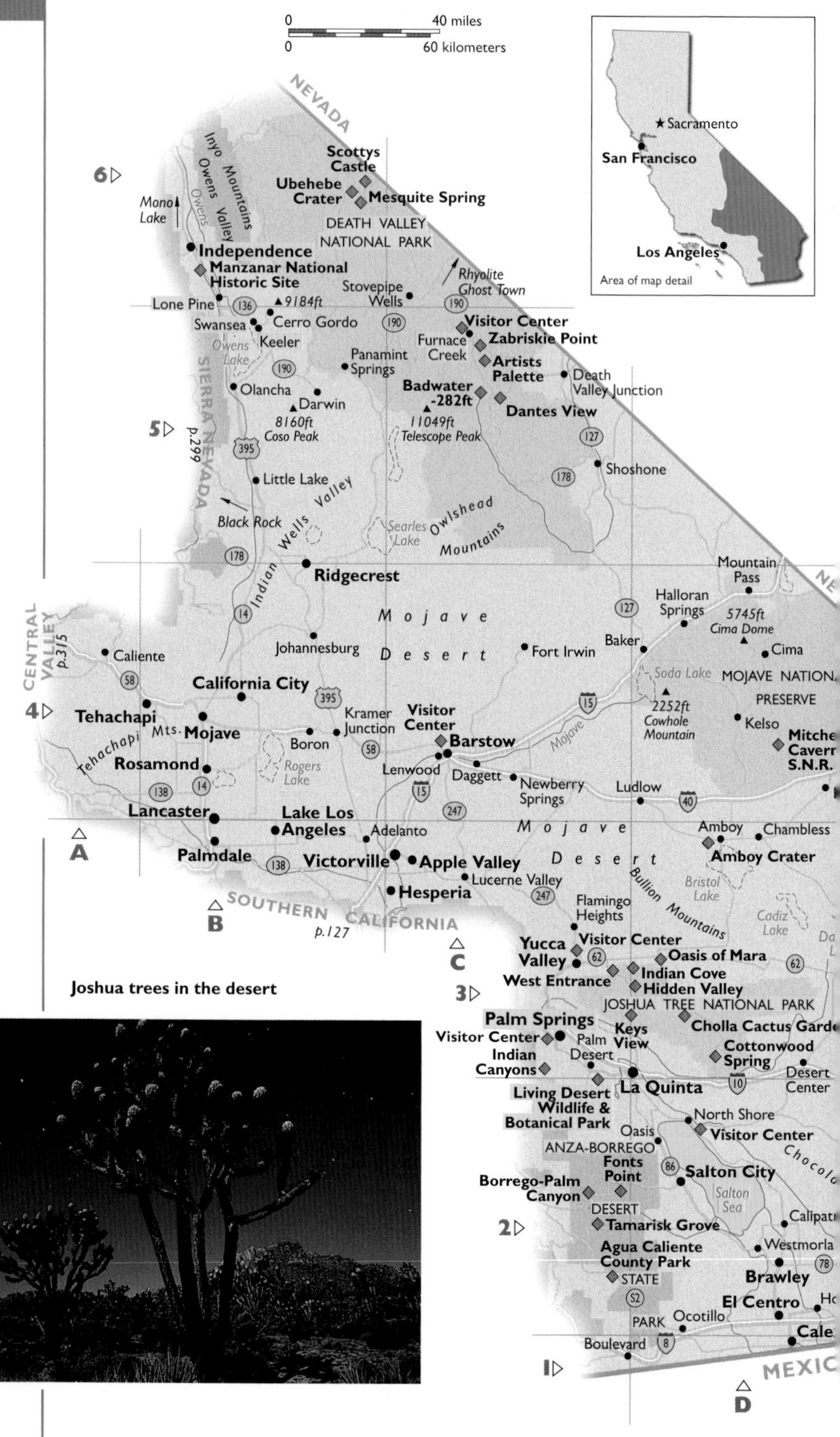
0 40 miles
0 60 kilometers
Sacramento
San Francisco
Los Angeles
Area of map detail
NEVADA
6
5
4
3
2
1
A
B
C
D
Inyo Mountains
Owens Valley
Owens
Mono Lake
Scottys Castle
Ubehebe Crater
Mesquite Spring
DEATH VALLEY NATIONAL PARK
Independence
Manzanar National Historic Site
Stovepipe Wells
Rhyolite Ghost Town
Lone Pine
136
9184ft
190
Swansea
Cerro Gordo
Visitor Center
Furnace Creek
Zabriskie Point
Owens Lake
Keeler
Panamint Springs
Artists Palette
Death Valley Junction
SIERRA NEVADA
p.299
Olancha
Darwin
Badwater -282ft
Dantes View
8160ft Coso Peak
11049ft Telescope Peak
127
395
Shoshone
178
Little Lake
Valley
Black Rock
Wells
Indian
Searles Lake
Owlshead Mountains
Ridgecrest
Mountain Pass
Halloran Springs
5745ft Cima Dome
14
Mojave Desert
CENTRAL VALLEY p.315
Caliente
Johannesburg
Fort Irwin
Baker
Cima
Soda Lake
MOJAVE NATIONAL PRESERVE
58
California City
15
2252ft Cowhole Mountain
Tehachapi
Mojave
Kramer Junction
Visitor Center
Barstow
Kelso
Mitchell Caverns S.N.R.
Tehachapi Mts.
Boron
Mojave
Rosamond
Rogers Lake
Lenwood
Daggett
Newberry Springs
Ludlow
138
40
247
Lancaster
Lake Los Angeles
Adelanto
Amboy
Chambless
Amboy Crater
Palmdale
Victorville
Apple Valley
Bullion Mountains
Bristol Lake
Lucerne Valley
Hesperia
Flamingo Heights
Cadiz Lake
SOUTHERN CALIFORNIA
p.127
Yucca Valley
Visitor Center
62
Oasis of Mara
West Entrance
Indian Cove
Hidden Valley
JOSHUA TREE NATIONAL PARK
Palm Springs
Keys View
Cholla Cactus Garden
Visitor Center
Palm Desert
Cottonwood Spring
Indian Canyons
Desert Center
10
La Quinta
Living Desert Wildlife & Botanical Park
North Shore
Visitor Center
Oasis
ANZA-BORREGO DESERT STATE PARK
Fonts Point
86
Salton City
Borrego-Palm Canyon
Salton Sea
Tamarisk Grove
Agua Caliente County Park
Westmorland
78
Brawley
S2
El Centro
Ocotillo
Boulevard
8

Joshua trees in the desert

The wind sculpts Death Valley dunes into a dramatic landscape.

The Desert

THE VAST AREA KNOWN TO MOST CALIFORNIANS AS THE DESERT IS actually two deserts. The northernmost, Death Valley and the Mojave, is kept dry by the rain shadow cast by the Sierra to the west. The southern desert of Joshua Tree and Anza-Borrego is a small part of the Colorado Desert, itself part of the Sonoran Desert. The rain shadow here is provided by the Peninsular Range.

This is a land of extremes. In summer, temperatures soar by day to 110 or 120° F, plunging by 40 to 50 degrees at night. Winds shape entire dune canyons in a single season. Water is a rumor for most of the year, except in spring, when flash floods can carve new landscapes overnight. These extremes, paradoxically, have made the desert even more enticing to Californians. Since the 1920s, Hollywood has been transfixed by the oasis of Palm Springs. In recent years it has again become fashionable, attracting not only the rich and famous but also New Age crystal-gazers and a small but growing contingent who come to see its modernist architecture.

Desert extremes have wrought a highly diverse ecology. In the far north is the Owens Valley, its beautiful pale dust the consequence of lands being drained by Los Angeles's thirst for cheap water. More superlatives are to be found in Death Valley National Park, while Joshua Tree National Park is the showstopper of the desert experience.

The basics of desert travel bear repeating. "Saved from dehydration" stories continue to feed local news stations. If you will be camping overnight, register at one of the sign-up boards, usually found at visitor centers and trailheads. Take at least one gallon of water per person per day just for drinking; for a strenuous trip, take two gallons each. If you are going *anywhere* except along well-known trails, take a map and compass. In spring and winter, check at ranger stations for flood alerts.

To appreciate the desert's natural wonders, pack a few extras. A small telescope will enrich the powerful experience of the desert night sky. Constellation maps and guides to local flora are available at major visitor centers. ■

Terrain north of Death Valley

Toward Death Valley

THE SITES AND TOWNS THAT DOT THE MOJAVE DESERT are a study in stubbornness, hinting at the tenacious if somewhat wistful pioneering mindset of those who struggled to arrive here, and settled the area, in the 1800s. Here, as Ambrose Bierce once said, the "horrible is allied with the beautiful." The inhospitable terrain permits few roads, but the intrepid with time to explore will find opportunities for many memorable hikes. Even from your car, there is beauty—wrapped in dust and wind, but beauty nonetheless—to see as you go to Death Valley.

Mojave Desert Visitor information

✉ 2796 Tanger Way, Barstow

☎ 760/253-4782

Edwards Air Force Base

www.edwards.af.mil

✉ 1 S. Rosamound Blvd.

☎ 661/277-8050 museum, 661/277-3517 Air Force tours by appointment 1st & 3rd Fri. each month

🕒 Closed Mon. & Sun.

The town of **Mojave,** gateway to the eponymous desert, is surrounded by intriguing sites, including **Edwards Air Force Base,** birthplace of supersonic flight and many other aviation firsts. The bases's Air Force Flight Test Center Museum provides a fascinating review, and free tours are offered of the NASA Dryden Flight Research Center. The Center's **Aerospace Exploration Gallery,** in nearby Palmdale, features exhibits tracing NASA's exciting past, present, and future in outer space. In springtime, the 1,745-acre **Antelope Valley California Poppy Reserve,** 25 miles west of Palmdale, bursts into

audacious color with its bloom of native wildflowers.

Hwy. 14 leads north to Death Valley National Park (see pp. 328–329) via **Red Rock Canyon State Park,** an archaeological wonderland and setting for the opening scenes in *Jurassic Park.*

The town of **Independence** stands not far from the ruins of old Fort Independence, where, in the 1860s, there occurred a number of often violent uprisings by the Paiute. The fort closed in 1872, after the Paiute were violently suppressed. Today the main attraction is the **Eastern California Museum,** which houses a detailed collection of pioneer and Native American history and a re-created village made from old buildings.

South of Independence is the site of the Manzanar Relocation Camp, where 10,000 Japanese Americans were interned during the years 1942–45, after the bombing of Pearl Harbor. This relic of a dark period in the nation's history has been marked as the **Manzanar National Historic Site.**

The little town of **Lone Pine,** established in the 1850s, is a base for climbers and skiers on **Mount Whitney,** whose peak soars to 14,495 feet some 25 miles to the west. **Whitney Portal,** several miles west of Lone Pine, is the start of several hiking trails including the one that leads to the summit. Movie enthusiasts know Lone Pine for its October film festival, featuring old cowboy movies *(tel 760/876-9103, www.lonepinefilmfestival.org).* The visitor information center has a map to movie sites. Among the classics filmed around here were *Gunga Din* and *The Lone Ranger.*

To reach Death Valley (see pp. 328–29) you turn east off US 395 onto Calif. 136 just south of Lone Pine. Near the junction is dry **Owens Lake,** named after Richard Owen, a member of Frémont's 1845 expedition. It was a viable waterway for steam-ships well into the early 1900s, but since the arrival of the Los Angeles Aqueduct in1913, which sapped most of the feeder streams, the lake has shrunk away to nothing. It contains some of the world's largest sodium silicate deposits.

Along Calif. 136 are several ghost towns, including Keeler, a still populated former mining town with a museum and ghost mines to explore. The **Cerro Gordo Ghost Town** *(tel 760/876-5030, www.cerrogordo.us)* itself was once known as California's Comstock, producing more than 4.5 million ounces of silver, lead, and zinc during the nineteenth century. It is being restored. ■

NASA Dryden Flight Research Center
www.dfrc.nasa.gov
☎ 661/276-2449
Tours 10:15 a.m.; reservations 3 weeks in advance, photo ID required; closed Sat. & Sun.

Aerospace Exploration Gallery
www.dfrc.nasa.gov
✉ 38256 Sierra Hwy, Palmdale
☎ 661/276-2662

Antelope Valley California Poppy Reserve
www.parks.ca.gov
✉ Lancaster Rd.
☎ 661/724-1180

Manzanar National Historic Site
www.nps.gov/manz
✉ Hwy. 395, 9 miles N of Lone Pine
☎ 760/878-2194

Lone Pine
324 A6

Visitor information
www.lonepinechamber.org
✉ 126 S. Main St.
☎ 760/876-4444

Red Rock Canyon State Park
www.parks.ca.gov
✉ Calif. 14, Ridgecrest
☎ 661/320-4001

Independence
324 A6

Eastern California Museum
✉ 155 N. Grant Street
☎ 760/878-0364
Closed Tues.

Death Valley National Park

PERHAPS MORE THAN ANY ONE OF ITS SINGULAR geological wonders, it is the ride down into Death Valley on Calif. 190, through the dusty Panamint Mountains, that lingers in the memory. It is a descent of grandeur. There is no better way to appreciate the entire sweep of Death Valley National Park. Take it slowly.

The best time to come is February through mid-April, when the desert wildflowers bloom and temperatures remain bearable. Winter is the most crowded season.Visitors coming in summer will need an air-conditioned car, a supply of water, and a carefully timed plan for their visit: Walking is bearable very early or very late in the day.

Furnace Creek is the center of traveler services in Death Valley. Here you will find accommodations, restaurants, and a store. In the far north of Death Valley, at **Mesquite Spring,** on a sharp turn in Calif. 267, is one of the stranger manifestations of émigré architectural fever in the state. It is **Scottys Castle,** a Moorish-style mansion built in the 1920s by Chicago insurance magnate Albert Johnson and his hustling, no-account, desert-rat buddy Walter "Scotty" Scott. Guides in period costumes give a lively account of the castle's builders. A few miles to the west is the **Ubehebe Crater,** thought to have been caused by volcanic activity.

Several popular natural wonders within a few miles of Furnace Creek (all well marked) include the **Devils Golf Course,** a huge salt pan where winds push boulders across the slick surface during rare rains. Farther east is the **Artists Palette,** a series of hills colored with a rainbow of various mineral hues. The colors are especially stunning around dawn and dusk. The same is true of nearby **Golden Canyon.**

If you have time and the heat is not too intense, explore the 4-mile **Gower Gulch Loop,** a trail through colorful badlands, multi-hued canyons, and old borax mines. Though it lacks the romance of silver and gold, borax—a chemical deposited when alkaline lakes evaporate—was one of Death Valley's few valuable resources. It was mined here from the 1880s. The **Borax Museum** at Furnace Creek tells the story of the mines through its collection of wagons and machinery. The **Harmony Borax Works Interpretive Trail**—at a quarter mile, manageable in all but the worst heat—starts at the Borax Works parking area north of Furnace Creek.

Don't leave Death Valley without visiting one of its spectacular viewpoints—ideally at sunrise or sunset. **Zabriskie Point** is the site of the 1970 Antonioni movie of the same name. One of the valley's most memorable sights, it has inspired dozens of well-known plein air painters from around the world.

About 20 miles south of Furnace Creek is **Dantes View,** which overlooks the entire valley from the Black Mountains. From here you can see two topographical extremes —the 14,495-foot peak of distant Mount Whitney, and **Badwater Basin,** site of the lowest point in the U.S. (282 feet below sea level). West of Badwater the land rises with impressive steepness, reaching 11,049 feet at the top of **Telescope Peak,** only a few miles away. ■

Death Valley National Park
www.nps.gov/deva
324 B6

Visitor information
Calif. 190, Furnace Creek
760/786-3200

Scotty's Castle
760/786-2392
$$$

Borax Museum
Furnace Creek Ranch, Harmony Borax Works Rd., W off Calif. 190
760/786-2345

Afternoon storm in Death Valley

Singing sands

With such place-names as Cowhole Mountain and Blind Hills, **Mojave National Preserve** *(tel 760/252-6100, www.nps.gov/moja)*, over three million acres of desolate terrain, lies south of I-15, southeast of Death Valley.

If you travel here, be sure to see the unique sand formation of **Kelso Dunes,** south of I-15 near Kelso. This sea of delicate, wind-created sand sculpture spreads out at the base of Providence Mountain. Golden-rose quartz grains, blown down from Afton Canyon over the course of 25,000 years, create a richly colored palette. Even more engaging is the unmistakable loud thrumming noise caused by loose sand sliding down the steep 600-foot dunes. Study of such dunes has led some anthropologists to link their subaural wavelengths to religious experiences by native peoples.

This part of the Mojave contains a number of other unusual geological sites. North from Kelso on Kelso Cima Road are extensive ancient lava flows traced by fossilized tube worms. This road takes you to **Cima Dome,** a high rounded hunk of rock thrust some 1,500 feet above the desert floor. Turning back south from Kelso on Kelbecker Road, visit the **Amboy Crater,** a 250-foot cinder cone. ■

Water, water

There is, indisputably, a lot of it: Every year, some 200 million acre feet (each enough to flood an acre of land under a foot of water) fall on California, two-thirds of it in the northern half of the state. And therein lies the rub. The water falls in the wrong place. It tends to evaporate or go where no one wants it to go. And most population growth occurs in the south, a land of few rivers and even fewer lakes and streams. "God," as sociologist Carey McWilliams eloquently put it more than 50 years ago, "never intended Southern California to be anything but a desert.... Man has made it what it is."

Humans have mainly made aqueducts. The story of the first is a familiar one to most Californians. A turn-of-the-century Los Angeles business cabal, worried about the impact of drought on land prices, convinced a panicked citizenry to underwrite a 230-mile water canal from Owens Lake. The visionary engineer William Mulholland built the aqueduct, the water from which was promptly used to "green up" the San Fernando Valley real estate holdings of the said business cabal. The fat cats may have profited, but the public still needed water. A new study was commissioned, and a new aqueduct built, this one from Sacramento. More water. More suburban growth. The story was repeated again and again.

The pattern persists to this day. Yet as suburban growth continues, many in California have come to question the belief that water needs can be filled by importing more and more water from far reaches of the state. Take the case of metropolitan Los Angeles. Today the region has 45 percent of the population on 6 percent of the state's habitable land—but only .06 percent of the state's total stream flow. With the population predicted to grow from 16 to 24 million over the next few decades, the region would seem ripe for yet another large-scale public works project.

Yet recent experience suggests otherwise, says UCLA's Martha Davis, who studies water-use issues and the environment. A drought that began in 1987 forced the change. Before then, L.A. water agencies had barely paid lip service to such concepts as water conservation, groundwater management, and water recycling. But in 1990, the three-year drought unexpectedly intensified. For the first time, the Metropolitan Water District mandated water rationing. "The response was dramatic," says Davis. "In 1990, water sales peaked at an all-time high of 2.6 million acre feet; by 1993, these sales had plummeted to 1.5 million acre feet.... We have fundamentally changed the water demand curve for the southland. We are supporting more people with less (not more) water."

But can such policies really meet the water needs of L.A.'s future population? Ultimately such questions are resolved not by public policy planners but by politicians who must balance the short-term needs of their constituents with the longer-term needs of the state as a whole. The former usually prevail.

Yet an enlightened public is beginning to

What water does in California

Left undirected and unrestrained, water has had a profound impact on the topography of California. Four interesting manifestations of this impact are:

Underground rivers (Mojave Desert): Created 15,000 years ago when sedimentation on above-ground rivers hardened to form a sandy "lid."

Alluvial fans (Death Valley): Formed when periodic downpours loosen hillside rubble and carry it to the bottom, creating fan-shaped mounds. *Bajadas,* also in deserts, are essentially spread-out, large-scale alluvial fans.

Badlands (statewide): Sharp features—thin spires, thick columns, and undulating folds—carved into soft sandstone hills by surface runoff.

Underground caves (throughout Sierra parks): Made by groundwater percolating through soluble rock. ■

alter water politics as well. A good example is the emergence of the Los Angeles River as an important political touchstone. For decades treated as little more than a giant drainage ditch, the river in recent years has become the focus of an intense debate over urban water use. A group named Friends of the Los Angeles River (FOLAR) has successfully fought to restore parts of the stream to its more natural state. The result is striking. In some parts, "it actually looks like a river, with ducks and everything!" an *L.A. Times* columnist pronounced. Yet whether that kind of sustained civic activism can alter the larger patterns of water use is still unclear. The hand of *Homo sapiens,* after all, has made southern California what it is today. ■

Below: In Death Valley, evaporation leaves a sunbaked pan. Right: El Pakina Cave in Mitchell Caverns, Providence Mountains

Joshua Tree National Park

ALTHOUGH THERE IS MUCH TO SEE WITHIN THIS 800,000-acre park, no one element has attracted as much comment, speculation, and even poetry as the Joshua tree, a plant so biomorphically abstract that it might have been designed by designed by a demented artist.

Joshua Tree National Park
325 C3
Visitor information
www.nps.gov/jotr
Oasis Visitor Center, Calif. 62 & Adobe Rd., Twentynine Palms
760/367-5500
$$

Not all have fallen in love with it. Capt. John C. Frémont, the first English-speaking traveler to record the trees, spoke of "their stiff and ungraceful forms...the most repulsive tree in the vegetable kingdom." To California Mormons, migrating back to Utah in the 1850s, the tree's branches, set at right angles to its trunk and then bent upward, as in prayerful supplication, seemed like prophetic guideposts. They promptly named the tree for the prophet Joshua. To naturalists such as Donald Peattie, the dean of California nature writing, they "look more like the blasted skeleton of a tree which has gone all awry..."

To many contemporary hikers, however, the Joshua tree's spareness, silhouetted against the bruised purple evening sky, seems to embody the natural solitude they seek in the park. In recent years one scenic canyon even hosted a kind of New Age wedding, where the groom's suit, all

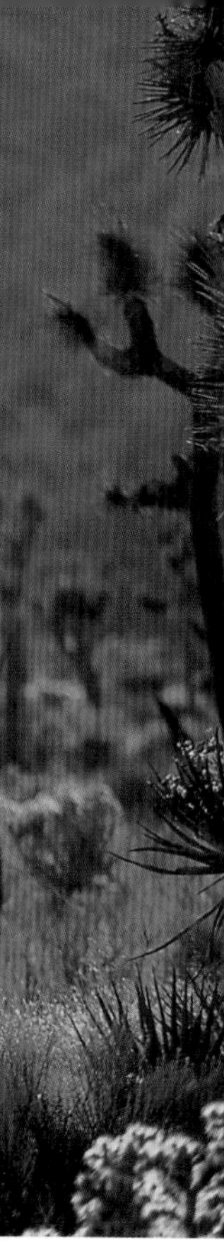

Hiking a trail among Joshua trees

pale sage green and powdery brown, was specially made to match the palette of the landscape. As national parks go, Joshua Tree is quite hip.

Perhaps the most important natural aspect of the park is its merging of two distinct deserts, the hot, dry Colorado at its eastern end with the slightly wetter, cooler Mojave in the west. In the former grow the ground-hugging creosote bush and the spread-eagled ocotillo bush. In the latter, Joshua trees proliferate, as well as several distinctive groves of fan palms. The park represents a wide diversity of geological activity, its stones and alluvial fans and varnished rock seeming to some to produce a kind of desert mosaic.

Most visitors spend their time in the (slightly) cooler west. The focal point near the northern entrance is the **Oasis of Mara,** for long the home of the Chemehuevi before becoming a popular stop for miners in the late 1800s. Later, cattle ranchers arrived. In the 1920s came homesteaders and the onslaught of cactus poaching—poaching that became so severe as to cause one prominent Pasadena matron, M. H. Hoyt, to lead a drive to win government protection, achieved in 1936 when the Roosevelt administration created Joshua Tree National Monument; in 1994 it was declared a national park.

If you plan on camping—and during the spring many do—the campground at nearby **Indian Cove** *(tel 877/444-6777)* is hard to beat. This is also the center of activity for the growing number of rock-climbing enthusiasts *(Joshua Tree Rock Climbing School, tel 760/366-4745, www.joshuatreerockclimbing.com)*. Not far away, off Canyon Road, is the **Fortynine Palms Oasis.** Here a 1.5-mile trail takes you to a desert oasis, replete with fan palms and animals slaking their thirst amid some rare desert shade.

Another favorite drive and hike begins at the west entrance on Park Boulevard. Go south from the entrance station and on to **Hidden Valley,** a onetime redoubt of cattle rustlers and colorful ne'er-do-wells. Farther south is the trailhead for **Lost Horse Mine,** about 2 miles away. (Do not go into this, or any other, mine.) Farther south still is **Keys View,** an overlook at 5,815 feet of the valley and mountain range. A number of the more ambitious trails also originate around here *(maps from the visitor center)*. Though walking is the best way to experience Joshua Tree National Park, there is also the well-marked **Geology Road Tour,** an 18-mile self-guided trek through some of the park's most dramatic rockscapes.

With more time, explore the central and eastern sections of the park. The former affords a rare glimpse at a desert-to-desert transition zone. A good place to stop is the **Cholla Cactus Garden.** Here grows the teddybear cholla, also called the jumping cholla, named for the tendency of its spiny needles to "jump" onto the clothes of hikers passing too closely by.

South from the Cholla Cactus Garden is **Cottonwood Spring** *(also accessible from I-10)*, one of the best kept secrets in the park and a welcome oasis. The spring, formed eons ago by an earthquake, was long used by Indians; their mortars, clay pots, and various other reminders of habitation can be seen throughout the spring area. Bighorn sheep can often be spotted in the Cottonwood Wash. For the hardy, the **Lost Palms Oasis Trail** more than rewards the 8-mile effort with amazing views and the largest grove of fan palms in the park.

Elite Land Tours *(tel 760/318-1200, www.elitelandtours.com)* offers in-depth naturalist-guided tours by Humvee. ■

Palm Springs

Palm Springs Desert Resorts
325 C3
Visitor information
www.palmspringsusa.com
70-100 Hwy. 111, Rancho Mirage
760/770-9000 or 800/967-3767

Palm Springs Aerial Tramway
www.pstramway.com
1 Tramway Rd., Palm Springs
760/325-1391 or 888/515-TRAM
$$$$

Palm Springs Air Museum
www.air-museum.org
745 North Gene Autry Trail, Palm Springs
760/778-6262
$$$

Palm Springs Art Museum
www.psmuseum.org
101 Museum Dr., Palm Springs
760/322-4800
Closed Mon.
$$

Agua Caliente Cultural Museum
www.accmuseum.org
760/778-1079
Closed Mon. & Tue.
$

McCallum Adobe
760/323-8297
Closed June–Sept.
$

THE ULTIMATE AMERICAN OASIS HAD ITS BEGINNINGS IN 1885, when a San Francisco lawyer established a health resort in the place that had always been the home of the Cahuilla. Revivified as a celebrity hideaway in the 1920s by the likes of Rudolph Valentino and Marlene Dietrich, remade again as a permanent home to the ultra-rich by Bob Hope and Frank Sinatra, Palm Springs owes its irresistible charms to one simple fact: It has water. Water from Mount San Jacinto, river water from the Colorado, and hot mineral water from deep in the earth—the springs that inspired its name. No wonder early Anglo settlers thought it exotic and wrote books with titles like *Our Araby: Palm Springs and the Garden of the Sun.*

Today, after an interregnum of benign neglect, Palm Springs has been revitalized with youthful vigor. The draw for the traveler can be summed up in five words: sun, pool, spa, golf, and more golf—over 110 courses carpet Palm Springs and the seven adjoining communities that make up the Coachella Valley, rimmed by dramatically sculpted mauve mountains. A sixth might be "shopping:" **Palm Canyon Drive** and **El Paseo,** in nearby **Palm Desert,** are both upscale shopping areas where people-watching during the high season (Oct.–May) is a draw in itself.

One of the few unashamed tourist traps in California truly worth seeing is the **Palm Springs Aerial Tramway.** Spanning the 2.5 miles between the desert floor and the top of Mount San Jacinto, the tramway, which has the single longest span of cable in the world, was completed in 1963. The air-conditioned tram, which revolves through 360-degrees, offers fantastic views of desert and mountains, as it ascends to cooler heights. At the top, 8,516 feet up, an upscale restaurant offers stupendous views, while **Mount San Jacinto State Park** *(tel 951/659-2607, www.parks.ca.gov)* offers more than 54 miles of trails.

Another magnificent aspect of the Palm Springs scene is the well-received **Palm Springs Air Museum,** which is, in its own words, "dedicated to the preservation, presentation and interpretation of the Air Power of World War Two...." It has one of the largest collections of flying World War II planes, along with rare and original combat photography and an extensive collection of World War II artifacts, uniforms, and memorabilia. Its programs regularly feature flight demonstrations.

Culture is definitely not one of the first things to dry up in a desert. The **Palm Springs Art Museum,** a public, privately funded, and nationally accredited art and natural science facility, has an outstanding art collection (see p. 337), along with a well-curated series of changing exhibitions. It also holds a number of interesting Native American artifacts, and offers concerts and lectures.

A small but engaging historical stop is **Village Green Heritage Center** *(219 S. Palm Canyon Rd., Palm Springs),* featuring the **Agua Caliente Cultural Museum** and the **McCallum Adobe,** displaying artifacts of Palm Springs's original settler, John Guthrie McCallum. Also named for McCallum is the **McCallum Theatre for the Performing Arts,** inside the **Bob Hope Cultural Center** in Palm Desert. The McCallum presents a full

Palm Springs, an oasis in the desert

and lively program including theater and music (classical and popular). It is an excellent way to pass a balmy desert evening—and to see the town's lively social life in action! Palm Desert's streets are enlivened by more than 150 public sculptures *(tel 760/568-5240; www.palmdesert art.org)*, notably along the ritzy El Paseo boulevard and in the 72-acre Civic Center Park *(San Pablo Ave.)*; not to be missed in the park are David Phelps's "The Dreamer" and Dee Clements's 88-foot-long granite "Holocaust Memorial." Pick up a map and booklet at the visitor center.

Superbly scenic Hwy. 111 links Palm Springs with Palm Desert and the other neighboring desert communities, including **La Quinta,** known for its premier golf courses and **La Quinta Resort & Club,** drawing Hollywood icons to the region's most illustrious spa. ■

Bob Hope Cultural Center

✉ 73000 Fred Waring Dr., Palm Desert

☎ 760/340-2787

Glamour in the desert

There was a time in the not-too-distant past when Palm Springs conjured not wealth and glamour but, rather, the old, the outdated, and the déclassé. But since the late 1980s, when the celebrity singer Sonny Bono was elected mayor (he later became its congressman before dying in a skiing accident in 1998), Palm Springs has staged an impressive comeback.

One reason is that a new generation of urbanites has discovered the blessings of the desert. The blessings come in the form of quietude, raw natural surroundings, and a relaxed style perhaps best characterized as "Desert Zen." Add to this the upsurge of interest in postwar modernist architecture, which the Springs has in abundance, and you have, as the trendy *Vanity Fair* recently put it, "a major revival."

Much of the renewed interest has been generated by younger bicoastal types who in recent years have snapped up and restored such architectural gems as the seven 1960s experimental steel houses *(Sunnyview Dr.)* by renowned architect Donald Wexler. This urban revival was epitomized by the purchase in 1993 of the famed Kaufman House *(470 W. Vista Chino)*, built in 1946 by the great Richard Neutra in the swanky old Las Palmas area. Following a long restoration by two Newport Beach professionals, in 2008, it was to be auctioned by Christie's as a work of art with a staggering pre-sale estimate of $15 to $25 million. The work of the late Albert Frey is also attracting attention. Near the Kaufman house stands one of his most engaging pieces of work, the Loewy house, commissioned in 1946 for Raymond Loewy, designer of the Coca-Cola bottle.

Celebrity, of course, fuels much of the scene (Palm Springs still hosts a number of celebrities, such as Barry Manilow and Jack Jones). Bob and Dolores Hope were the king and queen of the desert; their 1979 mansion was designed by architect John Lautner, a largely unsung genius of California modernism. The Hopes' first home *(1014 Buena Vista Dr.)* was just two blocks north of that of his inseparable sidekick Bing Crosby *(1011 E. El Alameda)*. Frank Sinatra's first Palm Springs house, on Alejo Road, is signaled by two palms the singer had planted so friends would know the house. Designed by Stewart Williams, the home is now known as Twin Palms.

Left: The Palm Springs Follies are an annual event. Above: Many roads in Palm Springs are named for celebrities. Right: Gary Cooper in riding gear at the El Mirador in Palm Springs, December 1932

Old-time celebrity homes abound. The local experts (see below) will guide the truly curious to several of them. De rigeur stops on the celebrity circuit include Liberace's Spanish-Revival-style home *(501 N. Belardo Rd.)*; and the Elvis Presley's honeymoon house, known as "House of Tomorrow" *(1350 Ladera Circle).* This dramatic structure was originally built for Donald Alexander, the mid-century developer responsible for building many of Palm Springs's Modernist homes.

The younger crowd—Chris O'Donnell, Donatella Versace—flocks to such places as the Korakia Pensione, a 1920s Hollywood getaway. Another place for the younger set is Miracle Manor in Desert Hot Springs *(tel 760/329-6641).* This low-slung 1940s motel was recently purchased and retooled by trendy L.A. architect Michael Rotondi and designer April Greiman. It is perhaps the sparest version of Desert Zen, with putty tones, floors of varnished plywood and concrete, linens of gauzy cotton. There are few of the traditional motel appliances—no TVs, phones, or clocks. But there is a natural spring-fed hot tub, an on-call masseuse, and plenty of delicious desert scenery and silence.

In Palm Springs itself, culture abounds, although much of it is the preserve of the locals, who have made fundraising parties an art form and their own homes into architectural shrines. Fortunately the Palm Springs Art Museum (see p. 335) offers a look into the collecting habits of this megaclass. Much of the museum's Western and Native American art was donated by film star Kirk Douglas and his wife, Anne, and author Sidney Sheldon. It includes some fine examples of work by members of the Taos Artists Society, including Walter Ufer, Joseph Henry Sharp, and Ernest Martin Hennings. Works by Maynard Dixon and Charles M. Russell are also represented in the collection. A treat awaits in the work of actor George Montgomery, who created a notable collection of sculpture and furniture.

Before setting out to see Palm Springs's celebrity homes, pick up a map of celebrity home locations at the Palm Springs Desert Resorts Visitors Bureau (see p. 334). Palm Springs Celebrity Tours *(tel 760/770-2700, www.celebrity-tours.com)* offers standard "talk and gawk" trips. Modernist expert Robert Imber offers guided architecture tours *(PS Modern Tours, tel 760/318-6118),* including by Segway. The publication "Palm Springs Architectural Highlights" is available from the Palm Springs Visitors Bureau and the Palm Springs Historical Society *(tel 760/323-8297).* ■

Indian Canyons

Indian Canyons
www.theindiancanyons.com
✉ South Palm Canyon Dr.
☎ 760/325-3400 or 800/790-3398
$ $$

Tahquitz Canyon Visitor information
www.tahquitzcanyon.com
✉ 500 W. Mesquite
☎ 760/416-7044
$ $$$

FOUR SPECTACULAR DESERT CANYONS LIE OUTSIDE OF THE town of Palm Springs. Although today traversed by outdoor types, from hikers to SUVers to mountain bikers, the area was once the domain of a single hardy people, the Agua Caliente band of the Cahuilla. Their imprint on the area remains in the form of pictographs, used to mark holy places, and bedrock mortars, which the Cahuilla used to grind the nuts, seeds, and berries that sustained them for centuries. Their descendants administer the canyons—which are considered sacred—and are major sponsors of a new, 50-acre Agua Caliente Cultural Museum complex *(www.aguacaliente.org)* to be built adjacent to the Indian Canyons. The dramatic new museum will replace the existing, tiny Agua Caliente Cultural Museum, in Village Green Heritage Center (see p. 335).

***Washingtonia* palms, Coachella Valley Preserve**

The four canyons each have a stream surrounded by steep rocky sides and are surrounded by barren hills. The 15-mile-long **Palm Canyon,** accessed via South Palm Canyon Drive, is the biggest of the four. The vast grove of *Washingtonia* palms that stretches for several miles along Palm Canyon is one of the biggest in the world. After visiting the **Trading Post,** where you can buy hiking maps plus Indian jewelry, pottery, and weavings, take the moderately graded trail into the canyon, which follows a beautiful palm-shaded stream before climbing up into the cacti-studded mountains.

Nearby **Murray Canyon** has herds of wild horses running through it. Bighorn sheep and deer are also numerous in the vicinity. An easy hike leads to **Andreas Canyon,** the site of another enormous grove of *Washingtonia* palms.

Closer to the city center, **Tahquitz Canyon** is setting for a huge natural amphitheater beneath Tahquitz peak. The snow melt from this peak feeds a spectacular waterfall. Ranger-led tours that depart the visitor center show visitors ancient pictographs and irrigation systems. ■

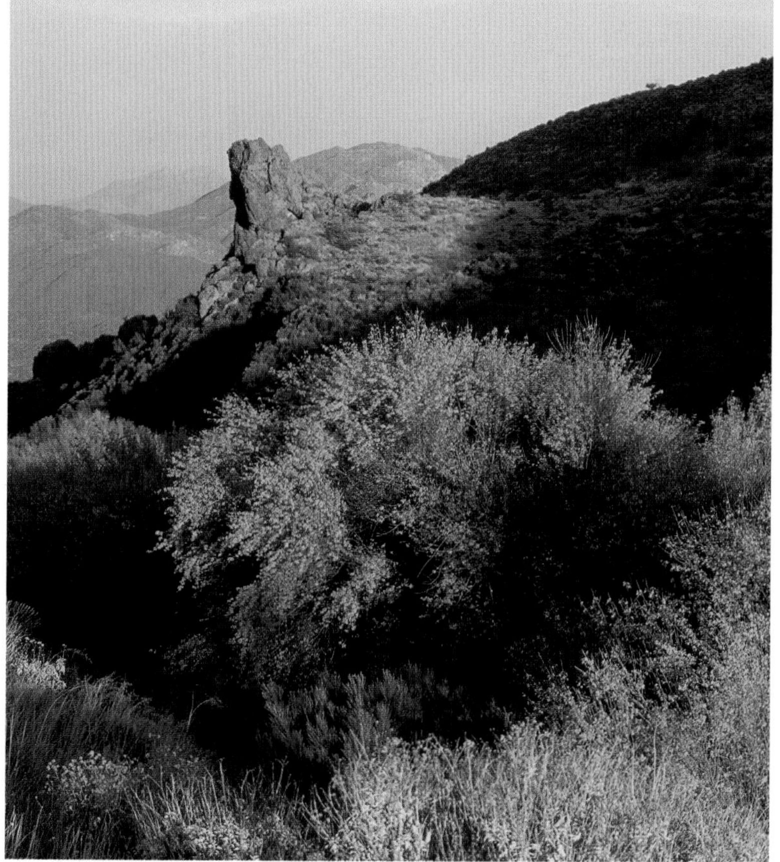

The Living Desert

The Living Desert Botanical Park shows a greener desert.

DESERTS HAVE LONG CAPTURED THE MINDS OF CURIOUS travelers and mystics but seldom seem to have inspired those charged with putting together parks and zoos. The Living Desert wildlife and botanical park is a rare exception.

Established in 1970, it has emerged as one of the most successful zoological parks in the nation dedicated to one task: a complete introduction to desert ecologies, both of North America and around the world. Spread over 1,200 acres of the Colorado Desert, part of the vast Sonoran Desert, the park contains nearly 400 species of animals and a wide array of desert flora. Although the **Discovery Room** near the entrance is ostensibly set up for children, it provides all ages with a tutorial on desert basics. Animal exhibits are interspersed throughout specialized gardens, among them the **Palo Verde Garden Center,** the (not to be missed) **Cahuilla Indian Ethnobotanical Garden**, and the **Upper Colorado Garden.** To the east is a section dedicated to African deserts and savannas, with animals ranging from gazelles and warthogs to giraffes and cheetah.

The big attraction is **Eagle**

Living Desert Wildlife & Botanical Park
www.livingdesert.org
325 C2
47900 Portola Ave., Palm Desert
760/346-5694
$$

Top: The delicate-looking desert smoketree
Above: The aptly named bighorn sheep

Fragrant trees of the desert

Although the spring bloom of the desert wildflowers gets all the press, much of the glorious fragrance that accompanies it is provided by the spring and early summer flourish of the desert trees. The most numerous species are all represented at the Living Desert Wildlife and Botanical Park.

Blue paloverde *(Cercidium floridum)* has a pale green trunk, spiny olive-green twigs, and sparse (if not entirely absent) foliage. Short and willowy, it is often found along stream and wash banks, performing a vital service in preventing erosion. Once a year it bursts into bright yellow bloom. Desert burros can be seen champing on its soft wood in stupid delight.

Desert smoketree *(Dalea spinosa)* is one of the great landscape treasures of the Palm Springs area. It owes its mystical image—a fog-shrouded tangle of wooden antlers—to its evanescent foliage. Until its third year its twigs are thickly coated with gray hairs, which explains the tree's ghostly appearance under the summer moon. It flowers precisely in the dead heat of summer, when tourists have departed.

Desert catalpa *(Chilopsis linearis)* was once used to make hunting bows. Fittingly known as the bow willow, it has long, thin, light green leaves and is willowlike in appearance. It often stands—hunches, rather—over washed-out culverts and ditches throughout the Colorado Desert. Its remarkable flowers are showy pink spikes with white and yellow spots in the throat. Later in the summer the heat draws out their subtle fragrance that resembles that of sweet violets.

Desert ironwood *(Olneya tesota)* more than lives up to its name. With a specific gravity of 1.14, a piece of it will sink in water. Its notable red-brown bark peels in long downward strips, and it has gray leaves. If you are in the desert in early summer you will witness its remarkable flowering, a flourish of thousands of indigo and rose-purple blooms with a subtle perfume.

True mesquite *(Prosopis juliflora)* is among the Colorado Desert's dominant flora. It has dark, reddish brown bark and slim, smooth twigs like tendrils waving at the bottom of the sea. Its usefulness to a range of inhabitants is legendary. Southwestern Native Americans used its strong wood to erect their homes; their children used it to make a wooden kickball; the elders made of its sugary fruit a nasty liquor. Spaniards fed their cattle on it; confectioners used it to make gum; the U.S. Cavalry fed it to their horses. Nevertheless, mesquite has rarely received its due praise, probably because it is one of the desert's most invasive plants. Its scent—piney and smoky—is the desert's own. ■

Canyon, at the end of the main pathway. The canyon contains a hiking trail network, streams, and native fauna in situ. Among them are the mountain lion, the bobcat, the Mexican wolf, and the golden eagle. One of the other exhibits explains the San Andreas Fault line and yet another is devoted to the desert bighorn sheep. And a new exhibit, **Amazing Amphibians: Frogs on the Edge,** opened in 2007 to educate visitors about the mass extinctions of amphibians worldwide. ■

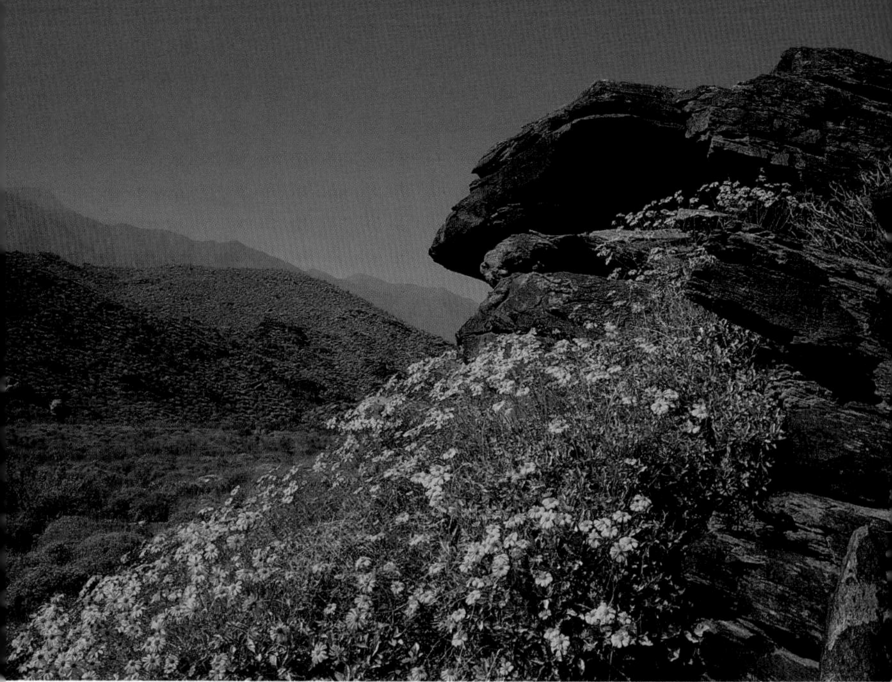

Anza-Borrego Desert State Park

Anza-Borrego Desert in bloom

THE FACT THAT THIS 600,000-ACRE PARK IS TUCKED INTO one of the most remote no-man's-lands in the state doesn't stop thousands of wildflower lovers from making their spring pilgrimage. And little wonder: Anza-Borrego is a capital of desert botanica. These blooms begin in February, when the blue sand verbena spreads like a rash over white-sand hillocks and golden-hued dunes. Then come the agave, the mallow, the ocotillo, and the brittlebush. By April the desert has become a vast—albeit temporary—wonderland of color.

Memorable places to go include the **Borrego-Palm Canyon Trail** *(trailhead on Borrego-Palm Canyon, W of Borrego Springs)*. The path first winds through a bamboo-filled grove before ending at a waterfall and a grove of 800 fan palms. The **Tamarisk Grove** *(Calif. 78 and Yaqui Pass Rd.)* has a number of palm canyons and spectacular gorges. **Agua Caliente County Park** *(Cty. Rd. S-2, S of Calif. 78)* is a site of the ancient Kumeyaay culture and a habitat for bighorn sheep and other desert wildlife. Ask for guides to archaeological sites at the visitor center.

For those staying in Borrego Springs, the one-hour round-trip east to see the views from **Fonts Point,** in the Borrego Badlands, is a must at sunset, when the great ball of fire boils dramatically down into the red-black horizon. If you really want to get to know the desert, naturalist Paul Johnson (reachable through the visitor center) conducts brilliant walking tours. ■

Anza-Borrego Desert State Park

325 C2

Visitor information

200 Palm Canyon, Borrego Springs

760/767-5311

ARE THE FLOWERS BLOOMING?

For up-to-date information on the Spring Bloom, contact the Anza-Borrego Desert State Park visitor center (see above), the Living Desert wildflower hotline *(tel 619/340-0435)* or the Payne Foundation *(tel 818/768-3533, www.theodorepayne.org)*. ■

Salton Sea

Salton Sea
325 C2
Visitor information
100-225 State Park Rd., North Shore
760/393-3052

Sonny Bono Salton Sea National Wildlife Refuge
Visitor information
www.fws.gov/saltonsea
Sinclair Rd. & Gentry Rd., Niland
760/348-5278
Visitor center closed Sat. & Sun.

ABOUT 30 MILES SOUTH OF PALM SPRINGS LIES ONE OF the most bizarre places in California. The Salton Sea was formed in 1905, when the Colorado River burst out of some badly constructed irrigation canals in nearby Yuma, Arizona, and ran, unchecked for almost two years, into a 35-by-15-mile desert basin with no natural outlet. The river water carried salt, which was left behind when the desert heat evaporated the water. More river water ran in and evaporated, leaving behind an increasingly high concentration of salt. This process has resulted in the Salton Sea's remarkably high salinity of 41 parts per million. The Pacific Ocean is about 35 parts per million.

The Salton Sea's unique biology has had remarkable consequences. On the one hand, it has become one of the West Coast's great bird-watching areas, with a huge population of pelicans and egrets, among others. The birds come to feed on the equally huge fish population, particularly the tilapia, which are so numerous that fishermen have been known to pull hundreds of the fish from the sea in just one sitting. (There is no limit on how many tilapia you catch.)

Salton flats

On the other hand, the sea is also a quagmire of ecological problems. Salt concentrations are increasing. For several summers both birds and fish have been found dying in large numbers. One theory is that fertilizers from farm water runoffs have fueled enormous blooms of algae. When these colorful (and very smelly) blooms die, they pull enormous amounts of oxygen from the water, killing the fish in large numbers. The dead fish rot, encouraging botulism, which is then passed on to the birds, with fatal results.

Nevertheless, the sea remains a popular destination for fisherfolk, water-skiers, and campers. Winter is the favorite season for campers and hikers. The **Mecca Beach** campground, about 1 mile south of park headquarters, is a perfect base camp for fishing fanatics.

And for bird-watchers the months from October through May are a delight. At that time, up to four million migrating birds flock about the sea. The **Sonny Bono Salton Sea National Wildlife Refuge** is the preferred destination for ornithologists.

Authorities are shaping a plan to rehabilitate the sea *(www.saltonsea.ca.gov)*, which is surrounded by the intensely irrigated farmland of the Imperial Valley—a lush Eden where avocados citrus, dates, grapes, tomatoes, and other vegetables are grown in astounding abundance. ■

Travelwise

California traffic, jamming

TRAVELWISE INFORMATION

PLANNING YOUR TRIP

WHEN TO GO

Is there really a bad time to visit California? It depends upon which California you mean. If northern California, then the late winter and early spring months are a chilly proposition. If southern California, late August and September can be too hot for some. The basic climatic signposts are: In summer, go north; in winter, go south. Of course, this means you will encounter heavy tourist traffic. One alternative worth the effort is to explore the various tourist "cusp seasons" (very early spring in Wine Country, for example, or very early summer in L.A.).

EVENTS & FESTIVALS

California is full of cultural events: colorful agricultural festivals, seasonal music fests, sporting and ethnic venues. Check out each city's website and/or visitor information bureau for an up-to-date listing. Some favorites are:

January On Jan. 1, the Tournament of Roses Parade and Football Game *(www.tournamentofroses.com)* makes Pasadena one big party; the flower-bedecked floats are viewable post-parade at Sierra Madre Park through Jan. 3.

February San Francisco's Chinese New Year Parade *(www.chineseparade.com)* still outclasses L.A.'s *(www.lagoldendragonparade.com)* by far.

March The Mendocino Whale Watch Festival *(www.mendowhale.com)* commences with great gusto, and with as much beer spouting as sea water.

April The Antelope Valley's blooming of native poppies is a good excuse for music, art, food, and fun at the California Poppy Festival, in Lancaster *(www.poppyfestival.com)*.

May Mark Twain buffs will love the Jumping Frog Jubilee in Angels Camp, Gold Country *(www.frogtown.org)*—a great place to drink up and tell a few "stretchers" of your own.

June It can get a bit snooty, but for pure Wine Country atmosphere you must experience the Napa Valley Wine Auction *(www.napavintners.com)*. Just don't overdo the wine before you start bidding.

July Right on the Central Coast, two great entertainment choices, the esteemed Carmel Bach Festival *(www.bachfestival.org)* and the Gilroy Garlic Festival *(www.gilroygarlicfestival.com)*.

August *Ee-ho-lay! Yi yi yi!* It's the Old Spanish Days Fiesta in old Santa Barbara *(www.oldspanishdays-fiesta.org)*, where you can get all dressed up and play Hidalgo for a day.

September The Russian River Jazz Festival *(www.russianriverfestivals.com)* competes with the San Francisco Blues Festival *(www.sfblues.com)*—and everybody wins!

October The Tor House Poetry Festival in Carmel *(tel 831/624-1813)* really brings out the old-time California characters.

November This is a good time to see the desert. What better excuse than the Art of Food & Wine Festival, in Palm Desert *(www.artoffoodandwine.com)*. Many of southern California's best chefs prepare treats.

December Multi million dollar yachts, small boats, and even kayaks bedecked in Christmas lights emblazon Newport Beach harbor during the Christmas Boat Parade *(www.christmasboatparade.com)*.

GETTING AROUND

AIRPORTS

Californians pioneered the use of small, agile, multi-passenger vans for to-and-from airport trips, and a number of companies ply their services (for example Shuttle Vans, Freeway Flyers, etc.) at all airports. Most are quite reliable, reasonable, prompt, and friendly. If you are staying at a major airport hotel, it will probably provide a free van ride to and from the airport; additionally, all the major car rental outfits provide a shuttle service to their outlets. Super Shuttle *(www.supershuttle.com)* offers a door-to-door service in L.A. *(tel 310/782-6600)* and San Francisco *(tel 415/558-8500)*.

John Wayne Orange County Airport Santa Ana *(tel 949/252-5200)* A growing regional airport, John Wayne is a reasonable alternative to flying into L.A., particularly if you are planning to spend the bulk of your time in southern California.

Los Angeles International Airport *(tel 310/646-5252)* A taxi ride will cost approximately $30 downtown, $25 to Beverly Hills.

Oakland International Airport *(tel 510/563-3300)* A taxi ride to Oakland city center will cost about $25.

Palm Springs *(tel 760/318-3800)* Taxi to center about $12.

Sacramento *(tel 916/929-5411)* Taxi to center about $25.

San Francisco International Airport *(tel 650/821-8211)* For a taxi, expect to pay $25–$30 for a one-way trip downtown.

San Jose Airport *(tel 408/501-0979)* If you are flying in for a bit of .com business, this is the preferred port of entry. Taxi to center approximately $10.

BY CAR

Unless you plan on landing in San Francisco and staying within the metropolitan area, get a car. The most powerful—and helpful—motorists' organization is the California State Automobile Association *(tel 800/922-8228, www.csaa.com).*

On most California freeways, the left-hand lane is reserved for the fastest drivers.

California has a huge array of car rental agencies. If you respond to a "bargain" ad, only to find there are no longer any cars of the "bargain" line left to rent, ask for a free upgrade.
Avis: tel 800/331-1212, www.avis.com
Budget: tel 800/527-7000, www.budget.com
Dollar: tel 800/800-3665, www.dollar.com
Hertz: tel 800/654-3131, www.hertz.com

PUBLIC TRANSPORT

Amtrak *(tel 800/872-7245, www.amtrak.com),* the nationwide rail network, has been enjoying good press and a revival among travelers who want to see the state more slowly. Greyhound Lines *(tel 800/231-2222, www.greyhound.com)* is the bus system, with fairly comprehensive, if slow, services to most cities.

In San Francisco, the Muni bus system is quite well regarded *(tel 415/701-2311, www.sfmta.com).* BART, the famous rapid transit train system (www.bart.gov), will whisk you fairly comfortably from downtown to the east, north, and south bays. Call the visitors bureau for details on passes.

In Los Angeles, the Dash bus system covers much of the city *(tel 213/808-2273, www.ladot transit.com).* The Metro system, currently fairly limited, is being extended *(tel 800/COMMUTE, www.metro.net).*

PRACTICAL ADVICE

- California is still paradise, but even paradise has a few rotten apples. Behave appropriately; do not walk alone in unknown districts; do not display expensive equipment or jewelry.
- Do not call it "Frisco."
- Do not call it "The Big Orange," "La La Land," "Tinseltown," or "El-Lay."
- Use common sense. Do not use an ATM machine if you are alone late at night.
- Do not expect everyone to speak English, particularly in some of the more interesting parts of L.A. and San Francisco. Do not "flip the bird" to any other drivers, regardless of how badly they may be driving.
- Do not pick up hitchhikers and, save for extreme emergencies, do not stop to help anyone along the freeway unless there is another person in the car with you and you can telephone for help (911) immediately.
- Buy some good maps.
- Carry bottled water with you in the car.

EMERGENCIES

In any part of the state, the 911 number is set aside for reporting all emergencies. If you are a victim of a crime, you may want to avail yourself of the counseling services at the Crime Victims' Hotline *(tel 800/394-2255).*

VISITORS WITH DISABILITIES

The California legislature has enacted a number of laws requiring restaurants, universities, municipal facilities, and all transport systems to provide wheelchair access. To find out about your rights, call 510/644-2555. The hearing impaired can get information by calling 800/622-3277.

VISITOR INFORMATION

The first resource is the California Division of Tourism *(1102 Q Street, Suite 6000, Sacramento, CA 95814, tel 916/444-4429, www.visitcalifornia.com)* which publishes a variety of helpful guides. Its website contains a list of regional convention and visitors bureaus and is linked to hundreds of region-specific sites, each in turn with hundreds of hotel, food, and attractions listings. The Division has 13 visitor information centers throughout the state.

An outstanding resource for outdoor folks is the National Parks Service; its website is highly useful, at www.nps.gov.

The three principal city visitor information bureaus are in Los Angeles *(333 South Hope St., tel 213/624-7300, www.discoverlos angeles.com),* San Diego *(2215 India St., tel 619/232-3101, www.sandiego.org),* and San Francisco *(900 Market St., tel 415/391-2000, www.onlyinsan francisco.com).*

BACKGROUND READING

To really get up on California culture and history, there is no better single volume in print than Carey McWilliams's classic *California: The Great Exception.* Unfortunately McWilliams's narrative ends in 1949, leaving the rest of the tale to countless imitators and others, many of whom cannot be trusted. One generally reliable commentator is the omni-intellectual state librarian, Kevin Starr. See any title under his name, particularly *Inventing the Dream* and *Material Dreams.* The essays of Richard Rodriguez, though sometimes a bit elliptical, are worthwhile and entertaining; his *Days of Obligation* is a good, meditative, and thought-provoking read. John Muir's *The Mountains of California,* is a must for all outdoor folk.

HOTELS & RESTAURANTS

California has an abundance of outstanding restaurants, with its two principal cities at the top of the national culinary tree. Wealthy areas, such as Hollywood in the south and Silicon Valley in the north, have helped to attract some of the world's great chefs to the region. But the real deals—and some of the best food—are to be found in the ethnic restaurants run by first-generation immigrants from Asia and the Middle East. There the ingredients are fresh, the food is prepared with familial vigor, and the prices are modest.

The state's hotels, inns, and bed-and-breakfast establishments span a wide range of styles and amenities, from the super-chic Peninsula in Beverly Hills or the traditional Mark Hopkins in San Francisco to the indulgently quiet and restful Manka's Inn in tiny Inverness. Save yourself some money—sometimes up to 50 percent—by looking in the *L.A. Times* Sunday edition, where many weekday and weekend bargains are advertised (available online at www.latimes.com).

WHAT TO EXPECT

Most California hotels operate what has become known as "the American plan," which simply means breakfast is not included in the price. What *should* be included is attentive, pleasant service, knowledgeable and pro-active staff, and a database of local and regional information about everything from local eateries to cultural and arts venues or sports teams. All of the hotels and inns listed below should be able to provide such, although the degree to which their staff will do so varies enormously. Service, even in the priciest of hotels, is a spotty commodity these days.

The listings attempt to strike a balance between chain hotels and regionally unique hotels. The major chains listed all do a good job of the basics. The better bed-and-breakfasts are a worthwhile alternative; you may have to do a bit more homework, but, in general, you will get cheerier staff—and also breakfast. The numbers for several bed-and-breakfast associations are included.

HOTEL CHAINS & GROUPS

Doubletree Hotels: tel 800/222-8733, www.doubletree.com
Hilton Hotels: tel 800/445-8667, www.hilton.com
Holiday Inn: tel 800/465-4329, www.holidayinn.com
Hyatt Hotels: tel 800/633-7313, www.hyatt.com
Marriott Hotels: tel 888/236-2427, www.marriott.com
Ramada: tel 800/272-6232, www.ramada.com
Sheraton: tel 800/325-3535, www.sheraton.com
Westin: tel 800/937-8461, www.westin.com
Wyndham Hotels: tel 877/999-3223, www.wyndham.com

BED-AND-BREAKFAST ASSOCIATIONS

California Association of Bed & Breakfast Inns: tel 800/373-9251, http://cabbi.com

CREDIT CARDS

AE American Express, DC Diners Club, MC Mastercard, V Visa.

PARKING

Where a hotel or restaurant has its own parking, the symbol P is included in the entry. Some hotels and restaurants offer valet parking, shown as P Valet.

RESTAURANTS

Closings for holidays may vary from year to year. It is advisable to check and to reserve a table.
L = lunch
D = dinner

Tipping

Except in rare situations (or when large groups are involved), tipping in California restaurants is, in theory, entirely voluntary. In reality, you are expected to leave 15 percent of the sub-total (before tax). Still, if you have a bad experience, do not hesitate to leave less, or even nothing.

PRICES

HOTELS

An indication of the cost of a double room without breakfast is given by **$** signs.

$$$$$	Over $280
$$$$	$200–$280
$$$	$120–$200
$$	$80–$120
$	Under $80

RESTAURANTS

An indication of the cost of a three-course dinner without drinks is given by $ signs.

$$$$$	Over $80
$$$$	$50–$80
$$$	$35–$50
$$	$20–$35
$	Under $20

HOTEL RESTAURANTS

Outstanding restaurants in hotels are listed separately and a cross-reference is made in the hotel entry. Where a hotel restaurant is above the standard one would expect for a hotel of that quality, the restaurant symbol is given as well as the hotel one, and the restaurant is described in the entry. No indication is given where the hotel has a restaurant of no particular merit.

SMOKING

Smoking is not allowed in restaurants in California. By law, hotels must have non-smoking rooms and non-smoking areas in the lobby. A few do not allow smoking at all, and this is indicated in the entry.

In the following selection, hotels are listed under each location by price, then in alphabetical order, followed by restaurants also by price and alphabetical order.

LOS ANGELES

AIRPORT—LAX

RADISSON
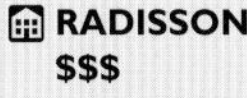
$$$
6225 W. CENTURY BLVD., 90045
TEL 310/670-9000
FAX 310/337-6555
The closest hotel to LAX, L.A.'s airport, has features that will endear it to anyone who must stay near the airport; these include deluxe soundproofing, spacious public areas, and recently redecorated rooms.
580 P All major cards

FROM THE BEACH

MARINA DEL REY

RITZ CARLTON MARINA DEL REY
$$$$$
4375 ADMIRALTY WAY, 90212
TEL 310/823-1700
FAX 310/823-2403
A luxury hotel with outstanding concierge service, tastefully decorated rooms, and quiet, impeccable service. The Ritz has the additional advantage of a fine restaurant, the Dining Room, where the French Provençal cuisine includes fresh pâtés and zesty bouillabaisse.
304 P All major cards

VENICE

JOE'S RESTAURANT
$$$
1023 ABBOT KINNEY BLVD.
TEL 310/399-5811
www.joesrestaurant.com
A favorite among locals, Joe's offers a delicately balanced California-French cuisine, showing the lighter dishes favored on L.A.'s Westside. The slow-roasted salmon with parsnip purée is a perfect complement to the asparagus with *frisée* and pancetta in tomato vinaigrette.
90 P All major cards

ROSE CAFÉ
$
220 ROSE AVE. (AT MAIN ST.)
TEL 310/399-0711
www.rosecafe.com
A big, airy cafeteria where the cappuccino is good, the breakfasts are satisfying, and the various cold salads are a favorite of the very trendy locals who hang out here.
150 P AE, MC, V

SANTA MONICA

LOEWS SANTA MONICA
$$$$$
1700 OCEAN AVE., 90401
TEL 866/210-9156
FAX 310/458-6761
www.santamonicaloewshotel.com
Another fine beachside hotel, the Loews features sun-filled atriums, tasteful guest rooms, and up-to-date business services for those who must tear themselves away from the beach to send something back to the office. The Loews restaurant, Lavande (see below), is notable.
359 P / All major cards

SHUTTERS ON THE BEACH
$$$$$
1 PICO BLVD., 90405
TEL 310/458-0030
www.shuttersonthebeach.com
Intimate, sun-filled, this is a luxury hotel on the coast. Rooms are spacious and bright, evocative of 1930s beachside cottages. Shutters is within walking distance of the Santa Monica Pier and other attractions. The One Pico restaurant is a regular for local celebrities like Mel Brooks and Anne Bancroft.
198 P Valet All major cards

FAIRMONT MIRAMAR HOTEL
$$$$
101 WILSHIRE BLVD., 90401
TEL 310/576-7777
www.fairmont.com
Located on a historic estate, this is by far the traditional favorite (President Clinton stays here when in town). The bungalows are swanky-plush; the up-top rooms have remarkable views of the coast. The Miramar is really quiet.
302 P All major cards

CHINOIS ON MAIN
$$$$
2709 MAIN ST.
TEL 310/392-9025
www.wolfgangpuck.com
Slick, breezy, and always crowded, Wolfgang Puck's family-style fusion cuisine (crab pot stickers with lemon chili oil dressing... is hard to beat. The charred tuna exemplifies Puck's puckish-ness with sauces.
100 P Valet Closed Sat.–Tues. L All major cards

OCEAN & VINE
$$$$
HOTEL LOEWS SANTA MONICA, 1700 OCEAN AVE.
TEL 310/576-3180
One of the more acclaimed new restaurants in L.A., retro-themed Ocean & Vine excels in California-fusion fare such as grilled Colorado rack of lamb with carrot cous cous and chocolate mint mop.
120 P All major cards

VALENTINO
$$$$
3115 PICO BLVD.
TEL 310/829-4313
For 25 years a revered L.A. institution, Piero Selvaggio's flagship is routinely rated among the best of the best. The wine collection warrants note for its depth and breadth of small specialty producers. Porcini mushrooms tend to pop up everywhere on this earthy menu. The oxtail ravioli hits the spot.
240 P Valet Closed Sun. All major cards

3-SQUARE CAFÉ & BAKERY
$$$–$$$$
1121 ABBOT KINNEY
TEL 310/399-6504
www.rockenwagner.com
Consistently rated as one of L.A.'s best places to eat. Restaurateur Hans Röckenwagner's latest fine-dining, yet casual, contemporary place is known for its sandwiches, salads, pastries, and such delights as crab soufflé with lobster butter sauce.
100 P Closed Mon.–Fri. L All major cards

BORDER GRILL
$$$
1445 4TH ST.
TEL 310/451-1655
www.bordergrill.com
Latin-influenced nouvelle cuisine comes from the kitchens of Mary Sue Milliken and Susan Feniger, hosts of the national TV cooking show *Too Hot To Handle*. The tacos filled with variously spiced meats (influences: Bombay, Santa Fe, Buenos Aires) are a bargain. You may want to float away on a cloud of the outrageous coconut flan.
246 P Valet All major cards

JIRAFFE
$$$
502 SANTA MONICA BLVD.
TEL 310/917-6671
www.jirafferestaurant.com
Another consistent performer, this one dishing up a version of California-French. Among the *plats* most desired are the roast rabbit in basil polenta and the seafood ragout with sweet white corn. Signature cocktails are a highlight.
85 P Valet Closed L All major cards

BROADWAY DELI
$$
1457 3RD ST. PROMENADE
TEL 310/451-0616
www.broadwaydeli.com
Eclectic deli cuisine combines the essentials—from matzo ball soup to rice pudding—with fine pastas, steaks, and salads. *The* place for people-watching on a summer evening. The take-out counter is extensive, with sweets and an array of cheeses, meats, and breads for picnics on the nearby beach.
150 P All major cards

MALIBU/SANTA MONICA MOUNTAINS

GEOFFREY'S
$$$$
27400 PACIFIC COAST HWY., MALIBU (4 MILES N OF MALIBU CANYON RD.)
TEL 310/457-1519
www.geoffreysmalibu.com
California cuisine dished up in the ultimate beachside location; some believe this is the only place where the food truly matches the quality of the view.
150 P All major cards

INN OF THE SEVENTH RAY
$$$
128 OLD TOPANGA CANYON RD., TOPANGA
TEL 310/455-1311
www.innoftheseventhray.com
The ultimate New Age dining experience, the venerable inn, its open-air seating perched on the side of a babbling brook, offers fine vegetarian and other specialties. The baked salmon and the pecan pie are two outstanding items.
200 P All major cards

SADDLE PEAK LODGE
$$$
419 COLD CANYON, CALABASAS (E OF MALIBU CANYON)
TEL 818/222-3888
www.saddlepeaklodge.com
The *ne plus ultra* of rustic California cuisine, this very woodsy and elegant canyon cottage offers adventurous game dishes, such as buffalo tartar with whole grain mustard aioli, and roasted elk tenderloin. For the tamer at heart, brunch on Sunday morning features delicious applewood-smoked bacon and waffles.
180 P Valet Closed L, & Mon.–Tues. AE, MC, V

WESTWOOD & WEST L.A.

HOTEL BEL AIR
$$$$$
701 STONE CANYON RD., BEL AIR, 90077
TEL 310/472-1211
www.hotelbelair.com
For over half a century the Hotel Bel Air has been charming guests with its blend of mission architecture, lush gardens, and fine food (its dining room is among the top California-French eateries in the city, with a much-requested lobster bisque). A good idea is simply to drop in for a drink at the terrace bar, perhaps in early evening, when the gardens turn to pure magic.
92 P All major cards

W LOS ANGELES
$$$–$$$$$
930 HILGARD AVE. WESTWOOD, 90024
TEL 310/208-8765
FAX 310/824-0355
www.starwood.com
This moderne-with-California-Spanish-overtones hotel is perfect for those who want to play on L.A.'s Westside at night while exploring inland during the day. Situated across the street from UCLA, the West offers a luxurious spa, spacious suites, and a fine lobby bar where the people-watching just goes on and on.
258 rooms & suites P All major cards

VINCENTI
$$$$$
11930 SAN VICENTE BLVD., BRENTWOOD
TEL 310/207-0127
www.vincentiristorante.com
Chef Nicola Mastronarti is

noted as one of the best Italian chefs in L.A. The fresh whole fish cooked over glowing embers is the main attraction, with such innovations as penne with *rapini* and pressed tuna roe done in a surprisingly light, fresh manner. For fans of the trendy *guanciale* (pig's jowl), this is the place.
90 P Closed L except Fri. & all Sun. AE, MC, V

ASAKUMA
$$
11701 WILSHIRE BLVD., WEST L.A.
TEL 310/826-0013
www.asakuma.com
A big fun sushi place, often packed with local Japanese businessmen and UCLA types. The sushi is very fresh and skillfully prepared, particularly the *toro,* like butter when in season.
103 P Valet All major cards

SOMETHING SPECIAL

BOMBAY CAFÉ

The brilliance of this well-known café was to blend various Indian street foods with modern preparation techniques, yielding a relatively low-fat but very flavorful cuisine. For lunch try the yummy frankies, a kind of chutney-fried burrito. The crispy shrimp, tandoori-chicken sausages, and smoked *bharta* (eggplant) are favorites.
$$
12021 W. PICO BLVD., WEST L.A.
TEL 310/473-3388
www.bombaycafe-la.com
112 P Closed L Sat. & Sun. All major cards

LA BRUSCHETTA
$$
1621 WESTWOOD BLVD., WEST L.A.
TEL 310/477-1052
www.labruschettaristorante.com
Northern Italian fare—osso buco, risotto Milanese, and veal scaloppini—combines with an impressive wine list to make this local favorite a reliable, festive affair.
78 P Valet Closed Sat. L & Sun. L AE, MC, V

PASTINA
$$
2260 WESTWOOD BLVD., WEST L.A.
TEL 310/441-4655
Tasty neighborhood Italian food that won't wreak havoc on a diet, despite the large portions of pasta, pizza, and gnocchi.
86 P Valet Closed Sat. L & Sun. L AE, MC, V

APPLE PAN
$
10801 PICO BLVD., WESTWOOD
TEL 310/475-3585
The old-fashioned U-shaped counter is always packed with locals waiting for their hit of hamburgers, fries, and apple pie. Great if you've been shopping and need sustenance.
23 P Closed Mon. Cash only

JOHN O'GROATS
$
10516 PICO BLVD., RANCHO PARK (NEAR BEVERLY GLEN)
TEL 310/204-0692
Just the greatest little down-home breakfast spot on the Westside, O'Groats is legendary among UCLA grad students, who succor themselves on the café's homemade biscuits and fries, only to return with their families years later—just to order the same thing!
65 P Closed D All major cards

MAURICE'S SNACK N' CHAT
$
5068 W. PICO BLVD., WEST L.A.
TEL 323/931-3879
Recently reopened as a take-out only after a few year's hiatus, this L.A. institution still serves soul food, pure and simple, prepared by octogenarian Maurice Prince. Fried chicken, southern style, is the local favorite, with baked chicken on Sundays. Save room for the apple or pecan pie.
P MC, V

CENTURY CITY

HYATT REGENCY CENTURY PLAZA
$$$$–$$$$$
2025 AVE. OF THE STARS, 90067
TEL 310/228-1234
FAX 310/551-3355
www.centuryplaza.hyatt.com
A city within a city, the swank, chicly contemporary Plaza, President Reagan's favorite campaign stopover, is perfectly situated between Beverly Hills and nearby shopping, live theaters across the street and in Westwood, and cultural happenings at UCLA and the Getty.
726 P All major cards

LA CACHETTE
$$$
10506 SANTA MONICA BLVD.
TEL 310/470-4992
www.lacachetterestaurant.com
California-French cuisine with a hearty rustic edge is what former L'Orangerie chef Jean-François Meteigner does best. Potatoes, cassoulet, and foie gras are prominent—happily so. Casual even at night.
120 P Closed Sat. L & all Sun. All major cards

FROM BEVERLY HILLS

BEVERLY HILLS

BEVERLY HILLS HOTEL AND BUNGALOWS
$$$$$
9641 SUNSET BLVD., 90210
TEL 310/276-2251
www.thebeverlyhillshotel.com
Recently revived by the Sultan of Brunei, the hotel has never seen better days than now. The gardens are lush, the service is very good, and the rooms are elegantly appointed with just about

every amenity known to Hollywoodkind. The Polo Lounge is still a fine place to eat, particularly at the ideal hour (1–2 p.m.), when you can observe the local wildlife devouring fresh shrimp salad and cool tomato soup.
183 rooms, 21 bungalows Valet All major cards

PENINSULA BEVERLY HILLS
$$$$–$$$$$
9882 LITTLE SANTA MONICA BLVD., 90212
TEL 310/551-2888
http://beverlyhills.peninsula.com
Without a doubt, the most elegant hotel in L.A. Rooms are the height of luxe—amazingly soft linens, deep soaking tub, tasteful period furniture. Outside are I.M. Pei's famous CAA headquarters, and a whole lot of shopping. Here a splurge is a splurge—in the splurge capital of the western world. The Belvedere restaurant (see this page) is the gilding on the lily.
196 Valet All major cards

SLS LOS ANGELES
$$$$
465 S. LA CIENEGA BLVD., 90048
TEL 310/247-0400
www.slslosangeles.com
Emerging in spring 2008, the former The Meridien has been given a complete transformation by Philippe Starck. If you like avant garde, this is the place. The hotel combines Japanese practicality and coolness with western luxury and Starck's signature colorful textures. There's even a meditation garden in the lobby, and the hotel's chic bar and restaurants are considered places to see and be seen.
297 All major cards

MOSAIC HOTEL
$$$–$$$$$
125 S. SPAULDING DR., 90212
TEL 310/278-0303
FAX 310/278-1728
www.mosaichotel.com
Recently reconstituted and now boasting a sumptuous contemporary elegance, this classy boutique option is comfortable, impeccable, and service oriented, earning raves for luxe at modest prices. The poolside tapas restaurant offers tantalizing international dishes.
49 All major cards

BELVEDERE
$$$$
PENINSULA BEVERLY HILLS HOTEL, 9882 LITTLE SANTA MONICA BLVD.
TEL 310/551-2888
The Belvedere not only does fine California fusion cuisine (sesame roasted prawns, New York steak with truffled hollandaise and fries), but also an outstanding brunch. A scene, but a quiet scene.
85 Valet All major cards

MATSUHISA
$$$$
129 N. LA CIENEGA BLVD.
TEL 310/659-9639
www.nobumatsuhisa.com
The place to eat sushi in *haute* Los Angeles, Matsuhisa is not a sushi bar, it's a sushi monument. Chef Nobu specializes in the most delicate of tastes, from sea urchin and shiso leaf to truffled sea scallops with caviar.
76 Valet Closed Sat. L & Sun. L All major cards

SPAGO BEVERLY HILLS
$$$$
176 N. CANON DR.
TEL 310/385-0880
www.wolfgangpuck.com
This is still one of the top five restaurants in the city (in the country, some would argue). Wolfgang Puck is at the top of his form here, with chef Lee Hefter dishing out amazing works such as ragout of sweet shrimp with chicken oysters (the morsels close to the backbone) and black truffles; seared foie gras with pigeon in quince-cranberry chutney; osso buco and *Knödel* stuffed with pork crackling.
300 Valet Closed Sun. L DC, MC, V

CUT
$$$-$$$$$
BEVERLY WILSHIRE, 9500 WILSHIRE BLVD.
TEL 310/276-8500
www.wolfgangpuck.com
Another chicly contemporary offering from Wolfgang Puck, CUT—a contemporary twist on the classic steakhouse—has proved itself a cut above since opening in 2006, garnering awards left, right, and center and drawing Hollywood's finest. Try the lobster and crab "Louis" cocktail with spicy tomato horseradish, followed by the signature Kobe beef short ribs with Indian spices.
140 Valet Closed L All major cards

HOLLYWOOD/WEST HOLLYWOOD

MONDRIAN
$$$$$
8440 SUNSET BLVD., WEST HOLLYWOOD, 90069
TEL 323/650-8999
www.mondrianhotel.com

PRICES

HOTELS
An indication of the cost of a double room without breakfast is given by **$** signs.

$$$$$	Over $280
$$$$	$200–$280
$$$	$120–$200
$$	$80–$120
$	Under $80

RESTAURANTS
An indication of the cost of a three-course dinner without drinks is given by $ signs.

$$$$$	Over $80
$$$$	$50–$80
$$$	$35–$50
$$	$20–$35
$	Under $20

Quintessential California chic draws the glamour set and hip executives to this sexy, showy, slightly surreal Ian Schrager hotel. The stunning lobby, with its diaphonous curtains and objets d'art, sets the urbane tone, as do full entertainment centers and well-chosen literature in lieu of Bibles in suave guest rooms. The acclaimed Asia de Cuba restaurant is quite the scene.
237 P Valet All major cards

SUNSET MARQUIS
$$$$$
1200 N. ALTA LOMA RD., WEST HOLLYWOOD, 90062
TEL 310/657-1333
www.sunsetmarquishotel.com
A tried and true industry favorite with quiet, impeccable service, this is the place the big executives send their families when they're in town for a deal. The Marquis is now in California-Mediterranean style. The rooms are perfect for breakfasting, perhaps after a dip in the outdoor pool, in which many a star has swum.
102 rooms, 12 villas P All major cards

LE PARC SUITE HOTEL
$$$–$$$$$
733 W. KNOLL DR., WEST HOLLYWOOD, 90069
TEL 310/855-8888
www.leparcsuites.com
Every suite has a sunken living room and a fireplace—and that's just the beginning of the amenities at this urbane yet somehow cozy getaway. With complimentary limousine service, very good rates, and a quiet location, it is a perfect spot from which to explore Lotusland U.S.A.
154 suites P All major cards

CHATEAU MARMONT
$$$
8221 SUNSET BLVD., WEST HOLLYWOOD, 90046
TEL 323/656-1010
www.chateaumarmont.com
If you want to experience a slice of true Hollywood, you can do no better than the Chateau. Over the years this 1929 castlelike mansion-hotel, with only 63 rooms, has hosted some of the great Hollywood eccentrics, from Christopher Walken (who once lived here) to John Belushi (who died here). The place has loads of charm and elegance, and the rooms are comfortable and well appointed, if a bit old. The Bar Marmont is a stylish hangout.
63 P All major cards

HOLLYWOOD ROOSEVELT
$$–$$$
7000 HOLLYWOOD BLVD., HOLLYWOOD, 90028
TEL 323/466-7000
www.hollywoodroosevelt.com
Another one-time stronghold of the famous and rich, the Roosevelt is a more modestly priced alternative to the Chateau Marmont. It has recently been restored to its original 1920s grandeur, with painted ceilings, ornate tile work, and a balconied mezzanine. Rooms are a little on the small side, but quite comfortable. Gable and Lombard once romped here.
333 P Valet All major cards

ASIA DE CUBA
$$$$
MONDRIAN HOTEL
8440 SUNSET BLVD.
WEST HOLLYWOOD
TEL 323/848-6000
Jeffrey Chedorow's outstanding nouveau Asian-Latino cuisine is reason enough to dine here, but the Strip's hippest eatery also serves up a soupcon of catwalk divas, rock stars, and Hollywood idols. Choose roomy banquets or an exquisite terrace with an arbor framed by terracotta pots on a Brobdingnagian scale. Try the chili-dusted pork with tasty tamal, and crispy yucca-coated mahi mahi in red wine miso, then end with the Bay of Pigs banana split sundae.
425 P Valet AE, MC, V

RED/SEVEN
$$$-$$$$
700 N. San Vicente Blvd.
TEL 310/289-1587
www.wolfgangpuck.com
The Pacific Design Center seems a perfect venue for Wolfgang Puck's red-themed lunch spot, with its fittingly minimalist decor and contemporary open design. Chef Yoshinori Kojima delivers superb Asian influenced dishes combining local ingredients with the freshest seafood available.
60 P Valet Closed D and Sat. & Sun. All major cards

AGO
$$$
8478 MELROSE AVE., WEST HOLLYWOOD
TEL 323/655-6333
Backer Robert De Niro and other Hollywood names help draw the hip industry crowd here for innovative Italian fare.
170 P Valet Closed L Sat. & Sun All major cards

MAROUCH
$
4905 SANTA MONICA BLVD., WEST HOLLYWOOD
TEL 323/662-9325
www.marouchrestaurant.com
This highly popular Middle Eastern restaurant does a little bit of Armenian, a little bit of Lebanese, a little Arabic—very well. The portions are huge, the pita bread freshly baked, and the attitude totally upbeat. Enjoy—this is a part of L.A. cuisine that is not much publicized, but well worth twice the modest price, not least for the belly dancing.
70–80 P Closed Mon. All major cards

MUSSO & FRANK GRILL
See Hollywood, p. 80

MELROSE AVENUE & AROUND

CAMPANILE
$$$$
624 LA BREA AVE.
TEL 323/938-1447
A foodie's dream, Campanile combines pure bold flavor with the freshest ingredients to produce some of the most satisfying cuisine in town. This is where the food critics go to get their fix of roasted black mussels in Meyer lemon aioli. It is also where the bitter almond panna cotta comes in a giant pool of coffee gelée. On Thursdays, chef Nancy Silverton gets out the old-fashioned Italian panini press and whips out staggeringly good grilled cheese sandwiches. Heaven.
160 Valet Closed Sun. D All major cards

CHIANTI/CHIANTI CUCINA
$$$
7383 MELROSE AVE.
TEL 323/653-8333
Chianti is 60 years old and still going strong, retaining much of its Old World ease amid the hectic pace of Melrose outside. The basics of northern Italian-American food—veal scaloppini, *pappardelle* in mushroom sauce, ravioli—coexist nicely with the lighter, faster fare next door at Chianti Cucina, where the basics are augmented with seared tuna and turkey osso buco. A good deal, two wonderful rooms.
Cucina: 40/Chianti: 50 Valet Chianti: Closed L All major cards

LUCQUES
$$$
8474 MELROSE AVE.
TEL 323/655-6277
www.lucques.com
The earthy, sensual fare at this recent addition to the L.A. food scene comes straight out of the kitchen of Suzanne Goin, one-time chef at Campanile and an aficionada of ingredients from local farmers' markets. Even the *L.A. Times* has raved about her "fat asparagus topped with fried egg and parmesan," her Tuscan bean soup and greens, and her saddle of rabbit with *pappardelle* and black cabbage. The blood-orange sorbet makes a perfect ending.
110 Valet Closed L Sun. & Mon. AE, MC, V

ANGELI CAFFÉ
$$
7274 MELROSE AVE. (W OF LA BREA AVE.)
TEL 323/936-9086
The little trattoria that launched a thousand wood-burning ovens. Austere but sensual Angeli cooked up one of *the* original modern southern Italian menus in L.A. Chef Evan Kleiman, a prolific cookbook author, bakes gorgeous breads and pizzas; appetizers like the *arrancini* (risotto balls) and antipasto plates (they change daily) are a delight, and the sandwiches are perfect for lunch. People-watching is good too.
150 Closed Mon. & L Sat. & Sun. All major cards

TOMMY TANG'S
$$
7313 MELROSE AVE.
TEL 323/937-5733
www.tommytangs.com
The original trendy Thai place, Tommy's continues to do some of the best Thai-moderne in L.A. The Malaysian clams in spicy mint noodles are a signature dish. Slurp some to see why.
75 Closed D Mon. All major cards

HANCOCK PARK & KOREATOWN

HOUSE OF CHAN DARA
$$–$$$
310 N. LARCHMONT BLVD., HANCOCK PARK
TEL 323/467-1052
http://houseofchandara.com
A Thai hangout, where the wait staff are at least as nice as the food, Chan Dara nevertheless is the best place to eat in Hancock Park. The *mee krob* is an old standard—and very good. Ditto the appetizers, particularly the shrimp in lemongrass.
115 Closed L Sat. & Sun. All major cards

WOO LAE OAK
$$
623 S. WESTERN AVE. (BET. 6TH ST. & WILSHIRE BLVD.)
TEL 213/384-2244
This traditional Korean barbecue house, where you grill your own meats and vegetables at your table, is a perfect introduction to the thriving world of Seoul food (sorry) of Koreatown, L.A.'s rising ethnic star.
285 All major cards

LOS FELIZ–GRIFFITH PARK

KATSU
$$–$$$
8636 W. 3RD ST.
TEL 310/273-3605
Once *the* trend-setting nouveau sushi joint, Katsu still makes some of the best, freshest sushi in L.A. The tuna (both *toro* and *maguro*) and the sea urchin are out of this world—certainly just out of the sea.
48 Valet Closed L Sat. & all Sun. All major cards

TRATTORIA FARFALLA
$$–$$$
1978 HILLHURST AVE.
TEL 323/661-7365
Small and cozy, Farfalla cooks

up consistently good southern Italian fare. The roasted chicken, the pasta in tomato-onion sauce, and the tiramisu are all delicious. No reservations—you may have to wait for a seat.
50 Valet Closed L Sun. All major cards

CHA CHA CHA
$
656 N. VIRGIL AVE.
(NEAR MELROSE AVE.)
TEL 323/664-7723
In trendy Silver Lake-Los Feliz, a short drive from Griffith Park's elegant southern side, Cha Cha Cha has been serving outstanding Caribbean food for a decade. The jerk chicken, the St. Bart's curried shrimp, and the "rasta wrap" are favorites.
90 All major cards

FAIRFAX DISTRICT

CANTER'S DELI
$
419 N. FAIRFAX AVE.
TEL 323/651-2030
www.cantersdeli.com
The original L.A. deli, complete with wise-cracking wait staff, garish lighting, and characters out of a Bernard Malamud novel. Open 24 hours a day, the food is acceptable, predictable deli food. You won't leave any on your plate.
450 MC, V

KOKOMO CAFE
$
FARMERS' MARKET, 6333 W. 3RD ST. (AT FAIRFAX AVE.)
TEL 323/933-0773
Southern cookin' with an L.A. twist, as in turkey hash and apple-smoked bacon, a great Cobb salad (if you haven't had one in L.A. yet, this is the one), and a festive, pleasant atmosphere where you're as likely to see a celebrity as a bunch of stagehands. Perhaps the best place to eat in Farmers' Market.
120 AE, MC, V

SAN FERNANDO VALLEY

SHERATON UNIVERSAL HOTEL
$$$$
333 UNIVERSAL TERRACE PKWY., UNIVERSAL CITY, 91608
TEL 818/980-1212
www.sheraton.com
The best place to stay in the valley, the hotel is located on the Universal lot. A good business hotel, it has spacious rooms and a giant lobby in which to meet friends before setting off for sight-seeing.
436 Valet All major cards

BEVERLY GARLAND'S HOLIDAY INN
$$-$$$
4222 VINELAND ST., N. HOLLYWOOD BLVD., 91602
TEL 818/980-8000
www.beverlygarland.com
Despite its size, this Holiday Inn is considered a homey place to stay. It sits on seven landscaped acres and has the usual Holiday Inn amenities, including a tennis court. Free shuttle to Universal.
1,135 All major cards

BISTRO GARDEN AT COLDWATER
$$$
12950 VENTURA BLVD., STUDIO CITY
TEL 818/501-0202
www.bistrogarden.com
Perhaps the prettiest location in the valley, the Garden offers Italian bistro food done to near perfection. Ravioli and the osso buco are favorites.
300 Closed Sat. L & Sun. L All major cards

SUSHI NOZAWA
$$$
11288 VENTURA BLVD. (NEAR VINELAND ST.)
TEL 818/508-7017
Cool slices of flavorful seafood, from salmon to mussels or shrimp, done with a skillful hand. The chef is known for his delicate flavor combinations, such as seaweed noodle on salmon or mussels in rice vinegar broth.
30 Closed Sat.–Sun. MC, V

MISTRAL
$$-$$$
13422 VENTURA BLVD., SHERMAN OAKS
TEL 818/981-6650
Outstanding Provençal cuisine with all the standards, from grilled entrecôte to the oniony French version of pizza, *pissaladière*. A good deal; an elegant place.
55 Valet Closed Sat. L & Sun. All major cards

LE PETIT BISTRO
$$
13360 VENTURA BLVD., SHERMAN OAKS
TEL 818/501-7999
www.lepetitrestaurant.net
Simple, authentic French food with the added benefit of charming surroundings. Try the eggplant and tomato tart.
80 Valet Closed L Sat. & Sun. AE, MC, V

PINOT BISTRO
$$
12969 VENTURA BLVD., STUDIO CITY
TEL 818/990-0500
www.patinagroup.com
Even well-seasoned fans of Joachim Splichal's more famous Patina (see p. 351) come here when they want just the essential City of Light fare. All the *plats du jour* are worth contemplating, if only to get a good dose of his irresistible *brandade* potatoes. Try the monkfish wrapped in bacon.
150 Valet Closed L Sat. & Sun. All major cards

FROM DOWNTOWN

LITTLE TOKYO

KYOTO GRAND HOTEL & GARDENS
$$$-$$$$

120 S. LOS ANGELES ST., 90012
TEL 213/629-1200
www.kyotograndhotel.com
Located in the heart of historic Little Tokyo, the former New Otani Hotel exudes simple Asian elegance and features a lovely oriental garden. Stylish rooms offer a choice of Japanese-style, with futons, tatami mats, and deep bath tubs; and Western, spare, impeccable, and very comfortable.
434 All major cards

R-23
$$$
923 E. 2ND ST.
TEL 213/687-7178
www.r23.com
Call ahead for *exact* instructions (you must drive here, even if in Little Tokyo). Fine sushi in tastefully decorated surroundings. This is a scene as well, with the trendy neo-industrial setting providing an interesting backdrop. Stick with the sushi.
48 Closed Sat. L & all Sun. All major cards

SOMETHING SPECIAL

FUGETSU-DO CONFECTIONERY
Step back in time, to an era when immigrant mom-and-pop candy shops made traditional Japanese sweet *manju* in hand-carved wooden forms, then wrapped them in maple leaves and ferns. The Fugetsu-do make their pastel-colored rice goodies exactly the way they did 100 years ago. A unique souvenir, a tasty treat.
315 E. 1ST ST.
TEL 213/625-8595
www.fugetsu-do.com
Closed D No credit cards

CHINATOWN

EMPRESS PAVILION
$–$$
988 N. HILL ST., 2ND FLOOR
TEL 213/617-9898
www.empresspavilion.com
The epitome of a giant Hong Kong restaurant, Empress Pavilion does the best breakfast and lunch dim sum in Chinatown. Dim sum, in fact, is the only reason to go there, the dinners being mostly lackluster.
700 All major cards

MON KEE
$–$$
679 N. SPRING ST.
TEL 213/628-6717
An old standby, Mon Kee does seafood better than anywhere in old Chinatown. Stir-fried rock cod, crab in ginger sauce, and shrimp in rock salt are the consistently outstanding mainstays. No reservations.
140 Valet AE, MC, V

AROUND MOCA

HILTON CHECKERS HOTEL
$$$$
535 S. GRAND AVE., 90071
TEL 213/624-0000
www.hiltoncheckers.com
A small, luxurious antidote to downtown's megahotels, Checkers has panache and quietude. Guest rooms are smallish but nicely appointed, with service—something these days rare at any price—among the best in town. The Checkers Restaurant is well known for its artful and satisfying California cuisine; the crab cakes are a favorite.
188 Valet All major cards

OMNI LOS ANGELES HOTEL
$$$–$$$$
CALIFORNIA PLAZA,
251 S. OLIVE ST., 90012
TEL 213/617-3300
www.omnihotels.com
Located just next to MOCA, the Omni Los Angeles offers luxury in a jumbo hotel. Somehow it seems to succeed, with spacious guest rooms and a fine eatery, the Noe' Restaurant, which fuses progressive American cuisine with Japanese aesthetics.
453 Valet All major cards

PRICES

HOTELS
An indication of the cost of a double room without breakfast is given by $ signs.

$$$$$	Over $280
$$$$	$200–$280
$$$	$120–$200
$$	$80–$120
$	Under $80

RESTAURANTS
An indication of the cost of a three-course dinner without drinks is given by $ signs.

$$$$$	Over $80
$$$$	$50–$80
$$$	$35–$50
$$	$20–$35
$	Under $20

MILLENIUM BILTMORE HOTEL
$$$
506 S. GRAND AVE., 90071
TEL 213/624-1011
www.millenniumhotels.com
If it's history and elegance you want, this is the place in downtown. Originally built in 1923, the Biltmore was one of the grandest hotels of its day. Now completely restored, it offers fine dining at Sai Sai, a top-rated Japanese eatery, well appointed guest rooms, and a sense of luxury, from old tiled fountains to a rococo-revival exterior.
473 Valet All major cards

WESTIN BONAVENTURE
$$$
404 S. FIGUEROA ST., 90071
TEL 213/624-1000
www.starwood.com
Unsurpassed as a convention hotel, the Bonaventure is huge and predictable. Located near

many downtown cultural attractions, its recently renovated rooms are stylish Like all downtown hotels, it offers its own nightlife, because walking around outside is sometimes unsafe. Great views, a fine bar.
1,354 All major cards

KAWADA HOTEL
$$
200 S. HILL ST., 90012
TEL 213/621-4455
www.kawadahotel.com
A budget alternative for downtown, close to Chinatown, MOCA, and various cultural venues, the Kawada provides serviceable rooms with TV, VCR, and two phones. The restaurant, Epicenter, makes for a good pre-concert outing. The hotel shuttle is extremely helpful for those who don't like driving.
116 All major cards

PATINA
$$$$
WALT DISNEY CONCERT HALL, 141 SOUTH GRAND AVE.
TEL 213/972-3331
www.patinagroup.com
Many consider the creations of chef Joachim Splichal to be the best food in Los Angeles, bar none. Here contemporary California meets primal French, as in venison foie gras and marscopone-polenta and quince sauce, with the roasted rabbit and potato dishes among the critics' favorites. Try the tasting menu.
160 Closed L Sat. & Sun. All major cards

CIUDAD
$$$
445 S. FIGUEROA ST.
TEL 213/486-5171
www.ciudad-la.com
Susan Feniger and Mary Sue Milliken virtually invented L.A.'s version of contemporary Southwestern cuisine. This restaurant wins rave reviews for its invocation of Buenos Aires and Barcelona, with the Argentine rib-eye steak and plantain gnocchi in tomatillo sauce.
230 Closed Sat. L & Sun. L All major cards

WATER GRILL
$$$
544 S. GRAND AVE.
(E SIDE OF LIBRARY)
TEL 213/891-0900
www.watergrill.com
This is the place to eat fish—bluefin tuna tartare, grilled rock bass, black sea bass with eel pot stickers. The sea bass in braised fennel is popular with the bankers and attorneys who keep coming back again and again and again…
140 Closed Sat. & Sun. L All major cards

THE ORIGINAL PANTRY CAFÉ
$
877 S. FIGUEROA ST.
TEL 213/972-9279
www.pantrycafe.com
The original downtown eatery, in continuous operation since 1924, the Pantry is now owned by Richard Riordan, the former LA mayor, who often eats here with constituents and staff. The menu is pure diner fare: huge pancakes, omelettes, steaks, and a daily blue plate special. Get in line, and bring a hefty appetite.
64 Cash only

FROM THE FOOTHILLS

PASADENA

THE LANGHAM HUNTINGTON HOTEL & SPA
$$$$$
1401 S. OAK KNOLL, 91106
TEL 626/568-3900
http://pasadena.langhamhotels.com
Pasadena has a long tradition as a winter haven for East Coast millionaires, so the luxury standards of this venerable hotel (the former Ritz-Carlton) for today's Croesus are, in keeping with the tradition, quite high: The rooms are ample, with marble bathrooms and cozy robes; the services are impeccable; and the ancillaries make the stay as engaging as it is restful. After a walk in the lovely gardens and covered bridges, their walls done in classic California scenes, get a bite to eat. The brunch is the best offering.
392 Valet All major cards

WESTIN PASADENA
$$$
191 N. LOS ROBLES AVE., 91101
TEL 626/792-2727
www.westin.com/pasadena
This solid business hotel is perfectly located right in the middle of the Plaza Los Flores. Stylish rooms are airy, the food at the Oaks Restaurant is quite good, and the overall feeling is one of glowing ease.
350 All major cards

PASADENA HILTON
$$-$$$
168 S. LOS ROBLES AVE. 91101
TEL 626/577-1000
www.hilton.com
This is Rose Bowl central come New Year's Day; during the rest of the year the Hilton is the old standby, relied upon by businessfolk, visiting Caltech types, and many smaller conventions.
296 All major cards

RESTAURANT DEVON
$$$
109 E. LEMON ST., MONROVIA
TEL 626/305-0013
Suburbia meets the frontier of urban cuisine at this 1890s carriage house. Some favorites: sautéed foie gras with mango, turtle-stuffed ravioli, monkfish in tomatillo-Grand Marnier sauce. Smallish portions and a pricey wine list, but flavors you won't find anywhere else.
70 Closed Mon. & L Sat. & Sun. All major cards

SHIRO
$$$
1505 MISSION ST.
TEL 626/799-4774
www.restaurantshiro.com
Shiro pulls off a tricky blend of French-Japanese cuisine and is rated one of L.A.'s best restaurants. The sizzling catfish in *ponzu* and the shrimp-salmon mousse in smoked salmon sauce are the reason so many go here for the most special of occasions. A decent (and reasonably priced) wine list too.
75 P Closed L and Mon. & Tue. AE, MC, V

TWIN PALMS
$$–$$$
101 W. GREEN ST.
TEL 626/577-2567
www.twin-palms.com
Pitched under two big palms and a giant tent roof, Twin Palms conjures a California version of a French market. The food is solid California cuisine with some Provençal overtones, particularly in the chef's use of goat cheese and Maui onions. The salads are superb. The atmosphere is one of the best in Pasadena, enhanced by live dinner jazz.
500 P Valet All major cards

SOMETHING SPECIAL

EURO PANE BAKERY

Former Spago pastry chef Sumi Chang brings a penchant for fine ingredients, fresh fruits, and traditional baking methods to this unassuming but wildly popular bakery. Try some brioche bread or a slice of the famous pear spice cake.
$–$$$
950 E. COLORADO BLVD.
TEL 626/577-1828
20 P Closed D
No credit cards

ARIRANG
$$
114 W. UNION ST.
TEL 626/577-8885
Cool, serene, elegant. Arirang offers the purest elements of traditional Korean barbecue. The appetizers are delightful, particularly the leek and onion pancakes.
280 P Valet All major cards

SALADANG
$–$$
363 S. FAIR OAKS AVE. (BET. CALIFORNIA BLVD. & DEL MAR AVE.)
TEL 626/793-5200
Artsy and moderne, this thriving Thai eatery has taken all the basics and serves them up with style. Try the green curry, the apple and chicken salad, the salad rolls, and the sweet rice dessert.
94 P All major cards

ALL INDIA CAFÉ
$
39 S. FAIR OAKS AVE. (JUST S OF COLORADO BLVD.)
TEL 626/440-0309
Intensely flavored Indian street fare done with a light use of traditional oils. The bargains, and some of the best cooking, are found in the lunch specials. These consist of a half-dozen filling meals—curries, tandooris, *thalis*, made of smaller dishes.
45 P All major cards

MONTEREY PARK–ALHAMBRA

See also the feature on Monterey Park, pp. 122–23.

EMPRESS HARBOR
$$
111 N. ATLANTIC BLVD., MONTEREY PARK
TEL 626/300-8833
www.empressharbor.com
The dim sum, the steamed daily catch, and the *juk* (rice porridge) are so good that even Westsiders make the trip to this Hong Kong–style eatery.
336 P All major cards

OCEAN STAR SEAFOOD
$$
145 N. ATLANTIC BLVD., #201, MONTEREY PARK
TEL 626/308-2128
This always crowded place serves some of the finest seafood in town. On a weekend, go for the dim sum feast, selecting *shui mai* (shrimp dumplings) and smoky steamed veggies from steam tables that roll by your table.
800 P AE, MC, V

SOUTHERN CALIFORNIA

LONG BEACH

HOTEL *QUEEN MARY*
$$
1126 QUEEN'S HWY., 90802
TEL 562/435-3511
www.queenmary.com
In its day (launched in 1936), the *Queen* set the standard for art deco luxury; today, largely because of preservationists, the *Queen* remains much the same. Guest rooms have ship-style bathrooms, wood paneling, and period furniture. Ask for an outside room with a view—and one of those swell round porthole windows!
365 P All major cards

FRENCHY'S BISTRO
$$$
4137 E. ANAHEIM ST.
TEL 562/494-8787
www.frenchysbistro.com
A (surprise) French restaurant without (really surprise) the attitude, Frenchy's is the place many locals love, and love to keep secret from outsiders. The sweetbreads are a treat.
40 P Closed Mon. & L Sat. & Sun. All major cards

ALLEGRIA CUCINA LATINA
$$
115 PINE ST.
TEL 562/436-3388

A festive atmosphere (live flamenco music and dancing on stage) and good tapas add charm here. If you have a big appetite, choose the paella.
175 Valet All major cards

CATALINA

HOTEL & RISTORANTE VILLA PORTOFINO
$$-$$$$
111 CRESCENT AVE.
AVALON, 90704
TEL 310/510-0555 OR 888/510-0555
www.hotelvillaportofino.com
Reliable and relaxed, the Portofino offers all modern amenities in a comfortable setting. Behind its classic Mediterranean exterior, rooms boast understated European elegance. It has a fine-dining restaurant and splendid waterfront views.
34 All major cards

ANAHEIM

DISNEYLAND HOTELS
$$-$$$$
www.disneyland.com
To extend the Disney experience, try one of the Walt Disney Company hotels. Of the three options: The **Disneyland Hotel** *(1150 Magic Way, 92802, tel 714/ 778-6600)* is located just off the Monorail. Disney's **Paradise Pier** *(1717 South Disneyland Dr., 92802, tel 714/999-0990)* has a spa, shopping, and a place that serves sushi. The **Grand Californian Hotel** *(1600 S. Disneyland Dr., tel 714/635-2300)* is done in an Arts and Crafts style. The park/hotel packages offer good deals.
All major cards

NEWPORT BEACH

THE RESORT AT PELICAN HILL
$$$$$
22800 PELICAN HILL RD. S., NEWPORT COAST, 92657
TEL 949/467-6800
www.pelicanhill.com
Opened in late 2008, this deluxe resort inspired by Italian Palladian architecture boasts a spectacular and serene seaside setting. Spacious and sumptuous rooms in bungalows and villas offer ocean views and lavish amenities. Other draws? A circular "Coliseum" pool, state-of-the-art spa, and a 37-hole Tom Fazio-designed golf course.
204 All major cards

THE ISLAND HOTEL
$$$$
690 NEWPORT CENTER DR., 92660
TEL 949/759-0808
www.theislandhotel.com
Jumbo rooms with rich appointments combine with top-of-the-line service at this former Four Seasons. Pavilion Restaurant offers one of the better dining experiences on this coast; the prix fixe specials are a fine deal.
295 All major cards

PASCAL
$$$
1000 BRISTOL ST. N.
TEL 949/263-9400
www.pascalnpb.com
Considered, at least by regulars, perhaps the best French cooking in Orange County. Sea bass is done with a deft hand; foie gras, ditto, comes with a rich duck confit.
100 Closed L Sat. & Sun. All major cards

COSTA MESA

LEATHERBY'S CAFÉ ROUGE
$$$$$
SEGERSTROM CONCERT HALL, 615 TOWN CENTER DR.
TEL 714/429-7640
www.patinagroup.com/caferouge
Sophisticates with deep pockets and an eye for aesthetics appreciate the sexy contemporary surrounds, including curvaceous glass wall and orange mohair booths. This stylish restaurant also delivers in the culinary arena, with an Asian-inspired fusion menu that offers such unusually innovative items as sea urchin brule over tile fish. The limited wine list is pricey.
120 Valet All major cards

LAGUNA BEACH

INN AT LAGUNA BEACH
$$$-$$$$$
211 N. COAST HWY., 92651
TEL 949/497-9722
www.innatlagunabeach.com
The true beach romantic's favorite, the inn, low slung and unassuming, offers some of the best views in southern California. From a roomy guest suite, one can watch morning sea mists, blue afternoon skies, and spectacular boiling sunsets.
70 All major cards

DIZZ'S AS IS
$$
2794 S. COAST HWY. (AT NYES PLACE)
TEL 949/494-5250
Just the best little restaurant in Laguna, the aptly named Diz serves up solid, honest fare. A great atmosphere in which to eat perfectly grilled fish, pink lamb chops, and steak au poivre. No reservations.
50 Closed Mon. All major cards

DANA POINT

RITZ CARLTON LAGUNA NIGUEL
$$$$$
1 RITZ CARLTON DR., 92629
TEL 949/240-2000
www.ritzcarlton.com
Watch the wealthy old-timers take on body-crunching waves below, then retire to the wood-paneled

elegance of the Ritz, where tea awaits. The Ritz's French restaurant, the Dining Room, has a knockout lobster soufflé.
393 Valet
All major cards

SAN DIEGO–LA JOLLA

W HOTEL
$$$$$
421 WEST B ST.
SAN DIEGO, 92101
TEL 619/398-3100
www.starwood.com
A suave downtown option, this newcomer brings a hip urban sophistication to San Diego. An unbeatable location, tasteful contemporary furnishings, and high-tech amenities combine with exceptional service. Its stylish Rice restaurant serves Asian-Latin fusion cuisine.
293
All major cards

SOMETHING SPECIAL

LA VALENCIA

Perched above the waters of La Jolla Cove, the historic Spanish-style La Valencia, onetime summer home to Charlie Chaplin and others, is still a great place to stay. Rooms and villas are old fashioned but comfortable, the lounge and bar have loads of hidalgo charm, and the views are unsurpassed.
$$$$–$$$$$
1132 PROSPECT ST.,
LA JOLLA, 92037
TEL 858/454-0771
www.lavalencia.com
117 rooms, 15 villas
All major cards

HILTON LA JOLLA TORREY PINES
$$$$
10950 N. TORREY PINES RD.,
LA JOLLA, 92037
TEL 858/558-1500
www.hilton.com
Close to the Torrey Pines Golf Course and to the Torrey Pines State Reserve, this is a top choice for comfort, service, and location. Guest rooms come with Egyptian cotton linens, down comforters, and butler service. The downstairs café is perfect for lunch, with flavorful salads and burgers galore.
394
All major cards

LOEWS CORONADO BAY RESORT
$$$$
4000 CORONADO BAY RD.,
CORONADO, 92118
TEL 619/424-4000
www.loews.com
Blessed with a spectacular location on the southern end of San Diego Bay, Loews, unlike the brassier Hotel Del across the way, specializes in elegant informality. Its in-house restaurant, Azurra Point, ranks among the city's finest dining spots. Try the lobster and goat cheese *chile relleno.*
440
All major cards

L'AUBERGE DEL MAR RESORT & SPA
$$$–$$$$
1540 CAMINO DEL MAR,
DEL MAR, 92014
TEL 858/259-1515 OR
800/245-9757
www.laubergedelmar.com
The place to stay if you can't get enough of either Torrey Pines State Reserve or the race track. Be pampered at this cozy inn where the atmosphere is quiet and the staff is helpful.
120 Valet
All major cards

MILLE FLEURS
$$$$
6009 PASEO DELICIAS
RANCHO SANTA FE
TEL 858/756-3085
www.millefleurs.com
Mille Fleurs is a delight for those who appreciate a chef's dedication to fresh ingredients and impeccable preparation. Fish—grilled, poached, and baked—is outstanding; so are game meats and (seasonal) suckling pig. The wine list just goes on and on and on…
120 Closed L Sat. & Sun. All major cards

PRICES

HOTELS
An indication of the cost of a double room without breakfast is given by $ signs.

$$$$$	Over $280
$$$$	$200–$280
$$$	$120–$200
$$	$80–$120
$	Under $80

RESTAURANTS
An indication of the cost of a three-course dinner without drinks is given by $ signs.

$$$$$	Over $80
$$$$	$50–$80
$$$	$35–$50
$$	$20–$35
$	Under $20

LAUREL
$$$
505 LAUREL AVE., SAN DIEGO
TEL 619/239-2222
http://sdurbankitchen.com
The cuisine of southern France is the star here, with peppery seafood dishes and cool poached fish entrées the pleasers. A great wine list; simple but decadent desserts.
130 Valet Closed L
All major cards

BERTA'S LATIN AMERICAN RESTAURANT
$
3928 TWIGGS ST., OLD TOWN
SAN DIEGO
TEL 619/295-2343
http://bertasinoldtown.com
It wouldn't be San Diego without *la cucina latina*, and if you're not heading south of the border, Berta's is the place. Big portions, ridiculously low prices, and remarkable breadth of menu are Berta's mainstays. Get the lamb—any lamb.
45 Closed Mon.
AE, MC, V

SANTA BARBARA & AROUND

FOUR SEASONS BILTMORE
$$$$$
1260 CHANNEL DR., MONTECITO, 93108
TEL 805/969-2261
www.fourseasons.com

Spanish-Mediterranean elegance, California amiability, and historic grandeur make this 21-acre resort a prime destination for Angelenos seeking respite from the city. The gardens, the mariachis in the sunset lounge, and the ever-pounding Pacific will lure you out of your impeccably appointed room. If you can't stay here, at least have lunch on the patio of the restaurant, La Marina.

207 rooms, 12 cottages P All major cards

TEMECULA CREEK INN
$$$$$
44501 RAINBOW CANYON RD., TEMECULA, 92592
TEL 909/694-1000
www.temeculacreekinn.com

Enjoying a lush golf-course setting in the heart of Southern California's wine country, this lodge offers spacious guestrooms with rich Southwestern decor combining cozy comforts and modern amenities.

130 P AE, MC, V

SAN YSIDRO RANCH
$$$$-$$$$$
900 SAN YSIDRO LN., MONTECITO, 93018
TEL 805/565-1700
www.sanysidroranch.com

Nestled among the foothills of Montecito, the ranch is a perfect place for living out the fantasy of the good Santa Barbara life. The cottages are beautifully appointed, with soft gauzy linens, fireplaces, and little gardens outside. Call for an in-room massage, then eat at the Stonehouse Restaurant, where lobster and a saffron-potato soufflé await your discerning tastebuds.

38 P All major cards

EL ENCANTO HOTEL
$$$-$$$$
1900 LASUEN RD. SANTA BARBARA, 93103
TEL 805/568-1357
www.elencantohotel.com

Overlooking the city from verdant hills, El Encanto is all charm, from its nine Craftsmen and 11 Spanish-Revival cottages to its breezy, sun-filled dining room, where you can sample classic California cuisine. The salads and soups in summer are simple, zesty, and beautifully presented. This exquisite hotel and restaurant are *slated to reopen in 2009 after being closed for a lengthy restoration.*

83 P All major cards

SANTA BARBARA INN
$$-$$$
901 E. CABRILLO BLVD., SANTA BARBARA, 93103
TEL 805/966-2285
www.santabarbarainn.com

Solid value, consistently good service, big rooms—and just across the street from the beach! The hotel's Fresco at the Beach restaurant (see below) is upstairs.

71 P Valet All major cards

FRESCO AT THE BEACH
$$$$
SANTA BARBARA INN, 901 E. CABRILLO BLVD., SANTA BARBARA
TEL 805/963-0111

Upstairs at the Santa Barbara Inn, Fresco at the Beach serves European comfort food and Chef du Cusine Jason Banks' Mediterranean inspired menu includes tapas. Live jazz adds to the hip ambience imbued with vibrant colors.

P Closed L Mon.–Sat. All major cards

HITCHING POST
$$$
406 E. CALIF. 246 (OFF US 101), BUELLTON
TEL 805/688-0676
www.hitchingpost2.com

Eat here when visiting the Santa Ynez backcountry, where wineries spring from land that once belonged to old California dons. Think cowboy steak house, then add a moderne penchant for fresh ingredients, spicy *chuilkes*, and simple desserts (almond pound cake with fresh blackberry sauce). The steaks are huge, the french fries award winning.

125 P Closed L AE, MC, V

ARIGATO SUSHI
$$-$$$
1225 STATE ST., SANTA BARBARA
TEL 805/965-6074

A small and unpretentious eatery, Arigato has the feel of a sushi bar in the older sections of the Ginza in Tokyo. The fish, particularly the various sushi rolls, keep the locals and out-of-town weekenders coming back again and again.

40 P Closed L AE, MC, V

DOWNEY'S
$$–$$$
1305 STATE ST., SANTA BARBARA
TEL 805/966-5006
www.downeyssb.com

Elegant Downey's serves up a changing mix of outstanding California cuisine with a touch of traditional French cooking. Look for cassoulets, entrecôtes, and a number of local fish offerings.

48 P Closed Mon. AE, MC, V

OJAI

OJAI VALLEY INN
$$$$
905 COUNTRY CLUB RD., 93023
TEL 805/646-5511 OR 888/697-8780

www.ojairesort.com
This 1930s establishment in mission revival architecture was restored in the 1980s and considerably expanded in 2003. Guest rooms are cozy and well appointed, many with antiques. The rolling grounds, spa, and fine dining at Maravilla enhance the charm.
308 P All major cards

THE RANCH HOUSE
$$$
S. LOMITA AVE.
TEL 805/646-2360
www.theranchhouse.com
Many credit the founders of this rustic eatery with the creation of modern California cuisine. The influence persists, with brasserie staples like lamb chops and artichoke salad. Stunning gardens.
140 P Closed L except Sun. & all Mon. All major cards

CENTRAL COAST

SOUTH

MORRO BAY

INN AT MORRO BAY
$$-$$$
60 STATE PARK RD., MORRO BAY, 93442
TEL 805/772-5651 OR 800/321-9566
www.innatmorrobay.com
Simple and quiet, the inn sits above Morro Bay's rocky shore, where the famous Morro Rock juts from the ocean floor. Guest rooms are equipped with state-of-the-art amenities, and the restaurant, the Paradise, offers fine fish and seafoods at decent prices.
108 P All major cards

PASO ROBLES

BISTRO LAURENT
$$
1202 PINE ST.
TEL 805/226-8191
www.bistrolaurent.com
If you're deep into cowboy wine country, you can't do better than this purveyor of rustic French cuisine, made with the freshest of local ingredients. The roasted squab is great, as is the roast chicken with garlic and rosemary.
50 P Closed L & all Sun. MC, V

SAN LUIS OBISPO

APPLE FARM
$$-$$$
2015 MONTEREY ST., 93401
TEL 805/544-2040
www.applefarm.com
Down-home coziness, in the form of fireplaces, canopy beds, and flowers, greets visitors to this happy abode. Located along sycamore- and live oak-dotted San Luis Obispo Creek, this Victorian also offers affordable, satisfying dining at its Apple Farm Restaurant. Don't miss the homemade ice cream.
103 P AE, MC, V

SYCAMORE MINERAL SPRINGS RESORT
$$-$$$
1215 AVILA BEACH DR., 93405
TEL 805/595-7302 OR 800/234-5831
www.sycamoresprings.com
A classic inland spa, complete with Mediterranean architecture, outdoor mineral spas (for soaking under the crystal-clear summer skies), and luxury suites with fireplaces. The Gardens of Avila Restaurant is cozy and romantic.
55 P AE, MC, V

SHELL BEACH

THE CLIFFS RESORT
$$$
2757 SHELL BEACH RD., 93449
TEL 805/773-5000 OR 800/826-7827
www.cliffsresort.com
Pacific elegance in a tranquil clifftop setting characterizes this favorite weekend haunt. Many rooms come with wonderful ocean views.
165 P All major cards

TEMPLETON

IAN MCPHEE'S GRILL
$$
416 MAIN ST.
TEL 805/434-3204
www.mcphees.com
If all the walking at Mr. Hearst's little getaway has left you hankering for a bit of pampering, try Ian's, a modernish grill room with absolutely inspired renderings of contemporary California cuisine. Locally raised meats make the steak offerings a good bet.
100 P MC, V

CENTRAL

BIG SUR

POST RANCH INN
$$$$$
CALIF 1, ACROSS FROM VENTANA, P.O. BOX 219, 93920
TEL 831/667-2200
www.postranchinn.com
The inn is the exact opposite of Deetjen's (see below, this page), from its Zen-ranch architecture to the spare California cuisine in the acclaimed Sierra Mar restaurant. Every known comfort is here: deep soaking tubs, thick terry robes, bedside massages, Indian slate bathrooms, stunning views of the ocean.
30 P AE, MC, V

VENTANA INN & SPA
$$$$-$$$$$
VENTANA, 93920
TEL 831/667-2331
www.ventanainn.com
Until the Post Ranch moved in across the way, the Ventana was considered the ultimate in Big Sur luxury; many people still consider it so. Giant guest suites, fully equipped kitchens, wonderful open-air decks and hot tubs, and a decent

restaurant. Don't count on much in the way of room service, but do make your way to the breakfast and the afternoon wine and cheese spread.
60 All major cards

BIG SUR LODGE
$$–$$$
CALIF. 1 (N SIDE), P.O. BOX 190, 93920
TEL 831/667-3100
www.bigsurlodge.com
Old-fashioned, basic family accommodations set in a scenic meadow surrounded by redwoods and pines make this an affordable and joyful destination. No TVs!
61 AE, MC, V

SOMETHING SPECIAL

DEETJEN'S BIG SUR INN
The ultimate in coastal rusticity, Deetjen's is a collection of wood-stove-heated cabins planted deep in the redwoods. For romantics, old Deetjen's is a must, if only for a night of listening to the wind rustle the trees and reading old books left for nature lovers. Breakfasts are particularly good.
$$–$$$
CALIF. 1, S OF BIG SUR, 93920
TEL 831/667-2377
www.deetjens.com
20 All major cards

CARMEL

PARK HYATT CARMEL HIGHLANDS INN
$$$$–$$$$$
CALIF. 1 (4 MILES S OF CARMEL), 93921
TEL 831/620-1234
www.highlandsinn.hyatt.com
More coastal luxury, this time perched above the rocks of Point Lobos, where seals frolic on jagged rock islands and mists float to and fro. Big guest room suites all have great views; in-room jacuzzis are perfect for after-hiking aches. Room service could be better, but the restaurant, Pacific's Edge, seems to have few coastal peers. Steer for the caramelized sea scallops and potato and basil salad.
142 All major cards

LA PLAYA HOTEL
$$$$
8TH AVE. & CAMINO REAL
P.O. BOX 900, 93921
TEL 831/624-6476
www.laplayahotel.com
Cool and serene, with beautifully tended central gardens and views of the Carmel coastline, this 60-year-old favorite has plenty of charm. It was originally built by Christopher Jorgensen for his new bride, who was one of the famed Ghirardelli chocolate clan. A sweet retreat still.
75 rooms, 5 cottages All major cards

QUAIL LODGE RESORT & GOLF CLUB
$$$$
8205 VALLEY GREENS DR., CARMEL VALLEY, 93923
TEL 831/624-2888
www.quaillodge.com
A luxury deal on the coast, the Quail has great service, outstanding dining at its Covey Restaurant, and everything the golf fanatic could ever want. Set in a serene and dreamy spot with rugged peaks and green valleys.
100 All major cards

ANTON & MICHEL
$$$
MISSION & 7TH STS.
TEL 831/624-2406
www.carmelsbest.com
Classic, elegant Continental cuisine with an emphasis on fresh ingredients makes Anton & Michel's one of the first dining stops for many coastal regulars. The wine list, featuring several area vineyards, has grown substantially in recent years.
90 All major cards

FRENCH POODLE
$$$
5TH ST. AT JUNIPERO ST.
TEL 831/624-8643
For more than 20 years now, some of the best French cuisine in town (try the duck and any of the sauced fish dishes) along with a quiet, restful interior. The chilled desserts are also a must.
36 Closed Sun. AE

TUTTO MONDO'S TRATTORIA
$
DOLORES ST. (BETWEEN 7TH & OCEAN AVES.)
TEL 831/624-8977
www.mondos.com
After a brisk walk on the beach, have lunch at this informal, cozy, and very skilled trattoria in old Carmel. The fish soups and traditional pasta are well worth the price; the hearty, welcoming service makes you want to come back for dinner.
70 All major cards

MONTEREY

CASA PALERMO
$$$$$
1518 CYPRESS DR.
TEL 831/647-7500 OR 800/654-9300
www.pebblebeach.com
Evocative of a lush Mediterranean village, this elegant enclave features sun drenched patios and lush landscaped grounds overlooking the Pebble Beach Golf Links. Lavish guest rooms feature wood burning fireplaces, oversize soaking tubs, and plush robes. Tennis and billiards are among the refined activities to enjoy.
24 All major cards

LODGE AT PEBBLE BEACH
$$$$–$$$$$
17 MILE DR., 92953
TEL 831/647-7500
www.pebblebeach.com
The luxurious lodge has been setting the standard for the haute golf world since 1919. The rooms are impeccably appointed with crisp linens and richly burnished decor. The Club XIX Restaurant, launched by Hubert Keller, is the place for French cuisine at its contemporary pinnacle. The Stillwater Bar & Grill is stuffier (jacket required) but legendary for seafood.
161 P
All major cards

SEVEN GABLES INN
$$$–$$$$
555 OCEAN VIEW BLVD., 93950
TEL 831/372-4341
www.pginns.com
The ocean view, the European antiques, the gilded age decor combine to make this clutch of yellow-gabled wood buildings a fine period hideaway.
14 P MC, V

PÈPPOLI
$$$$
THE INN AT SPANISH BAY, 2700 17 MILE DR.
TEL 831/647-7433
www.pebblebeach.com
Exuding cozy Tuscan ambience, Pèppoli also offers flavorful, rustic Italian dishes paired to classic Italian wines. Consider these favorites: mussels and clams steamed in a spicy shallot saffron broth, and slow braised veal shank with Pèppoli wine and gremolata. The sweeping views over The Links at Spanish Bay and the Pacific Ocean are dessert enough.
120 P Closed L
All major cards

MONTRIO
$$–$$$
414 CALLE PRINCIPAL
TEL 831/648-8880
www.montrio.com
For anyone who has grown impatient with the New American fad of recent years, this is where the form finds redemption in tasty, ingredient-savvy cooking by chef Tony Baker. Try the crab cakes or the rotisserie-cooked rib-eye steak.
200 P Closed L Sun.
All major cards

TARPY'S ROADHOUSE
$
2999 MONTEREY-SALINAS HWY.
TEL 831/647-1444
More American fare, but that would be to sell Tarpy's short. Inside the lovely ivy-shrouded stone house is some fine cooking, with the "American" menu including roast rabbit and a pecan barbecued duck that will drive you quackers for more.
300 P All major cards

PACIFIC GROVE

GREEN GABLES INN
$$$–$$$$
301 OCEAN VIEWS BLVD., 93950
TEL 800/722-1774
www.foursisters.com
A cross between an inn and a bed-and-breakfast, the Gables offers spacious rooms in its carriage house out back and more intimate, historic *chambres* in the main house, which was built, legend holds, by an enterprising sea captain for his mistress.
11 P AE, MC, V

FANDANGO
$$–$$$
223 17TH ST.
TEL 831/372-3456
www.fandangorestaurant.com
A fine mid-range alternative to the French fever that possesses the peninsula these days, Fandango's zesty Mediterranean fare (from Spanish paellas to Moroccan couscous) has locals lining up. The osso buco is heady with wine and veal stock, simmered just right.
140 P All major cards

PRICES

HOTELS
An indication of the cost of a double room without breakfast is given by **$** signs.

$$$$$	Over $280
$$$$	$200–$280
$$$	$120–$200
$$	$80–$120
$	Under $80

RESTAURANTS
An indication of the cost of a three-course dinner without drinks is given by $ signs.

$$$$$	Over $80
$$$$	$50–$80
$$$	$35–$50
$$	$20–$35
$	Under $20

NORTH

APTOS

APPLE LANE INN
$$–$$$
6265 SOQUEL DR., 95003
TEL 831/475-6868
www.applelaneinn.com
This 1870s farmhouse sits on two acres of lush rural back-country, where breezes whisper through giant pines and oaks. The breakfast is hearty enough to keep you going through a hike.
5 P Closed L
MC, V

BITTERSWEET BISTRO
$$$
787 RIO DEL MAR
TEL 831/662-9799
www.bittersweetbistro.com
Coastal bistro meets Mediterranean ristorante in a relaxed atmosphere. The rack of lamb is a feast for all senses.
100 P AE, MC, V

MA MAISON
$$$
9051 SOQUEL DR.
TEL 831/688-5566
One of the best eateries in the Santa Cruz area. Chef Lionel Le Morvan does outstanding

California-French cuisine at a reasonable price, served in an intimate atmosphere.
90 P Closed all Mon. & L Sat. & Sun. MC, V

CAPITOLA

INN AT DEPOT HILL
$$$–$$$$
250 MONTEREY AVE.
TEL 831/462-3376 OR 800/572-2632
www.innatdepothill.com
Depot Hill has 12 tastefully decorated rooms, each inspired by a different region, from the Mediterranean to jolly old England.
12 P All major cards

SANTA CRUZ

INN AT PASATIEMPO
$$–$$$
555 CALIF. 17, 95060
TEL 800/230-2892
www.innatpasatiempo.com
Set alongside Pasatiempo Golf Course, this fine country inn offers serene gardens, solid service, and rooms with fireplaces and jacuzzis. **Hollins House Restaurant** (at the golf course), with panoramic views of Monterey Bay, features no-nonsense (and very tasty) regional American cuisine.
54 P All major cards

SAN FRANCISCO

San Francisco is a grand city—and hard to beat for its wide range of hotels, inns, bed-and-breakfasts, and, of course, restaurants. Travelers also can consult the San Francisco Convention & Visitors Bureau *(tel 415/391-2000, www.onlyinsanfrancisco.com)*. One of the best-run such organizations in the country, it offers a variety of free lodging and food guides that are constantly updated by an ambitious, discerning staff.

GOLDEN GATE & AROUND

HAMA-KO
$$$$
108B CARL ST.
TEL 415/753-6808
This impeccable restaurant turns out some of the freshest sushi (especially the yellowtail and giant clam) in town. Traditional Japanese meals, too.
22 P Closed L & all Mon. MC, V

RESTAURANT CLEMENTINE
$$$–$$$$
126 CLEMENT ST.
TEL 415/387-0408
www.clementinesf.com
Culinary experiences here range from the leisurely (but well-attended) evening dinners to the luxury-ingredient tasting menus with California-French delicacies such as mussel and orange soup with saffron and fennel, lamb pot au feu, and monkfish in caraway and honey. A place for ingredient freaks and flavor hunters. Make reservations two to three weeks in advance.
49 P Valet Closed L AE, MC, V

KABUTO SUSHI
$$$
5121 GEARY BLVD.
TEL 415/752-5652
www.kabutosushi.com
Though his restaurant is plain plain plain, Kabuto's chef is considered one of the city's best sushi masters, carving up some of the finest fatty *toro* and briny *uni* found anywhere.
31 Closed L & all Mon. AE, MC, V

TON KIANG
$$$
5821 GEARY ST.
TEL 415/387-8273
www.tonkiang.net
One of the best Chinese restaurants in town. Ton Kiang is best known for its flavorful dim sum: veggie pot stickers with chili sauce, steam pork dumplings with lemongrass broth, *bun*—all steamy white and pure—touched with sweet pork on the inside and gingery glaze outside.
90 All major cards

MISSION DISTRICT

LA TRAVIATA
$$
2854 MISSION ST. (BETWEEN 24TH & 25TH STS.)
TEL 415/282-0500
A closely held secret of the younger, groovier folk now gentrifying the district, La Traviata offers affordable, classic Italian cuisine (tortellini, prosciutto, *zuppa di pesce*...) in a delightful atmosphere.
60 P Closed L & all Mon. AE, DC

LA TAQUERIA
$
2889 MISSION ST. (AT 25TH ST.)
TEL 415/285-7117
Truly an amazing deal: downright seductive Mexican food with zesty fresh salsas, tacos so yummy you'll want to take some back to your hotel room, and fast service. Stop here after touring the Mission.
70 No credit cards

PANCHO VILLA TAQUERIA
$
3071 16TH ST. (BETWEEN VALENCIA & MISSION STS.)
TEL 415/864-8840
http://panchovillasf.com
A friendly purveyor of such specialties as barbecued pork burritos, wonderful prawn tacos, and an array of Tex-Mex as well.
90 AE, MC, V

RUSSIAN HILL

LA FOLIE
$$$$$
2316 POLK ST.
TEL 415/776-5577
www.lafolie.com
Another top choice, La Folie

has garnered acclaim in several surveys as the city's preferred purveyor of New French cuisine; that the room is simply breathtaking and the service perfect makes it a "can't miss" for a night out. Chef Roland Passot never misses with such dishes as roasted Scottish salmon with braised escarole, gnocchi, smoked ham hock, and sweet onion sauce.
62 Valet Closed L & all Sun. All major cards

CIVIC CENTER

SOMETHING SPECIAL

JARDINIÈRE

A lively, elegant place presided over by the young Tracy des Jardins. Every detail of the cuisine is perfect, from the pan-roasted chicken with chanterelles (which will change your mind about chicken altogether) to the essence of verdure that permeates her pastas, and the amazingly refreshing sorbets and tortes.

$$$$
300 GROVE ST.
TEL 415/861-5555
www.jardiniere.com
200 Valet Closed L All major cards

FINANCIAL DISTRICT

JW MARRIOTT HOTEL

$$$$$
500 POST ST., 94102
TEL 415/771-8600
FAX 415/398-0267
www.panpacific.com
A wonderful place to stay in the city's theater district, the JW Marriott fuses the comfort and amenities demanded by today's luxe travelers with the services required by the business traveler (complimentary limousines, etc.). The rooms are soothing (pastels dominate), and the lunch menu at the Pacific Restaurant is tasty and diverse. Check for weekday deals.
329 All major cards

PALACE HOTEL

$$$$$
2 NEW MONTGOMERY ST., 94105
TEL 415/512-1111
FAX 415/543-0671
www.sfpalace.com
Another classic San Francisco hotel, with grand mahogany furniture, old-style ambience, and large, well-lit rooms, combined with many modern comforts. The Palace even has an indoor lap pool for chilly summer days. Diners in the Garden Court restaurant eat under a high domed glass roof hung with chandeliers.
552 All major cards

CLIFT HOTEL

$$$$
495 GEARY ST., 94102
TEL 415/775-4700
FAX 415/441-4621
www.clifthotel.com
Longtime tradition meets trendy style in this classic hotel given a makeover by Ian Schrager and his designer, Philippe Starck. Enjoy a cocktail in the Redwood Room (made from a single redwood tree, before such acts were considered abominations).
363 Valet All major cards

HOTEL NIKKO

$$$$
222 MASON ST., 94102
TEL 415/394-1106
FAX 415/394-1106
www.hotelnikkosf.com
Solid, upscale service, roomy guest suites, a great location, and the award-winning Anzu restaurant makes this a favorite. The spa services are worth checking out, particularly after a long plane flight.
533 All major cards

PRESCOTT HOTEL

$$$$
545 POST ST., 94102
TEL 415/563-0303
FAX 415/563-6831
www.prescotthotel.com
Plush (if smallish) rooms, a strong concierge desk, a great central location, and, best of all, room service from the downstairs restaurant Postrio (see this page) make this hotel popular with business travelers. The clublike atmosphere is enhanced by the lobby fireplace and plenty of dark wood.
164 Valet All major cards

WESTIN ST. FRANCIS

$$$$ (TOWER $$$$$)
335 POWELL ST., 94102
TEL 866/497-2788
FAX 415/774-0124
www.westinstfrancis.com
A fine old downtown standby, the St. Francis is a hotel for people who love to stroll the city, like the grand boulevardiers of old. Its lobby is sumptuous, its rooms warm and charming (some with original Victorian details), and its restaurant-bar, the Compass Rose, with skylights, marble columns, and exquisite wood-work, is downright delightful.
1219 All major cards

HOTEL TRITON

$$$
342 GRANT AVE., 94108
TEL 415/394-0500
FAX 415/394-0555
www.hoteltriton.com
Another boutique hotel, one with outstanding decor (a kind of neo-art deco), impeccable (but smallish) rooms, good service, and a great location: just steps from the old Chinatown Gate.
140 Valet All major cards

HOTEL VINTAGE COURT

$$$

650 BUSH ST., UNION SQ., 94108
TEL 415/392-4666
FAX 415/433-4065
www.vintagecourt.com
A cozy, jolly boutique hotel with a feeling of being in wine country, especially in the late afternoon, when the proprietors break out some of their most recent stash from Napa. Fireplaces, cozy quarters, and access to a health club come with the reasonable price—use the saving to eat at Masa's (see this page) in the hotel.
106 Valet All major cards

PETITE AUBERGE
$$–$$$
863 BUSH ST., 94108
TEL 415/928-6000, 800/365-3004
FAX 415/673-7214
www.jdvhospitality.com
Another "personal suite" set-up, this one with a tasteful French accent. Although the rooms are small, they are very comfortable. No con-cierge service to speak of, but the breakfast (included) and afternoon wine and cheese (free) are outstanding.
26 Valet All major cards

POSTRIO
$$$$$
PRESCOTT HOTEL,
545 POST ST.
TEL 415/776-7825
www.postrio.com
Wolfgang Puck's stylish San Francisco restaurant is just as exciting as his Los Angeles ones. In the impressive downstairs room feast on dishes such as stir-fried garlic lamb with chili and mint, Chinese-style duck with spicy mango sauce, and, of course, pasta.
180 Valet All major cards

MASA'S
$$$$–$$$$$
HOTEL VINTAGE COURT,
648 BUSH ST., UNION SQ.
TEL 415/989-7154
www.masasrestaurant.com
It is a rarity for a leading-edge restaurant to be this good for this long. At Masa's, California-French cuisine reaches its apex. The primacy of ingredients shows in such items as venison in caramelized apples and zinfandel sauce or spot prawns with fresh cranberry peas. Wines, cheeses, and desserts are equally good.
120 Valet Closed L, all Sun.–Mon., 1st 2 wks. Jan., & July 1–7 All major cards

AQUA
$$$$
252 CALIFORNIA ST.
TEL 415/956-9662
www.aqua-sf.com
As the name implies, this is *the* place in dressed-down San Francisco to get fish—glorious, fresh, briny, and tender. The prix fixe or the tasting menus are good investments (after all, you are in the Financial District), and if you're lucky you'll get the garlic black mussel soufflé or the potato crusted Idaho trout. But save room for dessert!
180 Valet Closed Sat.–Sun. L All major cards

CAMPTON PLACE
$$$$
340 STOCKTON ST.,
UNION SQ.
TEL 415/978-5555
www.camptonplace.com
Brilliant renderings of New American cuisine are the specialty of this seductive, restful, and yet somehow also stimulating restaurant. The Campton turns out stunning dishes like ribs with truffled potatoes or roasted fish in ginger port sauce. Star turns at breakfast and brunch, too.
75 Valet Closed Sun. L All major cards

FARALLON
$$$$
450 POST ST.
TEL 415/956-6969
www.farallonrestaurant.com
Designer Pat Kuleto pulled out all the stops with Farallon, a marine-themed restaurant with so many oceanic references that you have to go—if only for a drink at the jellyfish bar. Somewhat noisy, but the food is first-rate, particularly the oyster dishes. The pastry chefs have been voted best dessertmakers in the city.
225 Valet Closed L All major cards

FLEUR DE LYS
$$$$
777 SUTTER ST.,
UNION SQ.
TEL 415/673-7779
www.fleurdelyssf.com
This is the place to get a sure-fire, and very memorable, dose of *la grande cuisine*. The room is stunning, royal in its use of fleur-de-lys fabrics and elegant mirrors. The food rivals the best of Paris, ranging from delicate fishes to hearty Alsatian versions of quail, venison, and foie gras. An unforgettable experience.
80 Valet Closed L & all Sun. All major cards

MILLENNIUM
$$$$
580 GEARY ST.
TEL 415/345-3900
www.millenniumrestaurant.com
Healthy food for the gourmet—organic, vegan dishes such as Moroccan spice-roasted portobello mushroom, and almond-baked tofu with corn-garlic pudding.
150 Valet Closed L All major cards

GRAND CAFÉ
$$$
HOTEL MONACO,
501 GEARY ST.
TEL 415/292-0101
Even if the food were only so-so, the decor would warrant the name; very theatrical, it manages to take beaux arts style to new and elegant heights. Fortunately, the food

is outstanding. Try the sweetbreads if they are on the menu, and don't skip dessert.
244 Valet All major cards

LE COLONIAL
$$$
20 COSMO PL.
TEL 415/931-3600
www.lecolonialsf.com
With an atmosphere out of 1920s Vietnam, this stylish spot serves French-Vietnamese cuisine that might include scallop-ginger potstickers or pomegranate-glazed Peking duck. For a lively scene and good appetizers, head for the upstairs cocktail lounge.
320 Valet Closed L All major cards

ANJOU
$$–$$$
44 CAMPTON PL..
TEL 415/392-5373
www.anjou-sf.com
Authenic bistro cuisine in a quiet alley off Union Square. Lovely decor and first-rate daily specials keep the tables full.
42 Closed Sun.–Mon. DC, MC, V

CHINATOWN & TELEGRAPH HILL

HOUSE OF NANKING
$$
919 KEARNY ST.
TEL 415/421-1429
Not much to look at, and the service can be surly and abrupt, but aficionados of true Szechuan cuisine—fiery soups, even hotter sizzled eggplant—still come. Locals often bring their out-of-town friends here to show them that San Francisco Chinatown still has a few great eateries.
45 MC, V

HENRY'S HUNAN
$
924 SANSOME ST. (AT BROADWAY)
TEL 415/956-7727
www.henryshunanrestaurant.com
Hot and smoky—that's what great Hunanese food is all about, and that's what you get at this very popular eatery, where connoisseurs go when they just must have that steamed chili-tofu platter with deboned braised tilapia fish.
350 AE, MC, V

LUCKY CREATION
$
854 WASHINGTON ST.
TEL 415/989-0818
Lucky is the vegetarian who dines at Chef Kwok Lom's eatery. Try the various meatless meats—goose, pork, chicken—they're all good. Purists might stick with the mushroom-and-greens-stuffed dumplings or smoky oyster sauce broccoli.
40 Closed Wed. MC, V

PEARL CITY
$
641 JACKSON ST.
TEL 415/398-8383
When you're finished antiquing in Jackson Square, check out one of the city's better dim sum hangouts and consequently one that is always crowded. Try the shrimp-stuffed pot stickers and the crabmeat dumplings.
200 MC, V

NOB HILL

SOMETHING SPECIAL

THE HUNTINGTON

For the money, the best San Francisco experience around. The staff is excellent, rooms large, opulent, and quiet, and the extras don't stop, from limo service to personal modems to unbelievable room service; the spa has an indoor infinity pool and elegant treatment rooms. The Big Four restaurant is soothing and rich.
$$$$$
1075 CALIFORNIA ST., 94108
TEL 415/474-5400
FAX 415/474-6227
www.huntingtonhotel.com
136 All major cards

RITZ-CARLTON SAN FRANCISCO
$$$$$
600 STOCKTON ST., 94108
TEL 415/296-7465
FAX 415/291-0288
www.ritzcarlton.com
Pricey but, by most standards, one of the best hotels in the world. There is so much splendor: chandeliers, museum-quality oil paintings, flowers, chocolates, and personal maids. Staff is helpful, quiet, and stylish. And the dining room (see p. 368) earns equal accolades.
336 Valet All major cards

STANFORD COURT
$$$$$
905 CALIFORNIA ST., 94108
TEL 415/989-3500
FAX 415/391-0513
www.renaissancehotels.com/sfosc
Situated on the site of Leland Stanford's Nob Hill mansion, the Court takes its historical roots seriously, hence the amazingly elegant and grand

PRICES

HOTELS
An indication of the cost of a double room without breakfast is given by $ signs.

$$$$$	Over $280
$$$$	$200–$280
$$$	$120–$200
$$	$80–$120
$	Under $80

RESTAURANTS
An indication of the cost of a three-course dinner without drinks is given by $ signs.

$$$$$	Over $80
$$$$	$50–$80
$$$	$35–$50
$$	$20–$35
$	Under $20

lobby, with its high ceiling and stained-glass dome. Rooms are well appointed, and its restaurant, Fournou's Ovens, has fine American cuisine.
393 Valet All major cards

FAIRMONT
$$$$–$$$$$
950 MASON ST., 94108
TEL 415/772-5000
FAX 415/772-5013
www.fairmont.com
Of all Nob Hill's grand hotels, the Fairmont, with its gilded era lobby and soaring staircases, perhaps best evokes the city's golden age. Rooms are bigger in the new addition. The downright weird Tonga Room is worth investigation.
591 Valet All major cards

MARK HOPKINS INTER-CONTINENTAL
$$$$–$$$$$
999 CALIFORNIA ST., 94108
TEL 415/392-3434
FAX 415/421-3302
www.markhopkins.net
Built by one of the Big Four railroad barons, the Mark, with an infusion of investment from the Inter-Continental Group, maintains much of the elegance, service, and atmosphere of old San Francisco. The lobby is grand and lively, the service polished. The views from the Top of the Mark cocktail bar are hard to beat.
380 Valet All major cards

RITZ-CARLTON DINING ROOM
$$$$$
600 STOCKTON ST.
TEL 415/773-6168
www.ritzcarlton.com/hotels/san_francisco/dining
The brilliant, absolutely top-ranked New French cuisine (plentiful truffles, foie gras *sans pareil*) at the Ritz-Carlton Dining Room make it one of the best places on the West Coast, if not in the country, in which to dine. Try the warm wild mushroom strudel and the squab infused with sage and pancetta. Exquisite decor and the smoothest of service.
75 Valet Closed Sun. & Mon. All major cards

ACQUERELLO
$$$$
1722 SACRAMENTO ST.
TEL 415/567-5432
www.acquerello.com
Acquerello serves up grand and very modern Italian cuisine, in the style of the edgiest Roman ristorante, with such zesty chemistry as salmon with lemon oregano oil and black olive and parsley salad Siciliana. If the house gelato is on the menu, don't miss it.
55 Closed L & all Sun.–Mon. All major cards

NORTH BEACH

HOTEL BOHEME
$$$
444 COLUMBUS AVE., 94133
TEL 415/433-9111
FAX 415/362-6292
www.hotelboheme.com
Some fine Beat-generation atmospherics in a well-run old hotel right in the center of historic North Beach. What you save on the room you can spend on food—perhaps at the Rose Pistola along Columbus Avenue.
15 All major cards

SOMETHING SPECIAL

ROSE PISTOLA

The author's favorite Italian restaurant in San Francisco, the Rose serves up light but flavorful Ligurian fare. The Rose does roasted fish better than any restaurant in town. The appetizers, from garbanzo-flour breads to pungent olive and mini-sarsone plates, are astounding; the *pappa al pomodoro* (tomato bread soup) is worth returning for at lunch. A weekend treat: live jazz.

$$$
532 COLUMBUS AVE.
TEL 415/399-0499
FAX 415/474-6227
www.rosepistolasf.com
135 Valet All major cards

ENRICO'S
$$
504 BROADWAY (AT KEARNY ST.)
TEL 415/982-6223
www.enricossf.com
The key to Enrico's food is the perfect ingredients used in such dishes as: lobster and fennel and pea shoots in risotto, sautéed chicory in rhubarb chutney, house-cured pork chops arranged on creamy polenta. A wonderful, and decently priced, eating experience in old North Beach where great memories are still made—until late each day.
110 Valet Closed Mon.-Wed. L AE, MC, V

MARIO'S BOHEMIAN CIGAR STORE
$
566 COLUMBUS AVE.
TEL 415/362-0536
Just across from Washington Square, Mario's is the classic Italian coffeehouse. The foccacia sandwiches are as good as the wonderful cappuccino.
65 MC, V

MO'S GOURMET BURGERS
$
1322 GRANT AVE.
TEL 415/788-3779
The namesake burgers rank among San Francisco's best; also good chicken and steaks.
40 MC, V

PACIFIC HEIGHTS & JAPANTOWN

HOTEL DRISCO
$$$$
2901 PACIFIC AVE., 94115
TEL 415/346-2880
FAX 415/567-5537

www.hoteldrisco.com
A 1903 hotel located in the heart of Pacific Heights; views of the city, bay, and Golden Gate Bridge. Plush rooms and suites. No parking available.
48 All major cards

MAJESTIC
$$$–$$$$

1500 SUTTER ST., 94109
TEL 415/441-1100
FAX 415/673-7331
www.thehotelmajestic.com
Located between Japantown and Pacific Heights in the Cathedral Heights section, the Majestic is embedded in a sea of Victorian jewels. Edwardian in style, French Empire in decor, the hotel is old San Francisco on a small scale, with bed-and-breakfast-style personal service.
57 P All major cards

HOTEL KABUKI
$$$

1625 POST ST., 94115
TEL 415/922-3200
FAX 415/614-5498
www.jdvhotels.com/kabuki
A perfect compromise between bed-and-breakfast and the mega-hotel scene, this mid-size hotel was renovated in 2007 and features an exquisite decor blending Japanese and Western themes. Some rooms have their own Japanese-style soaking tubs.
218 P Valet All major cards

LAUREL INN
$$$

444 PRESIDIO AVE., 94115
TEL 415/567-8467
FAX 415/928-1866
www.thelaurelinn.com
Units with kitchenettes, free covered parking, and stylish spare decor create a place well suited to an extended stay, located on the margin of Pacific Heights. A chic cocktail lounge, the G Bar, is on the property.
49 All major cards

CAFÉ KATI
$$$

1963 SUTTER ST.
TEL 415/775-7313
www.cafekati.com
Neither fusion, Pacific Rim, nor exactly Asian, though Asian eclectic. Whatever you call it, folks come for the lemongrass beurre blanc, the roasted salmon with grilled portobello mushrooms, and the crème brûlée trio.
65 P Closed L & all Mon. AE, MC, V

MAKI
$$–$$$

1825 POST ST. (AT WEBSTER ST.)
TEL 415/921-5215
The place where aficionados go when they want Japanese cuisine cooked the old country way. Try the *wappa meshi*, a steamed-in-wood delight, or any of the grilled plates.
17 P Closed Mon. MC, V

BETELNUT PEJIU WU
$$

2030 UNION ST.
TEL 415/929-8855
www.betelnutrestaurant.com
Many foodies believe this is the *only* place to eat great Asian food in the city. Set in a noisy room, Betelnut specializes in the street food of Asia: anchovies with chilis and peanuts; savory lemon-grass broths and giant noodles; satay- or tea-smoked duck.
138 P DC, MC, V

ISOBUNE SUSHI
$$

1737 POST ST., JAPAN CENTER
TEL 415/563-1030
A fun "concept" restaurant, where little wooden boats float by in a tiny artificial brook, each bearing a different raw fish delicacy for your consideration. Decent, instant gratification. When it's quieter, in the late afternoon, the chef will custom-make special house rolls for you.
33 P MC, V

JUBAN
$$

1581 WEBSTER ST.
TEL 415/776-5822
www.jubanrestaurant.com
This lively Japanese barbecue, where you cook your own beautiful Kobe beef at your table, comes with rare praise from none other than the curmudgeonly author John Krich (author of *Around the World in a Bad Mood!*). The barbecue is great, he says, and be sure to try the cold noodles, which are "superb."
128 P AE, MC, V

THE WATERFRONT

ARGONAUT HOTEL
$$$$

495 JEFFERSON ST., 94109
TEL 415/563-0800
FAX 415/563-2800
www.argonauthotel.com
Occupying the old brick Del Monte warehouse, the hotel has a seagoing theme, right down to porthole-shaped windows and star-emblazoned blue carpeting in the guest rooms. Quiet retreat on Fisherman's Wharf.
252 P Valet

HARBOR COURT
$$$$

165 STEUART ST., 94105
TEL 415/882-1300
FAX 415/882-1313
www.harborcourthotel.com
A moderately priced business-tourist hotel with several outstanding amenities, including free area limousine service, a health club, and a pool with sauna. Rooms are comfortable, mid-size.
131 P All major cards

LE MERIDIEN
$$$$

333 BATTERY ST., 94111
TEL 415/296-2900
www.starwoodhotels.com
Freshly invigorated, this heart-of-the-financial-district hotel combines the Starwood

chain's competence with class, plus plenty of business services. The Park Grill offers splendid fine dining.
360 Valet
All major cards

MANDARIN ORIENTAL
$$$$
222 SANSOME ST., 94104
TEL 415/276-9888
FAX 415/433-0289
www.mandarinoriental.com
Perched on the top 11 floors of the First Interstate Bank, one of the city's tallest buildings, the Mandarin has views galore of the entire cityscape. Much acclaimed for comfort and attention to detail by some of the pickiest corporate travelers around.
158
All major cards

HOTEL GRIFFON
$$$–$$$$
155 STEUART ST., 94105
TEL 415/495-2100
FAX 415/495-3522
www.hotelgriffon.com
One of the better small hotels in the city, the Griffon is perfect for the couple who don't need the concierge services of a big hotel, nor the doting of a bed-and-breakfast. Rooms here are elegant yet conservative.
62 Closed L
All major cards

BEST WESTERN TUSCAN INN
$$$
425 NORTH POINT ST., 94133
TEL 415/561-1100
FAX 415/561-1199
www.tuscaninn.com
Don't be put off by the blank exterior. There is charm galore inside: modern Italian-style rooms, complimentary wine, and biscotti in the evening, and room service by the Café Pescatore next door.
221 Valet
All major cards

RESTAURANT GARY DANKO
$$$$$
800 NORTH POINT ST.
TEL 415/749-2060
www.garydanko.com
Flawless California-French cooking and beautiful fresh ingredients add up to the city's hottest dinner ticket, where the menu may include horseradish-crusted salmon with dilled cucumbers, or lemon-herb duck breast with duck hash and rhubarb compote.
65 Valet Closed L
All major cards

BOULEVARD
$$$$
1 MISSION ST., EMBARCADERO
TEL 415/543-6084
www.boulevardrestaurant.com
Boulevard, with its beautiful lush interior and memorable bay views, delivers some of the best brasserie cooking in town. At lunch try the fish du jour, particularly if it happens to be roasted sea bass. The appetizers alone are worth coming for: the potato cake napoleon is not only satisfying but also artfully pretty.
180 Closed Sat. & Sun. L All major cards

SOMETHING SPECIAL

GREENS
The mecca for the modern vegetarian, Greens shines as one of the best restaurants in the Bay Area. Its chef, the brilliant Annie Somerville, has shepherded Greens along the new vegetarian cooking with such dishes as griddle cakes with corn served with tomatoes, crème fraîche, and tomatillo sauce; melon and figs paired with goat cheese and peppery vinaigrette; and desserts like cherry pie with honey ice cream. Marvelous waterfront views. For a snack find a selection of bread and Italian sandwiches at Greens to Go up front.
$$$
BLDG. A, FORT MASON, OFF MARINA BLVD.
TEL 415/771-6222
www.greensrestaurant.com
200 Closed Sun. D & Mon. L D, MC, V

IL FORNAIO
$$$
1265 BATTERY ST.
TEL415/986-0100
www.ilfornaio.com
Italian food from "the Oven" consists of excellent pizzas, well-prepared pastas, and grilled meats. Leave room for one of their luscious desserts.
148 Valet All major cards

THE SLANTED DOOR
$$$
FERRY BLDG., MARKET ST. AT EMBARCADERO
TEL 415/861-8032
www.slanteddoor.com
Chef Charles Phan does a spicy, bold Vietnamese cuisine featuring items like "shaking beef" (stir-fried filet mignon with garlic), peppery Chinese squid with mustard greens, and chicken simmered in a clay pot with caramel sauce.
150 Valet AE, MC, V

PIPERADE
$$$
1015 BATTERY ST.
TEL 415/391-2555
www.piperade.com
Gerald Hirigoyen's Basque food is served among wine barrels and bright fabrics. Try the seafood and shellfish stew in red pepper sauce, or braised veal sweetbreadswith madeira.
60 Closed Sat. L & all Sun. All major cards

BEACH CHALET
$$
1000 GREAT HWY.
TEL 415/386-8439
www.beachchalet.com
If you've been hiking on scenic Ocean Beach, this renovated historic bungalow is the place for a great designer beer and your basic mini-brewery food.

It's noisy but pretty—and the view is unforgettable; behind, the adjacent park chalet has indoor/outdoor dining by a fire.
140 P MC, V

BAY AREA

EAST BAY

BENICIA

JEFFERSON STREET MANSION
$$$$$
1063 JEFFERSON ST.
TEL 707/746-0684
www.jeffersonstreetmansion.net
You will need to have made reservations to stay here. The reason? It has been rated one of the top three bed-and-breakfasts in the U.S. This Civil War-era mansion exudes period elegance throughout.
6 P All major cards

BERKELEY

BANCROFT HOTEL
$$
2680 BANCROFT WAY, 94704
TEL 510/549-1000
www.bancrofthotel.com
There are only 22 rooms in this historic Arts and Crafts hotel, originally built in the 1920s as a women's club, a fact that gives the Bancroft its unique sense of elegant intimacy. For a great price, too.
22 P All major cards

CLAREMONT RESORT
$$
41 TUNNEL RD., 94623
TEL 510/843-3000
This elegant and luxurious hotel in a giant white castle offers remarkable views of the bay. Originally built in the early 1900s, restoration has made it one of the Bay Area's top hotels. Its restaurant, Jordan's (see this page), adds the finishing flourish.
279 P All major cards

SOMETHING SPECIAL

CHEZ PANISSE
The temple, mecca, cathedral, and, just for fun, the Taj Mahal of modern California cooking, Chez Panisse has been turning out amazing food for more than 30 years. Legendary for its perfectionism and the insistence on only the freshest ingredients—from Sonoma-raised duck to Meyer lemons from Ventura or San Joaquin Valley lamb and olive oils. Reserve as far in advance as possible.
$$$$
1517 SHATTUCK AVE.
TEL 510/548-5525
www.chezpanisse.com
50 Closed Sun.
All major cards

CAFÉ ROUGE
$$$
1782 4TH ST.
TEL 510/525-1440
www.caferouge.net
With a lively ambience and a packed bar in the burgeoning 4th Street scene, Café Rouge can be counted on for a great steak, fresh oysters, and other bistro standards. Friendly service is refreshing.
85 P Closed Mon. D
AE, MC, V

JORDAN'S AT THE CLAREMONT
$$$
41 TUNNEL RD.
TEL 510/549-8510
Superb views and great service make a visit to the restaurant here worth an evening—and you can also check out the hotel without actually staying there! The New American cuisine is both delicate (in presentation) and hearty (in quantity and flavor).
175 P All major cards

BETTE'S OCEANVIEW DINER
$
1807 4TH ST.
TEL 510/644-3230
www.worldpantry.com
Classic '50s atmosphere complete with juke box add to this diner's popularity. For breakfast, wait in line for a down-home feast of beef hash and poached eggs, or soufflé pancakes, or even a cheesy herb omelette. If you can't wait, go next door to the bakery and dig in to superb muffins.
50 P Closed D
MC, V

OAKLAND

WATERFRONT PLAZA
$$$
10 WASHINGTON ST., 94607
TEL 510/836-3800
www.waterfrontplaza.com
Well-equipped modern hotel with spacious, light-filled guest suites, some with fireplaces, many with wonderful views across the bay.
154 P Valet All major cards

JACK LONDON INN
$–$$
444 EMBARCADERO W., JACK LONDON SQ., 94607
TEL 510/444-2032
www.jacklondoninn.com
A tidy inn situated on the lively waterfront, close to Yoshi's (see p. 372), with friendly staff and comfortable rooms. A bargain.
110 P
All major cards

BAY WOLF
$$$$
3853 PIEDMONT AVE.
TEL 510/655-6004
www.baywolf.com
For more than 20 years Bay Wolf has been serving up outstanding Mediterranean fare from its lovely converted old house. Check out its special "dishes of" series (Italy, France, Spain, Greece) for some flavorful memories.
80–90 P Closed Sat. L & Sun. L AE, MC, V

CITRON
$$$
5484 COLLEGE AVE.
TEL 510/653-5484
www.citronrestaurant.com
A friendly bistro with great service and delicate, albeit satisfying, fare. Try the roast chicken with chickpea, turnips, and pea shoots or the brilliantly crafted salads, such as butter-lettuce and celeriac with bacon and apple chips.
68 Closed Mon. L
All major cards

MILANO
$$–$$$
3425 GRAND AVE.
TEL 510/763-0300
www.milanooakland.com
Where the local money comes to enjoy California-Mediterranean cuisine with a creative edge. Red-brick walls and rich contemporary decor lend a glowing ambiance, and a removable storefront provides open-air dining on warm summer nights. Specialties include cioppinos, risottos, wood-oven pizzas, and such delights as grilled prawns stuffed with provelone wrapped in spinach and pancetta.
120 P Closed Sat. & Sun. L All major cards

YOSHI'S
$$–$$$
510 EMBARCADERO WEST
TEL 510/238-9200
www.yoshis.com
The Bay Area's top jazz venue also boasts a top-notch restaurant with classy contemporary decor. Take off your shoes in the traditional tatami seating and enjoy fresh sushi and classic Japanese dishes before taking in a show.
330 P Closed L
All major cards

LE CHEVAL
$$
1007 CLAY ST.
TEL 510/763-8495
www.lecheval.com
What a deal: beautifully prepared Vietnamese-French food in a lively, unpretentious setting. And the prices! Try the outrageously good Singapore noodles or the prawns in Vietnamese curry. Wash it down with decadent iced Vietnamese coffee.
385 P Valet Closed Sun. L All major cards

NAN YANG
$$
6048 COLLEGE AVE.
TEL 510/655-3298
Nan Yang offers an opportunity to savor Chinese cuisine created using excellent ingredients. A must is the garlic tomato spinach noodles with turmeric. The salads are also unforgettable.
20 P Closed Mon.
MC, V

WALNUT CREEK

LARK CREEK CAFÉ
$$$
1360 LOCUST ST.
TEL 925/256-1234
www.larkcreek.com
If you are visiting the East Bay, you can do no better than the Lark Creek Café, particularly if you liked the Lark Creek Inn in Larkspur (see this page). American cuisine prevails; grilled salmon and spoon bread is popular.
125 P AE, MC, V

HAVANA
$$
1516 BONANZA ST.
TEL 925/939-4555
www.havanarestaurant.net
A lively Cuban restaurant serving hearty, delectable dishes, including mango gazpacho, Havana crab cakes with pineapple aioli, and garlic studded pork with mojo sauce, mashed yuccas, and black beans. The Latin rhythms create just the right mood for enjoying killer mojitos and Cuban cocktails.
100 Closed Sat. & Sun. L All major cards

NORTH BAY

INVERNESS

MANKA'S INVERNESS LODGE
$$$$
ARGYLE & CALLANDER STS.
TEL 415/669-1034
www.mankas.com
A rustic Marin hideaway with a romantic atmosphere and views of Tomales Bay. Chef Benjamin Grade's American cuisine is topped by game and duck cooked on a wood fire.
14 80 P Closed D Mon.–Fri. in Feb.–Mar.
AE, MC, V

LARKSPUR

SOMETHING SPECIAL

LARK CREEK INN

The little yellow-and-white eatery that changed the Marin restaurant scene forever is still one of the best dining experiences in the Bay Area. Perhaps it's the setting (amid redwoods) or the staff (helpful and unpretentious). Certainly it is the food: Yankee pot roast with ravioli stuffed with chard and ham hock, oven-roasted Dungeness crab with lime butter, or grilled flank steak and endive.
$$$$
234 MAGNOLIA AVE.
TEL 415/924-7766
www.larkcreek.com
185 P Closed Sat. L
All major cards

MILL VALLEY

BUCKEYE ROADHOUSE
$$$
15 SHORELINE HWY.
TEL 415/331-2600
www.buckeyeroadhouse.com
Where foodies from the city come to PARTY! The Roadhouse's hearty, zesty, and impeccably prepared New American cuisine is the

reason; the bar, where you can eat a dish called Oysters Bingo, is packed most nights.
40 P MC, V

FRANTOIO
$$$
152 SHORELINE HWY.
TEL 415/289-5777
www.frantoio.com
Someone once called chef Giovanni Perticone's cuisine "Italian soul food"—a good description of such satisfying dishes as roasted mussels with thyme-scented tomato broth, or risotto with chanterelles and locally made foie gras.
196 P Closed L & all Mon. All major cards

POINT REYES

FERRANDO'S HIDEAWAY
$$$
31 CYPRESS RD.,
POINT REYES STATION, 94956
TEL 415/663-1966
www.ferrando.com
Set amid towering pines along the coast, Ferrando's, with cozy rooms and flowering gardens, is a home away from home for many vacationing San Franciscans, who love the interesting and friendly owners' dedication to detail and comfort.
6 P MC, V

SAN RAFAEL

GERSTLE PARK INN
$$$$
34 GROVE ST., 94901
TEL 415/721-7611
www.gerstleparkinn.com
Set among lovely gardens and a redwood grove, this inn was one of the first settlements in the area. The suites are full of fine linens and period antiques.
12 P AE, MC, V

INDIA VILLAGE
$
555 E. FRANCISCO BLVD.
TEL 415/456-2411
www.indianfoodsanrafael.com
One of the best Indian restaurants in the Bay Area, the village offers delicately prepared classics such as zesty and juicy tandoori prawns, non-greasy chicken *tikka masala,* and vegetarian samosas. All for an indecently low price.
85 P Closed Sun. L AE, DC

SAUSALITO

INN ABOVE THE TIDE
$$$–$$$$
30 EL PORTAL, 94965
TEL 415/332-9535 OR 800/893-8433
www.innabovetide.com
Sausalito is relaxing and quiet —especially at this waterfront hotel, which blends the charm of a bed-and-breakfast (the breakfast is elaborate and tasty) and the professional services of a hotel (massage, concierge, turn-down, and morning paper). A fine escape.
29 P All major cards

POGGIO
$$$$
777 BRIDGEWAY BLVD.
TEL 415/332-7771
www.poggiotrattoria.com
One of the broadest panoramic views of the bay can be caught from the portals of this classic Italian trattoria, where chef Chris Fernandez's soulful dishes include wood-roasted mussels with saffron tomato broth, and local Petrale sole with buttered spinach and poached potatoes with lemon caper sauce.
120 P Valet All major cards

CHRISTOPHE
$$
1919 BRIDGEWAY BLVD.
TEL 415/332-9244
http://french-restaurant-marin.com
Pure romance in a lovely old house decorated with art nouveau furniture. Christophe serves up French fare (duck-liver mousse, roast rosemary lamb, *profiteroles* to die for) at reasonable prices. The early bird prix fixe is excellent value.
35 P Closed L MC, V

SOUTH BAY

PALO ALTO

ELBE
$$
117 UNIVERSITY AVE.
TEL 650/321-3319
www.elbe-restaurant.com
Contemporary German is done in all of its nutty, earthy, smoky glory at appropriately named Elbe. Wild boar stew and Wiener schnitzel have won the chef acclaim.
75 Closed D Mon. & L Sat. & Sun. AE, DC

EMPIRE GRILL & TAP ROOM
$$
651 EMERSON ST.
TEL 650/321-3030
Unassuming and practical, the Empire, popular with everyone from Stanford professors to dating co-eds, serves up basic American comfort food at a reasonable price. The burgers are made from some of the best beef in the U.S.
150 P All major cards

SAN JOSE

FAIRMONT HOTEL
$$$$
170 S. MARKET ST., 95113
TEL 408/998-1900
www.fairmont.com
If you liked the luxe treatment you received at the San Francisco Fairmont, you'll love this equally comfortable—and much more modern—San Jose variant.
551 P Valet All major cards

HOTEL DE ANZA
$$$
233 W. SANTA CLARA ST., 95113
TEL 408/286-1000 OR

800/843-3700
www.hoteldeanza.com
If you must do business in Silicon Valley, this is the place. Relaxed atmosphere, art deco furniture, and communications technology galore.
100 Valet All major cards

EMILE'S
$$$
545 S. SECOND ST.
TEL 408/289-1960
www.emilesrestaurant.com
New owners have reinvented this romantic culinary shrine, instilling new elegance and black-vested service. Beloved of loyal patrons, the French-inspired fusion cuisine includes such temptations as crêpes stuffed with basil seasoned chicken and ricotta baked in tomato and Mornay sauce.
60 Closed L & Mon. D AE, MC, V

SARATOGA

RESTAURANT GERVAIS
$$$
14560 BIG BASIN WAY
TEL 408/867-7017
www.gervaisrestaurant.com
A wood-burning fireplace provides a warming backdrop for enjoying contemporary European fare, such as roasted veal chop with morel mushroom risotto and caramelized shallots, best followed by the trio of custards.
75 & 20 outside Valet Closed L & Mon. All major cards

WEST BAY

BURLINGAME

KULETO'S TRATTORIA
$$$
1095 ROLLINS RD., BURLINGAME
TEL 650/342-4922
www.kuletostrattoria.com
Restaurateur-designer (Boulevard, Jardinière, Farallon) Pat Kuleto's trattoria is jammed every night with diners clamoring for his wonderfully robust pizzas, vegetable-aioli combos, and roasted fish. Then there is the wine list.
250 Closed Sat. L & Sun. L All major cards

HALF MOON BAY

ZABALLA HOUSE
$$
324 MAIN ST., 94019
TEL 650/726-9123
www.zaballahouse.net
A converted farmhouse, almost engulfed in lush greenery and flowers, in a serene oceanside burg. If you want to get away from the crowds, this is a deal.
23 AE, MC, V

PRINCETON-BY-THE-SEA

PILLAR POINT INN
$$$
380 CAPISTRANO RD., 94018
TEL 650/728-7377
www.pillarpointinn.com
Try the supreme Pacific quietude and climate here, one of the best bed-and-breakfasts on the coast, and certainly one of the most luxurious. All the rooms have fireplaces, feather mattresses, and lots of romantic extras.
11 AE, MC, V

BARBARA'S FISH TRAP
$
281 CAPISTRANO RD.
TEL 650/728-7049
On the pier, this is the perfect place for a quick—but expertly executed—meal of fish and chips (or its local variant, calamari and chips).
38 No credit cards

WOODSIDE

BELLA VISTA
$$$
13451 SKYLINE BLVD., WOODSIDE
TEL 650/851-1229
www.bvrestaurant.com
Just out on Calif. 84 is this little rustic place offering French-Italian cuisine that will make you swoon. It is one of the few places to serve a decent Caesar salad made right at your table.
180 Closed L & Sun.–Mon. All major cards

WINE COUNTRY

Wine country has so many inns, hotels, and bed-and-breakfasts that many visitors rely on booking services to make reservations for them. This is particularly helpful during the high season (late spring through fall), when local wisdom (and a fee) will help you through the maze of available choices. Among the key services are: Bed & Breakfast Inns of Napa *(tel 707/944 4444, www.bbinv.com)*; Napa Valley Reservations Unlimited *(tel 800/251-6272, www.napavalleyreservations.com)*; and Wine Country Concierge *(tel 707/252-4472, www.winecountryconcierge.com)*.

NAPA VALLEY

CALISTOGA

MOUNT VIEW HOTEL
$$$
1457 LINCOLN AVE., 94515
TEL 707/942-6877
www.mountviewhotel.com
The Mount View is one of the area's most pampering getaways. Located in a historic setting, its guest rooms are big, cozy, stylish—just like the "Southern Calistoga American" cuisine served at the popular Catahoula Restaurant, where Cajun meets California.
32 AE, MC, V

DR. WILKINSON'S HOT SPRINGS RESORT
$$–$$$

1507 LINCOLN AVE., 94515
TEL 707/942-4102
www.drwilkinson.com
A wonderful, bare-bones, '50s-style motel that somehow seems almost elegant, particularly when taken with the on-site hot springs, volcanic ash mud baths, and extensive spa services. Mid-week specials offer "the works" (mud, aromatic whirlpool, mineral steam, and massage).
42 rooms, 17 cottages P AE, MC, V

BRANNAN'S GRILL
$$$
1374 LINCOLN AVE.
TEL 707/942-2233
Delicious, unpretentious, bountiful cooking. Try the ginger-honey braised short ribs with pumpkin risotto.
190 P All major cards

NAPA

OAK KNOLL INN
$$$$$
220 E. OAK KNOLL AVE., 94558
TEL 707/255-2200
Giant, airy rooms with vaulted ceilings, brass beds, wood-burning fireplaces, and marble-floored bathrooms. Breakfast is hearty and gourmet.
4 P MC, V

SILVERADO RESORT
$$$$$
1600 ATLAS PEAK ROAD, 94558
TEL 707/257-0200
Upscale 1,200-acre retreat centered on a white-pillared mansion exuding yesteryear elegance and sophistication. Modestly furnished cottage clusters encircle swimming pools and line the fairways of this acclaimed golf resort. The Royal Oak restaurant serves grilled prime steaks and fresh seafood over mesquite.
280 P All major cards

MUSTARDS GRILL
$$–$$$
7399 ST. HELENA HWY.
TEL 707/944-2424
www.mustardsgrill.com
The cradle of Napa California cuisine, Mustards has for more than 18 years served up a hearty menu including its famous smoked Peking duck, baby back ribs with corn pudding, and tempting hamburgers.
60 P DC, MC, V

RUTHERFORD

SOMETHING SPECIAL

MEADOWOOD

Perhaps California's best luxury destination, set amid groves of redwoods and firs, Meadowood is the kind of place you will tell your grandchildren about. Besides its huge guest cottages, it offers a spa, tennis courts, a golf course, and even a professional croquet court. The restaurant, rated among the state's top ten, has a menu with such delights as roasted rabbit with bay leaf gnocchi, crab and papaya confit appetizers, and seafood—steamed, fried, grilled—that will make you want to take up fishing. The cultural program aims high, too, with visiting performers including the Vienna Boys' Choir.

$$$$$
900 MEADOWOOD LN., 94574
TEL 707/963-3646 OR 800/458-8080
www.meadowood.com
85 P All major cards

AUBERGE DU SOLEIL
$$–$$$$
180 RUTHERFORD HILL RD., 94573
TEL 707/963-1211
www.aubergedusoleil.com
Hotel meets country estate in this elegant, flower-bedecked getaway, where you can take in stunning views of olive groves while feasting on the Provençal cuisine.
52 P All major cards

PRICES

HOTELS
An indication of the cost of a double room without breakfast is given by $ signs.

$$$$$	Over $280
$$$$	$200–$280
$$$	$120–$200
$$	$80–$120
$	Under $80

RESTAURANTS
An indication of the cost of a three-course dinner without drinks is given by $ signs.

$$$$$	Over $80
$$$$	$50–$80
$$$	$35–$50
$$	$20–$35
$	Under $20

ST. HELENA

WINE COUNTRY INN
$$$
1152 LODI LN., 94574
TEL 707/963-7077
www.winecountryinn.com
This inn sits on a delightful hilltop, its old stone tower conjuring the feeling of being in one of Robert Louis Stevenson's idylls about the place.
24 rooms & 5 cottages P Closed 3 weeks in Jan. MC, V

EL BONITA MOTEL
$$–$$$
195 MAIN ST., 94574
TEL 707/963-3216 OR 800/541-3284
www.elbonita.com
The budget alternative for those who want to spend their money on wine rather than luxurious suites, El Bonita is a pleasant, well-tended old motel within walking distance of a number of wineries.
41 P All major cards

TRA VIGNE
$$$
1050 CHARTER OAK AVE.
TEL 707/963-4444

www.travignerestaurant.com
This is the kind of Italian food—and surroundings—one would get in the very best Tuscan eateries: lots of fresh beans, fish, broths, and cracker-thin breads. The wine list is world-class.
65 P DC, MC, V

WINE SPECTATOR GREYSTONE
$$$
2555 MAIN ST.
TEL 707/967-1010
An absolute must, both for the food, which is bountiful, fresh, original, and always done perfectly, and for the wine, ditto. The restaurant of the Culinary Institute of America is in the old Christian Brothers Winery, a cavernous stone mansion. Dining here is akin to eating in a castle. The pastry chef is a genius; if the poached pears in zinfandel are on the menu, don't pass them by. A fine collection of cigars and aperitifs, many of the latter made in the valley, complete a wonderful experience.
125 P Valet All major cards

YOUNTVILLE

YOUNTVILLE INN
$$$–$$$$
6462 WASHINGTON ST., 94599
TEL 707/944-5600 OR 888/366-8166
A rustic community just minutes away from some of the valley's finest (read: French Laundry, see p. 376) dining, the inn offers luxurious amenities and your own patio.
51 P All major cards

SOMETHING SPECIAL

FRENCH LAUNDRY

A few years ago, a picky *New York Times* critic dubbed the French Laundry the best restaurant in America. So many people now agree that the only way you can get in is to call, between 10 a.m and 7 p.m., exactly two months before the day you want to dine here. No exceptions, save the occasional lurker who gets in by hanging about the front door all week. If you are a foodie, it's worth it. The 9-course lunch and dinner menus are prix fixe—$240—and and is an entire afternoon or evening's entertainment. The cuisine, dubbed California-French, offers entrées such as roasted rabbit saddles in pumpkin risotto and white truffle custard for an appetizer. Jackets are required for both lunch and dinner.

If you can't make a two-month commitment, but want to try chef Thomas Keller's fine food, go down the street to his equally raved about **Bouchon** *(tel 707/944-8037)* for a scaled-down version of the main act.

$$$$
6640 WASHINGTON ST.
TEL 707/944-2380
www.frenchlaundry.com
62 P Valet Closed Mon.–Thurs. L AE, MC, V

BISTRO JEANTY
$$$
6510 WASHINGTON ST.
TEL 707/944-0103
www.bistrojeanty.com
Phillippe Jeanty, the chef who put Domaine Chandon on the culinary map, has garnered outstanding reviews for his fine bistro fare here; the rabbit and the cassoulet are huge favorites with the foodie class.
50 P MC, V

SONOMA VALLEY

BOYES HOT SPRINGS

FAIRMONT SONOMA MISSION INN & SPA
$$$$–$$$$$
18140 CALIF. 12, 95416
TEL 707/938-9000
www.fairmont.com/sonoma
A sprawling, modern, mission-style inn with outstanding spa facilities and wonderfully cozy and well-appointed rooms. A fine base for a visit to Sonoma Valley. No smoking.
198 P All major cards

GLEN ELLEN

GAIGE HOUSE INN
$$$$
13540 ARNOLD DR., 95442
TEL 707/935-0237
www.gaige.com
A high-end country inn that prides itself on service and attention to detail. A great place from which to visit some wineries or to see Jack London State Historic Park.
14 rooms & 4 cottages P AE, MC, V

BELTANE RANCH
$$$–$$$$
11775 SONOMA HWY., 95442
TEL 707/996-6501
www.beltaneranch.com
For anyone who really wants to get back to the land, as they said in the 1960s, this is the place. Beltane is a working ranch, full of cattle and grapevines, set amid miles of oak-bordered trails. The charming ranch is family-run, which brings a warm feeling, particularly evident during long siestas on the old wraparound porch. No smoking.
5 rooms, 1 cottage P None

HEALDSBURG

MADRONA MANOR
$$$–$$$$
1001 WESTSIDE RD. (NEAR MILL ST.), 95448
TEL 707/433-4231 OR 800/258-4003
www.madronamanor.com
This late 19th-century house is more than the usual redone Victorian—it's a three-story mansion, set on eight acres of wooded splendor (and some gardened splendor as well). Most guests prefer the rooms in the main house, where the food action is.

23 P Closed Sun. AE, MC, V

BISTRO RALPH
$$$
109 PLAZA ST. (OFF HEALDSBURG AVE.)
TEL 707/433-1380
Another up-and-coming California-home-style bistro, with zesty Asian overtones. Try the peppery shrimp starter.
50 P Closed Sun. MC, V

KENWOOD

KENWOOD RESTAURANT
$$–$$$
9900 CALIF. 12
TEL 707/833-6326
The setting, right in the middle of Kenwood, draws locals from all around the valley to this bistro, where ingredients are just out of the ground and views are out of this world.
150 P Closed Mon.–Tues. MC, V

SONOMA

EL DORADO
$$–$$$
405 1ST ST. W., 95476
TEL 707/996-3220
RESTAURANT TEL 707/996-3030
www.hoteleldorado.com
This impeccable hotel overlooks the Plaza Sonoma. With sumptuous rooms and equally sumptuous breakfasts, it is a true find. Its Piatti restaurant serves decent Italian cooking.
26 P AE, MC, V

LA CASA
$
121 E. SPAIN ST.
TEL 707/996-3406
An old-fashioned Mexican food hangout not far from Sonoma Plaza. What better place to celebrate General Vallejo's wise decision, 150 years ago, to "help out" the American insurrectionists?
180 P All major cards

THE NORTH

ALBION

ALBION RIVER INN
$$$–$$$$$
3790 CALIF. 1, 95410
TEL 707/937-1919 OR 800/479-7944
www.abionriverinn.com
A Mendocino Coast wonder, this one with fantastic coastal view, deluxe amenities, and a very good restaurant that has won raves from locals and out-of-towners.
22 P All major cards

ALTURAS

BRASS RAIL
$
701 E. LAKEVIEW HWY.
TEL 530/233-2906
It may not be much to look at, but the Basque food just keeps on coming. And it's good: big rib-eye steaks, lamb chops, fried chicken, red beans, Spanish rice, garbanzo beans, ravioli.... For an amazingly low all-in price, you also get wine, homemade bread, soup, salad, coffee or tea, and ice cream.
200 P Closed Mon. MC, V

BOONVILLE

BOONVILLE HOTEL
$$–$$$$
14050 CALIF. 128 (AT LAMBERT LN.), P.O. BOX 326, 95415
TEL 707/895-2210
If you're out cruising the backwoods area, this is a good place to stay or to stop for lunch. The chef prepares a zesty Mexican menu with hints of New American cuisine.
10 P Closed Jan. & part of Feb. MC, V

CHESTER

SOMETHING SPECIAL

DRAKESBAD GUEST RANCH

Set on natural hot mineral springs in the midst of Lassen Volcanic National Park (see p. 286), Drakesbad is the last of the 19th-century country lodges. The owner-hosts make a stay here absolutely delightful, with an informal atmosphere and satisfying, unfancy cooking (three meals a day are included in the price). Horseback riding, volleyball, and trail hiking are among the offered activities—when you're not floating in the spring-fed thermal pool at night, gazing at the star-filled sky.
$$$
WARNER VALLEY RD., 96020
TEL 530/529-1512
www.drakesbad.com
20 P Closed Nov.–May MC, V

EUREKA

CARTER HOUSE
$$$$
301 L ST., 95501
TEL 707/444-8062 OR 800/404-1390
www.carterhouse.com
Actually three properties—a hotel, a bed-and-breakfast, and a separate cottage, itself with three rooms—the award-winning Carter is *the* place on the north coast. The decor is tasteful, with either period-perfect heirloom furniture or pleasing Southwesternalia. Big suites have all the right amenities, from whirlpool baths to jumbo beds.
No smoking.
33 P All major cards

RESTAURANT 301
$$$$
301 L ST.
TEL 707/444-8062
It would be an understatement to say the 301, at Carter House (see above), is Eureka's best—it's every bit as good as Café Beaujolais in Mendocino (see this page). The elegant candlelit dining room serves up impeccably

prepared dishes—fish, usually local, sautéed just right with chanterelle mushrooms brought in by a ranger from the nearby national forest.
45 Closed L All major cards

GARBERVILLE

BENBOW INN
$$$–$$$$
445 LAKE BENBOW DR., 95542
TEL 707/923-2124 OR 800/355-3301
www.benbowinn.com
Host to Hollywood stars from Charles Laughton to Joan Fontaine, the Benbow, with its grand Tudor architecture and up-country setting, has been completely restored. Guest rooms are cozy and full of period decor; the restaurant serves fine regional cuisine, and there's boating, tennis, golf, swimming, and hiking.
55 Closed Jan.–March All major cards

GUALALA

WHALE WATCH INN
$$$–$$$$
35100 CALIF. 1, 95445
TEL 800/942-5342
Large, airy modern rooms in a contemporary architectural complex perched high on a cliff overlooking the Pacific. A footpath takes you to a deserted beach. In the winter, watch whales through the telescope in the cozy lodge.
18 AE, MC, V

MCCLOUD

MCCLOUD HOTEL
$$–$$$$
408 MAIN ST., 96057
TEL 530/964-2822 OR 800/964-2823
www.mccloudhotel.com
Big, light-filled rooms with Victorian-era decor, heirloom furniture, in-room Jacuzzis, and an atmospheric lobby make the McCloud a unique place from which to explore Shasta country and beyond.
17 All major cards

MENDOCINO

SOMETHING SPECIAL

STANFORD INN
This is the kind of place we would all build if we were as single-minded, as energetic, and as creative as the Stanford family. The Stanford Inn is wonderful, from its modern but woodsy guest rooms to its vegetarian restaurant. The Stanford sits at the mouth of the Big River, an unspoiled estuary, home to great blue herons, ospreys, and harbor seals.
$$$–$$$$$
CALIF. 1 & COMPTCHE-UKIAH RD., 95460
TEL 707/937-5615 OR 800/331-8884
www.stanfordinn.com
41 All major cards

CAFÉ BEAUJOLAIS
$$$
961 UKIAH ST. (BETWEEN EVERGREEN & SCHOOL STS.)
TEL 707/937-5614
www.cafebeaujolais.com
For many years this rustic cottage set amid the wood and clapboard jumble of quaint Mendocino has attracted pickier diners from all over the country. The California country cuisine—with local wines, herbs, vegetables, and game—is a delight; the surroundings are intimate and memorable.
60 Closed L Mon.-Tue. All major cards

GOLD COUNTRY

Although not as organized as San Francisco or wine country, Gold Country has its own unique brand of help for travelers. Friendly, informal "tourists bureaus" are found in almost every small city and town. As well as the larger places like Sacramento, even tiny Angels Camp, Sutter Creek, and Sonora have their own helpful offices, staffed through the week. Just follow the "Gold Country" signs.

SACRAMENTO

DELTA KING
$$$–$$$$$
1000 FRONT ST., 95814
TEL 916/444-5464 OR 800/825-5464
www.deltaking.com
Of the 44 beautifully restored staterooms on this old riverboat, those toward the stern are the best, with views and elegant furniture. Breakfast is included.
44 Valet All major cards

AMBER HOUSE BED & BREAKFAST
$$$–$$$$
1315 22ND ST., 95816
TEL 916/444-8085 OR 800/755-6526
www.amberhouse.com
Three architectural motifs—mission, Mediterranean, and colonial—and three separate houses make up this lovely historic complex. Some rooms have hot tubs and fireplaces.
14 All major cards

HYATT REGENCY AT CAPITOL PARK
$$$–$$$$
1209 L ST., 95814
TEL 916/443-1234
www.sacramento.hyatt.com
The rooms are luxurious and airy, the service grand, the location (across from the scenic capitol) just peachy. For a chain, a good buy.
500 All major cards

BIBA
$$–$$$
2801 CAPITOL AVE.
TEL 916/455-2422
www.biba-restaurant.com

Biba Caggiano, cookbook author and TV host, is responsible for the delicate and flavorful pasta dishes here. Her roasted meats and game are also amazing.
100 P Closed Fri.–Sat. L & all Sun. All major cards

NORTH GOLD COUNTRY

GRASS VALLEY

HOLBROOKE HOTEL
$$–$$$
212 W. MAIN ST., 95945
TEL 530/273-1353
www.holbrooke.com
The rooms are spare but prim and clean; the atmosphere is artsy Gold Country fun; the food in Arletta's Restaurant is earthy, flavorful, and bountiful —New American with a sprinkling of local wild game and fruits (huckleberries, miners' lettuce, elderberries).
28 P All major cards

NEVADA CITY

THE PARSONAGE
$$–$$$
427 BROAD ST., 95959
TEL 530/265-9478
FAX 530/265-8147
http://theparsonage.net
A Victorian house built in the 1860s, the Parsonage has been restored to its gold rush grandeur. Breakfasts are hearty affairs. There is a cottage especially for families.
6 P Closed Jan. MC, V

COUNTRY ROSE CAFÉ
$$$
300 COMMERCIAL ST.
TEL 530/265-6248
Let's call the food at this unique and pretty bistro "Gold Country French." The patio is lush and serene. The lamb and ratatouille are highly recommended.
55 P All major cards

CENTRAL GOLD COUNTRY

COLOMA

COLOMA COUNTRY INN
$$$–$$$$
345 HIGH ST., 95613
TEL 530/622-6919
www.colomacountryinn.com
Set on five acres of prime Gold Country land, the inn is a beautifully restored 1852 Victorian, with period decor and antiques. The full breakfast is grand; the ballooning and rafting packages a deal.
5 P None

PLACERVILLE

ZACHARY JACQUES
$$$
1821 PLEASANT VALLEY RD.
TEL 530/626-8045
www.zacharyjacques.com
Jacques serves a memorable earthy, country-French menu. The roast rack of lamb is the pièce de résistance.
55 P Closed L & all Mon.–Tues. AE, MC, V

PLYMOUTH

AMADOR HARVEST INN
$$
12455 STEINER RD., 95669
TEL 209/245-5512 OR 800/217-2304
Situated in one of the most lovely spots in Gold Country (or for that matter the state), the inn is just next door to Deaver Vineyards and a deep blue lake. A full breakfast comes with the room price.
4 P AE, MC, V

SUTTER CREEK

FOXES BED & BREAKFAST
$$–$$$
77 MAIN ST., 95685
TEL 209/267-5883 OR 800/987-3344
www.foxesinn.com

PRICES

HOTELS
An indication of the cost of a double room without breakfast is given by **$** signs.

$$$$$	Over $280
$$$$	$200–$280
$$$	$120–$200
$$	$80–$120
$	Under $80

RESTAURANTS
An indication of the cost of a three-course dinner without drinks is given by $ signs.

$$$$$	Over $80
$$$$	$50–$80
$$$	$35–$50
$$	$20–$35
$	Under $20

With its elegant breakfast service, ornate period beds, and high ceilings, Foxes is a place where one can imagine what it was like to be a big-spending city slicker in gold rush times.
7 P MC, V

SOUTH GOLD COUNTRY

MURPHYS

DUNBAR HOUSE 1880
$$–$$$$
271 JONES ST., 95247
TEL 209/728-2897 OR 800/692-6006
www.dunbarhouse.com
This historic house is overflowing with Victoriana, the service is impeccable, and the nascent (but tasty) local wine country is worth exploring.
5 P AE, MC, V

SIERRA NEVADA

LAKE TAHOE

RITZ-CARLTON HIGHLANDS
$$$$$
NORTHSTAR
www.ritzcarlton.com

Opening in 2009, this top-of-the-line, ski-in, ski-out property promises to bring a whole new level of panache to Lake Tahoe with its deluxe condo units themed with logs and granite.
173 P All major cards

INN BY THE LAKE
$$–$$$$
3300 LAKE TAHOE BLVD., S. LAKE TAHOE, 96150
TEL 530/542-0330
www.innbythelake.com
The upscale motel is conveniently located just across the way from the swimming beach, close to Heavenly ski resort, accessed by free shuttle. Stay here and you can get a free ride to the casinos across the lake.
100 P All major cards

GRAHAM'S
$$$
1650 SQUAW VALLEY RD., OLYMPIC VALLEY, 96146
TEL 530/581-0454
Glowing with cozy intimacy, Graham's intimate pine-paneled dining room is warmed by log fires in river-rock hearths. The California-Mediterranean menu is typified by seared ahi with noodles appetizer, and three peppercorn crusted elk loin with lingonberry demiglaze. A vast wine list spans the globe.
125 Closed Mon.–Tues. AE, MC, V

SIX PEAKS GRILL
$$$
RESORT AT SQUAW CREEK, 400 SQUAW CREEK RD., OLYMPIC VALLEY
TEL 530/581-6621
Though the view of the Sierra Nevada is what may bring people here, it is the food at Six Peaks Grill that brings them back again and again. The Grill has also received accolades from serious foodies for its California-fusion cuisine and comfort foods, such as roasted corn chowded and grilled rib-eye steak. Leave room for the beehive-baked Alaska with meringue and raspberry sauce. The wine list is award-winning.
75 P All major cards

MAMMOTH LAKES

MAMMOTH MOUNTAIN INN
$$$–$$$$$
ONE MINARET RD., 93546
TEL 760/934-2581
FAX 760/934-0700
www.mammothmountaininn.com
At 9,000 feet, this modern alpine lodge offers cozy contemporary decor, blending comfort, convenience, and heaps of amenities, just steps away from the ski lifts. The Dry Creek Bar is the perfect spot for après-ski.
213 P AE, MC, V

WESTIN MONACHE
$$$$-$$$$$
100 CANYON BLVD.
TEL 760/934-2526
FAX 760/934-4686
Catering to outdoorsy folks with deep pockets, the all-suite, full-service Westin Monache opened in late 2007, bringing a new level of luxe to Mammoth. Rooms here have gas fireplaces and flat-panel TVs.
230 P All major cards

OAKHURST

SOMETHING SPECIAL

CHATEAU DE SUREAU & ERNA'S ELDERBERRY HOUSE

Next to the French Laundry, perhaps the closest thing there is to "destination dining." Erna's serves California-French with hints of the owner Erna Kubin. The dining room is elegant and dramatic, with dark beams on white walls and candles in the windows. Impeccable food. Chateau de Sureau, run by the same owners, is fabulously luxurious: goosedown pillows, stone fireplaces, and staff who just won't let you do a thing!

$$$$$
48688 VICTORIA LN., 93644
TEL 559/683-6860, 559/683-6800 (RESTAURANT)
www.chateaudusureau.com
12 Restaurant closed Mon. L & Tues. L AE, MC, V

SEQUOIA NATIONAL PARK

CEDAR GROVE LODGE
$
P.O. BOX 909, CEDAR GROVE, 93633
TEL 559/335-5500
www.sequoia-kingscanyon.com
Modest, functional, and right in the middle of some of the park's most spectacular scenery, this little lodge is perfect if you just want a burger and a bed. You can also picnic here, right on the river's edge.
21 P Closed mid-Nov.–May MC, V

YOSEMITE NATIONAL PARK

AHWAHNEE HOTEL & RESTAURANT
$$$$
1 AHWAHNEE WAY, YOSEMITE NATIONAL PARK, 95389
TEL 209/372-1407 OR 559/252-4848 (RESERVATIONS)
Make reservations several months ahead if you want to stay in this delightful 1920s mountain lodge, replete with Native American decor, stone and sugar pine construction, and cozy rooms with magnificent views of the valley's meadows and Half Dome. Also book ahead if you plan to luxuriate in the prettiest dining room in the state—the Ahwahnee's breathtaking light-filled restaurant, where the superb American cuisine comes with great service and memories to last a lifetime.

(Dinner for guests only.)
123 All major cards

TENAYA LODGE
$$$
1122 CALIF. 41 (S OF YOSEMITE S. ENTRANCE), P.O. BOX 159, FISH CAMP 93623
TEL 888/514-2167
www.tenayalodge.com
Big, very professionally run, and with cozy rooms, the Tenaya offers what people who stay here want: a comfortable, amenities-filled getaway offering rest, relaxation, and food for those long evenings after a day's hiking. Past patrons will appreciate a recent multi-million renovation. Its Sierra Restaurant is well regarded for its straight-forward American cuisine.
244 All major cards

WAWONA HOTEL & DINING ROOM
$$–$$$
CALIF. 41 (AT WAWONA EXIT), 95389
TEL 559/252-4848 (RES.)
www.yosemitepark.com
More modest than the Ahwahnee, the Wawona nevertheless holds its own on the Yosemite charm scale. The hotel consists of a sprawl of low-slung, whitewashed wooden cottages, with wraparound porches and views into a central meadow. Spend the day hiking, then come back to the restaurant's grilled trout and steaks—satisfying and tasty. Rooms are austere but comfortable.
104 All major cards

YOSEMITE LODGE AT THE FALLS
$$
YOSEMITE VALLEY, 95389
TEL 559/252-4848
Right in the heart of the valley, close to Yosemite Falls, the lodges offers motel rooms with Southwestern decor, as well as more rustic cabins.
245 All major cards

CENTRAL VALLEY

BAKERSFIELD

DOUBLETREE HOTEL
$$
3100 CAMINO DEL RIO COURT, 93308
TEL 661/323-7111
FAX 661/323-0331
One of a predictably competent, basic but useful, modern chain of business-traveler motels.
262 All major cards

CHALET BASQUE
$
200 OAK ST.
TEL 661/327-2915
People make a special trip just for the Chalet's wonderful roast lamb and pink beans special. Memorable Basque fare in a family atmosphere.
100 Closed Sun. L AE, MC, V

FRESNO

PICCADILLY INN WEST SHAW HOTEL
$$–$$$
2305 W. SHAW AVE., 93711
TEL 559/226-3850
www.piccadillyinn.com
The jumbo swimming pool will come in handy during the sweltering valley days; the amply sized guest rooms are neat, if austere, and even have their own refrigerators. No smoking.
194 All major cards

HANFORD

IRWIN STREET INN
$–$$
522 N. IRWIN ST.
TEL 559/583-8000
www.irwinstreetinn.com
A nicely restored, tree-shaded Victorian, the inn is a pleasant place to stop on the way north or south. Rooms feature antiques and period reproductions.
30 Closed Sun. D & all Mon. All major cards

VISALIA

SPALDING HOUSE
$$
631 N. ENCINA ST., 93291
TEL 559/739-7877
www.spaldinghouse.com
Another restored Victorian in farm country—this one complete with library, grand piano, and cozy sitting parlors. For those long evenings, lemonade, ice cream, and seats on the quaint wooden porch. Full breakfast is included.
3 AE, MC, V

THE DESERT

Accommodations and eateries of note are thin in the deserts, except for the Palm Springs region, known for its bounty of spa resorts, trendy boutique hotels, and private rentals—from golf course condos to deluxe villas. Visitors seeking rental lodgings should consult specialist online booking services, such as La Quinta Villa Rentals *(tel 760/327-9879, www.laquintavillarentals.com)*, McLeans Company Rentals *(tel 760/322-2500 or 800/777-4606, www.ps4rent.com)* and Vacationhomes *(www.vacationhomes.com)*. The Palm Springs Desert Resorts Convention & Visitors Authority *(tel 760/770-9000, www.giveintothedesert.com)* is a helpful resource.

DEATH VALLEY

FURNACE CREEK INN
$$$$
CALIF. 190, 92328
TEL 760/786-2345
www.furnacecreekinn.com
Cool off at this historic inn, where the pool is supplemented by a natural mineral spring, the food is climate-

adjusted, and the golf course equipped with plenty of refreshing sprinklers, beers, and umbrella drinks.
66 P All major cards

DESERT HOT SPRINGS

TWO BUNCH PALMS RESORT & SPA

$$$–$$$$
67 TWO BUNCH PALMS TRAIL, 92240
TEL 760/329-8791 OR 800/472-4334
www.twobunchpalms.com
It was here that director Robert Altman located the spa scene in his film *The Player,* about the Hollywood elite. Trendy and luxurious, Two Bunch is a wonderful, serene place, where the massages and mud baths are first-rate, the guest rooms stylish and calming, and the California-French cuisine in the intimate dining room is exquisite.
45 P AE, MC, V

INDIAN WELLS

LE ST. GERMAIN

$$–$$$
74985 CALIF. 111, 92210
TEL 760/773-6511
The California-French cuisine at this romantic little bistro has been getting good marks from picky foodies of late. The Grand Marnier soufflé is in itself a reason to be a sentient being. Chef/owner Michel Despras was recently named "Restaurateur of the Year" by the California Writer's Association.
250 P All major cards

PALM DESERT

CUISTOT

$$$$
72595 EL PASEO DR., 92260
TEL 760/340-1000
www.cuistotrestaurant.com
The menu has been officially dubbed California-French, but that's really a bit tame, a bit buttoned-up for the savvy, free-style cooking here. Try the quail stuffed with sweetbreads in white wine sauce to get a notion of the chef's deftness with essential flavors. The desserts are equally complex, unique, and, ultimately, satisfying.
290 P Closed Sun. L, all Mon., & July–Aug. All major cards

PALM SPRINGS

THE PARKER PALM SPRINGS

$$$$$
4200 E. PALM CANYON DR., 92264
TEL 760/770-5000
www.theparkerpalmsprings.com
Among the current crop of deluxe, retro themed desert spa hotels, The Parker has won accolades, many of which swoon over the hotel's cutting-edge chic and fine dining. The fun yet glamorous atmosphere is enhanced by the swank Palm Springs Yacht Club spa.
144 P All major cards

SOMETHING SPECIAL

VICEROY PALM SPRINGS

Exuding class, this luxurious boutique hotel is a perfect refuge from the woes of the world and is graced by Hollywood-Regency decor in a black, white, and lemon-yellow house motif. Hollywood's finest are often seen lounging beside the three pools, sipping signature fruit-infused mojitos at the stylish bar, or relaxing in the top-rated spa. Chef Stephen Belie conjures divine Californian fusion cuisine in the Citron restaurant. Try the pumpkin seed-crusted Chilean sea bass with lobster asparagus ravioli and uni butter.

$$$$$
415 S. BELARDO, 92264
TEL 760/320-4117
FAX 760/323-3303
www.viceroypalmsprings.com
68 P All major cards

MOVIE COLONY HOTEL

$$$$–$$$$$
726 N. INDIAN CANYON DR., 92262
TEL 760/320-6340 OR 888/953-5700
FAX 760/320-1640
www.moviecolonyhotel.com
With its minimalist designer furnishings and fabrics from the Modernist heyday, this chic compact hotel draws Hollywood mavens. Brushed steel, heaps of glass, and gray-white-and-canary-yellow colors set a 21st-century tone, and the open-air bar is a popular spot for martinis by the firepit.
17 P All major cards

SMOKE TREE RANCH

$$$–$$$$
1850 SMOKE TREE LN., 92264
TEL 800/787-3922
FAX 760/327-9490
www.smoketreeranch.com
The last of Palm Springs' venerable due-ranch lodges, this one still revolves around its stables while retaining the rusticity that drew erstwhile regulars Cary Grant and Walt Disney. Timber-beamed cottages are simply appointed and have fireplaces.
85 cottages P DC, MC, V

PEAKS

$$$$
ONE TRAMWAY RD.
TEL 760/327-1590
www.pstramway.com
At this elegant mountaintop eerie (accessed by the Palm Springs Aerial Tram), Chef David Le Pow delivers delicious California fusion dishes, such as rack of lamb with fresh peach compote and truffled mashed potatoes. Go not least for the peerless vistas from 8,560 feet.
125 All major cards

JOHANNES
$$$–$$$$
196 S. INDIAN CANYON DR., 92262
TEL 760/778-0017
Chef Johannes Bacher has created a masterpiece at his hip, high-end shrine to cosmopolitan dining. The minimalist decor—industrial piping, tiny halogens, lots of tomato bisque orange—is matched by precise service and attention to detail in the imaginative California-Asian-Austrian fusion cuisine.
Closed Mon. All major cards

FISHERMAN'S MARKET & GRILL
$–$$$
235 S. INDIAN CANYON DR., 92262
TEL 760/327-1766
www.gotofishermans.com
Whether it's classic English-style fish 'n' chips, charbroiled swordfish taco, or Ahi sashimi, you're guaranteed only the freshest seafood at this homey favorite of local cognoscenti. The oysters shooters are a hit at the adjoining Shanghai Red's hideaway bar, where live R&B music can be heard on Fri. and Sat. nights.
140 P All major cards

RICK'S
$–$$$
1973 N. PALM CANYON DR., 92262
TEL 760/416-0090
A friendly Cuban-American 1950s-style diner that packs in the locals for hearty American favorites, Cuban *ropa vieja,* and eclectic treats such as seared ahi tuna salad. If you like to sit at a counter, this is the place.
104 P Closed D AE, MC, V

RANCHO MIRAGE

DESERT SPRINGS JW MARRIOTT RESORT & SPA
$$$-$$$$$
74–855 COUNTRY CLUB DR., 92260
TEL 760/341-2211 OR 800/331-3112
FAX 760/341-1872
www.desertspringsresort.com
This large hotel combines stylish digs with all the amenities you could wish for, not least a massive state-of-the-art spa, the hottest night-club in the valley, and excellent dining options. Italian-style gondolas cruise right into the soaring atrium lobby to pick up and drop off guests.
884 P All major cards

RITZ CARLTON RANCHO MIRAGE
$$$$
68900 FRANK SINATRA DR., 92270
TEL 760/321-8282
www.ritzcarlton.com
Set on a plateau in the mountains, this sumptuous modern resort hotel emerged in 2008 from a $500 million remake and is now perhaps the desert's most luxurious hotel, with a clientele to match.
240 P All major cards

WALLY'S DESERT TURTLE
$$$$$
71775 HWY. 111, 92270
TEL 760/568-9321
www.wallys-desert-turtle.com
To some minds, this lavish restaurant serves the best cuisine in the desert, courtesy French chef Chef Pascal Lallemand. Try the pan-broiled Lake Superior whitefish, with mussels, leek fondue, and lemon beurre blanc apricot soufflé. This is one dinner you will want to dress up for.
180 P All major cards

LAS CASUELAS NUEVAS
$
70050 CALIF. 111, 92270
TEL 760/328-8844
An upbeat California-Mexican restaurant with everything the natives love: mariachi music (live), free-flowing Mexican beer (on tap), hearty Mexican-American classics (burritos, tacos, quesadillas), and some actual Mexican food as well (soups, *carne asadas*). Go a little early to get a good seat.
450 P All major cards

TWENTYNINE PALMS

29 PALMS INN
$$–$$$$
73950 INN AVE., 92277
TEL 760/367-3505
www.29palmsinn.com
After a long day of rock-climbing in Joshua Tree, there's no better place to cool off and relax than here. Each room has a patio, hot tub, and fireplace. The very acceptable restaurant means you don't have to leave the place for a good meal later on. The Inn is located on the famed Oasis of Mara, an attractive alternative to going to Palm Springs for the evening.
19 P All major cards

LA QUINTA

LA QUINTA RESORT & CLUB
$$$$$
49499 EISENHOWER DR., 92253
TEL 760/577-4800 OR 877/527-7721
www.laquintaresort.com
The quintessential desert escape, this legendary hacienda resort has for half a century lured luminaries, drawn to its calm and serenity. Lush grounds feature 41 swimming pools and 23 tennis courts, and guests can dine in a different restaurant each night of the week.
796 P All major cards

SHOPPING

Even the locals regard shopping as a recreation in California. This section suggests some places where you can find the unusual, the special, or the bargain.

LOS ANGELES

ANTIQUES

Rose Bowl Flea Market Rose Bowl, Pasadena, 2nd Sun. of month. From junk to jewels.

ART

Gagosian Gallery 456 N. Camden Dr., Beverly Hills, tel 310/271-9400, www.gagosian.com. Modern and contemporary art.
L.A. Louver Galleries 45 N. Venice Blvd., Venice Beach, tel 310/822-4955, www.lalouver.com. Contemporary art.
Latin American Masters 264 N. Beverly Dr., Beverly Hills, tel 310/271-4847, www.latinamericanmasters.com. Modern Latin American art.
Margo Leavin Gallery 812 N. Robertson Blvd., tel 310/273-0603. Contemporary art.

ARTS & CRAFTS/MISSION PERIOD PIECES

Gamble House Bookstore 4 Westmoreland Pl., Pasadena, tel 626/449-4178.
Jack Moore Craftsman Furniture 1419 N. Lake St., Pasadena, tel 626/577-7746.

BOOKS & MUSIC

Book Soup 8818 Sunset Blvd., West Hollywood, tel 310/659-3110, www.booksoup.com. Huge bookstore—classics to crime—plus a bistro.
Rhino Records 1720 Westwood Blvd., West L.A., tel 310/474-8685. What you'll hear next year, now.

FASHION & BOUTIQUES

Aardvark's 7579 Melrose Ave., tel 323/655-6769. Vintage clothing.
American Rag Company 150 S. La Brea Ave., Melrose District, tel 323/935-3154. Secondhand clothes and accessories.
Maxfield 8825 Melrose Ave., tel 310/274-8800. Designer clothes.
Tyler Trafficante 7290 Beverly Blvd., Melrose District, tel 323/931-9678. Tailor terrifico.
Y-Que 1770 N. Vermont Ave., tel 323/664-0021, http://yque.com. "Kitsch meets Mexican L.A."

FOOD

Grand Central Market 317 S. Broadway, tel 213/624-2378, www.grandcentralsquare.com. All manner of food and produce.
Pasadena Farmers' Market Washington St. & Sierra Madre St., www.smgov.net/farmers_market/, Wed. 8:30–1, Sat. 8–1, & Sun. 9:30–1.
Santa Monica Farmers' Market Wed. 8:30–1, Sat. 8–1, & Sun. 9:30–1.

FURNITURE & DESIGN

Pacific Design Center 8687 Melrose Ave., Melrose District, tel 310/657-0800, www.pacificdesigncenter.com. The Taj Mahal of Trend.
Sonrisa 7609 Beverly Blvd., Mel-rose District, tel 323/935-8438, www.sonrisafurniture.com.

HOLLYWOODALIA

Frederick's of Hollywood 6608 Hollywood Blvd., Hollywood, tel 323/957-5953, www.fredericks.com. Madonna's alleged choice.
Western Costume 11041 Vanowen Blvd., N. Hollywood, tel 818/760-0900, www.westerncostume.com. Studios' choice.

OUTLET STORES

The Grove 189 The Grove Dr., Los Angeles, tel 323/900-8080, www.thegrovela.com.

PAMPERING

Beverly Hot Springs 308 N. Oxford Ave., tel 323/734-7000, www.beverlyhotsprings.com.
Burke Williams Spas tel 310/587-3366, www.burkewilliamsspa.com. Four establishments: 1358 4th St., Santa Monica; 39 Mills Place, Pasadena; 8000 Sunset Blvd.; and 15301 Ventura Blvd., Sherman Oaks.
Frederic Fekkai Beauté de Provence 444 N. Rodeo Dr., tel 310/777-8700, www.fredericfekkai.com.

SOUTHWESTERNALIA

Arte de Mexico 5356 Riverton Ave., N. Hollywood, tel 818/769-5090, www.arteshowrooms.com.

SOUTHERN CALIFORNIA

ANTIQUES

Michael Haskell Antiques 539 San Ysidro Rd., Santa Barbara, tel 805/565-1121, www.michaelhaskell.com. Spanish and Spanish Colonial items.

ART

California Art Gallery 305 N. Coast Hwy., Laguna Beach, tel 949/494-7270, www.californiaartgallery.com. Plein air revivals.
Laguna North Gallery 376 N. Coast Hwy., Laguna Beach, tel 949/494-4324, www.lagunanorthgallery.com.
Santa Barbara Contemporary Arts Forum 653 Paseo Nuevo, tel 805/966-5373, www.sbcaf.org.
Scott White Gallery 2400 Kettner Blvd., San Diego, tel 619/501-5689, www.scottwhiteart.com.

BOOKS

Acres of Books 240 Long Beach Blvd., Long Beach, tel 562/437-6980, www.acresofbooks.com.

FASHION

San Diego Factory Outlet Center 4498 Camino de la Plaza, San Ysidro, tel 619/690-2999.

FOOD

Julian Pie Company 2225 Main St., Julian, tel 760/765-2400, www.julianpie.com. In fall, the apple of everyone's eye.

OLYMPICS
Arco Olympic Training Center 2800 Olympic Pkwy., Chula Vista, tel 619/656-1500, www.usoc.org/12181_19097.htm. Official U.S. Olympic merchandise and collectibles. Also free tours of official U.S. Olympic training facility.

CENTRAL COAST

FOOD
Casa de Fruta 10021 Pacheco Pass Hwy., Hollister, tel 408/842-7282, www.casadefruta.com. Fresh produce.
Pezzini Farms Hwy. 1 & Nashua Rd., Castroville, tel 831/757-7434, www.pezzinifarms.com. Artichokes.

FUNK
San Juan Bautista Peddlers Fair Mission San Juan, tel 831/623-2454. Sun.

OUTLET STORES
American Tin Cannery Factory Outlets 125 Ocean View Blvd., Monterey, tel 831/372-1442, www.americantincannery.com.

WINE GUIDES & MAPS
Chateau Julien Winery 8940 Carmel Valley Rd., Carmel, tel 831/624-2600, www.chateaujulien.com.

SAN FRANCISCO

ART & ANTIQUES
Gump's 135 Post St., Union Sq., tel 415/982-1616. Asian antiquities, jade, and much else.
Hang Gallery 556 Sutter St., tel 415/434-4264, www.hangart.com. Emerging Bay Area artists, for sale.
Isak Lindenauer Antiques 4143 19th St., tel 415/552-6436. American Arts and Crafts movement.
Kuromatsu 722 Bay St., tel 415/474-4027. Japanese arts and antiques.
Montgomery Gallery 353 Sutter St., tel 415/788-8300, www.montgomerygallery.com. Arts of California.
W. Graham Arader III 435 Jackson St., tel 415/788-5115, www.aradersf.com. Maps, prints, and books.

BEAUTY
Elizabeth Arden Spa 126 Post St., tel 415/989-4888, www.reddoorspas.com.

BOOKS
City Lights 261 Columbus Ave., North Beach, tel 415/362-8193, www.citylights.com. Landmark literary bookstore.
Green Apple Books 506 Clement St., tel 415/387-2272, www.greenapplebooks.com. Enormous variety of new and used books.
Museum Books S. F. Museum of Modern Art, tel 415/357-4000, www.sfmoma.org. Art-related books, posters, and souvenirs.

FASHION
Diesel 101 Post St., Downtown, tel 415/982-7077. High-end jeans, plus Italian fashions, spread across three floors.
Jeremy's 2 South Park, South of Market, tel 415/882-4929, www.jeremys.com. Labels like Prada, Barney's, and Armani at discounted prices.
Union Square. For serious shoppers, with Hermès of Paris, Gucci, Cartier, Celine, etc.
Wasteland 1660 Haight St., Haight-Ashbury, tel 415/863-3150, http://thewasteland.com. Vintage/trendy second-hand clothes at high prices.

FOOD
Ferry Street Farmers' Market Green St. & Embarcadero, Financial District, tel 415/353-5650, www.ferryplazafarmersmarket.com. Tue. 10–2 & Sat. 8–2.
Ghirardelli Chocolate 900 N. Point St.,Ghirardelli Sq., tel 415/775-5500, www.ghirardelli.com. Chocolate heaven.
ScharffenBerger Chocolates 1 Ferry Bldg., Embarcadero, tel 415/981-9150, www.scharffenberger.com. Gourmet chocolate.
Super Koyama 1790 Sutter St., tel 415/921-6529. Super fish.
Swan Oyster Depot 1517 Polk St., Polk Gulch,tel 415/673-1101. Little necks, bluepoints, and cherrystones since 1912.

FUNK
Aria 1522 Grant Ave., tel 415/433-0219. Furnishings and artifacts.

BAY AREA

ANTIQUES & ART
Alameda Flea Market Alameda Point, Alameda, tel 510/869-5428. Antique/collectibles market 1st Sun. of month.
Imari Gallery 40 Filbert Ave., Sausalito, tel 415/332-0245, www.imarigallery.com. Japanese antiques.
Oriental Corner 280 Main St., Los Altos, tel 650/941-3207. Orientalia.
Oveda Maurer Antiques 34 Greenfield Ave., San Anselmo, tel 415/454-6439, www.ovedamaurerantiques.com. Americana.
Telegraph Avenue Berkeley. World-famous street lined with off-beat stores and street vendors selling antiques, artwork, jewelry, and clothing.
Traywick Gallery 1316 10th St., Berkeley, tel 510/527-1214, www.traywick.com. Landscape works.

BOOKS
Cody's 1730 4th St., tel 510/559-9500, www.codysbooks.com.

FOOD
Civic Center Farmers' Market Marin Civic Center, San Rafael, tel 415/472-6100, www.marincountyfarmersmarkets.org. Thurs. & Sun.
Downtown Farmers' Market Festival 4th St., San Rafael, tel 415/472-6100. Thurs. & Sun. 8–1.
Johnson's Oysters Near Point Reyes Lighthouse (look for signs), tel 415/669-1149.
Paul Marcus Wines Rockridge Market Hall, 5655 College Ave., Oakland,

tel 510/420-1005, www.paulmarcuswines.com. Will ship all wines.
Oakland Farmers' Market 9th St. between Broadway & Clay, tel 510/745-7100. Fri. 8–2.
Tomales Bay Foods & Cowgirl Creamery 80 4th St., Point Reyes Station, tel 415/663-9335, www.cowgirlcreamery.com. Fresh cheeses, organic everything.

FUNK
Berkeley Flea Market 1837 Ashby Ave., tel 510/644-0744, www.berkeleyfleamarket.com.
San Jose Flea Market 1590 Berrysessa Rd., San Jose, tel 408/453-1110, www.berkeleyfleamarket.com.

MUSIC
Amoeba Music 2455 Telegraph Ave., Berkeley, tel 510/549-1125, www.amoeba.com. Thousands of titles from classical to hip-hop.

WINE COUNTRY

FOOD
Jimtown Store 6706 Calif. 128, Healdsburg, tel 707/433-1212, www.jimtown.com. From Brie to baguettes.
Oakville Grocery 124 Matheson St., Healdsburg, tel 707/433-3200, www.oakvillegrocery.com. Local cheeses, oils, etc.
Sciambra French Bakery 685 S. Freeway Dr., Napa, tel 707/252-3072.
Sonoma Cheese Factory 2 W. Spain St., Sonoma, tel 707/996-1931, www.sonomacheesefactory.com.
Sonoma Country Farm Trails P.O. Box 6032, Santa Rosa, 95606, tel 707/571-8288, www.farmtrails.org.
Vella Cheese Company 315 2nd St. E., Sonoma, tel 707/938-3232, www.vellacheese.com. Blue and Jack cheeses.

WINES
Napa Cellars 7481 St. Helena Hwy., Yountville, tel 707/944-2565, www.napacellars.com.
The Wine Room, 9575 Sonoma Hwy., Kenwood, tel 707/833-6131, www.the-wine-room.com.

WINERY GUIDES & MAPS
Napa Valley Vintners' Association 900 Meadowood Ln., St. Helena, tel 707/963-3388, www.napavintners.com.
Sonoma Valley Vintners' Association 783 Broadway, Sonoma, tel 707/935-0803, www.sonomavalleywine.com.

OUTLET STORES
Napa Premium Outlets 629 Factory Stores Dr., Napa, 64958, tel 707/226-9876.
St. Helena Premium Outlets 3111 N. St. Helena Hwy., St. Helena, tel 707/963-7282.

THE NORTH

FOOD
The Apple Farm 18501 Greenwood Rd., Philo, tel 707/895-2461, www.philoapplefarm.com.

WINE GUIDES & MAPS
Mendocino Winegrowers Alliance 525 S. Main St., Ukiah, tel 707-468-9886, www.mendowine.com.
Navarro Vineyards 5601 Calif. 128, Philo, tel 707/895-3686, www.navarrowine.com.

GOLD COUNTRY

See also the panel on Gold Country Shopping, p. 298.

ART
The Vault 42 S. Washington St., Sonora, tel 209/533-1384, http://vaultart.com. Local artists.

FLOWERS
Amador Flower Farm 22001 Shenandoah School Rd., Plymouth, tel 209/245-6660, www.amadorflowerfarm.com. Specializes in daylilies—650 varieties of them.

FRUIT
Boa Vista Orchards 2952 Carson Rd., Placerville, tel 530/622-5522, www.boavista.com. Fruit, wine, pies, and pastries.

WINE
Sutter Ridge Winery 14110 Ridge Rd., Sutter Creek, tel 209/267-1316, www.sutterridgewine.com.

CENTRAL VALLEY

FOOD
Sciabica and Sons 2150 Yosemite Blvd., Modesto, tel 800/551-9612, www.sciabica.com. Olives/olive oils.
Simonian Farms 2629 S. Clovis Ave., Fresno, tel 559/237-2294. More than 100 kinds of fruit and vegetable.

THE DESERT

FASHION
Trina Turk's 891 N. Palm Canyon Dr., Palm Springs, tel 760/416-2856. Bold designs for fashionistas.

FOOD
Hadley's Fruit Orchards 48190 Seminole Rd., Cabazon, tel 909/849-5255, www.hadleyfruitorchards.com. Dried fruit.

FURNITURE
John's Mid-Century Modern 891 N. Palm Canyon Dr., Palm Springs, tel 760/416-8876. Retro furniture from the 1950s and 60s.

OUTLET STORES
Desert Hills Premium Outlets 48400 Seminole Rd., Cabazon, tel 909/849-6641, www.premiumoutlets.com. One of the nation's largest outlet malls, with 130 stores from Armani and Burberry to Versace and Zegna.

ACTIVITIES

With a hospitable climate year-round, California has become the unofficial sports capital of the nation. The tourism bureaus, accessible through the California Division of Tourism Trade and Commerce (see p. 345), publishes guides and lists on all outdoor activities. Also useful are the Sierra Club *(85 Second St., San Francisco, tel 415/977-5500, www.sierraclub.org)*, the National Parks Service *(1111 Jackson St., Suite 700, Oakland, 94607, tel 510/817-1300, www.nps.gov)*, and the California Department of Parks and Recreation *(1416 9th St., Sacramento, 95814, tel 800/777 0369, www.parks.ca.gov)*.

BICYCLING

Backroads 801 Cedar St., Berkeley, 94710, tel 510/527-1555, www.backroads.com.

Getaway Adventures 2228 Northpoint Parkway, Santa Rosa, 95407, tel 800/499 BIKE, www.getawayadventures.com.

BIRD-WATCHING

Point Reyes Bird Observatory 4990 Shoreline Hwy., Stinson Beach, tel 415/868-1221, www.prbo.org.

San Francisco Bay Bird Observatory 524 Valley Way Milpitas, 95035, tel 408/946-6548, www.sfbbo.org.

CAVING

Caving expeditions Cave Loop Dr., Lava Beds National Monument, P.O. Box 867, Tulelake 96134, tel 530/667-2282.

DEEP SEA FISHING

H & M Landing 2803 Emerson St., Point Loma, San Diego, tel 619/222-1144, www.hmlanding.com.

Helgren's Oceanside Sportfishing Inc. 315 Harbor Dr. S., Oceanside, 92054, tel 760/722-2133, www.helgrensportfishing.com

GOLF

Los Angeles Area

Brookside Golf Course 1133 N. Rosemount Ave., Pasadena, tel 626/585 3594, http://brookside.lagolfclubs.com.

Rancho Park Golf Course 10460 W. Pico Blvd., Beverly Hills, tel 310/838-7373. Course located in the middle of Beverly Hills.

Southern California

Alisal Golf Course 1054 Alisal Rd., Solvang, tel 805/688-6411, www.alisal.com.

Balboa Park Municipal Golf Course Golf Course Dr., San Diego, tel 619/235-1184.

Sandpiper Golf Course 7925 Hollister Ave., Santa Barbara, tel 805/968-1541, www.sandpipergolf.com.

Torrey Pines Golf Club 11480 N. Torrey Pines Rd., La Jolla, tel 858/452-3226, www.torreypinesgolfcourse.com.

Central Coast

Del Monte Golf Course 1300 Sylvan Rd., Pebble Beach, tel 831/373-2700, www.pebblebeach.com. Short course but reasonable fees.

The Links at Spanish Bay North end of 17-Mile Dr., at Pebble Beach Resort, Spanish Bay, tel 831/624-6611, www.pebblebeach.com.

Pasatiempo Golf Course 18 Clubhouse Rd., Santa Cruz, tel 831/459-9155, www.pasatiempo.com.

Pebble Beach Golf Links At the Lodge at Pebble Beach (see p. 362), 17-Mile Dr., Pebble Beach, tel 831/624-3811, www.pebblebeach.com.

Rancho Cañada Golf Course Carmel Valley Rd., Carmel, tel 800/536-9459, www.ranchocanada.com.

San Francisco & Bay Area

Half Moon Bay Golf Links 2 Miramontes Point Rd., Half Moon Bay, tel 650/726-1800, www.halfmoonbaygolf.com. Two courses: Links and Ocean.

Presidio Golf Course 300 Finley Rd., Presidio NP, San Francisco, tel 415/561-4661, www.presidiogolf.com.

Desert Area

La Quinta Resort & Spa 49499 Eisenhower Dr., La Quinta, tel 760/564-4111, www.laquintaresort.com. Four courses.

PGA West 56150 PGA Blvd., La Quinta, 800/PGA-WEST, www.pgawest.com. Six courses.

Tahquitz Creek Golf Course 1885 Golf Club Dr., Palm Springs, tel 760/328-1005, www.tahquitzcreek.com.

HANG GLIDING

High Adventure 4231 Sepulveda Ave., San Bernardino, tel 909/883-8488, www.flytandem.com.

Torrey Pines Glider Port 2800 Torrey Pines Scenic Dr., La Jolla, tel 858/452-9858, www.flytorrey.com.

HIKING

Sierra Club tel 415/977-5500, www.sierraclub.org. Organizes hikes and sells detailed maps.

Yosemite Mountaineering School & Guide Service Curry Village, Yosemite Valley, tel 209/372-8344, www.yosemitepark.com. Rock climbing school, also guided hiking and back-packing trips.

HORSEBACK RIDING

Drakesbad Guest Ranch Lassen Volcanic National Park, tel 530/529-1512, www.drakesbad.com.

The Alisal Guest Ranch & Resort 1054 Alisal Rd., Solvang, tel 805/688-6411, www.alisal.com.

Los Angeles Equestrian Center 480 Riverside Dr., Burbank, 91506, tel 818/840-9063, www.la-equestriancenter.com.

Smoke Tree Ranch Stables 1850 Smoke Tree Ln., Palm Springs, 92264, tel 760/327-1372, www.smoketreeranch.com.

Yosemite Valley Stable Near Curry Village, Yosemite Valley, tel 209/372-8348, www.yosemitepark.com.

HOT AIR BALLOONING

Dream Flights 74181 Parosella St., Palm Desert, tel 760/321-5154, www.dreamflights.com.

Fantasy Balloon Flights 74181 Parosella St., Palm Desert, 92260, tel 760/568-0997, www.fantasyballoonflights.com.

Lake Tahoe Balloons S. Lake Tahoe, P.O. Box 19215, tel 530/544-1221 or 800/872-9294, www.laketahoeballoons.com.
Napa Valley Balloons 6975 E. Washington St., Yountville, tel 707/944-0228 or 800/253-2224, www.napavalleyballoons.com.

HOT SPRINGS

See also p. 255.
Golden Haven Hot Springs 1713 Lake St., Calistoga, tel 707/942-8000, www.goldenhaven.com.
Keough's Hot Springs 7 miles S of Bishop, off US 395, tel 760/872-4670, Closed Mon.–Tues.
Two Bunch Palms 67425 Two Bunch Palms Trail, Desert Hot Springs, 92240, tel 760/329-8791, www.twobunchpalms.com.

HOUSEBOAT RENTALS

New Melones Lake Marina Angels Camp, tel 877/468-7326, www.houseboats.com.
Shasta Marina Resort 18390 O'Brien Inlet Rd., Lakehead, 96051, tel 530/238-2284, www.shastalake.net.

KAYAKING

Mission Bay Sports Center 1010 Santa Clara Pl., San Diego, 92109, tel 858/488-1001, www.missionbaysportcenter.com
Monterey Bay Kayaks 693 Del Monte Ave., Monterey, 93940, tel 831/373-5357 or 800/649-5357, http://montereybaykayaks.com.
OARS P.O. Box 67, Angels Camp, 95222, tel 800/346-6277, www.oars.com.
Santa Barbara Adventure Company P.O. Box 208, Santa Barbara, 93102, tel tel 888/773-3239, www.sbadventureco.com. Also mountain biking.

MOUNTAIN BIKING

Bicycle Trails Council of the East Bay tel 510/466-5123. www.btceb.org.
Mammoth Mountain Bike Park tel 800/MAMMOTH, www.mammothmountain.com.
Palomar Downhill Bicycle Tour 16220 Hwy. 76, Pauma Valley, tel 800/985-4427.

MOUNTAINEERING/ROCK CLIMBING

Joshua Tree Rock Climbing School 760/366-4745, www.joshuatreerockclimbing.com
Shasta Mountain Guides 1815 Eddy Dr., Mount Shasta, 96067, tel 530/926-3117, www.shastaguides.com.
Yosemite Mountaineering School & Guide Service Curry Village, Yosemite Valley, tel 209/372-8344, www.yosemitepark.com.

SAILING

Marina Sailing 4633 Admiralty Way, Marina del Rey, 90292, tel 310/822-6617; 1551 Shelter Island Dr., San Diego, 92106, tel 619/221-8286; www.marinasailing.com.
Santa Barbara Sailing Center 133 Harbor Way, Santa Barbara, tel 800/350-9090, www.sbsail.com.

SKIING

Badger Pass Glacier Point Rd., Yosemite National Park off Calif. 41, tel tel 209/372-8430, www.yosemitepark.com.
Bear Mountain Ski Resort 433101 Goldmine Drive, E of Big Bear Lake City, tel 909/866-5766, www.bearmountain.com.
Lake Tahoe Contact the Lake Tahoe Visitors Authority, 169 Hwy. 50, Stateline, NV 89449, tel 775/588-5900, www.bluelaketahoe.com) for information on all of Tahoe's resorts (15 downhill resorts and 14 cross-country centers). The first three are the most popular:
Alpine Meadows 6 miles NW of Tahoe City, tel 800/441-4423 or 530/581 8374, www.skialpine.com.
Kirkwood Off Calif. 88, tel 209/258-6000, www.kirkwood.com.
Squaw Valley Squaw Valley Rd., off Calif. 89, 5 miles N of Tahoe City, tel 800/545 4350, www.squaw.com.
Mammoth Mountain Ski Area tel 760/934-2571, www.mammothmountain.com.
Mount Shasta Ski Park 104 Siskiyou Ave., Mount Shasta, tel 530/926-8610, www.skipark.com.

SKYDIVING

Perris Valley Skydiving Center 2091 Goetz Rd., Perris, tel 909/940-4290, www.skydiveperris.com.
Skydive California City 5999 Curtiss Pl., California City, tel 888/373-4007, www.skydivecaliforniacity.com.

SURFING

Club Ed Surf School & Surf Camp 5 Isabel Dr., Santa Cruz, tel 831/464-0177, www.club-ed.com.
San Diego Surfing Academy tel 800/447-7873, www.surfsdsa.com

UNDERSEA DIVING

Aquarius Dive Shop 2040 Del Monte Ave. Monterey, 93940, tel 831/375-1933, www.aquariusdivers.com.
Underwater Schools of America 225 Brooks St., Oceanside, 92054, 760/722-7826, www.usascuba.com.

WHITEWATER RAFTING

American River Touring Assoc. 2400 Casa Loma Rd., Groveland, tel 800/323-2782, www.arta.org.
Kern River Tours Lake Isabella, tel 800/844-RAFT, www.kernrivertours.com.
Whitewater Voyages 5225 San Pablo Dam Rd., El Sobrante, tel 510/222-5994, www.whitewatervoyages.com.

WHALE WATCHING

Cabrillo Whalewatch 3720 Stephen White Dr., San Pedro, tel 310/548-7562.
Dolphin Charters 1007 Leneve Place, El Cerrito, tel 510/527-9622 or 800/472-9942, www.dolphincharters.com.
Island Packers 1691 Spinnaker Dr. #105b, Ventura.
Monterey Whale Watching 96 Fisherman's Wharf, Monterey, tel 800/979 3370, www.montereywhalewatching.com.
Oceanic Society Expeditions Fort Mason Center, San Francisco, tel 800/326-7491, www.oceanic-society.org.

ENTERTAINMENT

San Francisco has some of the most way-out bars and clubs in the country and a theater scene that is in constant turmoil. L.A. is not far behind and San Diego seriously enjoys its theater. Taking in a game is part of California life whatever your passion. And music happens everywhere.

LOS ANGELES

COMEDY CLUBS

Comedy Store 8433 Sunset Blvd., 90046, tel 323/650-6268, www.thecomedystore.com.
Groundlings Theater 7307 Melrose Ave., 90046, tel 323/934-4747, www.groundlings.com.

MUSIC

Hollywood Bowl 2301 Highland Ave., 90068, tel 323/850-2000, www.hollywoodbowl.com. Classical.
House of Blues 8430 W. Sunset Blvd., 90069, tel 323/848-5100, www.hob.com. Popular.
Jazz Bakery 3233 Helms Ave., 90034, Culver City, tel 310/271-9039, www.jazzbakery.com. Big names in jazz.
L.A. Opera Dorothy Chandler Pavilion, 135 N. Grand St., 90012, tel 213/972-8001, www.losangelesopera.com.
L.A. Philharmonic Walt Disney Concert Hall, 111 S. Grand Ave., tel 323/850-2000, www.laphil.com.
Nokia Theater 777 Chick Hearn Court, Los Angeles, 90015, tel 213/763-6000, www.nokiatheatrelalive.com.
Roxy 9009 W. Sunset Blvd., 90069, tel 310/276-2222, www.theroxyonsunset.com. Rock.
UCLA Center for the Performing Arts 405 Hilgard Ave., 90024, tel 310/825-2101, www.uclalive.org.
Universal Amphitheater Universal City, 91608, tel 818/622-4440. Popular.
Whiskey A Go Go 8901 W. Sunset Blvd., 90069, tel 310/652-4202, www.whiskyagogo.com. Rock.
World Stage 4344 Degnan Blvd., 90008, tel 323/293-2451, www.theworldstage.org. Jazz.

NIGHTCLUBS

Bar Marmont 8171 W. Sunset Blvd., 90069, tel 323/650-0575.
Ritual 1735 N. Cahuenga Blvd., 90068, tel 323/463 0060, www.ritualsupperclub.com.
Viper Room 8852 W. Sunset Blvd., 90069, tel 310/538-1881, www.viperroom.com.

PUBLIC ARTS EVENTS

John Anson Ford Amphitheater 2580 Cahuenga Blvd., 90068, tel 323/461-3673, www.fordamphitheater.org.

SPECTATOR SPORTS

Anaheim Angels Angel Stadium, 2000 E. Gene Autry Way, Anaheim, 92806, tel 714/940-2000, www.anaheimangels.com. Baseball.
Hollywood Park 1050 S. Prairie Ave., Inglewood, 90301, tel 310/419-1500, www.hollywoodpark.com. Horse racing.
L.A. Clippers Staples Center, 1111 S. Figueroa St., 90017, tel 888/895-8662, www.nba.com/clippers. Basketball.
L.A. Dodgers Home Depot Center, 18400 Avalon Blvd., Carson, 90746, tel 877/342-5299, www.ladodgers.com. Baseball.
L.A. Galaxy Home Depot Center, 18400 Avalon Blvd., Carson, 90746,tel 877/342-5299, www.lagalaxy.com. Soccer.
L.A. Kings Staples Center, 111 S. Figueroa St., 90017, tel 213/742-7100, www.lakings.com. Hockey.
L.A. Lakers Staples Center, 111 S. Figueroa St., 90017, tel 310/426 6000, www.lalakers.com. Basketball.
Santa Anita Racetrack 285 W. Huntington Dr., Arcadia, 91007, tel 626/574-7223, www.santaanita.com. Horse racing.

TELEVISION AUDIENCES

Audiences Unlimited 100 Universal City Plaza, Building 3153, Universal City, 91608, tel 818/753-3470, www.tvtickets.com.

THEATER

Ahmanson Theatre 135 N. Grand Ave., 90012, tel 213/628-2772, www.centertheatregroup.org. In-house productions by Center Theatre Group, also touring Broadway productions.
Geffen Playhouse 10886 Le Conte Ave., Westwood, 90024, tel 310/208-5454, www.geffenplayhouse.com. Drama and comedy by prominent writers.
Japan America Theater Japanese Cultural & Community Center, 244 S. San Pedro St., 90012, tel 213/680-3700, www.jaccc.org.
Pasadena Playhouse 39 S. El Molino Ave., Pasadena, 91101, tel 626/356-7529, www.pasadenaplayhouse.org. Highly acclaimed professional theater.

SAN DIEGO

MUSIC

Belly Up Tavern 143 S. Cedros Ave., Solana Beach, 92075, tel 858/481-8140, www.bellyup.com. Rock and pop.
Brick by Brick 1130 Buenos Ave. , 92110, tel 619/275 LIVE, www.brickbybrick.com. Alternative.
Croce's 802 5th Ave., tel 619/233-4355, www.croces.com. Acoustic jazz.
Humphrey's 2241 Shelter Island Dr., Shelter Island, 92101, tel 619/244-3577, www.humphreysconcerts.com. Outdoor venue. Popular.
La Jolla Music Society 7946 Ivanhoe Ave., Suite 309, La Jolla, 92037, tel 858/459 3728, www.la-jolla-music-society.com. Classical.

NIGHTCLUBS

Cane's Bar & Grill 3105 Ocean Front Walk, tel 858/488-1780, www.canesbarandgrill.com. Rock.
Pacific Beach Bar & Grill 860 Garnet, Pacific Beach, 92109, tel 858/483-5212, www.pbbarandgrill.com.

SPECTATOR SPORTS

Del Mar Thoroughbred Club 2260 Jimmy Durante Blvd., Del Mar, 92014, tel 858/755-1141, www.delmarracing.com. Horse racing.

San Diego Chargers Qualcomm Stadium, 9449 Friars Rd., 92108, tel 619/280-2121, www.chargers.com. Football.

San Diego Padres 100 Park Blvd., tel 619/795 5000, www.sandiegopadres.com Baseball.

THEATER

La Jolla Playhouse 2910 La Jolla Village Dr., UC San Diego, 92109, tel 858/550-1010, www.lajollaplayhouse.org. Cirque de Soleil to Broadway.

Old Globe Theater Balboa Park, 92101, tel 619/234 5623, www.oldglobe.org. Contemporary and classic.

Cox Arena San Diego State University, 92112, tel 619/594-6947, www.as.sdsu.edu/cox_arena. Popular.

San Diego Opera Civic Center Plaza, 1200 Third Ave., 92101, tel 619/533-7000, www.sdopera.com. Classical.

San Diego Repertory Lyceum Theatre, 79 Horton Plaza, 92101, tel 619/544-1000, www.sandiegorep.com. Classic dramas to musicals.

SAN FRANCISCO & BAY AREA

In San Francisco unless indicated.

COMEDY

Cobb's Comedy Club 915 Columbus Ave., 94133, tel 415/928-4320, www.cobbscomedy.com.

Punch Line 444 Battery St., 94111, tel 415/397-7573, www.punchlinecomedyclub.com.

DANCE

San Francisco Ballet War Memorial Opera House, 301 Van Ness Ave., 94102, tel 415/865-2000, www.sfballet.org.

MUSIC

Boom Boom Room 1601 Fillmore St., 94115, tel 415/673-8000, www.boomboomblues.com. Venerable jazz and blues joint.

Bottom of the Hill 1233 17th St., 94107, tel 415/626-4455, www.bottomofthehill.com. Alternative.

Cal Performances Zellerbach Hall, Bancroft Way & Telegraph Ave., tel 510/642-9988, www.calperfs.berkeley.edu. Eclectic.

Enrico's 504 Broadway, 94133, tel 415/982-6223, www.enricossf.com. Jazz.

Fillmore 1805 Geary St., 94115, tel 415/346-6000. Rock.

Freight & Salvage Coffee House 1111 Addison St., W. Berkeley, 94702, tel 510/548-1761, www.thefreight.org. Folk.

Jazz at Pearl's 256 Columbus Ave., 94133, tel 415/291-8255, www.jazzatpearls.com.

San Francisco Opera War Memorial Opera House, 301 Van Ness Ave., 94102, tel 415/864-3330, www.sfopera.com.

San Francisco Symphony Davies Symphony Hall, 210 Van Ness Ave., 94102, tel 415/864-6000, www.sfsymphony.org.

Yoshi's 510 Embarcadero, Oakland, 94606, tel 510/238-9200, www.yoshis.com. Jazz.

NIGHTCLUBS

Café du Nord 2170 Market St., 94114, tel 415/861-5016, www.cafedunord.com. Everything from swing to salsa.

El Rio 3158 Mission St., 94110, tel 415/282-3325, www.elriosf.com. Salsa.

Starlight Room Sir Francis Drake Hotel, 450 Powell St., 94102, tel 415.395 8595, www.harrydenton.com. Stylish live-music lounge.

Tonga Room Fairmont Hotel, 950 Mason St., 94108, tel 415/772-5278, www.tongaroom.com. Kitsch.

PUBLIC ARTS EVENTS

Shakespeare in the Park, 415/558-0888, www.sfshakes.org. Various Bay Area venues. Summer weekends only. Free.

Stern Grove Summer Music Festival Sloat Blvd. & 19th Ave., 94132, tel 415/252-6252, www.sterngrove.org.

SPECTATOR SPORTS

Golden Gate Fields 1100 Eastshore Hwy., Albany, 94710, tel 510/559-7300, www.goldengatefields.com. Horse racing.

Oakland A's McAfee Coliseum, 7000 Coliseum Way, Oakland, 94621, tel 510/762-2255 (tickets), www.oaklandas.com. Baseball.

San Francisco 49ers AT&T Park, 24 Willie Mays Plaza, 94107, tel 415/656 4900, www.sf49ers.com. Football.

San Francisco Giants AT&T Park, 24 Willie Mays Plaza, 94107, tel 415/972-2000, www.sfgiants.com Baseball.

San Jose Earthquakes Buck Shaw Stadium, 500 El Camino Real, Santa Clara, 95050, tel 408/556-7700, http://web.mlsnet.com/t110. Soccer.

THEATER

American Conservatory Theater Geary Theater, 405 Geary St., 94133, tel 415/749-2228, www.act sf.org. Repertory.

Berkeley Repertory Theater 2025 Addison St., Berkeley, 94704, tel 510/647-2949, www.berkeleyrep.org. Eclectic productions.

Club Fugazi *(Beach Blanket Babylon)* 678 Green St., 94133, tel 415/421-4222., www.beachblanketbabylon.com Cabaret.

Curran Theater 445 Geary St., 94133, tel 415/551-2000. Large productions and musicals.

Exit Theater 156 Eddy St., 94102, tel 415/931-1094, www.sffringe.org. Experimental to classical offerings. Produces San Francisco Fringe in September.

Golden Gate Theater 1 Taylor St. at Market & 6th Sts., 94102, tel 415/551-2000. Host to nationally renowned productions.

Magic Theater Fort Mason Bldg. D, Fort Mason Center, Marina Blvd. at Buchanan St., 94123, tel 415/345-7575, www.fortmason.org New plays.

Theater Rhinoceros 2926 16th St., 94103, tel 415/861-5079, www.therhino.org. Gay and lesbian productions.

INDEX

INDEX

Bold page numbers indicate illustrations

N

O

P

ILLUSTRATIONS CREDITS

Abbreviations for terms appearing below: (t) top; (b) bottom; (l) left; (r) right.

Cover: (l), Images Colour Library; (center), Corbis/Philip James Corwin; (r), Gettyone/Stone.
1, Robert Harding Picture Library; 2/3, NGS/Keith S. Walklet; 4, Gettyone/Stone; 9, Corbis UK Ltd/Tom Bean; 11, R. Holmes; 12/13, Gettyone/Stone; 14/15, C. Karnow; 15, Gettyone/Stone; 16/17, Corbis UK Ltd/David Muench; 18 & back cover, Gettyone/Stone; 19t, Corbis UK Ltd; 19b, Gettyone/Stone; 20/21, NGS/Joe McNally; 22 & 23, C. Karnow; 24/25, Corbis UK Ltd/Tom Bean; 26, Corbis UK Ltd; 27, Bridgeman Art Library, London, Portrait of John Charles Fremont, by Charles Loring Elliot, Brooklyn Museum of Art, New York, USA; 28/29, Noella Ballenger & Associates; 30/31, Bridgeman Art Library, London, The Route to California. Truckee River, Sierra Nevada. Central Pacific railway, by N. Currier and Ives, J.M. Private Collection; 32, Gettyone/Stone; 34/35, Getty Images; 36/37, Bridgeman Art Library, London, Half Dome, Yosemite by Albert Bierstadt Private Collection/Christie's Images; 38, Bridgeman Art Library, Le Plongeur: the diver, 1971 by David Hockney. Bradford Art Galleries and Museums, West Yorkshire, UK © David Hockney; 40, Bridgeman Art Library, London, Robert Louis Stevenson, 1892 by Count Girolamo Pieri Nerli, Scottish National Portrait Gallery, Edinburgh, Scotland; 41, Brown Brothers; 42, CORBIS; 44/45, Corbis UK Ltd; 46/47, C. Karnow; 49, Magnum Photos/Steve McCurry; 51 & 52 C. Karnow; 54, PhotoFile; 56, C. Karnow; 57, AA Photo Library/M. Jourdan; 58, Corbis UK Ltd; 59, Arcaid; 60, Bridgeman Art Library, London, An Old Man in Military Costume (formerly called Portrait of Rembrandt's Father), c. 1630 (panel) by Rembrandt Harmensz. van Rijn (1606-69) J. Paul Getty Museum, Malibu, CA, USA; 62, J. P. Getty-Trust/CORBIS; 62/63, PhotoFile; 63, Corbis UK Ltd/Roger Ressmeyer; 64, Corbis UK Ltd/Phil Schermeister; 65, Photo File; 67, Skirball Cultural Center; 69, C. Karnow; 70, Corbis UK Ltd/Lyn Goldsmith; 71 & 72, C. Karnow; 73, Kaz Tsuruta/Asian Art Museum of San Francisco. Reproduced by permission; 75, Photograph © 2005 Museum Associates/LACMA. "The Cotton Pickers, 1876," LACMA, Acquistion made possible through Museum Trustees: Robert O. Anderson, R. Stanton Avery, B. Gerald Cantor, Edward W. Carter, Justin Dart, Charles E. Ducommun, Camilla Chandler Frost, Julian Ganz, Jr., Dr. Armand Hammer, Harry Lenart, Dr. Franklin D. Murp; 76, Corbis UK Ltd/W Cody; 77, PhotoFile; 78t, Getty Images; 78b & 79, C. Karnow; 80, Magnum Photos/Steve McCurry; 81, James Leynse/Corbis; 82, Corbis UK Ltd/Joseph Sohm; Chromosohm, Inc.; 85, Gettyone/Stone; 86, Peter Newark's Pictures; 87, C. Karnow; 88, Photovault; 91, Photovault; 92t, PhotoFile; 92b, Gettyone/Stone; 93, C. Karnow; 94, AA Photo Library/P. Wilson; 95, Corbis/Richard Cummins; 96, AA Photo Library/R. Holmes; 97, Corbis UK Ltd/Dave G. Houser; 98, Corbis UK Ltd/Shelley Gazin; 99, Woodfin Camp & Associates Inc.; 100, Richard Cummins/Corbis; 101, Corbis UK Ltd/Dave G. Houser; 102, Brown Brothers; 103, Corbis UK Ltd/Richard Cummins; 105, Corbis UK Ltd/Roger Ressmeyer; 107, AA Photo Library/P. Wood; 108, Frank Balthis; 109, Woodfin Camp & Associates Inc.; 110 & 111, Corbis UK Ltd/Michael Freeman; 113, Norton Simon Museum; 114, Henry Moore Foundation, Norton Simon Art Fondation, Norton Simon Museum; 114/115, Norton Simon Museum; 117, Karen Dardick; 118, Corbis UK Ltd/Francis G. Mayer; 119, Corbis UK Ltd/Richard Cummins; 120, Corbis UK Ltd/Vince Streano; 121, Corbis UK Ltd/Joseph Sohm; Chromosohm, Inc; 122 & 123t, Corbis UK Ltd/Phil Schermeister; 123b, Corbis UK Ltd/Nik Wheeler; 124/125, Corbis UK Ltd/Roger Ressmeyer; 126, Corbis UK Ltd/George Lepp; 127, PhotoFile; 130/131, PhotoFile; 131, Cabrillo Marine Aquarium; 133, PhotoFile; 134, © Disney Enterprises, Inc.; 135, © Disney Enterprises, Inc.; 136, Corbis UK Ltd/Neil Rabinowitz; 137, C. Karnow; 138/139, Kathleen Norris Cook; 140, PhotoFile; 141, Corbis UK Ltd/Ted Streshinsky; 143, Larry Ulrich; 144, Corbis UK Ltd/Richard Cummins; 144/145, Corbis UK Ltd/James L. Amos; 148/149, Gettyone/Stone; 149, NGS/Phil Schermeister; 150, Corbis UK Ltd/Richard Cummins; 151, Kathleen Norris Cook; 153, NGS/Phil Schermeister; 154, Corbis UK Ltd/Jim Sugar Photography; 154/155, NGS/Phil Schermeister; 156, AA Photo Library/M. Jordan; 157, Kathleen Norris Cook; 158, Corbis UK Ltd/Richard Cummins; 159, NGS/Phil Schermeister; 160, Gettyone/Stone; 161, Robert Harding Picture Library; 162, Frank Balthis; 165, C. Karnow; 166, Robert Harding Picture Library; 167, Corbis UK Ltd/Richard Cummins; 168, Corbis UK Ltd/David Muench; 169, Corbis UK Ltd/Dave G. Houser; 170, Images Colour Library; 173, Corbis UK Ltd/ Craig Aurness/Hearst Castle/CA Park Service; 175, Spectrum Colour Library; 176t, Corbis UK Ltd/Roger Ressmeyer; 176b, Corbis UK Ltd/The Brett Weston Archive; 177, Corbis UK Ltd/Ansel Adams Publishing Rights Trust; 178/179, Corbis UK Ltd/Robert Holmes; 180, Diane Cook & Len Jenshel/Getty Images 181, Kathleen Norris Cook; 183, Corbis UK Ltd/Bettmann; 184, Woodfin Camp & Associates Inc.; 185, PhotoFile; 187, NGS/Jonathan Blair; 188, Frank Balthis; 189, Corbis UK Ltd/Ron Watts; 192/193, Gettyone/Stone; 194, Corbis UK Ltd/Morton Beebe; 195, Fine Arts Museums of San Francisco, Gift of the Atholl McBean Foundation; 197, R. Holmes; 199t, Woodfin Camp & Associates Inc.; 199b, AA Photo Library/K. Paterson; 200/201, C. Karnow; 201l, Corbis UK Ltd/Richard Cummins; 201r, R. Holmes; 202, PhotoFile; 203, Images Colour Library; 204, Gettyone/Stone; 205, Corbis UK Ltd/Kevin Fleming; 206, Monica Lee; 207, Asian Art Museum of San Francisco. Used with permission.; 209, Floris Leeuwenberg/Corbis; 210, C. Karnow; 211, Getty Images; 212, C. Karnow; 213, Thomas Winz/Index Stock; 214, AA Photo Library/K. Paterson; 215, Frank Balthis; 216, Grantpix/Photolibrary.com; 218, R. Holmes; 220, Corbis UK Ltd/Richard Cummins; 222 & 223, R. Holmes; 224/225, Gettyone/Stone; 226, David Sanger Photography/Alamy; 227, National Park Service; 228, Gettyone/Stone; 229, Frank Balthis; 230, Frank Balthis; 232, Photovault; 234, R. Holmes; 235, AA Photo Library/R. Holmes; 237, R. Holmes; 238/239, Corbis UK Ltd/Robert Holmes; 238, © 1996 Franklin Avery; 239t, R. Holmes; 240, Corbis UK Ltd/Ted Streshinsky; 241, Corbis UK Ltd/Robert Holmes; 242, Spectrum Colour Library; 243, AA Photo Library/K. Paterson; 244/245, Gettyone/Stone; 246/247, R. Holmes; 247, PhotoFile; 248, R. Holmes; 249, C. Karnow; 250, Monica Lee; 251, C. Karnow; 254 & 255, C. Karnow; 256/7, NGS/Phil Schermeister; 258, R. Holmes; 259, Gettyone/Stone; 260/261, Robert Harding Picture Library; 261t, R. Holmes; 261b, Gettyone/Stone; 262, C. Karnow; 263, Kathleen Norris Cook; 264 & 265, C. Karnow; 266, PhotoFile; 267, C. Karnow; 268, C. Karnow; 270/271; Gettyone/Stone; 272/273, C. Karnow; 273 & 274, C. Karnow; 275, C. Karnow; 276/277, Gettyone/Stone; 277, Ardea London/B. 'Moose' Peterson WRP; 278/279, Photo Network; 281, Pictor International, London; 283, Spectrum Colour Library; 285, C. Karnow; 286, Frank Balthis; 287, C. Karnow; 288 & 289, AA Photo Library/R. Holmes; 291, Kathleen Norris Cook; 292/293, Kathleen Norris Cook; 294, Monica Lee; 295, Corbis UK Ltd/Phil Schermeister; 296/297, © John Elk III; 298, PhotoFile; 299, Gettyone/Stone; 300/301, Gettyone/Stone; 302, R. Holmes; 303t, PowerStock/Zefa; 303c, Mary Evans Picture Library; 303b, Bruce Coleman; 304/305, Phil Schermeister; 306, Gettyone/Stone; 307, Gettyone/Stone; 309 & 310/311, Kathleen Norris Cook; 311, Woodfin Camp & Associates Inc.; 312 & 313, R. Holmes; 315 & 316t, AA Photo

Library/R. Holmes; 316b, NGS/Sarah Leen; 318, Frank Balthis; 320, Frank Balthis; 320/321, NGS/Joel Sartore; 323, Kathleen Norris Cook; 324, NGS/Peter Essick; 325, Corbis UK Ltd/David Muench; 326/327, Gettyone/Stone; 328/329, NGS/Aurness Craig; 331t, Frank Balthis; 331b, Gettyone/Stone; 332/333, Gettyone/Stone; 335, Gettyone/Stone; 336, Woodfin Camp & Associates Inc.; 337l, PhotoFile; 337r, Corbis UK Ltd/Bettmann; 338, Kathleen Norris Cook; 339, Corbis UK Ltd/Raymond Gehman; 340t, Ardea London/Martin W. Grosnick; 340b, Ardea London/Kenneth W. Fink; 341, Frank Balthis; 342, Gettyone/Stone; 343, Gettyone/Stone

Founded in 1888, the National Geographic Society is one of the largest nonprofit scientific and educational organizations in the world. It reaches more than 285 million people worldwide each month through its official journal, NATIONAL GEOGRAPHIC, and its four other magazines; the National Geographic Channel; television documentaries; radio programs; films; books; videos and DVDs; maps; and interactive media. National Geographic has funded more than 8,000 scientific research projects and supports an education program combating geographic illiteracy.

For more information, please call 1-800-NGS LINE (647-5463) or write to the following address: National Geographic Society 1145 17th Street N.W. Washington, D.C. 20036-4688 U.S.A.

Visit us online at www.nationalgeographic.com/books

For information about special discounts for bulk purchases, please contact National Geographic Books Special Sales: ngspecsales@ngs.org

For rights or permissions inquiries, please contact National Geographic Books Subsidiary Rights: ngbookrights@ngs.org

Printed in China

Published by the National Geographic Society
John M. Fahey, Jr., *President and Chief Executive Officer*
Gilbert M. Grosvenor, *Chairman of the Board*
Tim T. Kelly, President, *Global Media Group*
John Q. Griffin, *President, Publishing*
Nina D. Hoffman, *Executive Vice President, President, Books Publishing Group*
Kevin Mulroy, *Senior Vice President and Publisher*
Marianne Koszorus, *Director of Design*
Leah Bendavid-Val, *Director of Photography Publishing and Illustrations*
Elizabeth L. Newhouse, *Director of Travel Publishing*
Carl Mehler, *Director of Maps*
Barbara A. Noe, *Senior Editor and Series Editor*
Cinda Rose, *Art Director*
Jennifer A. Thornton, *Managing Editor*
R. Gary Colbert, *Production Director*
Richard S. Wain, *Production Project Manager*
Bridget English, Caroline Hickey, Michael McNey, Christina Solazzo, Ruthie Thompson, Meredith Wilcox, and Mapping Specialists *Contributors to 2008 edition*

2008 updates by Christopher P. Baker

Edited and designed by AA Publishing (a trading name of Automobile Association Developments Limited, whose registered office is Norfolk House, Priestley Road, Basingstoke, Hampshire, England RG24 9NY. Registered number: 1878835).
Betty Sheldrick, *Project Manager*
David Austin, *Senior Art Editor*
Josephine Perry, *Editor*
Jo Tapper, *Designer*
Simon Mumford, Helen Beever, Amber Banks *Cartographers*
Richard Firth, *Production Director*
Picture Research by Zooid Pictures Ltd.
Drive maps drawn by Chris Orr Associates, Southampton, England
Cutaway illustrations drawn by Maltings Partnership, Derby, England
Tide pool illustration drawn by Ann Winterbotham

***National Geographic Traveler: California*, 3rd ed. (2008)**
ISBN: 978-1-4262-0324-4

The Library of Congress has cataloged the first edition as follows:
Critser, Greg.
California / Greg Critser.
p. cm.
Includes index.
ISBN 0-7922-7564-0
1. California—Guidebooks. I. Title.
F859.3 .C67 2000
917.9404'53—dc21 99-086464
CIP

CREDITS